D0208149

Shakespearean Intersections

# *Shakespearean Intersections*

*Language, Contexts, Critical Keywords*

Patricia Parker

UNIVERSITY OF PENNSYLVANIA PRESS

PHILADELPHIA

A volume in the Haney Foundation Series, established in 1961 with the generous support of Dr. John Louis Haney.



Published by
University of Pennsylvania Press
Philadelphia, Pennsylvania 19104-4112
www.upenn.edu/pennpress

Printed in the United States of America on acid-free paper
1 3 5 7 9 10 8 6 4 2

Library of Congress Cataloging-in-Publication Data
Names: Parker, Patricia A., author.
Title: Shakespearean intersections : language, contexts, critical keywords / Patricia Parker.
Other titles: Haney Foundation series.
Description: 1st edition. | Philadelphia : University of Pennsylvania Press, [2018] | Series: Haney Foundation series, | Includes bibliographical references and index.
Identifiers: LCCN 2017054846 | ISBN 978–0-8122–4974–3 (hardcover : alk. paper)
Subjects: LCSH: Shakespeare, William, 1564–1616—Language. | Shakespeare, William, 1564–1616—Literary style. | English language—Early modern, 1500–1700—Style. | English language—Early modern, 1500–1700—Semantics.
Classification: LCC PR3072 .P37 2018 | DDC 822.3/3—dc23
LC record available at https://lccn.loc.gov/2017054846

*For*

*my now extended family, with love*

*Contents*

## *Illustrations*

# Introduction

*Shakespearean Intersections: Language, Contexts, Critical Keywords* may call to mind other studies of Shakespeare in relation to the historical and contextual—as well as the term made famous in Raymond Williams's *Keywords: A Vocabulary of Culture and Society,* which began as an envisaged appendix to his influential *Culture and Society* (1958) but was published only later in 1976. However, the "critical keywords" in my subtitle here are meant not as a claim to words that were necessarily (or all) "key" terms in early modern English culture, but as words and phrases that provide a critical way into interpreting the language, contexts, and preoccupations of particular Shakespeare plays, together with issues and historical intersections that have been marginalized or have gone unnoticed by their editors and critics. The combination of "critical keywords" with historical intersections may also recall Roland Greene's recent study *Five Words: Critical Semantics in the Age of Shakespeare and Cervantes,* which in turn cites not only Williams's *Keywords* but also Leo Spitzer's "Historical Semantics," William Empson's *The Structure of Complex Words,* and Martin Jay's *Cultural Semantics: Keywords of Our Time.*[1] But unlike Greene's admirable study—which is structured around the five words of his title (*invention, language, resistance, blood,* and *world*)—this book stresses even more than his introduction does that any choice of "keywords" must acknowledge the impossibility of certainty about "which words are 'key' and which are not."[2] My deliberate choice of the term "critical keywords" stresses that the words and phrases foregrounded in different ways and contexts in the present study are "critical" in the sense that they are chosen from the language of particular plays themselves, as a heuristic methodology for particular critical analyses and interventions. And though—in the case of a critical keyword like "preposterous" (which runs through all of the chapters of this book), or "orthography" as opposed to "spelling backward," to which we will return with regard to race, religion, and sexuality later in this Introduction—the argument could be made that they were simultaneously part of an early modern English cultural semantics, other terms here function at a more local (or subtextual) level.

ᔕ

Each of the chapters engages with overlapping as well as different contexts and intersections, and involves a different ratio or distribution of attention in relation to language, contexts, and close reading. Chapter 1 ("Preposterous Reversals, Latter Ends: Language and Contexts in *Love's Labor's Lost*") begins with the "obscene and most prepost'rous event" (1.1.242) at the play's beginning, together with the verbal reversals and different senses of *post* and *pre*, "before" and "after," "front" and "back," and textual-bodily "latter ends" that are part of its "great feast of languages."[3] But it argues (in ways also important for the chapters that follow) that such apparently only linguistic, rhetorical, or verbal turns are crucially related to contemporary contexts of sanctioned order, position, and sequence. Its exploration of another of this book's critical keywords—the "continence" introduced in the King's "continent canon" (1.1.259), which is soon incontinently breached—involves not only this early play's frequently scatological language of bodily breaches, but also the generic breaching of its own "latter end," before turning to latter ends and breaching of other kinds, including of an "English" incontinently mixed with other tongues, geopolitical boundaries and borderlines, incursions by aliens or strangers, and racial as well as other interminglings and mixtures. This chapter then concludes by examining the scatological scapegoating—by the aristocratic men—of the "Judas" of the Pageant of Worthies, in the lines on the "latter end" of "Jude" whose "clipped" evokes circumcised Jews and the "Christian association of Jews with excrement and finally with sodomy."[4] In the process it examines the "sodomitical" application of "spelling backward" to the "Judaizing" of "preposterating" or turning "backward" to the Hebrew Testament, in ways important for a play where both "orthography" (or "right writing") and the language of biblical typology are prominently underscored. The broader contemporary contexts for preposterous reversals in this play thus make clear that what might seem the unconnected spheres of reading, writing, "orthography," sodomy, and biblical teleology were combined in the polemical abjection of religious (and racial) others; and that in this play and others of Shakespeare, the boundary between language and context is an incontinent divide.

Chapter 2 ("Mastering Bianca, Preposterous Constructions, and Wanton Supposes: *The Taming of the Shrew*") begins with the pivotal scene of translation or "construction" where Bianca appears with Lucentio (disguised as Cambio, master of "letters") and Hortensio/Litio, the master of music Lucentio calls a "Preposterous ass" for presuming to go "first"—exploring its relation to the stakes in the contemporary context of the proper order of the "arts" for the order of the genders, and the "cambio" or exchange within this play's subplot, where Bianca refuses both "masters" and finally emerges as anything but a tractable wife. It then proceeds to preposterous constructions throughout *The Taming of the Shrew*, from the micro-level of syntax and discourse to hierarchies of social position as well as of gender, and a major subtextual context that has gone almost entirely unnoticed by its editors and critics—the simultaneously "sodomitical," suppositional, and substitutive resonances of "supposes" it inherited from Gascoigne's *Supposes* and Ariosto's *I Suppositi*, which plays on both senses of the well-known term that could also mean "placed *under*." And it goes on to examine this major intertextual and interlingual context in relation to its importance for *The Taming of the Shrew*, including at its end, which leaves open to "suppose" or critical supposition (as well as *construing* or *construction*) the much-debated meaning of Katherine's final speech, along with reminders of other kinds of "supposition" (or "sub-position," in the Ariostan sense) in its concluding wordplay on target, "butt," and "Bianca" herself.

Chapter 3 ("Multilingual Quinces and *A Midsummer Night's Dream*: Visual Contexts, Carpenters' Coigns, Athenian Weddings") explores the continental and multilingual as well as English and contemporary visual contexts for the Athenian and marital "quince" so important for this Athenian marriage play—a crucial identification and connection that continues to be missing from even recent editions. It analyzes the implications of these multiple contexts and the repeated identification of the quince with weddings in Athens, love potions, and "fruitful issue" for *A Midsummer Night's Dream* as a whole—including the subordination of unruly women and female speech, the "tragical mirth" of the play Quince's actors come "to disfigure, or to present" (3.1.60–61), and the question of whether the quince itself could be queer, like the "medlar" or "open-arse" of *Romeo and Juliet* (2.1.36–38), the only other Shakespeare play that invokes quinces—in an Athenian "marriage" play "crisscrossed by all kinds of homo and hetero investments" (as Richard Rambuss puts it in *Shakesqueer*).[5] And it ends with the continuance, at and beyond this play's own "latter end" (4.1.217), of what Puck calls things that "befall prepost'rously" (3.2.121) and the tragic rather than "fruitful issue" to come from the Athenian marriage of Theseus and his conquered Amazon.

Chapter 4 ("'No Sinister Nor No Awkward Claim': Theatrical Contexts and Preposterous Recalls in *Henry V*") approaches *Henry V* from the perspective of the dual theatrical contexts in which it was preceded not only by *Richard II* and the plays of Henry IV but also by the often-ignored plays of his son Henry VI that had already "oft" been "shown" upon "our stage" (Epilogue 13), in a "preposterous" reversal of generational and chronological sequence. It then moves to the ramifications for *Henry V* itself of its "preposterous recalls" of these Henry VI plays, a perspective that has been missing from even recent criticism that stresses the role of "memory" and "forgetting" in Shakespeare's dramatic histories. Starting from the Cambridge rebellion of *Henry V* in a cause whose higher claim to the throne the Henry VI plays had already repeatedly foregrounded, it explores via these earlier plays what ironizes in advance this king's suppression of a rebellion he calls "preposterously" inspired. And it examines Exeter's presentation of Henry V's own claim to France as neither "sinister" nor "awkward" (2.4.85) as a striking rhetorical inversion of Henry's rhetoric of "right" and proceeding with a "rightful hand in a well-hallow'd cause" (1.2.293).

Chapter 5 ("What's in a Name? Brabant and the Global Contexts of *Othello*") starts from a question posed by Kim F. Hall ("What does it mean that Brabantio may be named after the Netherlands' Brabant, at the time ruled by Spain?") and the importance of thinking through this question at a time when Brabant is effaced by the name change to "Brabanzio" still continuing in the 2016 Oxford text and the widely used *Norton Shakespeare*'s 2016 third edition. Instead, however, of focusing on a narrow one-to-one correspondence between Brabantio and Brabant, this chapter widens the contextual lens to the contemporary geopolitical importance of Brabant itself, not only as a suggestive resonance for a play in which "Iago" evokes Sant'Iago Matamoros, Spain's patron saint, but also as a crucial global context for a plot in which the "Turk" so prominently figures, in a period when Brabant as the nearby center of Spanish rule was repeatedly linked to events involving the Ottoman power. It explores in detail this and other historical English intersections with Brabant important for this play—including the relation between London and Antwerp, and its famous Burse; the flooding into England of immigrants and refugees from Brabant; the years of English military involvement in Brabant and the Low Countries (from which the loanword *cashiering* important to *Othello* was brought back); the central role of

Brabant in the Spanish Armada (echoed in the storm that defeats the Turkish fleet in *Othello*); the installation in Brabant of the Spanish Infanta, Philip II's daughter, whose arguably more legitimate claim to the English throne than either Elizabeth or James continued to fuel fears of invasion from across the Channel; James's controversial 1604 peace with Spain; and the English plays that repeatedly foregrounded events in Brabant, including *A Larum for London, or the Siedge of Antwerpe*, which is strikingly echoed in the scene of carousing and drunkenness on Cyprus in *Othello*. The chapter then turns to a closer consideration of the importance of this geopolitical context for *Othello* as a whole—including "occupation," "fortification," and other terms from contemporary military science; "debitor and creditor" accounting as part of its cash and "credit" nexus; the importance of cloth (or "linens") as an index of female "low country" matters, in a period when "Low Countries" also designated the brothel district across the Thames, where women from Brabant and the Netherlands were frequently represented as prostitutes, or the "public commoners" that Brabantio's daughter is reduced to in the play itself; the recent argument by Ian Smith that the handkerchief of this tragedy is black rather than white;[6] and the role of the Spanish-named Iago, who refers ironically to himself as a "Turk" and becomes the play's "infidel within."

Chapter 6 ("Intimations of Ganymede in *Cymbeline*") takes as its subject the late play whose anachronistic palimpsest of ancient and early modern includes not only its own more global collocation of a "Dutchman" and "Spaniard" as well as a Briton, Frenchman, and Italians in its wager scene but also acknowledged echoes of the Spanish Armada and James's 1604 peace with Spain, though neither of these is named explicitly within it. Focusing on a name (Ganymede) that likewise appears nowhere in the play, this chapter suggests instead the possible "intimations" of Ganymede from contemporary contexts as well as the language and events of the play itself. It begins with the recall of Ganymede in the descent of Jupiter on his eagle in Act 5 (which has not been noted in previous criticism of this Jacobean play) and its contemporary contexts in relation to James's male favorites, including Robert Carr and James Hay, whose Scottish ancestor is directly recalled in the play's description of the old man and two boys who beat back the Roman invasion. Its exploration of the language of this play includes (as in other chapters) its intimations of "preposterous venery," or the "preposterous Italian way" of the "back-door'd Italian,"[7] not only in Posthumus's relation to the Italian Iachimo, but in its repeated references to the "back door" (5.3.45), "behind" (5.3.12), and "backside" (1.2.8), and the "ring" that is simultaneously associated with Innogen's female sexuality and a recall of the "ring" of transvestite boys from *The Merchant of Venice*. It examines the many passages of *Cymbeline* that resonate with the contemporary contexts for the Ganymede figure, from its opening allusion to the king's "Bedchamber" to the scenes involving Innogen cross-dressed as the "page" Fidele and the arresting metatheatrical moment in its final Recognition Scene where Innogen/Fidele remains clothed as a boy and the "woman's part" is revealed as a theatrical "part" played by a boy actor. And in doing so, it connects not only with the importance of transvestite theater and its "supposes" in other chapters, but also with the ways in which "recognition scenes" are ironized in relation to uncertain suppositions in Ariosto's *I Suppositi* and Gascoigne's *Supposes*, and dramatic "supposes" require a *both-and* or double vision, just as identity and desire remain open to supposition.[8]

ও

As the conclusion to this final chapter makes clear, *Cymbeline* gathers up a wide range of the preoccupations of the other chapters. But all of the chapters here are interconnected by shared language and intersecting contexts, as well as through particular "keywords." The contemporary contexts of literacy and humanist learning (along with marriage manuals and conduct books) and the inseparability of grammatical, rhetorical, and discursive structures from issues of gender, sexuality, and social status are central to Chapters 1 and 2 on *Love's Labor's Lost* and *The Taming of the Shrew*, but also to Chapter 3 on *A Midsummer Night's Dream*, where Quince's mispunctuated Prologue (characterized as "sound . . . not in government") joins the issue of sound elsewhere in this book, where oral/aural slippages undermine attempts at governance and "distinction." Geography and geopolitical issues link Chapter 5 on Brabant and the Low Countries to the invoking of Burgundy and Brabant in the history plays of Chapter 4 and the discussion in Chapter 1 of Spanish-held Navarre, the Dutch immigrants flooding into England, and "Did not I dance with you in Brabant once?" in *Love's Labor's Lost*, while both it and *Othello* (like *Cymbeline*) evoke the Armada in relation to different kinds of threatened invasion. Visual contexts are highlighted in the marriage paintings and emblem books of Chapter 3 on *A Midsummer Night's Dream* and the maps of Chapter 5 that make clear why Spanish-held Brabant across the Channel was such a repeated locus of invasion fears in England, while the famous painting in that chapter of the conference that led to James's 1604 peace with Spain makes visually apparent the major role played by Brabant in that peace.

In a canon where *Othello* begins as a comedy but becomes a tragedy after its first act and *Cymbeline*'s own generic status is mixed or open to question, the chapters are further connected by issues of genre or by mixed or frustrated generic expectations. *Cymbeline* is placed among the tragedies in the 1623 Folio, but has both comic elements and a nontragic end, in the kind of mixture or hybrid mingling involved in tragicomedy, in a plot where the coupling of Posthumus and Innogen incurs the king's wrath because of its mingling or mixing at the level of social estate, with the consequent danger of hybrid (or "bastard") issue. The conventional end of comedy is frustrated in *Love's Labor's Lost*, when "Jack" has not "Gill" (5.2.875), and complicated at the end of *The Taming of the Shrew*, where the Folio's "Kate" does not exit with Petruchio, leaving uncertain what will come after, while in *A Midsummer Night's Dream* the marriage of Theseus and Hippolyta is followed by hints of the tragic "issue" to come, and in *Henry V* the final Wooing Scene is shadowed by the Epilogue's reminder of the reign of the son who made "his England bleed" (Epilogue 12). The importance of incontinence and breaching introduced in Chapter 1, including in relation to the breaching of closure at a dramatic "latter end," is joined by the multiple senses of "latter end" throughout—from the repeated reminders of bodily ends and the exploitation of the "latter end" of Jud-as in a pageant in "the posterior of the day" in *Love's Labor's Lost* (5.1.91) to the evocation of a play's "latter end" by "Bottom" in *A Midsummer Night's Dream* (4.1.217); the end of *Henry V*, where the "latter end" (5.2.314) of the French princess is subjected to bawdy wordplay and a successful campaign that involved Henry's "Once more unto the breach" is followed by an Epilogue that breaches that king's own wishful closure; and *Cymbeline*, where the Roman invasion (like feared Scottish invasion in *Henry V*) is presented as a potential "sodomitical" breaching from behind.

"What's in a Name?"—in ways suggestive for the play as a whole—is explored not only in relation to "Brabant[io]" in Chapter 5 and "Quince" in Chapter 3, but also to "Judas" and other names in *Love's Labor's Lost*, to "Cambio" and "Bianca" in *The Taming of the Shrew*, and to the "memorable" names of the St. Crispin's Day speech of *Henry V*, which recall to "preposterous" dramatic memory what might otherwise be forgot. Similarly, in *Cymbeline*—where the name "Euriphile" evokes early modern Europe, "Iachimo" is the Italian counterpart of Spanish "Iago" (and English "James"), and "Fidele" raises the question of fidelity and faith, including with regard to the counterfeit or "simular"—the issue of (not) naming returns in a way that recalls *The Taming of the Shrew*, where the "absent-presence" of

Ganymede is felt in the relation between Sly and his page-boy wife, though Ganymede is never explicitly named in that play.[9]

The fact that so many of these names are translingual underscores another of the major interconnections between chapters, made explicit in the title of Chapter 3 on "Multilingual Quinces" but continuing throughout—from the polyglot wordplay of *Love's Labor's Lost* and the Latin lesson of *The Taming of the Shrew* (where the emphasis on "cambio" or exchange echoes the "*cambio*" of Ariosto's *I Suppositi* and its exploitation of Latin *suppone*) to *Henry V*, where translingual wordplay on "*Rex Angliae*," "*Angleterre*," and the play's hybrid "Anglish" is joined by the connection between "Angles" (or Englishmen) and "ingles" suggested in the description of Henry's "bedfellow" Scroop as an easily won "Englishman,"[10] and sotto voce reminders of the suppressed name of "March" associated with the borderlands or "marches" resonate with the French *marges* or margins that haunt this history play in another sense as well.

ɞ

In addition to *supposes* and *supposition*, *incontinence* and *breaches*, *awkward* and *sinister*, *occupation*, *cashier(ing)*, *cambio*, and *latter ends* of all kinds, the chapters are also connected by other critical "keywords." The simultaneously sexual, narrative, and bookkeeping sense of "(ac)count" foregrounded in the discussion of "debitor and creditor" accounting in *Othello* and *Cymbeline* is crucial to the double-meaning sense of "credit" in both plays, whose emphasis on the fidelity of "(ac)counts" is joined by the sexual sense of "arithmetic" suggested in both (including in Posthumus's "Spare your arithmetic; never *count* the turns"). The "ingle" evoked in *Henry V* in relation to Katherine as an "angel" (and boy player) is joined by *Cymbeline*, where "angel-like" and "By Jupiter, an angel" are descriptions of the beautiful "boy" Fidele, and *Love's Labor's Lost*, where "sore-L" may also suggest another bodily ingle, angle (or fault).

The King's "Conster my speeches better, if you may" in *Love's Labor's Lost* (5.2.341) reflects the importance of *construing* or *construction* as a key term in Shakespeare, including in *The Taming of the Shrew*, a play that not only features Lucentio's doubtful "construction" or translation in the Latin lesson and foregrounds the construction of gender and social position (including through performance) but also underscores the issue of fidelity that was frequently combined with what *Much Ado About Nothing* calls an "illegitimate construction" (3.4.50), when the Pedant responds, "Ay, sir, so his mother says, if I may believe her," to the question of whether Lucentio is his legitimate son (5.1.33).[11] Both construing or "construction" and the fidelity of "translation" resonate subtly once again with Chapter 6 on *Cymbeline*, where "translation" also involves a *translatio imperii*, since the issue of "fidelity" (raised in a different context through "Fidele") extends to the translation or "construction" provided by the Soothsayer, who may be an imperial spin-meister who adjusts his construings to the changing circumstances of the times, though his name evokes "sooth" or "truth."[12]

"Follow" and "following" are likewise important critical indices throughout —in *Love's Labor's Lost* in relation to the issue of what should "follow" what, from the level of discourse and rhyme to the aristocratic men's *imitatio* or sheep-like following and the sequence of male and female in Genesis 2; in *The Taming of the Shrew*, where Lucentio wrongly assumes the prescribed order of pedagogical following from his pupil; in the consequences to "follow" if France does not surrender in *Henry V*, in history plays where the teleological, chronological, and generational sequence of following is reversed; in the sequiturs of plausibility (or what should "follow" from assumptions about women and Moors) in *Othello*; and the ambiguous relation of "post" and "pre" in *Cymbeline*, where prophecy is simultaneously history. In ways underscored in the conclusion to Chapter 6, that famously "anachronistic" play—set in the past time of Augustus into which Christ was born but never reaching that typologically epochal future moment—is also extraordinarily suggestive in relation to what Jonathan Gil Harris has called "Preposterous Time,"[13] and the presumed teleology of biblical typology invoked in *Love's Labor's Lost* at this book's beginning.

Even apparently insignificant terms like "before" and "after" are critically important to the dilemmas of "service" that worry Grumio in *The Taming of the Shrew* (in relation to the ambiguous senses of coming "before" his "master"), in a play where "before" and "after," like "forward" and "backward," or "behind," simultaneously figure in their spatial, hierarchical, bodily, and sexual senses. These multiple senses resonate throughout *Love's Labor's Lost*, *Henry V*, and *Cymbeline* as well (including in the latter's reference to a "back door open" and "dead men hurt behind"), in a period when a crucial contemporary context for such intersections was provided in definitions like the one in Richard Huloet's Latin-English *Abcedarium* (1552) of the "Backedore or posterne, and which by circumlocution, signifyeth the Arse, or all thynges that is behynde vs, as Antica be all thynges before vs."[14]

This leads us to "preposterous"—the most pervasive "keyword" in this book, which was at the same time a major part of the "cultural semantics" of the period itself across multiple intersecting historical contexts. "Preposterous"—from *posterus* (behind or after) and *prae* (in front or before)—connotes a reversal of "post" for "pre," behind for before, back for front, second for first, and end or sequel for beginning. Like many other key terms in the period, it is also translingual—coming from Latin *praepostere* for "in a reversed order" or turned back to front. John Baret's multilingual *An Alvearie or Quadruple Dictionarie* (1580) has "*Prepostere*" for "Backward: ouerthwartly: arsieuersie: contrary to al good order" and French "*deuant derriere*" or "in front behind" (sig. E4r), while Huloet's Latin-English *Abcedarium* (1552) has "Preposterouse, out of order, overthwharth, transuerted, or last done which should haue ben first" (sig. Aa2v). Randle Cotgrave's *Dictionarie of the French and English Tongves* (1611) gives for French *préposterer* to "turne arsiuarsie: to put the cart before the horse" (sig. Sss2r), the familiar proverb for the "preposterous" strikingly registered in *King Lear,* where the "cart draws the horse" (1.4.224) appears in the Fool's reproach to the king who has preposterously made his "daughters" his "mothers."

In the contemporary discourse of rhetoric, "preposterous" was the rhetorical term for *hysteron proteron*—from the Greek *hysteros* (later or latter) placed first and *protos* (the former or first) put after or last.[15] Susenbrotus's continental description of this rhetorical figure made it a synonym for *praeposteratio*, or the reversal of *posterus* (behind or after) and *prae* (before or in front).[16] In England, George Puttenham's influential *Arte of English Poesie* (1589) used "Preposterous" itself as the English translation of this rhetorical term, describing "*Histeron proteron*, or the Preposterous" as that "disordered speach, when ye misplace your words or clauses and set that before which should be behind, & *e conuerso*," and noting that "we call it in English prouerbe, the cart before the horse"—the proverb still being cited for this inversion in Elisha Coles's *An English Dictionary* (1677), which has "Hysteron-proteron . . . a speaking or doing praeposterously, putting the Cart before the horse."[17]

But as the inverse of orders described as both "naturall and seemly," as Henry Peacham put it,[18] *hysteron proteron* or "The Preposterous" as a rhetorical form of "unnatural" disorder was inseparable from other forms of "preposterous" inversion—in ways that illustrate the methodological premises of this book with regard to the frequent inseparability in the period of terms and structures that appear to have to do only with language, rhetoric, or discourse, but at the same time underwrite much broader societal, cultural, and political orders and preoccupations. Thomas Wilson's *Arte of Rhetorique*

(1560), for example, chastises those who would "set the Cart before the horse" by placing woman before man or mother before father. Richard Taverner in 1569 translates Erasmus's adage on setting "the cart before the horse" as "thinges done preposteriously," as when "a wife would rule her husband" or the "commons" tell their "Prince what he had to do."[19] And Huloet's *Abcedarium* (1552) has "ouerthwarthly, or preposterouslye, as when the people commaunde the gouernour, the seruant, the master, or a fole, the wyse" (sig. J4v).

In relation to the disciplines of literacy and learning foregrounded repeatedly in this book (as well as different kinds of "latter end"), texts like John Hart's *Orthographie* (1569) stressed the importance of following the proper "order in writing," unlike discourses that "preposterously . . . begin at the latter end," while Richard Sherry's *A Treatise of Schemes and Tropes* (1550) echoed the biblical order of male and female from Genesis 2 in underscoring the "naturall" discursive order in which God is set before man and man before woman, rather than "backwards."[20] Ben Jonson, in *Discoveries*, repeated an important passage from John Hoskins's influential *Directions for Speech and Style* ("Neither can his mind be thought to be in tune . . . nor his reason in frame, whose sentence is preposterous") and opposed a "masculine" or virile style to the "preposterous" habits of contemporary "gallants," signs of the degeneracy of an age in which "wits grow downward, and eloquence grows backward."[21] And *hysteron proteron* or "The Preposterous" continued to function as a figure for other forms of "arsy-versy" inversion, including in William Rowley and Thomas Middleton's *A Fair Quarrel* (1612–1617), where a father observes that "Wise men begets fools, and fools are the fathers / To many wise children. *Hysteron proteron*, / A great scholar may beget an idiot, / And from the plough-tail may come a great scholar," and a later text that notes "All things are *Arsa versa, topsie turvie, hysteron, proteron*" when a character is asked to speak to another's "Back-Side."[22]

The "preposterous" in the period is repeatedly invoked as a key term in a strikingly wide range of different (but often intersecting) contexts. In the field of formal logic, *hysteron proteron* as a "preposterous" inversion included "the logical fallacy of assuming as true and using as a premise a proposition that is yet to be proved," or the proving of a proposition by reference to another one that presupposes it.[23] But it also connoted a reversal of cause and effect. George Thompson's *Aimatiasis* (1670), for example, charges its opponent with committing "a Hysteron Proteron in nature" after accusing him of confusing "primary precedent causes" with "consequents of the same," observing that it is "preposterous to take in that for a cause, which is but a meer effect, whose Posteriority plainly shews a dependency upon something going before."[24] As I have noted elsewhere and underscore in Chapter 5 here, *Othello* tragically exploits the "preposterous conclusions" that ensue when end or effect comes before cause, in the alleged sequiturs (or "it *follows* that") of Iago, as part of the pervasive recourse to logical as well as other structures of *hysteron proteron* within the entire Shakespeare canon.[25] In *Othello*, Iago's "if the beam of our lives had not one scale of reason to poise another of sensuality, the blood and baseness of our natures would conduct us to most prepost'rous conclusions" (1.3.326–329) evokes the kind of disorder or inversion in the "minde" that should be "ruled by reason, and not tyrannized by preposterous affection" (as Thomas Wright put it).[26] But it becomes (like "foregone conclusion" later in this play) a phrase that chillingly applies to the "preposterous conclusions" that result from Iago's own "preposterous" logic, which begins from foregone conclusions about women and Moors, in ways important in Chapter 5 in relation to Iago as that tragedy's "infidel within." The other explicit invocation of the "preposterous" in *Othello*—Brabantio's "For nature so prepost'rously to err . . . / Sans witchcraft could not" (1.3.62–64), from the discourse of witchcraft to which we will return—at the same time suggests an underlying inversion of cause and effect, or a perverse working backward from his daughter's elopement with a Moor to the assumption that she was bewitched by him.[27]

In relation to social and political disorder, "preposterous" was a key term for the elevation of "upstarts" above the social place or estate into which they were born, as in the description in Polydore Vergil of a ruler who "did preposterouslie exalte and honor the most obscure and servile persons." It figured in contemporary condemnations of the violation of sumptuary laws meant to distinguish different social orders, as in Philip Stubbes's complaint in *The Anatomie of Abuses* (1583) that the "mingle mangle of apparell" in England had reached such a "preposterous excesse" that "it is verie hard to knowe, who is noble, who is worshipfull, who is a gentleman, who is not,"[28] cited in relation to *The Taming of the Shrew* in Chapter 2. In ways important for multiple chapters in this book, it was also a keyword in texts on the "preposterous" transgressions of the English transvestite stage—on both sides of the antitheatrical debate—including its transgression of the biblical prohibition against cross-dressing, characterized by Stubbes as "*preposterous* geare, when Gods ordinance is turned topsie turuie, vpside downe," and what William Rankins described as the "unnaturall" monstrosity of players, "whether grounded by nature or insinuated by some *preposterous* education." The same term is used by Thomas Heywood in arguing against the antitheatricalists in *An Apology for Actors* (1612) that "To do as the Sodomites did, use preposterous lusts in preposterous habits, is in that text flatly and severely forbidden," but it is "not probable that plays were meant in that text" (sig. C3r–v).[29]

In relation to temporal sequence and succession as well as other conceptions of the "natural," the *preposterous* was a key term for the inversion of the order of the generations—invoked in Philip Massinger's *The Unnatural Combat*, where a father proclaims that it is "preposterous in nature" that he should "give account / Of [his] actions to [his] sonne." Inversion of generational priority and precedence is likewise registered in the collaborative play *Beggars' Bush*, which describes a father's kneeling to his son as a "preposterous" act (5.2.20),[30] and in the unnatural precedence of son over elders in lines often attributed to Shakespeare in *Sir Thomas More* ("I, in my father's life, / To take prerogative and tithe of knees / From elder kinsmen, and him bind, by my place, / To give the smooth and dexter way to me / That owe it him by nature").[31] As part of what Stephen Greenblatt has called the period's "deep gerontological bias,"[32] it is foregrounded in Shakespeare not only in *King Lear* but also in *The Taming of the Shrew*, where Tranio's generationally preposterous plan to beget his own sire (2.1.411) is joined by yet another "unnatural" proposition—a father's being willing to transfer all of his property to his son before his death—in ways discussed with regard to that play's "preposterous constructions" in Chapter 2. The reversal of the natural generational order and sequence of father and son is registered in comic fashion in *The Winter's Tale*, where after the Shepherd and his son are socially elevated to a "preposterous estate" (5.2.148), the son comments in unwittingly double-meaning lines that he was "a gentleman born before my father" (5.2.139–140), simultaneously evoking the preposterous generational reversal of a son coming before his father. In the different context of the reversed chronological order of the history plays, analyzed in relation to "preposterous recalls" in Chapter 4, the inversion of the natural order of the generations highlighted in the Epilogue to *Henry V* calls attention to the plays of the son Henry VI that had already come *before*, complicating in advance this king's suppression of what he describes as the "preposterously" inspired Cambridge rebellion (*Henry V* 2.2.112).

In ways important for the biblical rhetoric of Henry V's condemnation of that rebellion—as "another fall of man" (*Henry V* 2.2.142), and the work of a "cunning fiend" (2.2.111)—as well as for the repeated invocation of the "preposterous" in contemporary political contexts of insubordination and rebellion, the biblical origin of such rebellion was what one text termed the "preposterous pride" of Lucifer, the first rebel.[33] Atheists inspired by Lucifer were described as having "invert[ed] . . . the Order God hath disposed to the times preposterously, makeing the night day, and the day night."[34] And the rule of "Antichrist" (when "the rootes of the trees shulde growe upwarde") was repeatedly identified with rebellions accompanied by other societal disorders, where "children" ordered "their parentes, wyves their husbandes, and subjects their magystrates," so that "the fete ruled the head and the cart was set before ye horse,"[35] or the familiar proverbial instance of *hysteron proteron* or "the Preposterous."

The Fall itself was presented as an inversion in which Adam and Eve, by "a contrary movement and altogether backwards," attempted to place themselves above God, and Eve, the female subordinate or second, put herself "first," turning or perverting "this little world" both "upside down" and "backwards."[36] In the order of male and female as first and second in Genesis 2—cited in "The fourme of the Solemnization of Matrimonie" that is echoed in *The Taming of the Shrew*, including in the pivotal Bianca scene with which Chapter 2 begins—Eve as second in creation was meant to follow Adam as her precursor and head. But she was also the first to sin, as the New Testament stresses in 1 Timothy 2:12–14 ("I permit not a woman to teache, nether to vsurpe auctoritie ouer the man, but to be in silence. For Adam was first formed, then Eue. And Adam was not deceiued, but the woman was deceiued, and was in the transgression"), a passage for which the Geneva Bible marginal gloss has "The Woman was first deceiued, and so became the instrument of Satan to deceiue the man."[37]

The gender reversal involved in Adam's following Eve into sin provided the familiar paradigm for all such inversions of female and male, for which the "preposterous" in the period was a repeated keyword. In his influential *The Instruction of a Christen Woman* (1541), Juan Luis Vives described a woman who "presumeth to have mastery above her husband" as turning "backward the laws of nature"—"like as though a soldier would rule his captain or the moon would stand above the sun, or the arm above the head. For in wedlock, the man resembleth the reason, and the woman the body. Now reason ought to rule and the body to obey, if a man will live. Also St. Paul sayeth, 'The head of the woman is the man.' "[38] The argument from the "priority of creation"—in this Pauline text (from Ephesians 5:23) that itself relied on the order of male and female from Genesis 2—meant that since man was made "first, and as the more principal," it is "true from the beginning the woman was subjected, as in order of time she was created after man." To reverse this priority was to "suffer this order of nature to be inverted," as with the inversion that led to the Fall when "the Devil . . . made Eve Adam's mistress in God's matters."

The charge of such preposterous inversion was leveled not only against the "monstrous regiment" of female rule (as John Knox put it in 1558), but also against gender transgressions of all kinds. In his treatise on *Marriage Duties* (1620), Thomas Gataker observed that "where the wife maketh head against the husband . . . all things go backward." Francis Bacon condemned the "preposterous government" of the "Amazons" as against "the first order of nature," while Thomas Dekker termed female mastery a "preposterous" overturning ("what can be more preposterous, then that the Head should be gouerned by the Foote?"). In 1662, in *The Life and Death of Mrs. Mary Frith*, the purported memoirs of Moll Cutpurse, this unruly woman notorious for wearing male apparel is alleged to have said: "Let me be lay'n in my Grave on my Belly, with my Breech upwards . . . that as I have in my LIFE been preposterous, so may I be in my Death."[39]

The "prepost'rous event" that begins the analysis of *Love's Labor's Lost* in this book's first chapter depends on this prescribed biblical order of priority and *following* from Genesis 2, in Armado's condemnation of Costard (whose very name evokes Adam) for following a woman called "a child of our grandmother Eve" (1.1.264)—a reversal of the priority and proper ordering of the genders, where Eve (created *after* Adam, as her "head") is meant subordinately to "follow" *him.* But this play also reverses other forms of gender priority and hierarchy—including in the ways in which the aristocratic women teach the men (contrary to the strictures of 1 Timothy 2 as well as of contemporary conduct books and marriage manuals, like those also foregrounded in relation to the marital "Quince" in Chapter 3). And—as analyzed in Chapter 2—the echo of the "The fourme of the Solemnization of Matrimonie" in the pivotal Bianca scene of Act 3 simultaneously serves to measure Bianca's own departure from gender norms, including in relation to who should teach or instruct whom.

In ways that further exemplify the historical intersections constructed by the "preposterous"—including with regard to the "backward" or "contrary" inversion of a teleological sequence important in multiple chapters and specifically cited in Chapter 2 (for "A will make the man mad, to make a woman of him" in *The Taming of the Shrew*, 4.5.35–36)—the sequential biblical order of male and female as first and second in Genesis 2 was frequently combined with the teleological model of progression from "imperfect" female to "perfect male" from classical and other sources, the model echoed in George Chapman's *All Fools* (1605), where woman is pronounced to be "an unfinished creature, delivered hastily to the world before Nature had set to that seal which should have made them perfect" (3.1). As late as John Bulwer's *Anthropometamorphosis* (1650), the inversion of this "natural" teleology by the transformation of "male" into "female" was characterized as "a perverse regresse from more perfect to lesse," since "the perfection of all naturall things is to be esteemed and measured by the end" and "Nature alwaies intends the Generation of the Male."[40] But when the "preposterous" appears in texts that insist on the irreversibility of this "natural" teleological progression, it is frequently an index of anxieties surrounding such backward turning. George Sandys (for example) insists in his commentary on the sex change of Iphis in Ovid that "it is without example that a man at any time became a woman," since it is "*preposterous* in Nature, which ever aimes at perfection, when men degenerate into effeminacy," revealing in his very choice of terms a teleology haunted by its preposterous inverse. In the context of the related proper passive and active roles of male and female, William Harvey writes in his anatomical lectures: "Male *woo, allure, make love:* female *yeald, condescend, suffer:* the contrary *preposterous.*"[41]

The cultural semantics of the "preposterous" extended at the same time to both witchcraft and what was known as "preposterous *amor*," discourses that were, as Alan Bray and others have argued, frequently interconnected.[42] Stuart Clark records in *Thinking with Demons* that the assumption that "witches did everything backwards" was "a commonplace of scholarly demonology" and provides multiple instances of witches' backward, "sinistral or devillish acts" (inverting the course of rivers, kissing the backside, making the sign of the cross with the left rather than the right hand), or everything "preposterous and done in the wrong way," as Pierre de Lancre observed.[43] And the "preposterous" (as well as "sinister") inversions of witchcraft are reflected in the "magical dance" of the transvestite male witches in Ben Jonson's *Masque of Queenes*, "full of preposterous change" and "making their circles backward to the left hand"; in the backward "charm's wound up" of *Macbeth* (1.3.37); in Brabantio's "For nature so prepost'rously to err . . . / Sans witchcraft could not" in *Othello* (1.3.62–64), important in Chapter 5 for the spellbinding words of Iago, after Othello has said of his own tale-telling, "This only is the witchcraft I have us'd" (1.3.169); and in the "retrograde and preposterous way" of *The Late Lancashire Witches* (1634), where a wife rules a husband, a son commands his father, servants intimidate children, and the church bells are rung backward.[44]

Here again, multiple intersections in the period and in Shakespeare routinely extend beyond any single context or discourse. Beatrice is described in *Much Ado About Nothing* as able to "spell" a man "backward" (3.1.61), in lines that combine a witch's backward spells with an unmanning by a dominant woman, and the preposterous inversion of the orthodox teleology of gender from female to male.[45] In a period in which the "right" was identified with the male and the female with the "left" or "sinister,"[46] the biblical counterpart of the classical witch Medea's backward spelling was the "Siren" Eve, who (as Clark has noted) was frequently identified as the first witch. Conversely, in the context of the "forward" movement from "Old" to "New" Testament, Eve's backward spelling had its re-righting in the palindrome of "Eva" and the "Ave" (Maria) of the Gospels, described by Robert Southwell, for example, as undoing the "witching words" and spellbinding "charmes" that had led to the preposterous inversion of the Fall: "Spell *Eva* backe and *Ave* shall you find, / The first began, the last reverst our harmes, / An Angel's witching wordes did *Eva* blinde, / An Angel's *Ave* disinchants the charmes."[47] Here—in a way that underscores the methodological assumptions and diverse historical intersections in this book—a palindrome or verbal reversal is made to figure preposterous or "backward" inversions of other kinds, including in relation to the providential teleology of the Scriptures themselves.

Multiple different but intersecting contexts are also brought together in other explicit Shakespearean invocations of the "preposterous." In Sonnet 109, "Never believe, though in my nature reign'd / All frailties that besiege all kinds of blood, / That it could so preposterously be stain'd, / To leave for nothing all thy sum of good" (9–12) involves "putting that which should come last (*nothing*) ahead of that which should come first (*all thy sum of good*),"[48] a language of "last" for "first" (and vice versa) that joins the ironic echoes of the biblical "last shall be first" in *Love's Labor's Lost.* In *The Merry Wives of Windsor,* when Falstaff says to Master Ford (disguised as Master Brook), "Would it apply well to the vehemency of your affection, that I should win what you would enjoy? Methinks you prescribe to yourself very preposterously" (2.2.238–241), the "preposterous" figures not only the inverted arrangement in which Ford (as Brook) is directing his own cuckolding (in a sequence that involves Falstaff getting there *first*), but also—with "prescribe"—the sense of a preposterously inverted writing, as well as "pre-scription."[49] In the early history plays, Henry VI's "'Good Gloucester' and 'good devil' were alike, / And both preposterous" (*3H6* 5.6.4–5) invokes the familiar model of Luciferic inversion for the Gloucester who would later become Richard III. And in *Richard III* itself, his mother's "O, *preposterous* / And frantic outrage, end thy damned spleen" (2.4.63–64) joins his own earlier reference to his feet-first birth (*3H6* 5.6.71), in a period when Pliny's description of such a birth as "preposterous" ("*praeposteri natalis*") and "*contra naturam*," or contrary to the order of "nature," was echoed in contemporary midwifery handbooks.[50] Thomas Nashe referred to "those that are called *Agrippae*, who being preposterously borne with their feete forwarde, are saide to enter into the world with ill fortune, and to the great myschiefe of mankind, as with Marcus Agrippa and Nero."[51]

The "preposterous" thus connected multiple assumed forms of disorder or inversion in the period—including not only the rebellious or insubordinate reversal of ruler and ruled, or the "natural" order of father and son, elder and younger, and higher and lower social estate, but also inversions of discursive order, writing, and syntax; upside down, *contra naturam*, or feet-forward birth; the inverted rituals and "backward" spells of witches; and the hierarchy of gender, where the elevation of female over male and the reversal of the "natural" teleology from allegedly "imperfect" female to "perfect" male were figured as "preposterous."

But, as has long been observed, this term was also used for the allegedly "preposterous" in a sexual sense,[52] as it is in *Troilus and Cressida*, where Thersites's condemnation of Achilles and Patroclus (his "masculine whore") as "preposterous discoveries" (5.1.17–24) is part—as Mario DiGangi has importantly argued—of a scurrilous slander. The "preposterous" in the sense of "preposterous venery" or "preposterous *amor*"—like the word *praepostere* itself—had continental antecedents, in, for example, Etienne Dolet's *In Praepostera Venere Utentes* (Lyons, 1538) and Luigi Sinistrari's *De Sodomia*, which treats of coition in a "preposterous vase,"[53] and it frequently appeared in translations from continental sources. Sir Thomas Browne in *Pseudodoxia Epidemica* alludes to "unnaturall venery and degenerous effemination" in the species of "man," in a passage where "unnaturall venery" reflects the "sed etiam *praeposterae* libidinis" of his Latin subtext.[54] John Florio's translation of *The Essayes of Michael Lord of Montaigne* (1603) refers (in translating Montaigne's *desnaturées*) to "unnatural and preposterous loves" when "more by custome than by nature . . . men [do] meddle and abuse themselves with men."[55] But "preposterous" in this sense also crossed what Jonathan Goldberg has called the "homo/hetero divide,"[56] including in relation to the "preposterous Italian way" of back-door sexual entry, which could be what Celia R. Daileader has termed "gynosodomy" as well.[57] And—as Goldberg and others have stressed—"preposterous venery" or "preposterous *amor*" was inseparable in the period from multiple forms of societal and political disorder.[58] Michael Drayton, commenting in *Poly-Olbion* (1612) on the violent end of Edward II (what another text describes as the "Red-hot spit" that through his "Bowels . . . did gore"), remarks in a passage on his "Ganymedes" that he "For that preposterous sinne wherein he did offend, / In his posteriour parts had his preposterous end."[59] But such "preposterous" or posterior bodily inversion was the counterpart of this English king's elevation of upstart or "base" favorites to high estate ("Never did Princes more preposterate / Their private lives, and public regiment").[60] Similarly, verse libels against Buckingham as the "Ganymede" of James I invoked the familiar cultural code of preposterous *amor* in their charge that this "upstart love" has "turn'd / Love's pleasures arse verse" and converted Jove (or Jupiter) himself to "loving so 'gainst nature."[61] But the fact that such verses simultaneously depicted him as an upstart "Phaeton" makes clear at the same time (as Alastair Bellany comments) that "sexual and other apparently apolitical allegations . . . could carry powerful political meanings,"[62] a historical intersection important with regard to earlier favorites of James like Robert Carr and James Hay, discussed in Chapter 6 in relation to "intimations of Ganymede" in *Cymbeline.*

Jeffrey Masten in a brilliant study included in *Queer Philologies* has argued for the different model of the "Fundament" (and foundational or fundamental)—in contrast to the "preposterous"—also citing Bottom in *A Midsummer Night's Dream.*[63] I would add that the very name of "Bottom" not only suggests the "bottom of Gods secrets" from the biblical text he echoes when awakening from his dream,[64] but also the multiple and indeterminate body parts it evokes—not only the posterior (pace the *OED*) and bottom of the body more generally, but also the "bottom of thread" that could designate both the rounded ball of thread (or Latin *glomus*) that evokes the buttocks *and* the phallic shape of the elongated "bottom of thread" on contemporary weavers' looms, suggested (but also in an indeterminate fashion) in "beat me to death with a bottom of brown thread" in *The Taming of the Shrew* (4.3.136–137) and in *The Two Gentlemen of Verona* ("as you unwind her love from him . . . / You must provide to bottom it on me," 3.2.51–53).[65] "Bottom" in these multiple senses is thus (always) already "translated," simultaneously and indeterminately suggesting front, back, and the "unknown bottom" that cannot be "sounded" (to adapt a phrase from *As You Like It*, 4.1.207–208) as well as the logic of the "fundament" as foundational and fundamental that Masten so brilliantly explores.

In another classic piece in *Queer Philologies*, Masten also analyzes the inversion of orthography or "right writing" as a "skaiography" both "awkward" and "sinister" that moves in the opposite direction. And what I want to underscore in this book—from the opening chapter on preposterous reversal, "spelling backward," and the "latter" end of "Jud-as" in *Love's Labor's Lost* and beyond—is the often baleful effects of this and other rhetorics of "preposterous" inversion, including in the language of rectitude and "right" and the scapegoating of others.

In the contemporary context of orthography, spelling, and writing foregrounded so prominently in *Love's Labor's Lost*, but also in relation to other (including discursive, grammatical, humanist, and theological) disciplines of order and proper teleological sequence in other chapters, "orthography" (a word that shares its *orthos* with *orthodox*) was praised in Richard Mulcaster's *Elementarie* (1582) as the "right righting of our English tongue," in a passage that exploited the sense of "right" as the opposite of "left" as well as "wrong."[66] As Masten observes, the "*orthos*" of "orthography" means "straight, upright, standing, the opposite of crooked," and it was contrasted, in Alexander Hume's *Of the Orthographie and Congruitie of the Britan Tongue* (ca. 1617) to "*skaiographie*" (from *skaios*, "left, left-handed, awkward, crooked")[67] as the "perverse opposite to rectitude" and right-writing. Masten goes on to point out that "orthography" in *Much Ado About Nothing* (where Benedick says of Claudio "now is he turn'd ortography," 2.3.20) is aligned there with converting or turning to "what we would call 'heterosexuality.'"[68] But in addition, as already noted, "awkward" and "left" or "left-handed" as the inverse of the "right" are also exploited in "'Tis no sinister nor no awkward claim" in *Henry V*, explored in Chapter 4 in relation to Henry's rhetoric of "right" and "straight" or "forward" advance (including away from memories of Bolingbroke's "crooked" way to the throne), and the theatrically reversed sequence of English history plays, where so much depends on whether the dramatic series is read "forward" or to the right, or "awk," "backward" or in reverse.

In ways stressed in Chapter 1 and other chapters, the frequent early modern analogy between writing and sexual practices continues the combination of graphic and sexual familiar from medieval writers like Alanus de Insulis, where the "orthography" of "Nature" is contrasted to the "falsigraphie" associated with the "witchcraft" of Venus (regressing or degenerating from "male" to "female") and the perversion of Nature's "right" writing when men take the passive rather than active sexual role.[69] But the "preposterous" inversion of spelling backward in early modern contexts also repeatedly linked "sodomy" or "preposterous venery" to both Catholics and Jews (or Jewish *conversos*) accused of "preposterating" the biblical testaments themselves, reading Scripture "backward" (or leftward, like Hebrew) rather than "aright."

The lines in *Love's Labor's Lost* on "*a, b,* spell'd backward, with the horn on his head" (5.1.47–48) invoke the schoolboy's "hornbook" or "ABC," in a context where the tutor who "teaches boys the horn-book" (5.1.46) came with the contemporary associations of the *pedagogus* or schoolmaster with pederasty and *pedicare* or backwards sexual entry. But "spelling backward" in the period also resonated with Protestant polemics that combined Romans 1 on sexual practices *contra naturam* with the Epistle to the Galatians on Christians "bewitched" backwards to the Hebrew testament and circumcision, in ways discussed in Chapter 1 with regard to both the scapegoating of "Judas" as "clipt" and contemporary depictions of horned Jews and Mosaic Scriptures.

In the providential teleology of Christian typology that Milton described in *Paradise Lost* as moving from the Old Testament's "shadowy types" to gospel "Truth," Galatians centrally contributed, along with other New Testament texts, to the teleological model of reading the Scriptures themselves "aright" or in the "right" direction. Characterizing the "Hebrew" Testament itself as a *paedagogus* or "schoolemaster" (3:24), Galatians repeatedly stresses the importance of moving from Jewish "Lawe" to Christian "faith" rather than the reverse, an inversion on which the Geneva gloss comments "this were not to goe forward, but backward." To read scripture "aright" was thus to proceed from imperfect to perfect, spelling what the Geneva gloss terms the "ABC" of the Hebrew testament in a forward direction, from left to right, rather than the (sinister) reverse, including to circumcision as what an important commentary on Galatians called "the sinistre rooted persuasion of the Jewes."[70]

To read "aright"—from left to right, Old to New Testament—in a teleological and providential direction, rather than in the "backward" or "preposterous" reverse, was repeatedly stressed in Protestant polemics against a "preposterating" reversion to the Hebrew ceremonies.[71] These included condemnation in related contexts of anyone who, "praeposterous to God's order and method, will needs read his text backward, turning the heels to heaven, the head to earth," and what another text explicitly called the "preposterous

Hysteron Proteron" of turning back to the Hebrew testament from the "Grace" of the New[72]—or inversion of the teleology (and biblical typology) that Berowne invokes in his sophistical defense of the aristocratic men's perjury in *Love's Labor's Lost* ("It is religion to be thus forsworn: / For charity itself fulfills the law," 4.3.360–361). But in biblical and other commentaries that combined Galatians with Romans 1 on "unnatural" sexual use, the "preposteration" of the testaments was also associated with "preposterous *amor*" as another form of "spelling backward."

In the work of John Bale, for example, the preposteration of the testaments was inseparable from preposterous venery and the backward spelling of "Roma" itself that became contemporary slang for "back-door" sexual entry.[73] Bale's palindrome "Roma/Amor" ("If ye spell Roma backwarde . . . it is preposterus *amor*, a loue out of order or a loue agaynst kynde")[74] joined what he called "*arsewarde* procedynges" applied to turning backward from the Gospel to the Hebrew Law, or the inverse of reading "scripture a ryght."[75] But it also figured multiple other forms of "preposterous" inversion beyond what he calls the "preposterouse offyce of Venery" and so frequently identifies with the "Roman" church (including in the iterated palindrome of "Roma amor est. Amor est? qualis? Praeposterus" in *The Pageant of Popes*).[76] The "sodomitical" has been used as a conceptual framework for reading the work of Bale.[77] But Bale like others in the period strikingly demonstrates how a key term like "preposterous" enables the apprehension of multiple intersections and interconnections in early modern writing. In Bale himself, for instance, inversion of the providential movement of the testaments from "imperfection" to "perfection" (in the "sinister" reverse) was readily combined not only with "preposterous *amor*" but with a reversal of the left-to-right teleology of gender from "imperfect" female to "perfect" male (as opposed to the "witchcraft" of turning male into female, "he" into "she"), as well as inversion of the proper order of the generations. So in his *A Mysterye of inyquytie*, "Luciferic" inversion involves a *mundus inversus* of all kinds, culminating in "all in the feminine gender": "manye excellent writers in discribinge Anticristis kyngedome / hath called yt a false / fylthye / fleshley / whoryshe / preposterouse / . . . promiscuouse / and abhominable generacion. Here is the childe sayd to begett his father / or the sonnes childe his grandefather / & all in y femynine gendre."[78]

At the same time, contemporary descriptions of turning back from Gospel "truth" to the ceremonies of the Jews identified both idolatry and sodomy with a series of different but interrelated other figures for preposterous inversion, in ways that make it difficult to separate religious, racial, and sexual avatars in the period. Pauline paradigms of movement from "darkness" to "light," or from carnal circumcision to circumcision of the heart (Romans 2:29), were routinely combined with the baptismal figure of washing the "black Moor" or Ethiope white and with the Ethiopian "eunuch" of Acts 8, whose own conversion involved learning to read the Hebrew scriptures "aright." So going "backward" to the Hebrew Testament also reversed the racialized metaphorics of such baptismal washing or whitening.[79]

The fact that in Bale and others, a palindrome like "Roma/Amor" could simultaneously denote "preposterous venery" illustrates yet again what is repeatedly underscored in this book—the frequent inseparability in the period of graphic, rhetorical, linguistic, or grammatical forms from bodily, sexual, political, and other orders and implications. The assumption of writing from left to right as "right writing" impacted not only the representation of Hebrew itself as spelled "backward" but intersections like those reflected in John Earle's *Microcosmography* (1628), which has "men do with him as they would with Hebrew letters, spell him backwards and read him," or Thomas Palmer's citing of reading backwards "like a Jue" among examples of the "arsy-versy" in his emblem on "Preposterous or overthwart doings," a term ("doings") itself compounded with sexual overtones.[80] And leftward or "backward" writing is explicitly combined with preposterous venery in "*Italica*, this [. . .] / They put their pens the Hebrew way, methinks" in Middleton's *A Game at Chess* (1624), where "*Italica*" and backward or "Hebrew way" evoke back-door sexual entry (1.1.305–306), just as in other texts and contexts "Hebrew" and sodomy were connected as forms of turning "backward."[81]

In yet another early modern context that reflects the importance of such intersections, the combination of graphic and bodily or sexual in relation to another language written "to the left" rather than the "right" included the new arithmetic made possible by Hindu-Arabic numerals, which were written (like Arabic) allegedly "backwards," from right to left, or *sinistrorsum*,[82] while arithmetic itself (alternately spelled "arsemetric") was simultaneously assimilated to the bodily and scatological,[83] as well as to the sexual sense of "increase and multiply" made possible by its so-called "infidel O" or zero, which linked it to the dangers of female infidelity as well. It is precisely such intersections that make clear another of the reasons (beside the military) that Cassio in *Othello* is called an "arithmetician" (1.1.19) and why Posthumus in

*Cymbeline* cries "Spare your arithmetic; never *count* the turns. / Once, and a million!" (2.4.142–143) when he is convinced that his wife has been unfaithful.[84]

The "preposterous" was at the same time used in the period to characterize Turks as well as Jews, both identified with bewitching "backward" from baptism to circumcision, from Gospel liberty to the "bondage" of the "Hebrew" testament. Galatians (in the Geneva Bible translation) treats of those who "pervert the Gospel of Christ" (1:7)—a "pervert" that corresponds to the *convertere* of the Vulgate text—providing an exemplary instance of the ways in which the very language of "turning" could include (from its root in Latin *vertere*) not just "convert" but "invert" and "pervert," as well as an influential source for early modern descriptions of "turning Turk" (or "returning Jew") as a preposterous inversion and perversion as well as conversion. But it was also frequently combined with Romans 1:23–27 on reverting or turning back from "truth" to "lies," in texts that coupled the "uncleanness" of "idolatry" with a sexual "turning" from "natural vse" to "that which is against nature" (or *contra naturam*), as part of the condemnation of all such "preposterous practices."[85]

The combination of Romans 1 on sexual uses *contra naturam* and Galatians on Christians bewitched "backward" to circumcision pervaded multiple early modern texts on the Ottoman Turk and Christians "turning Turk." Despite what from our perspective is preposterous in the modern sense—transforming Islam or a later religion than the New Testament into a figure of "backward" turning or reversion to the Old Testament—early modern representations of Muslims (or "Hagarenes") as the "seede of Ishmael" and sharers in the "bondage" of Agar or Hagar, Ishmael's mother (described in Galatians 4 as a figure for the "Hebrew" testament), contrasted Christians as the heirs of the legitimate line of Sarah and the providential Abrahamic Promise to the bondage and circumcision that connected "Turk" and "Jew."[86] Thomas Gainsford comments in *The Glory of England* (1618) that Turks "circumcise the men . . . read backward as the *Iewes*, and obserue many other customes of *Moses Law*,"[87] Another text—echoing Galatians 1:7 on those who "pervert the Gospel of Christ" (or the "pervert" that corresponds to the Vulgate's *convertere*)—claims that "the Turks are preposterously zealous in praying for the conversion, or perversion rather, of Christians to their irreligious Religion."[88]

The association of the Turk with the "preposterous" in all of its overdetermined and intersecting senses pervades a wide range of early modern

English texts, in a period when (in contrast to an often-demonizing rhetoric) England also had diplomatic and trade relations with the Ottoman Porte, including those related to its conflicts with Spain and Brabant cited in Chapter 5 on *Othello*, where the "Turk," "turning Turk," and threatened invasion by the Turk most prominently figure. The inversion of "sense" over "reason" characterized by Thomas Wright as the mind "tyrannized by preposterous affection" was assimilated to Turkish sensuality as well as tyranny.[89] And "preposterous" is a repeated keyword in early modern descriptions of the Turk's "unnatural" family relations, akin to the killing of sons by fathers that Sir John Denham's *The Sophy* (1641–1642) condemns as "a preposterous gift, / An act at which inverted Nature starts." Samuel Purchas writes "*Solyman* as vnnaturall to his children, as Selim was to his father *Baiazet*" in the margins of his chronicle of "the succession of the Great Turkes."[90] The history of such unnatural, preposterous, or inverted familial relations fills the pages of texts such as Antoine Geuffroy's *Order of the Great Turk's Court* (1542), Francis Billerbeg's *Amurath* (1584), Richard Knolles's *Generall Historie of the Turkes* (1603)—one of the acknowledged influences on *Othello*—and Bartholomeus Georgijevic's *Ofspring of the house of Ottomanno* (1569), whose list of "the Emperours of Turkeye" includes the "marueilous cruel" Selimus who "poisoned his Father, and by that meanes obteined the turkish Empire."[91] Similarly, extending the repeated association of Lucifer with preposterous inversion, William Alexander's *Doomes-day, or, The Great Day of the Lords Iudgement* (1614) describes the "apostacie" or attempt to "usurpe heavens throne" by Lucifer ("puft up with preposterous aymes" and "with himselfe preposterously in love") as the original of everything that follows, from the Fall (where Eve the "Sirene" brought down Adam in turn) to the unnatural family of the "Turke" ("Proud Selimus, who with a monstrous spleene, / Thy father's ruine labour'dst to worke"; "Great Soliman, sole-man by Turkes thought still, / Whom could he spare who his own sonne did kill").[92]

Early modern texts on the Turk also frequently echo the familiar passages of Galatians and Romans I, combining turning "backward" to circumcision with "unnatural" sexual use and including both among the Turk's alleged "preposterous practices." The "bilious Bale" not only pairs Pope and Turk as the Gog and Magog of his apocalyptic writings but describes the "Turkes" as "relygyous buggerers to this present daye." Robert Burton—citing contemporary instances of men who, "leauing the naturall vse of women . . . burned in lust one towards another, and man with man wrought filthinesse" (a direct echo of Romans 1:27)—provides Italian and Papist examples (explicitly citing

Bale) but also notes that they make a practice of this among the Turks. And Thomas Coryat writes, "The Turkes are exceedingly given to Sodomie, and therefore divers keep prettie boyes to abuse them by preposterous venerie."[93]

The association of the Turk with "preposterous practices" was likewise extended to backwards or "arsy versy" representations of converting or *turning* Turk. A text of 1614 by William Davies, for example, not only repeats the familiar claim that Turks are "sodomites" but assimilates their doing "all things contrarie to a Christian" to a ritual of conversion or "manner of a Christian turning Turke" in which everything is done contrariwise or backward: "He is put upon a horse with his face towardes the tayle . . . then the picture of Christ is carried before him with his feete upwards, . . . and thus he rideth to the place of Circumcision . . . receiuing a name & denying his Christian name, so that euer after he is called a *Runagado*, that is, a Christian denying Christ and turned Turke."[94]

On the English stage—which frequently foregrounded more negative portrayals, despite other contemporary interactions that worked against such polar oppositions—representations of the Turk and turning Turk repeatedly associated both with multiple forms of the preposterous or inverted. The unnatural familial relations chronicled in early modern descriptions of the Turk and Turkish succession constitute a major preoccupation of *Selimus* and other Turk plays.[95] In Thomas Goffe's *The Raging Turke, or Baiazet the Second*, a father's kneeling to his son, "though filiall rites, / And morral precepts say the sonne must bend / Before the father," is explicitly classed among the Turk's "preposterous doings" (1.4.312–316).[96] But though it cites the normative "bond of dutie" which "the sonne" owes to "the father," *The Raging Turke* stages one after another of such "preposterous doings," dramatically highlighting the inverted familial relations identified with the Turk in contemporary descriptions.[97] Gender inversion is assimilated to other forms of every "false preposterous way" in Fulke Greville's *Mustapha*, which compounds unnatural family relations with the inversion of sense or sensuality over reason and an Eve-like female who exercises her "witchcraft" over Solyman the Great Turk.[98]

Turning Turk itself, in multiple English dramatic stagings, repeatedly involves not only the inversion of turning backwards to circumcision (as in Galatians) but also preposterous *amor* or "unnatural" sexual use from Romans 1. One of the most striking early dramatic conflations of turning Turk with both sodomy and circumcision occurs in Thomas Kyd's *Solyman and Perseda*, when the Christian Basilisco, captured by Turks and faced with death or conversion to Islam, quickly opts to "turne Turke" (3.5.10), and his religious "turning backward" from Christian to Turk is linked with "posterior" sexual entry, through the "back dore" (4.2.32–49).[99] But perhaps the English play that best illustrates the simultaneous relation of turning Turk to "preposterous *amor*," the witchcraft or enchantment of an "infidel" Eve, and circumcision as both the unmanning and turning backwards of a "bewitched" Christian is Robert Daborne's *A Christian Turn'd Turk* (1612). The anonymous *Newes from the Sea, Of two notorious Pyrats Ward the Englishman and Danseker the Dutchman* (1609) had already described the English Ward's "preposterous course" as a renegade in Tunis.[100] Daborne's play represents Ward's turning Turk and circumcision as a result of the Eve-like enchantress Turkish Voada, in a dumb show that closely resembles the preposterous or arse-varse description of a renegade's circumcision by William Davies, where the *mundus inversus* of unnatural social, familial, and other inversions joins the claim that "Turks" are "altogether Sodomites and doe all things contrarie to a Christian."[101] And in Daborne, Ward's turning Turk in response to the enchantments of this Turkish "sorceress" is compounded with the "preposterous *amor*" associated with both "back-doored Italian" and Turk: "Poor fellow, how he looks since Mahomet had the handling of him! He hath had a sore night at 'Who's that knocks at the backdoor?' Cry you mercy, I thought you were an Italian captain" (13.52–55).

At the same time, and at particular moments, however, the abjecting and scapegoating rhetoric of preposterous "inversion" in all of its senses could be destabilized as the binary logic of specular projection. In both *A Christian Turn'd Turk* and Philip Massinger's *The Renegado*—which both rewrites and ostensibly re-rights Daborne's plot through the re-turn of a renegade to the Christian faith and the baptism and conversion of another Turkish enchantress—there are passages that resist the simpler binary contraries of each play's reversible turning, assimilating their "Turk" plots briefly but tellingly to contemporary domestic satires and dramas on the same London stage (including of women who dominate men or wear the breeches) but also suggesting the instability of the binaries themselves.[102]

In Shakespeare, in ways that frequently work against such binary projections, descriptions of the "unnatural" family of the Turk repeatedly figure disorders within the *English* royal family, or the "civil butchery" (*1 Henry IV* 1.1.13) of troubled English succession and usurpation. In the English history plays—where the Bishop of Carlisle in *Richard II* delivers his striking "prophecy" of the woes to follow from Bolingbroke's usurping of Richard's crown

("The blood of English shall manure the ground, / And future ages groan for this foul act. / Peace shall go sleep with Turks and infidels, / And in this seat of peace tumultuous wars / Shall kin with kin and kind with kind confound," 4.1.137–141)—the "prophecy" itself is simultaneously ironic and "preposterous" because this English future of (un)civil butchery had already "oft" been "shown" (*Henry V,* Epilogue 13) in the earlier plays of the Wars of the Roses foregrounded in Chapter 4.[103] In *Henry IV Part 2*, the usurper's son (and future Henry V) assures his brothers at his father's death, "This is the English, not the Turkish court, / Not Amurath an Amurath succeeds, / But Harry Harry" (*2H4* 5.2.47–49), in a speech described by Richard Hillman as a specular "Playing Doubles."[104] And after he ascends the throne won by his usurper-father, Henry's "We are *no tyrant*, but a *Christian* king" (*Henry V* 1.2.241)—in a play that anachronistically invokes the Ottoman Turk in Henry's hope for a son who "shall go to Constantinople and take the Turk by the beard" (5.2.209)—is a distinction made in a reversed dramatic series where the son of the Earl of Cambridge executed by Henry V (his own kin) had already concluded that his father's "execution / Was nothing less than bloody tyranny" (*1 Henry VI* 2.5.99–100). In Chapter 5 on Brabant—where the more global widening of the contextual lens to the geopolitical includes the Ottoman Turk and contemporary encounters with Turkish power in the Mediterranean, as well as the Turkish invasion of Cyprus central to *Othello*—it is not the converted Moor accused of witchcraft or the enchantments of Desdemona that produce the tragedy's "preposterous conclusions," but rather the spellbinding effects of Iago, who not only claims, "We work by wit, and not by witchcraft" (2.3.372), but says, "Or else I am a Turk" (2.1.114), in lines that simultaneously disavow and convey the connection.

Preposterous representations of Turks, Jews, and others are part of a specular structure in which descriptions of aliens or foreigners (along with "preposterous" sexual practices) come from a lexicon of the preposterous that was already in place for alleged "inversions" within England. And such passages potentially destabilize, if only for a moment, the very binary oppositions on which the entire system of cultural, political, sexual, and religious contraries depends.

∽

The book that follows is, then, in one sense, an experiment in interconnection —treating of context(s) in ways other than historical reflection and of Shakespeare's language as intersecting with the language of his contemporary culture, while at the same time attending to more "global" historical intersections and events. It stresses the importance of attention to the translingual in every sense—including not only the polyglot resonances of early modern English that often go unnoticed by critics, but also the crossings and intersections between particular terms and discursive networks. It eschews a formalism that would separate the language of the plays from the social, racial, religious, and political, while at the same time underscoring the need for "close reading" (or as Harry Berger, Jr., calls it in *A Fury in the Words,* "close interpretation").[105] But it also stresses the importance of such close attention not only to the language of the plays but also to the very texts and discourses that might seem to belong only to the "contextual." In this sense, what connects its individual chapters most is a way or strategy of reading.

In its choice of particular plays, this book seeks to draw attention to contexts and subtexts, as well as complexities, that have been critically marginalized (or have gone unnoticed), and to provide new (including interdisciplinary) perspectives on particular works of Shakespeare—from early to late, and across different genres—in ways that reverberate beyond Shakespeare as well. Its engagement with historical intersections and the importance of particular historical contexts would seem to suggest a historicist perspective on Shakespeare and other writers. But it resists what is sometimes the historicist practice of setting a literary text against a largely inert background. Instead, its consideration of a wide range of historical contexts and intersecting discourses (including biblical typology, "orthography" or "right writing," double-entry bookkeeping, military science, medical handbooks, chronicle histories, arithmetic manuals, geopolitical treatises, and depictions of others) seeks to underscore the ways in which they themselves are rhetorically (and discursively) shifting and complex—complicating any simple opposition between "secondary" and "primary."

With regard to other criticism, as the endnotes make clear, this study engages with work whose wide range includes rhetoric and pedagogy; classical influences, temporalities, and histories (as well as history plays); theatrical performance; issues of gender, race, and "class"; and geographical/geopolitical interrelations. Though my approach here has some points of contact with what Mary Thomas Crane has called Shakespeare's "mental lexicon,"[106] it has fewer affinities with any intra-cranial approach (or claim of access to "Shakespeare's Brain") and more with the ideas of "distributed cognition" and "extended mind," or integrated cognitive and historical approaches, developed in work that has attended to language as well as to social, theatrical, and cultural environments and structures.[107]

The analyses in this book also intersect in multiple ways with work in queer studies, while at the same time stressing, in relation to the "preposterous," for example, the frequent inseparability of discourses of "sexuality" from other preoccupations and representations. Bruce Smith comments in *Shakesqueer* that "preposterous" has become "a key word in queer philology."[108] But as Jonathan Goldberg and I have both insisted, beginning from our separate publications on "preposterous *amor*" and "preposterous venery" in 1992, the preposterous (in the sexual sense) is inseparable from other contexts and discourses.[109] As Valerie Traub has recently noted, "In his 2009 book *The Seeds of Things*, Goldberg seeks the queer within the hetero by exploring, as he puts it in a related essay, the 'multiple materialisms to be found in early modernity,' extending the meaning of 'queer' to a consideration of physics because 'queer theory is not and never was just about sex in itself.'"[110] And in the pages of this book, the "preposterous" (including as spelling backward) includes not only sexuality, rhetoric, writing, and other early modern contexts but also the perverse (and potentially unstable) application of a speciously binary logic to the characterization and scapegoating of racial and religious others.

The "preposterous" itself—as Laurie Shannon notes in *Shakesqueer*—is one of the terms that "richly support queer reading"; but in lines like Brabantio's search in *Othello* for what caused "nature so prepost'rously to err" (1.3.62), a "preposterous flipped course" also "indexes an unsettled law that nevertheless is nature's," as "Nature is sufficiently free to move 'preposterously.'"[111] And—as Jonathan Gil Harris has so persuasively argued with regard to *Othello*—the "preposterous" can be not only linearly "first after, then before" but simultaneously "before and after," just as the unidirectional temporality of "before" and "after" in Pauline typology is unsettled in *Othello* itself by a "preposterous typological reversion" that sees the Moor as not only "*paganized*—made exotic, savage, barbarian," but also "*Islamicized* and *Judaized*," as Julia Reinhard Lupton so presciently observes.[112]

In the current debate over historicism and unhistoricism—largely prompted by Jonathan Goldberg and Madhavi Menon's "Queering History" (2005) and Menon's subsequent book *Unhistorical Shakespeare* (2008), and recently the focus of a carefully considered critique of "The New Unhistoricism in Queer Studies" in Valerie Traub's *Thinking Sex with the Early Moderns* (2016)—my explorations here of historical intersections and particular "critical keywords" may seem to come down on the side (in a familiar binary metaphor) of the historical.[113] But I agree with the 2016 special issue of the *Journal for Early Modern Cultural Studies* (edited by Ari Friedlander, Melissa E. Sanchez, and Will Stockton), on "Desiring History, Historicizing Desire," that the relation between past and present is always uncertain, chiastic, or *both/and*.[114] To adapt the title of Julia Reinhard Lupton's important 2011 study, "Thinking with Shakespeare" may always be an indeterminate palimpsest of "post" and "pre," both "presentist" and "historical" at once.[115] And, as in the final chapter (on "Intimations of Ganymede in *Cymbeline*"), "intimations" might best describe any historically contextual analyses and endeavors.

This book shares, finally, with recent collections of criticism like Ania Loomba and Melissa E. Sanchez's *Rethinking Feminism in Early Modern Studies: Gender, Race, and Sexuality* and Valerie Traub's *Oxford Handbook of Shakespeare and Embodiment: Gender, Sexuality, and Race*,[116] the conviction that these and other issues (and historical intersections) cannot be thought through in isolation from one another; and that it continues to be important to include careful analyses of language and discourse. I end this Introduction with the hope that the present book will add to that important work, and lead in turn to further critical explorations, conversations, and debates.

*Chapter 1*

# Preposterous Reversals, Latter Ends

## Language and Contexts in *Love's Labor's Lost*

Where, I mean, I did encounter that obscene and most
prepost'rous event.

—*Love's Labor's Lost* (1.1.241–242)

*Boyet.* And so adieu, sweet Jude! Nay, why dost thou stay?
*Dumaine.* For the latter end of his name.
*Berowne.* For the ass to the Jude; give it him. Jud-as, away!

—*Love's Labor's Lost* (5.2.626–628)

In past eras of criticism, *Love's Labor's Lost* was often characterized as an impossibly highbrow, academic, and stilted play, reveling in the "great feast of languages" (5.1.37) purely for its own sake, a more brittle, less "natural," and less successful example of early Shakespeare, preoccupied with rhetorical turns and antithetical sparring in ways that signaled its involvement in the artificiality of the "merely verbal."[1] Its performance has often been similarly stilted, ruled by a style that one of its directors has identified with "parasols" and that an actor in a Royal Shakespeare Company production called the "Harrods Window Approach."[2] What was not—or only rarely—seen or staged is the sustained evocation of the bodily and scatological within it that yields a very different (and far more important) play or the reversals that relate its notorious verbal turns and apparently only formal antitheses to inversions of social hierarchy as well.[3] What I want to do here, then, is not only to suggest that what has often filtered such perceptions of this play is a history of something like what Norbert Elias termed the "civilizing process," Pierre Bourdieu the articulation of "distinction," and Kenneth Burke an exclusion of the "thinking of the body," but to chart its "preposterous" reversals of gender, "class," and other forms of ordering and distinction as part of a different reading of its pyrotechnical wordplay and antithetical turns.[4] And to relate its simultaneous preoccupation with (in)continence, breaching, and latter ends of all kinds not only to its focus on bodily ends and its breaching of dramatic and other enclosures, but to the relation of its scatology and its focus on the "preposterous" to broader issues and contexts of race and religion in the period.

In the first act of *Love's Labor's Lost,* the Constable (Dull) enters with a letter from the "magnificent Armado" (1.1.191) accusing the lowly Costard of a crime the inflated Don terms an "obscene and most *prepost'rous* event" (1.1.242)—following a "female; or . . . a woman" (1.1.263–265), contrary to the all-male edict of Navarre, after the aristocratic men have sworn their "three years' fast . . . not to see a woman in that term" (1.1.24, 37). "Preposterous"—as noted in the Introduction—comes from *posterus* ("after" or "behind") and *prae* ("in front" or "before"), and it connotes, as we have seen, the reversal of "post" for "pre," back for front, after for before, posterior for prior, end or sequel for beginning. It was thus available not only for "backward" or "arsie versie" (John Baret) or for "last done which by rule [should] have been first" (Richard Huloet), but for any inversion of an order understood as "proper" and "natural."[5] The "prepost'rous event" that Armado here condemns is preposterous not only because it involves contravening the edict of the King but because Costard's "manner and form following" (1.1.201–218) involves a *man* following a *woman*—"a child of our grandmother Eve" (1.1.263–264)—a reversal of the priority and proper ordering of the genders in Genesis 2,[6] where Eve (created *after* Adam, as her "head") is meant subordinately to "follow" *him*:

*Costard.* The matter is to me, sir, as concerning Jaquenetta: the manner of it is, I was taken with the manner.
*Berowne.* In what manner?
*Costard.* In manner and form following, sir, all those three: I was seen with her in the manor-house, sitting with her upon the form, and taken following her into the park, which, put together, is in manner and form following. Now, sir,

for the manner—it is the manner of a man to speak to a woman; for the form—in some form.

*Berowne.* For the following, sir? . . .

*Costard.* Such is the simplicity of man to hearken after the flesh.

(1.1.201–212, 217–218)

To be "taken with the manner" here is the English equivalent of *capta cum manu-opere*—being caught "red-handed" or in the act, as Costard has been.[7] But it is also the "obscene event" referred to in the biblical Book of Numbers (5:18)—"So that another man lie with her fleshly . . . and there be no witness against her, nether she *taken in the maner*" (Geneva Bible); or "So that another man lye with her fleshly . . . and there is no witnesse against her, neither she *taken with the maner*" (Bishops' Bible).[8]

One example of being taken with or "in the manner" in this period was the apprehending of Venus and Mars *in flagrante delicto*: "when Venus and Mars were in bed together they were deprehended or taken in the manner, as we say."[9] But Costard's "taken with the manner" also summons the contemporary connection, noted by the *OED*, between "manner" (or *mainour*) and "manure" (interchangeable in sixteenth-century English spelling),[10] and hence the more scatological senses that will be picked up later in the play. Curious echoes of this "*manu-opere*" continue in the wordplay throughout on "*manu*," the manual, or what is done by "hand," not only in the letter to a "snow-white hand" (4.2.132) that passes instead through baser hands, but in the transformation of *ad unguem* or the "fingers' ends" to the "*ad dunghill*" and "I smell false Latin" of the final act (5.1.77–80), along with the implications of all the uses to which the "hand" is put.[11] "Taken with the manner" in this opening scene that includes Armado's indictment of an "obscene and most prepost'rous event" thus introduces the "flesh" and bodily hearkening after the "flesh" that anticipates so much of the play to follow.

Costard himself, the base or "shallow vassal" (1.1.253) in this scene, is the counterpart in the order of social hierarchy or class to Jaquenetta, the "weaker vessel" (1.1.272) in the order of gender, the "low . . . matter" (1.1.192) to which the high "style" (1.1.199) of Don Armado's letter stoops. And the lines leading from Costard's explication of this "matter" in his "manner and form following" (1.1.201–218) to Armado's "prepost'rous event" are preoccupied with the distance between "high" and "low," "high words" (1.1.193) and low things. The Spanish Don's inflated rhetoric (with its gap between "high" style and "low matter") introduces into the play the problem of the separation rather than the congruence between *verba* and *res*, words and things, a separation which will also rebound upon the pretensions of the aristocratic men, who repeatedly sever words from things, from deeds, or from more material substance. "Matter," here, in the sense of the thing concerned—as distinguished from the style or "manner"—is described in this scene in the parodied "high" language of a formal legal proceeding: "as concerning [Latin, *in re*] Jaquenetta," the "base wench" (1.2.59) or "thing" (*res*) in question here. But the letter's explicitly elevated style ("be it as the *style* shall give us cause to *climb* in the *merriness*")—with its sexual double entendres on "merriness" and the tumescent phallic swelling of Armado's "style" (as Shakespeare's Bottom put it, to a "point")—at the same time recalls the proverbial association of such a "low matter" or *res* with "women's matters" (*Julius Caesar* 1.1.22) or "country matters" (*Hamlet* 3.2.116), the "matter" that Iago in *Othello* explicitly sexualizes as a female *res* or "thing" (3.3.301–302). The connection is made even more explicit when Armado proceeds to stoop to this same Jaquenetta's "shoe," a term linked in *The Two Gentlemen of Verona* to the "shoe" with a "hole in it" that designates the sexual "shoe" or "show" of women as the "worser sole" (2.3.15–18). Armado's stooping first to this "base wench" and then further to her "shoe" and "foot"—"I do affect the very ground (which is base) where her shoe (which is baser) guided by her foot (which is basest) doth tread" (1.2.167–169), like his subsequent abasement to her "foot" ("profane my lips on thy foot," 4.1.85)—involves a reversal both of the order of gender and of social distinction. And this "foot" evokes not just the sexual double entendres on "foot/*foutre*" later exploited in *Henry V* (3.4.51–54) but a sense of downward movement in the body politic by one who had aspired upward. In the scene of Armado's accusatory "preposterous," in other words, if Costard is right that this particular "matter is to me," it is not for long. For Jaquenetta—the play's first representative of what Berowne will later call the "sign of she" (5.2.469)—will soon be taken up with the particular "manner" or "style" of the same "magnificent" Armado, who quickly turns from the high dudgeon of accusatory self-righteousness to pursue her lowly *res* as well.

From as early, then, as the opening of *Love's Labor's Lost*, the language of the "high" is contaminated or brought low by the "low matter" of the bodily and sexual.[12] The entire scene of Armado's rhetorically inflated letter, with its "manner and form following," is a parody of the "high words" and elaborate formalities of judicial arrest, formalities meant to separate the aspiring Armado from the "barbarous" (5.1.82), including the "shallow vassal" Costard described as an "unlettered small-knowing soul" (1.1.250). The letter the King proceeds to read to both onstage and offstage audiences unfolds through the "time When? . . . the ground Which? . . . the place Where?" (1.1.235–240) of a formal legal indictment, or the "circumstances most commonly requisite in presentments before Justices of peace,"[13] part of the new apparatus of a literacy linked with control and governance, reflected in contemporary treatises for officers of the Crown and law. But—as Lorna Hutson importantly notes in *The Invention of Suspicion*—the joke here is that while "Armado's letter labours about the circumstances of the offence," Costard "makes the proofs against him as manifest as possible" and "even pleads guilty," acknowledging "I confess the wench" (1.1.283) and quibbling instead on whether she was a "wench," a "damsel," or even a "virgin" (1.1.283–299), in a way that introduces the issue of forensic rhetoric and "evidential uncertainty" into the play as a whole.[14]

The "high" formalities of this opening scene are thus themselves deformed, not just in Armado's pretensions but by the "vassal" Costard, whose attempts to "vary the letter," as it was called (in lines that parody the textbook examples of such turning or varying), are motivated by a much more practical need to evade the "sentence" of the law (1.1.289–300).[15] The scene joins the deformation of the newly fashionable "lettered" formalities elsewhere in Shakespeare—in contexts where "Clowns" ostensibly too untutored to master the unfamiliar forms call attention to their structures and uses in the very act of deforming them. In *Love's Labor's Lost*, such deformations of grammar, logic, and what "follows" from them disorder what in *A Midsummer Night's Dream* is called the ordered "chain" of discourse (5.1.125), in a play in which so-called "rude mechanicals" (3.2.9) reveal both the mechanics of its construction and its connection with "governance" of all kinds. And the arrest of the "unlettered" Costard initiates what becomes in this earlier comedy an insistent foregrounding not only of the disordering "preposterous," as we shall see, but of the discipline and functions of literacy itself.[16]

The Spanish Armado's comic proceeding through the "who," "what," "when," and "how" of such "high words" provides an opportunity for the aristocratic men to mock him in this opening scene: but his manner is almost exactly echoed in the higher-born Boyet's rhetorically swollen address to the Princess in Act 2 (2.1.1–12). The elaborate or "high" formalities of logical division—meant to enable the activity of distinguishing or separating—are pilloried by the "base" (in rank) and "junior" (in age) servant Moth's *reductio ad absurdum* in Act 2, as he separates "melancholy" and "sadness" (1.2.7–8) and manages to reduce the "three years" of Navarre's forbidding edict to nothing more troubling than an "hour" (1.2.37), when his master Armado seeks to evade the restrictions of that edict without being technically forsworn. If from the perspective of the higher social orders in this play, the appropriate response to Costard's (or Armado's) imperfect mastery of "manner and form" is mockery and ridicule, from another perspective these deformations reflect on far more than the lower orders in the play: the "high" is brought "low" not only by the iterations of parodic mimicry but through exposures (like the cheeky servant Moth's) of how open to manipulation are the forms themselves—how "preposterously" led by bodily or material desire, rather than, more loftily, the other way around—when such turning or varying becomes a means through which the pretensions of the aristocrats are themselves deflated.

❦

> Contrary to thy established proclaimed edict and continent canon. . . .
>
> —*Love's Labor's Lost* (1.1.258–259)

> How follows that? . . .
>
> —*Love's Labor's Lost* (1.1.98)

Let us return, then, from this parody of juridico-discursive form in Act 1 to the "obscene and most prepost'rous event" that is its comic object. The "preposterous" crime for which Costard is imprisoned—having "sorted and consorted," with "a female; or for thy more sweet understanding, a woman" (1.1.264–265)—is not only "preposterous" in the sense of reversing the proper order of the genders (what should come *after* for what should come *before*) but pronounced contrary to the King's "proclaimed edict and *continent* canon" (1.1.258–260), a term generally glossed as a canon or law enforcing restraint.[17] The edict of the King that binds the little Platonic "academe" (1.1.13) of men is thus associated with "continence" in contrast to the incontinence that would result from consorting with women. As an edict meant to preserve an all-male enclosure and its inviolate integrity, it is therefore threatened by the incontinence or breaching associated with the (moral as well as bodily) "fault" of women, not only the "weaker vessel" (as Jaquenetta is called in 1.1.272) but traditionally an incontinent or "leaky" one, whose bodily openness, "fault," or "crack" is contrasted to male self-enclosure and bodily *integritas.*[18] The King himself echoes the danger of such "breaching" in his limitation on how far his liberality (2.1.167) will go in accommodating the new female incursion that threatens the undoing of the aristocratic men, when the Princess of France and her retinue arrive at the boundaries of his all-male retreat:

> *King.* . . . Mean time receive such welcome at my hand
> As honor (without *breach* of honor) may
> Make tender of to thy true worthiness.
>
> (2.1.168–170)

A breaching of the original "continent canon" and oath, however, is precisely what ensues, as each of the King's company follows in turn the model of the lowly Costard's defection.

That Jaquenetta is associated with Eve in the play's initial "prepost'rous event" already links this "weaker vessel" with the "fault" of the original generic "female; or . . . woman" (1.1.264–265). Eve was created *after* Adam (in the biblical story of male and female in Genesis 2), and should follow him in obedience as in sequence; but she becomes the leader in the "fall of man," an act in which Adam in turn—or *by* turning—becomes the first follower of "woman," the "sign of she" without whose "fault" the original paradise or park would still be unbreached.[19] Fittingly, then, for his Adamic role and the play's iteration of the original Edenic fault, Costard's name means both "apple" and slang for "head"; and this vassal's "hearken[ing] after the flesh" (1.1.217–218), in the lines on "manner and form following," directly echoes Adam's "flesh of my flesh" from the Genesis account, as well as the reversal in which this first-created "head" hearkened after that "flesh." The phrase attached to Jaquenetta—the "weaker vessel" here—aligns her explicitly with the tradition of woman as secondary and subordinate, while the inverse following that occasions Costard's imprisonment summons recollection of the "fault" that led to the original preposterous reversal of the genders, and with it the breaching of an Edenic enclosure. The "obscene and most prepost-'rous event" which begins the play's defections with a "man" (1.1.217) later called a "turf of earth" (4.2.88), here caught following "a child of our grandmother Eve" (1.1.264), thus becomes, within this early Shakespearean comedy, a recall of the original lapse or "fault" that breached the paradisal containment (another sense of "continent") of another "park"—one that long-standing misogynist tradition held would still be intact but for the creation of that sign of "she."

The "prepost'rous event" of Costard's following Jaquenetta, is, however, only the beginning of a series of such breachings, as it is of a series of reversals in the play of "high" and "low." Immediately following Costard's defection as the lowly "head" or first within this series comes the second, when Armado seeks "authorities" for his falling for this same "base wench" (1.2.59), in the exalted classical and biblical exempla of antiquity: Hercules overcome by Omphale, Sampson by Delilah, and Solomon by heathen women (1.2.65–76, 173–181). For all of his or the aristocratic men's subsequent attempts to find some "mighty president" (1.2.117) for their own defections, it is, however, the "base" vassal Costard who in this series *comes first*, providing the "president" or precedent (1598 First Quarto, "presedent") for the plot that ensues.[20] In what thus represents an inversion of social hierarchy as well as of gender, Costard, in a scene recalling Adam as both "head" and a man of "earth," becomes in retrospect a "president" set by the lowliest of the men—the "base" (rather than exalted or "mighty") head from which all else follows in the play as what Moth will call a "sequel" (3.1.134). The fact, for example, that Berowne's letter to Rosaline (condemning evidence of *his* defection) gets crossed with Armado's to the lowly Jaquenetta, implicates both "high" and "low" registers in this play in the original Adamic incontinence: not only parleying or speaking with but following a woman. It therefore undoes the play's elaborately constructed distinctions between "high" and "low," as both are brought low by the "weaker vessel" who is herself supposed to be mere subordinate, second, or sequel.

Don Armado's letter to Jaquenetta calls hyperbolic attention to the betrayal of his class or class aspirations such stooping involves, by invoking the emblem of "King Cophetua" (4.1.65) who stooped to love of a "Beggar Maid." At the same time, the language of Petrarchan servitude and self-abasement on which he calls appears to reverse the class relation into a gendered one, in which he waits on her as her servant in love, in ways the saucy mockery of this "country girl" (1.2.117) perpetually deflates. Armado's letter to Jaquenetta speaks in the polarized language of high and low, but also in this language of idealized self-abasement, at the same time as it exposes the more threatening underside of such a stooping, the possibility that a beggar's love, if not freely granted, might be "enforce[d]" (4.1.81): "I am the king, for so stands the comparison; thou the beggar, for so witnesseth thy lowliness. Shall I command thy love? I may. Shall I enforce thy love? I could. Shall I entreat thy love? I will. What shalt thou exchange for rags? robes; for tittles? titles; for thyself? me. Thus expecting thy reply, I profane my lips on thy foot, my eyes on thy picture, and my heart on thy every part" (4.1.78–86). For the moment, however, it confuses the roles of subject and object, conqueror and conquered, in its elaborate gloss on Caesar's *Veni, vidi, vici,* which when translated into the vulgar or "mother" tongue (the translational counterpart to the "base wench" who has so transported him) comes to rest in a catastrophic "nuptial" ("The catastrophe is a nuptial," 4.1.77)—one in which it is not clear who is marrying whom ("on whose side? the king's; no, on both in one, or one in both," 4.1.78).

This sense of preposterous reversal runs through a whole series of exchanges in the play—of young and old, female and male, low and high: from the "child" or "tender juvenal" Moth's instructing his "old man" or "tough signior" in wordplay on "senior" (1.2.11–12, 5.1.62), to the "boy" Cupid's commanding men (1.2.180–181); from the Princess's presuming to teach the King, her social and gender superior (2.1.108) or Jaquenetta's saucier mockery of the "magnificent" Armado (1.2.133–145) to the pageant of Worthies in which lower-caste players instruct their social betters, though the lessons appear lost on the aristocratic men. And as if to call attention to the "stooping" of "great" to insignificant (a trifling or insignificance suggested in the resonances of the name Moth or "mote"), Berowne invokes a whole series of parallels in his chastising of his fellows in Act 4:

> To see a king transformed to a gnat!
> To see great Hercules whipping a gig,
> And profound Salomon to tune a jig,
> And Nestor play at push-pin with the boys,
> And critic Timon laugh at idle toys! (4.3.164–168)

References to "following" and sequence or inversions of sequence are also everywhere in this early Shakespearean comedy, along with persistent harping on what comes *before* and what should follow or come *behind.* Moth answers Armado's command to "follow" him (3.1.133) with his flippant "Like the *sequel,* I" (134), in a scene packed with wordplay on what should come first and what at an end. Holofernes describes Berowne's letter to Rosaline as being to a "*sequent* [or follower] of the stranger queen's" (4.2.138–139). The play repeatedly parodies the period's new humanist disciplines of ordered sequence and what should "follow" what—from Costard's "in manner and form following" to the changes rung on how "*vidi*" follows "*veni*," while "*vici*" follows both (4.1.64–80). And in its opening scene, Dumaine and Berowne engage in an exchange on what might "follow" fittingly in the sequiturs of "reason":

*Longaville.* He weeds the corn and still lets grow the weeding.
*Berowne.* The spring is near when green geese are a-breeding.
*Dumaine.* How follows that?
*Berowne.* Fit in his place and time.
*Dumaine.* In reason nothing.
*Berowne.* Something then in rhyme.
(1.1.96–99)

The juxtaposition here—of "reason" and of "rhyme"—returns elsewhere in *Love's Labor's Lost*, with implications for women's "faults," as we shall see. But even before Costard's "manner and form following" in this same act, this early exchange between the two aristocratic men introduces the problem of "what follows" and by what form of "fitting."

The harping here on "following" continues in this comedy's repeated evocations of humanist *imitatio*, routinely translated into English as "following"—including as what Berowne derides as "base authority from others' books" (1.1.87). As the play proceeds, however, the more highbrow notions of *imitatio* and prior exempla soon become the less-exalted principle of sheep-like following enunciated by the perjured Dumaine ("Ill, to *example* ill, / Would from my forehead wipe a perjur'd note: / For none offend where all *alike* do dote," 4.3.122–124). And the humanist discipline of exemplary "following" invoked in Armado's search for "some mighty president" (1.2.117) among "great men" becomes, once the King's men are "all forsworn" (4.3.278), their own desperate search for some "authority" (4.3.283) as they repeat the example of Costard, a different kind of "base authority," when they post to what is called the "opposed end" (5.2.758) of their original oath. "Following" of this sort is suggested by the well-worn joke on "ship" and "sheep" ("Two hot sheeps . . . wherefore not ships?," 2.1.218), one so familiar by the time we reach the "sweet fellowship in shame" (4.3.48) of the perjured men that the ear may hear in this new male "fellow*ship*" the "fellow-*sheep* " of their own sheep-like following or pursuit, especially when the women of the play are so often described in the vernacular as "mutton" (1.1.302).[21]

The inversions involved in the play's initial "obscene and most prepost'-rous event" (of Costard's following a woman) and the aristocratic men's following his base "president" in turn (in posting to the "opposed end" of their original intent) are paralleled by the striking verbal reversals and rhetorical turns for which the play is famous—in lines such as Armado's "I love not to be cross'd" with Moth's "mere contrary, crosses love not him" (1.2.32–34), in Berowne's "They have pitch'd a toil; I am toiling in a pitch" (4.3.2–3), or the exchange in Act 5 between Berowne and Rosaline ("*Berowne*: Our states are forfeit, seek not to undo us. / *Rosaline*: It is not so, for how can this be true, / That you stand forfeit, being those that sue?," 5.2.425–427). What I want to suggest, however, from the perspective of the verbal, bodily, and structural inversions set in motion by this comedy's initial "prepost'rous event" is that its notorious verbal reversals and rhetorical turns—far from being marks of the "merely" verbal—are inseparable from the preposterous reversals of gender, class, and other forms of hierarchical ordering it proceeds to stage.

ꕥ

> Shall I teach you to know?
>
> —*Love's Labor's Lost* (4.1.108)

> The tongues of mocking wenches are as keen
> As is the razor's edge invisible . . .
>
> —*Love's Labor's Lost* (5.2.256–257)

> Did not I dance with you in Brabant once?
>
> —*Love's Labor's Lost* (2.1.115)

What may appear to be merely gratuitous verbal reversals or rhetorical turns in this play are, first of all, related to what it does to gender hierarchy and gender roles. *Love's Labor's Lost* involves not only the overturning of comic conventions in its unconventional end—in which "Jack" hath not "Gill" and the women impose a delay "too long for a play" (5.2.875–878)—but also the repeated reversal of contemporary stereotypes of female and male. The conventional Petrarchan topos governing, for example, *The Rape of Lucrece*—the male erotic siege of a female enclosure—is in this play explicitly reversed, as besieging "ladies" are placed outside the enclosure of an all-male "park." In a reverse, therefore, of the usual gender positions, the women of the play occupy the place and imagery of the aggressive male lover and the Princess of France and her attending Ladies present themselves as "humble-visag'd suitors" outside the King's "forbidden gates" (2.1.26, 34).[22] Though in ways not as explicitly irreverent as the responses of Jaquenetta to her male superiors and social betters, the Princess and her entourage also refuse to be subordinate or obsequious. The Princess, when addressing the King, says initially "pardon me, I am too sudden bold; / To teach a teacher ill beseemeth me" (2.1.107–108). But teaching the King and his followers is what she and the other Ladies proceed to do, as Eve Rachele Sanders, Kathryn M. Moncrief, and others have argued, including when Rosaline asks Boyet, "Shall I teach you to know?" (4.1.108).[23] And in ways that resonate with the issue of construing or construction underscored in the attempt to "master" Bianca in *The Taming of the Shrew* (discussed in the next chapter), the King's "Conster [i.e., Construe] my speeches better, if you may" (5.2.341) in the play's final act is an entreaty that recognizes the women's "right to construe meanings."[24]

*Love's Labor's Lost* foregrounds the misogynist topos of women's supposedly unstoppable tongues, as any woman caught within the enclosure of the park is to suffer the punishment of Philomel, her tongue cut out. But as the plot unfolds, it is the aristocratic men (or Armado, their ape) who most want "chat" (5.2.228), who are wordy, loquacious, or too copious of tongue. And although the penalty for the woman who intrudes into this all-male retreat is to have her tongue excised (1.1.124), the actual women in this play have tongues more cutting than they are cut, described as like "the razor's edge" ("The tongues of mocking wenches are as keen / As is the razor's edge invisible," 5.2.256–257).

The play's strikingly pointed speech is suggestively allied with its phallic counterpart; but in the exchanges between the Princess's retinue and the followers of the King, it is the women who are the possessors of the "pricks" and "points." When Berowne, for example, says to Rosaline, "Will you prick't [prick-it] with your eye?," she responds, "No point, with my knife" (2.1.189–90), playing on the double sense of "eye" as female genitalia (and hence her supposed lack of "point") but offering to "prick it." This same Rosaline, launching arrows at a target, indulges in bawdy dialogue with Boyet in which she identifies herself as the shooter/suitor who "hits" her "mark" (female "matter" or matrix) with a "prick."[25] In Holofernes's description of the hunt, it is the Princess who is described as having "pierc'd and prick'd a pretty pleasing pricket" (4.2.56). And when Berowne at last presents himself to Rosaline as a passive target and exclaims

Here stand I, lady, dart thy skill at me,
Bruise me with scorn, confound me with a flout,
Thrust thy sharp wit quite through my ignorance,
Cut me to pieces with thy keen conceit. (5.2.396–399)

the raped and mutilated Philomel envisaged in the men's initial pact and oath is replaced by something more suggestive of a passive male victim—an Orpheus or an Actaeon, cut down by Bacchantes or the instruments of the hunt.

At the level of rhetorical repartee, what may *seem* merely verbal sparring also forges connections between the play's reversing of letters and words and its reversals of the conventions of gender. When, for example, Berowne says to one of the Ladies, "Did not I dance with you in Brabant once?" (2.1.114), she replies to him in what *appears* to be an exact repetition or echoing of his question ("Did not I dance with you in Brabant once?" 115), apparently simply iterating, Narcissus-and-Echo fashion, the words of a male speaker who comes first. But her apparent repetition, with its pronomial shifters, also shifts the initial direction of Berowne's "I" and "you," changing the subject and object positions and hence making *her* into the one who danced with *him*, in "Brabant" or the *Low* Countries, with all of the sexual overtones of "danced," in a way that simultaneously complicates the gendering of this familiar contemporary double entendre:

*Berowne.* Did not I dance with you in Brabant once?
*Katherine.* Did not I dance with you in Brabant once?
(2.1.114–115)[26]

The Lady's response—far from being an example of "merely" verbal play—enacts a mocking reversal or shift *within* an apparently iterative "following," changing the position of subject and object, "I" and "you," in ways that connect this reversal with the later exchange on the sequences of letters and alphabetical literacy, where the positions of "U" and "I" are literally reversed (5.1.53–57).[27] As if to underline the reversibility of female and male, "I" and "you," in relation to sexual penetration and pursuit, a whole other bit of wordplay is devoted to the question of *who* pierces *whom*, in the paranomastic eliding of "person" or "pierce one" ("And if one should be pierc'd, which is the one?" 4.2.83–84), at the entrance of Jaquenetta or a "soul feminine" in Act 4 (4.2.81). In the exchange of position enacted in the responsive "Did not *I* dance with *you* in Brabant once?" or this play on which "one" should be "pierc'd," the issue in the context of the images of suitor/shooter, "pricks," and "marks" is one of the *reversibility* of subject and object, of *who* pursues *whom*, just as the concluding "Tu-whit, to-*who*" of the play's final song may, in its reminder of the sexual "wit" played on throughout, raise once again the question of the "who."

In relation to gender in this play, it is also important to examine its repeated pairing and opposing of "reason" and "rhyme," as well as its multiple references to the vernacular or "mother" tongue. Moth introduces a contrast between "father's wit" and "mother's tongue" as early as Act 1 (1.2.95). And much is made in the play of verbal "varying" or rhetorical turns as an analogue to the sexual "turns" of women—from the "maid" who serves Costard's "turn" (1.1.299), or the ladies who turn the aristocratic men from their original "intents" (5.2.758), to what Armado calls the "digression" (1.2.116) women represent from the male pursuits of "arms" and learning. But just as Adam (the "first to bear arms," as *Hamlet* puts it) was turned aside by the "fault" of "our grandmother Eve"—or as the sexual "fault" and "low matter" of Jaquenetta diverts the "high manner" of Armado's "style"—so there is a polysemous (and polymorphous) sense of female or sexual "fault" pervading the relation or opposition of "rhyme" to "reason." In the exchange between Berowne and Dumaine on what "follows" in Act 1, something that fails to follow in "reason" is said to follow in "rhyme" (1.1.99), in lines whose "green goose" (slang for "whore") and "fit" (1.1.98) convey a sense of sexual double entendre, even if we do not hear the sexually suggestive "fallows" in this form of "following."[28] "Rhyme" itself in the period was already associated (through the alternative spelling "rime" from Latin *rima*, "fissure, cleft, or chink") with the sexual "fault." (*OED* gives "chap, chink, or cleft" as one of the meanings of "rime," the spelling used in the play's early texts.)[29] It is not surprising, therefore, that the "verses" (from *vertere*, "to turn") that accompany the turning of the aristocratic men toward the lesser "matter" of the "sign of she"—verses addressed, after all, to mistresses—are called "guilty rhymes" (4.3.137); that Berowne (though claiming that he will not "groan for Joan" or be guilty of a "thing in rhyme," 4.3.179–180) has already confessed that "love" has taught him how "to rhyme" (4.3.12–13); that there is reference amidst the confessions of the Eavesdropping Scene to the "rhymes" that are "guards on wanton Cupid's hose" (4.3.56); or that the "love" there described as teaching both "rhyme" and "mallicholy" (4.3.13) calls attention to the confluence in sound between "rhyme" and "rheum," the latter, as in the "French disease," both an incontinent flowing and a proverbial consequence of following women.[30]

Armado's "falling" for Jaquenetta yields another reminder of the "fault" of "our grandmother Eve" when the Spanish Don proclaims his "most immaculate" love for this "base wench." His "My love is most immaculate white and red" (1.2.90) invokes the colors of love poetry from the biblical Song of Songs. But Moth's deflating rejoinder—"Most maculate thoughts, master, are mask'd under such colors" (1.2.91–92)—provides a reminder, instead, of the "maculate," spotted, or impure, the adulterating or duplicitous "colors" of cosmetics as well as of rhetoric (yet another long-standing connection between the bodily and the linguistic).[31] And the sense of duplicity is underlined in the "rhyme" Moth recites, which treats repeatedly of a woman's "faults" (1.2.100–101), in a sound that blends the impure or "false" with Eve's breaching and women's (moral and sexual) "faults." Such wordplay, accumulating as the play proceeds, adds to its developing lexicon of associations for the generic "sign of she": original "fault" or crack in a "continent" enclosure; impurity, maculation, or cosmetic coloring; "preposterous" subversion of the proper order of "head" and "foot." Armado adds to this series when he stoops to the same "weaker vessel" Costard had pursued, not only referring to his varying from the continent "edict" of Navarre as a "digression" (1.2.115–119) but identifying his turning to this "base wench" with translation or linguistic "turning," from Latin, the exalted *sermo patrius*, to the "base and obscure vulgar" (4.1.68–69) or vernacular "mother" tongue, in the letter he sends to proclaim his devotion to her "lowliness" (4.1.80).

Such rhetorical and poetic "turning" was associated by long-standing masculinist tradition with the turning, varying, and inconstancy of women.[32] The female alters, varies, and turns "tropically" in this model of the "soul feminine," and in so doing undoes the "continent canon" of male *integritas*. But this venerable identification of varying, turning, and troping with the stereotypes of variable and sexually "turning" women—a topos that appeals ultimately to the varying or turning of "our grandmother Eve"—is in *Love's Labor's Lost* revealed (like the stereotype of female *garrulitas*) to be simply part of the men's *image* of the "soul feminine," of all that is proverbially associated with the generic "sign of she." In fact—as the play goes out of its way to underscore—the actual women characters within it are much less interested in "varying" than the men, whose constancy of will is much more at issue.[33] What we encounter instead, for example, is Berowne's attempt to submit the terms of the edict of Navarre to a variation that better suits his will and appetite (4.3.286–362), in the exonerating exercise in rhetorical (as well as actual) variation that justifies the men's varying in Act 4, just as in Act 1 the first elaborate exercise in verbal "turning" or varying (from "wench" to "damsel" to "virgin" to "maid") forms part of Costard's attempt to evade the letter of the law by which he stands condemned (1.1.289–300). The traditional masculine topoi in which the "sign of she" is available both for the cosmetic or "maculate" and for the turns and "colors" of rhetoric are in this Shakespearean play turned around or on their ends: the women (proverbially associated in the period with incontinence and inconstancy) are concerned instead with the reining in of the "will," and the fidelity or "troth" that is the final measure of the "truth" of words. And by the end of the play that started by evoking Adam's temptation by a woman, "our grandmother Eve," we have instead clear reference to its reverse, *Adam's* tempting *Eve* ("Had he been Adam he had tempted Eve," 5.2.322).

ꝏ

> *Armado.* Some enigma, some riddle—come, thy l'envoy—begin.
> *Costard.* No egma, no riddle, no l'envoy, no salve in the mail, sir. . . .
> *Moth.* . . . is not l'envoy a salve?
>
> —*Love's Labor's Lost* (3.1.71–73, 79)

> *Costard.* . . . now you will be my purgation and let me loose . . .
>
> —*Love's Labor's Lost* (3.1.127)

"Preposterous" reversals are so insistent in this early Shakespearean comedy—and so frequently combined with bodily versions of the arsy-versy within it—that it does indeed become something like what Stephen Booth has called "a sustained, two-hour pun on *end.*"[34] And reversals of beginning and end, after (or behind) and before, inform not only passages of what might seem otherwise simply gratuitous wordplay but also the elaborate structuring of entire scenes. Literal reversal of sequence and direction occurs on a grand scale in the strikingly self-reversing Eavesdropping Scene of Act 4 (4.3), where each of the aristocratic men (first Berowne, then the King, then Longaville and finally Dumaine) appears, confesses his own perjury, and then hides and witnesses each new confession, before the scene literally turns upon itself and unwinds in reverse, as the defectors are brought out of hiding in exactly the opposite sequence and Berowne, the first to stray and first to appear on stage, becomes the last to be exposed.[35] The theatrical staging of this Eavesdropping or pivotal "recognition" scene—winding up in one direction and unwinding in reverse—involves both a structural *peripeteia* and an ironic fulfillment of Berowne's own pronouncement in Act 1, in one of the play's multiple variations on the biblical last shall be first. For the same Berowne who says there, "I am the last that will last keep his oath" (1.1.160), becomes the first here to view (from an "over-view," 4.3.173) the entire sequence of perjuries confessed, before he too is exposed at its final moment, caught by the "post" (4.3.187).

Reversal in the bodily and scatological sense of back for front, or latter end for beginning, also pervades the extraordinary scene of wordplay and stage play in Act 3 on "l'envoy" and "salve." This exchange begins as Costard, the imprisoned "Clown," is summoned to be an "embassador" for Armado to Jaquenetta ("*Armado*. Fetch hither the swain, he must carry me a letter. / *Moth*. A message well sympathiz'd—a horse to be embassador for an ass," 3.1.49–52), and Moth commences with this delaying "wonder" or "riddle":

*Moth*. A wonder, master! Here's a costard broken in a shin.
*Armado*. Some enigma, some riddle—come, thy l'envoy—begin.
*Costard*. No egma, no riddle, no l'envoy, no salve in the mail, sir.
O sir, plantan, a plain plantan; no l'envoy, no l'envoy,
no salve, sir, but a plantan!

(3.1.69–74)

The scene that ends in Costard's enfranchisement as an "embassador" starts off, then, with a "riddle" or "enigma"—on how a "costard" ("head" or "apple") could be broken in a "shin." But the lowly Costard's response quickly identifies this enigma to be solved with an "egma" or enema, and rejects "l'envoy" and "salve" in favor of the homelier remedy of a "plain plantan." What then follows is an extended verbal exchange on the reversing of "l'envoy" and "salve" ("*Armado*. Doth the inconsiderate take salve for l'envoy, and the word 'l'envoy' for a salve? / *Moth*. Do the wise think them other? is not l'envoy a salve?" 3.1.77–80). And in this exchange, the "l'envoy"—defined as an after-word or post-script ("an epilogue or discourse, to make plain / Some obscure *pre*cedence that hath *tofore* been sain," 3.1.81–82) and as something that should therefore "follow" or come at an end ("Now will I begin your moral, and do you *follow* with my l'envoy," 3.1.94)—is confused with the "salve" (or Latin "salv*e*") that should come at a beginning.

As the scene's complex wordplay proceeds, in increasingly dizzying reversals (including of speaking positions, exchanged midway), "l'envoy" is further described as "ending in" the "goose," an overdetermined bit of vernacular that suggests both a potential rude gesture and the slang for "prostitute" or venereal disease, introducing into what had seemed a more elevated academic debate about beginnings and ends an association with bodily "salves" and bodily ends. The entire exchange, once again, negotiates the distance between "high" and "low"—the social-climbing Armado introducing a definition of the formal epilogue or "l'envoy" (like the kind used notoriously by Gabriel Harvey) and the "base" Costard confusing it with a different kind of end, as well as rejecting what he takes to be high-class remedies with foreign-sounding names for the local remedy of the "plain plantan," homelier cure for ailments of both "head" and "shin."[36] The "enigma/egma" of a "costard broken in a shin" depends on the "costard" that is both "apple" and slang for "head"—producing a riddle involving the body's "opposed ends"—while "broken in a shin," apart from the physical breaking of shins common in an age when the "threshold" had to be high enough to hold the thresh ("I, Costard, running out that was safely within, / Fell over the threshold, and broke my shin," 3.1.116–117), also summons the contemporary sense of "sexual disappointment" (Costard is, after all, replaced as a suitor by the socially higher Armado here) and the slang for raising money, a resonance not inappropriate for a scene in which Costard is not only going to be "enfranchised" but will receive monetary "remuneration" (3.1.136) for his services.[37]

In this exchange on "l'envoy" and "salve," "costard" and "shin," the inflated or highbrow term "l'envoy" (as in Harvey's formal epilogue, afterword, send-off, or farewell) is thus associated with the "low matter" of the bodily. (We might also note here that in the most famous of satires on the pretensions of Harvey's own "Post-scripts" and "Lenvoyes," the "l'envoy" understood as "end" was already identified scatologically with the body's end, in a passage resonant for the "enigma/egma" of this scene.)[38] In ways that recall the original "obscene and most prepost'rous event" of Costard's following a woman, the linking of "envoy" and "goose" in the sense of loose or base wench finally prompts this same Costard's mistaking of Armado's announcement that he will "enfranchise" him for his intention to marry him off to "one Frances," stock name for a loose, "frank," or "liberal" woman: "I smell some l'envoy, some goose, in this" (3.1.121–122). "L'envoy," then, described as "ending in the goose" (3.1.99)—or "fat l'envoy" linked to "fat goose" (3.1.103)—already contaminate this academic and textual post-script or end with more bodily and bawdy implications, whether or not there is a hint of "buttocks" in "l'envoy," as Booth suggests.[39]

Costard's confusion of an "enigma" to be solved with an "egma" as another kind of loosing, at the beginning of this exchange, is thus picked up in its final lines, as Costard is to be "enfranchised" or let loose in order to become Armado's envoy or messenger (or as Moth puts it, "embassador for an ass," 3.1.52):

*Armado.* Sirrah Costard, I will enfranchise thee.
*Costard.* O, marry me to one Frances! I smell some l'envoy, some goose, in this.
*Armado.* By my sweet soul, I mean setting thee at liberty, enfreedoming thy person: thou wert immured, restrained, captivated, bound.
*Costard.* True, true, and now you will be my purgation and let me loose.

(3.1.120–127)

As editors of the play concur, the "purgation" or letting "loose" of something described here as "immured, restrained, captivated, bound" introduces an unmistakable bodily reference into the "purgation" that entails the freeing of this "embassador," one that follows from the sliding of "enigma" into "egma" at its beginning.[40]

This apparently gratuitous scene of wordplay in Act 3 depends, then, first on the reversal of what comes *after* for what should come *before*, a "l'envoy" that should come last, as "an epilogue or discourse, to make plain / Some obscure precedence that hath tofore [i.e., "before"] been sain" (3.1.81–82), with a "salve" or greeting that should come at the beginning, one that also suggests a "salvo" or discharge and hence even more scatological connections with a bodily "end,"[41] as when the departing "Wall" of *A Midsummer Night's Dream* says, "Thus have I, Wall, my part discharged so" (5.1.204), in a speech where the discharging could be before or behind.[42] And at the end of this exchange, on before and after, beginnings and ends, a loosing or opening up of something described as "immured, restrained, captivated, bound" (3.1.125) suggests connections both with the immured enclosure of the "continent edict" Armado is about to breach and with the "egma" that adds the purgative problem of an "end" to be loosed to the more highbrow riddle or "enigma" to be solved. The afterword that then accompanies the discharge of Costard as an envoy or "embassador" is Moth's response to this same master, that he will "follow" like the "sequel" (3.1.134).

"Envoy"—postscript or afterword—is aligned here with "embassador" (3.1.52), the messenger Armado is about to make of Costard by enfranchising him. But the entire scene of wordplay that begins with the enigma of a "costard" broken in a "shin" also turns out by its end to hint at a "purgation," "egma," or another kind of *envoi*, sending forth or enfranchising in a different sense. The sense in "enfranchising" of letting loose what was "immured" (3.1.124) or letting "out" what was held "within" (3.1.116) enables the bodily, scatological overtones at the end of this exchange. And, since "l'envoy" also meant dramatic end or catastrophe,[43] this scene in the midst of *Love's Labor's Lost* not only looks back to the original "continent" enclosure or immurement of the all-male "academe" Armado is about to breach, but forward to the latter end of the play itself, which involves not only envoys and sequels but another kind of breaching.[44]

The exchange on "envoy" and "salve" featuring lower-caste characters in Act 3 and the Eavesdropping Scene in Act 4 that exposes those higher up are explicitly connected when at the end of the latter Berowne is asked to find some "salve for perjury" ("*Longaville*. O, some authority how to proceed; / Some tricks, some quillets, how to cheat the devil. / *Dumaine*. Some salve for perjury," 4.3.283–285). In the lengthy justification that his famous exonerating speech constructs for the aristocrats' complete turnabout or volte-face to the "opposed end" of their original "intents" (5.2.758), what might from one perspective appear an offense is cleverly converted or turned into its opposite, and forswearing or perjury is reversed into what is claimed as a new kind of fidelity (4.3.287–362). When all of the King's men have (like the lowly Costard) been finally exposed, Berowne responds to their need for this saving "salve" (4.3.285) by the speech in which he sets out to prove that what they "first did swear unto" (287) should now be put behind, as they embrace the new "authority" and "books" of "women's eyes" (347). And this rhetorical about-face begets a whole series of reversals:

> For wisdom's sake, a word that all men love,
> Or for love's sake, a word that loves all men,
> Or for men's sake, the authors of these women,
> Or women's sake, by whom we men are men,
> Let us once lose our oaths to find ourselves,
> Or else we lose ourselves to keep our oaths. (4.3.354–359)

The echoes of a New Testamental language in Berowne's rhetorical "turn" or tour de force is the pivot on which the play itself turns—away from the initial "continent canon" of the Platonic "academe" and oath to a new vow to "woo these girls of France" (4.3.368). And the simultaneous recalls of the reversals and "salve" of the "envoy" scene are strengthened here by Berowne's "Light wenches may prove plagues to men forsworn" (4.3.382), when what is offered as a "salve for perjury" prompts remembrance of the "plagues" proverbially associated both with incontinence and with "girls of France," the danger that any who follow them may need another kind of "salve."[45]

> Thou hast mistaken his letter.
>
> —*Love's Labor's Lost* (4.1.106)

> he teaches boys the horn-book.
> What is *a, b,* spell'd backward, with the horn on his head?
>
> —*Love's Labor's Lost* (5.1.46–48)

Play on such "preposterous" reversal—of "opposed end" to initial intent, of back to front, after for before, latter end for beginning—is indeed so insistent in this play as often to appear to be repeated purely for this emphasis. In Act 3, for example, just after the wordplay on "l'envoy," there is the curious exchange in which Costard promises to appear "tomorrow morning" to receive instructions for a task he is to perform "this afternoon," swearing that he will know what to do only *after* he has done it, in opposition to Berowne's insistence that he must know "first" or before:

> *Costard.* When would you have it done, sir?
> *Berowne.* O, this afternoon.
> *Costard.* Well, I will do it, sir; fare you well.
> *Berowne.* O, thou knowest not what it is.
> *Costard.* I shall know, sir, when I have done it.
> *Berowne.* Why, villain, thou must know first.
> *Costard.* I will come to your worship to-morrow morning.
> *Berowne.* It must be done this afternoon.
>
> (3.1.154–161)

Here again, this sustained play on what comes *before* and what *after*, and their reversal, may seem simply gratuitous or only for the comedy of its apparent confusions. But it is important to attend not only to the hierarchical position of the interlocutors here but also to what subsequently follows. Berowne's commissioning of Costard is the second attempt (after Armado's) to enlist him as an envoy, "embassador" (3.1.52), instrument, or messenger. And when Costard first puzzles over the meaning of "remuneration" (the term Armado employs when he commissions him) and learns that it is less than the "guerdon" or "gardon" (3.1.169–173) Berowne can pay for a similar service, what he engages in is not abstract speculation over the relation of *verba* and *res* but a question with much more practical (and material) at stake: ("*Berowne*. . . . There's thy guerdon; go. / *Costard*. Gardon, O sweet gardon! better than remuneration, eleven-pence-farthing better," 3.1.169–171).[46] But in Costard's role as a carrier of letters for both of his social superiors—Armado and Berowne—each is subverted as the letters themselves are misdirected and crossed, either deliberately or as a result of his illiteracy or "unletter'd" status. The letter from Berowne to the "snow-white hand of the most beauteous Lady Rosaline" (4.2.132–133)—the one he thinks he delivers *first* (4.1.41–59)—is in fact exchanged or "mistook" (4.1.57), passing through the baser hand of Jaquenetta before it returns to its sender, embarrassingly, at the end of the Eavesdropping Scene (4.3.191). The emphasis in such crossing is not just on the "great feast of languages" (5.1.36) or antithetical verbal turns for their own sake but on social relations of precedence and priority, in a crossing in which the subordination of "low" to the socially higher or "high" that seeks to "employ" it (3.1.151) as messenger or envoy is subverted by a "misprision" in which the letters are "mistaken" (4.1.106) in every sense.

Letters themselves form a nexus in the plot in several senses—as the letters of the alphabet that can be reversed (in scenes that make much of the distinction between "book-men" and lowly "unlettered"); as the acquisition of literacy that supposedly separates the "Arts-man" from the "barbarous" (5.1.81–82); as the letter of the law (or formal legal proceeding); and as "post" or mail. The sense of letters as "post" or epistles includes the letter from Armado that accuses Costard in Act 1; the letter from Longaville described as "too long by half a mile" (5.2.54); the missive sent by Armado to Jaquenetta and Berowne's letter to Rosaline, which Costard promises to deliver "in print" (3.1.172)—a phrase that means "exactly" or "to the letter"—but which in fact is "miscarried" or misdirected, just as alphabetical letters are elsewhere in the play. References to literacy and the "letter(ed)" include the early description of Costard as "unlettered" (1.1.250), Armado's query to Holofernes ("Monsieur, are you not lett'red?," 5.1.45), the alliterative style of Holofernes's "affect the letter" (4.2.54) in the bawdy exchange on "sore L" and "pricket" in Act 4 (4.2.53–61), and the wordplay on letters in the banter of Rosaline and Katherine in Act 5 ("Fair as a text B in a copy-book. . . . My red dominical, my golden letter: / O that your face were not so full of O's!," 5.2.42, 44–45).[47] Letters as the alterers of meaning as of words are repeatedly foregrounded in this play, in its reminders of the instability of orthographic variants (5.1.19–25), sign of an only recently emergent literacy, where the varying of a single letter can transform meaning as well as form—not only varying "det" to "debt," "dout" to "doubt," or "abbominable" to "abhominable" (5.1.20–25) but enabling a slipperiness of homophonic play that is less the more modern form of punning (joining what was already discrete or separate) than the multiple possibilities for "misprision" or "miscarrying" when clear separation and standardization had not yet occurred.[48]

It is this comedy's repeated play on "post," however, that forges connections between the importance within it of letters—in all of these senses—and the reversal of "post" and "pre," "posterior" and front, introduced by the "prepost'rous event" at its beginning. The "post" shared with "pre*post*erous" is harped on relentlessly as the play proceeds—in the reference to the game of "post and pair" in the scene where the women one-up the men (5.2.67) and in the wordplay on "post" or letters that form so much of the criss-crossing between main plot and subplot, "high" and "low."[49] When Berowne's letter to Rosaline finally returns to its sender, overtaking him from behind at the end of the elaborately self-reversing Eavesdropping Scene, a single phrase calls attention to all that is brought together by this "post"—as "mail," as posting or speeding, and as coming *after*—when he attempts unsuccessfully to "*post* from love" (4.3.186).

The play on "post"—and the reversal of before and after—unleashed in the original "prepost'rous event" also pervades this comedy's emphasis on letters in the alphabetical sense. To be "lettered" is to be "singuled" or separated from the "barbarous" (5.1.81–82), in the hierarchy defended by the social-climbing "book men" in Act 5 and the disparaging of Costard as an "unlettered small-knowing soul" (1.1.250) when he first appears. But the iteration of this distinction in Act 5, in a scene that involves these "Arts-men," also comes in an exchange where letters themselves are "spell'd backward" (5.1.47) or preposterously reversed:

*Armado.* [*To Holofernes*] Monsieur, are you not lett'red?
*Moth.* Yes, yes, he teaches boys the horn-book.
What is *a, b,* spell'd backward, with the horn on his head?
*Holofernes.* *Ba, pueritia,* with a horn added.
*Moth.* *Ba,* most silly sheep, with a horn. You hear his learning.
*Holofernes.* *Quis, quis,* thou consonant?
*Moth.* The last of the five vowels, if "you" repeat them; or the fift, if I.
*Holofernes.* I will repeat them—*a, e, I*—
*Moth.* The sheep: the other two concludes it—*o, U.*
(5.1.44–57)

The "preposterous" reversal that turns "ab" into "ba" for sheep (in the context of allusions here to both the "horn-book" and the cuckold's "horn") recalls, in its "sheep," the scene of Costard's arrest for that "most prepost'rous event," following a woman referred to there, in the familiar slang, as "mutton" (1.1.302), as well as the "sheep" associated with instruction in literacy and the alphabet.[50] But it also introduces at the level of the "letter" the possibility of a volte-face of ordering or sequence, something turned "backward" or reversed (including in a bodily sense), in an exchange involving Holofernes the schoolmaster, whose services to the "commonwealth" were earlier described in lines whose inferences are decidedly sexual ("their sons are well tutor'd by you, and their daughters profit very greatly under you," 4.2.74–76), including with regard to the contemporary pederastic sense of "tutoring."

Jeffrey Masten, in *Queer Philologies,* has importantly added to earlier work on the combination of tutoring with the pederastic in these lines on the "horn-book" and "*a, b,* spell'd backward" the telling example of William Hornbye's *Hornbook*—or *Hornbyes Hornbook* (1622)—which combined teaching boys the hornbook or ABC with the schoolmaster's beating of boys' buttocks or "bare-bumbs" (sig. C1) studied by Alan Stewart and others.[51] And he notes in this text's reference to learning "the *Horn-booke* backward" (sig. C2v) "the correlation of discourses of alphabetical backwardness (for the married man as well as for the backward student boy) with sodomitical scenes (whether this is extramarital sex for men, or the hint of bare-bumb pederasty for the boy, linked in curious sequitur)," in a *Hornbook* whose title page shows the schoolmaster positioned "behind and around the boy," in a "resignification from hetero-reproductive to same-sexual (pedagogical reproduction)."[52]

Both spelling backwards and "post" in the sense of that which follows or comes preposterously "behind," moreover, are part of a play where the new disciplines of literacy and humanist pedagogy are part of the attempt to separate "high" from "low" in social terms, but where slippages of sound repeatedly undermine such distinctions. "Arts-man, preambulate, we will be singuled from the barbarous" (5.1.81–82) counsels the social-climbing Armado to Holofernes, the "arts-man," as they proceed to walk ahead of the others. But the speech itself calls attention to the frequently exploited closeness in sound of "arts" and "arse," and hence deflates the attempt to distinguish such "bookmen" from the "lowly asses" or *barbaroi* they pour contempt upon.[53] "Ass" is both a class word and a distinctly bodily reminder of the arsy-versy. And the play throughout this comedy on the "arsy-versy" or "preposterous"—turning back to front, behind to before—here literally informs the summoning of the familiar contemporary association of *ars* and *arse* (exploited in the use of "preposterous ass" for another "arts-man" in the Latin lesson of *The Taming of the Shrew*, foregrounded in the next chapter), as Armado issues the invitation to an "Arse-man" to "pre-ambulate" or go *before*.

Both the aristocratic men's about-face to the "opposed end" of their original "intents" and the earlier wordplay on an *envoi*, after-word, or postscript preposterously confused with a "salve" or beginning are reflected in the increasingly bodily reminders of the arsy-versy ("posterior" as well as "post") as the play proceeds from its initial "prepost'rous event" to its own unconventional latter end.

*Love's Labor's Lost* is not only filled with reminders of bodily functions and body parts (including "costard" or head broken in a "shin," and the "foot" of Jaquenetta, the "base" matter whose very name suggests close-stool or "jakes").[54] Its bodily emphasis is itself inseparable from its deflations of classical or learned *auctoritas*—as when the authority of "Horace," for instance, is heard as "Whore-Ass" in Act 4, in ways that remind us of the sounding elsewhere of "Ciceronianus," "Midas," or "Coriolanus" with scatological emphasis on their "latter end."[55] And the body so insistently foregrounded in this play is at the same time assimilated to dramatic structure, in the frustrating of comedy's traditionally consummating or phallic "point," underscored in Berowne's complaint that "Our wooing doth not *end* like an old play" (5.2.874),[56] to which we will return.

Even apparently throwaway lines keep body parts and latter ends continually in view, as they are also in the references to "Ovid the Nose" ("Ovidius Naso was the man. And why indeed 'Naso,' but for smelling out the odiferous flowers of fancy," 4.2.123–125) or Priscian's head ("Priscian a little scratch'd," 5.1.28–29). Act 5 begins with the book-men, the "abhominable" Armado (5.1.24), and the diminutive "Moth," whose polyvalent name evokes not only "mot" or "word" and "mote" as contrasted with "beam" (4.3.159–160), but the more earth-bound, material, and bodily—simultaneously "mound," "clod" or "turfe of earth," a "butt to shoot at," and the "gryne" or "groin."[57] It then proceeds to yet more reminders of the body's opposed ends, in lines that recall the digestive metaphorics of humanist *digestio* from the scorning of the illiterate "Dull" in an earlier scene ("*Nathaniel.* Sir, he hath never fed of the dainties that are bred in a book; / He hath not eat paper, as it were; he hath not drunk ink," 4.2.24–26) and the "taste" of "arts-men" in whom such matters "fructify" (4.2.29).[58] The sense of "fructifying" in this bodily metaphorics of consuming and digesting is joined by Moth's famous reference to the "scraps" of language which these book-men have only imperfectly digested ("They have been at a great feast of languages, and stol'n the scraps," 5.1.37), a "scraps" that joins the "orts" or scraps of orthography spelled as "ortagriphie" in both Quarto and Folio.[59] And Costard addresses the diminutive Moth or "Mot" as an *edible* word, ironically the longest and most difficult to spell ("*Costard.* O, they have liv'd long on the alms-basket of words. I marvel thy master hath not eaten thee for a word, for thou art not so long by the head as *honorificabilitudinitatibus*: thou art easier swallow'd than a flap-dragon," 5.1.38–42).

∽

> The posteriors of this day, which the rude multitude call the afternoon.
>
> —*Love's Labor's Lost* (5.1.89–90)

> For the ass to the Jude; give it him. Jud-as, away!
>
> —*Love's Labor's Lost* (5.2.628)

> Our wooing doth not end like an old play:
> Jack hath not Gill. These ladies' courtesy
> Might well have made our sport a comedy. . . .
>
> —*Love's Labor's Lost* (5.2.874–876)

Most strikingly, however, in the first scene of Act 5 (the scene that includes the spelling "backward" or inversion of alphabetical letters), the exchange extending from "Are you not lett'red?" to Armado's "Arts-man, preambulate" leads into an extraordinary series of double entendres on the "posterior," beginning with Armado's reference to a "show" to be presented before the Princess in "the posteriors of this day, which the rude multitude call the afternoon" (5.1.89–90). Holofernes repeats "posterior of the day" (5.1.91) and (with a play on *cul*) pronounces the phrase to be "well cull'd" (5.1.93): "The posterior of the day . . . is liable, congruent, and measurable for the afternoon. The word is well *cull'd*, chose, sweet and apt, I do *ass*ure you, sir, I do *ass*ure" (5.1.91–94). Armado continues, suggesting that they let "pass" what is "inward" ("I do *ass*ure ye, very good friend; for what is *inward* between us, let it *pass*," 5.1.96–97) and assist him to the "end" he requests. The refrain of "passing" in Armado's speech ("let that pass . . . let that pass," 5.1.101–105) is reiterated as he alludes to his intimacy with the King in lines notorious for their double-meaning "excrement" ("it will please his Grace . . . sometime to lean upon my poor shoulder, and with his royal finger, thus, dally with my excrement," glossed only belatedly as "my mustachio," 5.1.101–104), before he ends with talk of "eruptions and sudden breaking out of mirth" (5.1.114–115). Costard earlier in this scene confuses Latin *ad unguem* with "*ad dunghill*" for "at the fingers' ends" (5.1.77–78), in lines that prompt Holofernes's smelling of "false Latin" (5.1.79). And Holofernes again refers to the Pageant of Worthies as the "show" that is to be presented in "the posterior of this day" (5.1.119–122)—a show in which the lowly Costard "shall pass" (a famously puzzling phrase) the figure of Pompey the Great (5.1.128).[60] After the iterations of the "post" in its various senses throughout this play, the bodily sense of *posterus* in the opening act's "obscene and most prepost'rous event" returns, then, in Act 5, in the book-men's pretentious (or high) but finally scatological (or low) "posterior of this day" (5.1.119), in a passage packed with "arsy-versy" double entendres, justifiably translated into the stage gesture of a series of lower bodily emissions, a down-wind passing before which Nathaniel (with all the references to "smelling") might well be directed to hold his nose. The entire passage recalls the scene of wordplay in Act 3, with its reversal of prior and posterior, "l'envoy" and "salve," its "immured, restrained, captivated, bound," and its enfranchising "egma" or enema, and "purgation," even as it anticipates the "latter end" (5.2.627) and "passing" of the play itself.

In scenes such as this in *Love's Labor's Lost*, the bodily reference and scatology implicit within the "preposterous" as the "arse-varse" emerges unmistakably—not just reversing "posterior" for prior or front but revealing the bodily, "barbarous," or low within the apparently elevated or "high," even as the importance of "singulating" is most insisted on, in social (as well as linguistic) terms. And at such moments, the vernacular theatrical tradition—with its preoccupation with bodily orifices and emissions—erupts into the more academic or highbrow theater associated with "book-men" and "book-mates" (4.1.98).[61] But what is remarkable is that it was precisely such "singulation" that succeeded in establishing a decorum for much earlier criticism, in which it is difficult to ascertain even the existence of such excremental-scatological wordplay in *Love's Labor's Lost.*

The event presented in the "posterior of this day," or afternoon, is the Pageant of the Worthies to be played "before the Princess" (5.1.122) at the latter end of the comedy itself. It is here that the "posterior" sense of the preposterous or "arsy-versy" is even more insistently underscored, including in the reference to a "close-stool" that follows "Alisander the Conqueror" with Ajax or "A-jakes" (5.2.575–578), as in Sir John Harington's *Metamorphosis of Ajax* (1596) on the invention of the privy. But it also becomes part of a scapegoating in the scatological exchange that accompanies Holofernes's "Judas," the figure the aristocratic men seek to "out-face" or put "out of countenance" (5.2.607–623) by their ridicule:

*Boyet.* And so adieu, sweet Jude! Nay, why dost thou stay?
*Dumaine.* For the latter end of his name.
*Berowne.* For the ass to the Jude; give it him. Jud-as, away!
(5.2.626–628)

The exchange accompanying Holofernes's appearance as the pageant's "Judas" is relentless in its double entendres on the posterior, as it is on what comes after or behind—from the querying of what follows or comes after his first name (Iscariot or Maccabeus), to the equivoques on the traditional priority of the "elder" ("*Begin*, sir, you are my *elder*. / Well *follow'd*: Judas was hang'd on an *elder*," 5.2.605–606), in lines that invoke the proverbially stinking "elder" tree associated elsewhere in Shakespeare with scatological play on the "reverence" (or *faeces*) associated with "elders."[62] The lines also suggest a literal, and bodily, reversal of front and back in the interlingual wordplay that crosses English "face" with French buttocks or *fesses*, in the exchanges on the "face" of an "ass" (5.2.625), on "cheek" and "half-cheek in a brooch" (5.2.616), and on whether the "out-fac'd" actor can go "forward" once he has been put back "in countenance" (5.2.619–623).[63] And finally, the end of this exchange comes to the harping on the "latter end of his name" (5.2.627), producing "Judas" by adding an "ass" to "Jude" (5.2.628), rendering explicit the play on the "posterior" or "latter end" throughout and calling attention to the intrusion of the low vernacular into the "worthy" already lurking within the sound of "Horace" as "Whore-ass" in the scene of the "book-men" in Act 4 (4.2.102).

The pageant in Act 5 not only features this sustained "arsy-versy" play, culminating in an "ass" that comes at a "latter end," but underscores the embodiment of such obscene or lower-bodily references in the appearance of "Pompey the Great," the "Big," the "Huge" (5.2.550–557)—a simultaneous exaggeration and deflation that anticipates Alexander the Great or "Big" mispronounced in the Welshman's vernacular as "Alexander the Pig" in *Henry V* or the references to "Pompey Bum" in *Measure for Measure*, a play that also prominently features body parts.[64] "Greater than great, great, great, great Pompey! Pompey the Huge!" (5.2.685–686) is played or "parfected" in the pageant ("I am . . . to parfect one man in one poor man, Pompion the Great," 5.2.501–502) by none other than the "base" or lowly Costard himself, and the references to his "great limb or joint" (5.1.128) would justify his appearance on stage, as he enters to "stand for" (5.2.507) this "great," with the huge codpiece of vernacular stage plays and interludes.[65] The diminutive Moth (or "mote") appears as the "Great Hercules," in a disproportion so marked that it requires an "apology" that asks the audience to imagine Hercules in his infancy (5.2.588–594). The pageant as a whole, then, from the perspective of the aristocratic "great" or "magnificent," exposes lowly "asses" to their ridicule, as untutored actors unable to figure (so instead, as Peter Quince puts it, "disfigure") the exalted or "Worthy." In class terms, the insistent scatology of this Pageant Scene might appear to perform the same mockery on these unlettered players as that visited by a similar onstage aristocratic audience on artisan actors led by "Bottom" the "ass" in *A Midsummer Night's Dream*. But the perspective provided by Holofernes's plaintive "This is not generous, not gentle, not humble" (5.2.629) also enables us to see the supposed aristocratic "worthies" themselves as it were from underneath, from the perspective of the "asses" their mockery seeks to "singule" or distinguish them from, at the same time as the exalted biblical and classical "Worthies" of the pageant (including "Pompey the Huge") are deflated on stage by a performance that disfigures even as it "stands for," "passes," or represents, in the process making greatness "familiar."[66]

Act 5 also features the bringing down or deflating of the inflated Don Armado to the service both of the plow and of that "base wench" who had been the object or "low matter" of the play's initial "prepost'rous event." Armado speaks with the voice of class shame when—at the mention of the pregnant Jaquenetta, the "weaker vessel" he had stooped to conquer and who has conquered him—he accuses Costard of trying to "infamonize" him "among potentates" (5.2.678).[67] But there is also a sense of something more at work than simply the satiric or comic when this figure too (revealing that he possesses "no shirt," 5.2.710) proclaims that he has "seen the day of wrong through the little hole of discretion" (5.2.723–724) and announces that he has "vow'd to Jaquenetta to hold the plough for her sweet love three year" (5.2.883–884).

There is, finally, at this play's own "latter end," the abrupt entrance that breaks into and breaks off the expected conclusion of a comedy. In the midst of the pageant that includes reference both to "Jude-ass" and to the "giant limb" of "Pompey the Huge," Marcade enters as another "envoy" or "embassador" and delivers a different kind of "l'envoy"—the "tale" of death ("my tale is told," 5.2.720) that prompts the Ladies' "farewell," a message whose abruptness and finality paradoxically open up the play to an utterly different kind of sequel than the men expect. If the wordplay on a "Jude-ass" who is both "ycliped" and "clipt" (5.2.598–599) introduces the threat of cutting something short, this envoy's abrupt entrance also suddenly abbreviates or cuts short, a fact to which the exchange between the Princess and the King calls explicit attention (5.2.740–743). The harping throughout the play on what should come *after* and what first or *before* continues even in this end. The King begs the Princess to remember, in spite of this envoy's intrusion, that "loves argument" was "*first* on foot" and came *before* the "cloud of sorrow" that now appears as sad sequel to their merriment (5.2.747–748). And he argues for setting joy at "friends . . . newly found" *before* grief at "friends lost" or past (5.2.749–751). But though the Ladies are entreated at what is called not only "the latest minute of the hour" (5.2.787) but the "*extreme parts* of time" (5.2.740) to enable the play to "end" in the traditional consummation of comedy and Berowne complains that "Our wooing doth not end like an old play: / Jack hath not Gill" (5.2.874–875), the aristocratic men are forced instead to agree to an aftermath or sequel ("too long for a play," 878) that, like Jaquenetta's pregnancy, outlasts both this comedy's onstage end and another traditionally final consummating "point." If comedy's expected "catastrophe" (in the simultaneously Greek sense of an overturning or sudden turn as well as conclusion) is a "nuptial"—as Armado had reminded the audience earlier (4.1.77)—there is no "nuptial" at this end.[68] This generically unconventional open-endedness disrupts the expected comedic ending of the play itself and frustrates what the men had counted on as the "consummation devoutly to be wished" anticipated as their comic due. It involves, as one critic remarks, not only "a breach of theatrical promise" but a breaching of generic coherence—disrupting the conventional closure and enclosures of the classically well-made play.[69] And at the same time, as Lorna Hutson has observed, this nontraditional ending demonstrates "Shakespeare's brilliant inversion of the conventional use, in the classic catastrophe or dénouement of learned comedy, of a 'romantic' discovery of paternity," as the "truth of paternity" in the question of "who is the father of Jaquenetta's baby" remains unresolved, leaving the issue of evidence introduced in the legal language of the opening scene uncertain.[70]

This early Shakespearean comedy, then, comments explicitly on *dramatic* latter ends and the frustration of expected discoveries or resolutions even as it reaches what in the exchange on "Jud-ass" is termed a "latter end"—the phrase also used by "Bottom" in *A Midsummer Night's Dream* for the end of a play (4.1.217). Its final lines include lofty reminders of the gods (Apollo and Mercury). But it also ends after an event held in "the posterior" of the "day," and in ways that recall not just the exchange on "l'envoy" and "embassador" from Act 3 but the bodily play on "passing" in the scene of the arts (or *ars*)-men in Act 5. As earlier noted, "l'envoy"—as an "end"—was used in the period for a dramatic conclusion or "catastrophe." But "catastrophe" itself also appears elsewhere in Shakespeare in the contemporary slang sense of the bodily backside or posterior (*2 Henry IV* 2.1.60).[71] It may indeed then be appropriate to recall, at this play's own "latter end," the simultaneously bodily and structural variation on ends in the scene of the "enigma" or "egma" that produced the earlier "sequel" and "envoy" of Act 3, or the "enfranchisement" from "immured" containment (3.1.71–125) associated there both with "purgation" (3.1.126) and with the breaching of the continence and enclosures of the all-male "academe." For when in Act 5 Marcade, another "envoy," breaks into this comedy with the uncomic news of the "catastrophe" of death, and hence the tragic note of another kind of passing or enfranchisement, there is "catastrophe" in its other sense of "overturning," and an opening out onto more than comedy can contain.

The other traditional bodily metaphor for dramatic structure is catharsis, or literally a "purging," the Greek term translated into Latin as *purgatio*.

"Catharsis" in the dramatic sense is thus analogous to the bodily, even medical, activity of purging, in ways important to keep in mind when we consider the centrality of images of purging, purgatives, and purgation in *Love's Labor's Lost*, where the penance enjoined on these same young men as a sequel to its onstage end is a form of purgatorial or purgative cleansing—in Berowne's case associated directly with the ailing or "sick."[72] Purging, decay, and death, or final "passing," provide, in the period contemporary with the play, figures (along with women) for what looses or causes breaches in the "continence" and enclosure of the classical male body, in contrast to the "faulty" female one. Louis Montrose notes of this ending's breached enclosure, that "the ladies . . . perform a purgative function in the humorous world of Navarre."[73] Kathryn Moncrief observes that this deferred ending is also part of the "surprising gender reversal" in which women teach men in this play, since it is crucial to the aristocratic men's purgation as well as their maturation.[74]

Anticipating a sequel that will entail instead a new beginning, *Love's Labor's Lost*'s more provisional onstage ending announces the players' departure as Armado introduces something that "should have *followed* in the *end* of our show" (888). The first of the songs offered at its provisional close raises yet again the specter of another kind of female breaching—cuckoldry as the "word of fear" (5.2.901) that has been an undertone of all the play's references to "horns," "horn-books" and the dangers of associating with the "sign of she." And, after the songs, the interrupted play takes its leave with reference to Mercury, yet another "envoy" or "embassador" ("The words of Mercury are harsh after the songs of Apollo. You that way; we this way. [*Exeunt omnes*]). The comic ending of this early Shakespearean comedy is interrupted, then, by the arrival of the ambassador called "Marcade"—an "envoy" whose very name is linked with Mercury—and the play we have ends, as with the earlier scene of wordplay on "envoy" and "embassador" (3.1.52), in anticipation of what Moth there calls a "sequel" (3.1.134).[75] If the usual comic end or "catastrophe" is a "nuptial," what this play does is to open out rather than continently close off or contain. Adding a sequel "too long for a play," it ends with yet more emphasis on what follows or comes *after*, as its own epilogue or after-word is formed from the final motto or Mot ("The words of Mercury are harsh *after* the songs of Apollo," 5.2.930–931) that becomes the play's own enigmatic *envoi*, send-off, or farewell.

ᔓ

> *The Ladies turn their backs to him.*
>
> —*Love's Labor's Lost* (5.2.160 stage direction)

> Disguis'd like Muscovites.
>
> —*Love's Labor's Lost* (5.2.303)

> To do as the Sodomites did, use preposterous lusts in preposterous habits.
>
> —Thomas Heywood, *An Apology for Actors* (1612)

What, then, is at stake in all of this "preposterous" or "arsy-versy" play—on after and before, posterior and prior, back and front, an *envoi* or latter end anticipating a new beginning—that literally pervades this early Shakespearean play, not just at the level of the letter, or verbal turn, but in the structuring of stage gestures and entire scenes? And what is at stake in the repeated reduction of the decorous, elevated, or high to the "base," bodily, and low in a play that in the past had the reputation of being formal, stilted, and academic, concerned with "mere" rhetoric and "mere" words? It should be clear, first of all, from the class and gender implications of its antithetical turns and pointed repartee that a criticism that separates the linguistic or rhetorical from the bodily or "obscene"—or discursive structures from social ones—depends on historically anachronistic assumptions; and that what filtered an earlier era's perceptions of *Love's Labor's Lost* suggests the triumph of the very decorum (and "singulation" from the "barbarous") that is pilloried in this play, yielding readings in which its unmistakable bodily and scatological wordplay went either unnoticed or discreetly unmentioned.

In relation to this play's "preposterous" overturning of hierarchy and reversals of gender, it is important to stress that the body itself is cast in the plot in evocatively class and gender terms. In the opening scene of Navarre's "continent canon" and the all-male oath, Dumaine's "My loving lord, Dumaine is mortified: / The grosser manner of these world's delights / He throws upon the gross world's baser slaves" (1.1.28–30) introduces the mind-body hierarchy of high and low in which it is only "baser slaves" who embody enslavement to the "flesh," and trafficking with women is part of the "low matter" of this baser impulse. Dumaine's deprecatory class sneer is joined later in the play by reminders of class difference, in Berowne's "Some men must love my lady [i.e., a gentlewoman], and some Joan" (3.1.205)—the stock name for a peasant "wench," echoed in the "greasy Joan" of the final song

(5.2.929)—and the social-climbing Armado's "I am ill at reck'ning, it fitteth the spirit of a tapster" (1.2.40–41), reflecting the contemporary association of reckoning (or arithmetic) with the lower (or commercial) orders, in a play ironically filled with reckoning and calculation (including by the aristocratic men).[76]

As the play proceeds, however, as we have seen, the initial "prepost'rous event" for which the "base" Costard is imprisoned becomes the "president" or precedent for the series of defections to the "flesh" on the part of his social betters. The "obscene and most prepost'rous event" that stands at the opening of this comedy as the "head" or first of an entire series becomes, then, the emblem of its preposterous reversals of "high" and "low" in the body politic as well. Similarly, when in Act 4 of the play, Constable Dull confuses the high-flown Latin of Holofernes's *haud credo* with the like-sounding "old grey doe" of his lowlier vernacular or mother tongue and objects that the victim of the hunt was emphatically not a doe but a "pricket" (4.2.11–12), the emphasis is not so much on the "monster Ignorance" that Holofernes hastens to decry, or on sympathy for the learning it has thus "deformed" (4.2.23), as it is on the pretensions of the social-climbing "book-men" (4.2.34) and their imitative "following" of humanist discipline, just as it is on the "little academe" (1.1.13) of aristocratic "book-mates" (4.1.98). This comedy's multiple forms of mis-taking the word (*The Two Gentlemen of Verona* 3.1.284)—including the misprision and mistaking associated with the illiterate or "barbarous"—are closer to the continual verbal misprision that animates the play itself. Its parody-humanists stand exposed in their own deformations of learning when the "book-man" Holofernes sings the scale in the wrong order or out of turn (4.2.100). And the reduction of the *artes* to their bodily counterparts does not so much authorize a "high" or mocking reading of the "low" (a version of the "over-view" Berowne claims to have in the Eavesdropping Scene, before he too is brought low) as it exposes, by the very insistence on the bodily, the undoing of high "manner" or "stile" by lowly matters of all kinds.

Focusing on this play's initial "prepost'rous event" and its reflection in the (verbal and bodily) turns and "arsy-versy" reversals of "proper" ordering that fill it—together with its emphasis on latter ends of all kinds—makes it possible not only to become aware of more of this play's extraordinary verbal and rhetorical texture but to apprehend its relation to a range of different contemporary contexts, including gender and hierarchical position. For its sustained exploitation of the compound senses of the "preposterous" furnishes an important instance of a structure, and implications, that were to recur throughout the Shakespeare canon. And it provides an early Shakespearean example of the link of the apparently only verbal, logical, or rhetorical with the body (and body politic) in ways that enable reexamination of this canon in relation to the newly emergent (and soon to be dominant) disciplines of the new humanist elites, their production of a decorum of "singulating" or separating that was to become part of the attempt to eliminate "barbarisms" of all kinds.[77] To explore the Shakespearean resonances of the "preposterous," then, is to engage in a reconsideration of wordplay and structural play not simply for formal reasons (though historically informed close readings help counter a critical tradition shaped by this decorum) but for reasons that situate the play within that broader history.

There is even more, however, to be said about this play's exploitation of the arsy-versy or "preposterous," as it approaches its own latter end, including in relation to transvestite theater and "preposterous venery" (across the homo/hetero divide).[78] Preposterous reversal of "back" for "front" is enacted graphically on stage in Act 5 when Berowne's attempt to turn the men's "offence" into its saving reverse, or put a good face on their about-face, is rebuffed by the Princess and her entourage, who literally turn their "backs" to Moth when he reads the men's speech in praise of their "eyes" (5.2.161–162). Whether or not there are subtle reminders here of the familiar posterior or lower-bodily sense of "eyes" as what Chaucer, for example, called the "nether eye" (in a play where the "Ladies" themselves speak more bawdily than in any other Shakespearean play), the stage gesture of the Ladies as they literally turn back to front, presenting their "backs" to the young men's messenger, does abruptly divert the object (and subject) of his Petrarchan petition.[79] Moth is forced to change the referent of his speech from "eyes" to "backs" (5.2.160–161), when their bodily about-face necessitates a hasty emendation of his prepared address ("*Moth.* 'A holy parcel of the fairest dames [*The Ladies turn their backs to him.*] / That ever turn'd their—backs—to mortal views!' ")—prompting Berowne's anxious "Their 'eyes,' villain, their 'eyes' " (5.2.160–162). Though this turning is staged in the register of the aristocratic or "high"—rather than the "base" or social-climbing, as in the exchange with the "arts (or *ars*)-men" just before—what these "fairest dames" actually perform is the very reversal of "back" for "front" that the language of the bodily preposterous has harped on throughout. And this turnabout occurs in an exchange that simultaneously call attention to the hierarchy of gender, as Boyet counsels Moth to substitute "daughter-beamed eyes" for the "sun-beamed eyes" of his original address (5.2.169–172).

The Ladies, moreover, counter the men's volte-face or "changing" of their first intent (5.2.137) by the Princess's plan to "cross" their new intent (5.2.138), by having each lady "turn away her face" (5.2.148) and forcing each man to "Woo contrary" (5.2.135) to his intended aim, in the scene of the masquerade in which the Ladies are masked and the men, disguised as Muscovites, act out the fickleness that (in the Quarto text) had earlier characterized their relation to the "sign of she."[80] This crossing continues—in a final scene that seems a virtual enactment of the repeated wordplay on the name of "Longaville" for its length—when, having turned these "Muscovites" away, the Ladies follow Rosaline's advice to "mock them still," by wondering to the men's faces who these ridiculous Muscovites "were, and to what *end*" their "shallow shows" (5.2.304–305). And it is repeated in the reminders of the "prepost'rous event" of Costard's "following . . . a daughter of our grandmother Eve" in the "parleying" in which it is now "Adam"—or the men—who come to tempt "Eve" (5.2.322) to break a vow, in a scene in which even Berowne confesses that his "wit" is "at an *end*" (5.2.429). But this scene involving "Muscovites" in which the Ladies' backs are turned also suggests the other sense of "preposterous" as "preposterous venery," including the "sodomy" with which "Muscovites" or Russians were identified in the period.[81]

As already noted in the Introduction, the "preposterous" in the sense of the sexually "arsy-versy" (both "hetero" and "homo") appears frequently in early modern texts—in Florio's reference to "unnatural and preposterous loves" when "more by custome than by nature . . . men [do] meddle and abuse themselves with men," in Jonson's *Every Man in his Humour* ("for a more instance of their preposterous natures. . . . They have assaulted me . . . as I have walked alone in divers skirts i'the town"), and in the sexual "back door" or "posterne door" evoked in the "back-door'd Italian" of Middleton and Dekker's *1 Honest Whore* and the remark in Middleton's *Michaelmas Term* that it is "such an Italian world, many men know not before from behind,"[82] in a context that Celia R. Daileader has characterized as "gynosodomy."[83] It also appears in Thersites's invective in *Troilus and Cressida* (5.1.23–24) on Achilles and Patroclus, his "masculine whore," as "preposterous discoveries."[84]

Resonances of the "arsy-versy" in this sense would not be unexpected in a transvestite theater whose use of boys to play female roles was itself denounced in the period as trafficking in "preposterous" inversion.[85] Jaquenetta (the subject of the play's initial "prepost'rous event") was played, after all, not by a "wench" but by a transvestite boy. The Ladies who turn their "backs" to the "Muscovites" were boy players, in a play that repeatedly harps on the "preposterous" reversal of before and after, or behind. And in the wider context of contemporary English transvestite theater, this may be yet another reason why *Love's Labor's Lost* cannot end with the (hetero) consummation of "Jack" and "Gill." *Love's Labor's Lost* not only calls attention to Holofernes's tutoring in a culture where "tutor" had familiar pederastic overtones; it also begins by evoking the all-male circle of a Platonic "academe,"[86] where, with women excluded, the men's pastime is to come instead from the Spanish Armado. Early in the play, when Armado asks, "Who was Sampson's love, my dear Moth?" the answer comes back, "A woman, master" (1.2.76–77), as if that were not the only possible alternative.[87] Armado is himself the play's representative Iberian, a region associated with "preposterous venery" in contemporary projections of "sodomy" as *outside* England, as well as an outsider or "stranger." And, in ways that bring us back to the interrelated issues of boundaries or enclosures, incontinent breaches, and latter ends of all kinds, the "preposterous" (including preposterous venery and the multiple senses of spelling "backward") also have important implications within the wider contemporary contexts of religion and race evoked in this play as well.

∽

*Berowne.* It is religion to be thus forsworn:
For charity itself fulfills the law.

—*Love's Labor's Lost* (4.3.360–361)

*Holofernes.* Not Iscariot, sir.
"Judas I am, ycliped Machabeus."
*Dumaine.* Judas Machabeus clipt is plain Judas.

—*Love's Labor's Lost* (5.2.597–599)

If ye spell Roma backwarde . . . it is preposterous *amor*, a loue out of order or a loue against kynde.

—John Bale, *Englysh Votaryes*

The sinistre rooted persuasion of the Jewes . . .

—Erasmus's commentary on Galatians 3:1

Twenty-first-century criticism of *Love's Labor's Lost* has increasingly attended to its relation to contemporary geopolitical issues, including boundaries and borderlines, incursions of aliens or strangers, and racial as well as other interminglings and mixtures. In ways that parallel Louis Montrose's influential earlier description of the simultaneous marking and breaching of borders or enclosures in *Love's Labor's Lost*, Navarre itself was a permeable borderland or space between, as Elizabeth Pentland has recently argued with regard to the play's "Franco-Spanish setting." As Pentland points out, "Navarre's Franco-Spanish history" has been overlooked by critics who read the setting of this play as "an unambiguously French space" and "ignore the fact that in Shakespeare's day the greater part of the kingdom of Navarre was under Spanish rule—a fact that any informed Elizabethan would certainly have known."[88] And "Navarre's geographical, political, and cultural situation between two major European powers—Spain and France" included not only a "famed 'French' past" but also a well-known "annexation by Spain in 1512," which "Elizabethan writers like William Warner directly linked to the Spanish Armada of 1588," the more recent event the play directly evokes through the name of its Spanish Armado.[89] The Protestant Henry of Navarre (focus of so many topical readings of the play) was displaced and not in Navarre, though he retained that title. And he was strikingly depicted in Christopher Marlowe's *Massacre at Paris* (1593) as the "rightfull Lord and Souerayne" of Spanish-held Navarre who, it was hoped, would soon be crowned at Pamplona, its principal city, said to have been founded by Pompey the Great, the figure who is added to the traditional "Worthies" in *Love's Labor's Lost.*[90]

The play's setting in a Navarre that was itself a borderland or space between is reflected in its names, which are variously French, English, and Spanish—including French-sounding Boyet, Longaville, Berowne, and Dumaine, the English Costard, Nathaniel, and Dull, and not just the Spanish "Armado" but King Ferdinand himself (recalling the name of King Ferdinand II, who annexed Navarre for Castile in 1512, the event so often compared to the Armada). The name "Jaquenetta" evokes the patron saint of Spain in French form, along with the fact that the conquered portion of Navarre in 1512 had been joined to Castile on July 25, the "jour de S. Jacques" or feast day of St. James or Santiago,[91] which Shakespeare renders in French as "Saint Jaques" in *All's Well That Ends Well* (3.5.34, 3.5.95, 4.3.48) and evokes in the Spanish name of "Iago" in *Othello*. "Iaques, Iaques" is the "Spaniards choice" in Thomas Kyd's *Solyman and Perseda*, a few years before *Love's*

*Labor's Lost*. And François de Belleforest's *Grandes Annales* (1579)—a work well known in England—records "la feste de S. Iacques" as the day that "possession of the Kingdom of Navarre" by Castile was proclaimed by the Duke of Alba,[92] yet another way—I would add—that the geopolitics of Spanish-held Navarre were linked to Spanish-held Brabant, where a later Iberian Duke of Alba was so prominent in the English writing discussed in relation to Brabant and *Othello* in Chapter 5.

The hybrid or in-between status of Navarre has its counterpart in the multilingual and hybrid language of *Love's Labor's Lost*, which repeatedly takes advantage of what contemporary English critics decried as the mixed "gallimaufry" of English itself, its "borrowing the words of any foreigne language," or "Mingle-Mangle" of "sundry languages."[93] The "great feast of languages" (5.1.37) in this play is a polyglot "feast," including the Latin "*quis quis*" (5.1.52) potentially heard as English "kiss kiss," "*ad unguem*" as the scatological "*ad dunghill*" (5.1.77–80), "Moth" as French *motte, mot,* or *word* as well as English *Mote,* and multiple other interlingual crossings, including French *bransle* (for a dance), which becomes in English a "French brawl" (3.1.8–10),[94] and Holofernes's Latin "*haud credo*" ("I cannot believe it"), heard on the English ear of Constable Dull as "old gray doe." The disguised false Muscovites of Act 5 recall not only the Muscovy Company but also the use of Russian phrases by Thomas Nashe and others.[95] And in a play where the Princess of Aquitaine has traveled to Navarre to collect on a debt, even French *Aquitaine* may resonate translingually with English *acquit*.

The "*haud credo*/pricket" exchange on various kinds of deer (4.2.54–61) involves a "sore" (or "deer of the fourth year") and "sorel" ("a deer of the third year").[96] But "sorel" (or "sore L," the letter that suggests both the Roman numeral for fifty and a bodily or sexual "corner" or "angle") may also evoke other interlingual connections, including the Italian *sorella* (double-meaning "nun" or sister) that was a familiar byword for a less than "honest" woman,[97] and French "sore-*elle*," or the sound in French for what Berowne calls the "sign of *she*" (5.2.469). Given the "sodomitical" sense of "preposterous venery" already summoned in the "obscene and most prepost'rous event" (1.1.241–242) with which *Love's Labor's Lost* begins, and the reminders of its transvestite staging in the scene of the "Muscovites" where masked "Ladies" played by boys respond to an address to their "eyes" (or I's) by turning their "backs" (5.2.161–162), "sore-L" might also suggest another bodily ingle, angle (or fault),[98] just as the sound of English *doe* in Latin *haud credo* may summon to the ear French *dos* (or "back").

In a play that begins with the breaching of the King's "continent canon" and ends with an unexpected breaching of its own latter end, the permeability of boundaries or enclosures and the gallimaufry or linguistic mixture of borrowings (or incursions) into "English" have their counterpart in the permeable incontinence of sound itself—or the oral/aural capable of being heard in different languages at once, as in the case of the "sorel"/"sore L," "sore-ell" (or penis), and "sore-elle" or "sign of she."[99] And together they suggest a counterpart—in the language of the play—of what John Michael Archer has described as the contemporary context of a London that was both "polyglot" and preoccupied with the issue of "foreigners" and "strangers" (or "aliens"), both English subjects born outside of London and immigrants from other lands and tongues.[100]

The tensions in London involving French and Dutch refugees and immigrants that led to the Dutch Church Libel in 1593 provided the subtext for the dramatization of the earlier Ill May Day unrest in *The Book of Sir Thomas More*, the manuscript play in which Shakespeare is thought to have had a part.[101] "Dutch" resonances also surround both Falstaff and Shylock.[102] But *Love's Labor's Lost* even earlier exploited the interlingual sounding of Dutch, French, and English in the exchange between Katherine and Longaville (5.2.242–249) which combines the polyglot sounds of *long* and French *ville*, Dutch (or German) *viel*, and English *well*, *veil*, and *veal*, or the familiar contemporary joke about Dutch gluttony, in a passage that is dizzying in its interlingual border-crossings. Yet more Dutch connotations enter the play in the "Pompion" or pumpkin sounded in the naming of Pompey as "Pompion the Great" (5.2.502) in the Pageant of Worthies.[103] And—in ways highlighted in Chapter 5—the iterated naming of "Brabant" in *Love's Labor's Lost* ("Did not I dance with you in Brabant once?," 2.1.114–115) evokes not only the sexual "Low Countries" that were at once the "Netherlands" across the English Channel and contemporary slang for the brothel district in the suburbs of London, but also the Spanish-occupied territory from which refugees and other "strangers" were pouring into England in the years before the play, which was central to the recent threat from the Armada as well.

This play whose permeable borders, boundaries, or enclosures include linguistic interminglings or mixtures also famously foregrounds racial mixtures, in ways important to stress in relation to the wider contexts it evokes for the "preposterous." Armado is described as a traveler from "tawny Spain" (1.1.173), in a period when Spenser and others described Spain itself as the "most mingled" of nations, its racial and religious bloodlines intermixed with

Jews and Moors—the latter underscored by Armado's aligning himself more than once with King Cophetua, a legendary ruler from Africa (1.2.109–110, 4.1.65–80).[104] This Spanish "Don" is rendered as "Dun" (or dark) when Costard sounds his name as "Dun Adramadio, Dun Adramadio" (4.3.195). The striking language of blackness analyzed by Kim F. Hall and others in this play, where "blackamoors" also appear on stage with the "Russians" (5.2), is first introduced in the same part of the opening scene in which Don Armado's letter describes the initial "obscene and most prepost'rous event," in lines that include not only the blackness of his own melancholy but also the blackness of ink that was repeatedly used for racial and sexual blackness in the period: "So it is, besieged with sable-colored melancholy, I did commend the black oppressing humor to the most wholesome physic of thy health-giving air . . . where, I mean, I did encounter that obscene and most prepost'rous event that draweth from my snow-white pen the ebon-colored ink," 1.1.231–243).[105] The lines have to do with Costard and Jaquenetta, the figure who will be later described as most "maculate," stained or spotted, in ways that anticipate the language of both race and a female sexual blackness in *Othello*. And they anticipate the comedy's own subsequent foregrounding of blackness, maculation, and mixture—in a Shakespeare canon where blackness itself (both racial and sexual) was repeatedly combined with images of writing, books, and ink.[106] But given the transvestite context of this play, and its repeated suggestions of "preposterous venery," the image of blackness in these lines on a "most prepost'rous event" at the same time evokes the contemporary racialized connections between blackness and sodomy analyzed by Ian Smith and others.[107] As a consequence, they also bring us back to the lines on a "latter end" and the scapegoating of "Jude" as "Jud-as" by the aristocratic men in Act 5, and to important contemporary contexts for "preposterous" reversal and spelling "backward" in relation to race and religion.

Archer notes the "courtiers' cruelty" when the schoolmaster Holofernes appears in the pageant as Judas Maccabaeus, and the "scapegoating" of this figure that ensues—as he is "hooted off stage as 'Monsieur Judas,' a natural title from the French Boyet, perhaps, but redolent of Londoners' disdain for would-be-monsieurs from northern Europe," adding that "Holofernes, who is seen policing the borders of correct pronunciation at the start of act 5, has become assimilated to the 'perigrinate' outlandishness he attacked in Armado."[108] But in this pageant where the traditional Nine Worthies are reduced to five, the fact that four of them are classical figures (rather than the traditional three) further serves to "isolate the Hebrew, or rather Jewish component" Judas Maccabaeus, as "supernumerary."[109] And the aristocratic "Lords' expulsion of Judas Maccabaeus from the stage" at "the climax of the scapegoating process" is simultaneously evocative of the scapegoating of Jews—in lines where this "Judas" becomes both Judas "Iscariot" and "clipt," a short form of "ycleped" (or named) that evokes "clipped" or circumcised Jews as what Thomas Nashe called "foreskin clippers."[110]

> *Dumaine.* A Judas!
> *Holofernes.* Not Iscariot, sir.
> "Judas I am, ycliped Machabeus."
> *Dumaine.* Judas Machabeus clipt is plain Judas.
> (5.2.596–599)

The scatological scapegoating that ensues—where this "Judas" is ridiculed for the "latter end of his name" (5.2.627) and Berowne responds, "For the ass to the Jude; give it him. Jud-as, away!" (5.2.628: Q Judas, Folio "Iud-as")—adds to the "Christian association of Jews with excrement and finally with sodomy" that Jonathan Gil Harris has identified as one of the discourses of social pathology in early modern England.[111] And this association becomes part of what Archer describes as the attempt by "the members of the little academe" to "displace the taint of anality onto Holofernes" (as "Jud-ass" Maccabaeus / Iscariot) and "the other would-be Worthies in a manner that goes back to the Greek Old Comedy but which uses modern anti-Jewish stereotyping."[112] In the pageant scene itself, just before the "Judas" speech, "Holofernes presents Moth as Hercules, who killed Cerberus the 'canus' and strangled serpents in his—there is some suspense before the rhyme—'manus' " (5.2.589–591), in a play filled with scatological and sodomitical allusions to latter ends of all kinds. Earlier, Costard's reference to Moth as "my incony Jew!" (3.1.134) evokes both "cuny, a slang word for the female genitalia" and the "Jew" already sounded in Armado's address to Moth as a "tender juvenal" (1.2.8), the word paired with "Jew" in *A Midsummer Night's Dream* (3.1.95) and the name of Juvenal, the Roman "satirist most associated with scatology, catamites, and Jews." So the "play of syllable and signifier in *Love's Labour's Lost* links Jews with sodomy long before Hercules and Judas Maccabaeus make their appearance."[113]

Archer also notes that Armado—the Iberian Don "persistently linked with anal imagery in this play," who was "apparently slated to perform Judas Maccabaeus in the initial proposal for the Worthies scheme" (5.1.126–129)—may himself, as a Spaniard, have also been "associated with Jewish *conversos*, giving the portrayal even more point."[114] And after observing that in early modern England "Catholics were often lumped together with Jews because of both groups' supposedly literalistic adherence to law and ceremony,"[115] he cites the "play's central speech," where, in "justifying his friends' oath-breaking," Berowne "uses a theological metaphor to set them apart from such strict observers":

> It is religion to be thus forsworn:
> For charity itself fulfills the law,
> And who can sever love from charity? (4.3.360–362)

In these lines that Archer compares to the movement in *The Merchant of Venice* from Old Testament to New, the claim is that "the Lords enter a new dispensation of heterosexual 'love,'" while "The pedants are cast as spiritual Jews who remain immersed in the strict letter, useless knowledge, excremental self-absorption, and sodomy that their betters have abandoned," in a "device" of "scapegoating" reprised in the evocation of both sodomy and "clipped" or circumcised Jews in the ridicule of Holofernes as "Jud-as" in the final scene.[116]

Judith Hudson's characterization of what she calls Berowne's "feat of sophistry" here[117] joins the echoes of the New Testament already noted in Berowne's "Let us once lose our oaths to find ourselves, / Or else we lose ourselves to keep our oaths" (4.3.358–359), immediately before his "It is religion to be thus forsworn: / For charity itself fulfills the law" (4.3.360–361). The ironizing of Berowne's attempt to co-opt the teleological/typological language of progressing from a literal Old Testament to a New here further includes his questionable conflation of the "love" of the men now devoted to "Saint Cupid" (4.3.363) with the "*caritas*" (both love and charity) of 1 Corinthians 13. But it also brings us back to the wider religious and racial contexts for the "preposterous" and "preposterous" reversal (together with the sodomitical and scatological) in *Love's Labor's Lost* that are crucial to add, including with regard to spelling backward and the scapegoating of "Jud-as" in its final scene.

I noted earlier that "preposterous" reversals in *Love's Labor's Lost* are joined by the exchange on spelling "backward" in Act 5, where Moth's "What is *a, b*, spell'd backward, with the horn on his head" (5.1.47–48) is both a reference to the "horn-book" or "ABC" and evocation of the horns on the head of a cuckold, part of the anxiety of cuckoldry in this play that returns in the song of the "cuckoo" at its end (5.2.894–911). But—in ways that give to "horn" here a simultaneous Mosaic or "Jewish" resonance—spelling backward in multiple contemporary texts and contexts (including Shakespeare) was connected to "preposterous" inversions of other kinds. In *Much Ado About Nothing*, Beatrice is described as spelling men backward ("I never yet saw man, / How wise, how noble, young, how rarely featur'd, / But she would spell him backward"), in lines that go on to observe: "So turns she every man the wrong side out" (3.1.59–68). And these lines on spelling backward as a reversal of gender at the same time evoke the familiar backward spells of witches, recalled in the "charm" of the witches of *Macbeth* wound up in reverse, in Brabantio's "For nature so prepost'rously to err . . . / Sans witchcraft could not" in *Othello* (1.3.62–64), and the "praeposterous" dance "backward, to the left hand," of the male witches in Jonson's *Masque of Queenes*, in a period where "preposterous" was a keyword in the discourse of witchcraft itself.[118]

In the contemporary context of spelling and writing so prominently foregrounded in *Love's Labor's Lost*, "orthography" was praised in Richard Mulcaster's *Elementarie* (1582) as the "right righting of our English tongue," in a way that exploited not only the homophone of "right" and "write" but also the "right" as the opposite of "left" as well as of "wrong." Like other texts, John Hart's *Orthographie* (1569), whose title word shared its *orthos* with *orthodox*, further stressed the importance of following the proper "order in writing," unlike discourses that "preposterously . . . begin at the latter end."[119] Jeffrey Masten observes that the *orthos* of "orthography" (as "straight, upright, standing, the opposite of crooked") was contrasted in Alexander Hume's *Of the Orthographie and Congruitie of the Britan Tongue* (ca. 1617) to "*skaiographie*" (from *skaios*, "left, left-handed, awkward, crooked"),[120] as the "perverse opposite to rectitude" and right-writing. And he goes on to point out that "orthography" in *Much Ado* (where Benedick says of Claudio "now is he turn'd ortography," 2.3.20) is aligned there with converting or turning to "what we would call 'heterosexuality.'"[121]

The early modern analogy between writing and sexual practices—reflected in Nashe's complaint that "posterior Italian and Germane cornugraphers sticke not to applaude vnnaturall sodomitrie" (where "cornugraphers" combines the "posterior" use of the sexual "horn" with the schoolmaster's "hornbook" or "ABC")—continues the combination of sexual and graphic in medieval writers like Alanus de Insulis, where the "orthography" of "Nature" is opposed to the "falsigraphie" of the "witchcraft" of Venus, regressing or turning back from "male" to "female," and the inversion of

Nature's "right" writing when men assume the passive rather than the active sexual role.[122] But at the same time, spelling backward in early modern contexts also linked "sodomy" or "preposterous venery" to both Jews and Catholics characterized as "preposterating" the biblical testaments, or reading Scripture itself "backward" (or leftward, like Hebrew) rather than "aright."

The lines in *Love's Labor's Lost* on "*a, b,* spell'd backward, with the horn on his head" invoke the schoolboy's "hornbook" or "ABC," in a contemporary context where the tutor who "teaches boys the horn-book" came with the familiar associations of the schoolmaster or *pedagogus* with *pedicare* or backwards sexual entry, and boys' buttocks, that Masten has illustrated from texts like *Hornbyes Hornbook.* But in Protestant religious polemics in England, "spelling backward" as a "preposterous" inversion of writing (and reading) "aright" had at the same time a scatological and sodomitical religious inflection with regard to Papists and Jews. In the words of the "bilious" John Bale—who described the Pope as the "preposterouse vycar of the lambe" in a Rome filled with "buggeries"—"If ye spell Roma backwarde . . . it is preposterus *amor,* a loue out of order or a loue agaynst kynde" ("Roma amor est. Amor est? qualis? Praeposterus"),[123] an identification of the Roman Church with sodomy or the "preposterouse offyce of Venery" that was inseparable from the assumption of the Roman Church's Judaizing or turning backward to the "Hebrew" ceremonies, or what Bale called "*arsewarde* procedynges" applied to reverting from the Gospel to the Old Law, as the inverse of reading "scripture a ryght."[124]

In Bale and other Protestant polemicists, the preposteration of the testaments was inseparable from "preposterous *amor*" or the graphic and sexual backward spelling of "Roma" itself.[125] And it appeared in multiple texts of the period that combined Romans 1 on turning back to idolatry and sexual "use" *contra naturam* with Christians bewitched "backwards" to Jewish circumcision, in the influential passages of Galatians (and its early modern glosses) that described the Hebrew Old Testament itself as a *paedagogus* or "schoolemaster" (Galatians 3:24) and stressed the importance of reading the "ABC" of Scripture in a "forward" rather than "backward" direction, from left to right, rather than the (sinister) reverse.[126] As Laurence Tomson's influential translation of the New Testament put it in glossing Galatians 3:3, "If the Lawe be to be joyned with faith, this were not to goe forward, but backward,"[127] including to circumcision as what another important commentary on Galatians called "the sinistre rooted persuasion of the Jewes."[128] Going "backward" to the Hebrew Testament also reversed the racialized metaphorics of baptismally washing the "Blackamoor" or "Ethiope" white.[129]

To read "aright" was to move from left to right, Old to New Testament, in a teleological and providential direction, rather than in the "backward" or "preposterous" reverse—in ways repeatedly stressed in Protestant polemics that described reversion to Hebrew ceremonies as a "preposteration" or spelling backward of Scripture itself.[130] And, as noted in the Introduction, it included condemnation of those who, "praeposterous to God's order and method, will needs read his text backward, turning the heels to heaven, the head to earth,"[131] or what another text called the "preposterous Hysteron Proteron" of turning back to the Hebrew testament from the "Grace" of the New[132]—reversing the very teleology (and biblical typology) that Berowne invokes in his "sophistical" defense of the aristocratic men's perjury in *Love's Labor's Lost* ("It is religion to be thus forsworn: / For charity itself fulfills the law").

In ways that might never occur to modern audiences or readers, the period of *Love's Labor's Lost* thus contrasted reading, writing, and spelling in the "right" direction—rather than "preposterously" or "backward"—with sodomy, scatology, and the polemical abjection of religious and racial others, including Papists and Jews,[133] providing an important part of the wider contemporary context of the scapegoating and ridicule of "Jud-as" as "clipped" in lines that also exploit the sodomitical "latter end" of his name. And these early modern interconnections were registered in a broad range of English texts and dramatic productions—including in "men do with him as they would with Hebrew letters, spell him backwards and read him" (in John Earle's *Microcosmography* in 1628); in Michael Drayton's "Moone-calfe" (1627) on a figure ("Nor man nor woman, scarce Hermaphrodite") described as looking "like one for the preposterous sin, / Put by the wicked and rebellious Jewes, / To be a Pathique in their Malekind Stewes"; and in "*Italica*, this [. . .] / They put their pens the Hebrew way, methinks" in Middleton's *A Game at Chess* (1624), where "*Italica*" and backward or "Hebrew way" evoke back-door sexual entry (1.1.305–306), and "Sodomy, sixpence" is said to be a "sum" that should be on the "backside" of the book of the "Bishop," who acknowledges "There's few on's very forward, sir," 4.2.107–109).[134]

In the reversible "a, b" (or "abba") of *Love's Labor's Lost* ("What is *a, b,* spell'd backward, with the horn on his head?"), "horn" on the "head" (combined with a "backward" spelling of the "ABC" or hornbook and a sodomitical spelling backward) is thus capable of evoking not only the associations of the "horn" and "hornbook" with cuckoldry and the alphabetical "ABC" but also the contemporary depictions of Jews with horns (and the Jewish "horned hat") as well as the horns associated with the Mosaic scriptures themselves, especially since the Geneva gloss on Galatians stressed that the Hebrew testament was an "ABC" that must be read in the "right" direction, from left to right rather than the reverse.[135] The aristocratic men's scapegoating focus on the "latter end" of "Jude" may also recall the biblical Epistle of Jude that was famous for its lines on "Sodom and Gomorrhe" and following "strange flesh" (1:7), glossed in the Geneva Bible as "Moste horrible pollutions,"[136] at the same time as the sound of "Jew" in "Jude" underscores his association with Judas Iscariot as well as Maccabeus.

Beyond, then, John Michael Archer's important insight that the exchange on "Jud-as" in *Love's Labor's Lost* evokes the traditional connection between Judas and (sodomitical) Jews—in the lines where "ycleped" as "clipped" also evokes Jewish circumcision—the broader contemporary contexts for the "preposterous" and preposterous reversal (including as an inversion of "right writing" or spelling "backward") make clear that what might seem the discretely disparate or unconnected spheres of reading, writing, "orthography," sodomy, and biblical teleology/typology were combined in the polemical scapegoating and abjection of religious (and racial) others. Approaching the Shakespearean "preposterous" in this respect as well involves a labor that is at once historical, political, and linguistic. And in dramatic sites like this play and others of Shakespeare, the boundary between language and context is an incontinent divide.

*Chapter 2*

# Mastering Bianca, Preposterous Constructions, and Wanton Supposes

## *The Taming of the Shrew*

> Preposterous ass, that never read so far
> To know the cause why music was ordain'd!
>
> —*The Taming of the Shrew* (3.1)

At the beginning of Act 3 of *The Taming of the Shrew*, Lucentio (disguised as Cambio, master of "letters") and Hortensio (disguised as Litio, master of music) vie as rival "masters" for Bianca, the sister presented up to this point as exhibiting (in contrast to her sister the "shrew") the "Maid's mild behavior and sobriety" (1.1.71) that appears to guarantee that she will be a tractable, obedient, and subordinate wife. As the scene opens, Lucentio accuses Hortensio the "fiddler" of being too "forward" in putting music *before* letters or "philosophy" rather than the other way round, in lines that curiously echo the descriptions of the "forwardness" and frowardness of Kate the "shrew" herself:

*Lucentio.* Fiddler, forbear, you grow too forward, sir,
Have you so soon forgot the entertainment
Her sister Katherine welcom'd you withal?
*Hortensio.* But, wrangling pedant, this is
The patroness of heavenly harmony.
Then give me leave to have prerogative,

And when in music we have spent an hour,
Your lecture shall have leisure for as much.
*Lucentio.* Preposterous ass, that never read so far
To know the cause why music was ordain'd!
Was it not to refresh the mind of man
After his studies or his usual pain?
Then give me leave to read philosophy,
And while I pause, serve in your harmony.

(3.1.1–14)

"Preposterous" here is usually glossed by editors of the play as inverting "the natural order of things" or putting "the cart before the horse," the form of *hysteron proteron* or preposterous placing that was routinely available in the period for the inversion of allegedly natural orders of all kinds.[1]

This inversion or exchange of place is introduced in a contest between two rival masters which appears, at least initially, to be simply wrangling over which of the arts should have "prerogative," or come first. There is, however, much more at stake in the staging here of competing arts, in a scene in which the "preposterous" becomes the marker of much broader issues of order at work within the play as a whole. This prominently includes the "cambio" or exchange within the Lucentio-Bianca subplot itself, whereby Bianca (who at first appears to be the more tractable sister) becomes the master of both of her potential masters in this pivotal scene and finally emerges as an anything but tamed wife by the play's post-marital end.

That the proper ordering of rival arts appears to be the subject of the debate in this scene is consistent with the humanist emphasis on arts and learning that pervades *The Taming of the Shrew*—though it has often been easy to forget this emphasis in a play so often characterized as simply an early Shakespearean farce, in prior eras of its criticism. It might even be said that its combination of such traditionally elevated with lower (and lower-bodily) registers is part of the "cambio" of preposterous inversions it foregrounds. Lucentio opens the taming play proper by speaking of "the great desire I had / To see fair Padua, nursery of arts" (1.1.1–2), a reminder that Padua's university was famous throughout Europe. As the subsequent rhyming of "arts" and "hearts" and the competition of rival suitors for Bianca makes clear, however, the *ars amatoria* is the principal *ars* it pursues, however loftily disguised. Even the following of an "art" or *ars* itself within this play becomes part of the preposterous bodily reversals it both echoes and compounds. In a play that features a "tongue" in a "tail" (2.1.218) and in ways crucial for the Latin lesson used in this scene by Lucentio as a cover for his wooing of Bianca, Latin *ars* from the venerable *sermo patrius* or "father" tongue already came linked with preposterous, inverted, or lower bodily senses.

John Lyly's *Endymion* famously pairs "I am all Mars and Ars" with "Nay you are all Masse and Asse," but it is only one of the many translations from father to mother tongue that mingled high and low in the period. Thomas Nashe's lines on the "excrements of Artes" even more explicitly exploit the bodily and bawdy potential in any discussion of the learned *artes* or *ars*.[2] Within *The Taming of the Shrew*, Grumio's "O this woodcock, what an ass it is!"—in response to Gremio's "O this learning, what a thing it is!" (1.2.159–160)—is comically underwritten by such vernacular slippages, but so is Lucentio's "Preposterous ass" as an insult to a master of music who insists on the right of his particular *ars* to come first or before. Lucentio-Cambio's accusation against his "forward" rival—that he is "preposterous" for desiring to put *before* what should come *behind*—resonates with the scatology that from as early as Augustine identified the *ars musica* with the lower bodily or hindparts, as well as the sense of *preposterous* as arsy-versy that gives to Hortensio's placing of music first the stigma of turning back-to-front. In a scene that will soon suggest the bodily inferences of this "fiddler" teaching Bianca "fingering" and of the *re* (*res* or "thing") as a sexually double-meaning part of the musical gamut, it is impossible to separate the apparently high discourses of learning and the arts from the lower bodily and all it implies.[3] As modern readers or audiences, we may be distanced from the full implications of such preposterous play in *The Taming of the Shrew* by what Norbert Elias characterized as the historically intervening "civilizing process," or what Pierre Bourdieu has described as later developments of "distinction" between high and low.[4] But as with the scatological overtones of the "preposterous" and other apparently learned or mock-learned scenes in *Love's Labor's Lost*, explored in Chapter 1, we need to take time to learn the language of this historical vernacular in order to see what is at stake in the dramatic mise-en-scène of preposterous or arsy-versy exchanges of place and position in *The Taming of the Shrew*, not only in relation to gender but also for the other kinds of order and hierarchy it both stages and disrupts.

The sense of reversal introduced into this scene by Lucentio's "preposterous ass" soon involves subtle and not-so-subtle overturnings at the level of gender, but ones possible to track only if we are aware of the gender and other hierarchies already at work in the contemporary context of discussions of the arts, as well as what was at stake in the Latin texts employed by Lucentio as Bianca's would-be "master," in both a pedagogical and a marital sense. Debate over the hierarchy of rival "arts" was a major preoccupation not only in Baldassare Castiglione's *The Courtier* (translated into English by Thomas Hoby in 1561 and published in no fewer than four London editions by 1603) but also in the spate of books directed at upwardly mobile bourgeois families like Bianca and Katherine's in *The Taming of the Shrew*, concerned with what their merchant-father Baptista calls "good bringing-up" (1.1.99). Such manuals offered the aspiring merchant class the promise of access to the more gentle arts, while simultaneously foregrounding the cultural capital of such markers of distinction as something that (like clothing) could be acquired—as the tutoring of Bianca by hired masters suggests.

Maureen Quilligan (whose reading of the play is attentive to its emphasis on "class" as well as on hierarchies of gender) notes that the Induction—where Christopher Sly is schooled in how to address his Lady ("*Sly*: Al'ce madam, or Joan madam? / *Lord*: Madam, and nothing else, so lords call ladies")—draws "a quick conduct-book lesson in how to 'lord it,'" in a period when social identity itself was being shaped by these models of fashioning and "'self-fashioning.'" It thus stages in the process "the same social premise that underlies the courtesy books," that "social behavior is not a natural, biologically determined fact" but "can be learned (and unlearned)."[5] As so much feminist and other work has taught us, this same vogue for conduct literature was schooling young women on how to be "chaste, silent, and obedient," alongside a sprinkling of learning in music and other arts.[6] The conduct-book culture and context that the scene of rival "masters" and "arts" evokes in Shakespeare's *Shrew* should not, therefore, be unexpected in a play that repeatedly underscores the markers of upward mobility—or social hierarchies in a state of transition—including the double-meaning "titles" and "deeds" (3.2.123, 2.1.342) that hover between their older chivalric or aristocratic meanings and the new world of property transfers and marriage markets. In this sense, the "preposterous" (as a marker of the unnatural as well as the reversed), introduced into this scene of tutors hired by Bianca's upwardly mobile father, was itself a cultural keyword for all such "unnatural" acquisitions, as well as for social and gender reversals in the period.

In the scene that begins with the contest between Lucentio and Hortensio as supposed masters of arts who are rival masters for Bianca on the marriage market, Lucentio's "Preposterous ass, that never read so far / To know the cause why music was ordain'd" directly evokes such contemporary contexts. At the same time, the gendered invocation of "heavenly harmony" in these opening lines recalls contemporary debates over what should come *first* and what follow *after*, in a pivotal scene in which what seems to be simply a learned or mock-learned discussion of the priority of different arts has implications for the corresponding order of first and second, or subordinate, in the hierarchy of gender and social position. In advancing music's "prerogative" or right to come *first*, Hortensio (or Litio) invokes the Neoplatonic and Pythagorean tradition of "heavenly harmony," music as the cosmic *arche* or beginning of the world. Lucentio/Cambio, who reverses Hortensio's status and claim by denigrating this master of music, in social terms, as a mere "fiddler" (3.1.1), champions the inverse tradition in which music was characterized as subordinate or second, upbraiding his rival for not having "read" enough to know that music was to come only *after* more exalted studies. His "Preposterous ass, that never read so far / To know the cause why music was ordain'd! / Was it not to refresh the mind of man / *After* his studies or his usual pain?" (3.1.9–12) thus recalls texts like *The Courtier* itself, where music is cast in a subordinate or secondary role, as "a most swete lightning of our trauailes and uexations" or "a verie great refreshing of al worldlye paines and griefs." In Castiglione's influential text, which also had a major impact on conduct books for upwardly mobile or not-yet-gentle readers, the frequent or unsolicited performance of music by members of the aristocracy is rigorously condemned because such a pursuit would break down the distinctions between a nobleman and his music-performing servant (much less "fiddlers," or mechanical practitioners of the art).[7]

Sir Thomas Elyot's *The Boke named the Governour*—in its description of the "order" to be followed in "the bringing up of . . . children"—similarly counsels that music should come after more serious study, emphasizing that music "only serveth for recreation after tedious or laborious affairs." In ways that make clear the multiple hierarchies at stake in texts that have a noble audience in view, Elyot too warns that aristocratic practitioners of music risk being held "in the similitude of a common servant or minstrel," a term of opprobrium not unlike Lucentio's depiction of the music master as a "fiddler" here.[8] But even Thomas Morley's *Plain and Easy Introduction to Practical Music*—directed to a readership of the middling sort—makes clear that music is meant to "recreate" scholars only "*after* [their] more serious studies."[9]

Music in the context of such guides to "good bringing up" was thus understood as a diversion or form of recreation, not primary or first but subordinate and second. By contrast, to put music *first*—as Hortensio seeks to do, when he is ridiculed by Lucentio as a "fiddler" as well as a "forward" and "preposterous ass"—would also be preposterous in other senses, since it would involve a reversal of first and second, higher and lower on the social hierarchy reflected by the hierarchy of the arts themselves. "Fiddler" here evokes several of these subordinate positions at once. Contempt for musicians as practitioners of a "mechanical" art ranged from complaints such as Stephen Gosson's in *The Schoole of Abuse* against beggar companies of "fiddlers," to the use of the term "fiddler" both for the player of the violin (considered a rather vulgar instrument) and for the lower social status of musicians in the period. John Ferne, in *The Blazon of Gentrie*, treats of these "mechanicall practicioners" of "so base a profession" that the laws of the "Countrey . . . have determined them for roages and vagabonds, enemies to the publique good of our Countrey," and contrasts them to the "learned professor of that Science" commended by Pythagoras, Plato, Aristotle, and others. A similar social bias is reflected in Thomas Morley's reference to "ignorant *Asses*, who take upon them to lead others, being more blind than themselves."[10] Derogatory references to such musical "roages and vagabonds" in the period join contemporary sneers at players and other practitioners of "mechanic" arts. Hortensio complains that Katherine had branded him with this class sneer when he attempted to teach her music in an earlier scene. There, having had the "lute" broken on his head in her resistant "frets," he complains that "she did call me rascal fiddler / And twangling Jack, with twenty such vild terms, / As had she studied to misuse me so" (2.1.157–159).

Lucentio's ridicule of his rival tutor as ignorant of the proper order of the arts is thus a pedantic putdown grounded in one of the multiple indices of upward mobility in the period, reflected in texts such as Castiglione's *Courtier* and its bourgeois counterparts. Treatises such as Elyot's *The Governour* were directed to the governing classes broadly conceived, but handbooks such as Morley's joined the demand for tutors in the households of upwardly mobile merchants like Baptista who "had made fortunes . . . and who modelled their households on those of the social strata immediately above them."[11] At the level of contested social hierarchies, *The Taming of the Shrew*—which already calls sustained attention to the marriage-market "cambio" or exchange between landed gentry and merchant money—simultaneously reflects the market for schooling in the "arts" of proper "bringing up" in this contest between Bianca's rival masters.

Lucentio's "preposterous" in this scene of instruction is pronounced as a judgment on his rival's ignorance of this requisite order. But even more importantly for the place of this Bianca scene within the larger taming plot, what appears to be simply a pedantic discussion of the priority and ordering of the arts comes with important implications for the hierarchy of gender. For this is the scene in which Bianca will soon preposterously overturn the hierarchy of mastery itself—in a period when Vives, for example, in *The Instruction of a Christian Woman*, described female mastery over a husband as an inversion "which tourneth backewarde the lawes of nature, lyke as though a soudiour wolde rule his capitayne, or the moone wold stande above the sonne, or the arme above the heed."[12]

The casting of music as a diversion or recreation—to follow only *after* more serious pursuits—had its parallel in the contemporary context of the subordination of music, as handmaiden, to letters, philosophy, and the *logos* of words, the patroness of "heavenly harmony" not as *arche* or first but as literally ancillary (the etymological implication of its "handmaiden" status). In this respect, the subordination of music was frequently described in the period of *The Taming of the Shrew* in explicitly gendered terms. If Richard Wagner, much later, could make music female in the scale of gender—noting that "Music is the handmaid of Poetry [and] in the wedding of the two arts, Poetry is the man, music the woman; Poetry leads and Music follows"—the more contemporary witness of early modern texts such as *The Passionate Pilgrim* (1599) invoked the gendering of music and poetry as "sister" and "brother" ("If Music and sweet Poetry agree, / As they must needs, the Sister and the Brother"). Music is directly associated with women in *The Courtier*, which advises its readers that music is "meete to be practised in the presence of women" because their "sights sweeten the mindes of the hearers, and make them the more apt to bee pierced with the pleasantnesse of musicke, and also they quicken the spirits of the very doers" (Book II, 101). At the same time, music was feminized as something seductive that must be kept subordinate and under control. The same *Boke named the Governour* that counsels that male children should be "taken from the company of women" at age seven, lest they be imperiled by "sparks of voluptuosity which, nourished by any occasion or object, increase often times into so terrible a fire that therewith all virtue and reason is consumed" (Book I, ch. vi, 19), warns in its chapter on music that its "pleasant" diversion must not "allure" to "so much delectation" that it lead to "wantonness," "inordinate delight," or the "abandoning [of] gravity" and more serious pursuits (Book I, ch. vii, 21–22).

As a "thing to passe the time withall," music is further associated in *The Courtier* and other early modern texts and contexts with the making of womanish or effeminate men, along with "other vanities" that are "mete for women, & peraduenture for some also that haue the lykenes of men, but not for them that be men in deede: who ought not with suche delicacies to womannishe their mindes." Ascham writes that "The minstrelsie of lutes, pipes, harps, and all other that standeth by such nice, fine, minikin fingering is farre more fit for the wommanishnesse of it to dwell in the courte among ladies."[13] Music was thus not only associated *with* women but cast as able to turn male *into* female, a transformation highlighted in *The Taming of the Shrew* in multiple forms, not only in the transvestism that makes its first apparently tractable wife the Induction's transvestite page, but also in the later scene on the "sun" and "moon" (already highly gendered figures), where the patriarch Vincentio is pronounced a "maid" and Hortensio comments that it "will make the man mad, to make a woman of him" (4.5.35–36).

❧

> . . . the causes for whiche *Matrimonie* was ordeyned.
>
> —*The Booke of Common Prayer*

> *Bianca.* Now let me see if I can conster it. . . .
> I must believe my master, else, I promise you,
> I should be arguing still upon that doubt.
>
> —*The Taming of the Shrew* (3.1.41, 54–55)

There is, however, an even more striking echo evoked in the lines in which Lucentio claims that music should be not "forward" or first but subordinate or second, and that inversion of this order would be "preposterous"—an echo that comes with direct implications for the gendering of this hierarchy from even more authoritative contemporary contexts. The scene's invocation of the "preposterous" as a culturally loaded term that foregrounds the issue of what should have "prerogative" or precedence thus calls out for even closer scrutiny in relation to the marriage market and the hierarchy of male and female within it—with implications as well for the play's final scene and supposed "taming" of a "shrew." Lucentio's "Preposterous ass, that never read so far / To know *the cause why music was ordain'd*" directly echoes the "causes for whiche *Matrimonie* was ordeyned," from "The fourme of the Solemnization of Matrimonie" in *The Booke of Common Prayer*, the text that enjoins the woman as the "weaker vessell" to be "subiect" unto her husband in "quietnes, sobrietie and peace," or in other words, precisely what Bianca is assumed to be potentially when the play begins, in contrast to her sister the "shrew."[14] This unmistakable echo of the Ceremony of Matrimony—and with it the Pauline and other biblical assumptions of male prerogative and female subordination from the Genesis 2 order of Adam *before* Eve—has momentous implications for this pivotal scene in which Bianca will master both of her would-be "masters" in turn, extending the sense of preposterous overturning from the initial context of the order and hierarchy of the arts to a reconstruing (and reconstructing) at the level of gender.

Such a direct echo of the Ceremony of Matrimony sets up even further reverberations between this Bianca subplot scene and the larger shrew-taming play, which repeatedly recalls that ceremony (foundation of the Elizabethan homiletic tradition that counseled the subordination of women) and famously ends with Katherine's apparent iteration of the Pauline figure of the man as "head" (5.2.147) in her final speech. The Ceremony itself invokes the prescribed sequence of the genders among the "thinges set in ordre" in Genesis, and other biblical texts from which this order of priority was derived: man made in God's "owne ymage and symilytude," and woman, secondarily and "out of man." If music as handmaiden or subordinate is "ordain'd" to "refresh the mind of man / *After* his studies or his usual pain"—in the hierarchy of primary and secondary in which its "harmony" is to be "serve[d] in" only *following* the "prerogative" of "philosophy" or "letters"—then in the order derived from Genesis 2, matrimony is "ordained" to be similarly refreshing ("for the mutuall societie, help and comfort, that the one ought to have of thother, both in prosperitie and aduersitie"), with the helpmeet wife, or "weaker vessell," a clearly subordinate second.[15]

That there should be an echo of the Ceremony of Matrimony in the very lines that evoke a "preposterous" reversal at the opening of Act 3 thus gives to the question of order in this first major Bianca scene a much greater resonance than just a wrangling over rival arts, one with implications not only for the portrayal of the apparently tractable Bianca within it but also for the play as a whole. By the end of this play, as already noted, Bianca herself will be anything but subordinate or submissive, but will be chastised instead, like her sister before her, for being too "forward" as well as "froward" (5.2.119), a synonym for the "preposterous" that was routinely used for unruly wives. In this pivotal Act 3 scene, the echo of the Ceremony of Matrimony—and with it, the ordaining of matrimony in Genesis—is sounded in lines devoted ostensibly to a contest only between men, with Bianca the apparently passive object of their rivalry. But in this first major scene of the play to feature the supposedly submissive younger sister, this unmistakable echo invokes the Ceremony's strictures on the hierarchy of the genders at the very moment when Bianca will overturn and manipulate it, becoming not a submissive female but director of both would-be masters.

Textual editors from Theobald (1733) onward have emended what they see in this opening as a truncated line—"this is / The patroness of heavenly harmony"—to a formulation that identifies this "patroness" of "harmony" as Bianca herself, as distinguished from the discordant "frets" of her shrewish sister.[16] Far from providing a contrast to her elder sister, however, Bianca in this scene proves to be less tractable than her alignment with music as either handmaiden or heavenly harmony suggests. The scene's initial discussion of the proper order of the arts is cut short by Bianca herself. She refuses to be a "breeching scholar" (3.1.18) to either of her rival tutors, rejecting the master-pupil relationship of "following" or imitation prescribed in school texts such as Richard Mulcaster's *Positions* and the following of appointed "hours" and "times," in ways that pointedly recall the earlier rejection of "appointed hours" (1.1.103) by Katherine the *designated* shrew, in the scene that had contrasted Bianca's "mild behavior and sobriety" (1.1.71) to her more "froward" sister (1.1.69). Bianca puts an end to the wrangling of her would-be masters by reminding them instead of *her* prerogative:

> Why, gentlemen, you do me double wrong
> To strive for that which resteth in *my* choice.
> I am no breeching scholar in the schools,
> I'll not be tied to hours, nor 'pointed times,
> But learn my lessons *as I please myself.* (3.1.16–20, emphasis mine)

The scene that invokes the "preposterous" in relation to the appropriate order of the arts thus not only summons echoes of the proper order of the genders from the Ceremony of Matrimony (where women, like music, are to be secondary or subordinate), but already undercuts the taming plot's ostensible contrast between a "fretful" shrew and her apparently obedient younger sister, long before the final scene. This overturning is even clearer when this scene in Act 3 turns (after Bianca asks "Cambio" to "conster" or construe some Latin lines) into a lesson in translation—or what was known in early modern English as construing or construction. For this kind of linguistic construction was dominated by the very discipline of subordination, or obedient following of a "master," that Lucentio proceeds to assume.[17]

In a play that is literally filled with tags from grammar-school texts—including the *Grammar* of Lily and Colet whose "masculine gendre is more woorthy than the feminine"[18] was already a watchword for more than simply grammatical gender in the period—the lesson offered by the would-be "master" Lucentio/Cambio to Bianca as his intended pupil is based on precisely this contemporary order of following after, the pedagogical counterpart to the later textual description of Bianca as a supposed wifely "appendix" (4.4.104). This scene's staging of linguistic construing or construction foregrounds a term exploited repeatedly in Shakespeare—from the King's "Conster my speeches better, if you may" in *Love's Labor's Lost* (5.2.341) and Malvolio's "construction" (2.3.175) of the letter in *Twelfth Night* (including his telling "to crush this a little, it would bow to me," 2.5.140) to the impossibility of reading "the mind's construction in the face" in *Macbeth* (1.4.12) and the ambiguous "merciful construction of good women" in relation to how the play itself will be construed in *Henry VIII* (Epilogue 10). In relation to translation from Latin, it includes the "construction" provided by the "soothsayer" in *Cymbeline* (5.4.433, 442), whose "supposedly supernaturally inspired exposition" suggests instead that "meaning can be infinitely wrested to suit the agenda of the moment" through a "politically expedient" decoding.[19] And "construction" figures in relation to fidelity and gender in the "shrewd construction" to be made of Mistress Ford in *The Merry Wives of Windsor*, in the scene where her jealous husband "prescribe[s]" to himself "preposterously" (2.2.223, 241), and in the "illegitimate construction" of *Much Ado About Nothing* (3.4.50), a phrase that connects linguistic mistranslation or (mis)construing to the fear of infidelity and illegitimacy associated with women. "Illegitimate construction" figures in *Much Ado* as a suggestive double entendre for the connection between the infidelity of construings and the cultural anxiety evoked both there and in *The Taming of the Shrew* when the Pedant responds, "Ay, sir, so his mother says, if I may believe her," to the question of whether Lucentio is his legitimate son (5.1.33). Though it may be as foreign to us as modern readers as the multiple early modern implications of the "preposterous," this interconnection between the fidelity of translations and the fidelity of women was commonplace in Shakespeare and other contemporary works. In *Merry Wives*, for example, Mistress Quickly translates into ever-more-promiscuous vernacular constructions the Latin of the *sermo patrius* she fails to understand, in a play that makes clear that words, like wives, can be both unfaithful and out of a master's control.[20]

In *The Taming of the Shrew*, the disguised Lucentio/Cambio, who argues for the "prerogative" of going *first*, begins by expecting that his Latin lesson will unfold according to his own agenda and construing:

> "*Hic ibat*," as I told you before, "*Simois*," I am Lucentio, "*hic est*," son unto Vincentio of Pisa, "[*Sigeia*] *tellus*," disguis'd thus to get your love, "*Hic steterat*," and that Lucentio that comes a-wooing, "*Priami*," is my man Tranio, "*regia*," bearing my port, "*celsa senis*," that we might beguile the old pantaloon. (3.1.31–37)[21]

But in contrast to the schoolboy or "breeching scholar" who might be expected to follow the construction of a "master," Bianca produces her own very different construing, no more seconding or repeating his words than she consents to yield to "appointed times" or "hours." If from the perspective of the master's script, the role of the schoolboy is to follow after, this is precisely the subordinate or second position that Bianca here eschews.

Instead of iterating the translation of her would-be master (in both the pedagogical and the marital sense), Bianca responds:

> Now let me see if I can conster it: "*Hic ibat Simois*," I know you not, "*hic est* [*Sigeia*] *tellus*," I trust you not, "*Hic steterat Priami*," take heed he hear us not, "*regia*," presume not, "*celsa senis*," despair not. (3.1.41–45)

Some commentators have argued that Bianca's very different translation here is simply a way of raising her price in the marriage market, by withholding immediate assent from a suitor at the same time as adding that he should not "despair." But the implications of this translation lesson—and of Bianca's more ambiguous as well as divergent construings—are actually much more subtle and far-reaching than any such culturally commonplace reading of her demurring might suggest. Bianca turns the tables by providing a very different translation of the same Latin text that Lucentio or "Cambio" is attempting to make serve his turn with her. But strikingly, even feminist critics have missed the implications of the female complaint that provides the very basis of this Latin lesson—as well as the intertextuality that makes Bianca's doubts about Lucentio's constructions both more resistant and more complex.[22]

Such intertextual markers and contexts may often go unnoticed in *The Taming of the Shrew* because of lingering assumptions that it is part of a supposedly naive or simple "early Shakespeare." Some critics have even read Bianca as simply repeating the words of her "master" here, making this scene continuous with (rather than a striking departure from) the Bianca described by others earlier in the play as the tractably chaste, silent, and obedient woman of the conduct books.[23] However, the actual text that provides the basis for this translation lesson—from Ovid's *Heroides*, familiar to schoolboys, including Shakespeare, in Latin, and already translated into English by Turberville in 1567—is Penelope's anything-but-submissive or silent complaint against her own husband and master for taking so long to return home, a complaint that Shakespeare puts into the mouth not of a mild and tractable but rather of a "shrewish" wife in *The Comedy of Errors*, another early play.[24] The particular Latin lines presented for translation in this scene in Act 3 are from Penelope's complaining that other wives have heard the Troy story directly from their already-returned husbands, while she has had to get the story herself, and only at second hand, by sending her son out to find his father. But Bianca's "Where left we last?" (3.1.26) makes clear that Penelope's much longer female complaint—which initiates the entire series of female complaints that make up the *Heroides* and includes her anger at being left alone for twenty years, as well as her justified suspicion that Ulysses has been unfaithful—had already provided the text for a lesson begun even before this scene. The particular lines chosen for translation here—on the siege of Troy before the ultimate guileful breaching of its "walls" (or in Turberville's translation, "walles which you by breach haue brought to utter spoyle and sacke")—may themselves be part of the sotto voce commentary. For the disguised Lucentio has himself gained entry to Bianca's house only through guile, and the wooers in the sources for Lucentio's wooing use their disguised entry to breach the sexual walls of the corresponding female figures, a possibility suggested more indirectly in *The Shrew* in Hortensio's final lines in this scene ("Yet if thy thoughts, Bianca, be so humble / To cast thy wand'ring eyes on every stale, / Seize thee that list. If once I find thee ranging, / Hortensio will be quit with thee by changing," 3.1.89–92).[25]

The Latin text chosen by Shakespeare for Lucentio's supposed instruction of Bianca thus itself provides a highly suggestive context here. And the implications of such a well-known text for Bianca's resistance to Lucentio's instruction-construction in this scene become even more telling when the lesson moves on to the next line of the *Heroides*, which Lucentio presents in a translation he offers as authoritative or "sure":

*Bianca.* In time I may believe, yet I mistrust.
*Lucentio.* Mistrust it not, for sure Aeacides
Was Ajax, call'd so from his grandfather.
*Bianca.* I must believe my master, else, I promise you,
I should be arguing still upon that doubt.
But let it rest. Now, Litio, to you . . .

(3.1.51–56)[26]

This next line of the *Heroides* text, which Lucentio's "sure Aeacides / Was Ajax" appears to be translating, is "*illic Aeacides, illic tendebat Ulixes.*" But—contrary to the translation of "Aeacides" (or descendant of Aeacus) that Lucentio presses Bianca to believe is "Ajax"—both Turberville and modern translations of the *Heroides* agree that "Aeacides" in this line from Penelope's complaint is not Ajax at all, but Achilles. Turberville translates this line as "There fierce Achylles pight his Tents, / there wise Vlysses lay," while the modern Loeb translation has no index entry for Ajax at all, since *Aeacides* designates Achilles every time this phrase appears in the *Heroides*, even in its other female complaints.[27]

In ways equally suggestive for a subplot in which closing the marriage-market deal with Bianca's father requires Lucentio's own patrimony or inheritance from an only "supposed" father, Lucentio or "Cambio" here assures Bianca that his construction is "sure" by appealing to a supposedly sure male lineage for this connection ("for sure Aeacides / Was Ajax, call'd so *from his grandfather*"). But his attempt to assure as well as instruct Bianca in answer to her "yet I mistrust" is even at the level of purely textual translation a construing that is not in fact assured. In mistrusting the assurance of her would-be "master," in the pedagogical as well as the wooing sense here, Bianca not only takes over the direction of that wooing but proves to be clearly the better scholar,[28] since what he tells her to believe—on his assurance—is, like other supposes in this play of supposes, only his own very doubtful construction.

As part of an in-joke that those with grammar schooling might be expected to get, there is already every reason to mistrust this master's translation from Penelope's well-known *Heroides* complaint. But even more tellingly, Lucentio/Cambio's insistence that "Aeacides" is "Ajax" here actually abandons the *Heroides* text of justifiably complaining women for a different text and context altogether, one where there are no women present but only rival men competing for possession of a property or prize that is both passive and inert, as before she intervened, Bianca herself might have been supposed to be. In this different text—from the famous rivalry between Ajax and Ulysses over who will inherit Achilles' armor in *Metamorphoses* 13 (a debate that Shakespeare would later write large in *Troilus and Cressida* as well as echoing in *Hamlet*)—Ajax's claim that he is "Aeacides" and hence legitimate heir to this prize bases his right to inherit it as his property on the construing of a patriarchical line of descent and "title," while arguing that his rival can only by a "forged pedigree" ally himself to the "Aeacyds" (as Golding translated it) because Ulysses himself is a bastard—not his supposed father Laertes' son but offspring of his mother's coupling with another.[29] The text that the wooing "Cambio" here exchanges or substitutes for Penelope's introduction to the litany of complaints against men that fill the *Heroides* is, in other words, not only a rivalry exclusively between men for possession of a purely passive object but a text and wider context that once again draws attention to the very issues of property, patrimony, supposed fathers, or "illegitimate construction[s]" that pervade *The Taming of the Shrew* itself.[30]

In a scene that begins with such a clear echo of the Ceremony of Matrimony and its supposed "weaker vessell" who is to be "subiect" to her husband, Bianca not only intervenes but takes over the lessons offered by both "masters." And there is in her bringing of an end to the lesson in translation or construction a comment that is even more suggestive for the apparent shrew-taming trajectory of the play as a whole. When Bianca moves from "In time I may believe, yet I mistrust" to "I *must* believe my master" (in a line that may at first *appear* to signal her tractability or submission), it is not because Lucentio's is a "sure" construction or one she actually accepts. As this anything-but-passive female quickly makes clear, it is only a practical way of putting an end to what might otherwise continue interminably here: "else, I promise you / I should be arguing still upon that doubt. / But let it rest. Now, Litio, to you" (3.1.54–56).

Bianca's bringing Lucentio's proffered "lesson" to an end—in ways that make good on her promise to "learn my lessons as I please myself"—thus conveys something very different from acceptance of the conclusion that Lucentio himself presents as "sure," in a scene in Act 3 that forecasts the much less tractable Bianca of the play's post-marital end. It may even provide a suggestive advance gloss on her sister Katherine's apparent seconding of *her* shrew-taming master's constructions, when she makes the decision to iterate Petruchio's aberrant designations of the "sun" and "moon," and delivers what seems to be her apparently submissive final speech.[31] In a play full of such dramatic cross-references, as well as such "counterfeit supposes" (5.1.117)—beginning with the sotto voce witness of the Induction, where the play's first and perhaps only tractably obedient wife is a transvestite page following his master's designated script—perhaps Katherine's own apparent iteration of a culturally proffered script or construct is itself simply a way of bringing an otherwise endless debate to an at least temporary end, and nothing so straightforward as assumed assent.

Whatever the larger implications of this pivotal subplot scene—which begins by invoking the "preposterous" in the contemporary context of what should come *first* and what subordinately *second*—it is crucial in relation to the trajectory of Bianca within the play. Both of Bianca's putative masters here find the orthodox teacher-pupil relationship unexpectedly overturned. The evocation of Penelope not in her patient but in her complaining mode joins the echoing of the Ceremony of Matrimony from the lines on the preposterous overturning of other orders with which this scene begins, yielding not the simple subordinate Penelope but one used elsewhere in early Shakespeare for the speeches of a "shrew." And Bianca herself—described at the opening of the taming play as the wifely ideal so often represented by the more submissive Penelope—emerges through her own constructions of the *sermo patrius* or Latin text as a much less tractable figure, even while she continues to be described by others, who see her from the outside, as a wifely subordinate or "appendix" (4.4.104).

My reading of this scene of instruction and its would-be masters is thus that Bianca is here revealed to be neither a submissive Penelope nor the subordinate "weaker vessell" of the biblical texts on which the Ceremony of Matrimony itself depended. Characterizations of Bianca as only much later turning into a surprisingly "froward" wife, in the play's final scene, miss the implications of the "preposterous" overturning already displayed in this much earlier scene of a putative master's construing. Even a feminist critic as prescient as Karen Newman falls into this conventional reading of Bianca when she asserts of this language lesson in Act 3 that "far from the imaginative use of language and linguistic play we find in Kate, Bianca repeats verbatim the Latin words Lucentio 'construes' to reveal his identity and his love. Her revelation of her feelings through a repetition of the Latin lines he quotes from Ovid are as close as possible to the silence we have come to expect from her."[32] Amy L. Smith's "Performing Marriage with a Difference" ignores this scene of instruction in Act 3 and speaks of Bianca as only "finally" rebelling on stage in the final scene, though the earlier scene would be critically important to her argument about the destabilization of hierarchies and the role of performance and scripts in the play.[33] And strikingly, in a 2011 study of "Modeling Gender Education" in this play, Alyssa Herzog describes Bianca as representing "the ideal woman," like "the chaste, silent, and obedient women described by Suzanne Hull," while her sister "represents the unwanted woman—the scold"; and with regard to the play's male instructors, characterizes Bianca (in contrast to "the outspoken Katherina" who is unwilling "to take instruction from her tutor") simply as "apt to learn, and thankful for good turns" (2.1.165).[34] What, on the contrary, we encounter in this scene of supposed instruction is a very different Bianca from either the representations of her the play has already cast up, as the potentially chaste, silent, and obedient future wife, or the assumptions and constructions of otherwise astute interpretations.

ꕥ

> The oats have eaten the horses.
>
> —*The Taming of the Shrew* (3.2.206)

> A child shall get a sire, if I fail not of my cunning.
>
> —*The Taming of the Shrew* (2.1.411)

The language-lesson scene of construing or construction—with its denunciation of the music-master as a "preposterous ass" and the problematizing of "mastery" within it—has implications at the same time for a wider reading of the play and for the different kinds of preposterous construction within it. This includes implications for its underscoring not only of gender but also of "class" or social position (stressed by Amanda Bailey, David Evett, and others);[35] for the transvestite theatrical context (and "supposes") foregrounded from its Induction; for Katherine's final speech and the open-ended ending of its shrew-taming plot; for its repeated emphasis on backward and forward, before and behind; for Bianca as both "white" and boy player; and for "preposterous venery" and the sexual and other senses of "position" (along with "*cambio*" or changes of place) already highlighted in the sources of the Lucentio-Bianca plot in Ariosto's *I Suppositi* and Gascoigne's *Supposes*, though this crucial context has been generally overlooked.

The play as a whole is filled with the simultaneous invocation and inversion of orders of all kinds, not just with regard to male and female, but also in relation to masters and servants, elder and younger, and the generational priority of fathers over children. And strikingly, its preoccupation with "preposterous" reversals is so pervasive that it operates even at the level of the apparently throwaway line. When the servant Grumio says in Act 3 that the "oats" have eaten the "horses" (3.2.206) rather than the other way round, the sentence is one that some editors have tried to make sense of in a linear fashion.[36] But it also suggests a preposterous exchange of subject and object (oats eating horses, rather than the reverse), in a way that calls attention to the inversion of what should come after and what before in the play as a whole.

The sustained highlighting of various orders and their reversal starts with the Folio Induction that itself "goes *before*" the taming play, where the Lord is concerned that the sport to be had with the drunken Sly be *orderly* merriment ("haply my presence / May well abate the over-merry spleen, / Which otherwise would grow into extremes," Ind. 1.136–138). The beginning of the taming play proper is likewise in a scene in which the father Baptista insists on the order of elder and younger, with the accompanying problem for him of a shrewish elder sister who has the prerogative of being married *first* (1.1.50–51), before the apparently docile younger sister who declares that she knows her "duty" to her "elders" (2.1.7). In the wooing of her elder sister, Gremio warns the madcap Petruchio to "go to it *orderly*" (2.1.45), when he threatens to be too "forward" (51), the term that elsewhere is used not only for a "forward" (or "froward") woman but for the music master who is called a "Preposterous ass" (3.1.1, 9) in the scene where he proposes to teach Bianca the "order" of "fingering" and the "gamouth" (or "gamut") that is the basis of order and harmony in music (3.1.65, 67).[37] In the Tailor Scene of Act 4, the tailor who is to provide a cap for Katherine is instructed to make it "orderly and well, / According to the fashion and the time" (4.3.94–95). And the taming of "Kate" culminates in a final speech that at least seems on its surface to demonstrate the subordination of female to male advised in contemporary conduct books and other guides to harmony and order in marriage as well.

In a play that is filled with grammatical, musical, syntactical, and other forms of ordering and construction that were inseparable, in early modern contexts, from order on the societal and political level, the sequential order of male and female as primary and secondary in Genesis 2 (and other texts based on it) is combined with the striking textual figure of a woman's subordinate place when Lucentio receives "assurance" (albeit a "counterfeit" one) that his secret marriage to Bianca will guarantee him, as husband, his "sole right to print" ("Take you assurance of her, *cum privilegio ad imprimendum solum*," 4.4.91–93). This is the Latin phrase that combines the contemporary formula for a monopoly right of publication with the bridegroom's sole sexual right to the bride, and the concomitant sexual/textual metaphor for getting with child, reflected in "Your mother was most true to wedlock, Prince, / For she did print your royal father off, / Conceiving you" in *The Winter's Tale* (5.1.124–126).[38] Tellingly, it is in this same scene that Bianca is described as a wifely "appendix" (4.4.104), the term whose contemporary sense included both an addition and something that followed *after* as an afterword or postscript, or the textual counterpart of the order of first and second, Adam and *then* Eve, in that Genesis story.

Despite, however, its repeated emphasis on proper order and sequence across multiple contexts, including the proper order of the "arts" in the scene of rival "masters" for Bianca, *The Taming of the Shrew* literally bristles with "preposterous" exchanges of position—from the microlevel of rhetorical inversions to the larger hierarchies and orders of which it appears to provide "assurance" (one of its repeated keywords). And it does so in ways that make the name "Cambio" for Lucentio when he changes places with his servant Tranio into a byword not only for the marriage market of commercial exchanges that underwrite the financial bidding for Bianca or bring the landed Petruchio to "wive it wealthily in Padua" (1.2.75–76), but also for the hierarchical (and bodily) exchanges of place and position dramatized or suggested within it.

Contemporary avatars of "preposterous" or "arse-varse" reversal are highlighted even in passages where order is repeatedly stressed. In the scene of Katherine's arrival at Petruchio's country house, the servant Grumio (who is described as having been "sent *before*," in order to prepare for those who are "coming *after*," 4.1.4–5) demands that "every thing [be] in order" (4.1.51), and then proceeds to order his *narrative* account of the journey home of bridegroom and bride by invoking the familiar markers of discursive ordering or sequence ("Now I begin: *Inprimis*"—Latin for "in the first place," as *Riverside* notes). But what he narrates within this ostensibly ordered discursive frame simultaneously foregrounds a familiar figure for the preposterous inversion of female and male ("*Inprimis*, we came down a foul hill, my master riding *behind* my mistress," 4.1.66–68). The lines in this scene on his discursive ordering of his narrative or "tale" (4.1.54–72) evoke the sexual double entendres throughout this play on the reversal of "head" and (sexual) "tail." And his extended exchange with a fellow servant here includes not only the play's first reference to Katherine as a "shrew" (in Curtis's "Is she so hot a shrew as she's reported?" 4.1.21) but also his conclusion that Petruchio the "master" is "more shrew than she" (4.1.85).

Grumio's "I am sent *before* to make a fire, and they are coming *after* to warm them" (4.1.4–5)—when he has been sent ahead by Petruchio to prepare his master's lodging—itself turns on the paradox (and potentially hazardous position for a servant) of being preposterously placed "before" his master. "Before" in its multiple ambiguous senses then continues throughout this scene, including when Grumio responds to Petruchio's "Where is the foolish knave I sent *before*?" with "Here, sir, as foolish as I was *before*" (4.1.127–128), comically conflating the spatial sense of being sent "before" with the temporal sense of "before" as coming *first*. As a reminder of the inversion of *before* and *after* (or *in front* and *behind*) familiar from Puttenham's definition of *hysteron proteron* or "The Preposterous" as putting the "cart" before the "horse"—or Grumio's description of the *hysteron proteron* of gender that has his master "riding *behind*" his mistress—the series of changes rung in this scene on "before" and "after" joins the "preposterous" reversal of what should come *first* and what *after* or second in the subplot scene of instruction involving rival tutors in Act 3. But it also joins the paradoxes (and potential dilemmas) of "service" itself, faced in different ways by both Grumio (as Petruchio's servant) and Tranio (as Lucentio's), in a play that puts as much emphasis on the hierarchies of social position as it does on the hierarchies of gender.

The sustained verbal play in this scene where the servant Grumio, Petruchio's groom, comes "before" his master has its counterpart in Petruchio's own appearance as "groom" in the Wedding Scene immediately before it—where Grumio's "The oats have eaten the horses" (3.2.206) provides the grammatical inversion of subject and object that would be its counterpart at the micro-level. In the contemporary context where one of the primary monitors of social position were the sumptuary laws that made clothing a marker of place and degree, Philip Stubbes famously complained in *The Anatomie of Abuses* (1583)—whose setting in "Ailgna" is England or "Anglia" spelled backward—that the "mingle mangle of apparell" in England had reached such a "preposterous excesse" that "it is verie hard to knowe, who is noble, who is worshipfull, who is a gentleman, who is not."[39] And it is precisely such a "mingle mangle" or "preposterous" transgression of sumptuary markers that is both narratively recorded and staged in Petruchio's appearance at his own wedding, in a scene where even Grumio his "groom" (in the sense of his *servant*) is described as "a monster, a very monster in apparel, and not like a

Christian footboy or a gentleman's lackey" (3.2.69–71). "Mean apparell'd" (73) in his "mad attire" (124)—in a way that does "shame" to his "estate" or social place (100)—Petruchio the "mad-brain'd bridegroom" (163) of this scene is called "a groom indeed" (152), the double-meaning word used to chart his degraded social status,[40] to a "groom" in the sense of "menial" (New Oxford), serving man (*Riverside*), or "lower-class fellow" (New Cambridge; Arden 3)—the term that *Greene's Groatsworth of Wit* (1592) had used for Shakespeare himself in its contemptuous dismissal of that preposterously risen playwright as an "upstart crow." But elsewhere in Shakespeare's *Taming of the Shrew*, such "preposterous" transgressions are essential to the "cambio" of apparent gender and social estate behind its multiple "supposes" (as not just suppositions but changes or substitutions of place and position).

Precisely what Stubbes and others railed against as a "preposterous" transgression of the sumptuary laws is the basis of the initial "suppose" of the play's Induction, which introduces the socially "arsy-versy" transformation of the drunken Sly from a tinker to a lord, dressed in clothes befitting his change in position. This sartorial upward mobility comes with a new genealogy or patrilineage as well, in ways that comically anticipate the dubious patriarchal genealogy or descent in Lucentio's Latin lesson in Act 3, as "old Sly's son of Burton-heath, by birth a pedlar, by education a cardmaker, by transmutation a bear-herd, and now by present profession a tinker" (Ind. 2: 18–21) is transformed into "a mighty man" of great "descent" as well as property or "possessions" (Ind. 2: 14–15).[41] The Induction's corresponding gender transformation—of the transvestite boy page into Sly's obedient wife, instructed to deport himself with "soft low tongue and lowly courtesy" (Ind. 1.114)—not only joins its initial counterfeit "supposes" but underscores the construction of gender identity itself through performance,[42] in advance of the public performance by the boy player Bianca of "Maid's mild behavior and sobriety" (1.1.71) and the shrew-taming plot whose principal boy actor will embody the central fantasy or "suppose" of the taming of a shrew. It thus introduces—in an Induction where the Hostess is also called "boy" (Ind. 1.14)—the entire play's dependence on what early modern antitheatricalists condemned as the "preposterous" transgressions of the English transvestite stage, including its transgression of the biblical prohibition against cross-dressing, characterized by Stubbes as "preposterous geare, when Gods ordinance is turned topsie turuie, vpside downe," and what William Rankins described as the "unnaturall" monstrosity of players, "whether grounded by nature or insinuated by some *preposterous* education."[43] And the implication of "preposterous venery" that so often accompanied such antitheatrical writing is at the same time subtly evoked by the impatience for sexual "doing" in Sly's " 'Tis a very excellent piece of work, madam lady: would 'twere done!" (1.1.253–254), once the players have entered.

The striking "cambio" or changes of social position and apparent gender in the Induction are joined, when the "taming" play itself begins, by the reversal or substitution of place between master and servant in which Tranio becomes supposed "Lucentio" so that Lucentio (as "Cambio") can gain access to Bianca as a tutor, or the "suppose" essential to the subsequent Language Lesson scene of instruction and construction. And it is here that sustained attention is first given to the inverted form of "following" involved in a servant's following a master's command that his servant master him—beginning with Lucentio's "Then it *follows* thus: / Thou shalt be master, Tranio, in my stead" (1.1.201–202) and continued in Tranio's highlighting of this paradoxical shift ("I am tied to be obedient—/ For so your father charg'd me at our parting; / 'Be serviceable to my son,' quoth he, / Although I think 'twas in *another sense*," 1.1.212–215).

At the same time, however, what begins the series of preposterous inversions at the level of "class" or social position in this opening scene and the genesis of the Bianca-Lucentio subplot within it is a corresponding series of gender reversals, as Lucentio describes himself as captive to Baptista's younger daughter, in lines that include his own gender-shifting identification with Dido "Queen of Carthage" and Tranio with her sister Anna, from Virgil's *Aeneid*:

*Lucentio.* I found the effect of love in idleness,
And now in plainness do confess to thee,
That art to me as secret and as dear
As Anna to the Queen of Carthage was:
Tranio, I burn, I pine, I perish, Tranio,
If I achieve not this young modest girl. . . .
*Tranio.* Master, it is no time to chide you now,
Affection is not rated from the heart.
If love have touch'd you, nought remains but so,
"*Redime te captum quam queas minimo.*"

(1.1.151–162)

Tranio's Latin tag ("*Redime te captum quam queas minimo*," or "Ransom yourself from captivity as cheaply as you can," from Terence's *Eunuch*) is cited here from Lily's Latin grammar—yet another foregrounding of Latin grammar and "construing" in this play, as well as anticipation of the issue of mastery in the Latin lesson scene.[44] In the commercial context of the Paduan marriage market, "*Redime*" ("ransom" or "redeem") recalls the use in Terence of "redemption" in a monetary sense, already exploited by Shakespeare in the Ephesian market atmosphere of *The Comedy of Errors*.[45] But in this opening scene of a play whose "taming" plot depends on supposed mastery by a man, Lucentio's sense of himself as Bianca's captive (with Tranio's more cynical shift to the commercial sense that "Cambio" will have as well) is presented in an exchange where his characterizing of himself as Dido "Queen of Carthage" takes place in lines where the Folio's version of this well-known Latin tag (which has the feminine "*captam*" rather than male "*captum*") suggests yet another inversion of genders, at the grammatical level that was inseparable in the period from gender in another sense.[46]

In its immediate context, the line from Terence familiar from Lily's well-known grammar has to do (preposterously) with being mastered by a woman. And the setting of the Bianca-Lucentio subplot in motion here (with Lucentio's rhetoric of being captive to a woman) leads to other preposterous reversals or exchanges of position. Lucentio the master is transformed into a "servant" in this scene because he wants to be Bianca's "slave" ("let me be a slave, t'achieve that maid / Whose sudden sight hath thrall'd my wounded eye," 1.1.219–220)—part of the conventional Petrarchan rhetoric of courtship that was ultimately supposed to be reversed or re-righted in the Pauline hierarchy of marriage, in which the former "slave" or servant who idolizes his mistress would become her "master," in the kind of gender hierarchy he might expect from his "exclusive right to print" or the order and institution of matrimony from Genesis 2. But in the subplot that ensues—from this opening scene of the "taming" play to Bianca's "preposterous" overturning of both of her would-be "masters" in Act 3 and the final scene in which she emerges publicly as anything but successfully mastered—this Latin tag proves prophetic in a less promisingly redemptive sense for Lucentio at least.

The "cambio" or exchange of position between servant and master in this opening scene then leads to other forms of "preposterous" inversion as the subplot from Ariosto and Gascoigne's "Supposes" unfolds, including the scene of instruction that moves from inversion of the proper order of the "arts" to echoes of the Ceremony of Matrimony and Bianca's altering or doubting of her potential master's "construction." In the scene just before Lucentio's chastising of Hortensio as a "preposterous ass" for seeking to put *first* what should come *second*, and the language lesson's foregrounding of genealogy and patriarchal descent in the debate over whether Ajax deserves the patronymic "Aeacides," there is a series of strikingly "preposterous" reversals that have specifically to do with patrimony, generational sequence, and patriarchal descent, transferred (like so much in this play) from an aristocratic register to the kind of paternal underwriting Lucentio's wooing of Bianca as a wealthy burgher's daughter requires.

Here, Tranio (the servant who has already substituted for or assumed the position of his master) outlines in turn his inverted generational scheme to "(be)get" a "suppos'd" father for himself as "suppos'd Lucentio," in order to provide the patrimony necessary to underwrite his promises of property for Bianca:

> *Tranio.* . . . I have fac'd it with a card of ten.
> 'Tis in my head to do my master good.
> I see no reason but suppos'd Lucentio
> Must get a father, call'd suppos'd Vincentio;
> And that's a wonder. Fathers commonly
> Do get their children; but in this case of wooing,
> A child shall get a sire, if I fail not of my cunning.
> (2.1.405–411)

"Case" here doubly suggests not only the situation Tranio is in (of needing to "get" or beget his own "sire") but also the sexual "case" or place of begetting (as in the "lover's blessed case" or "in any case" of Act 4, in the scene involving the merchant-father "gotten" as the surrogate for Lucentio's actual father).[47] The wily servant Tranio's "cunning" used to "get" a sire in this "case" thus participates in two registers at once, the generative or sexual and the manipulative or sly. But what is noteworthy here is that this "getting" or begetting also involves the kind of generational reversal that is inscribed with the figure of the "preposterous" elsewhere in Shakespeare, not just in the "preposterous estate" of a son born before his father in *The Winter's Tale* (5.2.148, 139) or the scene in *King Lear* where the Fool's taunt that Lear has made his "daughters" his "mothers" (1.4.173) appears with the familiar exemplum of *hysteron proteron* as the cart placed before the horse, but also in the chronologically reversed tetralogies of English history plays, where sons come before fathers (in ways explored in Chapter 4).[48]

Tranio's preposterous scheme to "(be)get" a father, in a reverse of the natural order of begetting, is joined in these lines by another kind of inversion in "I have fac'd it with a card of ten," a reference to the card game "primero" (whose very name suggests primacy, priority, or coming *first*),[49] with which he prefaces the long shot of his plan to "get" a father's "assurance" for the promises made in bidding for Bianca. To "face" (or outface) it with a "card of ten"—in the game of "primero," which is also mentioned in Gascoigne's *Supposes*, where it is tellingly linked with turning "topsie turvie" (3.2)[50]—is to bluff that the lowest card will win the highest prize, yet another *cambio* or change of place between low and high. But the fact that the "gamester" (2.1.400) Tranio's "I have fac'd it with a card of ten" comes just before his lines on a "child" who will preposterously beget a "sire" not only underscores the importance of the repeated references to primero in this scene.[51] It also joins the wordplay throughout *The Taming of the Shrew* on "face" both as "outface" (or "brave") and as visage or "countenance," exploited in "face" in another sense in the Tailor Scene as well as the play on "countenance" and "face" (4.1.99–100) in the scene where Grumio is concerned about coming "before" his "master."[52] And it does so here in a context where "face" could mean both putting on a "front" or "face" and braving or brazening something out, as Tranio—the cunning servant (reminiscent of his predecessors in Plautus and Terence) who has already "fac'd" it as his "suppos'd" master, having put on his "count'nance" (1.1.229) as well as his "apparel" (1.1.228–229)—now plans to "face it out" further by preposterously (be)getting his own "sire."[53]

This final scene of Act 2—which leads directly from Tranio's speech on this preposterous begetting to the opening lines of the scene of instruction where Lucentio as "Cambio" calls Hortensio a "preposterous ass"—is already filled by reminders of other contemporary contexts of "unnatural" or preposterous reversal, including when Baptista insists that this "suppos'd Lucentio" obtain paternal "assurance" lest, contrary to the order of nature, this son should die *before* his father:

> *Baptista.* I must confess your offer is the best,
> And let your father make her the assurance,
> She is your own, else you must pardon me;
> If you should die *before* him, where's her dower?
> (2.1.386–389)

In the Padua marriage market—where Baptista has already confessed his "merchant's part" (2.1.326) and daughters are a negotiable "commodity" (2.1.328)—Baptista's shrewdness (a quality tellingly aligned with "shrew," at a time before that term was definitively gendered)[54] is to test this suitor's claim to being his "father's heir and only son" (2.1.364) against yet another "unnatural" (or preposterous) proposition: a father's being willing to transfer all of his property to his son before his death in order to provide him with such "assurance." The "Graybeard" rival Gremio understandably concludes that no father would brook such a generational inversion of power or position. And his response to the requirement that the supposed "Lucentio" obtain such "assurance" as a condition of Bianca's being granted to him is confidence that this condition cannot be fulfilled: "your father were a fool / To give thee all, and in his waning age / Set foot under thy table" (2.1.400–402).

In the contemporary context of what historian Keith Thomas has described as the "gerontocratic ideal" justified as "the law of nature,"[55] for a father to "set foot" under the "table" of his son would involve an unnatural overturning of the hierarchy of patriarch and heir, through a father's becoming his son's "dependent" (*Riverside*) or living on his "charity" (New Cambridge; New Penguin; Arden 2 and 3)—a reversal of the order of the generations (elder *before* younger, father *before* son) as preposterous or unnatural as a child's begetting a sire, in the plan devised by Tranio at the end of this same scene. Gremio's "your father were a fool / To give thee all" is an early forecast of Lear's position, when he preposterously turns his "daughters" into "mothers," transgressing the contemporary assumption that "by the will of God and the natural order of things, authority belonged to the old,"[56] and raising the fear that "if parents hand over their wealth or their authority to their children, those children will turn against them."[57] So it is not surprising that the scene where the Fool taunts Lear with this inversion of the "natural" order—"thou mad'st thy daughters thy mothers . . . when thou gav'st them the rod, and put'st down thine own breeches" (1.4.172–174)—is filled not only with the explicit invoking of *hysteron proteron* in the Fool's "May not an ass know when the cart draws the horse?" (224), but also with obscene play on the reversal of bodily position as well as more literally on what should "bear" what ("When thou clovest thy crown i' th' middle and gav'st away both parts, thou bor'st thine *ass* on thy back o'er the dirt," 160–162).

In the contrastingly comic context of this scene of preposterous or "unnatural" generational reversals in *The Taming of the Shrew*—where Tranio sets out to "get" a father and Gremio denies that a father would cede his patriarchal right to his son—the "assurance" required by Baptista involves the securing of a deed or title to property,[58] or the more material sense of "deeds" that Baptista's requirement demands: " 'Tis *deeds* must win the prize, and he of both / That can *assure* my daughter greatest dower / Shall have my Bianca's love" (2.1.342–344). In the marriage market where the joining of the Ceremony of Matrimony is inseparable from the material issue of an appropriate "jointure" or "jointer" (2.1.370), Gremio's "assurance"—as a man well "strook in years" (2.1.360)—is to offer Bianca his own property as her "dower" (343), in lines whose "only" ("And if I die to-morrow, this is hers, / If whilst I live she will be *only* mine," 361–362) subtly exploits the sound of "ownly" as well. But the disguised Tranio both picks up on and recasts this "only" ("That 'only' came well in. Sir, list to me: / I am my father's heir and only son," 363–364), in his offer of a jointure in the form of his "supposed" patrimony as his father's "only" son.

The reversal of positions in this scene is already suggested by the opposition embodied in these two suitors—of "age" and "youth," "Greybeard" and "Youngling" (2.1.337–338)—as well as in Gremio's insistence on his prerogative or priority ("I am your neighbor, and was suitor *first*," 2.1.334), reprised in the other suitor Hortensio's insistence on coming *first*, in the scene that comes immediately after. And in the rivalry over which of Bianca's suitors can "assure" the "greatest dower" (2.1.343), Tranio as the "suppos'd Lucentio" includes in the property of his "suppos'd" father to "*assure* her" (379) "two galliasses / And twelve tight galleys" (378–379). Given the repeated wordplay on "asses" in this play—including Katherine's "*asses* are made to bear" (2.1.199) earlier in this scene and the invocation of a "preposterous *ass*" in relation to Hortensio's *ars musica* in the scene that follows it—the repeated sounding of "ass" in "assure" (2.1.123, 343, 379), "galleasses," and "arras" (351) along with this "assurance" may itself compound the preposterous or "arsy-versy" inversion of place and position already foregrounded in this scene. It thus provides yet another link between the exchanges of generation and class through which Tranio's "assurance" is to be attained and the reversal of the genders as well as the "artes" or "*ars*" (in yet more wordplay on "ass") in the immediately following scene, where Bianca refuses to be a "breeching scholar" to either of her potential "masters."

∽

> Backedore or posterne, and which by circumlocution, signifyeth the Arse, or all thynges that is behynde vs, as Antica be all thynges before vs.
>
> —Richard Huloet's *Abcedarium Anglico Latinum* (1552)

> Backare! You are marvellous forward.
>
> —*The Taming of the Shrew* (2.1.73)

> Knock me here soundly. . . .
>
> —*The Taming of the Shrew* (1.2.8)

The exploitation of the arse-varse or preposterous in *The Taming of the Shrew*—explicitly sounded in Lucentio's denunciation of the too "forward" Hortensio as a "preposterous ass"—also includes its emphasis on "forward" (or "froward") and "back," as well as on what should come *before* and what *behind*, as in the scene where the servant Grumio describes his master as riding "behind" his mistress and worries about coming "before" his master, in the lines in Act 4 that turn on the temporal, spatial, and hierarchical as well as bodily ambiguity of "before" and "after." This repeated play on forward and back is strikingly underscored in the even earlier exchange when Petruchio introduces himself to Baptista as "Antonio's son, / A man well known throughout all Italy" (2.1.68–69), and Gremio comments:

> Saving your *tale*, Petruchio, I pray
> Let us that are poor petitioners speak too.
> [*Backare*]! [Folio, *Bacare*] you are marvellous *forward.*
>
> (2.1.71–73, emphasis mine)

Gremio's "forward" here plays both on the opposite of "backward" (including the possible place on stage where Petruchio may be, before he steps *ahead* of the others) and on "forward" in the sense of "presumptuous," the meaning it has frequently elsewhere in the play. And in his speech that ends with "Backare! you are marvellous forward," his "Saving your *tale*, Petruchio" resonates in turn with the sexualized pairing of "tales" and "tails" iterated elsewhere in *The Shrew* (including in the verbal sparring in this same scene between Petruchio and "Kate"). To Gremio's "Saving your tale" and the warning

"Backare!" Petruchio immediately responds, "O, pardon me, Signior Gremio, I would fain be *doing*" (2.1.74)—the term that combines the play's polyvalent emphasis on "deeds" (including as titles to property) with the sense of sexual "doing" that "tail" would imply, spoken by the character whose very name ("little Peter") may already evoke such bodily "doing," in a scene where he is anxious to get on with doing in every sense: to advance or move forward, with both marital and economic ends in view.[59]

"*Bacare*" or "Backare" is simply mock-Latin for "back" or "stand back."[60] But given the importance of "preposterous" play throughout *The Taming of the Shrew*—at the bodily as well as other levels—it is important at the same time to consider the contemporary contexts for this particular "backare." In Nicholas Udall's *Ralph Roister Doister* (I.2), it occurs in the context of rival wooers, where one is determined to come *first* (as Hortensio attempts in the scene where his rival calls him a "preposterous ass"). But it also figures in contemporary texts that aligned it with other orders and positions—bodily, sexual, and gendered—in relation to what should come forward or first and what back or behind. When it appears (repeated three times) as "Backare, quote Mortimer to his sow" in John Heywood's *Epigrams upon Proverbs*,[61] the responses it gets are a skeptical "Went that sow back at that bidding, trow you?" "Mortimer's sow speaketh as good Latin as he," and the even more distinctly gendered " 'The boar shall back first,' quoth she, 'I make a vow!' " (208). And intriguingly, when it is used in Lyly's *Midas*—a close contemporary of *The Shrew*—it is not just in the context of rivalry between servants who vie for which is "better," but in lines that invoke the grammatical "Masculine gender" (from Colet and Lily's *Grammar*) that is said to be more worthy than the feminine:

> *Licio.* Thou seruest *Mellacrites*, and I his daughter, which is the better man?
>
> *Petulus.* The Masculin gender is more worthy then the feminine, therfore, Licio, backare.
>
> (*Midas*, 1.2)[62]

"Backare" in Lyly's *Midas* (often cited for Gremio's "Backare" in *The Taming of the Shrew*) thus already comes loaded with a gender-inflected as well as social coding in relation to what should come "first" or forward and what should be positioned or placed back or behind.

In addition, however—in a play like *Midas* that abounds in sexual allusions (including "fiddle," "stick," "tongue," and "rope," which have their counterparts in *The Shrew*), a playwright like Lyly who elsewhere exploited the rhyming of "Mars" and Latin "Ars" with "Masse" and "Asse," and a period in which "Midas" (like "Judas" in *Love's Labor's Lost*) was repeatedly subject to wordplay on the "ass" at the "latter end" of his name—there may also be a sense in this "backare" from Lyly of the "backward" sexual position.[63] The relegation of "Licio," the addressee of his rival's "backare," to a "feminine" position, turns on a conflation of grammatical and sexual that was already familiar from Alanus de Insulis and other medieval as well as sixteenth-century writers.[64] And when "backare" appeared in John Grange's *Golden Aphroditis* in 1577, it was as follows: "yet wrested he so his *effeminate* bande to the siege of *backewarde* affection, that both trumpe and drumme sounded nothing for their Larum, but *Baccare, Baccare*."[65] The "siege of backewarde affection" here—with "trumpe," "drumme," and "effeminate"—suggests the possibility that "*baccare*" itself was already identified not only with the female or "feminine" as what should be subordinate rather than "forward" or first, but also with turning male into female, or putting a "man" in a "female" position.

Turning a man into a woman was already part of the cultural semantics of the "preposterous" in the period—as when George Sandys (for example) insisted that "it is without example that a man at any time became a woman," since it is "preposterous in Nature, which ever aimes at perfection, when men degenerate into effeminacy," or Sir Thomas Browne in *Pseudodoxia Epidemica* alluded to "unnaturall venery and degenerous effemination" in the species of "man" (where "unnaturall venery" reflected the "sed etiam *praeposterae* libidinis" of his Latin subtext).[66] And it is foregrounded in *The Taming of the Shrew* when Petruchio makes "Kate" address the old Vincentio as a "young budding virgin," and Hortensio protests that it "will make the man mad, to make a woman of him" (4.5.35–36)—or the kind of change from "male" to "female" that Sandys called "preposterous."

The music master Hortensio—who assumes the name "Litio" (or "Lisio") in the First Folio but "Licio" in the Second Folio,[67] or the same name as the character in Lyly's *Midas* who is told to "backare" (in an exchange that also includes reference to a double-meaning "fiddle" and "stick")—is called not only a "preposterous ass" but also a "fiddler," the cant term that served as a class sneer (as we have seen) but that also routinely crossed or elided the "homo/hetero divide," with a bawdy sexual inference that included "preposterous venery" as well. In multiple texts of the period, "fiddler" connoted a "sexual partner" and "fiddle" various kinds of sexual instruments (in both back and front), including the "fiddle-case" for Aretino's "*cassa de la viola.*" In *A Young-Mans Tryal* (1655), a later "Kate" is anxious "for one to play on her Fiddle"; and in John Fletcher's *The Woman's Prize; or, the Tamer Tamed* (ca. 1611), the sequel to *The Taming of the Shrew*, Petruchio comments on how some husbands are deprived of their conjugal rights while others "fall with too much stringing of the Fiddles."[68] But "fiddler" was also the contemporary English term for the Latin *cinaedus* (or "pathic" male).[69] Florio translates Martial's "*cinaedus*" in the text of Montaigne as "fiddler" ("*Et habet tristis quoque turba cynaedos,*" "Fidlers are often had / Mongst people that are sad").[70] And Ben Jonson cites the *cinaedus* from Juvenal's *Satires,* in attacking his enemies as *cinaedi* ("Not one of them but lives himself [if known] / *Improbior satyram scribente cinaedo*"), in *Poetaster*'s "Apologetical Dialogue" (53–54),[71] and features in *Every Man Out of His Humor* a boy called "Cinedo"—a term used for boy players elsewhere in the period, including in John Marston's *Scourge of Villainy* (3.49) on "fair Cinaedian boys," in the context of pederasty and "male stews." "Fiddler" in *Poetaster* has this overtone as well in the passage where Tucca says to Histrio the player, "we must have you turn fiddler again, slave, get a bass violin at your back and march in a tawny coat with one sleeve to Goose Fair" (3.4.112–113),[72] in the reference to the "villainous out-of-tune fiddler Enobarbus" (3.4.233),[73] and the later scene where Tucca says to the "minstrel" Momus, "When will you be in good fooling of yourself, fiddler?" (4.5.71–72),[74] in a plot in which players themselves are associated with "ingles" or catamites (including when Ovid Senior says to his son: "What? Shall I have my son a stager now? An ingle for players?" 1.2.12).[75]

"Backare" itself, then—like "preposterous ass" in the scene of Lucentio's rebuke to Hortensio, that his *ars musica* is to come *after* rather than *before*—already suggests the contemporary cultural semantics of the "preposterous" in this respect as well, not only a reversal of position at the level of "class" or gender (rival servants or the "sow" of Mortimer rather than the "boar") but the sense of "sub-position" already present in Ariosto's *I Suppositi* (source of Gascoigne's *Supposes* and Shakespeare's *Shrew*), to which we will return at the end of this chapter. The sexual double meanings that fill the scene of instruction involving the "fiddler" Hortensio—which exploits bawdy equivoques on musical "instruments," the "re" (*res*) or "thing" of the musical gamut, and the testicular (as well as sexually ambiguous) sense of "one cliff, two notes have I" (3.1.74, 77)—thus include overtones of preposterous venery as well as indeterminately crossing between "forward" (or front) and back, like "spit in the hole" (3.1.40), where it is not clear which orifice is intended.[76]

Preposterous constructions in this play repeatedly escape the binary logic of figuring in only one register, but are capable instead of a *cambio*-like shifting between multiple meanings and contexts, including of gender, class, or sexual position. And the emphasis on "back" in multiple senses, as well as the backside or reverse—in the exchange on "Backare" in Act 2, the subplot's "arsy-versy" exchange of place between master and servant, and the play's repeated harping on the different meanings of "before" and "behind," including in relation to servants and "service"—have their further counterpart in the scene where the master Petruchio orders his servant Grumio to "rap" or "knock" him ("Villain, I say, knock me at this gate, / And rap me well, or I'll knock your knave's pate," 1.2.11–12), in an exchange that resonates with the sense of social reversal—a servant "knocking" his master (as Thomas Moisan and others have suggested)[77]—but also with the kind of "arse-varse" sexual sense such "knocking" would imply.[78]

The entire passage turns on the verbal reversal or palindrome of "noc" and "con" that already gives to "[k]noc[k]" its familiar contemporary sexual sense, including in the ostensibly only heteronormative register sounded in the obscene double-entendres on "con" in the "tailor" scene (on taking up a mistress's "gown" for a master's use)—or the same sound that produces "con" or "count" from "gown" in the language lesson of *Henry V* (3.4.51–52). But here, as the "rap" or knocking of a "master" by his male "servant," it also conveys the sense of "preposterous venery" or "preposterous *amor*" that was itself exploited in the period as a palindromic reversal—in, for example, John Bale's "If ye spell Roma backwarde . . . it is preposterous *amor*," "a loue out of order or a loue agaynst kynde," in *Englysh Votaryes*, or "Roma amor est. Amor est? qualis? Praeposterous," in *The Pageant of Popes*, cited in relation to spelling "backward" in Chapter 1.[79]

The servant Grumio who is asked to "knock" his master registers his complaint against his master's command first in class terms, after he misunderstands the greeting in Italian between Petruchio and the just-entering Hortensio (1.2.24–25) as "Latin":

> Nay, 'tis no matter, sir, what he 'leges in Latin. If this be not a lawful cause for me to leave his service, look you, sir. He bid me knock him and rap him soundly, sir. Well, was it fit for a servant to use his master so . . . ? (1.2.28–32).

But "knock" and "rap"—which elsewhere in Shakespeare and his contemporaries include the bodily sexual sense of knocking at the "back door"—quickly shift to the sexual sense of "use" in this exchange before Hortensio's "gate," when Grumio goes on to complain:

> Knock at the gate? O heavens! Spake you not these words plain,
> "Sirrah, knock me here; rap me here; knock me well, and knock me soundly"? And come you now with "knocking at the gate?"
> (1.2.39–43)

The sense of the "preposterous" as a hierarchical status or "class" inversion—as the aggrieved Grumio complains, when he assumes that he has been asked to "knock" or assault the very master he is legally bound to protect—is thus quickly joined here by the sexual sense of the "preposterous." And this "preposterous" traversing of both class hierarchy and sexual position is part of a play where Grumio in Act 4 considers the different senses of coming "before" his master (rather than "after" or "behind"), in a period when Bale and others could describe reading Scripture "backward" as "arsewarde" and Richard Huloet's Latin-English dictionary could include both "Arse" and things that come "before" and "behind" in a temporal, spatial, and bodily sense in its entry on "Backedore or posterne, and which by circumlocution, signifyeth the Arse, or all thynges that is behynde vs, as Antica be all thynges before vs."[80]

Much by the play's end *seems* to involve the "righting" of such preposterously inverted hierarchies, including those of gender and social position (with the clever servant Tranio's obvious disappointment at his demotion).[81] Yet, in the contrary direction, Bianca, praised by Lucentio at the beginning for "Maid's mild behavior and sobriety" (1.1.71), becomes instead (along with the widow, a figure notorious in the period for such "preposterous" inversions) one of the "froward wives" (5.2.119) or "headstrong" (130) women, not meekly following like a subordinate wifely "appendix" but overturning the hierarchy of master and subordinate in ways that recall the pivotal scene of instruction and "construction" in Act 3 that sounded a telling echo of the Ceremony of Matrimony as well. The sense that she might also be unfaithful similarly recalls that same pivotal scene, which had ended with Hortensio's concern that she might be "ranging" (3.1.91), in lines that also include reference to a "stale" (3.1.90), the term used for Bianca's counterpart in Gascoigne's *Supposes*.[82]

Like the widow who "will not come" and bids her husband, instead, to "come to *her*" (5.2.92), this reversal of Lucentio's earlier sense of Bianca's tractability once again summons the cultural markers of the "preposterous," "backward," or "overthwart" overturning of the orthodox orders of gender (in ways picked up in Fletcher's subsequent rewriting and sequel).[83] And "Cambio," the adopted name cast off by Lucentio once it no longer serves *his* purposes, now continues in the change or shift within his apparently subordinate wife, who it is suggested will govern or master *him*—making the Latin tag from Terence on *Redime te* when he originally professed himself "captive" to Bianca an ironic prophecy of this trajectory. It therefore extends (rather than exercising an ultimate closural "re-righting" on) the sense of reversal, *cambio*, or change of position, even after "Cambio" has changed back into "Lucentio" and the particular *cambio* or exchange he had enacted with his servant has (from one perspective) been "righted."

In this final scene where Bianca is perceived as having changed or shifted (46), Katherine appears to be "chang'd, as she had never been" (5.2.115), in the other direction, into "another daughter" (114), as Baptista puts it. The formerly "shrewish" Katherine's final speech on the obedience owed by a wife to her husband as "head" (147)—lines that echo the Pauline glosses on the Genesis 2 text of female and male that were the underpinnings of the Ceremony of Matrimony (even though that text is not echoed here as explicitly as in the anonymous play *The Taming of a Shrew*)—is pronounced in this scene by Lucentio himself to be "harsh hearing when women are froward" (5.2.183). But whatever is made of her speech in the ongoing critical debate,[84] the fact that the final stage direction in the Folio has Petruchio exit without her may open their story as well into a more ambiguous sequel or "field of possibility"—as the play's most recent Arden editor, Barbara Hodgdon, has suggested—pointing "away from closure, and towards open-endedness," like the final lines of the dialogue itself, where Lucentio's " 'a wonder, by your leave, she will be tamed so' strikes a slightly hesitant note."[85] The unabated exchange of place that resists both righting and closure in this apparent ending figures place itself not as fixed or immutable but as subject to reversals to come, just as the declining of Bianca to follow the "construction" of Lucentio/Cambio in the Language Lesson scene had already altered a would-be master's apparently authoritative final word. And even critical certainty about the meaning (and intentions or motives) of Katherine's final speech itself remains open to "supposition" or uncertain "suppose."[86]

❧

Supposito, *a suppose, a thing supposed. Also vnder-set, or put vnder, put in the place of another.*

—John Florio, *A Worlde of Wordes* (1598)

Supposer. *To suppone; to put, lay, or set under; to suborne, forge, counterfeit, foist or thrust in false things among, or in stead of, true; also, to suppose, imagine, meane, understand, more then's expressed.*

—Randle Cotgrave, *A Dictionarie of the French and English Tongves* (1611)

and some I see smyling as though they supposed we would trouble you with the vaine suppose of some wanton Suppose.

—George Gascoigne, Prologue to *Supposes* (1566)

Given the clear foregrounding of transvestite theater and its (potentially misleading) "supposes" in the transvestite "boy" Hostess and boy "page" as Sly's wife in the Induction, and the fact that both Bianca and "Kate" are boy players, we might end on one other aspect of Shakespeare's play, which has gone almost entirely unnoticed by its editors and critics—the *sub*textual context of "Supposes" in a bodily, "suppositional," and sexual sense that is already part of the sources for the Bianca/"Cambio" plot in Ariosto and Gascoigne, but also important for both "supposes" and preposterous constructions in *The Taming of the Shrew*.[87]

"Suppose" in early modern English meant to believe or assume something to be true, including in a legal conjecture.[88] But it also had (as in Latin and Italian) not only the additional sense of substitute—or put in the place or position of another—but also to place (or be placed) *under* or below,[89] from Latin *supponere* and *suppositus* ("subjected"), which gave to Ariosto's *I Suppositi* its concomitant "sodomitical" inflection. Florio's Italian-English *Worlde of Wordes* (1598) has "Supponere, *as* Sottoponere. *also to suppose or surmise*," as well as "Suppositione, *a putting of a thing vnder another*, a supposition," "Supposito, *a suppose, a thing supposed. Also vnder-set, or put vnder, put in the place of another,*" and "Suppositiuo, *that may be supposed or counterfeite, suppositiue. Also put vnder*" (a range of meanings registered in his 1611 *Queen Anna's New World of Words* as well). And Randle Cotgrave's French-English dictionary of 1611 continues to reflect this contemporary semantic range, in its entries on "Supposé" as "*Supposed, imagined, meant, understood; also, underset, or put under; and suppositious, suborned; shifted, or put in for another; whence;* Enfant supposé. *A changeling*" and "Supposer" as "*To suppone; to put, lay, or set under; to suborne, forge, counterfeit, foist or thrust in false things among, or in stead of, true; also, to suppose, imagine, meane, understand, more then's expressed.*"[90]

Ariosto evokes not only substitution and supposition but also the bodily and erotic sense of "*suppositi*" (as sexual positions or postures) in both versions of his Prologue to *I Suppositi* (in prose in 1509; and verse in 1528–1531).[91] His prose version has "Non pigliate, benigni auditori, questo *supponere* in mala parte: che bene in altra guisa si *suppone* che non lasciò ne li suoi lascivi libri Elefantide figurato" (rendered in one translation as "Don't take these *substitutions* in a bad sense, my good audience, for they are not like the *substitutions* illustrated in the lascivious books of Elephantis")[92]—the famous erotic pictures of sexual positions (including preposterous or "sodomitical" positions) associated with the Greek poetess and courtesan Elephantis, cited in Martial, Suetonius, and other writers well known to Shakespeare.[93] But as other translations make clear, Ariosto's "*supponere*" and "*suppone*" here could as readily be translated as "supposing" in its multiple senses, including the sexual.[94] His verse Prologue has "E bench'io parli con voi di *supponere*, / Le mie *supposizioni* però simili / Non sono a quelle antique, che Elefantide / In diversi atti e forme e *modi* varii / Lasciò dipinte; e che poi rinovatesi / Sono ai dì nostri in Roma santa, e fattesi / In carte belle, più che oneste, imprimere, / Acciò che tutto il mondo n'abbia copia" (rendered in another translation as: "although I speak with you of *supposing*, my *suppositions* are not similar to the antique [i.e., ancient] ones, which in diverse acts and forms and various *positions* Elephantis had painted; and which then were revived in our time in Holy Rome, and printed in engravings more beautiful than decent, so that the whole world has copies of them,"[95] in lines where "supposing" for "*supponere*" and "suppositions" for "*supposizioni*" could also be translated as "substitutions."[96] This later verse Prologue thus adds to the "positions" depicted by Elephantis an unmistakable reference to the widely disseminated engravings of "*I modi*" (sexual positions or postures) published in 1524 by Marcantonio Raimondi from the erotic drawings of Giulio Romano, to which were added Pietro Aretino's *Sonnetti lussuriosi* (or "Lascivious Sonnets"), which famously also depicted "back-door" sexual entry.[97] As Bette Talvacchia notes in her discussion of Ariosto's deliberate invoking of such sexual "postures" (in *Taking Positions*), "Ariosto's sly reference" to

Elephantis and to the "small paintings, or *tabellae*, which displayed explicit sexual content, to which Ovid referred in the *Tristia*," evokes at the beginning of his *Suppositi* what were famous examples of "sexual tutoring."[98] And Lynne Lawner's translation of *I Modi*, or the "Postures" (or *posizioni*) of Aretino and Giulio Romano, renders Ariosto's "*supposizioni*" as "sup-positions," in an Englishing that underscores the sense of being placed *under* that made Ariosto's Prologue and his play famous for its exploitation of the "sodomitical" sense of "*suppositi*" as well.[99]

I quote here from different translations of *I Suppositi*, which variously render Ariosto's *suppone* and *supposizioni* as "substitutions," "supposes," "sup-positions," or inferred "sub-positions," because (as one widely used translation puts it), "There is no English word to convey adequately all the nuances of the Italian *suppositi*. The Latin participle, *suppositus*, itself translates into a number of possible Italian equivalents: *supposto* (supposed or assumed); *sottoposto* (submitted, subjected, or exposed); *sostituito* (substituted or interchanged); *finto* (pretended or feigned); *scambiato* (exchanged or mistaken); and even *posposto* (placed after or behind)." And it adds that "Ariosto was hoping that the minds of his audience would wander over a number of these meanings," in addition to "logical word substitutions" and the title's "sodomistic connotations," on which it placed "particular emphasis."[100]

Ariosto's prose Prologue already slyly evoked the "sodomistic" sense of his title, as of "*supporre*" as "*sottoporsi*" or placed *under*.[101] Although this prose Prologue to *I Suppositi* asks its audience not to take its "substitutions" (or "*supponere*") in a "bad sense," as a modern translation has it,[102] since they are not like those illustrated in "the lascivious books of Elephantis," "*I Suppositi*" could as easily be "an obscene allusion" as "substitutions," as its Italian editor notes,[103] just as "*supponere*" (as in Florio) could be "place under" (in the sexual sense of "*sottoponere*") and "*in mala parte*" could be "in a bad sense" but also a double entendre on a sexual "part" as well.

The verse Prologue to *I Suppositi* ends with yet more emphasis on the polyvalent meanings of *supponere*: "Vi potrà dar col suo nuovo *supponere* / Non dishonesta materia da ridere" ("it may give you, along with these substitutions [or supposes/suppositions], an honest subject for laughter"—or literally, "not dishonest material" for laughter).[104] And—at the same time—it introduces "*cambio*," Ariosto's term for changes and exchanges of position, adopted by Shakespeare as the supposed name of "Cambio" for Lucentio after he has exchanged position with his servant: "Questa *supposizion* nostra significa / Quel che in volgar si dice porre in *cambio*" ("This substitution [or supposition] of ours signifies what in the vernacular would be called *exchange*"), adding, "I'm explaining the meaning of the term in order to remove any evil thoughts and to make you understand that you haven't guessed correctly."[105]

As Ariosto scholar Sergio Costola notes, the title *I Suppositi* already "refers to male/male sexual relations" insofar as its actors interpreting female characters were part of a transvestite theatrical context, where gender is constructed through performance, though Ariosto's prologue includes "the author's explicit appeal to the spectator to focus attention not on the homoerotic aspect of the play" but on the "class switch between the master and the servant."[106] Moreover—in an ambiguity in Italian like the one exploited in *The Taming of the Shrew* with regard to the different senses of *before* and *after* or in Huloet's Latin-English dictionary entry on "Backedore or posterne, and which by circumlocution, signifyeth the Arse, or all thynges that is behynde vs, as Antica be all thynges before vs"—the prose Prologue's "li fanciulli per l'adrieto sieno stati suppositi, e sieno qualche volta oggidì" ("children have been substituted for one another in the past, and sometimes are today") exploits the ambiguity in "*adrieto*" or "*adietro*" as both "in the past" and "from behind," with "the latter giving to the rest of the prologue a quite explicit meaning focused on sodomy."[107] For it then moves from the suggestion of pederasty (in a "*fanciulli*" that could be rendered as "children" but also "male youths") to what it says must seem "new and strange" ("Ma che li vecchi sieno da li gioveni *suppositi*, vi debbe per certo parere e novo e strano; e pur li vecchi alcuna volta *si soppongono*, similmente": "But, to have young men substituted for old men must certainly seem new and strange to you; and, yet, this has occasionally been done")[108]—immediately before entreating the audience not to take "*supponere*" or "*suppositi*" in "a bad sense," for they are "not like the substitutions [or sup-positions] illustrated in the lascivious books of Elephantis."[109]

The Prologue to Ariosto's verse version of *I Suppositi*—which also suggests that any "*sporcizia*" (or bawdy meaning) is in the minds of his hearers—similarly begins with the ambiguity of "*soppongano*" (as both substitute and place *under*), as with the double-meaning "*adietro*" in lines having to do with "*I fanciulli.*"[110] And it moves to old men by youths "*sopposit*i" (rather than the other way round), again described as "new" and "strange" ("Ma che li vecchi siano / Similmente dai gioveni soppositi, / Nuovo e strano vi dee parer certissima- / mente . . ."),[111] before adding to the illustrations of ancient Elephantis the notorious contemporary depictions of sexual postures or positions by Giulio Romano (accompanied by the verses of Aretino), while assuring his audience that his "*supposizioni*" are different—simply "cambio" or exchanges, not "disonesta materia."

For all of the characteristic irony of Ariosto's simultaneous foregrounding and disavowal of the double meaning of his title and the play's substitutions or exchanges, the sotto voce implications were well known. As Laura Giannetti comments in her study of Ariosto's play and the transvestite theatrical context of which it was a part: "the author constructed a play on words based on the title of the comedy itself, a play on the multiple erotic implications of the term *suppositi* that he knew the audience would understand." After "affirming that *fanciulli* (male youths) were notoriously *suppositi* (exchanged / used / used anally) in ancient as well as in contemporary times, the author warned the audience that in the comedy they were about to see, even if it might seem strange, 'even old men are exchanged / used / used anally' (*si suppongano*)," clearly evoking in *si suppongano* the reversal in which "old men" took the passive part though—immediately after this—declaring that, "in this case, 'exchanging' (*supponere*) meant only mistaking one person for another."[112] And in his later verse Prologue, Ariosto "added a quip that seems to have been based upon the audience's reaction to the word play in earlier performances": with "subtle irony, he claimed that this explanation was necessary to avoid saying or drawing attention to 'certain dirty things' "—"Something, of course, that the prologue had just done and which apparently had evoked laughter: 'But you laugh. Oh, what have you heard from me that would cause you to laugh?' "[113] Giannetti also recounts the famous occasion in which one audience member who was amused was Pope Leo X, in a performance in Rome during Carnival in 1519, where Raphael provided the set; and cites the letter of Alfonso Paolucci to the Duke of Ferrara that recorded that when the narrator explained the comedy in the Prologue, "he played around with the title of the comedy which is *I suppositi* so cleverly that the Pope laughed very heartily with those around him. And according to what I heard, the French were quite scandalized by that title *Suppositi*."[114]

Even after the double-meanings of its Prologue, Ariosto's *I Suppositi* continues to suggest not just the *cambio* or change of hierarchical position between master and servant (basis of the subplot of Shakespeare's *Shrew*) but also the sexual overtones of *suppositi* and *suppone*, including in ways that underscore the transvestite theatrical context of its staging (in a scene involving the counterpart to the rivals' wooing of Bianca). In Act 3, scene 3, when the parasite Pasifilo enters and is asked, "Where the devil are you coming from?," he responds, "per l'uscio di dietro" ("from the back door")—a wording that recalls the "*dietro*" of the Prologue and "back-door" sexual entry as well as fitting with the parasite's "sodomitical" associations.[115] But even earlier, in Act 2, scene 3, both the "*gioveni*" or male youths that figure in the wordplay on "*suppositi*" and "*suppone*" or "*sottoponere*" in the Prologue and the transvestite theatrical context where the counterpart to Bianca is also a youthful male player are recalled and highlighted when the disguised counterpart to Lucentio baits his elderly rival (the lawyer Cleandro) by reporting that he is said to be "aperto di sotto" ("open down below," glossed as "*aperto*: sodomita")[116] and that the remedy for his "infirmity" is to be with "youths with their first beard," in lines rendered in the 1525 prose version with an added "*a le parte di dietro*" ("Che tu patisci una certa infermità, [a le parte di dietro] a cui giova et è appropriato rimedio a stare con *li giovani di prima barba*").[117] He also adds that this is the real reason his rival is wooing the sought-after daughter, in order to lure male youths (or "*giovani*") to their house, for his sexual use.

As Giannetti comments on this scene, in the context of *I Suppositi* as a whole: "The comedy, which turned on an exchange or switch of characters and roles and the misunderstandings that followed from this, at the same time employed sodomy and homoerotic desires as a means of making fun of the character of the old man Cleandro," the figure in Ariosto (I would add) who suggests a combination of both of Lucentio's rivals (the old Gremio and Hortensio or "Litio," whose very name evokes lawyers). And in the midst of other insults, he delivers "the final blow—at least on the comic plane—asserting that the only reason old Cleandro wants to marry a beautiful and rich young woman is because he has a greater desire for husbands than for a wife; a young and beautiful wife he can use as a hook to attract the young men he truly desires to his house," a motive (Giannetti notes) that was then also "taken up by Aretino in his *Marescalco*."[118]

Though the prose Prologue (with the familiar Ariostan irony) begs its audience or "hearers" not to take "questo *supponere* in mala parte" (or a bad sense), after he has spoken of "*li vecchi*" and "*li gioveni*," since he means "*suppone*" in a different way from what is pictured in the "lascivious books" of Elephantis, this scene's subsequent reference to Ganymedes or "*li giovani di prima barba*" in the play itself (where the old man who is a rival suitor for Bianca's counterpart is said to be more interested in male youths) "does not leave much to the imagination."[119] And Ariosto's verse version of *I Suppositi*—whose Prologue similarly suggests that any "*sporcitia*" (or indecent meaning) is in the minds of his hearers, immediately after its lines on the "new and strange" ("Nuovo, e strano") situation of "li vecchi . . . dai giovani suppositi" rather than the more usual pederastic way round—includes the "preposterous" sexual sense suggested by its title in other places as well.

Ariosto—a well-known and acknowledged source for other Shakespeare plays (including *Much Ado About Nothing* and the female-female desire and male twin of *Twelfth Night*)—thus prefaces his *I Suppositi* (the popular Italian play translated by Gascoigne as *Supposes*) with a characteristically ironic Prologue, which simultaneously evokes and disavows any connection with the sexual positions of the "Elephantis" or (in the verse version's addition) the erotic "postures" (or "*posizioni*") of Giulio Romano and Aretino, both of which included preposterous or "back-door" entry. Gascoigne's Prologue to his *Supposes* (1566)—in a translation that reflects his consultation of both of Ariosto's versions of *I Suppositi*—does not explicitly refer to either Elephantis or the sexual postures or positions of Giulio Romano's drawings and Aretino's accompanying sonnets.[120] But though he insists (in a way that subtly recalls Ariosto) that his "suppose" is "*nothing else but* a mystaking or imagination of one thing for another," Gascoigne's reference to "some wanton Suppose" in his own Prologue ("and some I see smyling as though they supposed we would trouble you with the vaine suppose of some wanton Suppose") would, as its editor G. W. Pigman III observes, be "hardly intelligible" without a recall of this underlying sexual or erotic sense (or as he puts it, "Without the reference to Elephantis the wanton meaning is hardly intelligible").[121]

In addition, Gascoigne not only explicitly added multiple scatological (bodily and "backside") touches but also continued Ariosto's frequent practice of leaving meanings up to the audience's own "supposes" or suppositions—including with regard to homoeroticism or preposterous venery—yet another way of subtly suggesting the uncertain status of evidence or proof that Lorna Hutson has analyzed as central to both plays, Italian original and English translation.[122] Gascoigne adds "arskisse" to Ariosto's wordplay on his own name (and that of Lucentio's counterpart Erostrato) in Act 2,[123] and exploits the sense of "purse" as "scrotum" as well as "female genitalia" (2.3) in relation to the marriage market where a father is negotiating with his daughter's rival suitors.[124] And his repeated scatological emphasis on the backside or "ass" continues in Act 3—with "What will you breake? Your nose in mine arse?" (3.1.11), a line that not only recalls the emphasis on the lower bodily in his earlier-added "arskisse" but simultaneously suggests the sexual sense of back-door entry from the corresponding passage in Ariosto, in an

English context where "nose" frequently had the sense of "penis" as well, including in Shakespeare.[125] This more explicitly sexual sense joins the repeated scatology of his *Supposes*' final act, where "hole in another place, I would your nose were in it" is added by Gascoigne to the traditional New Comedy discovery of an identifying "mole" (here on the "left shoulder").[126] And at the play's own end, Gascoigne also adds to Ariosto's wordplay on "*Suppositi*" his own concluding reference to an anal "suppositorie"—to make what he calls "a righte ende of our supposes" ("to make a righte ende of our supposes, lay one of those boltes in the fire, and make thee a suppositorie as long as mine arme," 5.10.44–48)[127]—joining the scatological combination of bodily backside and the play's latter end in Ariosto (whose prose ending has "*in culo*," or "up your ass," as Beame and Sbrocchi translate it) as part of an open-ended "Recognition Scene" that still leaves so much up to "supposition," or an ending that involves more "supposes" than definitive proof, as with *The Taming of the Shrew*.[128]

Even in the scene in Act 2 where Ariosto's Lucentio figure—disguised as his servant in order to woo (and sexually win) the counterpart to Bianca—reports to his rival the old lawyer that he is thought to be an "open-ended" sodomite ("*aperto di sotto*") and is wooing this young woman in order to attract male youths (or "*li giovani*") to their house, the issue of "suppose" or supposition is increased in Ariosto's verse version, used in this instance by Gascoigne, though he elsewhere draws on both versions, prose and verse. Ariosto's prose version is explicit about the "infirmity" whose "remedy" would be provided by these youths ("Che tu patisci una certa infermità, a cui giova et è appropriato remedio a stare con li giovani di prima barba" or "youths with their first beard," to which the 1525 prose version added "a le parte di dietro"). But in the verse version (which Gascoigne chose to follow here), the motive for wanting to attract "*giovani*" to his house is left up to "suppose" or supposition—"Li gioveni? A che effetto? . . . Imaginatelo / Voi pur" (or "Imagine it yourself"),[129] which appears in Gascoigne's *Supposes* as "Yong men? to what purpose? / . . . Nay, gesse you that" (or "guess you that").[130] But both the prose version's explicit lines on the "infirmity" that is the reason for his desire for Ganymedes or adolescent youths and the verse version of his desire for such "*giovani*," which (like Gascoigne's) leaves it up to supposing or supposition, glance simultaneously at the transvestite theatrical context of both stagings, where the young woman who is the object of the rivals' wooing is (like Bianca) a transvestite male player.

"Suppose" was therefore available for all of the senses exploited in *The Taming of the Shrew*—including for changes in class and gender position, for substitutions of the "counterfeit" or false for the true (or supposed), and for the uncertain status (including for its critics) of "supposition," but also for *cambio*-like changes in bodily and sexual position, including "preposterous venery." And it came in different ways from both sources with reminders of the "wanton Suppose" (as Gascoigne has it) of the sexual postures or positions associated with the *Ars amatoria* and "Elephantis," as well as with Aretino and Giulio Romano's wanton pictures.

The sexual positions or "postures" associated with Giulio Romano and Aretino were well known in early modern England and alluded to repeatedly in English writing, including in Robert Greene, Thomas Lodge, Thomas Nashe, and John Donne, and in Ben Jonson's *Sejanus* (1603) and *Volpone* (1605)—in which Shakespeare himself acted—as well as *The Alchemist* (1610).[131] Shakespeare also referred multiple times to "postures"—in *Coriolanus, Cymbeline,* and *Henry VIII,* but also in *Antony and Cleopatra,* in the transvestite theatrical context of "Some squeaking Cleopatra boy my greatness / I' th' posture of a whore" (5.2.220–221), and in *The Winter's Tale,* where that "rare Italian master" Giulio Romano himself (5.2.97) is said to be the sculptor of the statue of Hermione that closely resembles "Her natural posture!" (5.3.23).

Given the striking allusion to erotic postures in a transvestite theatrical context in *Antony and Cleopatra* and the explicit reference to Giulio Romano in *The Winter's Tale*—along with the fact that Shakespeare not only accessed sources for other plays in the original Italian, but made such prominent use of Ariosto's "*cambio*" in the name taken by Lucentio in the subplot from the "Supposes"—it is not at all impossible that the sexual sense of (sup)position and "*supponere*" in Latin, Italian, and English, including the "backward" position of preposterous venery (across the homo/hetero divide) is part of Shakespeare's *Shrew*—even after the Induction where Keir Elam has recently suggested an echo of such erotic postures in the allusion to "wanton pictures" (Ind. 1.47).[132] Elam persuasively suggests that the transvestite boy wife and the trick played on Sly in the Induction shows the further influence of Aretino's *Il Marescalco*, the play (well known in England) that provided the source for the plot and boy-wife of Jonson's *Epicoene*.[133] And the Induction itself evokes what Amanda Bailey describes as "the absent-presence of the 'best known myth of homoerotic desire in early modern England,' that of

Jupiter's seduction of his page Ganymede," as "Sly assumes the role of Jupiter by commanding his lady page to lie with him."[134] So *The Taming of the Shrew* more largely—beyond the Induction where "wanton pictures" are so strikingly alluded to (along with echoes of Ovidian *Metamorphoses* and the amorous *modi* of Ovid's *Ars Amatoria*)—may indeed echo the sexual resonances of Ariosto's "*I Suppositi*," and Gascoigne's own "wanton Suppose," including in the transvestite theatrical context it shares with the Induction (where, as Barbara Hodgdon notes, the addressing of the Hostess as "boy"—in the "single Shakespearean instance of addressing a woman as "boy"—may be "a typically Sly-like reference, calling attention to the boy actor's body beneath the role," as in " 'Some squeaking Cleopatra boy my greatness' ").[135]

In the Language Lesson scene itself, where Bianca claims she is no "breeching scholar in the schools" (3.1.18), the phrase at the same time evokes (as Bruce Smith notes in *Shakesqueer*) the contemporary context of Latin tutors and boys' buttocks that Alan Stewart and others have described as central to other sites and scenes of Latin learning and pedagogical instruction.[136] As this scene of rival tutors proceeds, its further reference to "the treble jars" (3.1.39) calls attention to Bianca's own boy player's voice as well.[137] And—in a play where the Induction calls such striking attention to the transvestite theatrical context where female parts were played by boys—the final scene's ambiguous references to Bianca's "bush" (in "I mean to shift my bush," 5.2.46) and to a "butt" (5.2.40) that is both "buttock" and a "target," culminate in concluding lines that exploit the meaning of Bianca's name not only as Italian for "white" but also as a homophone of "wight" and a target or "butt," in the multiple sexual senses of "you hit the white" (5.2.186).[138] They thus slyly raise the question of whether the play is a "comonty" (Ind. 2, 138)—in the double sense of involving the "common" female thing and the (hetero)consummation of comedy where each "Jack" has his "Gill" (already problematized in *Love's Labor's Lost*)—just as the transvestite "suppose" of the Induction leaves open the question of whether Sly knows (or cares) that his new "wife" is a boy. So perhaps in another way, the Induction that appears to disappear by the end of *The Shrew* (as distinct from *A Shrew*) is subtly reintroduced in another form, in the complexly ambiguous "suppose" (both "wanton" and sly) that is transvestite theater itself. Or, as Cotgrave put it, *supposer* as not only to "put, lay, or set under" and "counterfeit" or "thrust in false things among, or instead of, true," but "to suppose, imagine, meane, understand, more then's expressed."

*Chapter 3*

# Multilingual Quinces and *A Midsummer Night's Dream*

## Visual Contexts, Carpenters' Coigns, Athenian Weddings

> *Quince*, a kind of fruit, from French *Coing*. . . . Italian *Mela cotogna, pomo cotogno.* Latin *Malum cotoneum* . . . from *lasios* or *hirsutus* ("hairy" or "rough with down") and *melon*, or Latin *pomum* ("apple"). Portuguese *Marmelo.* Spanish *Membrillo*, from *membrum.*
>
> —John Minsheu, *Ductor in Linguas, The Guide into Tongues* (1617)

The first two chapters—on the comedies *Love's Labor's Lost* and *The Taming of the Shrew*—have already engaged with issues of transvestite theater, latter ends (both bodily and dramatic), wooing and marriage, and the disrupting or complicating of a heteronormative ending, as well as with the explicit invocation of the "preposterous," including suggestively with regard to "preposterous venery" and inversions of hierarchy and gender. Both have involved contexts that include literacy and learning, biblical and classical exempla, conduct books, female speech, unruly (or resistant) women, and prescribed orders of gender and "class" or social estate. And both have in different ways engaged with continental influences and the multilingual or interlingual nature of English itself. This third chapter—the last on a comedy before we turn to other genres—involves all of these, including the multilingual. But it also widens the lens to include important visual contexts in the period that are crucial to this comedy and the setting of this particular Shakespearean "marriage play" in Athens.

Editors and commentators often tell us that the name of Peter Quince in *A Midsummer Night's Dream* comes from carpenters' coigns or quoins, the wedge-shaped blocks used for building purposes at the corners of houses or walls, appropriately for an artisan-carpenter who appears in a "marriage play" concerned with constructing "houses" of another kind.[1] But rarely is anything said of the quince fruit itself, though it was part of a rich contemporary contextual network of associations with marriage, sexuality, love potions, and fruitful "issue," as well as of multilingual connections and metamorphic spellings that conflated it with coigns, quoyns, sexual corners or coining, and the *cunnus* or "queynte" its sound suggests.[2]

John Minsheu's well-known *Ductor in Linguas, The Guide into Tongues* (1617) clearly situates the fruitful English "Quince" within this suggestive multilingual network:

> *Quince*, a kind of fruit, from French *Coing*. . . . Italian *Mela cotogna*, *pomo cotogno*. Latin *Malum cotoneum*, *cydonium* ("quince apple, Cydonian apple") . . . *Malum Lanatum*, because of its wooly or downy covering ("*lanugine*"). Greek *melon kudonion*, from Cydonia (a city in Crete), and *lasiomelon* ("wooly apple"), from *lasios* or *hirsutus* ("hairy" or "rough with down") and *melon*, or Latin *pomum* ("apple"). Portuguese *Marmelo*. Spanish *Membrillo*, from *membrum*, . . . because of a certain similarity with the first pubic hairs of men and women.[3]

Minsheu's "Quince" entry makes clear not only its "wooly" or "downy" covering (reflected in the *lanatum* and *lanugine* of the Latin here) but also its connection to Crete, home of the Minotaur (offspring of Pasiphae's animal lust) and the labyrinth threaded by Theseus before his abandonment of Ariadne, all strikingly recalled within *A Midsummer Night's Dream* itself.[4] And it simultaneously foregrounds the sexual associations of this downy or "hairy" quince in its comment on *Membrillo* as its Spanish name (from Latin *membrum*)—a link that Covarrubias had already made in comparing the quince to "el miembro genital y femineo."[5] Both Cervantes and Góngora likewise exploited this sexually double-meaning *membrillo*, the latter in verses in the 1590s on "*membrillos*" as "so many members being eaten" (and on a river as a "great waterer of quinces"), the former in a story that features the quince as a love potion connected with "*una moresca*" or Moorish woman.[6] But even in English, quince (from French "*coing*") had a sexual double sense, figuring (for example) in a late medieval English verse where "Mos[s]y Quince, hanging by your stalke" is part of an address to the female pudendum.[7]

As a Cydonian "apple" as well as a heavily scented fruit of the pear family (which was used to perfume Roman bedchambers, according to a frequently cited passage from Pliny), the quince was identified not only with the golden fruit of the Hesperides and the bridal chamber of Hera and Zeus, but with the golden apples of Venus awarded by Paris.[8] The entry on "*Malum*" or "apple" in Thomas Thomas's Latin-English dictionary (1587) cited the "downy" *Malum Cydonium* or "quince apple," while Randle Cotgrave's *A Dictionarie of the French and English Tongues* (1611) observed that "*the Quince hath also beene called, Pomme d'Or,*" or "*golden apple,*" the "*amorous apple,*" or "*apple of Loue.*"[9] Even Venus herself was "often represented holding a Quince in her right hand," instead of the more usual golden apple,[10] while the "apple" thrown to a lover by the lascivious Galatea in Virgil's Third Eclogue (3.64) was identified or combined with the "quinces" ("pale with tender down") of Eclogue 2 (2.51).[11]

In a period (and Shakespeare canon) that repeatedly exploited the sexual suggestiveness of the medlar and other kinds of fruit, the quince evoked by the name of Peter Quince thus joins the sexually suggestive fruit fed by Titania to Bottom ("apricocks and dewberries," "purple grapes, green figs, and mulberries"). And the quince (like the mulberry) was also connected with exotic locations, including the "Ind" of the East as well as the West. It was identified with Persia in Vives's *Convivium* (included among Tudor schoolboy texts) and with Syria as well as its original Crete (by Henry Buttes), while Richard Eden's translation of Peter Martyr's *De Orbe Novo*, or *The Decades of the New World* (1555), compared the "color" (between white and black) of inhabitants of the "Indies" not only with the "purple" mulberry but also with the "tawny" quince.[12]

The quince as a "Cydonian apple," already identified with the golden apples of Venus, was, however, even more specifically connected with Eros or Cupid, with aphrodiasics or love potions, and with overcoming female resistance to marriage. Classicist Marcel Detienne—in describing these connections—notes that "the Greek word for 'apple' (*mélon*)," which "designates every kind of round fruit resembling an apple," is "used not only for the fruit of the apple tree but for the pomegranate and the quince, which was known to the Greeks as the 'Cydonian apple.' "[13] (He also connects the eating of the pomegranate by Persephone, sealing her marriage to Pluto or Dis, to the "quince" to be eaten on the wedding night by Athenian brides, to which we will return.) In ways suggestive for the love potion of Shakespeare's marriage play, which not only affects its young Athenian lovers but also overcomes the resistance of the unruly Titania, the quince was similarly identified with the golden apples of Venus used to conquer Atalanta, the Amazon-like huntress who is strikingly conflated with Hippolyta in both *The Two Noble Kinsmen* and *A Midsummer Night's Dream*, the independent female whose resistance to marriage is overcome by golden apples associated with the madness of Eros in Theocritus and with being "striken with the dart / Of Cupid" in Ovid's *Metamorphoses*.[14] And Erasmus's well-known adage *Malis ferire* ("to pelt with apples") combines these golden apples used to overpower Atalanta not only with the "apple" thrown by the lustful or saucy Galatea but also with Virgil's downy "quinces."

The "mosie" and "most sweetly fragrant" quince also had an important role in the contemporary context of continental and English herbals, which stressed (of this autumn-ripening fruit, shaped variously like "the round apple or the more elongated pear") that its southern variety (unlike the English) was most pleasant eaten raw, that it was called in Latin *Cotoneum* because it was "clad in a sute of white thin Coten," that it was a digestive for the "stomach," and that, as a hirsute or "hairy" fruit, it could be used to restore hair lost by the pox, qualities already noted in Pliny.[15] Well before *A Midsummer Night's Dream*—whose emphasis on fruitful issue extends from the "fruitless" and "barren" with which Hermia is threatened in its opening scene (1.1.72–73) to the blessing of Oberon on the "issue" of the Athenian marriages at its end (5.1.401–422)—the fruitful quince was also associated with both pregnancy and fortunate issue. Rembert Dodoens's *Histoire des Plantes* (1557), for example, translated into English by Henry Lyte as *A new herball, or historie of plantes* (1578), repeats (as do other herbals in the 1590s) the saying of Simeon Sethi that pregnant women should eat quinces in order to give birth to wise and understanding children. John Gerard's *The Herball or Generall History of Plants* (1597) likewise notes that "*Simeon Sethi* writeth, that the woman with childe, which eateth many Quinces during the time of hir breeding; shall bring foorth wise children and of good understanding." Henry Buttes's *Dyets dry Dinner* (1599) records in the "Storie for Table-talke" under "Malum Cydonium" or

"Quince" that "*Simeon Sethi*, counselleth women with child to eat many quinces, if they desire to haue wise children."

But the most striking association of "Quince" for Shakespeare's "marriage" play set in Athens is its widespread identification not only with marriage and "issue" in general but with Athenian weddings in particular. The emblem for "Matrimonium" in Henry Peacham's *Minerva Britanna or A garden of heroical deuises* (1612)—which features a man bearing a marital "yoke" and holding a quince in his hand—glosses the "fruitefull *Quince*" as the symbol of "wedlock" that "SOLON did present, / T'*Athenian* Brides, the day to Church they went," in a verse that cites "Plutarch" as its source (Figure 1).[16] And this marital *and* Athenian quince—connected with Solon the Lawgiver who mitigated Athens's harsh laws—appears in no fewer than three influential Plutarch texts, all familiar well before the time of *A Midsummer Night's Dream*. Plutarch's *Life of Solon* (readily available in Thomas North's translation of Plutarch's *Lives*, frequently consulted by Shakespeare as a source for other plays) mentions in its description of the Athenian Lawgiver's views on marriage (including that couples should not be mismatched in years or marry for property or wealth) Solon's mandate that "a newe maryed wife should be shut vp with her husband, and eate a quince with him,"[17] in relation to problems of fruitfulness and issue. In Plutarch's *Moralia*, the section known as "*Roman Questions*" records that "Solon in his Statutes ordeined, that the new married wife should eat of a quince before she enter into the bride chamber, to the end that this first encounter and embracing, should not be odious or unpleasant to her husband"—an influential passage on the quince as a breath-freshener for the bride that calls to mind the lines on Thisby's "breath" (and on "odious" for "odours" or "odorous" savors "sweet") in *A Midsummer Night's Dream* (3.1.82–85).[18]

The most influential text of Plutarch for this Athenian marital quince—also from the *Moralia* or "Morals"—was his *Conjugal Precepts*, which prominently featured this "quince" in the very first of its "Precepts of Wedlock." It begins with the need to combine Aphrodite (or sexual pleasure) with Hermes (or pleasant speech), in order to avoid "conflict or quarrelsomeness" in marriage, and goes on to record that "Solon gave order and commanded that the new-wedded bride should eate of a quince before that she came in bed with her bridegroom; signifying covertly in mine opinion by this dark ceremony, that first and above all, the grace proceeding from the mouth, to wit, the breath and the voice, ought to be sweete, pleasant, and agreeable, in everie respect."[19] The quince was thus associated

*Matrimonium*: 132

WHO loueth beſt, to liue in *Hymens* bandes,
And better likes, the carefull married ſtate,
May here behold, how *Matrimonie* ſtandes,
In woodden ſtocks, repenting him too late:
The ſeruile yoake, his neck, and ſhoulder weares,
And in his hand, the fruitefull *Quince* he beares.

The ſtocks doe ſhew, his want of libertie,
Not as he woont, to wander where he liſt:
The yoke's an enſigne of ſeruilitie:
The fruitefullnes, the *Quince* within his fiſt,
Of wedlock tells, which * *SOLON* did preſent,
T'*Athenian* Brides, the day to Church they went.

* Plutarch.

Sed

Figure 1. *Matrimonium* emblem from *Minerva Britanna* by Henry Peacham. London, 1612. By permission of the Folger Shakespeare Library.

not only with fruitful consummation on the wedding night and with concord or harmony between bride and groom, but also with making the breath, and mouth, of the bride in particular sweeter and more agreeable, advice that Plutarch reiterates at this text's conclusion by reminding the bride to "haue alwaies in your mouth the good word."

*Conjugal Precepts* goes on from its opening "quince" to give other advice which strikingly resonates with Shakespeare's Athenian marriage play: to beware of love potions (capable of transforming a man into an "ass"), to avoid the lustful choice of Pasiphae with the bull (which produced the cross-species Minotaur), to find future husbands by the ear rather than the eye (as Hermia finds Lysander in Act 3), to refuse expensive trifles or gifts from suitors (as it says "Lysander" did for his daughters), and (for wives) to imitate Phidias's statue of the domesticated rather than the lascivious or unruly Venus, whose foot resting on a "turtle" signified that a wife should remain silently at home, speaking only words agreeable to her husband.

Plutarch's *Conjugal Precepts* exerted an enormous influence on writing devoted to female conduct as well as to marriage in the sixteenth century—including Vives's *Instruction of a Christian Woman* and Edmund Tilney's *Flower of Friendship*, which are filled with passages from it, and Erasmus's *Conjugium* or "Marriage" Colloquy, whose English translation in *A Mery Dialogue, declaringe the properties of Shrewd Shrews and Honest Wives* (1557) reflects its precepts on a wife's sweet and acceptable speech in the very name of Eulalia (literally "sweetly speaking"), the "honest wife" who counsels the shrewish Xantippa on how to use mild words and behavior with her husband.[20] Solon's mandate to brides in Athens, on the eating of a quince on the wedding night, was at the same time a staple of continental marriage treatises, which stressed that it made the mouth more "odorous" in every sense.[21]

Because the *Moralia* was originally in Greek and not apparently available in English in its entirety until Philemon Holland's translation in 1603, it might be assumed that at the time of *A Midsummer Night's Dream* Shakespeare could not have known about the mouth-sweetening quince of either these "Precepts of Wedlock" or the passage of Plutarch's "Roman Questions" on ensuring that the bride's breath would not be "odious" or unpleasant to her husband. This often-adopted assumption, however, would be false. Within the sixteenth century, in England as in Europe, the *Moralia* was one of the most frequently translated and cited collections of "moral" texts, while *Roman Questions*—known as *Quaestiones Romanae* or *Problemata*—was available in Latin translation as early as 1477, as well as in Amyot's French translation of the whole of the *Moralia* in 1572. *Conjugal Precepts* was translated into Latin as early as 1497, and had appeared in many other Latin translations before the 1590s, as well as in multiple vernacular translations, some of which were produced for particular wedding occasions.[22] Even before Amyot's translation of the *Moralia*, these marital "Precepts" had been translated numerous times into French, starting as early as 1535—including a translation in 1559 occasioned by the marriage of Mary Stuart to the French Dauphin, which included an anagram of her name as its dedicatee, and another by Estienne de la Boétie entitled *Les Règles de Mariage*, composed before 1563 and published in 1571 through his friend Montaigne.[23]

Like Plutarch's other works, the *Moralia* was extraordinarily popular not only on the Continent but also in England, where as Martha Hale Shackford observed long ago in her study of Plutarch's English influence, "if Sir Thomas North had not translated Plutarch's *Lives*, in 1579, there is strong probability that Shakespeare would have read the biographies in French or in Latin versions," since "Plutarch's popularity had increased steadily in the sixteenth century until a knowledge of his *Lives* and his *Morals* was almost presupposed on the part of the reading Englishman."[24] Debts to different parts of the *Moralia*, or "Plutarches holesome Morrals," as they were called by Gabriel Harvey in 1592, can be seen in a wide range of English writers, including Sir Thomas Elyot, Philip Sidney, Thomas Lodge, Nicholas Udall, Stephen Gosson, Edmund Spenser, Francis Bacon, and others.[25]

The influence of Plutarch's *Conjugal Precepts* in particular (along with other versions of Solon's mandated quince) was itself registered in England well before *A Midsummer Night's Dream*. An anonymous English *Praise of Musicke* (1586), for example, cited among the "rites and ceremonies of marriage" the "eating of a quince peare, to be a preparation of sweete & delightful dayes betweene the maried persons, the ioyning, of Mercury and Venus togither, as a token that love must be preferred & fostered by curteous speeches." But perhaps most strikingly in relation to Shakespeare's exposure to this Athenian quince, Plutarch's "Precepts of Wedlock" (long before Holland's translation) were not only Englished but incorporated at length in John Lyly's *Euphues and his England*, in the advice of Euphues to his friend Philautus on the occasion of his marriage—which notes that "*Solon* gaue counsel that before one assured himselfe he should be so warie, that in tying himselfe fast, he did not vndo himselfe, wishing them first to eat a Quince peare, yt is, to haue sweete conference with-out brawles."[26] The advice given by Lyly's Euphues (who is explicitly represented in this text as an "Athenian" and reminds his friend that "it is as farre from *Athens* to *England*, as from *England* to *Athens*") goes on to rehearse Plutarch's familiar conjugal precepts, including not only their advice to choose with the "ear" rather than the "eye" but also their counsel to husbands to "suffer the wranglyngs of young maryed women" common "in the first moneth" before they can be made more "tractable," an influential aspect of Plutarch's text on the domesticating of "curst wiues" that might also have influenced, directly or indirectly, plays such as *The Taming of the Shrew.*

ᔕ

> Poma nouis tribui debere Cydonia nuptis
> Dicitur antiquus constituisse Solon.
> ("Solon of old is said to have ordained that quinces be given to newly-weds")
>
> —Andrea Alciato, *Emblemata* (Lyons, 1550)

> Coing: m. *A wedge; also, a quince; also, an angle, nooke, or corner; also, a coyne, or stamp, upon a peece of coyne.*
>
> —Randle Cotgrave, *A Dictionarie of the French and English Tongues* (1611)

The textual tradition identifying the "quince" with weddings and the mandate of Solon also continued well beyond the date of *A Midsummer Night's Dream*—including in an English poem by William Cartwright in 1641 on the marriage of the "Lady Mary" to the Prince of Orange, which described the bride on the wedding night as "Soft as the Wooll, that Nuptiall Posts did crowne, / Or th'Hallowd Quince's Downe, / That Ritual Quince, which Brides did eate, / When with their Bridegrooms they would treat."[27] But the connection between the "Quince" and weddings was also a visual commonplace by the time of Shakespeare's play. A mid-sixteenth-century painting by Paris Bordone (Figure 2) is clearly identified as a marriage portrait by the bride's picking a quince, characterized by Erwin Panofsky as "the wedding fruit *par excellence*."[28] Edgar Wind likewise identified Giovanni Bellini's *Feast of the Gods* as a wedding painting because its central female figure is shown holding a quince (Figure 3), "a symbol of marriage" common in "Venetian marriage paintings," in which (as Wind notes) "the fruit is generally held or touched by the bride."[29] But for the simultaneously marital and Athenian quince, the most widely disseminated visual *and* textual source was the

Figure 2. Allegory (Mars, Venus, Victory, and Cupid) by Paris Bordone. By permission of the Kunsthistorisches Museum, Vienna.

extraordinarily popular *Emblemata* of Andrea Alciato (or Alciati), which strikingly featured a *Cotonea* or "Quince" emblem that explicitly identified this "Cydonian apple" with the matrimonial mandate of Solon of Athens:

Poma nouis tribui debere Cydonia nuptis
Dicitur antiquus constituisse Solon.
Grata ori & stomacho cum sint, ut & halitus illis
Sit suauis, blandus manet & ore lepos.

("Solon of old is said to have ordained that quinces be given to newly-weds, since these are pleasant both to mouth and stomach. As a result their breath is sweet, and winning grace drops from their lips.")[30]

The emblem also appeared in the 1621 edition of the *Emblemata* complete with an illustration of Hymen and Cupid (carrying a basket of quinces under a tree laden with these "Cydonian apples") and a detailed commentary on weddings,

Figure 3. Detail from *Feast of the Gods* by Giovanni Bellini. By permission of the National Gallery, Washington, DC.

beginning with Plutarch's *Conjugal Precepts* (Figure 4). But right from its first appearance, in much earlier sixteenth-century editions, Alciati's "Quince" was already the emblem of matrimony its Latin verse suggests. The 1577 edition (Figure 5), which featured luscious pear-shaped quinces with the influential commentary of Claude Mignault, combined all three of Plutarch's texts on Solon's Athenian mandate with references to the familiar passages from Pliny on its fragrant taste and smell, as well as its benefits for the "stomach."[31]

Sixteenth-century vernacular and other versions of Alciati's widely disseminated "Quince" emblem varied between the different Plutarch texts, as

Emblemata. 861

# Cotonea.

## EMBLEMA CCIV.

*POMA nouis tribui debere Cydonia nuptis*
*Dicitur antiquus constituisse Solon.*
*Grata ori & stomacho cùm sint, vt & halitus illis*
*Sit suauis, blandus manet & ore lepos.*

## COMMENTARII.

I. *Mali Cydoniæ cõsideratio.* MALVS Cotonea haud magna est arbor, sed humilis, frequenter etiam instar fruticis nascitur, cortice vestitur asperiusculo, squamas quasdam quandoq; dimittente: ramos explicat aliarum arborum modo, circa quos folia subrotunda, veluti vulgaris pomi, superna parte virentia & glabra, prona verò mollia & albicantia. Flores ex purpureo candidi sunt; fructus, de quo solùm hic sermo, pomo similis, nisi incisuris quibusdam quandoque crispetur; tenui pubescit lanugine, colore auri lutei, odore fragranti. Appinguntur hic etiam, hinc Amor, poma Cydonia gestans; illinc Hymenæus, nuptiarũ præses.

II. *Cotoneæ cur à nouis nuptis ederetur.* PLVTARCHVS in *γαμικοῖς παραγγέλμασιν* ita scribit: *Ὁ σόλων ἐκέλευε τὴν νύμφην τῷ νυμφίῳ συγκατακλίνεσθαι μῆλον κυδωνίου κατατραγοῦσαν, αἰνιττόμενος ὡς ἔοικεν, ὅτι δεῖ τὴν ἀπὸ στόματος καὶ φωνῆς χάριν εὐάρμοστον εἶναι πρώτην καὶ ἡδεῖαν.* Solon iubebat

Figure 4. *Emblemata* by Andrea Alciati. Padua, 1621. By permission of the Folger Shakespeare Library.

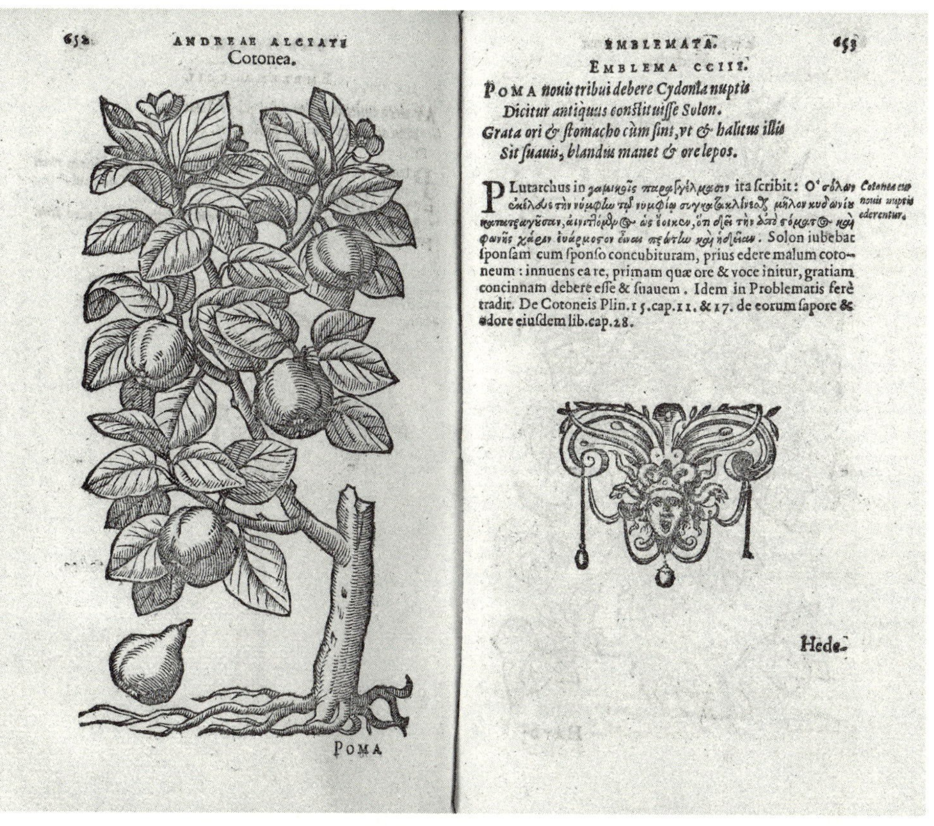

652. ANDREAE ALCIATI

Cotonea.

POMA

EMBLEMATA. 653

EMBLEMA CCIII.

*POMA nouis tribui debere Cydonia nuptis*
*Dicitur antiquus constituisse Solon.*
*Grata ori & stomacho cùm sint, vt & halitus illis*
*Sit suauis, blandus manet & ore lepos.*

Plutarchus in γαμικοῖς παραγγέλμασιν ita scribit: Ὁ Σόλων ἐκέλευε τὴν νύμφην τῷ νυμφίῳ συγκατακλίνεσθαι, μῆλον κυδώνιον κατατραγοῦσαν, αἰνιττόμενος ὡς ἔοικεν, ὅτι δεῖ τὴν ἀπὸ στόματος καὶ φωνῆς χάριν ἐνάρμοστον εἶναι πρώτην καὶ ἡδεῖαν. Solon iubebat sponsam cum sponso concubituram, prius edere malum cotoneum: innuens ea re, primam quæ ore & voce initur, gratiam concinnam debere esse & suauem. Idem in Problematis ferè tradit. De Cotoneis Plin. 15. cap. 11. & 17. de eorum sapore & odore eiusdem lib. cap. 28.

*Cotonea cur nouis nuptis ederentur.*

Hede-

Figure 5. *Emblemata* by Andrea Alciati, with commentary by Claude Mignault (Claudius Minos). Antwerp, 1577. By permission of the Folger Shakespeare Library.

to whether this golden Cydonian apple was a gift to both bride and groom in Athens or just to be eaten by the bride—as the 1549 French edition (Figure 6), for example, suggested in its recording that "Les Coingz" were mandated by Solon to be given to the new bride ("la nouuelle espouse"), to render her mouth more "odorous" or fresh smelling ("de bonne odeur") and her words more "modest" and "honest."[32] But the commentaries on Alciati's marital "Quince" in sixteenth-century annotated editions all repeatedly stress its relation to Plutarch's *Conjugal Precepts*, the good words esssential not just to marital concord but to the bride in particular, as well as its value as a breath-freshener.

254 LES ARBRES. EMBLEMES

*Le Coing.*

A la nouuelle eſpouſe donnoit l'on
Iadis des coingz, par la loy de Solon.
Bons ſont au cœur: & rendent bonne aleine
Pour bien penſer: ſans parolle villaine.

Les Coingz cõfortent le cœur, & inſpirent doulce aleine à la bouche. Et d'iceulx les preſens iadis faictz aulx nouuelles eſpouſes, les admonneſtoient de auoir le cœur net en bonne, & honneſte penſee: & la bouche de bõne odeur, en pudicques, & honneſtes parolles.

Figure 6. *Emblemes d'Alciat.* Lyons, 1549. By permission of the Folger Shakespeare Library.

The *Matrimonium* emblems of Alciati's popular collection at the same time incorporated other influential parts of *Conjugal Precepts*, together with the tradition connecting this "Cydonian apple" to the golden apples of Venus associated with female sexuality, unruliness, and overcoming Atalanta's resistance to marriage. One of these, in 1534, actually depicted Phidias's statue of Venus holding an apple in her right hand and resting her foot on the turtle (Figure 7), an emblem of domesticity contrasted in the commentaries with shrewish, garrulous, or gadding women. Another in 1566—under *Matrimonium*: *In fidem vxoriam* or "On the fidelity of a wife"—glossed the apples of Venus in the tree above its married couple (Figure 8) in a verse that featured both the lascivious Galatea who threw the sexually suggestive "apple" at her lover and the resistant Atalanta (*Scheneida* or "Schoeneus' daughter"), who was finally conquered ("uicit") by Hippomenes, her competitor-suitor, through the distracting golden apples of Venus or Cupid. And the commentaries on this Matrimony emblem refer the reader both to the golden apples awarded by Paris and to the influential *Malis ferire* adage of Erasmus that had already combined the apples of Galatea and Atalanta with Virgil's "quinces."[33]

The tradition linking quinces with sexuality and matrimony—as well as the marital mandate of Solon of Athens—continued in the 1593 edition of Cesare Ripa's *Iconologia*, which described as its emblem of "Matrimonio" a young man with a marital yoke and the quince that "by the commandment of Solon" was presented to newlyweds in Athens, because "it is dedicated to Venus, mother of fecundity" (as well as pleasant to the taste and "odore" or smell). Noting that the quince appears in depictions of young lovers as well as of Venus, Ripa's 1593 edition links it both with consummation or coitus, which outside of marriage would be a "grave sin," and with its familiar resemblance to the body's "secret" parts ("qualche similitudine con le parti secrete del corpo"). The 1603 edition of Ripa (Figure 9) features the illustration that Peacham clearly adapted for his own "Matrimonium" quince emblem of 1612, with its young man bearing the visual yoke and constraints of wedlock and carrying the emblematic quince, accompanied by the text's reminder of Solon's Athenian mandate. In treating of the serpent or "viper" to be placed under the married man's feet, Ripa also associates the quince of Eros or "Amor" (and the potentially excessive sexuality of the wife) with the frequently exploited contemporary wordplay on *malum* (or evil) and the paradisal "apple" itself, symbol of the first marriage as well as the Fall associated with the seductions of Eve.[34]

104 ANDREAE ALCIATI

Mulieris famam non formam
uulgatam eſſe oportere.

Alma Venus quæ nam hæc facies, quid denotat illa
Teſtudo, molli quam pede diua premis?
Me ſic effinxit Phidias, ſexumq; referri
Fœmineum, noſtra iuſsit ab effigie,
Quodq; manere domi, et tacitas decet eſſe puellas,
Suppoſuit pedibus talia ſigna meis.

Figure 7. *Emblematum Libellus* by Andrea Alciati. Paris, 1534. By permission of the Folger Shakespeare Library.

MATRIMONIVM. 205

MATRIMONIVM.

In fidem vxoriam.

*Ecce puella, viro quæ dextra iungitur. Ecce*
*Vt ſedet: vt catulus luſitat ante pedes?*
*Hæc fidei eſt ſpecies: Veneris quam ſi educat ardor,*
*Malorum in læua non malè ramus erit.*
*Poma etenim Veneris ſunt, ſic Schenëida vicit*
*Hippomenes. petijt ſic Galatea virum.*

Figure 8. *Emblemata* by Andrea Alciati. Paris, 1566. By permission of the Folger Shakespeare Library.

306 ICONOLOGIA

MATRIMONIO.

tenendo nella medesima mano vn cotogno, & sotto à piedi hauerà vna vipera.

Per lo giogo, & per li ceppi si dimostra, che il Matrimonio è peso alle forze dell'huomo assai graue, & è impedimento al caminare in molte attioni di libertà, essendo il maritarsi vn vendere se stesso, & obligarsi à legge perpetua, con tutto ciò è caro, & desiderabile per molti rispetti, & particolarmente per lo acquisto de' successori nelle sue facoltà, le quali siano veri heredi della robba, & della fama, per l'honore, & credito che s'acquista nella Città, prendendosi questo carico per mantenimento d'essa, & per lo piacere di Venere che lecitamente se ne gode, però si fà con l'anello, il quale è segno di preminenza, & di grado honorato.

Il coto-

Figure 9. *Iconologia* by Cesare Ripa. Rome, 1603. By permission of the Folger Shakespeare Library.

"Quince" in *A Midsummer Night's Dream* thus came with a rich visual as well as textual network of contemporary contexts and associations—with Athenian weddings as well as with sexuality and fruitful issue, aphrodisiacs or love potions, exotic locations, and the homelier qualities of a breath-freshener and digestive for the "stomach"; but also with female speech and overcoming the Amazon-like resistance of Atalanta, who is conflated with Hippolyta in Shakespeare's marriage play as well as in *The Two Noble Kinsmen.* That Shakespeare, moreover, was familiar by the mid-1590s with the long-standing connection between quinces and weddings is even further suggested by the fact that the only other place in the canon where quinces appear is in the scene of preparation for Juliet's wedding to Paris in *Romeo and Juliet* (4.4.2), the play of the same period that presents the correspondingly tragic version of the Ovidian *amor* of Pyramus and Thisbe.

But what about the quince in relation to the carpenters' "quoyns" or "coigns" with which we began? Here, both similarities of sound and the metamorphic variety of early spellings—along with the multilingual heritage of English itself—collapse any distance we might anachronistically assume between the fruitful quince and the quoins, coigns, and coins with which Quince's name has already been connected. Quince itself is spelled "quoyne" and quincetree as "Coyn-tree" in thirteenth- and fourteenth-century English writing, showing the influence of French "*coing*," as does the spelling of quinces as "Coynes" in Chaucer's translation from the French of *The Romaunt of the Rose.* Quince in French is spelled "quoyn" and "Quynce tree" as "quoynier" in John Palsgrave's French-English *Lesclarcissement de la Langue Francoyse* (1530),[35] while the variable sixteenth-century spellings of English "quince" make clear that "coyns," "quoyns," and "quynes" could be "quinces" as well as monetary "coins," carpenters' "coigns," printers' wedges or "quoyns," and the corners, coigns, or quoyns of houses and walls.[36] In relation to "coynes" and "corners" of all kinds, the "quince" associated with consummation on the wedding night was thus simultaneously part of the sexually suggestive network of "coining" and "coigns" (including *conio*, *cuño*, coiner, or "wedge") and of "con" words that included (in John Florio's Italian-English rendering, for example) "*coniugio*, marriage matrimonie, wedlock, copulation" and the "*conno*, a womans privie parts or quaint as Chaucer calles it," which the sounding of quince as "coynes" or "coin-tree" suggested.

Contemporary interlingual dictionaries are highly suggestive sources for this network of contemporary cognates (including "cognate" itself, which—as Florio comments of *cognato*—meant both related by marriage and "cleaved or coyned"). Florio's "Quinces" (for Italian "*Cotogni*") in *A Worlde of Wordes* (1598) appear in a list that includes "*Cotone*, cotton, bumbace, a nappe or a thrum," reminding us of the cottony *Cotoneum* behind the "Quince" who directs the Athenian "hempen home-spuns" (3.1.77) in Shakespeare's play, where the weaver Bottom invokes the cutting by the weaver "Fates" of "thread" and "thrum" (5.1.285–286). But the most suggestive—and most revealing for the combination of corners, coins, and carpenters' coigns or quoins with the simultaneously sexual and marital "quince"—is the French "*Coing*" from which English "Quince" itself derives, which (as Cotgrave's French-English dictionary makes clear) combines all of these into a single sound:

> Coing: m. *A wedge; also, a quince; also, an angle, nooke, or corner; also, a coyne, or stamp, upon a peece of coyne.*[37]

"*Coing*" (source of the spelling of quinces as "Coynes" and quince tree as "Coyn-tree") is thus simultaneously a quince, a carpenter's wedge or coign, an "angle, nooke, or corner," and the "coyne, or stamp, upon a peece of coyne," just as the "*coignier*" or quince tree in Cotgrave's definitional series is a homophone of "*Coigné*" ("wedged; driuen, or knocked in; stamped, coyned"), in a list where "*Coignaufond*" (driving or wedging into the bottom or "*fond*"), used by "Rab." or Rabelais for "Knocking, leacherie, Venerie" (from "*Coigner*. To wedge, to fasten with a wedge; to driue hard or knocke fast in, as with a wedge" as well as "to stamp or coin"), comes immediately after "*Coignasse*: f. A female Quince, or peare Quince, the greatest kind of Quince."

The Shakespearean corpus itself exploits different parts of this homophonic network, even beyond *A Midsummer Night's Dream*. Helge Kökeritz in *Shakespeare's Pronunciation* sees a sexual "pun on *quoin* 'wedge'" in Hal's "so far as my *coin* would stretch" in *Henry IV Part 1* (1.2.51–55), in lines whose "Did I ever call for thee to pay thy part?" strengthens the sexual connotations of his having "paid all" as well as of this stretching "coin."[38] "Coiner," like corner, has a sexual sense elsewhere in Shakespeare—in Othello's "keep a corner in the thing I love / For others' uses (3.3.272–273) and Posthumus's "We are all bastards. . . . Some coiner with his tools / Made me a counterfeit" in *Cymbeline* (2.5.2–6), lines that evoke not only the monetary "Coyne" used for consummation or coitus on the wedding night, but also the cuckolding "tool" of an adulterous phallic stamping. The "quoin" or "coign" that was variously a "cornerstone" and "the external angle of a wall or building" similarly appears in the "coign of vantage" in *Macbeth* (1.6.7) and the "coign a' th' Capitol, yond cornerstone" of *Coriolanus* (5.4.1).

In *A Midsummer Night's Dream*, the name of Peter Quince already recalls the name of the one married apostle, together with the network of bodily and biblical "stones" that included the Peter or "rock" on which a different or counter-structure was founded and the "living stones" of 1 Peter 2. But the choice of "Quince" for Shakespeare's Athenian marriage play manages at the same time to combine the quince associated with Athenian weddings in both visual and textual contexts in the period with the rejected biblical cornerstone or "coign," in a play whose artisanal Bottom recalls the "bottom of Goddes secretes," from the text of 1 Corinthians that also emphasizes the wisdom of fools beyond the comprehension of reason and (Athenian as well as other) rulers of this world.[39]

This brings us, then, to the sound of Peter "Quince" itself and the relation of the nuptial "present" of Shakespeare's Quince to the Athenian newlyweds (and Athenian ruler) of this "marriage" play. We are accustomed to pronouncing the "Qu" of "Quince" the way anglophones rather than francophones (for example) pronounce the "Qu" of "Quebec" (for "Québec"). But in a period in which English "quinces" were spelled "coynes," it may well have sounded closer to the "coingz" of its own French connections—as in "Les Coingz" in the 1549 French edition of Alciati in Figure 6. Kökeritz implies the sounding of "qu-" as "co-" in his gloss on Hal's stretching "coin" as "quoyn" and comments on the sound of "qu" as "k" or hard "c" in the bawdy sexual double entendres of "qui's, quae's, and "quods" (as "keys, case, and cods") in Shakespeare's *Merry Wives of Windsor* or the "kiss kiss" of "quis quis" in the multilingual context of *Love's Labor's Lost*.[40] If Peter "Quince" sounded closer to "coigns" or French "coingz" than to modern English "quince," it would make even more sexually suggestive the repeated sounding of his name as a virtual refrain in the roll call of the other suggestively named artisans (including Snug the Joiner, his fellow carpenter), in the scene of the casting of the "enterlude" to be performed on Theseus's "wedding-day at night" (1.2.6–7), in which he advises them to "con" their "parts" (1.2.99–100) before their rehearsal in the Athenian woods, where (as Bottom puts it) they will rehearse "most obscenely" (1.2.108).[41] But whatever the sound of this Athenian artisan-director's name, all of the connotations of the sexual and marital "quince" as well as of wedge, coign, or "coyne" converge in Bottom's "First, good Peter Quince, say what the play treats on; then read the names of the actors; and so *grow to a point*" (1.2.8–10). For these lines exploit not only the sexual connotations of coining, driving, or wedging in (as in Cotgrave's "coignau*fond*") but also the "growing" (as well as the genital-vegetal onomastics) already associated with the quince itself—a phallic "growing" reiterated in Lysander's amorous protestation to Helena on his "growing" love for her instead of Hermia ("Things growing are not ripe until their season," 2.2.117), after the love potion has transformed the object of his desire.

ൕ

*Quince.* . . . say he comes to disfigure, or to present . . .
—*A Midsummer Night's Dream* (3.1.60–61)

*Puck.* . . . those things do best please me
That befall prepost'rously.
—*A Midsummer Night's Dream* (3.2.120–121)

*Philostrate.* Hard-handed men that work in Athens here . . .
And now have toiled their unbreathed memories
With this same play, against your nuptial.
—*A Midsummer Night's Dream* (5.1.72–75)

*Puck.* . . . Jack shall have Jill;
Nought shall go ill:
The man shall have his mare again, and all shall be well.
—*A Midsummer Night's Dream* (3.2.461–463)

There is, as always, much more that could be said about the rich textual, visual, and cultural network that came to Elizabethan writers—or the playwright of *A Midsummer Night's Dream*—bearing quinces. Both their presentation at actual weddings and the tradition of translating Plutarch's "Precepts of Wedlock" for particular wedding occasions may suggest that some kind of wedding occasion (if only *staged*) is being evoked by Shakespeare's choice of this culturally overdetermined name. But in a way that also fits with what is oxymoronically called the "tragical mirth" (5.1.57) of the artisans' play of "Pyramus and Thisby," as well as the rich classical network that connected quinces with famous lovers and marital pairs, F. W. Clayton points out that the only quinces in all of Ovid appear in the story of Cephalus and Procris, the *Othello*-like tragedy of suspected infidelity and jealousy that is directly evoked in Quince's nuptial play, in "Not Shafalus to Procrus was so true" (5.1.198), immediately after the substitution of the notoriously unfaithful "Helen" (5.1.197) for the paradigmatically faithful "Hero."[42] Even the multilingual networks we have traced do not exhaust the possibilities: Clayton himself adds, when "quinces are ripe, *carpentur*, they'll be plucked,"[43] a connection that may seem far-fetched until we reflect on Shakespeare's similarly interlingual metamorphosis of the sound of Latin "*Nini*" ("of Ninus") from Ovid's *ad busta Nini* (or "at Ninus's tomb")—in the narrative of Pyramus and Thisbe—into the English "ninny" or fool of the unlearned artisans' performance (3.1.97–98, 5.1.202).

What might we conclude, then, with respect to the implications of the choice of "Quince" for Shakespeare's Athenian marriage play? Recent major editions continue to recycle the usual gloss that limits the implications of this name to carpenters' coigns or quoins. Jonathan Bate and Eric Rasmussen's Royal Shakespeare Company edition of 2007–2008 simply notes that Quince comes "probably from 'quines' or 'quoins,' a carpenter's wooden wedges."[44] And the 2016 New Oxford Shakespeare just has: "The name 'Quince' seems to allude to 'quoins,' corners of a building, wedges."[45] In the widely used 2016 *Norton Shakespeare* edition, Stephen Greenblatt's introduction to the play makes no mention of the Athenian wedding tradition that so prominently featured the fruitful "Quince." Lukas Erne's new Norton gloss once again cites only carpenters' quoins ("The artisans' names recall their occupations. Quince's name is probably derived from 'quoins,' wooden wedges used by carpenters who made buildings such as houses and theaters"). And this *Norton Shakespeare* third edition continues to use Henry Peacham's emblem from *Minerva Britanna* (1612) of "A man trapped in the yoke of matrimony" as an illustration for *Much Ado About Nothing* rather than *A Midsummer Night's Dream*, with no mention that the married man depicted in it is holding a quince or of the verse on quinces, Solon's mandate from Plutarch, and Athenian weddings that this Peacham Matrimony emblem so prominently included.[46]

Here—as in the last chapter on the name of "Cambio" in *The Taming of the Shrew* and Chapter 5 to come on Brabant as part of the wider global contexts of *Othello* (in ways effaced by the Oxford and Norton editions' change of name from Brabantio to Brabanzio instead)—"What's in a Name?" is not a matter of a one-to-one correspondence with a particular character but rather suggestive of the ways in which name choices in Shakespeare so often introduce much wider and more important resonances for the play as a whole, including from the multiple early modern contexts they simultaneously evoke. And in *A Midsummer Night's Dream*, the contemporary visual, textual, and multilingual contexts so unmistakably evoked by the choice of "Quince" are crucial to this marriage play set in Athens, which places so much emphasis on love potions, sexuality, unruly women, and female speech, as well as on the question of fruitfulness and fruitful issue.

Within the matrimonial tradition of *Conjugal Precepts* in which Athenian quinces so prominently figured, the "quince" identified with Athenian weddings was, as we have seen, a commonplace in the conduct literature on marriage and marital "concord" as well as on wifely chastity, silence, and obedience. From that perspective, the progression of the play as a whole, with its matrimonial ending, its language of "harmony" and "concord," and a final wedding scene in which its formerly feisty or unruly young Athenian brides, Hermia and Helena, are completely silent, may suggest (as to an earlier era of critics it *did* suggest) the traditional harmonies and hierarchies produced by that trajectory, even as it raises the issue for feminist and other critics of the ways in which the genre of such "comedies" depends on the question of for *whom* they are providing a satisfying comic ending.

The initially rebellious Hermia who had vowed in the opening scene not to "yield my virgin patent up / Unto his lordship, whose unwished yoke / My soul consents not to give sovereignty" (1.1.80–82) insists, as Laurie Shannon notes, on a resistance to a paternally designated marriage before which she prefers to remain unmarried (in lines—I would add—where "unwished yoke" resonates ironically with the Ripa and Peacham Quince emblems where the marital yoke is borne by the married man, while at the same time invoking the crucial matter of a woman's "consent").[47] By the end of the play, once she (like Helena) has gained the husband she originally wanted, the final scene leaves up to the audience's (and critics') "suppose" (as at the ending of Shakespeare's *Shrew*) whether the silence of these two formerly unruly young women represents the achievement of their own goals (including consent) or the conclusion and desired trajectory of the conduct books of the period that so frequently cited Plutarch's "Precepts of Wedlock" and the mandated "quince" in relation to the bride and the subject of female speech.

Even the play's comic reflection of the quince's homelier associations as a breath-freshener has a distinctly different edge in relation to what these "unbreathed" artisan actors present in its final marital scene. The familiar Athenian quince that was to prevent discord and sweeten the breath and mouth is echoed not only in the "odious" of the lines on Thisby's "breath" in the artisans' rehearsal in the woods (where it is "Quince" who intervenes to correct "odious" to "odorous" as well as "sweet") but also in the advice to the "dear actors" themselves (once Quince's play has been "preferr'd") to "eat no onions nor garlic, for we are to utter sweet breath; and I do not doubt but to hear them say, it is a *sweet comedy,*" as Bottom puts it, just before his "No more words . . . away!" (4.2.38–45). What Quince and company "present" at the final Athenian wedding banquet is an "interlude" (between "after-supper and bed-time," 5.1.34) described to Athens' ruler as the "labor" of "hard-handed men that work in Athens here," who "now have toiled their unbreathed memories / With this same play, *against* your nuptial" (5.1.72–75). And in the "Pyramus and Thisby" play that both ends in death and is filled with allusions to cuckoldry and infidelity, it is unclear (as that ambiguous phrasing suggests) whether Quince's nuptial offering is presented for or "against" the happy occasion, in the performance of yet "unbreathed" actors whose words may be something other than what *Conjugal Precepts* describes as "sweete, pleasant, and agreable, in everie respect"—including in Quince's own mispunctuated Prologue, which turns a compliment to their onstage aristocratic audience into an insult.

Fruit in the period (as in Shakespeare) also famously crossed the "homo/hetero divide"—as Jonathan Goldberg has shown with regard to the "medlar" of *Romeo and Juliet,* in the speech of Mercutio that leads to Juliet as an "open-arse" and Romeo as "a pop'rin pear" (2.1.36–38), in the one other play in the canon that invokes quinces (for Juliet's projected wedding to Paris) and a speech that at the same time calls attention to Juliet as a transvestite boy player.[48] So it raises the question of whether the quince identified with Athenian weddings could also be queer. Laura Giannetti Ruggiero has detailed the multiple Italian texts of the period where melons and apples (like the peach) were explicitly associated with the erotics of "sodomy" because of their "rounded shape," identified with "a youth's bottom" or buttocks (and assumed "passive"or "female" sexual role) but also, as in Aretino, with preposterous or back-door sexual entry in male-female erotics as well.[49] These texts also exploit the different meanings of "before" (*innanzi*) and "after" (*dietro*) or "behind," in ways we have already encountered in the *I Suppositi* of Ariosto in Chapter 2 as well as the English-Latin dictionary of Huloet there on the "Backdoore."

Such erotic play on melons and apples (like peaches) because of their "rounded shape" and "the bodily parts they represented" (Giannetti Ruggiero

41) might be dismissed as specifically Italian—as in the multiple references to the "preposterous Italian way" of "backdoor" entry in Middleton and others in the period.[50] But—in a Shakespeare canon that includes the "medlar" of *Romeo and Juliet*, an Athenian play where Oberon's use of the love potion is to obtain possession of the "lovely boy" (2.1.22), and a play-within-a-play where it is not clear whether "wall's hole" in Thisby-Flute's "I kiss the wall's hole, not your lips at all" (5.1.201) is "before" or "behind"[51]—it is worth remembering that descriptions of the "quince" fruit repeatedly identified it as both "melon" and "apple," including in Minsheu's definition of the English "Quince," which also records its equivalent in Spanish as "*Membrillo*, from *membrum*," because of "a certain similarity with the first pubic hairs of men and women," so not restricted to the female body. And the already-cited Second Eclogue of Virgil that has "Come hither lovely boy. . . . My own hands will gather quinces, pale with tender down" is famously homoerotic, as well as employing the Latin for "downy" (*lanugine*) that was also used to suggest a youth's first beard.[52] So—in a play where "Thisby" is performed by Flute, who is reluctant to play a woman because "I have a beard coming" (1.2.48) and the name of "Bottom" can suggest both "front" and "back" (as noted in the Introduction)[53]—it is not at all out of the question that the "quince" so often compared to the "rounded shape" of both "apple" and "melon" may also cross or elide the "homo/hetero divide."

Puck's "things do best please me / That befall prepost'rously" in Act 3 (3.2.120–121) seems to have to do only with the play's disordered middle in the woods outside Athens, before the final act, in which (as he crudely puts it) "Jack shall have Jill; / Nought shall go ill: / The man shall have his mare again, and all shall be well," 3.2.461–463). But as Amanda Bailey has recently commented, "the man shall have his mare again" at the end of this line "turns the patriarchal prerogative on its head by recommending as a resolution an erotic pairing that broaches the human-animal divide."[54] What might seem the simply orthodox heternormative coupling of "Jack" and "Jill" both here and in the final wedding feast at the play's own "latter end" (as Bottom calls it [4.1.217]) not only involves in Puck's own formulation the cross-species pairing of "man" and "mare" that Bruce Boehrer and others have analyzed, but is subject—as in *Love's Labor's Lost* and the "supposes" of *The Taming of the Shrew*—to the multiple erotic possibilities of transvestite theatrical supposition. And what Richard Rambuss, in *Shakesqueer*, calls "Shakespeare's Ass Play" is "crisscrossed by all kinds of homo and hetero investments"—something I would add could extend to the apparently only heterosexual associations of the "quince,"[55] whose *both-and* indeterminacy could also be "fundamental" (as Jeffrey Masten has said of "Bottom").[56]

What Quince and his artisan-players (including Bottom) come "to disfigure, or to present" (3.1.60–61) in this Athenian marriage play is also important to the play's own "latter end."[57] In one way, their performance is already a disfiguring of contemporary theater practice—since, as Tiffany Stern has pointed out,[58] early modern artisans are not known to have performed classical stories—though it might be added that the "tragical mirth" of their "Pyramus and Thisby" performance from the story told by artisan-weavers in Ovid's *Metamorphoses* crosses genres from narrative to dramatic primarily to suggest how this ultimately tragic subject from Ovid at the wedding of Theseus to his conquered Amazon might figure "*against* [their] nuptial" (5.1.75), in an overall play that "seems rather to *problematize* than to celebrate marriage."[59] But Quince's "disfigure" in this marriage play that rings so many changes on "figure" itself (the word that in Latin includes both "form" and "shape")—from Theseus's reminding the rebellious Hermia of a father's power to "disfigure" as well as "figure" (1.1.51) to Hippolyta's imagining of "all their minds transfigur'd so together" (5.1.24)—also involves disfiguring in another sense as well, in ways that refigure, transfigure, and disfigure the "fruitful" association of the well-known marital quince, in a play where Quince himself uses "disfigure" as an apparently only malapropping synonym for "present" in the artisans' rehearsal in Act 3.

In Act 5, Quince's own misplacing of punctuating "stops" in his Prologue to the artisans' performance not only involves "sound" not "in government" (5.1.124), as Hippolyta puts it, which transforms (or disfigures) what might have been a compliment into an insult instead.[60] It at the same time introduces the function of punctuation, at the play's "latter end," and the question there (as in other open-ended Shakespeare plays) of where generically to place the "stop." The name choice of "Quince" evokes not only Athenian weddings and marital consummation or coitus (as its contemporary visual and textual contexts make clear) but also its repeated association with hoped-for fruitful issue, as we have seen. But after this comedy's final Athenian wedding feast, what is suggested is not comic closure, containment, or conclusion but the return of the night world outside Athens.[61] And Oberon's blessing on the marriage bed—with its hope that "the issue, there create, / Ever shall be fortunate" (5.1.405–406)—not only evokes (while warding off) the disfiguring "blots of Nature's hand" (5.1.409) but also shadows the ending itself with a reminder of the well-known tragic "issue" of the marriage of

Theseus and the Amazon Hippolyta: the death of Hippolytus evoked by the very name choice of Hippolyta (rather than Plutarch's alternative "Antiopa"), familiar not only from Seneca's tragedy *Hippolytus* but from Ovid's *Metamorphoses* as well, or yet another way in which things turn out "prepost'rously" (here turning comedy to tragedy) beyond the play's own wishful punctuation or "stop."[62]

The "tragical" subject of Pyramus and Thisbe from Ovid's weavers, which "Quince" and his artisan-players come "to disfigure, or to present" to newlyweds in Athens, already evokes the shadow of a tragic disfiguring or deforming of generic expectation, as well as the fruitful "issue" (in its double sense of both "offspring" and Athenian marital outcome) identified with the fruitful Athenian quince. But here, the more discordant and tragic hints of the unfortunate Hippolytus who was the issue of Theseus's marriage to his conquered Amazon and the echo of the ambiguous "Not Shafalus to Procrus was so true" (5.1.198) in this final blessing ("So shall all the couples three / Ever *true* in loving be," 5.1.407–408) import more discord than concord into the ending of a play where broken oaths and infidelities have already been so prominently featured. And the hopefully fruitful blessing on the "marriage bed" simultaneously evokes the tragic sequel to come, in which Hippolyta will be replaced by Phaedra and her lust for her stepson, and Theseus himself will bear responsibility for Hippolytus's tragic death.

The difference between "tragedy" and "comedy" in this open-ended ending is thus itself a question of where the final punctuation, or "stop," is placed; and the misplaced punctuation, "points," or "stops" of "sound" not "in government" (5.1.118–124) in Quince's "if we offend, it is with our good will" (5.1.108) find a curious echoing in Puck the English actor's "if we shadows have offended" (5.1.423), in the Epilogue to the larger play's audience that Theseus has already said no blameless play needs. If the issue of female speech is left open to "suppose" (or critics' suppositions)—as at the end of *The Taming of the Shrew*—the sequel to come from this Athenian ruler's marriage disfigures or deforms the expected fruitful ending and "issue" of comedy itself, as well as shadowing the fruitful "issue" identified with the Athenian quince. For this "nuptial" or wedding occasion, the "Quince" of Shakespeare's "marriage" play may introduce an entirely different kind of present, disfiguring as well as presenting, so to speak, an entire cultural, marital, and "moral" tradition.

*Chapter 4*

# "No Sinister Nor No Awkward Claim"

## Theatrical Contexts and Preposterous Recalls in *Henry V*

My rightful hand in a well-hallow'd cause.

—*Henry V* (1.2.293)

'Tis no sinister nor no awkward claim,
. . . He sends you this most memorable line.

—*Henry V* (2.4.85–88)

The order was revers'd.

—*Richard III* (2.1.87)

Shakespeare's *Henry V* has, in its Folio version, a crucially important double ending. First, there is the sense of triumphant *telos*, brought about by the successful conquests of the ruler Hall called "the mirror of Christendome," Holinshed a "paterne in princehood" and "mirrour of magnificence," and the Chorus to the play the "mirror of all Christian kings" (*H5* 2.Chorus.6).[1] However, there then follows the little Epilogue that not only forecasts the historical *sequel* to Henry V's success but looks simultaneously two ways at once—forward in *chronological* time to this triumphant king's successor, Henry VI, the son who would lose all that his father had won, and backward in *theatrical* time to the plays that had already dramatized the losses of that son, a history the Epilogue recalls as having "oft" been "shown" upon "our stage":

Thus far, with rough and all-unable pen,
Our bending author hath pursu'd the story,
In little room confining mighty men,
Mangling by starts the full course of their glory.
Small time; but in that small most greatly lived
This star of England. Fortune made his sword;
By which the world's best garden he achieved,
And of it left his son imperial lord.
Henry the Sixt, in infant bands crown'd King
Of France and England, did this king succeed;
Whose state so many had the managing,
That they lost France, and made his England bleed;
Which oft our stage hath shown; and for their sake,
Into your fair minds let this acceptance take.

The Epilogue to *Henry V* that starts with reference to "Our bending author" both anticipates the disastrous history to follow from Henry V's union with Katherine of France (so hopefully forecast in the Wooing Scene just concluded) and reminds the audience that this later history had dramatically been "shown" *before*.[2] The "last word" of *Henry V* is therefore not one of definitive triumph or closure, but rather a strangely recursive circling back, to the plays of the son who lost not only France but also the throne of England itself, in the conflict of Lancastrian and Yorkist that became the Wars of the Roses. Though the rhetoric of lineal succession is here invoked ("Henry the Sixt . . . did this king *succeed*"), it is simultaneously countered by the reminder that in the *theatrical* context of these dramatic histories, there is instead a reversal of linear sequence, in which the son who was to succeed this father had already appeared on stage.

The Epilogue to *Henry V* (coming at the end of the dramatic series) thus calls attention to what E. M. W. Tillyard termed the "curious procedure" of the series itself, the fact that the first tetralogy of plays (*Henry VI Parts 1–3* through *Richard III*) dealt with a historical period that is chronologically later than the theatrically later or second tetralogy (*Richard II* through *Henry IV 1 and 2* to *Henry V*).[3] In this reversed ordering—as the Epilogue to *Henry V* goes out of its way to underscore—sons precede fathers, and successors come before ancestors, rather than following the order of the chronicles structured by reign. Tillyard and others in an earlier generation of Shakespeare criticism attempted to rationalize this strange reversal—and rescue the order of chronology—by postulating the possible prior existence of lost earlier versions of the second tetralogy plays, a speculation that would realign the *dramatic* series with the chronicles' chonological succession.[4] The pull of chronology, indeed, is so powerful that the 1623 Folio famously printed Shakespeare's histories according to the sequence of reigns—from Richard II to Richard III; while even otherwise canny modern commentators on these plays frequently revert to what we might call the "default position" of chronology, forgetting (or simply ignoring) the fact that the historical aftermath to *Henry V* had already been the subject of its popular dramatic precursors. There is, however, no evidence of the prior existence of "lost" plays that might explain away the "curious procedure" of what we in fact have—two groups of history plays in which chronology itself (as Marjorie Garber put it, quoting *Richard III*) is part of an "order" that is "reversed."[5] There is thus no proof that the dramatic series followed the succession of reigns in Holinshed and Hall, whose accounts are otherwise often followed so closely in these plays that an older generation of critics viewed Shakespeare's histories as a simple reflection of the chronicles themselves.

The pertinent chronological or historical sequence moved from the deposition of Richard II by the usurper Bolingbroke (son of John of Gaunt, Duke of Lancaster) and the subsequent Lancastrian rule of Henry IV, Henry V, and Henry VI, to the reign of the Yorkists from Edward IV to Richard III and the defeat of Richard by Richmond, the future Henry VII, whose marriage to Edward's daughter ended the Wars of the Roses and inaugurated the Tudor line. The chronicles follow this sequential order, as well as developing, as often noted, a concomitant historiography of cause and effect. In the *theatrical* context of the history plays' reversed order, however, the plays of the son, Henry VI, precede the play of the father, *Henry V*, and *Richard III*, the end of the chronological sequence, leads dramatically into *Richard II*, its historical beginning.[6] These dramatic histories place particular emphasis on the reigns Hall's chronicle termed "The victorious actes of Kyng Henry the fifth" and "The tragical doynges of Kyng Richard the thirde." Yet the inverted order in which they do so yields "curious" effects, producing echoes of the dramatically earlier *Richard III* in the later *Henry V*, even though the Tudor archvillain Richard III came historically well after Hall's "mirror of Christendome."[7] In the "curious procedure" of this reversal, early follows late, and *after* precedes *before*, rather than the "natural" or temporal sequence, just as other parts of the Shakespeare canon play on an unnaturally "preposterous" reversal in which "post" precedes "pre," a son is "a gentleman born before

[his] father" (*The Winter's Tale*), "successors" come before "ancestors" (*Merry Wives*), children beget their own sires (*The Taming of the Shrew*), "daughters" become "mothers" to their father (*King Lear*), and a daughter "begets" the father who begot her (*Pericles*). Yet far from glossing over this "curious procedure," Shakespeare's dramatic histories call attention to this reversal, in ways whose implications for *Henry V* I propose here to explore.

Once we take seriously the reversal of chronological order in which the play of the father (*Henry V*) comes after rather than before the plays of the son (Henry VI), certain passages begin to appear in a different light. One of the most striking is the "prophecy" by the Bishop of Carlisle in *Richard II* of the woes to follow from Bolingbroke's usurpation of Richard's crown (that "in this seat of peace tumultuous wars / Shall kin with kin and kind with kind confound," *R2* 4.1.140–141), a prophecy reminiscent of the paradigm of English history in Hall—as a fall from unity (and legitimacy) because of Bolingbroke's act to the ultimate discord of the Wars of the Roses, before the apocalyptic *telos* of Tudor peace. Yet what this prophecy projects onto "future ages" still to come, in a passage literally studded with "shall" and "will," is the history of civil discord that had already been "shown," in the earlier plays of Henry VI and the Wars of the Roses.[8] Carlisle's prophecy of this dire future ends with an appeal that it be "prevented" ("Prevent it, resist it, let it not be so"). But part of the irony of the speech is that it *had* been (in an early modern sense of this term that is frequent in Shakespeare) "pre-vented" or preceded by what theatrically had come *before*.

Yet another striking effect of the reversed order of these dramatic histories is the sense of recursive return or circling back created by the fact that the death of Henry V, projected as a future event in the Epilogue to *Henry V*, had already occurred at the beginning of *Henry VI Part 1*, which starts with the funeral of this triumphant king:

> *Dead march. Enter the Funeral of* KING HENRY THE FIFT, *attended on by the* DUKE OF BEDFORD, *Regent of France, the* DUKE OF GLOUCESTER, *Protector, the* DUKE OF EXETER, [*the* EARL OF] WARWICK, *the* BISHOP OF WINCHESTER, *and the* DUKE OF SOMERSET. . . . (*1 Henry VI*, opening SD)[9]

*Henry VI Part I* begins (like *Hamlet*) just after the death of a father, and repeatedly evokes the conjuring of the spirits of the already dead; *Henry V* begins with a reference to "flat unraised spirits" and brings Henry V himself back to life within its "wooden O" (*H5* Prologue 9, 13). In a curious variation, perhaps, on this uncanny raising and its reversal of the "natural" sequence from life to death, the chronologically *later* "Falstaffe" (Folio spelling)—the historical Sir John Fastolf who is presented as cowardly and dies in the dramatically *earlier* play (*1H6* 1.1.131, 1.4.35, 3.2.104)—is revived in the name of "Falstaff" substituted for Oldcastle in the dramatically later (but chronologically earlier) tetralogy,[10] or the Falstaff who comically rises from the dead at the end of *1 Henry IV* and continues to haunt *Henry V* even after the report of his death on the threshold of the French campaign. And the "crooked" figure of Richard III (whose chronologically later reign had already been dramatized in the play that bears his name) is recalled (along with the "crooked" Bolingbroke from *2 Henry IV*) in the "crooked figure" with which *Henry V* itself begins (Prologue 15), though he is supposed to be the antithesis of this "mirror of all Christian kings" (2.Chorus.6).[11]

To call attention to the strikingly recursive relationship between the Epilogue to *Henry V* and the dramatically earlier opening of *1 Henry VI* is not to suggest that such a "preposterous" recursive design was already present in the earliest histories. To make such a claim about the early history plays, for which the precise original order of composition and authorship are still open to question, would be utterly unnecessary to the present argument. It is also not to suggest that my use of the term "tetralogy" in this chapter (to distinguish between the plays that were early and those that were late) in any way presumes a prior design or plan. It is, however, to observe that by the time the little Epilogue or tail-piece to *Henry V* directs attention *backwards* to the plays of Henry VI, there is a deliberate sense of ouroboros-like recursivity or circling back, like the "O" or "crooked figure" of the Prologue to *Henry V* or the Epilogue's own reference to "our *bending* author" (Epilogue 2). Fluellen's allusion in *Henry V* to a tale in his "mouth" that is taken out of his mouth "ere it is made and finished" (4.7.43) evokes simultaneously an ouroboros figure and the breaching of the "finished," closed, or complete, and joins the sense of the "fracted and corroborate" (*H5* 2.1.124) that Christopher Pye sees as a defining one for the play as a whole.[12] This recursivity, bending back from end to beginning rather than proceeding in linear or sequential fashion to a definitive teleological, providential, or eschatological end, also fractures the language of "perfection" (or "how things are perfected") in the bishops' praise of the new-reformed king at the beginning of *Henry V* (1.1.69), reversing the progression from multiplicity to unity encapsulated in Canterbury's self-serving parable of the bees (1.2.187–208)[13] and undermining the play's own apparently triumphant conclusion with a reminder of the earlier plays' dramatization of what subsequently undid it. What I want to explore, then, in what follows, is the difference this recursivity might make to our apprehension of the rhetoric of straightforward "advance" and "right" in *Henry V* itself.

This issue is even more important in light of the fact that *Henry V* is often presented in splendid isolation, or only in relation to *Richard II* and *Henry IV*, the plays of the second tetralogy that immediately precede it, without reference to the simultaneous "pre" *and* "post" of the Henry VI plays its Epilogue so pointedly recalls. Such isolation from the "ill neighborhood" (*H5* 1.2.154) or contaminating reminders of these earlier dramatic histories seems to reflect what this "mirror of all Christian kings" (as the Chorus has it) himself wants to establish—clear and impermeable boundaries around the beginning and end of his exemplary reign, unbreached by undermining reference to what is excluded. But the play itself—in marked contrast to this bounded self-enclosure—pre-vents the forgetting of this larger theatrical context through the Epilogue that calls attention, at the very height of Henry's triumph, to the reversed dramatic order in which what is suppressed or omitted in *Henry V* had already been "shown" before its beginning.

> . . . whatsoever cunning fiend it was
> That wrought upon thee so preposterously
> Hath got the voice in hell for excellence.
>
> —*Henry V* (2.2.111–113)

> The signs of war advance!
> No king of England, if not king of France!
>
> —*Henry V* (2.2.192–193)

In order to suggest the importance of this prior theatrical context for what is suppressed or left unsaid in *Henry V*, what I propose is to focus first on a scene from this play that explictly invokes the "preposterous" used elsewhere in Shakespeare for precisely such inversions of successor and ancestor, end and beginning—the scene of the exposure at Southampton of the conspiracy against Henry by Richard Earl of Cambridge, Thomas Grey, and Lord Scroop of Masham, the "English monsters" (as he calls them) who are executed as a result:

These English *monsters*! My Lord of Cambridge here,
You know how apt our love was to accord
To furnish him with all appertinents
Belonging to his honor; and this man
Hath, for *a few light crowns*, lightly conspir'd
And sworn unto the practices of France
To kill us here in Hampton. To the which
This knight, no less for bounty bound to us
Than Cambridge is, hath likewise sworn. But O,
What shall I say to thee, Lord Scroop, thou cruel,
Ingrateful, savage, and inhuman creature?
Thou that didst bear the key of all my counsels,
That knew'st the very bottom of my soul,
That (almost) mightst have coin'd me into gold,
Wouldst thou have practic'd on me, for thy use?
May it be possible that foreign hire
Could out of thee extract one spark of evil
That might annoy my finger? 'Tis so strange,
That, though the truth of it stands off as gross
As black and white, my eye will scarcely see it.
Treason and murther ever kept together,
As two yoke-devils sworn to either's purpose,
Working so grossly in a natural cause
That admiration did not hoop at them;
But thou ('gainst all proportion) didst bring in
Wonder to wait on *treason* and on *murther*;
And whatsoever *cunning fiend* it was
That wrought upon thee so *preposterously*
Hath got the voice in *hell* for excellence. . . . (2.2.85–113)

Henry's invocation of the "preposterous" here is glossed by editors as "contrary to nature" (*Riverside*), "unnaturally" (New Cambridge; Oxford; *Norton Shakespeare*), "inverting the natural order" (New Penguin), or "contrary to the natural order of things" (Old Cambridge).[14] It also carries with it, in Henry's apocalyptic rhetoric and reference to a "cunning fiend," the sense of a "damned enterprise" (164) or infernal rising up, a *mundus inversus* or overturning of the sanctioned order inspired by "devils" from "hell" against heaven's anointed king. The treachery of Scroop in particular (identified in the play as well as in Holinshed as Henry's "bedfellow" and presented here in terms that simultaneously evoke the language of sodomy or "preposterous venery" linked with the demonic) is described as at once a Judas-like betrayal and the diabolical emblem of such "preposterously" inspired rebellion ("this revolt of thine, methinks, is like / Another fall of man," 141–142).[15] "English monsters" itself invokes a term that was frequently part of the lexicon of "preposterous venery," in a period when it could be used to figure preposterous inversions of all kinds, including the political and hierarchical—in a scene where Henry's religious rhetoric is summoned to authorize suppression of a rebellion of "traitors" characterized as an infernal and unnatural act.

Henry's "preposterously" thus appears in its combined early modern sense of inverted and unnatural in his condemnation of the rebellion at Southampton, on the very threshold of the war in France. And exposure of what Henry terms "this dangerous treason lurking in our way" (2.2.186) serves pivotally as the prelude to his "advance" on France, once the rebels are sent off to their execution:

> Now, lords, for France; the enterprise whereof
> Shall be to you as us, like glorious.
> We doubt not of a fair and lucky war,
> Since *God* so graciously hath brought to light
> This *dangerous treason* lurking in our way
> To *hinder* our *beginnings*. We doubt not now
> But *every rub is smoothed on our way*.
> Then *forth*, dear countrymen! Let us deliver
> Our puissance into the hand of *God*,
> Putting it *straight* in expedition.
> Cheerly to sea! The signs of war *advance*!
> *No king of England, if not king of France*! (2.2.182–193)

Suppression of this "treason" and "preposterously" inspired rebellion thus immediately leads to the ringing religious and patriotic rhetoric of the war itself, enabling the "advance" on France to be put "straight in expedition," without further hindrance or "rub," now that what had threatened to "hinder our beginnings" has been removed and the way "smoothed" of such impediments.

"Preposterous" in Henry's use of the term thus participates in the rhetoric of infernal and divine in which he casts the legitimacy of his rule as medieval mystery, loyalty to it as to an order that is divinely sanctioned, and the quelling of "unnatural" rebellion as what would be, from a providentialist perspective, the first of the "Victorious acts of Henry V." With these boundaries established, and this problem (apparently) contained, other perspectives on this rebellion are here suppressed. Henry's condemnation of these "monsters" depends on his purely static characterization of their rebellion as "preposterously" inspired, understood synchronically as a vertical or hierarchical antithesis. But "preposterously" itself—as the contemporary term for the reversed as well as unnatural—simultaneously conjures up a very different way in which Henry's wished-for new "beginnings" are "hindered," by the elliptical hints that undermine both this self-enclosure or containment and Henry's legitimizing rhetoric of "right." The ostensible motive of this rebellion—that the conspirators agreed to "sell" their "sovereign's life to death and treachery" for a "foreign purse" (2.2.10–11), a "few light crowns" or coins offered by the king of France (2.2.89)—supports Henry's representation of the rebellion as a Judas-like betrayal, of "traitors" (2.2.1) seduced by "foreign hire" (100). Modern audiences viewing *Henry V* in isolation would have no sense of what Henry's rhetoric here both constructs or forges and suppresses. But the buried pun on "crowns" subtly evokes the real motive for this rebellion, left unsaid throughout the entire scene: not "crowns" as coins of France but rather the "crown" of England. And these hints—along with the Epilogue's reminder of the plays of the son that had been "shown" *before*—undermine not only Henry's rhetoric of straightforward "advance" and "right" but also the boundaries or enclosures of a history that might otherwise move in self-contained, "straight," forward-looking, or linear fashion from beginning to end.

Commentators on this scene note that it is strangely "cryptic" as to the real motive of the rebellion,[16] the motive that surfaces only in the double meaning of a "few light crowns" or in Cambridge's own terse ellipsis ("For me, the gold of France did not seduce, / Although I did admit it as a motive / The sooner to effect what I intended," 2.2.155–157). Editorial footnotes inform the reader of the political motive that is suppressed within the Rebellion Scene but outlined in the chronicles of Holinshed and Hall, who emphasize that Cambridge had married the sister of Edmund Mortimer, Earl of March (the line designated by Richard II as rightful heir to England's throne) and that "after the death of which earle of March, for diverse secret impediments, not able to haue issue, the earle of Cambridge was sure that the crowne should come to him *by his wife*, and to his children, of hir begotten."[17] The real motive behind the rebellion was thus the right to the throne through the female by which Cambridge and his heirs would be England's legitimate rulers, instead of Henry V and the usurping Lancastrian line. And Henry V's own claim to France through the female (Edward III's French mother Isabel), which forms the basis of his "right" in the Salic Law speech of Act 1 (1.2.96), would likewise be invalidated by the higher Cambridge claim through the female to both England *and* France—suppressed in the Salic Law Scene as well as the Rebellion Scene where Cambridge and his co-conspirators are sent to their deaths as traitors.

Hall and Holinshed also inform their readers of Cambridge's preservation of the future of his heirs and their claim to the crown by his silence, as well as the momentous aftermath of his rebellion—the ultimate rise of his heirs to possess their right to the throne and unseat the Lancastrian line, or (as Hall put it) the destruction of the "walles" of Henry's own house.[18] In ways opaque to modern audiences or readers for whom this rebellion is viewed only within the isolated enclosure of *Henry V*, the apparently minor Cambridge of the Rebellion Scene is no less a figure than the ancestor whose successors would ultimately supplant the Lancastrian usurpers, replacing Henry VI, the unsuccessful son of Henry V, with Cambridge's grandson as Edward IV, a new Earl of March and England's first Yorkist king. And as outlined in what follows, it is in the plays of Henry VI that the Epilogue recalls that this aftermath of the Cambridge rebellion had already "oft" been "shown," undermining Henry's rhetoric of "right" by recalling something that "hinders" it in a different, *theatrical*, sense. What is striking, however, is that critics of *Henry V* frequently ignore this larger theatrical context. And even editors who refer to the aftermath of the Cambridge rebellion outlined in the chronicles may tend to forget (or omit) that this is what had already been highlighted in plays so popular by 1592 that Philip Henslowe's *Diary* recorded the profitable box-office returns of "harry the vj [i.e., the vi]," Thomas Nashe wrote that Talbot's death had been seen by "ten thousand spectators at least (at several times)," and *Greene's Groatsworth of Wit* adapted a line from *3 Henry VI* (on a "tiger's heart wrapp'd in a woman's hide," *3H6* 1.4.137) in its condemnation of Shakespeare as an "upstart crow."[19]

In his New Cambridge edition of *Henry V* (1992, updated 2005), Andrew Gurr argues that Cambridge's motive—along with the Marches' greater claim—is suppressed within *Henry V* by Shakespeare himself, and stresses that the "best account of what Shakespeare suppressed" was the "specific corrective" to *Henry V* provided in the later *Sir John Oldcastle* play, commissioned in 1599 by Philip Henslowe for the rival company at the Rose.[20] Gurr notes that the "lineage issue behind the Cambridge conspiracy"—omitted in the Rebellion Scene of *Henry V*—is fully outlined in that non-Shakespearean play, as the greater right to England (as well as France) of Cambridge and his Yorkist heirs, because of descent through the female from the third son of Edward III, in contrast to the Lancastrian line from the fourth son, John of Gaunt ("this Harry, or his father king, / Who fetcht their title but from Lancaster, / Fourth of that royall line").[21] Gurr sees the suppression of this more legitimate title in the Rebellion Scene as a more general sign of "what Shakespeare suppressed" in *Henry V*, a suppression later exposed and corrected in the rival *Oldcastle* play. And his case against Shakespeare as the agent of this suppression is furthered by his observation that "even the fact that Cambridge was younger brother to the York who dies at Agincourt is omitted from Shakespeare's play, although it is specified in Holinshed. Since York's identity as the Aumerle of *Richard II* is also omitted, a minor irrelevance given the exclusively symbolic function of York's valour in the battle, that may simply have been streamlining, polishing out irrelevant details. But the elimination of an alternative dynastic claim to the English crown in favour of Henry's claim to the French crown cannot have just been streamlining."[22]

I mention Gurr's emphasis on the later *Oldcastle* play not to single out what is in so many respects a remarkable edition of *Henry V*, but rather to suggest that the importance of the Epilogue's reminder of the plays of the son that had already been "shown" before *Henry V* still has not permeated our more general critical consciousness, particularly in relation to this play's notorious omissions. Katharine Eisaman Maus, for example, noted in her *Norton Shakespeare* introduction to *Henry V* (in 1997 and 2008) that in the Salic Law Scene, "Henry decides to press his claim on the French throne through the female line of descent. Shortly thereafter, he executes three erstwhile friends for conspiring against his life. In fact their plot was inspired by the conviction that Henry's title to the English throne was obstructed by the Earl of Mortimer's daughter, the Earl of Cambridge's wife. In other words, Henry employs against the French a principle that, if it were enforced against him, would strip him of both English and French kingdoms. Yet *the point is made so obliquely that only a spectator cognizant of the tangled Plantagenet genealogy is likely to catch it*."[23] In her rewritten introduction to the third edition of *The Norton Shakespeare* (2016)—where this passage is omitted—there is a partial notice that *Henry V* "refers constantly to events before and after its own temporal limits, events familiar to Shakespeare's audience from plays they had already seen performed" (1534); but only the "earlier plays" (1536) of *Richard II* and *Henry IV* are discussed, with no mention of the Henry VI plays, including in the section on the Rebellion Scene, or in that scene's notes.[24] The New Folger edition of *Henry V* (1995; reissued 2009) likewise makes no mention of the *Henry VI* plays in glossing the Rebellion Scene, including Cambridge's cryptic line there on his "motive"—commenting instead that "Cambridge's motivation, according to *historians*, was to advance the Earl of March's claim to the English throne."[25] And its genealogy of "Henry V's French Descent" (xv) shows only the lines of Richard II and Edward III's fourth son John of Gaunt from Edward III's French mother—completely omitting the higher claim to both France and England, through the third son (and female descent), of the Earl of March as well as of Cambridge and his heirs. More recently, the 2010 Royal Shakespeare edition of *Henry V*—though it notes the Epilogue's reference to the plays of Henry VI and comments that "There is a strong possibility that Shakespeare played the part of the Chorus himself" (xvi)—does not include the importance of what is revealed in those earlier plays but suppressed or omitted in *Henry V*.[26]

Similarly, among twenty-first-century critical treatments, Nicholas Grene's *Shakespeare's Serial History Plays* (2002)—though its chapter "Looking Back" begins with Carlisle's prophecy in *Richard II* as looking "forward" to the Wars of the Roses while "theatrically it looks back to Shakespeare's dramatisation of those wars"—does not consider those earlier plays in relation to what is suppressed in the Rebellion Scene or elsewhere in *Henry V*.[27] Garrett A. Sullivan, Jr.'s *Memory and Forgetting in English Renaissance Drama* (2005) does not include *Henry V* or the early histories.[28] James Shapiro's *A Year in the Life of William Shakespeare: 1599* (2005) simply notes in its discussion of *Henry V* that Cambridge's higher claim to the throne was emphasized in the later *Oldcastle* play.[29] Peter Holland's *Shakespeare, Memory and Performance* (2006), though it begins with memory and the "memorable" in *Henry V*, does not include its striking explicit remembrance of the Henry VI plays.[30] The chapter on *Henry V* in Warren Chernaik's *Cambridge Introduction to Shakespeare's History Plays* (2007), though it frequently mentions the plays of the second tetralogy, cites only one link to the earlier plays—Henry VI's soliloquy at the Battle of Towton (*3 Henry VI* 2.5) as a possible parallel to Henry V's soliloquy on "ceremony" on the night before Agincourt (*H5* 4.1)—with no mention of their relevance to Cambridge or the Rebellion Scene.[31] Lina Perkins Wilder's 2010 book on *Shakespeare's Memory Theatre* does not mention the *Henry VI* plays anywhere in its chapter "Wasting Memory: Competing Mnemonics in the Henry Plays," even though she stresses that "theatrical memory" is as important as "the nationalistic common memory identified by Anthony Dawson" and refers to "a remembering theatrical community."[32] Janette Dillon's *Shakespeare and the Staging of English History* (2012)—though its treatment of the *Henry VI* plays includes scenes that are relevant to what is suppressed or omitted in *Henry V*—does not examine their importance in relation to what is notoriously missing with regard to Cambridge's higher claim from its Salic Law speech and the Rebellion Scene. And though Hester Lees-Jeffries's *Shakespeare and Memory* (2013) cites the possible recall in the Prologue to *Henry V* of the funeral that began *1 Henry VI* and briefly refers to York's claim in the early plays,[33] it does not connect either to Cambridge or what the Rebellion Scene suppresses. Frequently, not even ironic readings mention what in the Henry VI plays had already foregrounded what in *Henry V* is left out. So strikingly, what Karl Wentersdorf over forty years ago called a "conspiracy of silence" regarding these omissions and suppressions has largely continued.[34]

I mention such instances here in order to underscore in what follows the costs of effacing from our critical consideration of *Henry V* the popular earlier history plays its Epilogue so directly recalls. Apart from the fact that these plays are much less studied, part of the problem may be the influence of chronology itself (already reflected in the 1623 Folio, where the *Henry VI* plays come after *Henry V*), an influence so strong that even treatments that trace the dynastic motives behind the Cambridge rebellion often present this aftermath in its chronological rather than its dramatic sequence. If we attend to the reversed theatrical order of these histories, however, in which the political motive and aftermath of the Cambridge rebellion had already been "shown" in advance, this dramatic anticipation provides a crucially important perspective on *Henry V*, not only in the Salic Law and rebellion scenes but elsewhere in the play, including the elliptical summoning of the Duke of York, whose title passed after his Agincourt death to the heirs of the executed Cambridge. And it ironizes in advance Henry's repeated rhetoric of proceeding with a "rightful hand in a well-hallow'd cause" (1.2.293), curiously inverted in the presentation of Henry's "memorable line" (2.4.88) to the French as "no sinister nor no awkward claim" (2.4.85), to which we will return.

Jonathan Baldo has shown that "in spite of officialdom's extraordinary deployment of a rhetoric of remembrance in the play, reminding characters and viewers alike of the sacred, moral, and patriotic obligations to remember, *Henry V* bears more powerful testimony to the advantages of forgetting," a pattern of strategic forgetting and remembering "intimately connected to the exercise of power."[35] The king's prayer on the night before Agincourt—entreating the "God of battles" to "think not upon the fault / My father made in compassing the crown!" (4.1.288–294)—is the only openly voiced reminder in this play of Bolingbroke's usurpation and murder of Richard II, and it is spoken when Henry is alone on stage. What I want to suggest is not only that strategic forgetting and remembering apply to Henry V's attempt to put the "fault" of his father Bolingbroke in the past, along with Falstaff, the other "bad father" from the Henry IV plays; but also that what we might call "preposterous recalls" of the period *after* Henry V's death, from the earlier plays of Henry VI, likewise make clear what in this final play of the series is suppressed or omitted, undermining speech after speech through haunting reminders of what has been left out and what breaches the containment of its wishful enclosures.

Much is made in the Rebellion Scene itself of the fact that what Henry terms a "preposterously" inspired rebellion has been successfully "prevented" (*H5* 2.2.164), in lines that iterate the thanks given for its "prevention" (2.2.158). But the rebellion described as inspired "preposterously," in Henry's wishfully static sense of fiendishly or unnaturally, continues to undermine Henry's own rhetoric of straightforward and "rightful" advance by having been pre-vented, in the familiar Shakespearean sense, by the plays of the son that had already come *before*, simultaneously complicating a more innocent or straightforward reading of Henry's and his supporters' rhetoric of "right," as well as differently "hindering" his new "beginnings."

ꟹ

*Plantagenet*. . . . declare the cause
My father, Earl of Cambridge, lost his head.
—*Henry VI Part 1* (2.5.53–54)

*Mortimer*. . . . I was the next by birth and parentage;
For by my mother I derived am
From Lionel Duke of Clarence, third son
To King Edward the Third; whereas he
From John of Gaunt doth bring his pedigree,
Being but fourth of that heroic line. . . .

But as the rest, so fell that noble earl,
And was beheaded. Thus the Mortimers,
In whom the title rested, were suppress'd.
—*Henry VI Part 1* (2.5.73–92)

*Plantagenet.* . . . methinks, my father's execution
Was nothing less than bloody tyranny.
—*Henry VI Part 1* (2.5.99–100)

The first of these advance theatrical exposures of a radically different perspective on Henry V's suppression of the Cambridge rebellion is staged in a memorable scene of *Henry VI Part 1*, the play that began with the funeral of Henry V and dramatized the post-Agincourt losses in France, as well as the growing civil conflict that (as the Epilogue puts it) "made . . . England bleed." Here, the son of the executed Cambridge (Richard "Plantagenet," soon to become the new Duke of York, the title left vacant at Agincourt by the death of Cambridge's elder brother) has explained to him—and thus to the audience—by Mortimer, the imprisoned Earl of March himself, the greater "right" through the female that the Lancastrians have "suppress'd" and the real motive behind the Cambridge rebellion:

*Plantagenet.* Therefore, good uncle, for my father's sake,
In honor of a true Plantagenet,
And for alliance sake, *declare the cause*
*My father, Earl of Cambridge, lost his head.*
*Mortimer.* That cause, fair nephew, that imprison'd me
And hath detain'd me all my flow'ring youth
Within a loathsome dungeon, there to pine,
Was cursed instrument of his decease.
*Plantagenet.* *Discover more at large what cause that was,*
For I am ignorant and cannot guess.
*Mortimer.* I will, if that my fading breath permit
And death approach not ere my tale be done.
*Henry the Fourth, grandfather to this king* [i.e., Henry VI],
*Depos'd his nephew Richard,* Edward's son [i.e., Richard II],
The first begotten, and the lawful heir

Of *Edward king, the third of that descent*;
During whose reign *the Percies of the north*,
Finding his *usurpation* most unjust,
*Endeavor'd my advancement to the throne.*
The reason mov'd these warlike lords to this
Was, for that (young Richard thus remov'd,
Leaving no heir begotten of his body)
*I was the next by birth and parentage*;
*For by my mother I derived am*
*From Lionel Duke of Clarence, third son*
*To King Edward the Third*; whereas he
From *John of Gaunt* doth bring his *pedigree*,
Being but *fourth* of that heroic line.
But mark: as in this haughty great attempt
They labored to plant the *rightful heir*,
I lost my liberty, and they their lives.
Long after this, when *Henry the Fift*
(Succeeding his father Bullingbrook) did reign,
*Thy father, Earl of Cambridge* then, deriv'd
From famous Edmund Langley, Duke of York,
*Marrying my sister that thy mother was*,
Again, in pity of my hard distress,
Levied an army, weening to redeem
And have install'd me in the diadem.
But as the rest, *so fell that noble earl,*
*And was beheaded. Thus the Mortimers,*
*In whom the title rested, were suppress'd.*
(*1 Henry VI* 2.5.51–92)

What Mortimer here rehearses at length, in advance of the later plays that included *Henry V*—to the audience as well as to the executed Cambridge's son—is the entire past history of Bolingbroke's deposing of Richard II (later staged in *Richard II*); the uprisings of the Percies during his reign as Henry IV to replace the usurper-king by Mortimer as Richard II's designated heir (a claim later dramatically underscored in *1 Henry IV*, where Mortimer appears as a *younger* man and is called the rightful "owner" of Bolingbroke's throne);[36] and Henry V's suppression of the Cambridge rebellion motivated by this same cause, dramatized later in *Henry V*. In addition, Mortimer crucially foregrounds the descent through the female from Edward III that made the Marches' "title" more legitimate than the Lancastrian Henries' and gave Cambridge's heirs a higher right to the throne. It therefore does not take knowledge of the chronicles or a later "corrective" to *Henry V* like the *Oldcastle* play to expose what is suppressed about this greater dynastic right in *Henry V*. For this prior theatrical "discover[y]"—in the earlier plays the Epilogue recalls—already provided this "corrective" in advance.

Cambridge's son (revealed in this scene to be the "heir" through the female of the dying and issueless Earl of March, from Mortimer's "sister that thy mother was") concludes from this revelation of how the rightful "title" was "suppress'd," that his "father's execution" by Henry V was "nothing less than bloody tyranny" (*1H6* 2.5.99–100)—inverting in advance of *Henry V* not only Henry's rhetoric of divine and demonic in the Rebellion Scene, but his "We are *no tyrant*, but a Christian king" (1.2.241) in the Salic Law Scene as well.[37] Mortimer's rehearsal of the more legitimate right "suppress'd" in Henry's execution of the Earl of Cambridge is recounted as past history in this scene from *1 Henry VI*, contributing to that play's sense of coming after crucial prior events to which it is a sequel. But, in the reversed *dramatic* ordering of these histories, the higher "right" that the Earl of March already exposes "at large" in this earlier play precedes Henry's own rhetoric of proceeding with a "rightful hand in a well-hallow'd cause" in *Henry V* (1.2.293), providing a very different advance perspective not only on the Cambridge rebellion but on Henry himself.

This inverse perspective on the Lancastrian rhetoric of "right" is staged again and again in these early history plays, including in *1 Henry VI* itself, together with the inversion of "wrong" for "right"—the term whose other opposite is "sinister," in ways important for the presentation in *Henry V* of Henry's right to France as neither "awkward" nor "sinister" (*H5* 2.4.85).[38] Cambridge's son vows after Mortimer's "discover[y]" that he himself will right these "wrongs" (*1H6* 2.5.124), by taking up the suppressed March cause to which he is heir. But even before he enters in this scene, Mortimer the Earl of March comments on the ill treatment by the Lancastrians of this son, whose "*wrong* doth equal mine, / Since Henry Monmouth [i.e., Henry V] first began to reign" (*1H6* 2.5.22–23). And in the famous invented scene of "red" and "white" roses that anticipates the Wars of the Roses to come—where Suffolk and Somerset pluck the "red" rose symbolic of the

Lancastrians—not only the son of Cambridge and the "Lawyer" but strikingly also the Warwick who will appear in the St. Crispin's Day speech of *Henry V* (4.3.54) pluck the white rose instead, holding the Lancastrian claim to be in the "wrong" rather than the right (*1H6* 2.4.36, 57).

Warwick himself defends the son of the rebel Cambridge executed by Henry V, rehearsing even in advance of the imprisoned Mortimer his high descent ("thou *wrong'st* him, Somerset; / His grandfather was Lionel Duke of Clarence, / Third son to the third Edward, King of England," *1H6* 2.4.82–84) and promising to wear the white rose that will become the emblem of the suppressed March-York cause.[39] When, soon after, the son of Cambridge is created Duke of York, the title left vacant by the Agincourt death of Cambridge's elder brother, it is again Warwick who urges not only the "right" of Cambridge's son but the righting of "his father's wrongs" (*1H6* 3.1.148–160), done to him by Henry V, by the conferring on him of this title.[40]

The rhetoric of "right" and "rightful hand" (simultaneous opposite of both "wrong" and "sinister"), sounded repeatedly in *Henry V*, had therefore already been inverted in one of the earlier plays its Epilogue invokes, and Henry V himself emerges from this play—in advance of the dramatic *Henry V*—as a double or ambivalent figure: the king whose successes in France stand as reminder of a heroic past but also a king whose "tyranny" and "wrongs" had "suppress'd" a more legitimate "right." At the same time, the advance exposure of the Marches' suppressed "right" provides a very different perspective not only on the Cambridge rebellion but on Henry's own hierarchical rhetoric of low and high in the later scene of the rebellion he characterizes as "preposterously" inspired, since here it is the Lancastrian line of Henry himself that is discovered to be of the "meaner sort" (*1H6* 2.5.123)—arrivistes lower down in the hierarchy of descent, without a right to the throne.

ᔕ

*York.* . . . My mother, being heir unto the crown,
Married Richard Earl of Cambridge . . .
By her I claim the kingdom. . . .

—*Henry VI Part 2* (2.2.44–47)

*Warwick.* What plain proceedings is more plain than this?
Henry doth claim the crown from John of Gaunt,
The fourth son, York claims it from the third. . . .

—*Henry VI Part 2* (2.2.53–55)

*Salisbury*. . . . I have considered with myself
The title of this most renowned duke,
And in my conscience do repute his Grace
The rightful heir to England's royal seat.
—*Henry VI Part 2* (5.1.175–178)

*Henry VI Part I* thus provides a radically different perspective on what is suppressed or omitted in *Henry V* itself, including the link through the female that would undo Henry's right to both England and France. But in the other Henry VI plays its Epilogue recalls as having already "oft" been "shown," this higher "right" is staged again and again in other memorable scenes as well. In the play known in the Folio as *The second Part of Henry the Sixt*,[41] when news comes of the territory lost in France, Cambridge's son, now Duke of York, laments the loss of these French lands as *his*—not the Lancastrians'—by right ("So York must sit, and fret, and bite his tongue, / While *his own lands* are bargain'd for and sold," *2H6* 1.1.230–231; "Cold news for me; for I had hope of France, / Even as I have of fertile England's soil," *2H6* 1.1.237–238).[42] His "A day will come when York shall claim his own" and "when I spy advantage, claim the crown"—so that no longer will "proud Lancaster usurp my *right*" (239–244)[43]—therefore already precedes (or pre-vents) the language of "well-hallow'd cause" and "right" to France as well as England in the Salic Law and other speeches of *Henry V*, including Henry's "The signs of war advance! / No king of England, if not king of France!" (*H5* 2.2.192–193) immediately after he sends the Cambridge conspirators to their execution.

The March-York claim suppressed by Henry V is further highlighted in *2 Henry VI* by the servant's accusation of his master "of high treason" for saying "that Richard Duke of York" is "rightful heir unto the English crown" and that Henry VI is but "an usurper" (*2H6* 1.3.183–185).[44] And soon after—as with Mortimer's extended "discover[y]" in *1 Henry VI*—the higher right "suppress'd" in the dramatically later *Henry V* is disclosed again on stage "at full" (*2H6* 2.2.6), by Cambridge's son York himself, in a scene that stresses his claim through the female, and a "title / Which is infallible, to England's crown" (*2H6* 2.2.4–5):[45]

*York*. . . . Edward the Third, my lords, had seven sons:
The first, Edward the Black Prince, Prince of Wales;
The second, William of Hatfield; and the third,
Lionel Duke of Clarence; next to whom

Was John of Gaunt, the Duke of Lancaster;
The fift was Edmund Langley, Duke of York;
The sixt was Thomas of Woodstock, Duke of
Gloucester;
William of Windsor was the seventh and last.
Edward the Black Prince died before his father,
And left behind him Richard, his only son,
Who after Edward the Third's death reign'd as king
Till *Henry Bullingbrook, Duke of Lancaster,*
The *eldest son and heir of John of Gaunt,*
Crown'd by the name of *Henry the Fourth,*
Seiz'd on the realm, *depos'd the rightful king,*
Sent his poor queen to France, from whence she came,
And him to Pomfret; where, as all you know,
*Harmless Richard was murthered traitorously.*

*Warwick.* Father, *the Duke hath told the truth;*
*Thus got the house of Lancaster the crown.*

*York.* Which now they hold *by force* and *not by right;*
For Richard, the first son's heir, being dead,
The issue of the next son should have reign'd.

*Salisbury.* But William of Hatfield died without an heir.

*York.* The *third son,* Duke of Clarence, *from whose line*
*I claim the crown,* had issue, Philippe, a *daughter,*
Who *married Edmund Mortimer, Earl of March;*
Edmund had issue, Roger Earl of March;
Roger had issue, Edmund, Anne, and Eleanor.

*Salisbury.* This *Edmund,* in *the reign of Bullingbrook,*
As I have read, *laid claim unto the crown,*
And but for Owen Glendower, had been king,
Who kept him in captivity till he died.
But, to the rest.

*York.* His eldest *sister,* Anne,
My *mother,* being *heir unto the crown,*
*Married Richard Earl of Cambridge,* who was
To Edmund Langley, Edward the Third's fift son, son.
*By her I claim the kingdom. She* was heir
To Roger Earl of March, who was the son
Of Edmund Mortimer, who married Philippe,

Sole *daughter* unto Lionel Duke of Clarence;
So, if the issue of the *elder son*
Succeed before the *younger*, I am king.
*Warwick.* What *plain proceedings* is more plain than this?
Henry doth claim the crown from *John of Gaunt*,
The *fourth son*, York claims it from the *third*. . . .
(*2 Henry VI* 2.2.10–55)[46]

Warwick's "plain proceedings" here carries the combined sense of "pedigree" and lawful and legitimate succession,[47] in a scene that leads to his conclusion that Cambridge's son York has a greater "birthright to the crown" (2.2.62) and is the more "rightful sovereign" (2.2.61) than the usurping Henries ("which now they hold by force and not by right," as York had put it). In other words, the usurpation by Bolingbroke and murder of Richard II that surfaces explicitly only once in *Henry V*—in Henry's prayer before Agincourt that his father's "fault" will not be thought on (4.1.288–305)—along with the higher claim through the female that would undo Henry's "right" to France as well as England, are outlined at length in yet another of the earlier plays its Epilogue recalls, exposing in *advance* what is suppressed or left unsaid in *Henry V* itself.

The claim of the Marches or Earls of March, linked with the marches or borderlands that haunt all three Lancastrian reigns, gets associated with Ireland in particular in *2 Henry VI*, as the son of the Cambridge whose rebellion is not actually dramatized until *Henry V* announces in this earlier play his plan to return from Ireland to "claim" his "right / And pluck the crown from feeble Henry's head," *2H6* 5.1.1–2),[48] after he has made use of the rebellious Jack Cade. As the play proceeds, the Cade rebellion—with its own pseudo-genealogy of descent from the Mortimers (4.2)—brings to the fore the claim of "the house of York, thrust from the crown / By shameful murther of a guiltless king / And lofty, proud, encroaching tyranny" (*2H6* 4.1.94–96),[49] in lines whose evocation of the sun breaking through the obscuring clouds (4.1.98) invokes the badge of Edward III himself for the suppressed March-York right. The Cade rebellion is countered by Lancastrian Clifford's strategic reminder of the martial successes of "Henry the Fift" ("Is Cade the son of Henry the Fift, / That thus you do exclaim you'll go with him? / Will he conduct you through the heart of France, / And make the meanest of you earls and dukes?," 4.8.34–37).[50] But *2 Henry VI* ends with Cambridge's son York returning "from Ireland . . . to claim his right" (5.1.1) and proclaiming that he is "England's lawful king" (5.1.4)[51]—a return from Ireland that was historically joined by the return invasion from France of Warwick, Salisbury, and Cambridge's grandson Edward, the new Earl of March, who would ultimately reign as England's first Yorkist king.[52]

Once again, in the final act of *2 Henry VI*, the claim by the son of the executed Cambridge to a higher birth than that of the Lancastrian usurpers ("I am far *better born* than is the King," *2H6* 5.1.28), like the conclusion in *1 Henry VI* that the *Lancastrians* are of the "meaner sort," inverts—in advance—the language of a *mundus inversus* (or "preposterously" inspired rebellion) invoked in the putting down of the Cambridge rebellion in *Henry V*. The opening of the last act of *2 Henry VI* puts repeated emphasis on this reversal of perspective—as York says to the reigning Henry VI, "By heaven, thou shalt rule no more / O'er him whom heaven created for thy ruler" (5.1.104–105) and, accused by Lancastrian Clifford of leading "a brood of *traitors*" (5.1.141), responds, "Look in a glass, and call *thy* image so. / *I* am *thy king*, and *thou* a false-heart *traitor*" (5.1.142–143).[53] And it is here that the suppressed March-York claim is definitively concluded by Salisbury—Warwick's father—to be the more legitimate and "rightful" one ("My lord, I have considered with myself / The *title* of this *most renowned duke*, / And in my *conscience* do repute his Grace / The *rightful heir* to England's royal seat," 5.1.175–178), a language echoed as the play ends in the battle of St. Albans waged and won by York in the name of "justice and true right" (5.2.25), with Salisbury fighting on the Yorkist side.[54]

❧

> *King Henry*. [*Aside*.] I know not what to say, my title's weak,—
>
> —*Henry VI Part 3* (1.1.134)

> *King Henry*. Art thou against us, Duke of Exeter?
> *Exeter*. His is the right, and therefore pardon me.
> *York*. Why whisper you, my lords, and answer not?
> *Exeter*. My conscience tells me he is lawful king . . .
>
> —*Henry VI Part 3* (1.1.147–150)

Finally—joining the other major dramatic anticipations or "preventions," in these early histories, of Henry's language of "a well-hallow'd cause" and "rightful hand" in *Henry V*—there is the extraordinary opening scene of *Henry VI Part 3*, where the suppressed "right" of the Marches inherited by Cambridge's son York is publicly proclaimed. For here, this Duke of York, acknowledged by Warwick to have a more legitimate title to the throne "Which now the house of Lancaster usurps" (*3H6* 1.1.23), returns to "take possession of my right" (*3H6* 1.1.44), sits in Henry VI's throne, and pronounces his greater "right" to the crown (*3H6* 1.1.148), in the play's dramatic counterpart to the famous oration of York's superior claim in Holinshed and Hall.[55] What is particularly striking in this scene—once again, from the very plays the Epilogue to *Henry V* recalls—is that the language of "right" (and the "natural" as opposed to "unnatural") on which the dramatic Henry V will later draw in ordering the executions of the Cambridge "traitors" at Southampton, is here repeatedly inverted, as York takes the throne of Henry VI and is commanded by the latter to "descend":

*King Henry.* . . . Thou factious Duke of York, *descend* my throne,
And kneel for grace and mercy at my feet:
*I am thy sovereign.*
*York.* *I am thine.*
*Exeter.* For shame, come down. He made thee Duke of York.
*York.* It was my inheritance, as the earldom [i.e., of March] was.
*Exeter.* Thy *father* [i.e., Cambridge] was a *traitor* to the crown.
*Warwick.* Exeter, *thou art a traitor* to the crown,
In following this *usurping Henry.*
*Clifford.* Whom should he follow but his *natural* king?
*Warwick.* True, Clifford, *that's Richard Duke of York.* . . .
(*3H6* 1.1.74–83)[56]

Henry VI in this scene appeals to the genealogy of *male* succession ("I am the son of Henry the Fift," 1.1.107),[57] but has to support his weaker legitimacy by appeal to Henry V's military successes (as the king "Who made the Dolphin [Dauphin] and the French to stoop," 1.1.108) as well as to the threat of force. But in the exchange that follows, not only does this last Lancastrian monarch admit "my title's weak," but Lancastrian "Exeter" acknowledges the greater "right" of Cambridge's son:

*King Henry.* Think'st thou that I will leave my kingly throne,
Wherein my grandsire and my father sat?

No; first shall war unpeople this my realm;
Ay, and their colors, often borne in France,
And now in England to our heart's great sorrow,
Shall be my winding-sheet. Why faint you, lords?
My title's good, and better far than his.

*Warwick.* Prove it, Henry, and thou shalt be King.
*King Henry.* Henry the Fourth by conquest got the crown.
*York.* 'Twas by *rebellion* against his king.
*King Henry.* [*Aside.*] *I know not what to say, my title's weak,*—
Tell me, may not a king adopt an heir?
*York.* What then?
*King Henry.* And if he may, then am I lawful king;
For Richard, in the view of many lords,
Resign'd the crown to Henry the Fourth,
Whose heir my father was, and I am his.
*York.* He rose against him, being his sovereign,
And made him to resign his crown perforce.
*Warwick.* Suppose, my lords, he did it unconstrain'd,
Think you 'twere prejudicial to his crown?
*Exeter.* No; for he could not so resign his crown
But that the next heir should succeed and reign.
*King Henry.* *Art thou against us, Duke of Exeter?*
*Exeter.* *His is the right*, and therefore pardon me.
*York.* Why whisper you, my lords, and answer not?
*Exeter.* *My conscience tells me he is lawful king* . . .

(*3H6* 1.1.124–150)[58]

Henry VI's "I know not what to say, my title's weak" (which may or may not be an "aside") anticipates his agreement later in this scene from *3 Henry VI* to entail the crown to York and his heirs (1.1.194–195), disinheriting his own son.[59] And Lancastrian Exeter's "*His* is the *right*" (1.1.148) and finding in his "conscience" that Cambridge's son is the "lawful king" (1.1.150) join the conclusion of Warwick reaffirmed in this scene and of Salisbury earlier in *2 Henry VI* ("I have considered with myself / The title of this most renowned duke, / And in my *conscience* do repute his Grace / The *rightful heir* to England's royal seat," *2H6* 5.1.175–178).

Intriguing here is the fact that it is an "Exeter" who concludes against the Lancastrian "right," since this figure—though a different *historical* personage—bears the same title (Duke of Exeter) as the "Exeter" of *Henry V*, who presents Henry V's "pedigree" to the French as "evenly deriv'd" (*H5* 2.4.91) and insists that it is "no sinister nor no awkward claim" (*H5* 2.4.85), in the speech to whose inversions we will return in more detail later in this chapter. For—in plays that famously conflate historical personages, including ones that successively hold the same title—the fact that in *3 Henry VI* it is an "Exeter" who cannot in his "conscience" defend the Lancastrian "right" (though he himself is a Lancastrian) may further complicate the rhetoric of "right" in *Henry V*, "preposterously" anticipating the historically earlier Exeter whose inverted phrasing presents Henry V's "pedigree" as neither "sinister" nor "awkward." Nothing in Part 3 identifies this "Exeter" as a different person from his namesake in *Henry V*, or in *Henry VI Part 1*, where he stands somewhat apart from both factions.

If there is a dramatic echoing of "Exeters," this could also suggest a reason for the anomalous inclusion of "Huntington" in the Wooing Scene of *Henry V* (5.2.85)—though nowhere else in that play or the other histories—since Huntington is the father of the "Exeter" of *3 Henry VI* who had already dramatically acknowledged that the executed Cambridge's son has a greater "right" to the throne than the usurping Henries, as well as the son of the Earl of Huntington executed after an abortive plot to assassinate the usurping Bolingbroke, or Henry IV.[60] But whether or not there is a subtle *dramatic* elision of this earlier "Exeter" with the "Exeter" of *Henry V* who presents Henry's "pedigree" to the French (*H5* 2.4.90–91), the dramatically later "Exeter" *had* already appeared (as the same historical personage) in *Henry VI Part 1* as both the young king's "special governor" (*1H6* 1.1.171) and the figure who says, "And now I fear that fatal prophecy / Which in the time of Henry nam'd the Fift / Was in the mouth of every sucking babe, / That Henry born at Monmouth should win all, / And Henry born at Windsor lose all" (*1H6* 3.1.194–198), a prophecy uttered on stage in the earlier *1 Henry VI* and "preposterously" recalled in the Epilogue to *Henry V* itself.[61]

In this memorable opening scene of *3 Henry VI*, therefore, both a Lancastrian Exeter and in a different way Henry V's own son acknowledge the more legitimate claim or "right" of the March cause behind the Cambridge rebellion that is later staged in *Henry V* with this name omitted and higher "right" suppressed. The repeated recitation in these earlier plays of the female link through which Cambridge's son York claims his greater "title" and "possession of my right" (*3H6* 1.1.44, 104) not only "corrects" in advance what is left out or suppressed in the Salic Law and Cambridge rebellion scenes of *Henry*

*V* but openly underscores the claim through the female that would undo Henry V's right to France as well as England. At the same time, Warwick's challenge to Clifford's "Whom should he follow but his *natural* king?" ("True, Clifford, that's *Richard Duke of York*," *3H6* 1.1.82–83), in a scene where Henry VI himself admits that his "title's weak," ironizes in advance his father Henry V's own appeal in the Rebellion Scene to the natural as opposed to the unnatural. Perhaps this is one of the reasons why, in Henry's condemnation of the rebels in that scene of *Henry V*, the conspiracy itself is contradictorily described as a "natural cause" ("Treason and murther . . . / As two yoke-devils sworn to either's purpose, / Working so grossly in a *natural* cause," *H5* 2.2.105–107), a word that editors have had to scramble to explain is meant to designate its "infernal" inverse.[62]

The prior staging of this earlier play also complicates the Mystery Play rhetoric of infernal and divine invoked in the Rebellion Scene, in Henry's suppression of a "preposterously" and "fiend[ishly]" inspired uprising against his rule. For the buffeting and scourging of Christ clearly evoked in the mocking and death of York himself at the hands of his Lancastrian enemies in *3 Henry VI* (*3H6* 1.4; 2.1) already calls attention to the language and iconography of demonic and divine—in reverse—*before* the dramatic Henry V uses it to justify the execution of the Cambridge "traitors."[63]

The dramatic Henry V's execution of Cambridge marks a wishful punctuation or boundary-drawing, an attempt to cordon off his new "beginnings" from a rebellion he describes as threatening to "hinder" them. But the Cambridge rebellion against this new king so anxious to separate himself from his father Bolingbroke's "crooked" history is shadowed not only by the Henry IV plays that immediately precede it but also by the earlier plays of Henry VI recalled by its Epilogue as already "shown" upon "our stage." And the play that directly recalls those earlier plays of Henry V's son simultaneously suppresses and calls attention to its suppressions, hinting at what is left out, just as it undermines Henry's claim that Agincourt was won "without stratagem" (*H5* 4.8.108–109) through memories of the palpable "device" (Hall) or "politike invention" (Holinshed) by which it was famously won.

Proceeding "preposterously"—against the order of chronology, in ways authorized by the "bending author" of the Epilogue to *Henry V*—would lead backwards, then, from Henry's condemnation of what he characterizes as a "preposterously" inspired rebellion in *Henry V* to the multiple prior disclosures of its higher motive in the plays of Henry VI, the historical aftermath or sequel that had already dramatically come before. The fact that it is left unsaid in *Henry V* does not mean, within this larger theatrical context, that it is unknown (or dependent on knowledge from the chronicles or the later "corrective" of the *Oldcastle* play). The emphasis is thus thrown upon the motives and mechanisms of suppression in *Henry V* of what had already been exposed in advance.

ల

> . . . people on the marches of Wales, for the favour which they bare to the Mortimers lineage.
>
> —Holinshed, *Chronicles* (1587)

> To make that worse, suff'red his kinsman March
> (Who is, if every owner were well plac'd,
> Indeed his king) to be engag'd in Wales . . .
>
> —*Henry IV Part 1* (4.3.93–95)

> We give express charge that in our marches through the country there be nothing compell'd from the villages.
>
> —*Henry V* (3.6.108–110)

One of these suppressions in *Henry V* is the name of "March" itself—the higher claim behind the Cambridge rebellion—in a play that also both invokes and questions the loyalty of the marches or borderlands to Henry (Irish, Scots, and Welsh). The claim from the excluded Marches or Earls of March is already linked in the earlier plays with the "marches" or borderlands of England. Cambridge's son York—through his mother Anne Mortimer, the female link that was the basis of his higher claim—had lands in the Marches of Wales as well as in Ireland.[64] The threat from the "Marches" in both senses is in the *Henry VI* plays repeatedly underscored, from the initial disclosure of his suppressed "title" and "right" by Mortimer, the imprisoned Earl of March in *1 Henry VI*, to the triumph of Cambridge's grandson, the new "Earl of March," in *3 Henry VI* (*3H6* 2.1.179), described as "in the marches . . . / Making another head to fight again" (*3H6* 2.1.140–141), in lines whose "marches" the New Cambridge edition (where "Marches" is capitalized) glosses as the "Borders (of Wales)," where he had support from "the loving Welshmen" (*3H6* 2.1.180). Coming from those "marches" or borderlands (*3H6* 2.1.140), this new Earl of March entered with "triumphant march" (*3H6* 2.6.87) into London in *3 Henry VI* to be crowned as Edward IV, the first Yorkist king. He was also the king who not only supplanted Henry V's own weaker son but annulled the sentences of Henry V against the "traitors" Cambridge, Scroop, and Grey, reversing Henry's rhetoric of "right" into the Yorkist language of usurping Lancastrian "wrong."

Shakespeare's linking of the "marches" with this heir of the March claim and triumphant grandson of the executed Cambridge (in plays that come before the suppression of the Cambridge rebellion in *Henry V*) thus resembles the account in Holinshed (*Chronicles,* 3:269), which treats of this finally triumphant "earle of March" as supported by the "people on the marches of Wales, for the favour which they bare to the Mortimers lineage" and of the raising of this "Edward earle of March, sonne and heir to Richard duke of Yorke" to the status of "king and governour of the realm."[65] In *Henry IV Part 1*, Mortimer, the Earl of March (1.3.84), is repeatedly linked with Wales in particular—in Act 1 ("Whose daughter, as we hear, that Earl of March / Hath lately married," 1.3.84–85), Act 4 ("suff'red his kinsman March . . . to be engag'd in Wales," 4.3.93–95), and again in Act 5 ("towards Wales, / To fight with Glendower and the Earl of March," 5.5.39–40), in a play where Mortimer is called the "next of blood" to Richard II (1.3.145–146) and rightful "owner" of the crown (4.3.94).[66] The threat he poses to the former Bolingbroke who reigns as Henry IV can be summoned there so briefly because this claim had already been prominently presented in the earlier dramatic histories, including in the scene of *1 Henry VI* where this same Mortimer, as an imprisoned older man, had outlined the suppressed March right to Cambridge's son. And once again, the links are underscored between the March claim to the throne and the borderlands or Marches, including the Welsh borderlands at the boundaries of England, where the Battle of Shrewsbury (with which *1 Henry IV* ends) was fought.

In *Henry V* itself, though the rebellion of Cambridge, Grey, and Scroop is motivated by the usurped March claim, the name is suppressed both within and beyond the Salic Law speech and Rebellion Scene. But it continues to sound sotto voce in the "marches" or borderlands linked with the "pilfering borderers" of England (1.2.140–142), and in the iteration of "marches" and "march" throughout Henry's military "march" on France, in pursuit of his questionable claim after he has executed the Cambridge rebels ("To-morrow for the *march* are we address'd," 3.3.58; "if they *march* along / Unfought withal," 3.5.11–12; the "soldiers sick and famish'd in their *march,*" 3.5.57; the "*march* on" to Calais, 3.6.141; "*March* to the bridge," 3.6.170; and "I thought upon one pair of English legs / Did *march* three Frenchmen," 3.6.149–150).

Such a haunting resonance to Henry's forward advance or "march" through France should not be unexpected, given that a foreign war was itself counseled as a deflection from the illegitimacy of Henry's claim to England (*2H4* 4.5.213–214), the result of Bolingbroke's usurpation, theft, or "conveyance" of the crown. The link with theft is subtly sounded in the notorious pilferer Pistol's departure for the war in France ("Touch her soft mouth, and *march*," *H5* 2.3.58) and even more subtly in the bishops' self-interested support of the war, in the parable of the bees and the "pillage" which "they with merry *march* bring home" (1.2.195). And once in France, the Boy's comment on Bardolph and the others who "will steal any thing, and call it *purchase*" (3.2.42) echoes the very term for Bolingbroke's "crooked" path to the crown ("What in me was *purchas'd*," *2H4* 4.5.199), in the speech that had advised the busying of "giddy minds" by "foreign quarrels" (*2H4* 4.5.213–214), lending a telling undertone to Henry's "we give express charge that in our *marches* through the country there be nothing compell'd from the villages" (*H5* 3.6.108–110), in the scene in which he orders the execution of Bardolph for stealing a "pax."

❧

*Canterbury.* . . . this Salique law
To bar your Highness claiming from the female,
And rather choose to hide them in a net
Than amply to imbar their crooked titles
Usurp'd from you and your progenitors.

—*Henry V* (1.2.91–95)

*King Henry.* May I with right and conscience make this claim?
*Canterbury.* The sin upon my head, dread sovereign!
For in the book of Numbers is it writ,
When the man dies, let the inheritance
Descend unto the daughter.

—*Henry V* (1.2.96–100)

There are multiple aspects of *Henry V* itself that point (like the Epilogue) to the reversed order of the dramatic histories by their "preposterous" recalls or are affected by this reversal, including with regard to the prior exposure in the Henry VI plays of what in *Henry V* is omitted or suppressed. In the Salic Law Scene (1.2) the entire argument against the "law Salique" (1.2.11) prohibiting inheritance to France through female descent is provided in response to Henry's desire to satisfy his "conscience" and his "right"—first in his request that the Archbishop of Canterbury not "*fashion, wrest, or bow your reading*, / Or nicely charge your understanding soul / With opening *titles miscreate*, whose *right* / Suits not in native colors with the *truth*" (1.2.14–17), and then in his "May I with *right* and *conscience* make this claim?" (1.2.96) after the archbishop's presentation of the French kings' "crooked titles / Usurp'd" (1.2.94–95). But Canterbury's response to the king's requirement that he unfold "justly and religiously" (1.2.10) his right to France makes clear that legitimacy here depends upon the exigencies of power, as it charts a history of usurpation and "conveyance" that, while purporting to be about *French* usurpers, reflects the "crooked" path to the title of the former Bolingbroke himself:

*Canterbury.* . . . King Pepin, which *deposed* Childeric,
Did, as heir general, being descended
Of Blithild, which was daughter to King Clothair,
Make claim and title to the crown of France.
*Hugh Capet* also, who *usurp'd* the crown
Of Charles the Duke of Lorraine, sole heir male
Of the true line and stock of Charles the Great,
To *fine his title* with some *shows of truth*,
*Though in pure truth it was corrupt and naught*,
*Convey'd* himself as th'heir to th' Lady Lingare,
Daughter to Charlemain, who was the son
To Lewis the Emperor, and Lewis the son
Of Charles the Great. Also *King Lewis the Tenth*,
Who was *sole heir to the usurper Capet*,
Could not keep quiet in his *conscience*,
Wearing the crown of France, till satisfied
That fair *Queen Isabel*, his grandmother,
Was lineal of the Lady Ermengare,
Daughter to Charles, the foresaid Duke of Lorraine;
By the which marriage the line of Charles the Great
Was re-united to the crown of France.
So that, as clear as is the summer's sun,
King Pepin's title and Hugh Capet's claim,
King Lewis his satisfaction, all appear

To hold in *right and title of the female*;
So do the kings of France unto this day.
Howbeit, they would hold up this Salique law
To *bar your Highness claiming from the female*,
And rather choose to hide them in a net
Than amply to imbar *their crooked titles*
*Usurp'd* from you and your progenitors.

(1.2.65–95)

The archbishop's recital of this history of French kings—including their own claims "in right and title of the female"—is presented as definitively authorizing Henry's right to France, through a "female" descent not barred by any "law Salique." It thus provides the basis for Henry's claim to the throne of France through another "Queen Isabel," French wife of Edward II and mother to Edward III, who here is never mentioned, perhaps because this female link would be a reminder of the Marches' higher claim to France as well as England. As with the later omissions in the Rebellion Scene (whose interstices manage to hint at what is suppressed), the Salic Law speech's justification of Henry's "right" suggests, however, between the lines, what remains unsaid. The history of French dynastic struggles rehearsed by Canterbury is of "crooked titles / Usurp'd," ostensibly intended to heighten the contrast with English Henry as France's lawful king. But it also repeatedly mirrors or mimics the English situation of Henry himself. The mention of "King Pepin" who "*deposed* Childeric," and sought retroactively to legitimize his claim, cannot but recall the deposing of Richard II (and hence the "fault" of Henry's father), as well as anticipating the post-facto attempts by Henry to rectify Bolingbroke's "crooked" path to the throne, by a "penitence" he says in his pre-Agincourt prayer comes only "*after* all" (4.1.304). The "usurper Capet"—who "convey'd himself as th' heir to th' Lady Lingare" in order to "*fine* his *title* with some *shows of truth*, / Though in pure truth it was corrupt and naught"—recalls the "conveyor" Bolingbroke, thief of the crown in the sense of "convey" as "steal" established by Pistol in *Merry Wives* (1.3.29) and by the deposed Richard in the "Conveyers are you all" of *Richard II* (4.1.317).[67] The theft or "conveyance" of the crown had already been paralleled by the emphasis on pilfering in the scenes of Hal's tavern companions in the plays of *Henry IV*, where Mortimer the Earl of March was called the rightful "owner" of the crown (*1H4* 4.3.94) and rebellions in the cause of the Marches had troubled the English usurper's unquiet reign. But remembrance of the dying Mortimer from the plays the Epilogue invokes also complicates in advance this speech about *French* usurpers, since Bolingbroke's conveying of the "title" not only from Richard but from Richard's designated heir had already been "discover[ed] . . . at large" by Mortimer in *1 Henry VI*. "King Lewis the Tenth"—"sole heir to the *usurper Capet*," who "Could not keep quiet in his *conscience*, / Wearing the crown of France" until he could legitimize it by reference to "Queen Isabel, his grandmother"—comes closest in this rehearsal of French usurper-kings to the situation of Henry V himself, son of a usurper whose own legitimacy is open to question. For Henry requires the Salic Law speech to "satisfy" *his* "conscience" (1.2.31, 96), by legitimizing *his* claim to the "crown of France" (1.2.68) through the other (unnamed) Isabel, mother of Edward III.

The archbishop's concluding reference to French "crooked titles / Usurp'd" (*H5* 1.2.94–95) thus tellingly echoes both the repeated references to Bolingbroke's usurpation in the Henry VI plays and this usurper-father's own confession of his "indirect crook'd ways" to the "crown" (*2H4* 4.5.184–185), from the scene of *2 Henry IV* in which he advised his son to deflect attention from that "crooked" title by a foreign war. And both disrupt or compromise attempts to banish memories (historical *and* theatrical) in *Henry V*—along with this son's attempts to close off or insulate his new reign from memories of this "crooked" path, making it "even," "straight," or "smooth." The Quarto's "fine his title"—used for the usurper Capet in the Salic Law speech—is glossed by the *Riverside* editor as "embellish" or "furbish" (as it is by other editors who choose this text over the Folio's "find"). But "fine" in the familiar Shakespearean sense of "end" (invoked in other plays as *respice finem* or "look to the end" and in *Henry V* itself by the archbishop's marveling at "how things are perfected," or completed, 1.1.69)[68] also marks Henry's attempts not only to furnish or "furbish" his title with some "shows of truth"—including by the elaborately constructed legal argument of the Salic Law speech—but to bring closure, end, or "fine" to the question of *his* title.

Commentators on the Salic Law Scene point out that what remains unspoken in this speech was made clear not only in the chronicles of Holinshed and Hall but also in the *Mirror for Magistrates*, which prominently featured the Marches' claim to greater legitimacy through this female link.[69] But, as we have seen, contemporary audiences would not have to rely on having knowledge from these sources because the female basis of the claim of the Earls of March (and hence of Cambridge's heirs) had already been dramatized in the very plays the Epilogue recalls. The conclusion of Cambridge's son in *1 Henry VI* that his father's execution by Henry V was an act of "bloody tyranny" (*1H6* 2.5.100) reverberates within the Salic Law Scene itself, in Henry's own "We are *no tyrant*, but a Christian king" (*H5* 1.2.241). His "May I with *right* and *conscience* make this claim?" (1.2.96)—in the midst of Canterbury's urging of his claim to France by "right and title of the female"—resonates with multiple "preposterous" echoes from the plays the Epilogue recalls as well as with memories of the plays of Henry's "crooked" father. And this compound theatrical memory of what remains unspoken or "suppressed" in *Henry V* complicates in advance the torturous justifications of the Salic Law speech itself.

Equally intriguing with regard to the "preposterous" recall of the plays of Henry VI is the biblical authority from the Book of Numbers invoked by the archbishop in response to Henry's question in this scene:

> *King Henry.* May I with *right and conscience* make this claim?
> *Canterbury.* The sin upon my head, dread sovereign!
> For in the *book of Numbers* is it writ,
> When the man dies, *let the inheritance*
> *Descend unto the daughter.* Gracious lord,
> Stand for your own, unwind your bloody flag,
> *Look back* into your *mighty ancestors*;
> Go, my dread lord, to *your great-grandsire's tomb,*
> *From whom you claim*; invoke his warlike spirit,
> And your great-uncle's, *Edward the Black Prince,*
> Who on the French ground play'd a tragedy.
> (1.2.96–106)

The invocation of the biblical Book of Numbers here is consistent with the chronicles from which this part of Canterbury's speech is taken. Numbers does indeed provide biblical authority for the tracing of title or inheritance from a "daughter," used here (as by Edward III) to claim an English king's right to the crown of France.[70] But the insertion of this biblical authority between Henry's question concerning his "conscience" and "right" and Canterbury's immediate shift from the female to a patriarchal line suggests another deflection of attention (like the "foreign" war itself), since the same text from the Book of Numbers used here to argue that Henry is acting with what he terms in this scene a "rightful hand" in a "well-hallow'd cause" (1.2.293) was the biblical authority used to argue the greater "right" of the

Marches and of the executed Cambridge's Yorkist heirs. John Hardyng's second (Yorkist) version of his chronicle, prepared under the patronage of Cambridge's son York (after he received unsatisfactory treatment at the hands of his original patron, Henry VI), outlined "York's right to the throne as heir to Edward III through the female line," arguing that "God gave to Moses in the Book of Numbers the law that a daughter is able to inherit, and that since Christ himself claimed the right to kingship through his mother's descent, there is no reason why *York* should not be the *true king*."[71] The very text of "Numbers" used to justify Henry V's claims to France was, in other words, an authority that would undo the Lancastrian right to the crown of "England" as well as "France," even further ironizing Henry's "No king of England, if not king of France" (2.2.193) in the Rebellion Scene to come.

Canterbury's counsel to Henry here, that he "Look *back* " to his "mighty ancestors," urges this new king to draw inspiration from the past, from the examples of Edward III ("your great-grandsire's tomb, / *From whom you claim*," 1.2.102–104) and Edward the Black Prince, whose French campaigns this play will repeatedly invoke. Bishop Ely repeats the call of this new king to "remembrance" in his urging of Henry to this foreign war ("Awake *remembrance* of these valiant dead, / . . . You are their heir, *you sit upon their throne*," 1.2.115–117). But what enables awareness of the verso to the recto of Henry's rhetoric of "right" and the Salic Law speech is remembrance of what had already been "shown" upon "our stage," the advance "discovery" of the suppressed claim through the female in the plays of the son. Exeter's "Rouse yourself, / As did the former lions of your blood" (1.2.123–124) summons the phallic imagery of conquest (introduced in Henry's reference to "our sleeping sword of war," 1.2.22) as well as the heraldic "lions" of the English royal house. But it leaves unmentioned—in its evocation of a masculine English patrimony and heraldry—the French "flower de luce" with which these "lions" had been quartered by Edward III, the sign of the female link already theatrically invoked as a symbol of the losses that "made his England bleed" (Epilogue 12) in the earlier plays of Henry VI ("Cropp'd are the flower-de-luces in your arms, / Of England's coat one half is cut away," *1H6* 1.1.80–81).

As in the archbishop's "Look back into your mighty ancestors," to "your great-grandsire's tomb . . . / And your great-uncle's, Edward the Black Prince" (1.2.102–105), mention of the female on which the entire claim to France depends is replaced in Ely's reminder of the "valiant dead" by a purely male line of descent. And once again, in a play where what is suppressed or banished from memory is as important as what is memorialized or remembered, emphasis on "remembrance" is shadowed by strategic forgetting. But at the same time, the invocation of "remembrance," "ancestors," and the Black Prince summons the more troubling remembrance that the direct English line from this same "Black Prince" went not to the usurping Lancastrians but to that prince's "sole heir male," the deposed Richard II, and then to the Earl of March designated by Richard as his heir. Ely's "*You* are *their heir*, you sit upon *their throne*" (1.2.117), in such close proximity to the history of usurpers in the Salic Law speech and the invocation of descent through the "daughter" from the Book of Numbers, is one of those lines in the play capable of looking simultaneously two ways at once—a reminder not only of this heroic male line but also of the higher right through the female that had already "oft" been "shown." Canterbury's legitimizing of Henry's war follows the chronicle sources in deriving his claim to France through the female and specifically through the authority of the Book of Numbers. But in the theatrical context of the history plays' reversed order, the clue to the unspoken inverse of this entire speech and scene had already been provided in advance, by the repeated rehearsal in those earlier plays of the suppressed March-York claim, and its dependence on female descent from Edward III.

"Right" is reiterated in Canterbury's urging of Henry's expeditious advance to France ("With blood and sword and fire, to win your *right*," 1.2.131). But the lines further recall the bishops' own self-interested motives in legitimizing the war, in the reminder, in the reference to the "mighty sum" (1.2.133) raised by the clergy to finance the campaign, of their already privately disclosed desire to divert attention from the Commons's "bill" against their lands (1.1.1–19). The very assembly, in other words, that is convoked to impart legitimacy, authority, "conscience," and "right" to Henry in this early scene contains—or rather fails to contain, in the sense of concluding or closing off with an end or "fine"—its own theatrical memories of his more questionable "right," in the midst of a passage that calls the king to a (selective) "remembrance." Henry Ansgar Kelly notes that "Holinshed . . . follows the practice of historians before him in side-stepping the issue of possible culpability in Henry V's tenure of the throne in place of the rightful heir, and follows them also in not adverting to the incongruity of urging the God-sanctioned right of females to inherit upon the French, when this very right was what entitled Mortimer to all that Henry V claimed for himself both in England and in France" (*Providence,* 146). But Shakespeare's play—while including the Salic Law speech from the chronicles that *elides* mention of this suppressed right—simultaneously hints at what is left unsaid, including in its "preposterous" recalls (or a different kind of "remembrance") of the prior dramatic rehearsal of the rival claim from the Marches that would undo Henry's legitimacy and "right."

ᔕ

> They of those marches, gracious sovereign,
> Shall be a wall sufficient to defend
> Our inland from the pilfering borderers. . . .
>
> —*Henry V* (1.2.140–142)

> Those that were your father's enemies
> Have steep'd their galls in honey. . . .
>
> —*Henry V* (2.2.29–30)

Returning to the Rebellion Scene of *Henry V* from the already-staged Henry VI plays also makes clear the rebellion's own "preposterous" recalls. "Richard Earl of Cambridge" (*H5* 2.2.66) is an obscure or unknown name if *Henry V* is viewed in isolation—just as the real motive behind the Cambridge rebellion is omitted by Henry and only cryptically alluded to by Cambridge himself. But "Richard Earl of Cambridge" is repeatedly invoked in the plays that had "oft" been "shown" before it, including in *1 Henry VI*—from Somerset's taunt to Cambridge's son ("Was not thy father, Richard Earl of Cambridge, / For treason executed in our late king's days?," *1H6* 2.4.90–91) and the plea by that son to the imprisoned Earl of March to "declare the cause / My father, Earl of Cambridge, lost his head" (*1H6* 2.5.53–54) to Mortimer's "discover[y]" (2.5.59) of the suppressed higher "right" of Cambridge and his heirs, since Mortimer's sister had married the "Earl of Cambridge" (*1H6* 2.5.84). His name is reiterated in *2 Henry VI*, where Cambridge's son as Duke of York outlines his claim through his mother Anne Mortimer's marriage to "Richard Earl of Cambridge" (2.2.45), when presenting his "title, / Which is infallible, to England's crown," *2H6* 2.2.4–5). And it reverberates through the striking opening scene of *Henry VI Part 3*, where Cambridge's son sits on the throne of Henry VI, and his more legitimate right to the crown is not only acknowledged by Lancastrian Exeter but suggested by Henry VI himself—first in "I know not what to say, *my title's weak*" (1.1.134) and then by his entailing of the crown to York and his heirs.

The repeated connection between the March claim and the borderlands or marches of England is itself important in relation to the Rebellion Scene of *Henry V*. The threat from England's borderlands if Henry advances on France is a central preoccupation of its opening act, where Henry fears "the Scot, who will make road upon us / With all advantages" (1.2.138–139), but is assured by Canterbury that "They of those marches, gracious sovereign, / Shall be a wall sufficient to defend / Our inland from the pilfering borderers" (1.2.140–142). The scene soon after of the Cambridge rebellion in the (unspoken) name of the suppressed March cause features among its nobles Westmorland, the "Warden of the Marches against Scotland,"[72] the figure who in Hall warns Henry V of the danger from "enemies behind at your backe when you go to conquere adversaries before your face" (54) and reminds the English of the long-standing links between the danger from these Scottish marches and the "unstable Welshmen" of "unruly Wales" (53). Already a major character in the *Henry IV* plays, Westmorland in the Rebellion Scene of *Henry V* thus comes with links to the defense of England's marches or borderlands, as the figure in charge of the "frontiers and Marches adioyning to Scotland" (Hall, *Union,* 55; see also Holinshed, *Chronicles,* 3:69), along with Scroop. But Scroop (among those of the "marches" who are to be "a wall sufficient to defend / Our inland from the pilfering borderers," 1.2.140–142) has by his joining of the Cambridge conspiracy become identified instead with those who present a threat to the (simultaneously) territorial and royal body of "Harry England" (3.5.48), in a rebellion described as the "fault" in the "little body" of "England" that "France" has "found out" (2.Chorus.16–20), in a play that repeatedly aligns France with the troublesome borderers of England. And the sodomitical discourse of preposterous venery introduced into this play (as Jonathan Goldberg and others have noted) in the description of the "Scot" pouring at the frontiers or "marches" into England's "breach" (1.2.149), or what Hall calls "enemies behind at your backe when you go to conquere adversaries before your face," is sounded most explicitly in Henry's denunciation in the Rebellion Scene of his former "bedfellow" Scroop, the "Englishman" on whom a "cunning fiend" has "preposterously" worked (2.2.125, 111–112).

In the Rebellion Scene, each of the Cambridge conspirators comes with connections to the earlier rebellions in the Marches' suppressed cause, including Scroop, whose description as Henry's "bedfellow" (*H5* 2.2.8) may also bring with it echoes of the "crown" itself as a "troublesome . . . bedfellow" (*2H4* 4.5.22), from the scene of *2 Henry IV* where the former Bolingbroke had warned his son to "waste the memory of the former days" (*2H4* 4.5.215).[73] Scroop's uncle, Richard le Scroop (or Scrope) was the Archbishop of York (or "prelate Scroop") who appeared as a major figure in the Henry IV plays. *Henry IV Part 1*—which reminds its audience that Mortimer the Earl of March was "proclaim'd / By Richard, that dead is, the next of blood" (1.3.145–146) and is rightful "Heir to the crown" (1.3.157)—ends with the king's telling his son John and Westmorland, warden of the northern Marches, to go toward York to "meet Northumberland and the prelate Scroop, / Who, as we hear, are busily in arms. / Myself and you, son Harry, will towards Wales. / To fight with Glendower and the Earl of March" (*1H4* 5.5.37–40). Scroop's uncle, the Archbishop of York, was also a major figure in the rebellions against the king in *Henry IV Part 2* (1.3; 4.1–2) and was executed by Henry IV (*2H4* 4.2.122) "in defiance of the precedents and the canon law against the execution of ecclesiastics,"[74] a pivotal event in the reign of the former Bolingbroke and the act seen as divinely punished by the illness that plagued Henry IV until his death.[75] Scroop's uncle's rebellion is in turn presented in *Henry IV Part I* as related to the still earlier death of William Scroop, the Earl of Wiltshire who had been a favorite of Richard II (*Richard II* 2.1.215; 3.2.122), one of the "caterpillars" of the commonwealth put to death by Bolingbroke—an act referred to in *1 Henry IV*, where the "prelate" Scroop is described as "bear[ing] hard / His brother's death at Bristow, *the Lord Scroop*" (1.3.267–271). What predates the denunciation of the rebel Scroop in *Henry V* is thus an entire dramatic pre-history associated with the Lancastrian usurpation of Richard II's throne and the cause of the Marches' greater "right."

The rebel Scroop executed by Henry V is also intriguingly linked with Henry's relation to his father in another sense. Scroop was not only Henry's intimate and "bedfellow" (*H5* 2.2.8) but an earlier boon companion, part of the younger generation that had joined Henry (as Prince of Wales) while Henry IV was still upon the throne and the figure installed as treasurer during that period.[76] He was thus identified with Henry's (or Hal's) own riotous youth, part of the pre-history that the bishops remark, at the beginning of *Henry V*, this former Prince of Wales put behind him when he became king, as *novus homo* or reformed prodigal son. Scroop's connection with the king's past riotous life may be one of the reasons why the Rebellion Scene itself is surrounded by two scenes reminiscent of that earlier tavern world, including the scene recounting Falstaff's death (2.3). Strangely, at this point, as has often been noted, both the play's and Henry's own attempts to "advance" are countered by a recursive return to London and these past tavern characters (2.1), in contradiction to the opening Chorus to Act 2, which promises that the scene will advance directly to Southampton ( "Unto Southampton do we shift our scene," 2.Chorus.42).

Thomas Grey as a cousin of Hotspur is yet another reminder of these past challenges to the legitimacy of the Lancastrian "right," dramatized in the plays of the former Bolingbroke as Henry IV. When Grey says to the new king at the beginning of the Rebellion Scene—before the rebels' conspiracy has been exposed—"those that were your father's enemies / Have steep'd their galls in honey" (*H5* 2.2.29–30), the image recalls the crucial scene of *Henry IV Part 2* where the former Bolingbroke had counseled the waging of a foreign war, in lines where he warns his son that the rebels in his own reign for the suppressed March cause are bees whose "stings" are but "newly ta'en out" (*2H4* 4.5.205). Since the Cambridge rebellion itself has as its unspoken motive the continuation of that "gall," Grey's words thus also retrospectively ironize Canterbury's pious fable of the bees in the opening act of *Henry V*, where the bees are cited as an image of the "many" working harmoniously under this new king as "one" (*H5* 1.2.183–213).

Henry V's cryptic reference in the Rebellion Scene to what his "love" had done for Cambridge in elevating him to his earldom ("You know how apt our love was to accord / To furnish him with all appertinents / Belonging to his honor," *H5* 2.2.86–88) provides a between-the-lines reminder that the rebellious Cambridge was the younger brother of Aumerle, who had conspired against the former Bolingbroke on behalf of the March claim (as he did dramatically in *Richard II*), since Henry had elevated this conspirator to the earldom of Cambridge in order to heal old wounds with Aumerle as the present Duke of York.[77] The Earl of Cambridge at the head of the rebellion that threatens, as Henry V puts it, to "*hinder* our beginnings" (2.2.187) is therefore linked both to the *past* threats to Henry's father's reign and to the ultimate success of the March right in the *future* reign of Henry's son, already dramatized in the plays the Epilogue recalls, where his name is repeatedly invoked and Cambridge's grandson becomes England's first Yorkist king.

The so-called "English monsters" that Henry condemns for "treason" in the Rebellion Scene of *Henry V* thus bring with them connections that exceed the boundaries of this play, from both the "pre-" and "post"-history of this scene, the past history of Bolingbroke's usurpation and rebellions against Henry IV (dramatized in the second tetralogy) and the theatrically past but historically future history of the higher "right" through the female and ultimate unseating of the Lancastrian line that had already been such a major part of the plays the Epilogue reminds its audience had preceded it. Peter Saccio's remark that the Cambridge plot is "epilogue to an old struggle" and "prologue to a later contention" (*English Kings,* 73) for this reason aptly describes its pivotal *historical* importance, though Saccio does not mention the overdetermination by both sets of past *theatrical* productions of the threat that is suppressed or left unspoken in all but the interstices of the Rebellion Scene itself.

The dramatic execution of the Cambridge rebels marks an attempt to cordon off the French campaign from memories of a past that is both chronological and theatrical. But like the similarly cast-off Falstaff (or Oldcastle by his earlier name, the historical figure connected not only with the Lollard uprising against Henry but also with the conspiracy against Henry for the Marches' cause and the Marches of Wales, to which he had escaped)—whose reported death (2.3) immediately follows the execution of these rebels (2.2)—the threats from the Marches both past and to come continue to haunt *Henry V* itself, even as Henry at the end of the Rebellion Scene proclaims that an end has been definitively put to this hindrance or "rub" (*H5* 2.2.182–188). Henry's forward "advance" to the campaign in France, once this "rub" has been smoothed out, is already compromised in his "no king of England, if not king of France!" (2.2.193) through the preposterous recalls of the plays of his son. And the rhetoric of "right" employed by this king in pursuit of his claims in France "in the right / Of [his] great predecessor, King Edward the Third" (*H5* 1.2.247–248)—supported by Canterbury's Salic Law speech and urging of Henry to advance with "blood and sword and fire, to win your right" (*H5* 1.2.131)—is inverted in the very scene in which that right is presented to the French king, soon after the Rebellion Scene itself.

ᔕ

*Exeter.* . . . 'Tis no sinister nor no awkward claim . . .
And when you find him evenly deriv'd
From his most fam'd of famous ancestors,
Edward the Third, he bids you then resign
Your crown and kingdom, indirectly held
From him, the native and true challenger.
*French King.* Or else what follows? . . .

—*Henry V* (2.4.85, 91–96)

Here, only two scenes after the rebellion is suppressed, Exeter presents Henry's "pedigree" to demonstrate that he is France's rightful king "by law of nature and of nations" (2.4.80), demanding that the French king resign his "borrowed glories" (2.4.79) and the "crown of France" (2.4.84). But Exeter's demand comes in a speech whose inverted phrasing manages to suggest its own other side, even in the very language in which it presents that claim:

> He wills you, in the name of God Almighty,
> That you divest yourself, and lay apart
> The borrowed glories that by gift of heaven,
> By law of nature and of nations, 'longs
> To him and to his heirs, namely, the crown,
> And all wide-stretched honors that pertain
> By custom, and the ordinance of times,
> Unto the crown of France. That you may know
> 'Tis *no sinister nor no awkward claim*,
> Pick'd from the worm-holes of long-vanish'd days,
> Nor from the dust of old *oblivion* rak'd,
> He sends you this *most memorable line*,
> In *every branch* truly demonstrative;
> [*Giving a paper.*]
> Willing you *overlook* this *pedigree*;
> And when you find him *evenly deriv'd*
> From his most fam'd of famous ancestors,
> *Edward the Third*, he bids you then resign
> Your crown and kingdom, indirectly held
> From him, *the native and true challenger*.
>
> *French King*. Or else what follows? (2.4.77–96)

"Memorable" (in Exeter's rehearsal here of Henry's "most memorable line") is a term "used by Shakespeare only four times, all in this play," as Gary Taylor points out.[78] In this scene, it is invoked twice in relation to Henry's patrimony—first by the French in their remembrance of the battle of Crécy ("He is bred out of that bloody strain / That haunted us in our familiar paths. / Witness our too much *memorable* shame / When Cressy battle fatally was struck," 2.4.51–54) and then in Exeter's recitation of Henry's "most *memorable* line" (2.4.88). But the Folio's "haunted" here, which the Arden editor T. W. Craik stresses in its sense of *being* haunted rather than simply the "pursued" or hunted suggested by Gurr,[79] also summons the memory of something that haunts the presentation (and "right") of this "line" itself. And the iteration of "memorable" in Exeter's "most memorable line" (2.4.88) simultaneously makes possible the perception of what is strategically forgotten.

Exeter's speech before the French is the counterpart in the play of the elaborate legal justification of the Salic Law speech in Act 1, where female descent is offered to support Henry's "conscience" and "right" (*H5* 1.2.96), in a scene already dramatically preempted by the disclosure of a higher female link than Henry's in the Henry VI plays. Here, Exeter's presentation of Henry's "most memorable line" (2.4.88)—in a speech that contrasts this memorializing with "oblivion" (2.4.87)—is presented in the inverted form of "no *sinister* nor no *awkward* claim" (2.4.85), a rhetorical turn that simultaneously evokes its opposite. "Sinister" in the period meant not just "left-handed" (the inverse, in other words, of Henry's rhetoric of proceeding with a "*rightful hand*," 1.2.293) but also both "crooked" and "illegitimate," product of a "bastard line," the taint of illegitimacy that made the "bar" or "bend sinister" its heraldic sign.[80] It thus evokes the combined contemporary resonances of the opposite of "right," including the inverse of the straight, upright, or legitimate.[81] "Sinister" was also routinely combined with "preposterous," as when the "malice of men," for example, was described as "so greate, that they . . . think sinisterlie and preposterouslie of all the good deedes which are wrought."[82] And "awkward" (which appears in the Folio as "awk-ward") was in early modern English a term for the preposterously or "awkly" reversed, not just the "Awkward, lefthanded, *gauche*" (fitting counterpart of "sinister") but the "preposterous," "upside down," "back to front," *revers*, awry.[83] To receive something "awkly" involved "turning to the left side" rather than "on the right hand,"[84] while to write "awklie"—as Golding put it, for example—was to write backwards or in a reverse direction.[85] Shakespeare himself uses "awkward" elsewhere in the reversed or "awkward wind" of *2 Henry VI* (3.2.83) and the "awkward action" of Patroclus's theatrical mimickry in *Troilus and Cressida* (where Achilles and Patroclus themselves are called "preposterous discoveries").[86] "Awkward," in other words, meant not just "oblique" (as Gary Taylor suggests),[87] but "preposterous," inverted, awry, or wrong way round, the opposite of the direct, linear, or "straightforward." In this sense, then, Exeter's " 'Tis no sinister nor no awkward claim" uses precisely the contemporary terms that would suggest its other side.

Though Henry V's "pedigree" is here presented by Exeter as "evenly deriv'd" (*H5* 2.4.91)—glossed by editors as "directly," "justly," "accurately" or "truly descended"[88] and contrasted with the French king by whom the "crown and kingdom" are only "*indirectly* held" (2.4.94)—the rhetorical turn that states that Henry's "most memorable line" is neither "sinister" nor "awkward" (rather than simply "right") thus subtly evokes, even as it denies, its own preposterous reverse. And at the same time, Exeter's presentation of this English king as the "native and true challenger" (2.4.95) depends on the contradictory logic in which Henry is both already the rightful ruler of France—from whom all others usurp their "borrowed glories" (2.4.79)—*and* the challenger who has to be designated as the French king's heir in the final Wooing Scene in order to secure that right, even after he has won the battle.[89]

The underside of this rhetorical *occupatio* on the threshold of the English occupation of France, managing to evoke the "sinister" or illegitimate inverse of Henry's claim to be proceeding with a "rightful hand," may also be subtly compounded by a specifically Shakespearean invention, the fact that (contrary to the chronicle sources) this entire speech is put into the mouth of Exeter rather than the "pursuivant at Armes" who outlines the king's claim in Holinshed and Hall (or the "Herald" in *The Famous Victories of Henry the fifth*).[90] For as a Beaufort—ancestors of the Tudors whose own illegitimacy had to be bolstered by Henry VII's (or Richmond's) strategic marriage to the daughter of a more legitimate king—Exeter was part of an illegitimate or "bastard" Lancastrian line, legitimated post facto after Gaunt married his former mistress Catherine Swynford but still carrying the taint of illegitimacy that allows Gloucester to call Exeter's brother Cardinal Winchester "thou *bastard* of my grandfather" in *Henry VI Part 1* (3.1.42).[91] (In the late 1590s, the challenge to James as a legitimate successor to the English throne was also based on *his* Tudor-Stuart Beaufort lineage, in contrast to the Spanish Infanta who was legitimately descended from John of Gaunt, to whom we will return in Chapter 5.)[92] Dramatically, it is understandable that the figure used to present Henry's claim to the French is the Exeter who plays such a prominent role in this play. But the presentation of Henry's own "memorable line" as neither "awkward" nor "sinister" (i.e., illegitimate) is also ironically put into the mouth of a Beaufort already associated with a Lancastrian illegitimacy, in a dramatic series in which the taint of illegitimacy more generally continues to haunt the Lancastrian line, however Henry V labors to legitimize or make it "right."

The "pedigree" offered by Exeter in this speech places Henry within the direct line of descent from "Edward the Third" (2.4.93), proclaiming it as a descent through which he is "evenly deriv'd" from his "famous ancestors" (2.4.91–92). But this "most *memorable* line" simultaneously assigns to "oblivion" (2.4.87) what it strategically evens or smooths out, effacing the "crooked" Bolingbroke and the deposition and murder of Richard II (Edward III's *direct* heir) and omitting the higher March title through the female (from Edward's third son) that had already been repeatedly foregrounded in the plays of Henry VI.[93] "Evenly-deriv'd" in Exeter's presentation of this "pedigree" joins the image of the "smooth" or even in Henry's own speech after the Cambridge rebellion is suppressed ("We doubt not now / But every rub is smoothed on our way," 2.2.187–188). But it also joins other speeches in the play (including the Salic Law speech, with its "crooked titles / Usurp'd," 1.2.94–95) that suggest the *making* smooth or even of what is crooked or awry, including Bolingbroke's "indirect" and "crook'd" way to the throne (*2H4* 4.5.184). Significantly, the "pedigree" provided by Exeter—which traces Henry's claim back to Edward III after the French king has already traced him to that patriarch's son "Edward, Black Prince of Wales" (2.4.56)—simultaneously recalls to memory (in this scene that twice invokes the "memorable") the Prince of Wales who was father to Richard II, and hence the very different construction of descent (to the Earl of March and *Cambridge*'s heirs) that would make Henry's claim not "evenly" but "crookedly" derived, its own "awkward" or preposterous reverse. It is also emblematic of other parts of the play where this effacing occurs, including the scene of Fluellen's Welsh "slip of the tongue" not only in comparing Henry V to "Alexander the Pig" (4.7.13), but in effacing Bolingbroke altogether, as Henry stands by and affirms Fluellen's erasure of his "crooked" father by making Edward III Henry's "grandfather" rather than *great*-grandfather (*Flu.* "Your grandfather of famous memory, an't please your Majesty, and your great-uncle Edward the Plack Prince of Wales, as I have read in the chronicles, fought a most prave pattle here in France. / *K. Hen.* They did, Fluellen," 4.7.92–96).

I have already noted that it is a "Duke of Exeter" (designated by that same title and hence easily confused with the Exeter of *1H6* and *Henry V*) who, in the reversed dramatic order of these histories, had acknowledged before this scene of *Henry V* that the Henrys' claim was neither legitimate nor rightful—in the opening of *3 Henry VI* where that Exeter concludes in his "conscience" that York, the son of the executed Cambridge, is the rightful "heir" (1.1.146–148) and "lawful king" (1.1.150)—and also that this dramatically earlier Exeter's father (Huntington) is referred to in the Wooing Scene of *Henry V* itself. But even without this specific resonance, Exeter's speech in *Henry V* on Henry's "pedigree" as "evenly deriv'd" and his right to France as "no sinister nor no awkward claim" had already been doubly undermined in advance of *Henry V*, both by the rebellions against the "crooked" former Bolingbroke in *Henry IV Parts 1 and 2* and by the preposterous echoes from the Henry VI plays as a whole.

Immediately after his presentation of Henry's "pedigree," Exeter's demand that the French king "resign" his "crown and kingdom" (2.4.93–94) is followed by his threat of violence, yet another reminder of the throne and power held by the Lancastrians "by force and not by right," as Cambridge's son had put it in *2 Henry VI* (2.2.30):

> *French King.* Or else *what follows?*
> *Exeter.* Bloody constraint; for if you hide the crown
> Even in your hearts, there will he rake for it.
> Therefore in fierce tempest is he coming,
> In thunder and in earthquake, like a Jove,
> That if requiring fail he will compel;
> And bids you, in the bowels of the Lord,
> Deliver up the crown, and to take mercy
> On the poor souls for whom this hungry war
> Opens his vasty jaws; and on your head
> Turning the widows' tears, the orphans' cries,
> The dead men's blood, the privy maidens' groans,
> For husbands, fathers, and betrothed lovers,
> That shall be swallowed in this controversy.
> This is his claim, his threat'ning, and my message.
> (*H5* 2.4.96–110)

The French king's "Or else *what follows?*" serves here as a pivotal phrase—turning from Exeter's presentation of what properly follows or succeeds in Henry's "most memorable line" to the dire consequences that Exeter announces will follow for the French if "requiring" fails and is replaced by force (2.4.101). Though this speech is not generally accorded the critical attention given to Henry's own speech and threats before the gates of Harfleur

(3.3.1–43), it makes similarly clear the destructive "force" attached to this claim of "right." "What follows?" is echoed immediately after Exeter's presentation, in the "Follow, follow!" of the Chorus to Act 3 ("Holding due course to Harflew. Follow, follow!" 3.Chorus.17), as prelude to Henry's rousing "Once more unto the breach" (3.1.1). But the very speech by "Exeter" that lays claim to France—and threatens the violence that will "follow" if Henry's demand is not granted—itself calls attention to the inverse or underside of Henry's rhetoric of "right" and the "oblivion" on which its selective remembering depends. And it subtly echoes (even as it inverts) the rhetoric of "rightful hand" and "well-hallow'd cause" that provided the legitimizing basis of the Salic Law speech and suppression of the Cambridge rebellion.

∽

Then shall our names,
Familiar in his mouth as household words,
Harry the King, Bedford and Exeter,
Warwick and Talbot, Salisbury and Gloucester,
Be in their flowing cups freshly rememb'red.

—*Henry V* (4.3.51–55)

*Westmorland.* Perish the man whose mind is backward now!

—*Henry V* (4.3.72)

*King Henry.* Take it, brave York. Now, soldiers, march away.

—*Henry V* (4.3.132)

Other inconvenient memories accompany the French campaign itself, as its "advance" proceeds. The scene on the night before Agincourt contains a reminder of the Rebellion Scene in the invented exchange where the dissenting "Williams" responds, "That's more than we know" (4.1.129), to the disguised king's claim that his "cause" is "just and his quarrel honorable" (4.1.127–128). And the punning "crowns" (monetary and royal) associated with the Cambridge rebellion in Act 2 are recalled in the repeated references to "French crowns" (4.1.226, 228) or coins in this scene, just before the king's own prayer on "the fault / My father made in compassing the crown" (4.1.293–294), as well as in the "crowns" of the later scene involving the alleged "traitor" Williams (4.8.15, 25, 57–60), whose subversive questioning is never adequately answered in the play.[94]

The latter end of *Henry V*—which might otherwise simply resound with the heroic theme of the outnumbered English and the ultimate triumph of the Agincourt victory—is thus shadowed by Williams's dissent and inclusion of the other commoners in this invented exchange, on the same night that Henry prays that his father's "fault" will not be remembered (4.1.293). But it is also filled with "preposterous" recalls of the plays that had already "oft" been "shown," together with "anachronisms" that beg to be seen in relation to the theatrical context of the reversed dramatic histories. I have already mentioned the *post*-Agincourt appearance in *1 Henry VI* of the Warwick whose name appears in the ringing roll-call of the St. Crispin's Day speech. But what is remarkable about this speech as a *whole* is that the names it memorializes from Agincourt itself are also (as Gurr notes) a "roll-call of the figures made famous in *1H6*,"[95] including at least one who did not appear at Agincourt at all. And this comes in the midst of a speech that rousingly appeals to what will be *remembered*:

> This day is call'd the feast of Crispian:
> He that outlives this day, and comes safe home,
> Will stand a' tiptoe when this day is named,
> And rouse him at the name of Crispian. . . .
> Old men *forget*; yet all shall be *forgot*,
> But he'll *remember* with advantages
> What feats he did that day. Then shall *our names*,
> Familiar in his mouth as household words,
> Harry the King, *Bedford* and *Exeter*,
> *Warwick* and *Talbot, Salisbury* and *Gloucester*,
> Be in their flowing cups freshly *rememb'red*.
> This story shall the good man teach his son;
> And Crispin Crispian shall ne'er go by,
> From this day to the ending of the world,
> But we in it shall be *remembered*. (*H5* 4.3.40–59)

The rhetoric of this famous speech is the invigorating rhetoric of prophecy, looking forward in time to the Apocalypse itself ("This story shall the good man teach his son; / And Crispin Crispian shall ne'er go by, / From this day to the ending of the world," 4.3.56–58). But the sequence here envisaged as a linear movement from father to son to the final apocalyptic end of history had already been dramatically bent or curved by the fact that this entire subsequent history of sons to come—presented here as the *aftermath* of Agincourt—had already been shown before, in the plays the Epilogue will explicitly *remember*.

Even more strikingly, the "names" (4.3.51) so resonantly summoned in this heroic roll-call are the very figures whose subsequent careers (and roles in the losses in France under Henry V's son) had already been "shown" upon "our stage." "Salisbury" is the warrior whose post-Agincourt history had already been dramatized in *Henry VI Part 1* (1.4),[96] as well as the name of the different historical figure who concludes in his "conscience" (in *Henry VI Part 2*) that the Marches' suppressed cause is in the "right" and the executed Cambridge's son is "rightful heir to England's royal seat" (5.1.175–178). "Gloucester" is the younger brother of Henry V, whose post-Agincourt career and ultimate fall as Protector of England (one of the "many" who had the managing of the "state," as the Epilogue puts it) had already been a major preoccupation of *Henry VI Parts 1 and 2*, where he delivered a memorable speech on the losses in France of what Henry V had won ("Blotting your names from books of memory. . . . / Undoing all, as all had never been!," *2H6* 1.1.78–103).[97] "Bedford" is the other brother of Henry V whose battles against Joan la Pucelle or the Maid of Orleans had already "oft" been "shown" in *1 Henry VI*. "Exeter"—the same duke who proclaims to the French in *Henry V* that Henry's is "no sinister nor no awkward claim"—is one of the "many" responsible for the dead king's son in that earlier play of French losses, as well as the figure who speaks there the "fatal prophecy" ("That Henry born at Monmouth should win all, / And Henry born at Windsor lose all," *1H6* 3.1.194–198) dramatically recalled in the Epilogue itself.[98] And he bears the same title as the Exeter who had already dissented in his "conscience" from the rightfulness of the Lancastrian claim in *3 Henry 6*, in the face of the greater "right" of Cambridge's son York.

Two figures in this St. Crispin's Day roll-call of Agincourt's memorable "names" (4.3.51) are particularly telling in relation to its "preposterous" recalls, since at least one of them did not even appear at the Agincourt "memorialized" in this rousing speech. "Talbot"—who (as Arden 3 editor Craik observes) "did not in fact take part in the French wars until 1419" (291) and so could not have been at Agincourt—is the military hero who was the "virtual protagonist" of *Henry VI Part 1*,[99] and the hero whose memorable death, before "ten thousand spectators at least (at several times)," was recorded by Nashe. "Warwick"—who was also not at Agincourt (according to Craik, Peter Saccio, and Holinshed)[100]—was already not only part of the reversals in France dramatized in *1 Henry VI* but, as we have seen, the figure who in the emblematic scene of "white" rose and "red" (*1H6* 2.4) had plucked the "white rose" associated with the suppressed March-York cause and subsequently promoted the righting of the "wrong" done to the executed Cambridge by the elevation of his son to the title of York left vacant at Agincourt (*1H6* 3.1.148–160). In *1 Henry VI*, he had also defended the Cambridge lineage ("His grandfather was Lionel Duke of Clarence, / Third son to the third Edward, King of England," *1H6* 2.4.83–84), even before Mortimer outlined the title of the more "rightful heir" that was "suppressed" by Henry V in the Cambridge rebellion (*1H6* 2.5.80–92). And he shares the "name" of the Warwick who in *Henry VI Parts 2 and 3* was instrumental (as "kingmaker") in the rise of Cambridge's son the new Duke of York (though he later deserted Edward IV) and was conflated or confused with that other memorable Warwick.[101]

Within the St. Crispin's Day speech, "Be in their flowing cups freshly *rememb'red*" (4.3.55) is said of "names" that are to be made "familiar" as "household words" (4.3.52) by the Agincourt battle that is still to come. But in a speech that places so much emphasis on remembrance, these very names simultaneously enable a "preposterous" *dramatic* remembering of figures whose historically future links with the post-Agincourt losses and the rise of the March-York claim had already been "shown" upon "our stage"—including the heroic Talbot done in not only by the French but also by civil conflict in England and the Warwick who had championed the right of the executed Cambridge's son. The speech itself pointedly contrasts *remembrance* with *forgetting* ("Old men forget; yet all shall be forgot, / But he'll remember with advantages / What feats he did that day," 4.3.49–51). But the great "names" that are to be "rememb'red" (4.3.55) in time to come also recall to memory what in *Henry V* might otherwise be forgot, and hence work in the opposite direction from the suppression of those memories in the Rebellion Scene and elsewhere in the play. And the appearance of Westmorland as well in this St. Crispin's Day scene—though he was not historically at Agincourt, having remained in England as warden of the Scottish marches[102]—keeps in mind the figure intimately linked with the rebellious "Marches" (in both senses) in the plays of the "unquiet reign" of Henry IV.

The preposterous recalls in this cast of characters and roll-call of names on the eve of Agincourt itself thus gives an intriguing resonance to Westmorland's "Perish the man whose mind is *backward* now" (4.3.72) immediately following the forward-looking rhetoric of Henry's St. Crispin's Day speech (with its simultaneously backward-looking "memorable" names). This is a scene that already summons a perspective that is both *after* and *before*, in the French "herald" (4.3.122) who arrives before Agincourt and will "once more come again" (4.3.127)—in a play whose iterations of a "back-return" (5.Chorus.41) have often been noted, not only in the Chorus to Act 5 but in the recursive movements of other scenes.[103] And the ringing roll-call of names in the St. Crispin's Day speech—in a play whose Prologue invokes a "conjuring" back from the dead—includes the (*theatrically*) "backward" reminder of something that is "once more *come again*," made possible through the reversed dramatic order in which their later fates on less successful battlefields in France had already been "shown."

It is here, at precisely the point in *Henry V* where the subsequent history of the Agincourt victory and suppressed March-York claim has been recalled in the names already famous from those earlier dramatic histories, that there appears on stage for the first and only time in *Henry V* (4.3.130–133) the Duke of York who would die at Agincourt, taking the mind "backward" in a double sense—both back to the "Aumerle" of *Richard II* (and hence to the "fault" of the usurper Bolingbroke) *and* back to *1 Henry VI*, where the title of "Duke of York" had been assumed after Agincourt by Cambridge's son (*1H6* 3.1.172). Editors have puzzled over York's brief appearance here, which is in no way necessary to the plot of *Henry V*, and over the lack of mention within this play that he is the elder brother of the executed Cambridge (though that is specified in Holinshed).[104] But the cameo appearance of this pivotal figure here, at the end of the scene whose St. Crispin's Day speech has recalled so many memorable figures from the plays the Epilogue explicitly remembers, inserts a reminder of what in this play has been suppressed, including the unspoken March claim in Henry's suppression of the Cambridge rebellion, in a scene that ends with Henry's instruction to York, who craves "the leading of the vaward" (4.3.131), "Take it, brave York. Now, soldiers, *march* away" (4.3.132).[105]

Another scene in Act 4 of *Henry V* that might be seen within the perspective of "memorable" names and the Epilogue's pointed recall of the plays of Henry VI is Exeter's elegiac description of the deaths at Agincourt of Suffolk and York himself (4.6)—yet another invented scene added by Shakespeare to his chronicle sources (which appears in both Quarto and Folio texts of this play). The pairing here of York and Suffolk (from the simple juxtaposition of their names in Holinshed in the list of the noble English dead) begs the question of why what Gurr calls this "fanciful" or invented scene is in the play at all but also the choice of these two names in particular.[106] The "brave York" (4.3.132) who dies at Agincourt, as earlier remarked, is the bearer of the title ("Duke of York") that passed after his death to Cambridge's son, already dramatized in the scene of *1 Henry VI* where Warwick asks Henry VI to "right" his executed "father's wrongs" (*1H6* 3.1.149–160). And becoming the new "York" had been in those earlier plays of Agincourt's aftermath the first major act toward regaining the higher "right" to the throne suppressed by Henry V. "York" is thus a highly resonant name from the plays that have been staged before, iterated here in this purely invented scene.

Even more suggestive in this regard is the entirely invented *pairing* of "York" with "Suffolk" in this elegiac description, since this Suffolk was a historically insignificant figure who appears nowhere else in *Henry V*; and in the chronicle of Monstrelet, it is Henry V himself—not a Suffolk—who was involved at York's Agincourt death, with danger to his "crown."[107] But the much more memorable "Suffolk" (brother of the Suffolk who dies at Agincourt—here fictively represented in the embrace of "York") is the Suffolk who was the bitter antagonist of the York of those earlier plays,[108] the Lancastrian who in the invented emblematic scene of white and red roses in *1 Henry VI* had plucked the "red" rose (with Somerset) and whom York there vows to "note" in his "book of memory" and "scourge" when the time comes to claim his right to the throne (*1H6* 2.4.100–103). This is also the Suffolk who in *2 Henry VI* implicates Cambridge's son York in the charge of "high treason," in the claim of the "master" that he is the "rightful heir" (*2H6* 1.3.177–185), and the Suffolk that York there wishes were "suffocate" (*2H6* 1.1.124) for his crucial role in losing the French lands in Anjou and Maine that York considers rightfully *his* (*2H6* 1.1.231–232). The Suffolk of these "oft"-shown earlier plays is thus a major figure not only in relation to the loss of territories in France that York considers "his own lands" (*2H6* 1.1.231) but also in relation to the cause of the Marches suppressed by Henry V's execution of the Cambridge conspirators—since it is in the scenes of rivalry with Suffolk that York vows to no longer let "proud Lancaster usurp my right" (*2H6* 1.1.244) and to bring about the "day" when "York shall claim his own" (*2H6* 1.1.239), as he does at the beginning of *3 Henry VI*.

"York" and "Suffolk," then—presented in *Henry V* in an invented Agincourt embrace—are the "memorable" names of the figures whose rivalry had been such a major part of the earlier plays of the aftermath of Agincourt, the Lancaster-York rivalry that contributed there to the death of the Talbots and increased to make York and Suffolk the principal rival-antagonists following the Talbots' deaths. And the possibility of a "preposterous" recall here is strikingly increased by the fact that the very description of their deaths in this invented scene echoes (as Dover Wilson and subsequent editors have noted) the deaths of the Talbots in *1 Henry VI*.[109]

This invented scene thus recalls not only the memorable names of the "Suffolk" and "York" intimately related to the losses in France and rise of the suppressed March-York "right," already "shown" upon "our stage," but also the deaths of the Talbots that had been such a signal dramatic event—and does so at the high point of Agincourt itself. As several of the play's editors point out, the account of York here as "larding the plain" (*H5* 4.6.8) simultaneously evokes as well yet another memory of Falstaff, the figure who "lards the lean earth as he walks along" (*1H4* 2.2.109) in the plays where "Oldcastle" had been his original name.[110] A reminder of the banished Falstaff whose "name" is ostensibly "forgot" in the very next scene (*H5* 4.7.50) is as a result kept alive in this invented memorializing elegy, together with the name of "York" that looks two ways at once—back to the Aumerle of Bolingbroke's "fault" in *Richard II* and forward to the post-Agincourt history that had already been "shown."

The description here of the Agincourt deaths of "York" and "Suffolk" ends with Henry's being moved, like Exeter, to tears and his "I must perforce *compound* / With mistful eyes, or they will *issue*" (*H5* 4.6.33–34). Gary Taylor has argued that this line should read not as Warburton's emended "mistfull" but the "mixtfull" of the Folio text, an argument he makes from the sense of mixture elsewhere in these lines.[111] But perhaps another argument for this Folio "mixtfull" is its anticipation (in "compound" and "issue") of the mingling or mixing of the "compound . . . boy" ("half French, half English," 5.2.207–208) that Henry himself will project as the hopeful "issue" of his union with French Katherine in the Wooing Scene (5.2), the mixed or mingled "issue" Henry VI (5.2.349), whose disastrous subsequent history had already been staged in the plays of the other Suffolk and York. The Folio's "mixtfull" as a portmanteau term would thus recall (as well as anticipate) the already-dramatized "issue" of that mingling (as both "successor" and "consequence"). But it also joins the repeated invocation of mixtures and interminglings in *Henry V* itself (including illegitimate or "bastard" mixtures)—not only the sense of mixture or hybridity conveyed, for example, in the reference to "bastard Normans, Norman bastards" (3.5.9) or in the "basterd" of the scene invoking Ireland through "Macmorris" (3.2.123), but also the specter of bastardy or illegitimacy that might stand (as in Exeter's "No sinister nor no awkward claim") as a sign for all that complicates Henry V's attempts to cordon off or separate, including the contamination or "ill neighborhood" of the plays he seeks to banish from memory, and with them reminders of the illegitimacy of his own line.

ꟹ

> Go forth and fetch their conqu'ring Caesar in . . .
>
> —*Henry V* (5.Chorus.28)

> *French King.* Take her, fair son, and from her blood raise up
> Issue to me . . . that never war advance
> His bleeding sword 'twixt England and fair France.
>
> —*Henry V* (5.2.348–355)

> *King Henry.* Prepare we for our marriage; on which day,
> My Lord of Burgundy, we'll take your oath,
> And all the peers', for surety of our leagues. . . .
>
> —*Henry V* (5.2.370–372)

At what will ultimately be (with the Epilogue) the play's own breached or open end, there are yet more preposterous recalls, including what may be—in light of the return of York himself from Ireland in the "oft"-shown earlier plays—yet another layer to the already complexly overdetermined Chorus to Act 5. This Chorus is famous for its comparison of Henry, returning from Calais as a "conqu'ring Caesar" (5.Chorus.28), to the expected return of the Earl of Essex or Mountjoy from Ireland ("the general of our gracious Empress, / As in good time he may, from Ireland coming, / Bringing rebellion broached on his sword," 5.Chorus.30–32), in lines linking France with the rebellious Ireland to which both had been dispatched by Elizabeth (as York in the earlier plays had been by Henry's son).[112] As we have seen, the York dispatched to Ireland in *2 Henry VI* returns from Ireland (as his supporters Salisbury and Warwick and his son the new Earl of March do from Calais) to claim the throne from the Lancastrian usurpers, openly asserting the claim from the Marches that Henry V had suppressed. The Chorus's description of Henry's return from France (and its pairing with an anticipated return from Ireland) is already resonant, as Gurr observes, with echoes of the return from France of the exiled Bolingbroke in *Richard II* (5.2.3–21).[113] But Cambridge's son York—returning from Ireland to claim his "right" from the usurpers—also famously invoked the figure of "Iulius Caesar" for the usurping Bolingbroke, in the very oration from the chronicles that formed the basis for the opening scene of *3 Henry VI*.[114] Thus, even at the moment of Henry's greatest triumph, this Chorus to the final act of *Henry V*—with its invocation of returns to England from both directions, Ireland and France (or "Calais")—may be filled with compounded echoes not only of the usurping Bolingbroke dramatically linked with Henry as a "conquering Caesar" but of the aftermath of the cause of the Marches already dramatized in the plays its Epilogue will soon recall.

The scene that immediately follows this Act 5 Chorus subtly recalls the issue of female descent or the "law Salique" in the "salt" and "leek" of the comic exchange between (English) Pistol and (Welsh) Fluellen,[115] even as the image of a "leek" in a mouth suggests another ouroboros figure as the play nears its end. In this same interposed scene, Pistol's "All hell shall stir for this" (5.1.68) significantly echoes the famous lines from Virgil's epic *Aeneid* (7.312), where what seemed to be certain peace, conclusion, or closure had been broken or breached yet again, as the cycle of war and revenge continues.[116]

Immediately after this scene of "salt" and "leeks," the "law Salique" invoked at the threshold of the French campaign returns in its importance for the play as a whole, since the weak link in the Treaty of Troyes with which the play concludes, in its final Wooing Scene between Henry and French Katherine, is that the "dangers of the Salic Law" are reintroduced in this "covenant, whereby the marriage left the French crown to Henry's heirs," thus opening the son they "compound" to the same problem that had surfaced in the Salic Law Scene in Act 1, of a king of England claiming the right to France through a female link.[117] And this is precisely the problem that the plays the Epilogue recalls had already "oft . . . shown," in the claim by the French Dauphin (pointedly excluded from the Wooing Scene of *Henry V*) to be France's true king. One of the many dramatic ironies overhanging this final scene of *Henry V*—from the plays of his son that had earlier been "shown"—is that the Dauphin (or French king's son) who is conspicuously missing from the Wooing Scene itself had already been shown as triumphing over the English in the plays that had been staged before.[118]

The Wooing Scene is indeed filled with such "preposterous" recalls, even at what seems to be the apex of Henry's triumph—in a scene that also provides a reminder of "preposterous venery" (and the play's own transvestite theatrical context) in the reference to catching Katherine by the "latter end" (5.2.314).[119] Henry's wooing of Katherine—that favorite of romantic stagings—is already anticipated by the fact that, earlier in the play, when Katherine was offered to Henry with only "to dowry, / Some petty and unprofitable dukedoms" (3.Chorus.30–31), rather than the territories over which the war is fought and ultimately won, the union was rejected by Henry out of hand. The scene of the wooing itself in Act 5 is prefaced by Henry's clear signal to the French that if they want "peace" they must "*buy* that peace / With full accord to all our just *demands*" (5.2.70–71), together with his unromantic description of Katherine as "*our capital demand*, compris'd / Within the fore-rank of our articles" (5.2.96–97). The emphasis, in this wooing, on "deeds" that are more honest than "words" summons the martial-chivalric persona of the "plain soldier" who knows "no ways to mince it in love" (5.2.126, 149), but it also evokes (as in *The Taming of the Shrew*, whose possible though uncertain "taming" is recalled by Henry's repeated reference to Katherine as "Kate") the sense of "deeds" as titles to property, in a wooing whose aim is territorial and dynastic.[120] The end of the wooing relentlessly emphasizes the "buying" and negotiating that has taken place offstage, when the French and English lords re-enter, having done the real bargaining involved.[121] Even after the romantic language of the wooing, Henry makes clear that "Kate" is to be his wife only if the cities he wants come with her ("I am content, so the *maiden cities* you talk of may wait on her"; "*I love France so well that I will not part with a village of it*; I will have it all mine. And, Kate, *when France is mine . . . you are mine*," 5.2.326–327, 173–176).[122] And the Katherine who participates in some of the banter of the wooing exchange is significantly silent (with no speaking lines after her "mouth" is "stop[ped]" with a "kiss," 5.2.272–275), as the real compact becomes an affair between men.

Critics have observed the overshadowing of this final Wooing Scene by awareness of the historical aftermath of this marriage and its mingling or compounding of English and French in the disastrous "issue" that was Henry VI. But its underlying sense of irony is even more powerfully underscored by its larger *theatrical* context, the fact that the plays of this aftermath had already been staged, and by its pervasive "preposterous" theatrical recalls, a dramatic irony emphasized in its reference to what is only "*hereafter* to know" (5.2.212) so close to the Epilogue's reminder of what has already "oft" been "shown." Henry's promise to Katherine, "the elder I wax, the better I shall appear" (5.2.229), is uttered before an audience that knows that this king will not wax "elder": his funeral had been solemnly staged at the opening of *1*

*Henry VI*, which begins not only with "*Dead march. Enter the Funeral* of KING HENRY THE FIFT" but also his brother Bedford's praise of "King Henry the Fift, too famous to live long" (*1 Henry VI* 1.1.6). Henry's forecast that Katherine will prove "a good soldier-breeder" and that they will "compound a boy . . . that shall go to Constantinople and take the Turk by the beard" (*H5* 5.2.206–209) had already been belied by the earlier plays of this weak and "effeminate prince" (*1H6* 1.1.35), who not only does not go to Constantinople (invoked here in Henry's anachronistic reference to the Turk) but loses all that his father had won. And "broken English," in a wooing where that phrase might seem simply part of its charm ("Come, your answer in broken music; for thy voice is music and thy English broken; therefore, queen of all, Katherine, break thy mind to me in broken English," 5.2.243–246), more ominously resonates with the memory of the already-staged plays that had repeatedly "shown" the "English broken."

Henry's description of Katherine as his "fair flower-de-luce" (*H5* 5.2.210) similarly recalls the losses in France dramatized in *1 Henry VI* as the cutting from "England's coat" of the "flower-de-luces" (*1H6* 1.1.80–81) associated with Edward III's and Henry V's victories. And in the rise in those earlier plays of the March claim suppressed by Henry V, York's return with his "army of Irish" in *2 Henry VI* "to claim *his right*, / And *pluck the crown from feeble Henry's head*" (*2H6* 5.1.1–2) includes "I cannot give due action to my words, / Except a sword or sceptre balance it. / A sceptre shall it have, have I a soul, / On which I'll toss the flow'r-de-luce of France" (*2H6* 5.1.8–11). In *Henry V*—where Michael Neill and others have stressed that France is joined by Ireland (as England's territorial *before* and *after*), including in the Wooing Scene[123]—even Henry's promise to Katherine that "*England* is thine, *Ireland* is thine, *France* is thine" (*H5* 5.2.239–240) if she says "Harry of England, I am thine" (5.2.237) is preempted by the earlier-staged claim of Cambridge's son York to be the "lawful king" (*2H6* 5.1.4) rather than the Lancastrian usurpers, since his claim (in the Duke of York's oration from Holinshed used as the basis for the opening scene of *Henry VI Part 3*) included not only England but Ireland and France: "the said Richard duke of Yorke, verie true and rightfull heire to the crownes, roiall estate, and dignitie of the realmes of England and of France, and of the lordship of Ireland aforesaid."[124] Once again, such a preempting does not depend on knowledge of the chronicles, since York himself, in *Henry VI Part 2*, had not only lamented the lost French lands as *his* (*2H6* 1.1.230–238) but said that *he* is the legitimate "owner" of "England, France *and* Ireland" as well (*2H6* 1.1.232).

When the Wooing Scene—like *Henry V* as a whole—is seen in isolation, a French woman being taught to speak the language and ultimately yield to the dominion of her country's conquerer may seem part of the triumphant "perfections" of this English "mirror of all Christian kings," who dominates this "maid" as he takes possession of a symbolically female territory.[125] But this relation of male to female, ruler to ruled, is reversed in the historical "sequel" to Henry's triumph that had "oft" been dramatized before, in the inversion of the hierarchy of gender by Henry VI's wife, the French "Amazon" (*3H6* 4.1.106) Margaret of Anjou, who reverses or overturns the relation between ruler and ruled in the reign of Henry V's son. The reference in the Wooing Scene to the "witchcraft" in the French princess's "lips" (5.2.275–276), rather than simply conventional or romantic, likewise preposterously recalls not only the witchcraft said by some to be responsible for Henry V's death (evoked at the beginning of *1 Henry VI* in Exeter's "shall we think the subtile-witted French / Conjurors and sorcerers . . . contriv'd his end?," *1H6* 1.1.25–27), but also the "witching" power of Joan of Arc, or La Pucelle, the Maid of Orleans who is the scourge of the English after Agincourt, described in *1 Henry VI* as "that witch, that damned sorceress" (*1H6* 3.2.38).[126]

Even the final apocalyptic conclusion to the compacted union of Henry V with his French princess resonates with striking recalls of the "sequel" that had already been "shown," qualifying its rhetoric of movement from discord to unity with the "preposterous" dramatic memory of its subsequent reversal:

*French King.* Take her, fair son, and from her blood raise up
Issue to me, that the contending kingdoms
Of France and England, whose very shores look pale
With envy of each other's happiness,
May cease their hatred; and this dear conjunction
Plant neighborhood and Christian-like accord
In their sweet bosoms, that *never war advance*
*His bleeding sword 'twixt England and fair France.*
*Lords.* Amen! . . . .
*Queen Isabel.* God, the best maker of all marriages,
*Combine your hearts in one, your realms in one!*
As man and wife, being two, are one in love,
So be there 'twixt your kingdoms such a spousal,
That never may ill office, or fell jealousy,
Which troubles oft the bed of blessed marriage,

Thrust in between the paction of these kingdoms,
To make *divorce* of their incorporate league;
*That English may as French, French Englishmen,*
*Receive each other.* God speak this Amen!

*All.* Amen!

*King Henry.* Prepare we for our marriage; on which day,
My Lord of *Burgundy, we'll take your oath,*
*And all the peers', for surety of our leagues.*
Then shall I swear to Kate, and you to me,
And *may our oaths well kept and prosp'rous be!*

(5.2.348–374)

This is the end of the Wooing Scene before all exit (and the Epilogue begins), and it rings with the hopefulness of a triumphant conclusion—but only if *Henry V* is viewed in isolation or simply as the culmination of the second tetralogy rather than in its larger theatrical context. Katherine's mother's prayer in this scene—"So *happy be the issue* . . . / Of this good day and of this gracious meeting" (5.2.12–13)—carries with it, from this larger dramatic perspective, the theatrical memory that the double-meaning "issue" to come from this meeting and marriage is the son (and consequence) whose disasters have already been shown, as this seeming culmination becomes part of the "fracted and corroborate" form of a play breached by recursive reminders of what has already undone its resonant rhetoric of "union."

The most strikingly "preposterous" character in these final lines is the figure of Burgundy himself, made co-regent with Bedford at the Treaty of Troyes and presiding dramatically over the negotiations at the end of *Henry V*.[127] For, in the already "oft"-shown plays of the aftermath of this apparently final "union," the same Burgundy who is the joiner of French and English in this concluding Wooing Scene had already been the principal figure in its disjoining or "divorce," the very "divorce" ominously invoked (as something to be avoided or warded off) in the Wooing Scene's own final "spousal" (*H5* 5.2.362–366).[128] In one of the most memorable scenes of the plays the Epilogue recalls, Burgundy—still united with the English and co-regent with Bedford in *1 Henry VI*—is taunted by La Pucelle for this "joining," as a union that benefits only the English: "Who join'st thou with, but with a lordly nation / That will not trust thee but for profit's sake? / When Talbot hath set footing once in France / And fashion'd thee that instrument of ill, / Who then but English Henry will be lord, / And thou be thrust out like a fugitive?"

*1H6* 3.3.62–67). Indeed, La Pucelle's "enchanting" and successful appeal to him in that earlier play to return to the cause of the formerly "fertile France" (*1H6* 3.3.44)—now ruined by the English despoilers—is preposterously "echoed" in Burgundy's own lament in this final Wooing Scene for the ruined "garden" of France,[129] a connection the Epilogue itself suggests when it calls the France that Henry V won and Henry VI lost the "world's best garden" (*H5* Epilogue 7). By the time of the concluding "spousal" of *Henry V*, this same Burgundy had already "oft" been "shown" as enticed by La Pucelle to uncouple this union by defecting from the English cause, siding instead with the Dauphin he concludes to be "the rightful King of France" (*1H6* 4.1.60). And he had already become, in that earlier play of the aftermath of the Treaty of Troyes, part of the French forces who "compass" Talbot and lead to his memorable death—an act that Gloucester there called "monstrous treachery" (*1H6* 4.1.61). The Burgundy who presides over the union of French and English in the final Wooing Scene of *Henry V* had thus dramatically already been the instrument of the "breaking" of the English which the language of "broken English, English broken" ominously recalls, part of the irony imported into this concluding apocalyptic "union" from the sequel that had come before.[130]

To highlight the theatrical contexts and "preposterous" recalls that reverberate throughout this play, even in this final scene of *Henry V*, is not to argue that all audience members would have seen or remembered the plays the Epilogue so pointedly recalls. But it is to stress how important it is to take seriously the recursive "bending" of the Epilogue itself, both with regard to what is suppressed or strategically forgotten in *Henry V* and with regard to the breaching of its own wishful (self-)containment or enclosure. Sometimes "once more unto the breach" means moving "awk," or in reverse.

*Chapter 5*

# What's in a Name?

## Brabant and the Global Contexts of *Othello*

> What does it mean that Brabantio may be named after the Netherlands' Brabant, at the time ruled by Spain?
>
> —Kim F. Hall

The principal source for *Othello*, Giraldi Cinthio's *Hecatommithi*, provides only one name—that of Desdemona—and considerable critical work has been done on glossing not only her name (from Greek *dusdaimon* ["unfortunate"], with its "daimon" underscored by "Desdemon" in *Othello*) but also the play's other names, including Cassio, which might have been sounded as "Cashio," as Michael Neill suggests.[1] In relation to the invoking of Spain in this play set in Venice and Cyprus, important work has been done on the Spanish names of Roderigo (whose name may recall the legendary fighter against the Moors) and Iago, the name that strikingly evokes *Sant'Iago Matamoros* or "Slayer of Moors,"[2] the patron saint James in whose name the Moors were driven out of Spain—whose familiarity in England is registered by the reference to St. James's in London as "Saint Iagoes Parke" in Thomas Dekker's *Whore of Babylon* not long after *Othello*'s own first performance.[3] The evocation of Spain provides for this tragedy a wider or more "global" geography beyond Venice and Cyprus (including for its mercenary soldier Iago, in a period when Italy was rife with Spanish mercenaries). But with the exception of the question raised by Kim F. Hall that provides the epigraph for this chapter, even most recent editors do not comment on the name of "Brabantio" (noting simply that he is a Venetian senator and father to Desdemona), though it too is a name that Shakespeare invents and adds to his source from Cinthio.[4] And like the Oxford *Complete Works* text before it (repeated in the New Oxford Shakespeare of 2016), the much-used *Norton Shakespeare* has continued (even in its 2016 third edition, which is no longer tied to the Oxford text) to efface "Brabant" altogether by substituting the name "Brabanzio" instead.[5]

Eric Griffin in his 1998 study of Roderigo, Sant'Iago, and the "Spanish Spirits" of Shakespeare's play remarks (but only in a single sentence) that "Brabantio's name bears its own telling cultural significance: its root is 'Brabant'—as in that occupied kingdom of the Spanish Netherlands."[6] He also cites the 1985 essay by Frederick M. Burelbach that observes that "Brabantio" is "reflective of the divided history of Brabant, a duchy in the Low Countries."[7] But what Burelbach goes on to sketch—again only briefly—is an unnecessarily literalistic one-to-one correspondence between the history of Brabant and what happens in *Othello* to Brabantio in particular.[8] What I want to suggest in what follows is a more capacious and less literalistic attempt to respond to Kim F. Hall's thought-provoking question, by laying out a series of associations the evocation of "Brabant" might summon, as part of the wider global context of *Othello* as a whole.

This will include this play's preoccupation not only with "country matters" but also with a simultaneously sexual and territorial "occupation"; the cash nexus evoked in Iago's repeated "put money in thy purse" (in a mercenary context where, as Michael Neill remarks, "cash is the key to all relationships");[9] the importance of "credit" in the combined senses it shares with *The Merchant of Venice*, including most ominously in Iago's plan to "undo" Desdemona's "credit with the Moor" (2.3.359); and the "debitor and creditor" or double-entry bookkeeping identified with "Florentine" Cassio in the opening scene. But the chapter will also explore at greater length the multiple interconnections between Brabant and England in the years leading up to *Othello* (first performed in 1604); the parallels drawn by contemporaries between London and Antwerp (the city that Dekker called the "eldest daughter of *Brabant*");[10] the importance of Brabant to the "theoric" of the new military science (invoked in *Othello*'s opening scene); the long years of English military involvement in the Low Countries, where Brabant was the center of Spanish rule; and the far-flung theaters of war that repeatedly connected Brabant with campaigns against the Turk in the Mediterranean and elsewhere.

Virginia Mason Vaughan, in her chapter "Global Discourse: Venetians and Turks" in *Othello: A Contextual History*, makes no mention of Brabant as part of this wider context, though it was such a crucial part of the increasingly global network of commerce, credit, and war in the period. By the time of *Othello*, "Brabant" was a familiar name in England for immigrants and refugees from Brabant itself, like "John Brabant" and "Philip Brabant, weaver," and readily available for variants like "Brabantio," as John Foxe's *Actes and Monuments* and other contemporary texts make clear. It had already been used for the names of "Brabant Junior" and "Brabant Senior" in John Marston's *Jack Drum's Entertainment* (1601), the latter likely modeled on Ben Jonson, who had done military service in the Low Countries in the 1590s.[11] Ernst Honigmann in his Arden 3 *Othello* (without mentioning the Low Countries as a context) suggests that not only Marston's "Brabant Senior" but also the "Duke of Brabant" in the anonymous play *The Weakest Goeth to the Wall* (published in 1600) may have suggested Brabantio's name.[12] But it is important to add that the Duke of Brabant in that play is not only, on the personal level (like Brabantio), a father angry at the elopement of his daughter, but part of a play that repeatedly evokes contemporary Elizabethan stereotypes of the Low Countries and the ruthlessness of Spanish soldiers there—managing at the same time to summon in its reference to saint "Jacob's staff" (sig. E4v) yet another familiar form of the Spanish Sant'Iago.

Though its setting is in Venice and Cyprus, *Othello* itself explicitly evokes the Low Countries in the pivotal night scene of carousing and drinking on Cyprus, where Iago refers to "your swag-bellied Hollander" as well as "your Dane, your German," and "your English" as excessive drinkers (2.3.77–79), lines on which editors have commented that "English drunkenness was often blamed on 'the bad habits brought back by soldiers returning from the wars in the Netherlands.'"[13] Even Iago's reference to "cashier'd Cassio" (2.3.375) in this drinking scene—like his earlier "and when he's old, cashier'd" (1.1.48)—foregrounds a term that was brought back to England from the "Low Country campaigns" for a dismissed soldier or disbanded military company. Sir Roger Williams—the professional soldier who did extensive military service in Brabant and the Low Countries and was prominently identified with the new military science invoked in *Othello*—uses the term in its variant form of "cashed" in his *A Briefe Discourse of Warre* (1590), for cashiered officers and regiments. And Shakespeare himself, before *Othello*, had already used this Low Countries term in *The Merry Wives of Windsor*, where Falstaff is urged to "cashier" his followers (1.3.6), and "the gentleman . . . was (as they say) cashier'd" (1.1.174–179) suggests both "dismissed" and eased of his "cash."[14] In the context of *Othello*—where the cash nexus includes not just the "cashiering" of Florentine "Cass[h]io" and the Spanish-sounding Iago's "put money in thy purse" (1.3.341) but also the collocation of mercenary soldiers in the service of Venice—this loanword from the Low Countries campaigns manages at the same time to strengthen the simultaneously financial and military associations that "Brabant" itself (and Antwerp, its financial center) would evoke.

By the time of *Othello*, Shakespeare had referred more than once to Brabant, including in *Henry V*, from the French king's reference to "the Dukes of Berri and of Britain, / Of Brabant and of Orleance" (2.4.4–5) and "Dukes of Orleance, Bourbon, and of Berri, / Alanson, Brabant, Bar, and Burgundy" (3.5.41–42) to Henry's own citing of "Anthony Duke of Brabant, / The brother of the Duke of Burgundy" (4.8.96–97) among the French killed at Agincourt, the dynastic link between Brabant and Burgundy that by the time of the play had made Brabant one of the Spanish king Philip II's Habsburg dominions.[15] ("Burgundy" in the Low Countries—long since in Spanish Habsburg control—itself figures prominently in other plays, independent of the "Duke of Burgundy" who appears in *Henry V* and *1 Henry VI*, including as a place of refuge and political alliance in *3 Henry VI* and *Richard III*, and as France's "waterish" rival for Cordelia in *Lear*.)[16] In *Love's Labor's Lost*, the repeated "Did not I dance with you in Brabant once?" (2.1.114–115) summons not only the name of this well-known part of the Netherlands or Low Countries, but also the sexual sense of "country matters" (*Hamlet* 3.2.116) already invoked in *The Comedy of Errors*, where the mapping of different geographies onto a female body includes "Where stood Belgia, the Netherlands?" and the response is "O, sir, I did not look so low" (3.2.138–139).[17] In *Henry IV Part 2*, Hal's "The rest of the low countries have made a shift to eat up thy holland" (2.2.21–22) explicitly compounds the sexual sense of "Low Countries" with the revolt of the Netherlands against Spanish occupation and the military campaigns in which England was centrally involved in the period leading up to *Othello*—as well as the traffic in cloth to which we will return. At the same time, the occupied Brabant evoked through the name of Brabantio was subjected not only to the familiar sexual equivoques on the Low Countries but to the sexual-territorial language of invasion, occupation, siege warfare, and conquest associated with Brabant in particular as the center of Spanish power there.[18]

Brabantio in the first act of *Othello* accuses the Moor of "witchcraft" ("She is abus'd, stol'n from me, and corrupted / By spells and medicines bought of mountebanks; / For nature so prepost'rously to err . . . / Sans witchcraft could not," 1.3.60–64), in lines that summon the familiar association of witchcraft with Moors and Turks as well as with backward spells—before Othello tells his "story" to the Venetian Senate, in the convincing speech that ends "This only is the witchcraft I have us'd" (1.3.169).[19] And by the end of this scene, the "preposterous" is invoked again in Iago's "If the beam of our lives had not one scale of reason to poise another of sensuality, the blood and baseness of our natures would conduct us to most prepost'rous conclusions" (1.3.326–329), a phrase that gains a different and more ominous resonance as the play turns to tragedy, in his vow to bring a "monstrous birth" to "the world's light" (1.3.404).

But Brabantio himself in this scene also makes the comparison between the sexual occupation of his daughter by a Moor and the Turk's invasion of Cyprus (1.3.210–211), in a context in which what Peter Stallybrass has called "patriarchal territories" readily elided the sexual occupation of a woman with the invasion or occupation of territory as well. It is this combination of bodily, territorial, and military that is repeatedly suggested in the play by the assimilation of Desdemona to the simultaneously military and erotic language of a "land carract" (1.2.50) and an "alarum to love" (2.3.26), and by Othello's inspecting a "fortification" (3.2.5) just before the Temptation Scene that convinces him that his place has been taken by his "lieutenant" ("For sure he fills it up with great ability," 3.3.247) and his own "occupation's gone" (3.3.357).[20] For the name of Brabantio to evoke Brabant as a famously occupied territory in the "Low Countries" would thus be consistent with the combination of sexual and territorial "country matters" that pervades *Othello* itself.

✣

> The moste fayre & famous citie of *Antvverp* . . . the principal in trafike & opulence, not only of this country of *Brabant,* but of all the netherland prouinces.
>
> —Abraham Ortelius, *An epitome of Ortelius his Theater of the vvorld* (ca. 1601)

> The place at *Andwarp* whiche they call the Burse, or at London the Roiall Exchange, and at *Venice la piazza del riuo alto.*
>
> —Jerome Turler, *The Traveler* (1575)

> By debitor and creditor—this counter-caster,
> He (in good time!) must his lieutenant be.
>
> —*Othello* (1.1.31–32)

In the years leading up to *Othello*, references to Brabant abound in English writing,[21] along with engagements with Antwerp, whose famous Burse provided the model for Thomas Gresham's (and the Royal) Exchange in London. The "notable Mart towne, in Brabant, called Antwerpia" (as it was called in the popular collection *Batman vppon Bartholome* in 1582), was a central focus of the increasingly global network of financial, credit, and trade relations as well as military campaigns. The Medici bank of Florence already had agents in "Antwerp and Bergen-op-Zoom" by the mid-fifteenth century. Barabas in Marlowe's *Jew of Malta* has debts owing in "Florence, Venice, Antwerp, London, Seville" (4.1). Even earlier in the sixteenth century, Antwerp, the city that William Cuningham in *The Cosmographical Glasse* (1559) called "the noblest" in "all Europe," had for decades (as Jerry Brotton observes) been "overtaking Venice as the commercial capital of Europe."[22] And—like Venice—it was a major center of book publishing as well.[23]

The global importance of Brabantian Antwerp was also stressed in the well-known *Theatrum orbis terrarum* published in Latin in 1570 by "Abraham Ortelius Citizen of Antwerpe, and Geographer to Philip the Second, king of Spain,"[24] famously used by Marlowe and others. Translated as a whole into English soon after *Othello*, it was not only available in Latin but already redacted in a shorter English *Epitome* in 1601–1603 (Figure 10), whose entry on "BRABANT" described "the most fayre & famous citie of Antwerp lying on the riuer of *Skeld*" as "the principal in trafike & opulence, not only of this country of *Brabant*, but of all the netherland prouinces & inferior to no citie in Christendom," before it went on to mention "Bruxels" (or Brussels, "the court of the Prince"), "Macklyn" (or Mechelen, "the highest court of Law"), and "Louaine" (or Louvain, site of Brabant's famous "vniuersitie").[25] The fuller *Theatrum* description of Brabant, which included it among the dukedoms in the Low Countries that "King Philip, sonne to Charles the fifth, challenged by right of inheritance," likewise stressed the importance of Antwerp ("the most famous mart . . . of all *Europe*") and went on to list the other most notable Brabantian cities, including Brussels (where "for the most part resideth the Prince"), Louvain ("habitation of the Muses"), "Machelen" (or Mechelen, "famous for the court of Parliament here"), 's-Hertogenbosch, "Bergen ap Zoom" (or Bergen-op-Zoom), Breda (where "stands the Palace of the Earles of *Nassau*"), "Maestright" (or Maastricht, "a large, populous, and rich citie, which though it seemeth to lie without the bounds of *Brabant*, acknowledgeth the Duke of *Brabant* as her soueraigne Lord"), Liere,

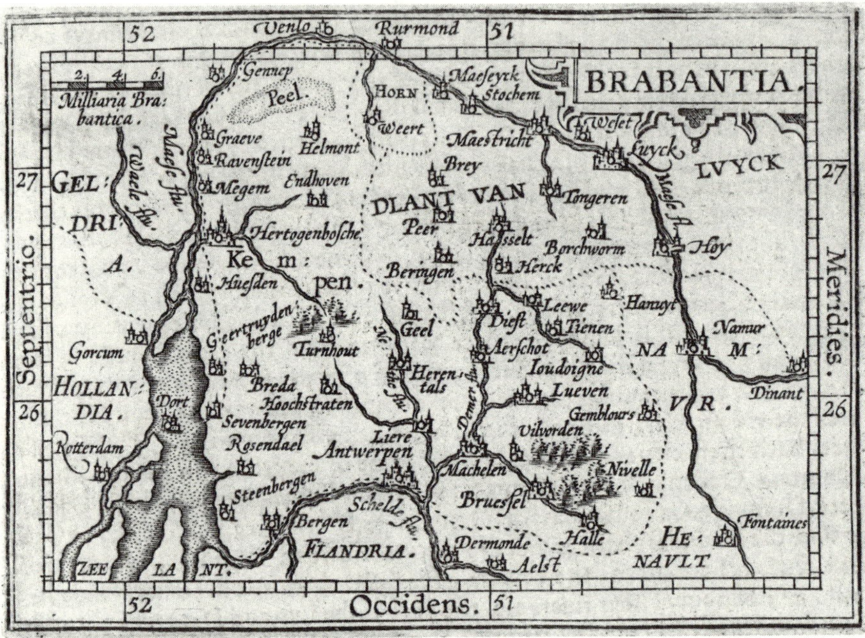


Figure 10. Map of Brabant (Brabantia) in Abraham Ortelius, *An epitome of Ortelius his Theater of the vvorld*. London (i.e., Antwerp), 1603. By permission of the Huntington Library.

Vilvoorde, Diest, and the "Freetownes" of Brabant, includng Turnhout and Hoogstraten (*Theatrum*, 34ff.). All of these names and more resonated in repeated English reports of and from Brabant in the period leading up to *Othello*, including Breda, Bergen-op-Zoom, Mechelen, and Turnhout in relation to English involvement in the Low Countries' military campaigns. At the same time, the strategic location of Spanish power in the Low Countries just across the English Channel (Figure 11) made it a repeated source of invasion fears in England as well.

Brabant was also prominently described in Lodovico Guicciardini's much-read description of the Low Countries, which Ortelius cites as one of his own principal sources (where "you shall not only reade of these places, but euen behold them with your eyes, so curiously hath he described them"). Guicciardini was himself an example of the more global geographical networks of the period. A Florentine by birth and nephew of Francesco Guicciardini, author of a history of Florence and the history of Italy translated into

Figure 11. Frans Hogenberg, *Leo Belgicus* (1583). By permission of Den Haag, Koninklijke Bibliotheek, shelf number KW 1710 B 11.

English by Geoffrey Fenton in 1579,[26] he lived primarily as a merchant and writer in Antwerp, where he died in 1589. And it was in Antwerp that he published his influential account of the Low Countries in 1567, as *Descrittione di M. Lodovico Gvicciardini patritio fiorentino, di tvtti i Paesi Bassi, altrimenti detti Germania Inferiore.*

The "epitome" of Guiccciardini—published in English in 1593 as *The description of the Low countreys and of the prouinces thereof, gathered into an epitome out of the historie of Lodouico Guicchardini*—provided a detailed description of Brabant, from its geographical extent to the importance of its principal cities, including Louvain and Brussels (where is "also resident, the Court Feudale of Brabant"). But it was most lavish in its description of Antwerp and its famous Burse (whose name it explains as "purse" in ways suggestive for Iago's "Put money in thy purse"), the model in England of

Gresham's Burse in Lombard Street, still known by that name despite its renaming as the Royal Exchange by Queen Elizabeth.[27]

This "epitome" of Guicciardini on Brabant details "the causes of the great wealth that Andwerp is grown to," including its famous "Marts," and its key position in relation to global "traffique." Its description of the change "in the yeare 1503," when "the Portugales began to bring spices out of their *Indias*, and from *Calicut* into *Portugale*, & from thence to *Andwerp*, which before that time were wont to be broght by the Red sea to *Barnt* & thence to *Alexandria*, & so to *Venice*" (27), provides a contemporary account of the early sixteenth-century shift from Venice to Antwerp that Jerry Brotton and others record. Its report of how, after 1516, Antwerp became "greatly frequented" by "diuers Marchants strangers," including "Spaniards and Italians," who "departed from *Bruges* to go and dwell at *Andwerp*" (27), likewise provides a contemporary remarking of the shift from Bruges in Flanders (medieval site of English "traffique" and Florentine bank branches) to Antwerp in Brabant that is noted by modern economic historians as well as by Fernand Braudel, who observes that Antwerp became "the center of the *entire* international economy, something Bruges had never been even at its height."[28] And it describes in detail the "Marchandice" coming out of "dyuers Countryes to Andwerpe" and "sent into those Countries from Andwerp," including "Barbarie" and "Tapistrie of Turkie" and other goods from Venice (34), cloth and other commodities from Florence, and goods coming "by Sea out of England itselfe" (34–38), commenting that "the traffique between England and the Low countryes, of that which is reciproquely bought & sold betweene these two Nations, amounteth yearly to aboue twelue Millions of crownes, in such sort that hardlye can they liue the one nation without the other" (40).

English writing in the decades before *Othello* is likewise filled with references to Antwerp in Brabant and its famous Burse. Andrew Borde's *Introduction to Knowledge* (ca. 1548) observes in its chapter on "Braban" (which also notes its reputation for "good fellowes the whyche wyll drynke all out") that "Handwarp" or Antwerp is "a well-favoured marchaunt towne," with a fine "Burse" and "fayre place" for "englyshe marchauntes."[29] George Gascoigne's *Glass of Government* (1573/5), in a scene set in Antwerp (1.2), includes "going towardes the *Bowrce* [i.e., Burse] to harken of entertainment."[30] *Thomas Lord Cromwell* by "W.S."—classed among Shakespeare's "apocryphal plays" and advertising on the title page of its 1602 printing, "As it hath beene sundrie times *publikely Acted* by the Right Honorable the Lord Chamberlaine *his*

*Servants*," that is, Shakespeare's company—asks the audience to imagine "Young Cromwell, / In *Antwarpe* Ledger for the English Marchantes" with "*Cromwell in his study with bagges of money before him casting account.*"[31]

"Brabant"—as the locus of Antwerp and its famous Burse—was thus identified with accounting and "credit" as well as with commodities, "traffique," money, and the "purse," all important parts of the cash and credit nexus sounded in *Othello.* Gresham himself had increasingly become head of his family's commercial operations in Brabant, in Antwerp as well as in Brussels, trading not only in cloth but in armory and weapons and functioning, as military historians note, as Elizabeth's mid-century arms supplier.[32] He served as royal agent in the Netherlands in 1551 at "a particularly critical juncture in the operations of the English crown on the Antwerp money market" and worked to reduce English royal indebtedness at Antwerp, both in the reign of Edward VI and intermittently during the reign of Mary I (which ended with "the English crown's debts at Antwerp again hovering about the third of a million pounds sterling mark"),[33] before finally succeeding, under Elizabeth, in all but eliminating the English crown's debts to Antwerp financiers. For "the first third of her reign," as Ceri Sullivan writes in *The Rhetoric of Credit,* Elizabeth "looked to the continent's money markets, in particular to Antwerp," where Gresham "fostered her credit by careful attention to repayment on due dates, in the meantime manipulating exchange rates in a successful effort to reduce the crown's overall debt."[34] Brabant—with its financial center at Antwerp—was thus central to the network of global "credit" in which not only Florence and Venice but also England itself were crucially involved.

Gresham's Burse or Exchange in London—opened in 1568 and renamed the Royal Exchange by Elizabeth in 1571—was not only called the "Burse" in ways that directly recalled Antwerp's (on which it was modeled) but was repeatedly mentioned in descriptions of the Turk, as well as compared to the Rialto in Venice. John Lyly still called it the "Burse" in his description in *Euphues and his England* (1580) of the "*Burse* which they call the *Royall Exchange,* for the meeting of Merchants of all countries, where any traffique is to be had," and (like many later texts) Holinshed was still referring to Gresham's "Burse" in 1587. Hugh Gough, who dedicated to Gresham his 1569 translation of Bartolomej Georgijevic's *The ofspring of the house of Ottomanno,* wrote in his dedication not only of the "great Turkes power" and the Ottoman "Empire" that "hath spredde it selfe so farre" but also of "the infinite riches geuen to the buildinge of that princely woorke, commonly called the Burse" in London. The 1585 translation of Nicolas de Nicolay's *The nauigations, peregrinations and voyages, made into Turkie* included both Antwerp's Burse and Gresham's in its description of the "Burse" where merchants assemble in a tributory city to the Turk, as they do at the "burse of Antwerp, & royal exchange of London" (37). Jerome Turler's *The Traveler* (1575) combined in a single sequence "the place at *Andwarp* whiche they call the Burse, or at London the Roiall Exchange, and at *Venice la piazza del riuo alto*,"[35] while Robert Greene, in his 1590 translation of *The Royal Exchange* ("written in Italian, and dedicated to the Signorie of Venice"), claimed in its prefatory address "To the right honourable Cittizens of the Cittie of London" that the "Exchange in London, euerie way duelie weyed, excelleth all the Burse reales in the world."

The history of the "Burse" or "Exchange" testified not only to the importance of Antwerp for London but also to the major role of those who had come from Brabant to England. The architect of Gresham's Exchange—Hendryck van Paesschen—was based in Antwerp (where he built fortifications and other structures) and responsible for the Duke of Brabant's palace in Brussels.[36] But at the same time as the Exchange "retained its affiliation with Antwerp," of whose Burse it was a copy, "London's appropriation of the architecture that symbolized Antwerp's economic progress"—particularly when it was renamed the Royal Exchange—"signaled to London's merchants and their prosperous northern European neighbors that London was prepared to surpass Antwerp's more powerful position in an increasingly global world market."[37]

Plays and other works before and contemporary with *Othello* likewise not only cite or include Gresham's Burse or the Royal Exchange but also its "global" interconnections. The "Exchange" is cited in relation to "Usury" (Sc.17.9–10) in a plot involving a Levantine Jew and Italian merchant who threatens to "turn Turk" (as well as reference to Venice and other far-flung places) in *The Three Ladies of London* by Robert Wilson, who was originally associated with Leicester's Men and with "Will Kempe visited Leicester and a company of his old patron's players in 1585–1586 while Leicester was in the Low Countries."[38] Thomas Nashe in *Pierce Penilesse* (1592) describes an old "Usurer" at the Exchange, in a passage that begins with its cosmopolitan "confusion of languages."[39] And an entire scene (1.3) is set in the Exchange (alternately called the Burse) in William Haughton's *Englishmen for My Money* (1598), whose preoccupation with both commerce and sexual traffic or low "country matters" includes wordplay on the keeping of "accounts"

(1.1.147–148) that depends on the bawdy senses of "[ac]count." The broader global context of Haughton's city comedy includes references to the Turk (e.g., 4.1.285) and three merchant-suitors from outside England—a Frenchman, an Italian, and a "Dutchman" named "Vandalle" in the 1616 Quarto, who refers to "Antwerp" where "cloth" is "dear" (2.3.6), is described in stereotypes that include the "drunken" Dutch (3.2.137), and speaks in "Dutch-French terms" (2.3.3) that suggest the hybrid language of Brabant (including a Spanish "diabolo," 5.1.181). The scene (1.3) that Haughton sets in London's Burse or Exchange includes not only the "Dutchman," "Frenchman," and "Italian" but also a Spanish merchant, the play's Portuguese usurer-father, and other merchants and "Strangers." And it is filled with references to vessels "laden with the wealth of ample Spain" (1.3.33), far-flung credit networks (including a "bill of exchange," 1.3.42), a "factor" in "Venice" (1.3.246), and "Barbary sugar" (1.3.101) with other "commodities" on ships in the Mediterranean headed to "Turkey" but reportedly "set upon" by "Spanish-galley pirates" (1.3.107–113)—a danger ultimately avoided by a storm that for audiences would recall the 1588 Armada (to which we will return, since it crucially involved Spanish-occupied Brabant as well).[40]

Earlier in the same year (1604) as the November performance of *Othello* at the court of King James—whose prior coronation in 1603 had been held on Sant'Iago's Day (July 25)—James's royal entry into London on March 15 included an arch erected near or "by the Royall Exchange" by the "Dutch" community (a capacious term that included exiles from Brabant as well as other parts of the Low Countries). James "was the first king for whom the Royal Exchange was incorporated into a royal progress and he was the first whose royal progress included an arch sponsored by the Dutch stranger community."[41] The architect of the arch was a Protestant refugee from 's-Hertogenbosch in Brabant who had arrived in England in 1567. The account in Dekker's "The Magnificent Entertainment: Given to King James" (1604) moves from the Italians' pageant (or "*Italian* shore") to "the Land of the 17. Provinces" (the original Burgundian lands of the Habsburg Netherlands), where the "*Belgians*" of the pageant describe themselves as "a Nation banisht from our owne Cradles" (664–701), a reminder of the exile that is simultaneously reflected in their address to the king and "implicit request that their status as strangers in the realm be accommodated and protected."[42] At the same time, with London's Royal Exchange in the immediate background, the backside of the Dutch arch featured the Antwerp Burse, symbol of both cultural and commercial exchange with London, foreshortening "the distance between Antwerp and London and their commercial centers" and "challenging the new king" to "experience London as a 'world city'" through that striking juxtaposition.[43]

Soon after *Othello*, the Exchange also figured prominently in Thomas Heywood's *If You Know Not Me, You Know Nobody* (1605–1606)—which included "Brabant" in Part 1 as part of the dominions of England's Queen Mary I and Spain's Philip II, and cited in Part 2 the "great Burse in Antwerpe" as that which most resembles "Greshams Burse" in "Lumber-street" (or Lombard Street), in a plot preoccupied with "cash" and "credit" that featured Gresham himself as a major character.[44] Published in 1606 but possibly performed as early as 1604–1605, its famously unhistorical connection of Gresham with Morocco on the Barbary Coast—when his actual history was so bound up with Antwerp in Brabant (where he "made his money carrying on his father's business in the English cloth trade"[45] as well as managing England's "credit")—not only redirects attention from Antwerp as London's rival but reflects the more global connections of which *Othello* itself was a part. As Jean E. Howard observes, the play's unhistorical association of Gresham with North Africa and the Levant "anachronistically connects Gresham to events that primarily occurred after his death, namely, the rise of the chartered companies, especially the Turkey Company in 1581, the Barbary Company in 1585, and the Levant Company in 1592. . . . If the historical Gresham was not directly connected to this trade, by 1605 Heywood nonetheless is not able to separate the Royal Exchange—and hence its builder—from such associations."[46] Gresham's "pearl"—recalling the biblical "pearl of great price" that figures so strikingly in *Othello* (5.2.347)—not only foregrounds that biblical figure but highlights the exoticism and lavish expenditure such global traffic could involve,[47] while the play's two main events, the building of the Royal Exchange and defeat of the Armada, connect this more far-flung global network to London's rivalry with Antwerp and the invasion threat from Spain in which Spanish-occupied Brabant so strategically figured.

Antwerp in Brabant was at the same time central to the language of accounting and double-entry bookkeeping foregrounded at the beginning of *Othello*, in the lines on the "arithmetician" (1.1.19) Cassio as both "countercaster" and "debitor and creditor" (1.1.31)—a language that continues in Iago's "I stand accomptant [i.e., accountant] for as great a sin" (2.1.293) and Othello's invoking of a final judgement, audit, or "compt" (5.2.273). "Debitor and creditor" (the English term for double-entry accounting) was identified not only with Florence, where the term for the ledger was *libro dei debitori e creditori*, and with Venice in its facing-pages form, but also with Antwerp, where Simon Stevin (who would go on to apply the new "arithmetic" to military science and write his own double-entry treatise) began as a "bookkeeper and cashier." Double entry itself was a product of increasingly global networks of commerce and "credit transactions" and the need to control agents, factors, or "lieutenants," following the rise of the "sedentary" merchant who used "partners, agents or correspondents to secure representation abroad."[48] Venetian Alvise Casanova's manual on double-entry bookkeeping, published in 1559 using the "Venetian method" of facing debits and credits, included a "ledger [that] follows the mercantile ventures of two brothers from Antwerp . . . when they come to Venice to open a branch of the family business."[49]

Antwerp—the commercial center whose Burse was the model for London's Exchange—was crucial to the transmission of "debitor and creditor" or double-entry accounting to England. Tuscan Luca Pacioli's *Summa de arithmetica, geometria, proportioni et proportionalità* (Venice, 1494)—the text that made him the "father of double-entry bookkeeping" through its codification of long-standing practice in Venice, Florence, and elsewhere—was redacted in 1543 by Antwerp merchant Jan Ympyn Christoffels, who also passed on Pacioli's urging of accountants to put "at the head of the Inventory a Cross and the name of Jesus or some other Christian symbol to distinguish you from Turks, Jews and others."[50] This influential redaction at Antwerp was quickly translated into French and then into English, as *How to Kepe a Boke of Accomptes* (1547). And it was incorporated by James Peele (father of Shakespeare's fellow-dramatist George Peele) into *How to Keepe a Perfect Reconyng after the order of the moste worthie and notable accompte, of Debitour and Creditour* (1553), in turn expanded in *The Pathe waye to Perfectnes, in th'Accomptes of Debitour, and Creditour* (1569). Antwerp also produced Valentin Mennher de Kempten's *Practique . . . pour cyfrer et tenire Liures de Compte* (1550), a work by this "teacher in Antwerp" that was well "known and often quoted in England"; John Weddington's *Howe to kepe Merchantes Bokes of accomptes. After the order of Debitor and Creditor* (Antwerp, 1567); and Jan de Raeymaker's *Comptes pour les Cassiers* (Antwerp, 1603), a "small manual of commercial arithmetic" published for "Cashiers."[51] And in England, John Mellis's *Briefe Instruction and Maner how to Keepe Bookes of Accompts after the order of Debitor and Creditor* (1588)—which revised the earliest English version of Pacioli—repeatedly stressed (like other "debitor and creditor" treatises) the crucial importance of an account's "Fidelitie" as well as "honesty" and "truth" (10), a language that was applied in the period to the fidelity and honesty of the female sexual (ac)count as well.[52]

In a play set in Venice where Florentine Cassio—called both an "arithmetician" and "debitor and creditor" (1.1.19, 31)—is finally "cashier'd" (2.3.375), and Iago's plan to undo Desdemona's "credit" (2.3.359) with the Moor succeeds through his provision of a false account that alleges her adulterous preference for her "country forms" (3.3.237), this set of global connections between Florence, Venice, Antwerp in the Low Countries, and London (where the theater and brothel district itself was a locus of arithmetic and "debitor and creditor" accounting)[53] is an important part of the broader interconnections between *Othello* and Brabant, including in relation to the sexual "Low Countries," to which we will return.

ര

> "The Martyrdome and burning of William Tyndale in Brabant."
> —Illustration in *The whole workes of W. Tyndall, Iohn Frith, and Doct. [Robert] Barnes, three worthy martyrs* (1573)

> Cardinall *Poole* came out of *Brabant* into *England*, and . . . was by Parliament restored to hys olde dignitie, that he was put from by King *Henrie*.
> —John Stow, *The chronicles of England* (1580)

> My departure oute of *Brabante*, (myne owne naturall Countrey) into youre Maiesties Realme of *Englande* . . . to escape the handes of the bloud-thirsty.
> —Jan van der Noot, *Theatre for Voluptuous Worldlings* (1569)

There were, however, even further connections of different kinds between England and Brabant throughout the century leading up to *Othello*, including with regard to the reign of Mary and Philip that took England back to Catholicism after Henry VIII's break with Rome, the pouring of Brabantian refugees into England, the broader geopolitics of the threat from the Ottoman Turk, and fears in England of a Spanish invasion. Thomas Nashe begins *The Unfortunate Traveller* (1594) by setting it "About that time that the terror of the world, and feauer quartan of the French *Henrie* the eight . . . aduanced his standard against the two hundred and fifite towers of *Turney* and *Turwin*, and had the Emperour and all the nobility of Flanders,

Holland, and Brabant as mercenarie attendants." Anne Boleyn was sent as a teenager in 1513 to the prestigious Habsburg court of Margaret of Austria in Mechelen between Antwerp and Brussels, the court in Brabant in which Margaret ruled as governor of the Netherlands and the future Habsburg Holy Roman Emperor Charles V was brought up.[54] In the wake of the Reformation, Brabant figured centrally in the history of religious and doctrinal conflicts. It was the site, for example, of the martyrdom of William Tyndale, who was captured in Antwerp and put to death for heresy in 1536 at Vilvoorde, near Brussels, memorialized in the Protestant polemics of John Bale and others and in an illustration of "The Martyrdome and burning of William Tyndale in Brabant" that accompanied the account from Foxe's *Acts and Monuments*, in a collection of martyrdoms and sufferings among "infidells" in Brabant in 1573. On the opposite side of the religious divide, John Donne's maternal grandfather, the Catholic playwright and epigrammatist John Heywood, went into exile to Brabant in 1564, when a commission was set up to enforce the Act of Uniformity against Catholics during Elizabeth's reign.[55]

John Stow's *The Chronicles of England* (1580)—which refers repeatedly to the long history of "English Marchants goodes in Brabant" (252) and the residence in Brabant of Charles V, the Holy Roman Emperor—includes Brabant among the united dominions of Charles's son Philip and England's "Queene Mary" (1092), at their marriage in 1554 on "Saint James day" (July 25, the feast day of "Sant'Iago," Spain's patron saint). Stow notes as well that as part of the restoration of Catholicism to England, "Cardinall *Poole* came out of *Brabant* into *England,* and . . . was by Parliament restored to hys olde dignitie, that he was put from by King *Henrie*" (1093). Brabant had already been the place of Philip's triumphal entry into Antwerp as ruler of the Netherlands in 1549. And Brabant was repeatedly the center of attention during Mary's reign, since Philip (about whose prolonged absence Mary herself was bitter) resided in Brussels, rather than England, holding court from there as sovereign of the Netherlands even during England's loss of Calais in 1558, as well as negotiating from Brussels the far-flung Habsburg engagements with the Turk.[56] (The crucial triangulation of Brabant, England, and engagements with the Turk was dramatically foregrounded in relation to Philip and Mary's union, since the "Tunis tapestries" celebrating Charles V's victory over the Ottoman Barbarossa in Tunis in 1535, commissioned in Brussels by Charles's sister the Regent Mary of Hungary, were made in Brussels with silk thread from Granada, facilitated by an Antwerp financier, and sent from Brussels to London for their first public appearance at their wedding, before being displayed in Antwerp and Brussels and finally hung in Philip's palace in Spain in 1556.)[57] As historian M. J. Rodríguez-Salgado observes, "Philip's evident preference for the Netherlands drove a deeper wedge between him and his English subjects," because of his desire to protect Habsburg interests there.[58] In 1556, when Charles V abdicated in favor of his son, Philip II was declared king of Spain in Brussels, the center in Brabant of Habsburg rule, where he also was when Mary died in 1558. Even his subsequent agreement to propose marriage to Elizabeth was made from Brabant.[59]

In the decades of religious struggle between Catholic and Protestant in the Low Countries as well as England, Brabant was also a major source of "Dutch" refugees flooding into London—from artisans like "Philip Brabant the weaver" in Foxe's *Actes and Monuments* to writers like Jan van der Noot, who began his *Theatre for Voluptuous Worldlings* (1569) with a dedication to Queen Elizabeth that records "my departure oute of *Brabante*, (myne owne naturall Countrey) into youre Maiesties Realme of *Englande* . . . as well for that I would not beholde the abhominations of the Romyshe Antechrist, as to escape the handes of the bloud-thirsty" (sig. Aiiir).[60] As Marjorie Rubright notes in *Doppelgänger Dilemmas: Anglo-Dutch Relations in Early Modern English Literature and Culture*, "Among the immigrants whose places of origin are recorded in the historical record, Brabant (including the city of Antwerp), is the 'most frequently mentioned,'" and "immigrants from Antwerp would go on to play an important role in the management of the Dutch, French, and Italian Churches in London during the second half of the sixteenth century."[61] Ortelius's nephew Emanuel van Meteren of Antwerp, whose influential *Historia Belgica* was frequently cited by English writers, spent most of his life in England and (as Andrew Pettegree observes) was involved with the stranger churches.[62] Still others—like "Hans Pemable of Antwerp," who listed "religion" and "work" as the reason for his coming to England—were examined out of concern about the legitimacy of those who "pretend to be here for their conscience,"[63] a fear that, decades later, would be part of the Dutch Church Libel of 1593, which included the charge of immigrants "counterfeiting religion" to enable their "flight" to England (line 42), as well as their being "infected" with "Spanish gold" (lines 43–45) and "using membership in the Dutch Church as a cover for all manner of nefarious activities,"[64] including usury and spying.

In the years leading up to *Othello*, however, in ways that suggest why Brabant is evoked in a play preoccupied with the Turk, Brabant was not only the focus of attention in England as a site of Protestant struggle against

Spanish occupation, but repeatedly foregrounded as part of the more global network of Spain's interconnected dominions and military engagements—including against the Turk at Cyprus and Lepanto. The revolt of Brabant and the Low Countries against Spanish occupation started in 1566 when the minor nobility presented Philip II's designated regent of the Netherlands, his half-sister Margaret of Parma, with a petition for religious toleration (known as the "Request"), and the so-called Iconoclastic Fury or smashing of Catholic images broke out at Antwerp and other parts of Brabant, including Breda, 's-Hertogenbosch, Mechelen, and Turnhout.[65] It soon led to Philip's sending "the Duke of Alva to Brussels with a force of 10,000 men to take control and execute reprisals."[66] But these and ensuing events in Brabant and the Low Countries were also part of a much broader geopolitical context that included the Turk in the Mediterranean and Adriatic, the Moors of North Africa, and the Moriscos or converted Moors of Spain itself.[67] Even in the crucial initial period, Philip II's plans to make a personal visit to the Low Countries in 1565 had to be suspended because of the siege of Malta, and in 1566, when "the Turks' main effort for the year would be directed against Hungary, leaving the west Mediterranean relatively safe and the king free at last to deal with some of his other problems," Philip's intention to visit as well as "send financial and military assistance to the government in Brussels" was interrupted by news of the nobility's petition.[68]

In the second half of the century, "the Low Countries became the scene of the most ruthless warfare which western Europe had ever seen," while "the Mediterranean was the scene of battles between Christian and Turk, both by sea and land."[69] Of the close interrelationship between the campaigns in these widely separated territories, historian Geoffrey Parker notes in *The Army of Flanders and the Spanish Road* that "in 1567 . . . the Duke of Alva drew the 8,652 Spanish infantry that he led to the Netherlands from the *tercios* stationed in Sicily, Naples, Sardinia and Milan and brought 7,614 new recruits from Spain (*bisoños*) to replace them. In 1571 these troops, now seasoned and experienced themselves, boarded the galleys of both Philip and Venice and featured prominently at the victory of Lepanto against the Turks. Two years later, 5,000 of them marched to the Netherlands to fight the Dutch."[70] In more detail, Parker also writes of these far-flung and costly military engagements:

> An unfavourable international situation, and especially the campaigns of the Turkish fleet in the Mediterranean, obliged Philip II

> to temporize and offer concessions in the Netherlands between 1559 and 1566. The decision of Sultan Suleiman to campaign in Hungary, and his death there, in 1566 reduced the pressure on Spain's Mediterranean possessions and enabled Philip II to send the Duke of Alva and 10,000 veterans from the garrisons of Italy to the Netherlands the following year. . . . Although it took longer and cost more than expected, Alva managed to defeat an invasion of the Netherlands by William of Orange and his allies before the Ottomans attacked again. The duke defeated the last rebel army at the end of 1568 and paid off most of his victorious troops, albeit at inordinate cost, the following year. The Netherlands almost "paid their own way" in 1570 and 1571 . . . to the delight of Philip II who faced the revolt of the moriscos and a new phase of Turkish aggression in the Mediterranean: both made heavy demands on his treasury. The main fleet that fought at Lepanto cost Spain 2.5 million florins.[71]

Brian M. Downing observes, in *The Military Revolution and Political Change*, that the Low Countries thus "benefited from Turkish attacks in the Mediterranean and revolts in Spain, which diverted Habsburg soldiers from the northern fronts"; and writes with regard to the Morisco revolt in Spain and the Turkish threat (including to Cyprus, the threat from the Turk that is foregrounded in *Othello*):

> Spain's attention was diverted from the Dutch Revolt by another revolt, this one from the remaining Moors in southern Spain. The Morisco Revolt, as it is called, was thought to signal a Turkish invasion. Though this was not forthcoming, the Porte being content with annexing Cyprus from Venice, the rebellion nonetheless altered strategy in Madrid, and resources had to be diverted at a critical period in the Dutch Revolt. In 1574 the Turks (after, but not necessarily because of, Dutch encouragement) went over to the offensive in the Mediterranean, seizing Tunis and requiring a withdrawal of resources from the Army of Flanders. This strain on Spanish resources led to complete fiscal collapse and the securing of Dutch independence, at least for a while.[72]

As Jonathan I. Israel records in *The Dutch Republic*, "The combined burden of paying for the war against the rebels in the Netherlands and that against the Ottomans in the Mediterranean had, by the autumn of 1575, stretched Philip II's finances to the point where he could no longer service his mounting debt to his Genoese bankers."[73] Unable to pay the soldiers of his Army of Flanders unless he abandoned his defense of the Mediterranean (something he was unwilling to contemplate), he made the decision to break credit with his bankers, from whom he was unable to obtain more loans. And after abortive peace negotiations at Breda in Brabant (which Philip entered into in part because the reconquest of Tunis by the Turkish fleet in 1574 once again focused his attention on the Mediterranean), a Spanish Decree of Bankruptcy was issued in September of 1575.[74]

Not just modern historians but Shakespeare's own contemporaries repeatedly commented on this extended theater of war and the cash and credit crises it engendered, including with regard to the "Spanish Fury" in 1576 of unpaid, mutineering Spanish soldiers in Antwerp and elsewhere in Brabant. Among other texts, *A discourse of the vsage of the English fugitives, by the Spaniard* (1595), issued anonymously but likely authored by Sir Lewis Lewkenor, whose 1599 translation of Gasparo Contarini's *De magistratibus et republica Venetorum* (as *The Commonwealth and Government of Venice*) is thought to have influenced Shakespeare's representation of Venice, described the vast extent as well as cost of Spain's widespread territories and military engagements—from the Indies to the "Low countries" (which have "cost him one with another two millyons and more yeerely above the revenuewe and other commodities received thereout") to Portugal, Naples, Sicily, and campaigns against the "Turke" (of "whome hee standeth mightily in feare")—commenting that "his provinces stande so seuered and disunited, that the transporting of his Navie from one to another is infinite chargeable vnto him."[75] Another English tract, published just after Philip II's third 1596 Decree of Bankruptcy, also described the extraordinary cost of Spain's far-flung campaigns.[76]

ꟹ

> The noble citie of *Antwerpe* most tyrannously and most lamentably was thus taken, burnt and spoyled by the Spaniards, euen then the same day *Don Iohn de Austria* the bastard sonne of *Charles* the 5. Emperour . . . came into the *Netherlands* to gouerne the same.
>
> —Emanuel van Meteren, *A true discourse historicall, of the succeeding gouernours in the Netherlands,* trans. Churchard and Robinson (1602)

> "Is not the Lowe Countries the Rise, by which shee [i.e., Spain] may leape into England?"
>
> —Robert Devereux, second Earl of Essex, "Apologie" (1598)

The interconnected sites of war as well as the broad territorial reach of the Habsburg dominions were likewise reflected in the major figures involved in the struggles in Brabant itself, in ways repeatedly recorded in texts published in England prior to *Othello*. Margaret of Parma, the illegitimate daughter of Charles V who resided as regent at the court in Brussels, was first married to Alessandro de' Medici, Duke of Florence, and then (after his murder) to Ottavio Farnese, the Italian Duke of Parma, and ultimately retired to Italy from Brabant. The Duke of Alva (or Alba)—a knight of the order of Santiago who had fought against the Turk under Charles V—marched his soldiers in 1567 across what became known as "the Spanish Road," Philip II's territories (and those of his allies) from Lombardy in northern Italy to Brussels in Brabant, stopping in Lorraine to celebrate the Feast of Sant'Iago on July 25.[77] Don John of Austria, illegitimate son of Charles V and half-brother of Philip II, joined the Knights Templars in the relief of Malta (1565), led the Spanish forces against the revolt of the Moriscos in Spain in 1568–1569, was made admiral of the Spanish and Austrian fleet after the Turk's conquest of Cyprus, and led the Christian forces to victory against the Turk at the Battle of Lepanto in 1571 (the event celebrated—but not without denigrating Don John as a "forraine Papist bastard"—in the *Lepanto* of King James himself, published in Edinburgh in 1591 and again in London in 1603 to commemorate James's succession).[78] Don John temporarily conquered Tunis in 1573 and continued to fight Muslim pirates in the Mediterranean from 1572 to 1574, but (hoping ultimately to invade England and marry the captive Mary Stuart) was appointed governor of the Netherlands in 1576, the year of the violent sack of Antwerp that provoked so many outraged English responses. The Duke of Parma (Margaret's son Alessandro Farnese), who was born in Rome, was sent as a child to the court of Philip II of Spain in Brussels in Brabant, fought successfully against the Turk at Lepanto, and became (after Don John's death in 1578) the new governor-general of the Netherlands, whose victories included the successful siege of Antwerp in 1585 that led to even more Brabantian refugees in London.

In the decades leading up to *Othello*, Brabant was not only a source of refugees and a battlefield between Protestant and Catholic but the focus of ongoing anxiety in England regarding possible Spanish invasion from across the Channel. As a result of Alva's attempts to stamp out heresy, "some 60,000 Protestants fled abroad, to England, France, and Germany," and "the Protestants who arrived in London as well as English merchants who were working in Antwerp (England's main trading partner) did much to publish the horrors of the Duke of Alva's regime."[79] Brussels became the center of Alva's repressive rule and the location of the notorious "Council of Troubles" or "Council of Blood," as it was popularly known. Antwerp had a bronze statue in honor of Alva erected by its governor. And Mechelen (where Anne Boleyn had been sent as a maid of honor at the Habsburg court) was brutally sacked in 1572 after it welcomed the troops of Prince William of Orange, prompting the surrender of other rebellious towns in Brabant and Flanders. In the decades that followed, St. Geertruidenberg in Brabant was captured by the Orangists in 1573, taken by the Spanish in 1589, and recaptured by the Dutch in 1593. In 1588 it had been betrayed to Parma by the English garrison.[80] Antwerp was subjected to the "Spanish Fury" of 1576 and finally fell after Parma's siege in 1585. Vilvoorde was captured by Parma in 1584, as part of his strategy to isolate Antwerp and the surviving rebel centers in Brabant, while Grave in Brabant was recaptured by the Spanish in 1586. And even closer to the date of *Othello*, Hoogstraten in Brabant was the site of a famous mutiny in 1602, and the Dutch lay siege to 's-Hertogenbosch in 1603.[81]

Brussels, as the center of Habsburg rule in Brabant, repeatedly figured over many years in English accounts of Spanish occupation, including as the court of Charles V, Philip II, and Margaret of Parma and the locus of Don John's "joyeux entrée" as the new governor of the Netherlands in 1576,[82] after years of fighting the Turk. It was the site of the "Union of Brussels" between the Spanish authority and leaders of the revolt in 1577, but in 1585 was also besieged and taken by Parma. It was Parma's center of power in the 1588 Armada invasion scare. And throughout the 1590s—as R. B. Wernham has recounted in *The Return of the Armadas*—it was the center of Habsburg power from which other plots and potential invasions were coordinated. The accusation by the Earl of Essex against the queen's Portuguese-born physician Roderigo Lopez for plotting to poison her (for which he was executed in 1594) crucially involved Brussels—since it implicated Philip II's principal ministers there. Another plot against Elizabeth's life—"devised at Brussels by a number of English exiles maintained there at the King of Spain's charge"—was uncovered that same year.[83] In 1596, Calais had been taken for Spain by the troops of the archduke Albert, who ruled from Brussels, and fears were aroused of a new Armada in revenge for the sack of Cadiz in which Anglo-Dutch troops from the Low

Countries were involved. Another Armada scare was sounded in 1597, involving mistaken reports of English and Dutch ships. In 1598, the Treaty of Vervins that made peace between Spain and France was negotiated by the archduke in Brussels, where English spies were dispatched to gather information on this and other events crucial to England. Elizabeth herself also insisted on negotiating with the archduke who ruled from Brabant.[84]

In 1599—after Philip II's death—Brussels in Brabant became even more alarmingly the center of the rule of Philip's daughter the Infanta Isabella, who after marrying Archduke Albert and arriving there from Spain as his co-regent, became the focus of her brother Philip III's desire to act on her claim to England itself. Isabella's claim to the throne of England—as a more legitimate descendant of John of Gaunt than the "bastard" Tudor-Stuart line—had already been advanced by Philip II in Spain, fueling the earlier fears of an Armada invasion to enforce it. And it had been prominently put forward in *A Conference about the Next Succession to the Crowne of Inglande* (printed in Antwerp under the pseudonym R. Doleman in 1594 but commonly ascribed to Robert Parsons, leader of the English Jesuits) as greater than that of Scottish James and other potential claimants.[85] Isabella's move from Spain to a position of power in Brabant across the Channel only strengthened that feared threat. As Susan Doran comments in "James VI and the English Succession": "As a result of *A Conference* James came to believe he might well have to fight for the English throne on Elizabeth's death" and "This anxiety was intensified in 1599 when the Infanta Isabella arrived in Brussels with her new husband Albert to be joint sovereign rulers of the Spanish Netherlands, because it would be relatively easy for them to send troops to England from that geographical base."[86]

The year 1599 saw an even more dramatic "Armada" scare in England, where "reports of the armada's imminent arrival grew ever more strident," "London was awash with rumours," and expectations of "a major landing of the Spanish-Netherlands army" led to proposals of building "a bridge of boats across the Thames . . . 'in apeish imitation of Antwerp'" in 1585.[87] Though this so-called Invisible Armada turned out to be a false alarm, this alarm was sounded in the same year as England was unsettled by the rebellion in Ireland (to which Essex was dispatched, and a substantial number of English troops were redirected from the Low Countries), where Tyrone was "writing to Philip III of Spain as 'Your Majesty's faithful servant.'"[88] Essex himself—who had accompanied his stepfather Leicester to the Low Countries in 1585 (where he was appointed "colonel-general of the cavalry"), sought military advice from Sir Roger Williams, and was a major supporter of Dutch interests in England, as well as maintaining correspondents in Florence and agents in Venice—wrote, "Is not the Lowe Countries the Rise, by which shee [i.e., Spain] may leape into England?" in his 1598 "Apologie," which circulated widely in manuscript before its authorized print edition in 1603 (which was quickly translated into Dutch).[89] And, in 1600, he wrote to James in Scotland that his enemies "practiced to supplant James and secure the succession of the Infanta of Spain to the throne of England," and accused Elizabeth's principal secretary, Sir Robert Cecil, of asserting that "he could prove the Infanta's title to be better than the title of any other competitor to the crown."[90] In 1601, at the Essex rebellion trial of Essex and Southampton, Shakespeare's patron, Essex once again "took the chance to counter-attack with his allegation that Cecil had told a fellow Councillor that the Infanta had as good a claim as anyone to the English succession," a charge refuted by Essex's own uncle, Sir William Knollys, who testified that "what Cecil had said, during a discussion about Dolman's (that is Father Robert Parsons's) book on the succession, was in fact 'is it not strange impudence in that Dolman to give an equal right in the succession of the crown to the Infanta of Spain as any other.' "[91] In the crucial years immediately before the composition of *Othello* (which Michael Neill dates as likely from 1602–1603),[92] not only the wielding of Habsburg power from Brabant, but the arrival in Brussels of the Spanish Infanta who had such a prominently discussed claim to the English crown, made Spanish-occupied Brabant a continual focus of English attention. And in the same period—as a reminder of the more global networks of which these events were a part—attempts were made to "raise money from Florence and Venice" to alleviate the problem of the queen's own stretched finances in 1600, after so many years of English involvement in the Low Countries and fears of Spanish invasion.[93]

ꝏ

> The Battaile of Giblou in Brabant, fought betwene Don Iohn of Austria, and Mounsieur de Gugny, Generall of the armie of the States.
>
> —John Polemon, *The second part of the booke of battailes* (1587)

> The inuesting of the Duchie of Brabande in the person of the Lorde Frauncis, onelye brother of the Frenche King, Duke of Aniow.
>
> —*The ioyful and royal entertainment* . . . , trans. Arthur Golding (1582)

> The ouerthrowe of the Armie of the king of Spaine, at *Turnhaut* in *Brabant.*
>
> —Newsletter published in London (1597)

> It is also written from *Antwerp*, that the Infanta is in person come into the Campe.
>
> —*Newes from Ostend of . . . Archeduke Albertus his forces* (1601)

With regard to the decades-long history of English military involvement in Brabant, after the sack of Antwerp in 1576 and Don John of Austria assumed authority in Brussels, it was hoped by many in England that Elizabeth might send an English army under Leicester; and, though this did not happen, a small English force was sent in 1578 under Leicester's protégé John Norris, who would, in 1580, lead his men in "storming the important city of Mechelen" in Brabant.[94] In 1578, Don John won a successful battle at Gembloux, a town near Louvain, an event reported in numerous English accounts. John Polemon's *The second part of the booke of battailes* (1587), for example, described what it called "The Battaile of Giblou in Brabant, fought betwene Don Iohn of Austria, and Mounsieur de Gugny, Generall of the armie of the States,"[95] beginning with Don John's taking of "the Castell of *Namur*, a place of great consequence for the recept of forraine forces and entrance into Brabant" and ending with Don John's taking not only of this "toune of Giblou" (or Gembloux) but Louvain itself. In yet another of the many links between the Spanish military campaigns in the Low Countries and the Turk, the Spanish cavalry—crucial to this victory in Brabant—"Dressed in turbans like the Turkish light horse, whose tactics were successfully emulated."[96] But although Don John "won a spectacular victory over the States-General at Gembloux in January 1578, forcing them to abandon Brussels, and although his troops went on to capture several nearby towns," gradually "the army of the States-General forced Don John to fall back on his fortified camp at Bouge, near Namure," and there "in October 1578 the victor at Lepanto and Gembloux died."[97]

Brabant and Antwerp in Brabant continued to figure in a major way in English accounts in the years that followed Don John's death, in Elizabeth's relationship with Hercule François de Valois, Duke of Alençon and Anjou (the younger son of Catherine de' Medici and Henry II of France and brother to French king Henry III, with whom she entered into a marriage contract in 1579), which dominated English foreign policy between 1580 and his death in 1584 because he was central to an alliance with France over the Low Countries and Portugal. When Prince William of Orange and the States-General decided to make Anjou "prince and lord of the Netherlands" in 1581, and Anjou had spent part of that year in England, Elizabeth sent him in early 1582, in the company of Leicester and a large party of English nobles and gentlemen (including the queen's cousin Lord Hunsdon, Secretary Walsingham, and Philip Sidney), to his "joyeuse entrée" into Antwerp as "Duke of Brabant."[98] The event was described in detail in contemporary texts, including Arthur Golding's translation of *The ioyful and royal entertainment of the ryght high and mightie Prince, Frauncis the Frenche Kings only brother by the grace of God Duke of Brabande, Aniow, Aláunson, &c. Into his noble citie of Antwerpe. 1582.*[99] And when Anjou was ultimately opposed by the citizens of Antwerp, in his attempt to seize more absolute power, in what became known as the "French Fury" of January 17, 1583, and left Brabant for good, dying the next year,[100] this too was prominently reported in England.

Other locations in Brabant were sites of battles that were not only reported in England but included English involvement. "Breda in the lande of Brabant" (as it was referred to in Johannes Carion's *The Thre Bokes of Chronicles*, published in England in 1550)—which was identified with the Prince of Orange as part of his family's estate and described by Ortelius as the site of "the Palace of the Earles of Nassau"—was repeatedly in reports in England with regard to struggles against the Spanish. In 1575, it was the site of the aborted peace talks that Philip II had entered into in the face of new pressure from the Turk in the Mediterranean and North Africa. These negotiations were recorded in numerous English publications of the period, including Thomas Stocker's influential translation of *A Tragicall historie of the troubles and ciuile warres of the lowe Countries* in 1583, which cited "the Treaty of peace at Breda broken of 1575" in its account of "the barbarous crueltie and tyrannie of the Spaniard."[101] As a rebel town in Brabant, Breda was captured for Spain by the Duke of Parma in 1581; and recaptured in 1590 by the army of the Dutch Republic, led by Maurice and William Louis of Nassau and aided by English forces led by Sir Francis Vere, a loss for Spain that Lewkenor's *A discourse of the vsage of the English fugitives by the Spaniard* (1595) ascribed to the king of Spain's ongoing cash crisis.[102]

Brabant was also repeatedly in the news in England in the years leading up to *Othello* because of the English garrison at Bergen-op-Zoom. In 1588, when the Spanish sought to compensate for the Armada's defeat earlier that year by attacking it, "The successful Anglo-Dutch defence of Bergen-op-Zoom against Parma's 30,000-man strong field army" showed the English, as David Eltis records in *The Military Revolution*, "how effectively they could perform with foreign advice and assistance."[103] As Paul E. J. Hammer observes in *Elizabeth's Wars*, "For the first time, Parma—widely acknowledged as the best general of his day, leading Europe's most famous army—had been defeated in open battle," making that Anglo-Dutch victory in Brabant "a major blow to the myth of Spanish invincibility."[104]

Reports from battlefields in Brabant and elsewhere in the Low Countries—and of English involvement—continued throughout the 1590s, when Ben Jonson served there under Sir Francis Vere. The Dutch recaptured St. Geertruidenberg in north Brabant from the Spanish army in 1593. There was yet another mutiny of soldiers at Zichem (or Sichem) in Brabant in 1594–1596, a history of mutinies among Spain's troops that also included Diest in 1590–1591 and 1599–1601.[105] Even closer to the date of *Othello*, the major battle at Turnhout in Brabant in 1597 inspired not only newsletters published in England but a play on the London stage that featured Vere himself. The campaigns of Orange's son Count Maurice of Nassau against the Spanish army of occupation were increasingly gripping English attention, "especially since English troops were fighting alongside him," and contemporaries were particularly impressed by "his two most famous battles, Turnhout in Brabant and Nieupoort in Flanders."[106] In addition to the recounting of his victories in ballads and broadsides, his 1597 victory at Turnhout was celebrated in two newsletters published in London that same year. A translation from the French entitled *A Discourse more at large of the late ouerthrowe giuen to the King of Spaines army at Turnhaut, in Ianuarie last, by Count Morris of Nassawe, assisted with the English forces*, celebrated victory over "the armie of the king of Spaine, at Turnhaut in Brabant." Another anonymous newsletter—*A true discourse of the ouerthrowe giuen to the common enemy at Turnhaut, the 14. of Ianuary last 1597, by Count Moris of Nassaw and the states, assisted with the English forces*—hailed this battle as "the greatest and most notable victorie" in the civil wars against Spain and attributed "the greatest part of the honor of that day's victory" to Sir Robert Sidney, the lord governor of Flushing (i.e., Vlissingen, at the mouth of the Schelde River, the crucial passageway to Antwerp), as well as commending Sir Francis Vere.[107] And in 1599, in a context in which plays could also "perform the function of newsletter or news-ballad," this victory at Turnhout in Brabant was "acted upon a Stage" in London, with Sir Francis Vere appearing as a character ("in a

Beard resembling his") and Sir Robert Sidney seconding him in "Killing, Slaying, and Overthrowing the *Spaniards*."[108]

That there was so much English military involvement in Brabant made it the focus of English attention over an extended period. In 1583, after Elizabeth's suitor Alençon-Anjou had been rejected as governor (including in the uprising in Antwerp against his attempted military coup), Sir John Norris, who had led his men in storming Mechelen in 1580, was appointed "general of all the states' forces in Flanders until the crisis was resolved."[109] And in 1585, in the wake of the assassination of William of Orange and the Spanish siege of Antwerp, when Elizabeth signed the Treaty of Nonsuch and officially dispatched English forces to the Low Countries under Leicester in the expedition in which Philip Sidney died at Zutphen the next year (an official intervention reported in the pages of Holinshed, Camden, and others), she made Norris "colonel-general and governor of the Queen's forces."[110] Leicester himself subsequently made "his fateful decision to accept appointment as governor-general of the Netherlands from the states-general, and was sworn in on 15 January 1586."[111]

Sir Francis Vere was repeatedly involved in major engagements in Brabant over many years. Originally serving as a mercenary in the early 1580s under the Welsh professional soldier Sir Roger Williams, Vere joined the English army under Leicester after the siege of Antwerp in 1585. In 1586, he was prominently with the English company in Brabant at Bergen-op-Zoom, where he and the English garrison were victorious over the Duke of Parma in 1588, and Vere was knighted by Lord Willoughby, a figure whose campaigns were also celebrated in ballads. Valued by Maurice of Nassau for his mastery of siege warfare, Vere led the English forces in the army that stormed Breda in 1590. And in 1597 he was "instrumental to the complete rout of the Spanish army in the battle of Turnhout,"[112] the famous victory in Brabant that was staged in London in 1599, with Vere himself as a character. As John S. Nolan comments on Vere and his brothers in "The Militarization of the Elizabethan State": "Young Englishmen of military bent warmed to the Veres' command, which nearly became an academy for the training of officers." Sir Francis Vere, as "the Elizabethan officer who founded the system of tactics and discipline used in England,"[113] was repeatedly associated with campaigns and sieges in Brabant in the final decades of the sixteenth century. He was also centrally involved in the protracted Low Countries siege at Ostend, which began in 1601 (close to the Battle of Kinsale, which put an end to Spanish involvement in Ireland) and did not end until 1604, the year that *Othello* was first performed.[114]

In the years immediately prior to *Othello*, the siege at Ostend (famously referred to in *Hamlet*) kept Brabant repeatedly in the news, since it was waged by the archduke Albert, co-regent (with the Infanta Isabella) in Brussels,[115] the well-known archduke who would later appear as a character in Chapman's *Conspiracy and Tragedy of Charles Duke of Byron* (1608). "Eloquent testimony to the sensational character of the news from Ostend in early 1602 is the fact that the *Short-Title Catalogue* . . . lists no less than seven pamphlets concerned with the siege and the assault of the Archduke": one of these pamphlets—published anonymously—"caused an enormous sensation at the time, as witnessed by contemporary correspondence."[116] John Manningham's *Diary* for January 1602 records it as "*a booke of Newes from Ostend.* Touchinge the parly which Sir Fr. Vere held with the Archduke there."[117] Bearing the full title *Extremities vrging the Lord Generall Sir Fra[ncis]: Veare to the anti-parle with the Archduke Albertus. Written by an English gentleman of verie good account from Ostend, to a worshipfull gentleman his friend heere in England . . . VVith a declaration of the desperate attempt made since, by the sayde Archdukes forces, for the winning of the ould towne* (London, 1602), this news bulletin from Ostend not only described the opposition of Sir Francis Vere and the English to the archduke Albert, but also noted the ongoing cash crises that would ultimately lead Albert and the Infanta to be prime movers of the peace with James in 1604 ("Newes came that the Archduke hath nowe at last pacified, and reconciled all his mutinous soldiers which haue béen long time in *Brabant,* holding for none but themselves . . . their discontent growing from want of pay," 18).[118]

The archduke who ruled from Brabant was repeatedly foregrounded by name in the titles of other news bulletins from Ostend, including *The Oppugnation, and fierce siege of Ostend by the Archduke Albertus his forces* (London, 1601), and its updating that same year in *Newes from Ostend of, the oppugnation, and fierce siege made, by the Archeduke Albertus his forces, . . . whereunto are ad[d]ed such other newes and accidents as haue lately hapned at Ostend,* which records that "it is also written from *Antwerp,* that the Infanta is in person come into the Campe" (sig. B3) as well as describing Sir Francis Vere's defense against Albert's siege. Another pamphlet naming the archduke (with the Infanta) in its title—*A dialogue and complaint made vpon the siedge of Oastend, made by the King of Spaine, the Archduke, the Infanta, the Pope, the Prince Morrice, and the eldest sonne of Sauoye* (London, 1602)—begins with the cost of the siege in "men and money" (sig. A2).[119] *A short report of the honourable iourney into Brabant by his excellencie Graue Mauris, gouernour and*

*Lord Generall of the vnited Netherlandish Prouinces* (also published in London in 1602) again treats of the archduke's siege and the sending of opposing forces "as well for the reliefe of *Ostend,* as also to deliuer the rest of the Netherlandish Prouinces from the yoke of the tyrannous Spanyards" (2), in addition to providing news from Brabant, including Turnhout, "*Hertigenbosche,*" and "the Towne of *Grave.*" And still other accounts highlighted the heroism of Vere and his brother Horace against the archduke who ruled with the Infanta from Brussels.[120] After Ambrosio Spinola was finally victorious in 1604, "Albert and Isabella entered Ostend in triumph, but it was a Pyrrhic victory" since the town was "in ruins."[121]

*Othello* has been repeatedly linked to James's peace negotiations with Spain that led to the Treaty of London in 1604, the same year as its performance at James's court. But in fact the archduke and Infanta, governors of the Spanish Netherlands in Brabant, were central to this peace. As historian Pauline Croft notes in "*Rex Pacificus,*" the "conclusion of the treaty of London confirmed the success of the archdukes in gradually transforming the contacts between England and Spain into a trilateral relationship" between England, Spain, and Brabant. And in the famous painting (Figure 12) of the Somerset House conference of negotiators of the peace that was ultimately enshrined in the Treaty of London in August, 1604, it is not the Spanish delegates who are seated opposite Cecil, Northampton, and Devonshire (i.e., Mountjoy), but rather the delegates from the Spanish Netherlands—Louis Verreyken (Audiencier of Brussels), Jean Richardot (President of the Council of State in Brussels), and Charles de Ligne, Prince-Count of Arenberg (a leading aristocrat of the Habsburg Netherlands who participated in the siege of Antwerp in 1585 and served the archduke in Brussels, including as an ambassador).[122] As Paul E. J. Hammer notes, the treaty also still allowed both the Dutch and the archduke "to recruit English volunteers for their armies," since there was no peace between Spain and the Dutch, and "the war in the Low Countries continued, although now with English troops on both sides."[123] So in 1604—when *Othello* was performed before James—"Brabant" continued to be a major focus of English attention and engagement.

∽

> Alarums in the Campe, surprises of Townes, Camisadoes, &c. I haue in the low Countries, vnder *Don Iohn,* seene pollitikely put in practise. . . .
>
> —William Garrard, *The Arte of Warre* (1591)

Figure 12. Painting of the Somerset House Conference commemorating James I's 1604 Peace with Spain. By permission of the National Portrait Gallery, London.

> I haue serued these sixteene yeeres in Ireland, and in the Low Countries.
>
> —Giles Clayton, *The Approued Order of Martiall Discipline* (1591)

> So are the gentlemen, and worthie people of our nation that haue pursued the defensory warres in the lowe Countrie, specially to be praised . . . with . . . their seruice in *Brabant* against the *Spaniards.*
>
> —Geffrey Gates, *The Defence of Militarie Profession* (1579)

> *Spanish* discipline is verie gratefull vnto the men of warre. . . .
>
> —Sir Roger Williams, *A Briefe Discourse of Warre* (1590)

In ways crucial to the contemporary contexts for a play that begins with Iago's contempt for the "arithmetician" Cassio (1.1.19) and the "bookish theoric" (1.1.24) of a "soldiership" (1.1.27) "That never set a squadron in the field, / Nor the division of a battle knows" (1.1.22–23), it is also important to note that Brabant was a central focus not only in relation to particular battles but in relation to the art of warfare itself as part of the new military science (and its arithmetic), reflected in the repeated sieges and building of fortifications at St. Geertruidenberg, Zevenbergshen Hoek, and elsewhere. And the varied history of English military involvement in Brabant and the Low Countries significantly contributed to the new "theoric" of war invoked in *Othello*'s opening scene (1.1.24).[124] Florentine Machiavelli's *Dell'arte della guerra* (*Art of War*) had a substantial impact not only in England but also in the Low Countries, influencing Maurice of Nassau and other military leaders there. In addition to Barnabe Rich and others in England, it also had a major influence on Henry Percy, the Earl of Northumberland,[125] whose military enterprises were mainly in the Low Countries, as it did on one of the most influential military texts of the period, Fourquevaux's *Instructions sur le faict de la guerre* (1548), which Paul Ive translated into English as *Instructions for the Warres* (1589).[126] Ive himself, the military engineer whose *Practise of Fortification* (1589) provided details that Marlowe inserted into *2 Tamburlaine* (3.2.55–92),[127] had been sent to the Low Countries with Leicester's expeditionary force in 1585, in the wake of Parma's siege of Antwerp. In 1600, "he was again on military tour in the Low Countries, now with Henry Percy, ninth earl of Northumberland, to whom he dedicated a 1600 manuscript translation of Simon Stevin's Dutch treatise on fortification, *De sterctenbouwing*."[128] (As the example of Stevin makes clear, the new technologies of double-entry bookkeeping and military science—both foregrounded at the beginning of *Othello*—could be combined in the same person.)

Similarly important were direct English encounters with the Spanish army in Brabant and the Low Countries. As John Hale writes in *The Art of War and Renaissance England*, "the Spanish army had seen constant active service and had become a model of organization, discipline, and striking power for the rest of Europe." And though "it was galling for the English to have to learn about war from their arch enemies both in politics and religion, the Spaniards," even Bernardino de Mendoza's *Theorique and Practice of War* (which "gave an excellent account of the Spanish army under the Duke of Alva in the Netherlands") was translated in 1597 by Sir Edward Hoby, who had himself seen service in the Low Countries.[129]

As Hale observes, "Knowledge of Spanish methods also came from English soldiers who fought in the Netherlands, both on the Catholic side as soldiers of fortune and on the Protestant side as soldiers of the crown" and "The best account from an English observer is *A Brief Discourse of War*, by Sir Roger Williams (1590)," the Welsh soldier who has been suggested as a possible model for Shakespeare's Fluellen in *Henry V*.[130] Returning to England through Brabant in 1573, Williams "was arrested but the Spanish commander who interviewed him . . . offered Williams the chance to enlist in his regiment," which Williams accepted; he then served with the Spanish army of Flanders, before returning to England in 1577.[131] In 1578 and after, he served in the Low Countries under Sir John Norris, and returned there after the 1585 siege of Antwerp spurred Elizabeth to send English forces, becoming lieutenant general under Colonel General Norris and governor of the port town of Sluys (or Sluis), which he fought to defend in 1587. His *A briefe discourse of warre* in 1590—frequently cited in relation to the new military science in *Othello*—reflects this long experience. It tells how when "passing throgh *Lier* in *Brabant*" in 1573 he had originally entered into "the Spaniards wars" under "*Iulian Romero*" (27), recounts the cruelty of the Duke of Alva and of "Davila" and the Spanish in Antwerp, and (as noted earlier) repeatedly uses the loanword from the Low Countries campaigns that is foregrounded in *Othello*, for soldiers, officers, and companies that have been "cashed," "cashiered," or dismissed.[132]

Multiple influential English contributors to the growing "theoric" of military science likewise had experience in the Low Countries' wars, including in Brabant.[133] William Garrard, author of *The Arte of Warre* (1591), had "served as a mercenary for fourteen years in the Low Countries,"[134] and cites "Guichardines discriptions of the low Countries" (26) and the military strategems that "I haue in the low Countries, vnder *Don Iohn,* seene pollitikely put in practise" (344), as well as those of the Duke of Parma. Giles Clayton, in his address to readers of *The approued order of martiall discipline* (1591), writes, "I haue serued these sixteene yeeres in Ireland, and in the Low Countries, and haue seene many peeces of seruice in both places." Matthew Sutcliffe, author of *The Practice, Proceedings, and Lawes of Armes* (1593), was "judge-advocate general under Leicester in the Low Countries." And Robert Barret, whose *The Theorike and Practike of Modern Warres* (1598) ranked with the work of Garrard and Clayton as one of the most authoritative contemporary military treatises, writes that his work derives from his military service "among forraine nations, as the French, the Dutch, the Italian, and Spaniard."[135]

Thomas Digges—whose publication in 1579 of his and his father Leonard Digges's *Stratioticos* is routinely cited with regard to the lines on the "theoric" and "arithmetic" of war in *Othello*—dedicated it to the Earl of Leicester and wrote it in the midst of hopes during 1577–1578 that Leicester would lead an English force against the Spanish after the sack of Antwerp in 1576. Digges himself visited the Low Countries in the autumn of 1578, observing the troops and inspecting fortifications.[136] When Elizabeth finally sent the English forces under Leicester in response to the siege of Antwerp in 1585, Digges was appointed both trench-master and muster-master of that expeditionary force, though his attempts to check abuses in the distribution of soldiers' pay ultimately led to increasing disputes and his official discharge in early 1588. Before publishing the revised and augmented version of *Stratioticos* in 1590 and *Pantometria* in 1591, Digges also defended Leicester's reputation in *A Briefe Report of the Militaries Services done in the Low Countries, by the Erle of Leicester* (1587) and *A Briefe and True Report of the Proceedings of the Earle of Leycester for the Reliefe of the Towne of Sluce* (1590), which notes that he "went in person to Berghen vp zome" (i.e., Bergen-op-Zoom in Brabant) to "recure all seditious wounds, and to drawe all in one line to the reliefe of this besieged Towne" (6) and that "Count Hollock" (the Dutch army commander Philip of Hohenlohe-Neuenstein) "had at that time it is said six thowsand men in Brabant in Armes" (6).

Brabant at the same time figured not only in the careers of English diplomats and spies but in the published works of prominent English soldier-writers. Thomas Wilson, the humanist who implicitly compared Philip II of Spain to the tyrant Philip II of Macedon in his edition of Demosthenes's *Orations*, was active as a diplomat in the Low Countries, treating with Philip II's governor, Don John of Austria, and sending back information from Brussels. He was also a principal secretary to Elizabeth while she was considering both whether or not to intervene in the Low Countries and possible marriage to Alençon, the Duke of Anjou. George Chapman, who fought in the Low Countries in 1585–1586 under Captain Robert Sidney in the wake of the siege of Antwerp and referred to the Duke of Parma as the "Italian Duke" in his poems, included Elizabeth's French suitor Alençon-Anjou as a chararacter ("Monsieur") in *Bussy d'Ambois* (1603–1604; printed 1607 and 1608) and *The Revenge of Bussy d'Ambois* (1610–1611; published 1613), where Act 1 stages his taking "his leave for Brabant" (when he was declared Duke of Brabant) and he refers to the "new-upstarted state in Brabant / (For which I am bound)."

George Whetstone, whose *Promos and Cassandra* (1578) provided a major source for *Measure for Measure*, reported on his military service in the Low Countries in *The Honorable Reputation of a Soldier* in 1586 (and perhaps indirectly in *The Rocke of Regard*). And after he was appointed as "commissary of musters" in the Low Countries under Thomas Digges in 1587, he was killed in September 1587 in a duel outside the English Brabant garrison town of Bergen-op-Zoom.[137]

Detailed accounts by such writers make clear, yet again, the awareness in England of the interconnected theaters of war of which Brabant was a part, including in relation to the Turk. Geffrey Gates's *The Defence of Militarie Profession* (1579)—which is filled with references to the "Turke" ("the most cruell and noyfull spoylers and destroyers that euer were vpon the earth"; "mightie, dreadfull, and inuincible in Armes, for the lamentable spoile, ruine, and extirpation of many Empires, states, kingdomes, & nations")[138]—juxtaposes such descriptions with the "false promises" of the "faithlesse Regent, the Dutches of Parma" in Brussels (23), the "tirannous purpose" (24) of "King Philip" of Spain, and the "Duke of Alva," whose "gouernement in *Belgia*" (26) included building "the Castell of *Antwerp* for mastering that proud citie" (23). Gates praises the "Brabanders and Flemings" who joined the revolting Hollanders and the "Prince of Orange" to "redeme their countrey from the power of ye oppressers, and driue the *Spanyards* with their adherents out of the lande" (25). And he singles out as "specially to be praised" the "gentlemen, and worthie people of our nation that haue pursued the defensory warres in the low Countrie" (58) and "their seruice in Brabant against the Spaniards" (58)—including against Don John of Austria—adding, "I haue here made mention of the service of our nation in Brabant, that it may breede further encouragement vnto others that are likewise wel minded vnto Martiall occupation" (58). Gates also describes the Machiavellian guile of Don John, victor at Lepanto, at his coming into Brabant as governor of the Netherlands in 1576—writing that he at first gave "credite" to his hidden intentions by comporting himself "so sweetly, that hee woulde seem of faithfull intent and devoir to reduce the common welth to peace, concord, and obedience by gentlenes & liberal dealing," but that by this "device" he meant to delude the States and the Prince of Orange "til he had snared them al in his power, and then to execute his bloudy intention." At the end of his narrative, he gives thanks that "the Lorde God frustrated this plan" to the "vtter ouerthrowe of theire porpose" and the "everlasting shame and discredite of the Lord *John*" (34).

In the years leading up to *Othello*, repeated prolific reports of Brabant were likewise provided by Thomas Churchyard, who saw extensive military service in the Low Countries, including as a mercenary, and in 1577 (the year after the sack of Antwerp) was in Brussels as a letter-bearer between Francis Walsingham and the English ambassador Thomas Wilson. Early in the Low Countries' revolt against Spain, Churchyard was "hired to lead an uprising of protestants in Antwerp in March 1567, but eventually had to flee," and "he was in Antwerp again in 1582 with the duke of Alençon and Anjou," witnessing Anjou's "honourable entertainment" there.[139] In addition to writing an epitaph for Sidney in 1587, Churchyard repeatedly included Brabant in his works on campaigns in the Low Countries as well as on war in general. In his "Epistle Dedicatorie" to *A Pleasant discourse of court and wars* (1596), he referred to himself as "the chiefe captaine" in "Anwerpe" (or Antwerp) in "Brabant." Much earlier, his *A Generall Rehearsall of Warres, called Churchyardes choise* (1579) made clear to its readers the extent of Philip II's far-flung dominions and military engagements—chronicling the "warres betweene kynge Phillippe, and the great Turke" and the role of Don John ("Dom Iohn de Austria") "against the Turkes" in the Mediterranean, including at Malta, as well as "the tyme of Don Ihons gouernment" in Brabant and the Low Countries after 1576. Churchyard also provided an up-to-the-minute account of the Duke of Parma's siege of "Mastricke" or Maastricht in 1579, the "large, populous, and rich citie" that Ortelius had included in his description of Brabant because it "acknowledgeth the Duke of *Brabant* as her soueреigne Lord."

The year before this, in 1578, Churchyard's *A lamentable, and pitifull description, of the wofull warres in Flaunders*, from the final years of "*the Emperor Charles the fifth . . . vntill this present yeare, and death of Don Iohn*" (1578),[140] described the whole course of the Low Countries' revolt against Spanish occupation as beginning in Antwerp in the mid-1560s ("where they threwe down Images, and made a great vproare among the common people," 17), in the uprising in which its citizens "saide I should be theyr leader" (19). He named "Sir Thomas Gresham" as a "Witnesse" (19) in a narrative that frequently mentioned Antwerp's Burse, the Prince of Orange's "Toune of his owne called Breda" in Brabant (24), Philip II's sending of the "Duke of Alva" (34) to replace "the Dutches of Parma" (34), and the fleeing of refugees "in great numbers" to "England" (37). And he included a detailed description of the 1576 sack of Antwerp, laying blame on the city's feasting and drunkenness ("quaffing and bibbing," 59–60)—immediately following his account of the sack of Antwerp with the arrival of "Don Iohn de Austria" (61), "triumphantly receeiued" into Brussels (63).

In addition to his own works on these events, Churchyard produced (with Richard Robinson) an updated translation in 1602 of Emanuel van Meteren of Antwerp's influential *Historia Belgica*—which chronicled "*the succeeding gouernours in the Netherlands, and the ciuill warres there begun in the yeere 1565 with the memorable seruices of our honourable English generals, captaines and souldiers, especially vnder Sir Iohn Norice knight, there performed from the yeere 1577 vntill the yeere 1589.*"[141] This adapted translation repeatedly foregrounded the multiple sites in Brabant in which these wars were engaged, including Louvain, "Liere in Brabant" (39), Mechelen or "Machlin in Brabant" (39), Brussels, Antwerp, Breda, and Bergen-op-Zoom, and the involvement of English and Welsh soldiers, including "Captaine George Gascoyne" (9), Sir Thomas Morgan (Governor of Bergen-op-Zoom), Sir Roger Williams, and Sir Francis Vere, in addition to Leicester, Lord Willoughby, and the Earl of Essex. In a mixture of van Meteren's original with passages of his own (and from Stow), it once again included Churchyard's involvement in the 1567 uprising in Antwerp. It recorded the infamous sack of the "noble citie of Antwerpe" in 1576 as on the "same day Don Iohn de Austria the bastard sonne of Charles the 5. Emperour" came "into the Netherlands to gouerne the same" (23), after years spent fighting the Turk, followed by his entry in "triumph" into Brussels, as "Gouernour General for the Spanish King ouer all those Netherlands" (26). And as with the many reports that connected the campaigns in Brabant with those against the Turk, it drew a direct link between Don John's victory at Lepanto and his subduing of Louvain in Brabant in 1578—"Vpon the first day of August (amongst vs English commonly called Lammas day) in the yeere of Christ our Sauiour 1578 (which day the Spaniards doe highly honour, especially Don Iohn, who [on] this day ouercame the Turks in a battell by sea)" (31).

Van Meteren's text and its 1602 English translation simultaneously reflected not only the familiar triangulation of Brabant and the Low Countries with campaigns against the Turk but also the comparison of Spain itself to the Turk that was a staple of contemporary Protestant writing:

> Manifestlie thus it appeareth in the sight of God and all the world, what impietie, malice, mischiefe and crueltie the Pope and Spanish king hath with foxlike subtiltie, & lyonlike force practised against the nobles and States of the Low Countries, infringing their ancient

> priuiledges, breaking fidelitie in contracts, violating the bonds of amitie, and violentlie oppressing al integritie of loyal subiects and faithfull seruants of God, seeking to make hauocke of high and low, rich and poore, young and old, with more than Turkish tyrrany in those dominions most vntollerable. (67)

It then moved directly from this passage on the threat to the Low Countries of this lethal combination of Machiavellian force and guile with "Turkish tyranny" to the threat to England itself: "against the most lawfull, naturall, christian, and religious *Phenix* of feminine sexe, and the most peerelesse Paragon of true professing Princes, *Elizabeth* Quéene of *England* her gratious Royall person, her noble lawfull kingdomes, naturall faithfull subiects, and happie peaceable estate and gouernment" (68).

Once again, Churchyard's 1602 translation of events in Brabant and the Low Countries provided a detailed account of Elizabeth's receiving the Duke of Alençon and Anjou "at Whitehall, with princely feastings and banquettings" in late 1581, and sending him in the company of Leicester, "Master Philip Sidney," and "many other Gentlemen" (43), to his formal entry into "Antwerpe in Brabant," together with his return "into Brabant" in 1583 with his French forces (44) and his subsequent attempt to seize "absolute authoritie" (49), before the uprising of "the Citizens of Antwerpe" (50), who stopped his way "at Macklin in Brabant" (51). It also included his desire before his death to "be buried as Gouernour and Duke of Brabant" (53).

Brabant at the same time figured in this text as the site of the two assassination attempts against William of Orange in Antwerp (in 1582 and 1583) before he was finally assassinated at Delft in 1584, and in its description of Parma's siege of Antwerp in 1585 (69ff.), which prompted Elizabeth to send the army under Leicester that included "Lord Robert Deuoreux Erle of Essex" (75) and Philip Sidney, together with the falling out between Elizabeth and Leicester after he was made governor by the States-General (75–77). It devoted many pages to the Duke of Parma's siege in 1588 of Bergen-op-Zoom (105–111), describing it as "a very large and commodious citie" with a "Garrison" of "Englishmen" (107), which was ultimately "deliuered from the siege of the enemies" (109). And it drew repeated connections between events in Brabant and England, including the Spanish Armada of 1588, ascribing the death of the formidable Duke of Parma the year after (1589) not only to the "sickness" he contracted after his fall "as he was riding [from] Berghen to Machlin" but to "the sorrow which he conceiued by the euill successe of the

Spanish Nauie in the inuasion of England a little before in that last yeere 1588" and his failure in Brabant at "the siege of Berghen, from when he was enforced to depart without any thing done by him" that same year (111).

ᔕ

> Within three daies Antwarpe, which was one of the rychest Tounes in Europe, had now no money nor treasure to be found therein.
>
> —George Gascoigne, *The spoyle of Antwerpe* (1576)

> Let Brabant bragge what gaines they get, that liues in secure sort.
> But Antwerpe thou thy woful wracke, thy spoyle hath proued plain
> where martiall mindes do want, no state in safety may remaine.
>
> —Barnabe Rich, *Allarme to England* (1578)

> Send such Reuellers into the roome,
> As some of them shall haue caroust their last . . .
> . . . thought no harme, but drinking health to health.
>
> —Anon., *A Larum for London, or the Siedge of Antwerpe* (1602)

If news of the campaigns against the Turk was repeatedly reported in England—in accounts of "military battles at Malta, Lepanto, Cyprus, and elsewhere,"[142] as the work of Daniel Vitkus and others has made clear—news from Brabant was thus also repeatedly disseminated in England in a multitude of different forms. In the years immediately leading up to *Othello*, on top of the many accounts of English military involvement in Brabant—including at Bergen-op-Zoom in 1588, Breda in 1590, and the 1597 Battle of Turnhout dramatized in London in 1599—what provoked repeated "alarums" for England and London itself was what was happening in Antwerp, where English financial and other interests were so directly engaged. It was the principal site not only of the "Iconoclastic Fury" of the mid-1560s to which Thomas Churchyard and others were English eyewitnesses, but also of repeated mutinies related to Spain's ongoing cash crises. In 1574, when Antwerp mutineers were owed over three years in wages, Don Luis de Requesens, Spanish governor-general of the Netherlands, lamented that "mutineers had driven money out of Antwerp and destroyed all credit and reputation."[143] And following the Spanish Decree of Bankruptcy in 1575 and Requesens's death in 1576, another mutiny of unpaid Spanish soldiers spread across Brabant, threatening Brussels as well as other centers and leading to a violent storming of Antwerp by "the main body of mutineers," during which "Europe's greatest commercial and financial centre was subjected to slaughter, pillage and rape" for days.[144]

The sack of Antwerp on November 4, 1576, was thus not a siege but a violent sacking of wealthy Antwerp in a mutiny of Spanish soldiers after the 1575 Spanish Decree of Bankruptcy (so closely bound up with his campaigns against the Turk) that left Philip II unable to send money to the Low Countries. But in the years prior to *Othello*, it frequently got combined (as both a traumatic event in Brabant and a warning or "alarum" bell for England) with Parma's siege of Antwerp in 1585, which resulted in the fall of Antwerp that even Elizabeth's signing of the Treaty of Nonsuch and sending in forces under Leicester were unable to prevent. Together, these two "sensational examples of the protracted troubles of the Low Countries with Spain" both "created a sensation in England."[145]

As G. Geoffrey Langsam comments in *Martial Books and Tudor Verse*: "The fall of Antwerp served inexhaustibly as the basis for a homiletic example to London in contemporary prose and verse." John Stow described the sending in 1585 of Leicester and the English forces in his *Annales* of 1592 and 1600 (and in a later edition of 1631, added a detailed description of the military siege of Antwerp). Thomas Nashe lamented "the destruction of Antwerpe" (as a simultaneous warning to London) in *Christ's Teares over Jerusalem* in 1593. And the "Martiall exploits" evoked in Marlowe's *Doctor Faustus* included the vow to "levy souldiers" with "coyne" and "chase the Prince of Parma from our land, / And raigne sole king of all our provinces, / Yea stranger engines for the brunt of warre, / Then was the fiery keele at Antwarpes bridge" (124–129)—a direct allusion to the famous "fireships" devised by the Italian engineer Federico Giambelli to prevent Parma's mid-1580s blockade of Antwerp.[146]

The earlier sack of Antwerp in 1576, known as the "Spanish Fury," quickly became a major part of the Black Legend of Spanish cruelty. It produced responses across Europe, in ballads, paintings, engravings, and books, while in England, "horrified English merchants and soldiers then present in Antwerp first passed on the news to friends and contacts in London" and "a spate of ballads and pamphlets were written telling of the terrible destruction, looting and murders."[147] The sack provoked not only an immediate account by English eyewitness George Gascoigne, numerous contemporary English ballads, and responses by Barnabe Rich, Geffrey Gates, Thomas Churchyard, and others but also a play performed by Shakespeare's own company, the

Lord Chamberlain's Men, and published in 1602—*A Larum for London, or the Siedge of Antwerpe*, whose subtitle ("the Siedge of Antwerpe") suggests a recall of the 1585 siege of Antwerp as well.

Gascoigne, who had already set part of his *Glass of Government* in Antwerp and served as a mercenary in the Low Countries (as well as writing a masque in 1572 that included the Turk's siege of Famagusta in Cyprus and the Battle of Lepanto), was on the crown's payroll as an agent and observer for Walsingham and Lord Burghley in Antwerp at the time of the sacking in 1576, and was a "defender in skirmishes around the English House, a residence used by merchants abroad, where he was staying at the time."[148] His eyewitness account of the sacking in *The spoyle of Antwerpe* (1576), published anonymously after his return to London that November, has been described by his biographer Charles Prouty as "the finest extant example of Elizabethan reporting."[149] But it also sounded an alarm by drawing a parallel between Antwerp and London, casting this "rewfull tragedie" as a warning to the English "to detest & avoyde those synnes, and prowde enormyties, which caused the wrath of God to be so furiouslye kindled and bent against the Towne of Antwerpe" in Brabant and "to learne to looke better about vs for good order & dyrection, the lacke whereof was theyr overthrow" (C7r–v).[150] Using the stock name for Spanish soldiers ("Dom Diego," a familiar variant of Spain's patron Sant'Iago), it recounted their "barbarous cruelty" in a "pitifull massacre" leading to the death (it claimed hyperbolically) of 17,000 people, with "heapes of dead Carcases whiche laye at every Trench where they entred," "shamful rapes," and "the wylfull burning and destroying of the stately Towne houses, & all the monuments and records of the Citie." It cited the Spaniards' "greedie mindes" in pillaging the wealthy Brabant city (so that "within three daies Antwarpe, which was one of the rychest Tounes in Europe, had now no money nor treasure to be found therein," and no "creditte" could be found), in an account that repeatedly referred to Antwerp's "Bource" (and its proximity to the "English house"), including the Spanish soldiers' turning this famous place ("which was wont to be a safe assemblie for Marchants") into one surrounded by "dycing tables."[151] But at the same time, Gascoigne's eyewitness report (as Patricia Cahill observes) combined "a gripping account of violence and bloodshed—including brutal attacks on Englishmen—with an homage to Spanish military discipline." Thus, while Gascoigne "describes the ferocity of the Spaniards after winning control of Antwerp, he also writes that they 'were to be honored for the good order and direcction which they kepte' in charging and entering the city" (B3r), in contrast to the "'carelessness and lack of foresight' of the Antwerp citizens."[152] And he pictures the Walloon and German mercenaries responsible for the city's defense as coming to the surprise night attack on the city "from drinking and carousing" (sig. B3r). As Cahill concludes, "In Gascoigne's account, the story of Antwerp is the story of a people so lacking in military expertise that they were utterly powerless when the Germans and Walloons who had been charged with the city's defense began to flee," and "*The spoyle of Antwerpe* hints at a sentiment that by the late sixteenth century would be ubiquitous in Elizabethan martial discourse: ruin will come to Londoners unless they prepare themselves for Spanish invasion."[153]

The alarm was also sounded in contemporary English responses to the sack of Antwerp by "the journalists of the times, the broadside balladers," whose titles in the Stationers' Register included "A warning songe to Cities all to beware by Andwerps fall" (January 25, 1577), "Heavie newes to all Christendom from the woofull towne of Antwerp comme" (July 1, 1577), and "A godlie exhortacon unto Englande to repent him of the evill and sinfull waies / shewinge thexample and distruccon of Jerlm and Andwarp" (November 15, 1578), a comparison of the Spanish sack of Antwerp in Brabant with the destruction of Jerusalem by the Romans in 70 A.D.[154] Ralph (or Rafe) Norris's ballad *A Warning to London by the Fall of Antwerp* (1577)[155] also sounded the alarm bell: "Let *Antvverp* warning be, / thou stately *London* to beware, . . . The scourge which late on *Antvverp* fel: / Thy wrack and ruine dooth foretel." Once again it blamed the vulnerability of Antwerp on drunkenness ("Forsake thy Deuilish drunken trade: / Which almoste hath the entrance made"), urging instead the importance of vigilance and proper military order ("Watch well"; "Be vigilant, sleepe not in sin"; "Erect your walles, giue out your charge / Keep wel your [ar]ray"). It also warned ominously not to trust the Spaniard's Machiavellian "craft" or guile, "fine flattery" or "fair face" ("Trust not a ciuil foe, / Which vnder coulour wisheth good: / For ere thy self doost knowe, / by craft he seeks to haue thy blood").

The alarm was soon sounded by other English writers, including writer-soldiers who (as Nick de Somogyi remarks) found in the Spanish sack of Antwerp "the grounds to reinforce their calls for military reform" in England itself.[156] Barnabe Rich, who had seen military service in the Low Countries and incorporated parts of Whitehorne's translation of Machiavelli's *Art of War* into his own military writing, responded to the 1576 sack of Antwerp with his *Allarme to England* in 1578.[157] It urged the need for English military readiness, warning the reader to "remember what happened to Antwerpe" (sig. F1r)—"let Brabant bragge what gaines they get, that liues in secure sort. / But Antwerpe thou thy woful wracke, thy spoyle hath proued plain / where martiall mindes do want, no state in safety may remaine" (**iii v–*iiii r). Casting himself in "the part of some poore belringer" who "hath rong the larum bell, or hath runne through the campe in great haste, crying Arme, arme, arme," Rich thus sounded the "alarum" bell to English readers and warned of the parallels between the Low Countries and England: "I will therfore put such in remembrance, of ye state & condition of *Holland, Zeland, Flanders, Brabant* and other partes of the lowe countries: How many yeares continued they in peace and quietnesse, in dronkennesse, in lecherie, in riot, in excesse, in gluttonie, in wantonnesse (I will not say in the like predicament that we nowe remaine in *Englande*)" (sig. F4 r–v).

In 1578, Thomas Churchyard's *A lamentable and pitifull description of the wofull warres in Flaunders* had also responded to the Spanish sack of Antwerp as an alarm or "warning to all wanton Cities, hereafter to give and keepe better watche of their libertie and wealth" and described the attack as happening "aboute dinner time when some have more mind of their belly, than their safetie; and fall to quaffing and bibbing, when greedie hunger and thirste shoulde be moderated with sober diet."[158] The next year, Geffrey Gates's *Defence of Militarie Profession* (1579) cited recent events in "low *Duchland*" (23) as proof of the importance of military readiness: "Then should *London* be martial against the day of war, and able upon the sodain to put it selfe in armes" (54).[159]

But closest to the time of *Othello* itself was the play performed by Shakespeare's own company and published in 1602—*A Larum for London, or the Siedge of Antwerpe*, which drew on Gascoigne's 1576 eyewitness account of the sack of Antwerp and, like Rich's *Allarme to England* in 1578, explicitly sounded "A Larum" (both alarm bell and a call to arms) in its very title. As Patricia Cahill observes (in an analysis that relates this play to earlier Shakespeare history plays in the repertory of the Chamberlain's Men, though it does not mention *Othello*), this anonymously authored play's subtitle, *The Siedge of Antwerpe*, may well have "summoned up bitter memories of the victory of the Spanish forces in their year-long siege of Antwerp in 1585," and by the time of the play's Quarto publication in 1602, it would in addition "surely have summoned up one of the longest and bloodiest sieges of all—namely, the Spanish siege of the Anglo-Dutch garrison at Ostend," which had begun in June 1601 and was continuing. As Cahill notes, the "lame soldier" ("Stump") who is central to the play is given the name "Lieutenant Vaughan" ("both a family name associated with the earl of Essex and the name of a Welsh commander who served in the 1585 siege of Antwerp").[160] At the same time, given the "alarm" being sounded in England in 1599 (when Roslyn L. Knutson thinks it might have been performed, since the English feared an invasion by Spain's Philip III)[161] and the "widespread interest in (and opposition to) the English/Spanish peace negotiations in the summer of 1600," the fact that "the play was registered for print in May 1600 may well suggest an effort on the part of the publisher to exploit a hot topic," providing a warning that "unless Londoners recognize the dangers of peace and the need for defense of the realm, they, too, will suffer Spanish invasion."[162] The topic would be even more pressing after the accession of King James in 1603 and his controversial peace with Spain in 1604 (the year of the court performance of *Othello*), the initiative in which Brabant was so central.

As William S. Maltby has observed, *A Larum for London* as a play about bloodthirsty Spanish troops sacking Antwerp in Brabant contributed greatly to the "Black Legend,"[163] the demonization in England of the Spanish identified with Sant'Iago. In a plot in which the Spanish are called "more couetous than deuils of hell," two in particular stand out—"Sancto Danila" or the Spanish commander Sancho D'Avila (called "deuilish and vnchristian," sig. Br) and the anachronistically included Duke of Alva, the "damned fiend" and "deuill" (sig. B2r) who (like Danila, who lulls Antwerp's citizens into "a false sense of security" by ordering his soldiers to "hide behind the castle walls")[164] disarms the "credulous" through a dissembling Machiavellian dishonesty and guile.

In *A Larum*'s striking combination of erotic and military language, Antwerp itself is feminized by Danila as "that flower of *Europe*" whose "breath" is "as sweete as the Arabian spice," who "is amorous as the wanton ayre, / And must be Courted," and "beckons vs vnto her sportfull bed / . . . To Reuell in that bower of earthly blisse" (sig. A3r)—in a plot that by contrast to this language of amorous invitation involves rape, torture, and the forceful occupation of the city. And a different kind of traffic is foregrounded in its references to wealthy Antwerp's "rich coffers" as well as its famous "Market place" and "Burse,"[165] a mercenary motive underscored even further in the scenes involving an English factor, who is tortured by Alva and Danila for cash, and the "English Governor," who protests to Alva that "we are not heere great Lord, to ioyne with them / In any bolde confederacie of warre, /

But for the trafficke, which all nations else, / (As well as England) haue within this place," and is forced by Alva to produce "money" for "ransome of your house" (sig. D3r).

By contrast to the Spanish soldiers, Antwerp's inhabitants are described not only as used to "soft effeminate silks" (with their "nice mindes set all on dalliance" rather than "feates of armes," sig. A2v) but as carousing and drinking ("Send such Reuellers into the roome, / As some of them shall haue caroust their last," sig. A4r). They are called "Bouzing Bacchanalian centures," "Bouzing Be[l]gians," and "swilling" or "drunken Dutch" (in the familiar conflation in which inhabitants of the Low Countries, including Brabant, could all be referred to as "Dutch"), who as they were "banqueting" and in "a drunken Bacchanall" and "thought no harme, but drinking health to health," were on this night unprepared (in "deepe carouse" and "drunke"), disorderly, and ("vndone for want of discipline") completely overcome by their attackers.[166]

The play repeatedly reminds its audience that this attack happened in Brabant—referring not only to Antwerp but to the help brought to Alva from other parts of Brabant, including from Liere by Julian Romero, the commander under whom Sir Roger Williams had served for the Spanish. It refers to the citizens of Antwerp as "Brabanters"—from its account of the Spanish soldiers who deride as a "Brabant bitch" a mother who tries unsuccessfully to save her children, to the speech of the lame soldier featured on its title page, who calls "Antwerpe" his "native place," laments that "Ther's not a towne almost in Brabant now / That giues a man the safetie of a night" (sig. F3r), and is one of "two fierce assailing Brabanters" (sig. G1v) who emerge as heroes though they die in their unsuccessful attempt to save Antwerp itself. An "Alarum" bell sounds strikingly in this play set in Brabant, on the night of this famous attack on the most prosperous city in the Low Countries. And (as its title makes clear) it sounds an "alarum for London" as well—that what happened to Antwerp "May be a meane all Citties to affright / How they in sinne and pleasure take delight" (sig. G2r).

Nick de Somogyi suggests multiple connections between *A Larum for London, or the Siedge of Antwerpe* and *Othello*, though he nowhere mentions the evocation through the name of "Brabantio" of the well-known location of Antwerp foregrounded by *A Larum*'s repeated references to "Brabant" and "Brabanters." He also points to the important parallel between the Spanish in this play and the Turk:

> Otherwise slavish in its rendering of Gascoigne's source, the play's author makes two significant additions, by which those lessons are translated into dramatic form. Firstly, the direct responsibility for the massacre is transferred from Gascoigne's mutinous "common Souldiers" (Alv) to the Duke of Alva, unhistorically introduced. Secondly, he presents a one-legged soldier, Lieutenant Stump, whose "ventrous actes and valorous deeds" are proclaimed on the play's title-page. In short, he invents a villain and a hero: the Scourge of God and the Just Warrior. . . . In sixteenth-century Christian tradition, Satan was cast as the instrument of that divine indignation . . . but "the most consistent invocation of the traditional theory was made in connection with the Ottoman empire" (Patrides, 130). "Solimanne," wrote Theodor Buchmann in 1542, "is onely the whippe with the whych the holy and rygteous Lorde doth beate and scourge us for owre vicious lyvinge" (Patrides, 133). . . . But though the Turkish threat sporadically induced a pan-Christian defence (notably at Lepanto), as the ramifications of the Reformation widened, it was the Catholic empire which replaced the Turk as the new scourge of God. Sidney referred to Philip II as "this Spanish Ottoman" (Howell, 40).[167]

In this play where the Spanish are compared to fiends from hell, and the "Devil" and Alva are conflated, "*A Larum for London* embodies in Alva, the instrument of 'royall Phillip' (903), 'the sharpe scourge, that fond securitie, / Hath justlie throwne on Antwerpes wilfulness' (657–8)." His Captain Danila is explicitly described as wielding the "sharpe point" of an Ottoman scimitar or "Semiter" (949), as well as practicing torture and championing "the hellish technology of gunpowder,"[168] both identified with the Turk and Spain.

As De Somogyi points out, the Spanish "devil" Alva's role in this play further "allies military tactics with theatrical villainy" by making Alva himself into a Machiavel, whose use of fraud and guile, or the " 'better cullor' of policy" (107), makes it possible for him to " 'delude' " Antwerp's " 'credulous inhabitants' " by causing it " 'to be publisht' " that he is dead and disguising his army as a funeral cortege.[169] Commenting that he might even "owe a debt to Marlowe's Barabas, who also pretends death to be 'reveng'd on this accursed Towne' (5.1.63)" and to *The Jew of Malta*'s "Chorus ('Albeit the world thinke *Machevill* is dead . . . ')," De Somogyi observes that in *A Larum to London*, Antwerp is exposed in Alva to a compendium of Elizabethan villainy—another 'hellish Dragon' poised on the walls of its 'bower of earthly blisse' (90)."

Though he does not make the connection with *Othello*'s evocation of Brabant, in this play on the sack of Brabant's most famous city, De Somogyi suggests even more connections between *A Larum for London, or the Siedge of Antwerpe* and *Othello*—including between the one-legged soldier "Lieutenant Vaughan" or "Stump" and "Lieutenant Cassio," who in the final act of *Othello*, his "leg . . . cut in two" (5.1.72) when he is "maym'd" by Iago (Folio), is carried on stage in "*in a Chaire*" (in the 1622 Quarto), a reflection of the source in Cinthio where he has lost a leg. And in relation to the demonization of the Machiavel Alva as a "damned fiend" and "devil," he points out that in *Othello*, the outward signs in Iago of a "devil" or "Divinity of Hell" are not visible ("I look down towards his feet; but that's a fable," 5.2.286).[170]

᪥

*Iago*. Away, I say; go out and cry a mutiny . . .
Who's that which rings the bell? *Diablo*, ho!
The town will rise . . .

—*Othello* (2.3.157, 161–162)

And let me the canakin clink . . .
Why then let a soldier drink . . .

—*Othello* (2.3.70, 73)

what impietie, malice, mischiefe and crueltie the Pope and Spanish king hath . . . practised against the nobles and States of the Low Countries, . . . with more than Turkish tyrrany in those dominions.

—Emanuel van Meteren, *A true discourse historicall, of the succeeding gouernours in the Netherlands* (1602)

It is difficult to read *A Larum for London, or the Siedge of Antwerpe*—or the earlier English descriptions of the "mutiny" and sack of Antwerp that repeatedly emphasize the carousing and drunkenness of Antwerp's unprepared citizens and defenders on the night of the attack—and not think of *Othello*, given that *Othello* adds to its source in Cinthio a night of "feasting" (2.2.9) and "drinking" (2.3.34) and Iago refers contemptuously to those that are supposed to be keeping "watch" as a "flock of drunkards" (2.3.59), before instructing Roderigo to "go out and cry a mutiny" (2.3.157). This night of drinking, military unreadiness, and "mutiny" in *Othello* is filled with the ringing of an "alarum" bell (as in the "alarums" rung as warnings to England in the many responses to the sack of Antwerp in Brabant)—in a scene where Desdemona herself is called by Iago "an alarum to love" (2.3.26), as part of its own combination of erotic and military. Iago bears not only the name of Sant'Iago Matamoros, Spain's patron saint, but the familiar name for Spanish soldiers, as Gascoigne's use of "Dom Diego" for the soldiers who sacked Antwerp and robbed it of its "money" and "treasure" makes clear. And when the sounding of the alarm bell prompts Iago's "Who's that which rings the bell? *Diablo*, ho! / The town will rise" (2.3.161–162), "*Diablo*," as editors point out, is a strikingly Spanish oath used here for the only time in all of Shakespeare, by the Spanish-named Iago,[171] who becomes not only the Machiavel but the undiscerned *diablo* or "devil" of the play itself.

The night scene of carousing in *Othello*, of course, is not in Brabant or the Low Countries but in Cyprus, and the threat is not from the Spaniard but from the Turk. But it is the scene of *Othello* in which the Low Countries are explicitly recalled—in the drunkenness associated with the "English" through "the bad habits brought back by soldiers returning from the wars in the Netherlands" (Neill, *Othello*, 263)—and Cassio is "cashiered," the Low Countries' loanword recently adopted (like other military terms) into English. Even Iago's drinking song in this scene ("And let me the canakin clink . . . / Why then let a soldier drink," 2.3.69–73) recalls the stage-Dutch song about drunkenness in Dekker's *The Shoemakers Holiday* ("Fill up the canniken drink"), yet another loanword from the Southern ("Flemish and Brabantic") Dutch that was "most likely also the variety that Dekker was familiar with," since "it may be assumed that his family left the Low Countries for England in the early stages of the Dutch revolt."[172]

Just such a geographical palimpsest or wider global context would not be unexpected, given how how often Spain itself was conflated with the Turk and how frequently Brabant as the nearby center of Spanish power was linked to events in the Mediterranean and the threat from the Turk—including through Don John, the victor at Lepanto who figured so prominently in both. Gascoigne's depiction of "the Turke that Prince of pride" in his account of Cyprus and Lepanto in the wedding masque of 1572 came just a few years before the alarum he sounded in *The Spoyle of Antwerpe*, the principal source for *A Larum for London*, the play in which a Turkish "scimitar" is wielded by a "devilish" Spanish commander. And in *Othello*, Iago the seasoned soldier and "true machiavel of the play" (Neill, *Othello*, 197) not only bears the quintessential Spanish name but says when he is accused of slander by Desdemona, "Nay, it is true, or else I am a Turk" (2.1.114).

Given the interconnected theaters of war and repeated combination of threats from the Mediterranean with "alarums" from Brabant, it would not be surprising if the name of Brabantio evoked this more extended global context in a play whose principal focus is the Turk, without having to entail any literalistic one-to-one relation with the character himself. Or that the scene of carousing and drinking on Cyprus that has no counterpart in Cinthio—where the Low Countries are directly invoked and Othello, awakened by the "alarum" of the "dreadful bell" (2.3.175), asks, "Are we turn'd Turks, and to ourselves do that / Which heaven hath forbid the Ottomites?" (2.3.170–171)—might have as one of its resonances the *A Larum for London* sounded from Brabant and already staged by the Chamberlain's Men by the time of *Othello*.

*A Larum for London*—published in 1602, as the writing of *Othello* itself was beginning—is by no means the only play in the years leading up to *Othello* in which the Low Countries prominently figured. Dekker's *Shoemakers Holiday* (1599) had already reflected the presence of "Dutch" strangers in London, and featured the drinking song echoed in the scene in which Cassio is "cashiered." *The Weakest Goeth to the Wall* (1600) had featured a "Duke of Brabant," along with reminders of the Low Countries' wars. Marston's *Jack Drum's Entertainment* had included in "Brabant Senior" a possible avatar of Jonson, who had fought in those wars. And—most strikingly in relation to Shakespeare himself—*The Book of Sir Thomas More*, whose assumed revision by Shakespeare with others is dated by its Arden editor to after 1600 (and even as late as 1603–1604, as James sought peace with Spain, or contemporary with *Othello*), contains scenes ascribed to Shakespeare that directly evoke the strangers from the Low Countries residing in London as a result of the Spanish occupation.[173] To evoke "Brabant" in a play that already invoked the Low Countries through the "swag-bellied Hollander" (2.3.78) of the scene of carousing that recalls the drunkenness of English soldiers returned from the wars, would not only widen the range of geographical reference *Othello* is famous for but relate it more closely to its contemporary theatrical context as well as the multiple "alarum[s] for London" that were sounded from Brabant through the decade before.

∽

> Great and extraordinary preparations made by sea as well as in Spayn by the king there as in the Lowe Countreys by the duke of Parma.
> —Queen Elizabeth to Admiral Lord Howard (December 1587)

> The Spaniards . . . feared lest they were like vnto those terrible ships, which *Frederic Ienebelli* three yeeres before, at the siege of *Antwerpe*, had furnished with gun-powder, stones, and dreadfull engines, for the dissolution of the Duke of *Parma* his bridge.
> —Richard Hakluyt, "The Spanish huge Armada sent in the year 1588 for the inuasion of England" (*Principal Navigations*, 1599–1600)

Even the "storm" or "tempest" that defeats (and "drowns") the Turkish fleet, celebrated on this night of carousing on Cyprus, in yet another addition to Cinthio, recalls the alarm of the major invasion from Spain coordinated from Spanish-occupied Brabant—the Armada of 1588, first of the series of Armada invasion scares whose continuation in the 1590s contributed to *A Larum for London*. Eric Griffin joins Emrys Jones in seeing a reminder of Lepanto in the ultimately avoided threat to Cyprus in *Othello*. But Griffin also notes that "Shakespeare's improvisation upon Cinthio" recalls England's "1588 'deliverance' from Philip's Armada,"[174] an echo recorded as well by editors of the play. Nowhere has it been noted, however, how central Brabant—and events in Brabant, including the siege of Antwerp a few years before—were to the Armada itself, though this was repeatedly foregrounded in contemporary English writing.

Parma's siege of Antwerp in 1585 had spurred Elizabeth to effectively declare war on Spain by signing the Treaty of Nonsuch, and the Armada a few years later was Spain's retaliation, a planned invasion of England across the English Channel by Parma himself, which aimed both to end English support for the Low Countries and to conquer England for Spain.[175] Brabant was central to its preparation—between Spain and Parma in Brussels, where Walsingham sought to secure "intelligence." Elizabeth in December 1587 sent instructions to her admiral (Lord Howard) that began: "Being sondry wayes most credibly given to understand of the great and extraordinary preparations made by sea as well as in Spayn by the king there as in the Lowe Countreys by the duke of Parma."[176] Her famous speech at Tilbury (where Leicester's forces were sent to defend the Thames estuary) repeated the reference to Parma: "I know I have the body but of a weak and feeble woman; but I have the heart and stomach of a king, and of a king of England too, and think foul scorn that Parma or Spain, or any prince of Europe, should dare to invade the borders of my realm."[177] Cardinal Allen's tracts intended for circulation among English Catholics, calling on them to "offer every assistance to the 'liberators' when they arrived and to abandon their allegiance to Elizabeth," were taken from Rome to Antwerp for printing, and were from there to "cross to England for distribution with Parma's troops."[178] At the same time—in yet another reminder of the complex interrelations between the Turk, Spain, Brabant, and England—Elizabeth in 1587 "made use of every opportunity to curry favour with the sultan" through her representative in Constantinople, managing to "persuade the Turks that they had nothing to gain from renewing the truce with Spain"; and rumors circulated (though they later proved false) that the sultan "had promised Elizabeth that he would attack Spain if Philip attacked England (January 1588), and that his fleet had set forth for a campaign in the Mediterranean (June 1588)."[179]

The close interrelationship has already been noted earlier in this chapter between events in Brabant and the aftermath of the Armada, including later in 1588, when the Spanish hoped to wipe out the stigma of the Armada's defeat by attacking Bergen-op-Zoom, which was successfully defended against Parma's powerful field army by the Anglo-Dutch defense that included the English under Sir Francis Vere.[180] Churchyard's 1602 translation of van Meteren related Parma's death in 1589 both to the unsuccessful Armada ("the sorrow which he conceiued by the euill successe of the Spanish Nauie in the inuasion of England a little before in that last yeere 1588") and to his failure in Brabant at "the siege of Berghen, from whence he was enforced to depart without any thing done by him" in that same year (111).

But events in Brabant (including the siege of Antwerp in 1585) were also part of contemporary accounts in England of what ultimately led to the defeat of the Armada itself, the scattering of its fleet and ultimate "drowning" of its forces.[181] The Armada's route through the English Channel was chosen so that the Spanish fleet could anchor off the coast of Flanders, and coordinate with Parma's formidable army for his invasion of England. But, as Paul Hammer records in *Elizabeth's Wars*, when the Armada was a "sitting target" anchored off Calais and "Parma's major warships were trapped at Antwerp," the English admiral Howard launched fireships against the Spanish fleet that resulted in "panic and the scattering of the Armada."[182] As other historians repeatedly comment, James McDermott notes in his study of *England and the Spanish Armada* that the panic these English fireships caused at this key moment in 1588 was the result of the traumatic memory for the Spanish of

Federico Giambelli's legendary fireships—the "hell-burners" or "explosive-packed rebel barges that had destroyed Parma's bridging works at Antwerp three years earlier"—particularly since Giambelli, "the inventor of these infernal devices[,] was known since to have become an English pensioner."[183] As military historian Steven A. Walton has detailed in a study of military science and foreign expertise in England, Giambelli—an Italian Protestant exile from Mantua who served as "master of the pioneers (trench construction engineers) in the War of the Dutch Rebellion"—had been "postmaster general for Leicester in the Netherlands in the 1580s" (where he was famously responsible for the fireships at Antwerp in 1585), before coming to England and being "hired to fortify the Thames in 1588." And Thomas Bedwell, who had "served under Leicester in the Netherlands," from 1585, was "asked to collaborate with him "on the defenses of the Thames estuary in the run-up to the Armada crisis."[184] In 1588, as Colin Martin and Geoffrey Parker write in *The Spanish Armada*, "No Spaniard could forget Giambelli's terrible 'hell-burners of Antwerp' " and Elizabeth's lord admiral "was consciously playing on these fears," since although those earlier fireships had ultimately not succeeded in preventing Antwerp's fall to Parma in 1585, "the 'hellburners of Antwerp' entered the vocabulary, and the irrational fears, of every Spanish soldier."[185] These "hellburners" or fireships of Antwerp in Brabant—vividly recalled in Marlowe's *Doctor Faustus*—were a major part of contemporary narratives of the Armada in England as well.

The extended account of "the Spanish huge Armada sent in the yeare 1588 for the inuasion of England" in Hakluyt's *Principal Navigations* (1599–1600)—incorporated from "Emanuel van Meteran in the 15. booke of his history of the low Countryes"—at the same time made clear the connections to the Turk as well as Brabant (including the siege of Antwerp in 1585), and the central role of Parma in the planned invasion of England, observing that this plan would enable the Spanish king "to conquere England and the lowe Countreys all at once" (592). Noting that "Pope *Sixtus quintus* for the setting forth of the foresaid expedition, as they vse to do against *Turkes* & infidels, published a *Cruzado*, with most ample indulgences which were printed in great numbers" (594), the account in Hakluyt described the Pope's dispatching of Cardinal Allen to the Low Countries and the plan to have the Pope's bull (confirming the excommunication of Elizabeth) taken to England, where the queen's subjects would be enjoined to "performe obedience unto the duke of Parma and vnto the Popes Legate" (595). In the familiar representation of the Spanish as Machiavels, the story in Hakluyt reported how, in guilefully offering peace with England and misleadingly claiming that "the whole expedition might seem rather to be intended against the Low countries than against England . . . the duke of *Parma* by these wiles enchanted and dazeled the eyes of many English & Dutch men that were desirous of peace" (595). (The counterpart in *Othello* would be the false report of the Turkish fleet by "Signor Angelo," who puts the Venetians in "false gaze," anticipating the guile and false accounts of Iago himself.)

The description of the Armada in Hakluyt repeatedly foregrounded the central role of the Duke of Parma from his seat of power in Brussels—the formidable Spanish opponent already familiar to the English from the campaigns in Brabant in which English soldiers were involved and the siege of Antwerp that led to the fall of that city and alarms to London. Hakluyt's narrative records that "it was commonly giuen out that the *Spaniard* hauing once vnited himselfe vnto the duke of Parma, ment to inuade by the riuer of Thames" (595) and that the Spanish fleet expected "to ioyne with the duke of *Parma* his forces, without which they were able to do litle or nothing" (600). It notes that Parma expected that "hee should be crowned king of *England*" (600), assuming that, once landed, "he might easily haue wonne the Citie of *London*, both because his small shippes should have followed and assisted his land forces, and also for that the Citie itselfe was but meanely fortified and easie to ouercome by reason of the Citizens delicacie and discontinuance from the warres" (601)—a striking parallel to the delicacy and military unreadiness of the citizens of Antwerp in the sack of 1576 that led to so many English "alarums." And it explicitly recalls the siege of Antwerp (including Giambelli's "hellburners") in describing how Elizabeth's lord admiral turned eight of his "woorst & basest ships" into fireships by loading them with gunpowder and "other combustible and fiery matter" and sending them "against the Spanish fleet," which "put the Spaniards into such a perplexity and horrour (for they feared lest they were like vnto those terrible ships, which *Frederic Ienebelli* three yeeres before, at the siege of *Antwerpe*, had furnished with gun-powder, stones, and dreadfull engines, for the dissolution of the Duke of *Parma* his bridge, built upon the river of Scheld)." It triumphantly records, however, that—in contrast to Antwerp, where this ultimately did not prevent the city's fall—the ships of the Armada, in fear of the English fireships, cut "their cables whereon their ankers were fastened" and "betooke themselues very confusedly vnto the maine sea," where the greatest of the Spanish ships ("in this sudden confusion"), "falling fowle of another ship, lost her rudder" and was assaulted by the English. It then goes on to recount—after this breaking up of the Armada by the famous strategem used at the siege of Antwerp—how the invasion of England was ultimately evaded and so many of the Spanish were "drowned" upon the "Irish coast" (605).

Brabant—together with the memory of events in Brabant, including in Antwerp and the "alarum" sent to London—was thus central to accounts of the Spanish Armada, already acknowledged as recalled in the threatened Turkish invasion of Cyprus in *Othello*. And, like the many reports from Brabant as the center of Spanish power in the Low Countries, which made clear how closely linked events there were to engagements with the Turk, the preparation for the Armada itself involved complex interconnections between England, Brussels, Spain, and the Ottoman sultan.[186]

ઌ

> This fortification, gentlemen, shall we see't?
>
> —*Othello* (3.2.5)

> A warning to all good Wives, that they look well to their Linnen.
>
> —Thomas Rymer on *Othello*

> handkerchief
> Spotted with strawberries . . .
>
> —*Othello* (3.3.434–435)

> The worms were hallowed that did breed the silk . . .
>
> —*Othello* (3.4.73)

In the new era of gunpowder, siege warfare, and "fortification," fears of invasion by Spain—as in *Othello*, of Cyprus by the Turk (the Ottoman power that in fact had already successfully occupied it)—were directly linked across these far-flung theaters of war to the rise of the new military science explicitly evoked in *Othello*'s opening scene. In addition to the sieges in the Low Countries witnessed by English soldiers, the need for fortification had already spurred the application of what was known as *trace italienne* to the fortifying of bastions in England—the "scepter'd isle" (as John of Gaunt put it in *Richard II*) vulnerable, like Cyprus, to invasion. Peter Whitehorne had added a treatise on "fortification" to his frequently reprinted translation of Florentine Machiavelli's *Art of War*, one of the texts evoked in the reference to the new military science in *Othello*.[187] And "fortification" in the military sense had already, by the time of *Othello*, been stressed as part of the armory of war in the earlier history plays, including—with a glance at the new "bookish theoric" invoked in *Othello*—*Henry IV, Part 2* ("or else / We fortify in paper and in figures," 1.3.55–56).[188] The threatened siege of Harfleur in *Henry V* (and determination afterwards to "fortify" it against the French) had been modeled on the siege of Damascus against the Turk in Part 1 of Marlowe's *Tamburlaine*, whose plea of its virgins for mercy (5.2.4–10) is reflected in the conflation of fortified walls and virgin walls in Shakespeare's play ("maiden walls that war hath never ent'red," 3.3.20–21, 5.2.321–322). Part 2 of *Tamburlaine* had "famously paraphrase[d] military engineer Paul Ive's treatise *The Practise of Fortification*," directly inspired by the Low Countries' wars—as well as invoking the "Jacob's staff" (3.3.42) in the siege of Balsera,[189] the military instrument named after the pilgrim's staff of Sant'Iago.

In Act 3 of *Othello*—after celebration of the storm that prevents the invasion of Cyprus by the Turk—Othello prepares to inspect the "fortification" of the isle (3.2.5). But this explicit allusion to the military fortification of Cyprus against invasion and occupation comes suggestively just before the pivotal Temptation Scene, where, in an ironic echo of *Hamlet* (where Barnardo warns Horatio that he will "assail your ears, / That are so fortified against our story," 1.1.31–32), Iago, the "machiavel" who had earlier compared himself ironically to the "Turk" (2.1.114), begins his siege on Othello's unfortified "ear" ("I'll pour this pestilence into his ear—/ That she repeals him for her body's lust," 2.3.356–357). And in a tragedy where Brabantio had already conflated the sexual and territorial in comparing his daughter's occupation by a Moor to the Turk's feared invasion of Cyprus (1.3.210–211), Iago's story of Desdemona's sexual occupation by Othello's "lieu-tenant" convinces Othello that his "occupation's gone" (3.3.357), in the simultaneously military and sexual senses.

In the Temptation Scene itself, Desdemona is linked more than once to sexual "country matters"—in Iago's "I know our *country* disposition well: / In Venice they do let God see the pranks / They dare not show their husbands" (3.3.201–203) and "Her will, recoiling to her better judgment, / May fall to match you with her *country* forms" (3.3.236–237), lines that evoke the familiar "obscene play on 'country'" and the female "count."[190] And as the focus shifts from martial to domestic, the increasing obsession with cloth centrally includes the silk handkerchief that evokes associations with the Low Countries (both geographical and sexual) as well as reminders of the global "traffic" from Venice through Antwerp to London.

As Susan Frye observes in *Pens and Needles: Women's Textualities in Early Modern England*, "The earliest pattern book in English was published in 1530 in Antwerp," and by 1600, the "domestic culture of the Netherlands . . . closely paralleled that of England in a number of ways, as is evident in the books of needlework patterns and other self-help books that passed steadily across the channel in both English and Dutch."[191] Antwerp (with its Burse, where Italian was a lingua franca) was crucial to the transmission of luxury textiles between Venice and London. Cited for its "silks" in *A Larum for London*, it was also a major center of silk production as well as supplier of silks to England. Jane Schneider observes in Lena Cowen Orlin's *Material London, ca. 1600*, that "ambassadors from the Spanish court of Philip II flaunted silk, albeit in black, while Italian merchants displayed this luxury fabic in an array of beautiful colors." And Antwerp was the crucial go-between: "There were, as well, competing coalitions of merchants, the most powerful of whom, the Merchant Adventurers, mediated the export of undyed woolens, manufactured in the rural districts, to nearby Antwerp, returning home with silks and spices acquired from Italian and other merchants in this important center of 'world trade.' "[192] As Jean E. Howard notes, "As long as Antwerp remained the clearing-house for English textiles, Italian merchants were active in promoting north-south commerce. English cloth moved south through Antwerp, and oil, currants, spices, and luxury fabrics such as velvets and silks moved north."[193] At the same time, the influx of "strangers" from Brabant and other parts of the embattled Low Countries prominently included silk weavers like "the widow Catherine Payne, silk weaver and resident of England for twenty years, [who in 1593] reportedly specified that she was from 'Andwerpe (Antwerp) in the Province of Brabande (Brabant)."[194]

According to Lien Bich Luu, the immigrant "strangers were concentrated overwhelmingly in the clothing industry,"[195] including in silk, linen, and lace (or "open work"), as well as the "New Draperies" (*neiuwe draperij* in Flemish) that were such a prominent part of the English cloth and clothing market.[196] As Natasha Korda remarks, Ben Jonson's allusion in *Poetaster* (1601) to "pure" linen and bleaching or whitening by "pure laundresses out of the city" (4.1.16–20) "is probably a reference to the Protestant refugee laundresses and starchwomen from the Low Countries who plied their trade in the suburbs," like "Widow Stedon of Maastricht, who employed eight English women, and Dionis Welfes of Antwerp, who employed nine" (both from Brabant) or the women from the Low Countries whose "religious and sexual 'purity' was often mocked or called into question."[197] "Mistress Dinghen van den Plasse" was described in Stow's *Annales* as a refugee from Tienen in Flemish Brabant to whom the "best and most curious wives" of London repaired because of the reputation of "the dutch for whitenesse & fine wearing of Linnen" (in a context in which "although the majority of refugees were Flemings and Walloons from the Spanish Netherlands, the term 'Dutch' was loosely employed during the period to refer to anyone from the Low Countries or regions directly adjacent").[198]

As Korda observes in *Labors Lost: Women's Work and the Early Modern English Stage*, the association of cloth with the Low Countries was bound up with female sexual "honesty," in a period when "Low Countries" was simultaneously a term for the brothel district in the suburbs of London, where women from Brabant and other parts of the "Nether-lands" (the bawdy pun used in *The Comedy of Errors*) served both the city and the commercial theaters. Marston's *The Dutch Courtesan* opens with the familiar identification of the "Low Countries" with the brothel district, combined with reference to the Low Country wars ("I would have married men love the stews as Englishmen love the Low Countries; wish war should be maintained there lest it should come home to their own doors," 1.1.58–68).[199] Korda chronicles (and critiques) the often negative portrayal of these women for "trafficke," "businesse," and taking "accompts," or "accounts," as well as the stereotype of the "wanton" woman, in a context where women from the "Low Countries" were polarized between virgin and whore, and sexual purity or "honesty" was identified with the "whiteness" and purity of their linens. Edward Grimeston's *Generall Historie of the Netherlands* (1608)—which draws on van Meteren's *Historia Belgica*—praises their "spinning and weaving of Holland cloth" and their keeping of "accounts" without "any touch of lightnesse or dishonestie," linking these virtues as well to their resistance to the Spanish in the Low Countries wars.[200] But the "visibility of Netherlandish working women in London's immigrant community, and in the networks of commerce surrounding the commercial theaters" met with "a mixed response in contemporary dramatic literature, where they were at times portrayed as promiscuous commercial agents (if not as prostitutes) and, at other times, as paragons of domestic virtue renowned for their thrift, chastity, and industry—or some combination thereof."[201] In a period when the theater and brothel district was also the major locus of the "debitor and creditor" accounting (and "arithmetic") invoked in *Othello*, and textiles, because they could be "recycled and refashioned . . . were a medium of exchange, almost as fluid as money,"[202] cloth itself could figure both "country matters" and "traffic" both monetary and sexual (or the terms on which Iago's slander of

Desdemona tragically turns), as well as the obscene sense of the female "(ac)count" familiar from Haughton's *Englishmen for My Money* and other contemporary texts.

"Cleane lynnen [is] commendable in a wife" advised George Whetstone, the writer whose *Promos and Cassandra* provided a major source for *Measure for Measure*, who saw military service in the Low Countries and died in a duel outside Bergen-op-Zoom in Brabant.[203] The contemporary erotic (rather than virtuous) association of cloth with women's bodies, or low "country matters," however, had already been foregrounded before *Othello*, including on stage. As Susan Frye observes, "The printer William Barley opens his reproduction of a Venetian pattern book, *A Book of Curious and Strange Inventions* (1596), with verses in English addressed to a female readership that quickly stray into sexualized language." And Dekker's *The Shoemaker's Holiday* (1599) features a voyeuristic scene in which the cloth goods of a seamstress—handkerchief, ruffs, and band—are identified with her eroticized "hand," while the anonymous play *The Wisdome of Doctor Dodypoll* (1600) suggestively makes an "embroiderer" the "object of desire in a painted portrait."[204] Famously in Middleton and Dekker's *The Roaring Girl* (1611), "the low countries" as both "foreign wenching" and keeping a "whore i' th' suburbs" are combined with "hollands" or fine linen, in an exchange between Master and Mistress "Openwork" that simultaneously evokes "a fabric whose origin is in the Low Countries," the geographical Netherlands, the female body or "country matters," and London's brothel district, in the familiar identification of the "sexual geographies of London with the Low Countries."[205] At the same time, the name of Mistress Openwork "demonstrates a similar association of her sexualized body literally displayed as 'open' by her public, mercantile activities, with her needlework, because 'open' or 'cut work' is produced by taking out the horizontal threads in a piece of cloth and then using the needle to collect the remaining threads into lacy patterns characterized by holes in the fabric."[206]

In Shakespeare, even before *Othello*, where cloth is so intimately bound up with female "low country matters," "holland" is used for the cloth in Mistress Quickly's juxtaposition of "a true woman" with "holland of eight shillings an ell" (*1H4* 3.3.71–72), lines that simultaneously associate trafficking in linens with the issue of whether a woman is sexually honest or "true." And in *Henry IV Part 2*, Hal's taunt to Poins ("the rest of the low countries have made a shift to eat up thy holland") aligns the fine linen cloth of the Netherlands, the Low Countries' wars, and the sexual-commercial "traffic" of the brothel district, where women from the Low Countries who worked in cloth were associated with prostitution. The identification of the whiteness of "linens" with sexual purity had also, before *Othello*, involved allusions to the Low Countries (and suburbs of London) in *The Merry Wives of Windsor*, where sexually "dishonest" associations are deflected away from the " 'pure,' native wives who send their linens" to the "whitsters" or whiteners (3.3.12–14) and the "basket used to convey the dirty laundry (along with Falstaff) offstage was in all likelihood the hamper used by the Chamberlain's Men to store costumes and convey their own foul linens and attires to laundresses like the Widow Stedon and Dionis Welfes," the Brabantian refugees from Maastricht and Antwerp.[207]

Sexual low "country matters" are famously bound up with cloth in *Othello*—whose moral Thomas Rymer notoriously reduced to "a warning to all good Wives, that they look well to their Linnen"—from the "handkerchief / Spotted with strawberries" (3.3.434–435) that becomes a fetishized substitute for the female "common thing" (3.3.302) that cannot be seen, to the bed sheets Desdemona is accused of contaminating (4.1.208), in a parallel to the image of ink stains on a paper or book.[208] And both are joined by the cloth purse that connects Desdemona's sexual orifice and its "secret sale" to the play's pervasive cash and credit nexus.[209] Desdemona's "purse" is linked with the handkerchief itself when she asks, "Where should I lose the handkerchief, Emilia? . . . / Believe me, I had rather have lost my purse / Full of crusadoes" (3.4.23, 25–26). It is also bound up with the sense of "credit" as good name or reputation that *Othello* shares with *The Merchant of Venice*, as Iago proceeds to "undo" Desdemona's "credit with the Moor" ("Who steals my purse steals trash; 'tis something, nothing; / 'Twas mine, 'tis his, and has been slave to thousands; / But he that filches from me my good name / Robs me of that which not enriches him, / And makes me poor indeed," 3.3.157–162). In a context where textiles were "a medium almost as fluid as money," the cloth purse that figures Desdemona's sexuality simultaneously figures the "use" (or "usury") to which it can be put, in a play where Iago's "fairness and wit, / The one's for use, the other useth it" (2.1.129–130) includes the "obscene innuendo" (Neill, *Othello*, 249) that a woman will make "her body available for use, i.e. sexual 'use' for a usorious return (prostitution)." Desdemona's "purse" becomes the place where the cloth, cash, and credit nexus combine.

In *Othello*, as Dympna Callaghan observes, "Desdemona's nightshift, like her wedding sheets, is the symbolic obverse of 'the stinking clothes that fretted in their own grease' (3.5.113–14) in the buckbasket of dirty laundry in which Sir John Falstaff is dispatched in *The Merry Wives of Windsor*."[210] But as Iago assumes control of the narrative about cloth in *Othello*, the language of this tragedy set in Venice and Cyprus increasingly resembles the idiom of the brothel district, as the aristocratic Venetian senator Brabantio's daughter is reduced to a "public commoner" (4.2.73) or whore, with Emilia her "bawd" (4.2.20), and Iago's convincing of Othello that Cassio has "cope[d]" his wife (4.1.86) evokes yet another loanword from the Low Countries, one in which the sexual and monetary combined.[211]

Emilia herself evokes the traffic in textiles in London and its consumption of foreign fashion when she insists that she would not betray her husband "for measures of lawn, nor for gowns, petticoats, nor caps, nor any petty exhibition" (4.3.73–74). And she "implicitly distances herself from those women who, like Bianca, exchange sexual favors for desirable material objects—sheets, shirts, handkerchiefs, lingerie, and trimmings."[212] But in the scene where she offers the handkerchief to Iago, Emilia is herself reduced to a "common thing" (3.3.302) even before she is taken by Othello to be a "bawd" (4.2.20). And the ambiguous, manipulable language of "work" —as well as the doubleness of "huswife" as "housewife" and "hussy"—encompasses both women. Lynda Boose has noted that the embroidery on the handkerchief in *Othello* is most frequently referred to as "work."[213] Emilia says, "I'll have the work ta'en out, / And give't Iago" (3.3.296–297). Cassio entreats "Sweet Bianca, / Take me this work out" (3.4.179–180) and then more forcefully, "I like the work well; ere it be demanded / (As like enough it will) I would have it copied. / Take it, and do't" (3.4.189–191). Bianca later rebels with "A likely piece of work. . . . This is some minx's token, and I must take out the work?" (4.1.151–154). But even before the "spotted" handkerchief becomes the focus of attention, Iago taunts Emilia with the charge that all women are "Players in your huswifery, and huswives in your beds . . . / You rise to play, and go to bed to work" (2.1.113–115).

Bianca herself is described by Iago as "a huswife that by selling her desires / Buys herself bread and cloth" (F, "Cloath"; Q, "cloathes," 4.1.94–95), a combination of cloth work with a reputation for prostitution that may be simply his own slander, as with the reputation of cloth workers in the "Low Countries" of the London suburbs. Bianca's appellation as a "courtesan" in the character list does not directly equate her with a prostitute in "a brothel in Southwark"; but women in the period were frequently forced to combine "needletrades with prostitution" because "textile industries did not pay women even subsistence wages."[214] In the contemporary context of the

"Low Countries" of London's suburbs where cloth was sent to "whit[e]sters" or whiteners" (as it is in *Merry Wives*) even Bianca's own name might suggest such an ambivalent whitening, in a play where her presence on Cyprus simultaneously recalls the camp followers familiar from the Low Countries' wars.[215]

In the source of *Othello* in Cinthio, the color of the handkerchief embroidered "*alla moresca*" (or in the "Moorish fashion") is not given.[216] But recently Ian Smith has argued that the handkerchief "dy'd in mummy" in *Othello* (3.4.74) is black rather than white, aligning it with the black body of the Moor—as well as the sexual blackness associated with Desdemona's "virtue" turned into "pitch" (2.3.360)—and further rendering it "a visible, material manifestation of Iago's mental monstrosity unpacked."[217] This—I would add—may be a reason why Othello includes in its history that "the worms were hallowed that did breed the silk" (3.4.73), immediately before that it was "dy'd in mummy" (3.4.74), since the mulberry tree from which silk was produced was known in the period as the "Moor" tree, from its Latin name *morus*—the same Latin word that included "black" and meant that Sir Thomas More (or *Morus*) could be represented as a Moor as well as in depictions surrounding him with mulberry leaves on which silkworms were feeding.[218] And, if the silk handkerchief is black, there would (in addition to the link Smith has suggested with Iago) be even more connections with Spanish-held Brabant, since black silk in the period was associated with Spain, and Antwerp in Brabant was the principal locus of the transmission of silk to England.

The geographical palimpsest that makes it possible to evoke Brabant and the Low Countries through the family name of Brabantio and Desdemona herself—in a context in which events in Brabant and the Low Countries were so bound up with events on the Barbary Coast and engagements with the Turk—was, it should be added, shared by the contemporary geocultural palimpsest in which the "Low Countries" of the brothel district in the suburbs of London were also known as the "Barbary Coast" and "Turkish shore," where women sexually "turned Turk,"[219] as Othello accuses Desdemona of doing (4.1.252–254). And the silk handkerchief that Paul Yachnin has characterized as registering "the theatre's participation in English society's fetishized trade in textiles"[220] itself becomes a global material object, identified with sexual Low Country matters as well as the far reaches of North Africa and Egypt (3.4.55–57) and through "the worms . . . that did breed the silk" (3.4.73) with the global traffic that brought silk from Venice and Antwerp to London.

ꕥ

Nay, it is true, or else I am a Turk.

—*Othello* (2.1.114)

For nature so prepost'rously to err . . .
Sans witchcraft could not.

—*Othello* (1.3.62–64)

Conduct us to most prepost'rous conclusions.

—*Othello* (1.3.329)

Kim F. Hall observes that "while popular views of Venice and Cyprus are woven into *Othello*'s action, allusions to other geographical spaces like Barbary, Aleppo, Africa, and Florence deepen the texture of the play."[221] To suggest that Brabant is evoked through the name of "Brabantio" and contributes in multiple ways to deepening the texture of this play is to suggest that it too provides, like Lepanto and the Armada—neither of which is cited by name—part of this play's wider global context, without any need for a one-to-one correspondence between the character of Brabantio and what was known for so long in England to be part of engagements that included the Low Countries, Cyprus, and the Turk. As Barbara Everett remarks of "Shakespeare's dramatic nomenclature" more generally, though she does not mention Brabantio, it "reflects certain harsh facts in the world outside the plays; and these facts help to extend" the "imaginative resonance possessed by mere names."[222]

The evocation of Brabant joins the already far-flung geographies that *Othello* both directly and indirectly evokes—from the Black or Pontic Sea (3.3.453) and Aleppo in Syria (5.2.352) to the Spanish Armada threatening the invasion of England. It is part of the broader canvas of "a world which could not be at all adequately described in private and domestic terms" in the scenes that "evoke a world of public events: affairs of state, war, and military heroism," before it is replaced by "confinement to the private and domestic sphere" or the "peculiarly private or even domestic nature of its action" (as Emrys Jones puts it in arguing for *Othello*'s evocation of Lepanto).[223] And like the play's other global resonances, it simultaneously provides a larger context for and throws into even bolder relief the ultimate narrowing of the play's focus to the domestic and personal—as the scene on Cyprus in which the drunken Cassio is cashiered, Desdemona is described as "an alarum to love," and Iago's "We work by wit, and not by witchcraft" (2.3.372) echoes Brabantio's accusation of the Moor ("For nature so prepost'rously to err . . . / Sans witchcraft could not," 1.3.62–64), moves toward the great Temptation Scene of Act 3; and "honest" Iago—the unrecognized "machiavel" who bears a Spanish name and refers to himself ironically as a "Turk"—manipulates the "credit" market of the play, works by a different kind of spellbinding toward "prepost'rous conclusions" (1.3.329), and becomes the tragedy's infidel within.

*Chapter 6*

# Intimations of Ganymede in *Cymbeline*

*Iupiter descends in Thunder and Lightning, sitting uppon an Eagle . . .*

—*Cymbeline* (First Folio, 1623)

The King of Goddes did burne erewhyle in love of Ganymed.

—Ovid, *Metamorphoses* 10 (trans. Arthur Golding)

Other chapters in this book have discussed the language of the plays in relation to particular historical intersections and contexts. Many—including Chapter 5 (which has "What's in a Name?" in its title)—have engaged with the wider importance of particular characters' names within the plays in which they appear. And many have foregrounded the language of the *preposterous* and of "preposterous venery" across the "homo/hetero divide." What I propose to do in this final chapter is to focus on a name ("Ganymede") that nowhere appears in the play under discussion; but to consider the possibility of "intimations" of Ganymede from contemporary contexts as well as the language, events, and internal relations of the play itself, including its opening reference to the King's "Bedchamber" (1.1.42), the role of "Fidele" as both wife and transvestite page or boy actor, and the descent of Jupiter with his eagle.

In approaches to Shakespeare's *Cymbeline* that stress the link between King James and the Roman emperor Augustus (in whose reign the play is ostensibly set), a central connection is the figure of Jupiter, who descends on his eagle in Act 5—since not only Virgil but other Roman writers, including

Suetonius, record Augustus's aligning himself with Jupiter as the preeminent Roman god, and James had already been figured as Jupiter in Jonson's *Hymenaei* and his own self-representations.[1] The speech of Jupiter to the Leonati at this crucial moment in *Cymbeline* clearly recalls Jupiter's prophecy of the ultimate happy ending of Aeneas's travails in Virgil's *Aeneid*, which ends with the *pax Augustus*,[2] while at the same time evoking James's fulminating descents on Parliament when it resisted the naturalization of the Scots, as well as his cherished cause of the Union of the Kingdoms.[3] But at the same time—and in ways illustrative of the double (or multiple) perspectives at work in this late play—the references to "greatness' favour" (5.3.192) and unreliable "courtiers" (5.3.200) that follow Jupiter's descent also subtly ironize both.

In contrast to readings that see *Cymbeline*'s Jupiter as the play's deity or Divine Providence,[4] Leah Marcus and others have argued that the descent of Jupiter on the eagle not only recalls James—whose imperial ambitions were figured as a Roman eagle flown westward to London at his coronation[5]—but emerges as one of the fault lines in the play's own relation to Jacobean iconography and propaganda:

> Like the episode of Imogen's misguided grief over Cloten's headless body, the Descent of Jupiter is perilously balanced between the compelling and the ludicrous. It is "double written" or overwritten in a way that calls special attention to it and invites political decipherment but also provides a mechanism by which the "authorized" political reading can be dispersed or ridiculed. To use James I's own complaining language for such abuse of the clear royal intent, the Descent of Jupiter is contrived in such a way that it can easily be "throwne" or "rent asunder in contrary sences like the old Oracles of the Pagan gods." In London, 1610, before an audience for whom the play's political meaning was at least potentially legible, how and whether the episode got "read" according to the Jacobean line would depend in large part on how it was brought to life in the theater.[6]

Marcus continues by arguing:

> The same is true of the play as a whole. By embedding *Cymbeline*'s "Jacobean line" within various structures which at least potentially call it into question, Shakespeare partially separates the play from

> the realm of authorship and "Authority," reinfuses its topicality with some of the evanescence and protean, shifting referentiality that were still characteristic of the Renaissance theater as opposed to authored collections of printed *Workes*. If King James I made a practice of beating off the subversive proliferation of meaning in order to communicate his "clear" political intent, Shakespeare in *Cymbeline* can be seen as one of those jangling subjects who scatter language and signification, dispersing the king's painstaking crafting of a unified whole nearly as fast as the royal author can put it together.[7]

The descent of Jupiter with its echoes of the *Aeneid* and Roman *imperium*—including the *pax* or peace of Augustus, the emperor of *Cymbeline*'s putative Roman setting—is part of a play that is an anachronistic palimpsest of ancient and early modern, which simultaneously includes the bourgeois sources of its wager plot from Boccaccio's *Decameron*[8] and its anonymous Dutch translation in *Frederyke of Jennen* or Genoa. In *Cymbeline*, the wager plot itself begins in a scene that includes on stage "a *Dutchman*" and "a *Spaniard*" (1.4.0SD), as well as a "Frenchman," a "Briton," and two Italians—reminders of early modern Europe joined by the name "Euriphile" in Act 4 (4.2.233). And its references to "Rome" and empire throughout repeatedly resonate with reminders of the new Rome of the Habsburg empire that included both the Low Countries and Spain (as in the silently present "Dutchman" and "Spaniard" of the wager scene) and Charles V, the Habsburg Holy Roman Emperor, together with his son Philip II of Spain, whose Armada has already been acknowledged as evoked by this play's Roman invasion—just as Cymbeline's peace with Rome at its conclusion has been aligned with James's controversial 1604 peace with Spain discussed in the previous chapter, though none of these are named explicitly in this late play.

What I would like to suggest in this chapter is another aspect of *Cymbeline* that works by indirection or intimation and another dimension of "protean, shifting referentiality" in the descent of Jupiter on his eagle, which has gone without comment in relation to James or the play as a whole—namely its reminder of Jupiter's eagle and descent in the story of Ganymede, the beautiful Trojan boy whose *raptus* and elevation as Jupiter's favorite was central to the entire history of empire and the revenge of Juno wreaked upon Aeneas, the Trojan charged with the project of founding Rome.[9] That a reminder of Ganymede could be evoked by Jupiter's descent on the eagle would thus be germane to the relation of *Cymbeline* to the "translation" of empire itself from Troy to Rome (and ultimately to Britain and early modern Europe), since "Trojan" Ganymede was linked to the revenge of Juno against Troy and its descendants so prominently chronicled in the *Aeneid*, the epic of empire echoed in Jupiter's own speech. In a way important for this play of multiple revenge plots, Juno's reason for revenge—foregrounded in "with Juno chide, that thy adulteries / Rates and revenges" (*Cymbeline* 5.3.125–126)—thus centrally involved Jupiter's relation with this beautiful Trojan boy as well.

Familiar accounts of the *raptus* or "rape of Ganymede" were readily available in Virgil (*Aeneid* 1.28, 5.250–257) and Ovid's *Metamorphoses* (10.155, 11.756).[10] As James M. Saslow notes in *Ganymede in the Renaissance*, the influential reference to Ganymede and Jupiter in the first book of the *Aeneid* (the book that Shakespeare would soon after recall in the opening of *The Tempest*) stresses Juno's anger at Jupiter's love of the boy as "contributing to the goddess's role in provoking the Trojan War."[11] Ganymede's Trojan origin is underscored again later in the *Aeneid*, in the description in Book 5 of a cloak into which the story is woven of the beautiful boy caught up in the talons of Jupiter's eagle. The Trojan link (and revenge by Juno) also figures prominently in Ovid's *Metamorphoses* (10.155–161) and *Fasti* (6.43), both well-known sources for Shakespeare, and Jupiter's *raptus* of Ganymede is cited again in *Metamorphoses* 11,[12] immediately following the end of the Ceyx and Alcyone story that Shakespeare used for the description of Posthumus's sailing away from Innogen in *Cymbeline* itself (1.3.8–22).

Ovid's most influential retelling of the Jupiter and Ganymede story in Book 10 comes, tellingly for *Cymbeline* (where Cloten's severed head recalls Orpheus's), in the midst of Orpheus's rejection of women and tales of "prettie boyes / That were the derlings of the Gods": "The King of Goddes did burne erewhyle in love of Ganymed / The Phrygian and the thing was found which Jupiter that sted / Had rather bee than that he was. Yit could he not beteeme / The shape of any other Bird than Aegle for to seeme / And so he soring in the ayre with borrowed wings trust up / The Trojane boay who still in heaven even yit dooth beare his cup, / And brings him Nectar though against Dame Junos will it bee."[13]

In Spenser's *The Faerie Queene*, an important source for *Cymbeline* (as Martin Butler and others point out), Ganymede's Trojan origin is likewise recalled in a context devoted to Jupiter's (or Jove's) love for this "lovely boy": "The first was Fancy, like a lovely boy, / Of rare aspect, and beautie without peare; / Matchable either to that ympe of Troy, / Whom Jove did love, and chose his cup to beare."[14] And Ganymede appears in a tapestry that "depicts Jove's eagle abducting the lovely shepherd boy as his frightened companions gaze up in wonder," in a passage in which male homoeroticism is in tension with the marital chastity the book itself takes as its virtue.[15]

As Bruce Smith has observed, "the story of Jupiter and Ganymede was the best known myth of homoerotic desire in early modern England," and Ganymede (origin of English "catamite") was "the commonest epithet in early modern English for a homosexual male."[16] For antitheatrical writers like William Prynne, English transvestite theater itself had affinities with the Ganymede story, including the virtual sex changes it supposedly enacted. In Prynne's words, sodomites clothed their Ganymedes "in woman's attire, whose virilities they did oft-times dissect, to make them more effeminate, transforming them as neere as might be into women, both in apparel, gesture, speech [and] behavior."[17]

The Jupiter and Ganymede story was familiar not only from classical sources but from myriad references in contemporary writing, including Christopher Marlowe's *Dido, Queen of Carthage* and *Hero and Leander*. As Mario DiGangi has stressed, the story of Ganymede also had its context in "a familial drama involving Jupiter's wife Juno and their daughter Hebe," as well as in a misogynistic rejection of women. Disgust at the "woman's part" (subject of Posthumus's misogynistic tirade in *Cymbeline*) is foregrounded in Thomas Cooper's influential classical dictionary, which tells of how when Hebe one day "chaunsed to fall, and disclosed further of hir neather partes, then comeliness woulde have to be shewen, Jupiter, to the great displeasure of his wife Juno, removed her from that office, and appointed Ganymedes to serve hym at his cuppe." In *Dido, Queen of Carthage*—where "Jupiter has no qualms about risking the public display of Ganymede's nether parts," "dandling Ganymede upon his knee," and "playing" wantonly with him—when Juno expresses her "hate of Trojan Ganymede, / That was advanced by my Hebe's shame" (3.2.42–43), she "reinforces the sense that it is the display of 'shameful' female parts (the 'pudendum') that provokes Jupiter's ire" in a story that "reveals a great deal of anxiety about female sexuality."[18] The gender tensions within the Ganymede story had already been foregrounded in Arthur Golding's 1567 translation of Ovid, where Jupiter advances Ganymede "against Dame *Junos* will."[19] And in a play closer to the date of *Cymbeline*, John Mason's *The Turke* (published in 1610), an older male tells his youthful page, "I will turne *Jupiter*, hate the whole sexe of women, and onely embrace thee my *Ganimede*."[20]

As DiGangi comments, "Jupiter's love for Ganymede constitutes a single homoerotic affair among numerous heteroerotic affairs that angered Juno. Yet because Jupiter replaces his female servant with a male servant and his wife with a boy, the story of Ganymede uniquely links the offense of a husband's marital infidelity with his rejection of women."[21] As James Saslow puts it in his influential account of the Ganymede story: "Jupiter's preferment of Ganymede over Hebe and Juno's consequent jealous resentment were often interpreted as a parable of two closely connected social phenomena"—"the subordinate status or worth of women and the potentially disruptive effect of a man's homosexual infidelities on the relations between husband and wife."[22]

ᔕ

> by the fount
> Where first you took me up . . .
> The love of boys unto their lords is strange.
>
> —Beaumont and Fletcher, *Philaster, or Love Lies A-Bleeding*

The association of Jupiter and his eagle with the Ganymede story—including in the imperial context of the translation of empire from Troy to Rome—was well known from other sources as well as more generally in the period. That Ganymede could be recalled in Jupiter's descent on the eagle in *Cymbeline*'s last act is rendered even more likely by the fact that Thomas Heywood's *The Golden Age* (ca. 1609–1611)—printed in 1611 with a title page indicating that it had "beene sundry times acted at the Red Bull, by the Queenes Maiesties Seruants"—featured the ascent of Jupiter and Ganymede to heaven on an eagle.[23] And in Beaumont and Fletcher's *Philaster, or Love Lies A-Bleeding*, the King's Men play routinely cited in relation to *Cymbeline*, Ganymede is prominently evoked, in a plot that simultaneously glances at James. Jeffrey Masten has argued in *Queer Philologies* for the pervasive echoes of the Jupiter and Ganymede story in that play, including in relation to its "boy" Bellario, even though it never mentions Ganymede by name.[24] Masten sees reference to "the story of Ganymede, a figure hovering over the whole play" (115), in the lines in which Bellario says to Philaster, "Sir, you did take me up / When I was nothing, and only yet am something / By being yours" (2.1.5–7),[25] a "taking up" that recalls Jupiter's *raptus* of Ganymede in lines that simultaneously call attention to the relation of master and servant, and stress "his availability for pedagogic instruction and transformation" (116).

And after the revelation in the final scene that this "boy" is a girl (Euphrasia), Philaster's request ("tell me why / Thou didst conceal thy sex," 5.5.145–146) "produces another narrative that is *simultaneously* a genealogy of Bellario's/ Euphrasia's true gender *and* a second version of Philaster's earlier speech explaining the love of boys unto their lords," since "Euphrasia's now 'female' version of her story is nevertheless still structured by the rhetoric of 'taking up,' associated with the shepherd Ganymede" (119):

> Euphrasia's story, ostensibly the backstory of her true gender, simultaneously restages the shepherd Ganymede's flight, legible, as Leonard Barkan has pointed out, as his ravishment and/or his education: the story of awakened desire here is also the story of rising thoughts. Having dressed herself "[i]n habit of a boy," Euphrasia continues, she sat "by the fount / Where first you *took me up*" (5.5.173, 182–83). Discovered to be a woman, Euphrasia's rhetoric and narrative continue to mark her as a boy. (120)

Because she also remains in boys' clothes even at the play's end, and the ambiguities persist, Masten then asks, "Is this why Philaster must 'call [Bellario] still so'? Is it the persistence of the boy clothing that she still wears—the force of 'habit'? Or what Orgel describes as her 'deci[sion] to remain permanently in drag'?" (120).[26] And he goes on from the persistence of echoes of Ganymede in *Philaster* to stress that Ganymede and Jupiter's eagle constituted a ubiquitous sign in the culture itself, in the 1590s and beyond.[27]

Suzanne Gossett's 2009 edition of *Philaster* not only cites Masten's argument (from its earlier published form in 2006)[28] but suggests a topical application to James and his favorite Robert Carr in the very exchange on the "boy" taken "up" that Masten cites as a reminder of Ganymede taken "up" by Jupiter. Glossing boys "preferred" to "greater men" (in the sense of social advancement), she writes: "This description of *boys* being preferred to *greater men* (*prefer* appears three times from 15 to 25) suggests King James's well known penchant for beautiful male favourites and in particular for Robert Carr, who came to James's attention in 1607 and was given increasingly important titles" (145).[29] Gossett also comments on the "saucy" of these lines that "Carr's arrogance was notorious" and draws a further parallel between James and the anonymous king of the play, including in relation to James's claims to "a manner or resemblance of Diuine power vpon earth" (involving tensions with Parliament) and to Philaster's saying he is "no minion": "Philaster's assertion that he is 'no minion' would have resonated as James's predilection for young men became increasingly apparent; the king ceased to cohabit with his wife after the birth and death of the Princess Sophia in 1607, and his special relationship with Robert Carr, his first truly conspicuous 'minion,' began in that same year" (26). Although she does not explore the broader implications for Shakespeare's play, she draws (in this same scene) a comparison with the boy "Fidele" (*Cymbeline*'s cross-dressed Innogen) in Philaster's "The love of boys unto their lords is strange": "The 'love of boys unto their lords' is shown as unreliable, if not *strange*, in *Cym*: in 4.2 the disguised Innogen's tale of affection for her 'master / A very valiant Briton' moves Lucius to take 'Fidele' as a page because 'Thy name well fits thy faith,' yet Innogen has invented this master and is actually lying on the body of Cloten. Later, when Lucius assumes that 'Fidele' will use the boon offered by Cymbeline to beg his life, the page informs him, 'Your life, good master, / Must shuffle for itself' and Lucius concludes that 'Briefly die their joys / That place them on the truth of girls and boys' (5.5.104–7)" (146).[30]

This play by Beaumont and Fletcher that has been so closely linked to *Cymbeline* also repeatedly suggests a critical perspective on James—including not only his penchant for male favorites but in addition his creation of knighthoods and the claimed prerogative of the king to wield Jupiter's "thunder" (4.4.53), in ways suggestive for the evocation of carpet knights and the descent of Jupiter in *Cymbeline* as well.

ေ

The King he takes the babe
To his protection, calls him Posthumus Leonatus,
Breeds him, and makes him of his Bedchamber,
Puts to him all the learnings that his time
Could make him the receiver of. . . .

—*Cymbeline* (1.1.40–44)

Boy,
Thou hast looked thyself into my grace,
And art mine own. . . .

—*Cymbeline* (5.4.93–95)

Haie with his sonnes, supposing they might best staie the flight,
placed themselues ouerthwart the lane. . . . The Danes being here

staied in the lane by the great valiancie of the father and the sonnes, . . . fled backe in great disorder . . .

—Holinshed, *The Description & History of Scotland* (1587)

James's favorites had already been assimilated to the Jupiter and Ganymede story prior to his accession to the English throne in 1603, including through Marlowe's *Edward II* and the representation of the "girle-boy" Gaveston as a "shamelesse *Ganimed*" in Drayton.[31] But *Cymbeline* also makes a clear reference to James's "Bedchamber" favorites in its own opening scene. The Gentleman who says he cannot "delve" Posthumus "to the root" (1.1.28) goes on to recount that he was elevated to the royal "Bedchamber" by the king who "Puts to him all the learnings that his time / Could make him the receiver of" (1.1.42–44), a detail that simultaneously suggests potentially more complex (or additional) reasons for Cymbeline's anger about the union of Posthumus and Innogen. Martin Butler comments in his New Cambridge edition (81): "As so often in this play, the practices of Cymbeline's court reflect seventeenth-century Whitehall rather than first-century Camulodunum. At the Stuart court the Gentlemen of the Bedchamber were the king's most personal attendants, serving in his private lodgings and sleeping by his bed; a prestigious and intimate office. Under James the Bedchamber was the focus for a group of elite courtiers, who notoriously received the richest favours and rewards." Butler also points to the link between this opening reference to the king's "Bedchamber" and the final scene, where Cymbeline—not knowing that "Polydorus" and "Cadwal" are his own sons Guiderius and Arviragus—raises them (with Belarius) to the position of "knights o'th'battle. . . . / Companions to our person" (5.4.20–21), in lines where "Companions" is "*Cymbeline*'s version of the Jacobean office of Gentlemen of the Bedchamber, personal attendants on the king who served him on intimate terms" but in an ancient context where "the honour goes to the worthiest men" (226). And in this same final scene, when Cymbeline himself is taken by the looks of the "page" Fidele ("Boy, / Thou hast looked thyself into my grace, / And art mine own," 5.4.93–95), Butler, glossing these lines with "won my favour merely by your looks," draws a specific comparison to James's reigning favorite Robert Carr: "In 1607 Robert Carr, the future Earl of Somerset but then a mere page, won favour when he caught King James's attention at a tilt" (228).

Another of the Gentlemen of the Bedchamber in James's court was his other Scottish favorite James Hay—who was elevated to the king's Bedchamber soon after James's accession in 1603.[32] This favorite of James is already known to be directly pertinent to *Cymbeline* because the heroism of his ancestor at the battle of Luncarty (AD 976) between the Scots and Danish invaders—described in Holinshed's *History of Scotland*—provided the basis of the description in Act 5 of the heroism of the "old man and two boys" who beat back the Roman invasion at the narrow "lane" (5.3.3–51). Holinshed records this ancient example in *The Description & History of Scotland* (1587) already used for *Macbeth*:

> [P]erceiuing that there was no hope of life but in victorie, [the Danes] rushed foorth with such violence vpon their aduersaries, that first the right, and then after the left wing of the Scots, was constreined to retire and flee backe, the middle-ward stoutly yet keeping their ground: but the same stood in such danger, being now left naked on the sides, that the victorie must needes haue remained with the Danes, had not a renewer of the battell come in time, by the appointment (as is to be thought) of almightie God.
>
> For as it chanced, there was in the next field at the same time an husbandman, with two of his sons busie about his worke, named Haie, a man strong and stiffe in making and shape of bodie, but indued with a valiant courage. This Haie beholding the king with the most part of the nobles, fighting with great valiancie in the middle ward, now destitute of the wings, and in great danger to be oppressed by the great violence of his enimies, caught a plow-beame in his hand, and with the same exhorting his sonnes to doo the like, hasted towards the battell, there to die rather amongest other in defense of his countrie, than to remaine aliue after the discomfiture in miserable thraldome and bondage of the cruell and most vnmercifull enimies. There was neere to the place of the battell, a long lane fensed on the sides with ditches and walles made of turfe, through the which the Scots which fled were beaten downe by the enimies on heapes.
>
> Here Haie with his sonnes, supposing they might best staie the flight, placed themselues ouerthwart the lane, beat them backe whome they met fleeing, and spared neither friend nor fo: but downe they went all such as came within their reach, wherewith diuerse hardie personages cried vnto their fellowes to returne backe vnto the battell, for there was a new power of Scotishmen come to their succours, by whose aid the victorie might be easily obteined of

> their most cruell aduersaries the Danes: therefore might they choose whether they would be slaine of their own fellowes coming to their aid, or to returne againe to fight with the enimies. The Danes being here staied in the lane by the great valiancie of the father and the sonnes, thought verely there had beene some great succors of the Scots come to the aid of their king, and therevpon ceassing from further pursute, fled backe in great disorder vnto the other of their fellowes fighting with the middle ward of the Scots.
>
> The Scots also that before were chased, being incouraged herewith, pursued the Danes vnto the place of the battell right fiercelie. . . . [I]n the end the Danes were constreined to forsake the field, and the Scots egerlie pursuing in the chase, made great slaughter of them as they fled. This victorie turned highlie to the praise of the Scotish nobilitie, the which fighting in the middle ward, bare still the brunt of the battell, continuing manfullie therein euen to the end. But Haie, who in such wise (as is before mentioned) staied them that fled, causing them to returne againe to the field, deserued immortall fame and commendation: for by his meanes chieflie was the victorie atchiued.[33]

Glynne Wickham points out that this original tenth-century "Haie" whose heroism is echoed in *Cymbeline* received "a peerage for his services" and that "the incident that thus brought the family land, wealth, and status was preserved pictorially in their coat of arms."[34] And John Kerrigan, in *Archipelagic English* (2008), seeing his descendant Sir James Hay as a "potential Scottish patron" for Shakespeare himself, argues that the "likely occasion" for *Cymbeline*'s use of Holinshed's account of his "farming ancestor" was "the admission of Sir James as a Knight of the Bath at the 1610 investiture of the Prince of Wales—the probable context . . . for the first performance of *Cymbeline*."[35] But what goes without comment in most analyses of *Cymbeline* that record this historical connection is that James's favorite Hay, who became a Scottish knight before becoming a naturalized Englishman in 1604 and rising to Lord Hay in 1606, was notorious for the extravagance with which he lived and, as master of the robes whose responsibility was to provide the king with clothing, ran up huge debts.[36] As Martin Butler notes, not in his edition of *Cymbeline* but in an essay on Ben Jonson, "Royal finances had been in disarray virtually since James's accession, not the least because James was a spender rather than a saver, who had a large household, an entourage of Scots and a temperament inclining towards liberality"; and though his problems were not entirely of his own making, the ways in which he "exacerbated his problems" included "appointing James Hay as head of the Wardrobe despite his penchant for consuming vast sums of money in displays of courtly ostentation," the penchant that led to Francis Osborne's later comments on Hay as a "Monster in Excess."[37] Hay the Jacobean favorite provided the courtly opposite, in other words, to the heroism of the Scottish ancestor whose valor Holinshed records, suggesting the kind of historical contrast evoked later in the play, in the final scene's allusion to "knights o' th' battle" (5.4.20), between such ancient heroism and contemporary "carpet knights."[38]

Complaints about Scots in the Bedchamber predate *Cymbeline* by several years—along with complaints about financial extravagance and James's concept of *imperium*. Jonson's *Sejanus*—devoted to Tiberius's favorite—though dating from an earlier period, increasingly took on a more topical resonance. And by 1610, the likely date of *Cymbeline*, Samuel Lewkenor was interpreting Xenophon's story of Cyrus and Croesus in the *Cyropaedia* (one of James's favorite texts) as "a tale of lavish spending on wanton favorites."[39] Already, in 1605, Jonson and Chapman had been imprisoned for satirizing the Scottish favorites in *Eastward Ho*.[40] And Beaumont and Fletcher's *The Woman-Hater* (1606) may have glanced at James's favorites in the same period as Dekker's *Whore of Babylon* provided a critique of his pacificism and unpopular peace with Spain.[41] In the years between 1603 and 1610, as Neil Cuddy has observed, English resentment of James's Scottish favorites and their lavish spending was also inseparable from resistance to his Union project and the naturalization of the Scots—major contemporary contexts invoked in topical readings of *Cymbeline*, though without reference to James's Scottish favorites and the issue of the "Bedchamber" (where Scots predominated).[42]

The Gentleman's report, at the beginning of *Cymbeline*, that Posthumus himself was raised to the king's "Bedchamber," and put by the king to "all the learning that his time / Could make him the receiver of," is most reminiscent of Robert Carr, the page with whom James fell in love in 1607, casting himself "in one of his favourite roles, the kindly schoolmaster" and giving him "Latin lessons every morning."[43] (James also cast himself as a "father" to his favorites, making it clear that Roman Lucius's "rather father thee than master thee" when he takes the "boy" Fidele as his "page" in Act 4 would not preclude his also becoming Jupiter to his Ganymede).[44] Carr rose quickly in the years leading up to *Cymbeline*—already made Gentleman of the Bedchamber by the end of 1607; given by James "a tablet of gold set with diamonds, and the King's picture," in March of 1608, which Alan Stewart observes was "a token more often given between lovers than master and servant"; and the following January, given estates that had been seized from Sir Walter Raleigh.[45] But, as Stewart observes, "It was not long before James's infatuation with Carr was a source of open mockery," in a context in which at the same time "to get on at court now meant being able to praise the new favourite."[46]

In the years following 1607, the description of the "smooth-faced" Carr repeatedly fit the image of the youthful Ganymede.[47] ("Smooth" and "soft" were also familiar terms for the *mollis* male, something we might remember in relation to *mollis aer*, made to stand for "*mulier*" or wife in the Soothsayer's heteronormative construing or "construction" of Jupiter's enigmatic text in *Cymbeline*'s final scene, where the "page" Fidele remains clothed as a "boy" on stage). By 1612, two years after the likely date of *Cymbeline*, Carr was still the reigning royal favorite when Peacham's Ganymede emblem was published, an emblem directly linked to James's bedchamber favorites by Curtis Perry, in *Literature and Favoritism*:

> Henry Peacham's emblem book *Minerva Britanna* (1612) offers a pictorial representation of King James's list of unforgivable crimes from *Basilikon Doron*. The emblem features Ganymede "the foule Sodomitan" riding on a cock (which Peacham tells us represents incest), and carrying Circe's wand (witchcraft), a cup of poison, and some counterfeit coins. Though Peacham's emblem is based directly on James's text, the invocation of Ganymede invokes an underground figuration of James and his bedchamber favorites as sodomitical. For Ganymede, by virtue of his office in the household of Jove, is a figure specifically of court service, which means that Peacham's figuration transposes James's rather general list of crimes into a specifically courtly context. Whether or not Peacham intended it, this adds a critical or satirical dimension not present in James's writing; court corruption reflects poorly on the king.[48]

Perry observes that "English resentment of Scottish interlopers helped shape the initial jealousy created over the bedchamber privilege," and, though "the cupbearer is actually a privy chamber position, Peacham's Ganymede is in some sense an iconic shorthand for the discontents that accompanied this development" (117). In a way pertinent to the likely date of *Cymbeline*, he also dates this discontent to years earlier than the emblem itself: "James's generosity to Robert Carr and other members of the Scottish Bedchamber prompted grumblings, by 1610, that the public cisterns were being drained for the use of 'private cocks,' a remark with the same risqué double-meaning it might have today" (131–132). As Perry points out in an earlier piece, "Direct accusations of sodomy were dangerous and so tend to be muted, but there is a bass-rumble of such gossip linking James with his Bedchamber favorites which nevertheless survives," including with regard to Carr.[49]

Peacham's Ganymede emblem is very different from the "transcendent" tradition of Alciati's earlier emblem, where Jupiter's *raptus* and Ganymede's ascent were figured as reflecting the love of God, a tension not unlike the difference between religious or "transcendent" readings of Jupiter in *Cymbeline* and more skeptical ones.[50] As Mario DiGangi comments, the "more subversive reading" of Peacham's Ganymede emblem—published years after complaints against Carr and the Bedchamber favorites had already begun—is further corroborated by two accompanying Latin quotations from Tibullus and Ciprian that were more applicable to James than to Peacham's nominal patron Prince Henry, the first of which warned, "O flee the foolish effeminacy of boys, who as trusting a whirling top, always have passions for an unjust cause," and the second admonishing, "By that vice which you do not correct you will be punished, O King."[51]

All of these contemporary contexts—including the ascent of Jupiter and Ganymede on an eagle in Heywood's *The Golden Age*, the importance of Ganymede for *Philaster*, and Peacham's implicit critique of James in the Ganymede emblem, in the years just before and after *Cymbeline*—suggest that the Ganymede story might well be evoked, sotto voce, in the descent of Jupiter on his eagle in *Cymbeline*, in addition to the ways in which the implied Ganymede figure pervades (as in *Philaster*) other parts of the play, from the opening allusion to James's "Bedchamber" favorites to the final scene in which the "page" Fidele remains in the clothing of an attractive "boy." The likelihood of Ganymede's hovering around the edges of *Cymbeline* is also increased by the hints of Ganymede in the "Cesario" of *Twelfth Night* (still, like "Fidele," dressed in boy's clothes at play's end) and by the reference to "Ganymede" as "Jove's own page" in *As You Like It* (1.3.124),[52] a play whose ending includes the heteronormative ("Wedding is great Juno's crown," 5.4.141) but also foregrounds the role of "boys" playing the "woman's part" in English transvestite theater, as *Cymbeline* does in its final scene, to which we will return.

ᔕ

What false Italian,
As poisonous tongued as handed, hath prevailed
On thy too ready hearing?

—*Cymbeline* (3.2.4–6)

Thy Caesar knighted me; my youth I spent
Much under him.

—*Cymbeline* (3.1.67–68)

Having found the back door open
Of the unguarded hearts, heavens, how they wound!

—*Cymbeline* (5.3.45–46)

*Cymbeline* itself repeatedly crosses what Jonathan Goldberg has called the "homo/hetero divide."[53] Its insistent images of penetration are frequently heterosexual, including the rape of Lucrece and Philomel, in the scene in Innogen's "chamber" (2.2), and the bawdy wordplay that immediately follows it, in which Cloten seeks to "penetrate" Innogen through the ear with his "music" as a prelude to being able to "understand" her ostensibly female sexual "case" (2.3.70). But when the image of penetration is repeated in Act 3, it is in lines that recall Iago's penetration of Othello's ear, as that pair displaces Othello's relationship with the slandered Desdemona. Pisanio, reading the letter in which Posthumus accuses Innogen of infidelity, comments: "O master, what a strange infection / Is fall'n into thy ear? What false Italian, / As poisonous tongued as handed, hath prevailed / On thy too ready hearing?" (*Cymbeline* 3.2.3–6).[54]

Goran Stanivukovic has argued that the "Posthumus-Iachimo bond, centered around the figure of the Italian sodomite-merchant, suggests both the economic and sexual anxieties of the early modern society and theatre."[55] Figured as "Italian," sexual penetration the "preposterous Italian way"—or a "sodomitical" reversal of before and after or behind—was repeatedly foregrounded in the period, in the "back-door'd Italian" of Middleton and Dekker's *1 Honest Whore*, in Middleton's " 'tis such an Italian world, many men know not before from behind' " in *Michaelmas Term*, and the sexually suggestive "key given after the Italian fashion, backward" in *A Mad World, My Masters*. In Mason's *The Turke*, a gentleman usher whose office is normally to come "before" remarks that his "office" (a standard sexual term) has been "italianated, I am faine to come behind" (5.1.2156).[56] It was also, however, figured as "Roman" (including in the more contemporary sense evoked in *Cymbeline*'s anachronistic reference to a "Romish stew"), as in John Bale's "If ye spell Roma backwarde . . . It is preposterous *amor*, a loue out of order or a loue against kynde," and the "Rome backwards" that was a familiar euphemism for backwards sexual entry, including in Barry's *Ram-Alley*.[57] In the lines in which Cymbeline says to Lucius of his own youthful experience under Augustus in Rome—"Thy Caesar knighted me; my youth I spent / Much under him" (3.1.67–68)—there may not be an explicit reminder of ancient Roman sexual practice. But that practice was well known, even in relation to Julius Caesar, whom Suetonius taunts as "Queen of Bithynia" for his alleged pathic role as a youth under King Nicomedes in Asia Minor.[58] "Preposterous *amor*" or "preposterous venery" extends in the canon of Shakespeare from the sexual overtones of the "preposterous" in *Love's Labor's Lost* to Thersites on the "preposterous discoveries" Achilles and Patroclus (his "masculine whore") in *Troilus and Cressida*, in the years before *Cymbeline*.[59] And, as I have argued elsewhere, the "preposterous" or "backward" turning of the young male actors playing the "witches'" in Jonson's *Masque of Queenes* may summon, sotto voce, the "preposterous venery" associated with James's own male favorites.[60]

What Joel Fineman called the logic of the "post" in Shakespeare has been explored in relation to the "Post" of Posthumus's own name—in topical readings devoted to the contemporary political and legal context of the "post nati," or Scots born *after* James's accession to the English throne,[61] a temporal sense of "pre" and "post" that could make all of the difference. In ways that recall the preposterous temporal reversal in which sons come before fathers in the English history plays discussed in Chapter 4, the temporal sense of the "preposterous" is exploited in *The Winter's Tale*—like *Cymbeline*, another late play—when the Shepherd Son says, "I was a gentleman born before my father" (5.2.139), in the scene where the shepherds' upwardly mobile rise to a "preposterous estate" (5.2.148) is simultaneously a malapropism for "prosperous," or the kind of upward mobility Posthumus has experienced, in ways that make him the object of Iachimo's scorn and the king's rejection in *Cymbeline*. *Cymbeline* likewise resembles the "preposterous" *temporal* situation of *Henry VIII* and Virgil's epic celebration of Augustus, where what is presented as "prophecy" is a history that has already occurred.[62] But in relation to the critical importance of birth at a particular date—before or after, "post" or "pre"—the fact that *Cymbeline* takes place in the period just *before* the birth of Christ also involves a historical date that made a crucial difference, though this epochal distinction between "*pre*" and "*post nati*" has gone largely ignored in relation to the potential critique it makes possible of James's imperial emulation of Augustus, as well as ambitions to empire itself.

The contemporary context and pertinence of the Jacobean "*post nati*" to *Cymbeline* has been extensively discussed. But the importance of the play's multiple references to preposterous venery has gone largely ignored, except for a small handful of critics, and the question of its importance (or even why it is included) in this play remains unclear. Ros King has drawn attention to what she sees as repeated images of "buggery" in *Cymbeline*—in Innogen's "needle" as inflicting a "prick" or "wound in the rear of the 'goer-back' " (1.1.165–169), which she remarks "carries more than a hint of the act of buggery";[63] in the "strain of effeminizing buggery" she describes as "confirmed" in the ensuing scene between Cloten and two lords of the court, where it is remarked, "His steel was in debt, it went o'th'backside the town' (1.2.8–9); and in "another, amazing image of buggery" in the exchange between Cymbeline and his daughter involving "aural puns" on "puttock" and "beggar" (1.1.139–143).[64] She stresses, however, that "what I am describing is a dark and corrupting shadow constructed by the playwright for the audience to discern, no matter how dimly, not for the characters primarily to intend" (103). And she adds, "Buggery, in this play, is less the marker of homosexual identity and practice than the ultimate expression and denigration of 'the other,' the 'not us' " as well as a marker of "the brutalizing effect of war" (103–104).[65]

With regard to the Roman invasion of Britain that provides its scenes of war, Linda Woodbridge in an earlier study observed that the female body of Innogen is used to figure "Britain," in ways that cast the Roman invasion as parallel to the invading by Iachimo of Innogen's "chamber" in the bedroom scene in Act 2 or the earlier Elizabethan figure of an intact female body resisting such incursions.[66] But in relation to the "homo/hetero divide," the terms in which that invasion is actually described repeatedly suggest preposterous venery, in ways that recall the earlier lines of *Henry V* on a Scottish invasion as a "sodomitical" rape or breaching from behind (*Henry V* 1.2.149). In *Cymbeline*, the description of the Roman invasion, where the "backs of Britons [were] seen, all flying / Through a strait lane" (5.3.6–7) and "the strait pass was dammed / With dead men hurt behind" (5.3.11–12), echoes the earlier reference to the "backside" of the "town" with regard to Cloten ("His steel was in debt, it went o'th'backside the town," 1.2.8–9). And when the heroic defense of that narrow lane "miraculously closes off these male bodies to penetration and submission to Roman invaders," the "Britons penetrate the now cowardly Romans," in a dramatic turnaround described as a "back door" wounding from behind: "Having found the back door open / Of the unguarded hearts, heavens, how they wound!" (5.3.45–46).[67]

With regard to other parts of *Cymbeline*, both Goran Stanivukovic and more recently James Bromley have revisited the "ring" that figures so prominently in the wager plot. Traditionally the ring has been associated by critics with the "woman's part," including through its origin from Innogen's mother and its gifting to Posthumus from Innogen in the lines "This diamond was my mother's. Take it, heart, / But keep it till you woo another wife, / When Innogen is dead" (1.1.112–114). But Stanivukovic points out that what Iachimo desires is "Posthumus's ring":

> It is Posthumus's ring that he desires. The ring is an object of bonding, and Iachimo's insistence on possessing the ring emphasizes the value Iachimo places on his bond with Posthumus. This value, I would argue, is an intimate one, and it is enabled here through the ambivalent erotic implication of "ring" as both vagina and anus (whose literal translation from Latin . . . is "ring"). This double erotic meaning of "ring" introduces illicit desire in the private agreement between Iachimo and Posthumus. The queer meaning of this scene, in which the ring features as a site of crisis, associates the silent agreement over an invalid contract with privacy in which an improper erotic exchange between men takes place. What Iachimo does in the wager scene in which he plays "dry usurer" is what Renaissance men did on their route to power: they negotiated their access to power by creating strategies that would disrupt the order, order which in *Cymbeline* is represented in male bonding and structured through the exchange of women and promotion of marriage.[68]

In his more recent book *Intimacy and Sexuality in the Age of Shakespeare* (2012), James Bromley argues that reference to "the woman's part" in Posthumus's famously misogynist speech (2.5.22) also opens up "a conditional space of possibility where, if he 'could . . . find out the woman's part' in him, he might find there the possibility of pleasure in the sexual penetration of his body" (66), and he extends this to the larger structure of the play "wherein Posthumus's relations with men that depend on a potentially eroticized submission conflict with and are supplanted by the prior claims of his reproductive relation with Innogen" (66), in a plot that ultimately "embraces reproduction while rejecting and leaving behind the potential pleasures of submission, pleasures related to, though not completely congruent with, anal penetration" (78). Bromley argues that Posthumus's voyeuristic envisioning of Iachimo as a "full-acorned" German "boar" mounting Innogen (2.5.16) "points to a relation between a man and the husband he cuckolds, the eroticism of which is routed through the wife" (67). And he points out that in yielding the "ring" to Iachimo as winner of the wager, he "opens up his 'woman's part' to the Italian when he gives him the ring because it is a 'part' given to him by a woman and it places him in the submissive position traditionally occupied by women in Renaissance culture" (71). Bromley concludes that "the vaginally-coded ring Innogen gives to Posthumus becomes an anally-coded one when he gives it to Iachimo" (71) and that "Posthumus's submission is only reversed when Iachimo, after being disarmed by him, admits 'the heaviness and guilt within my bosom / Takes off my manhood' (5.2.1–2). The specter of his eroticized submission to another man exorcised, Posthumus can reunite with his wife" (71).[69]

Though neither Bromley nor Stanivukovic mentions this striking earlier instance, the participation of the "ring" of Innogen in both sides of the "homo/hetero divide" is made even more suggestive by memories of the "ring" of Portia from *The Merchant of Venice*, a character who is already recalled in Iachimo's reminder to Innogen that she is bankrolling Posthumus (1.6.123). The ending of *The Merchant of Venice* directly calls attention to this ring in relation to the sexual "ring" of boys—not only the male figure that the cross-dressed Portia pretends to be in the Trial Scene, but also the figure of the boy player.[70] And "ring" in its male bodily sense may be suggested even earlier in *Titus Andronicus* as well.[71]

❧

By Jupiter, an angel—or, if not,
An earthly paragon. Behold divineness
No elder than a boy!

—*Cymbeline* (3.6.42–44)

I will not say
Thou shalt be so well mastered, but be sure
No less beloved. . . . Ay, good youth,
And rather father thee than master thee.

—*Cymbeline* (4.2.381–383, 393–394)

> Shall's have a play of this? Thou scornful page,
> There lie thy part.
>
> —*Cymbeline* (5.4.228–229)

Cleopatra's "I shall see / Some squeaking Cleopatra boy my greatness" in *Antony and Cleopatra* (5.2.219–220) is frequently recognized as a striking reminder of that play's transvestite staging. But just as arresting a "transvestite theatrical" moment in *Cymbeline* comes in the Recognition Scene of Act 5, in connection with "Fidele," the "page" or beautiful boy. The "woman's part" as a *theatrical* part performed by a transvestite boy player had already been foregrounded in *The Two Gentlemen of Verona*.[72] But in *Cymbeline*, it takes the form of a sudden metatheatrical disclosure, at the very moment when "Innogen" comes forward to reveal "herself" (in one of the final scene's many "recognitions") but Posthumus sees only the "page" in boy's clothes:

> Shall's have a *play* of this? Thou scornful *page*,
> There lie thy *part.* (5.4.228–229)

It is an extraordinary—and (from the perspective of the plot) wholly *unnecessary*—metatheatrical moment: Posthumus could simply have struck "Fidele" without using a language that so pointedly underscores the play's own transvestite theatrical context. And it creates a more ambiguous double-vision (simultaneously boy player *and* wife) at the very moment that "Innogen" comes forward.[73] It also looks back not only to the "woman's part" as theatrical part when the boy actor playing the cross-dressed Julia in *The Two Gentlemen of Verona* spoke of playing "the woman's part" dressed in "Madam Julia's gown" (4.4.160–161) but also to the simulative in Orsino's comment to Cesario that "all is *semblative* a woman's part" in *Twelfth Night* (1.4.34).

"Acting" a "part" in the double sense of "perform" (as theatrical performance but also as accomplishment or execution) had already been sounded in Posthumus's letter ordering Innogen's murder as his revenge for her assumed infidelity—"That *part* thou, Pisanio, must *act* for me, if thy faith be not tainted with the breach of hers" (3.4.24–25), lines that curiously link the "breach" of Innogen's "dearest bodily part" as well as her faith with the question of whether Pisanio will faithfully accomplish the act he is being enjoined to perform. And performing a theatrical "part" is suggested elsewhere in the play—including in Posthumus's description of the Roman invasion, where "These three, / Three thousand confident, in act as many—/ For three performers are the file when all / The rest do nothing" (5.3.28–31) recalls not only the old man and two boys of the just-staged scene in which a few actors stand for the entire battle but also the metatheatrical Prologue to *Henry V* (24–25).

"Part" itself is sexualized earlier in *Cymbeline* as the "dearest bodily part of your mistress" (1.4.122)—the obsessive focus of the entire wager plot—or the female sexual "part" or "count" reflected in the "country" of "country mistresses" (1.4.46), the "count" of Posthumus's anguished "Spare your arithmetic; never *count* the turns. / Once, and a million!" (2.4.142–143), and his reference to what Innogen should "from en*count*er guard" (2.5.19) in his misogynist speech on "the woman's part" (2.5.20) after he has been convinced of her infidelity. But—in a play that is the only one in Shakespeare other than *Othello* to invoke both "arithmetic" and "debitor and creditor" (5.3.228) accounting by name—the double-meaning sense of "(ac)count" exploited by other writers of the period (including Shakespeare) simultaneously evokes the problem of the fidelity of both kinds of (ac)count, in yet another slander plot, where Iachimo (like Iago) provides a falsified account that directly recalls the language of debitor and creditor accounting, and presents it with what he calls "simular proof enough" (5.4.200).[74]

The sudden metatheatrical "Recognition" in Act 5, however, in which the "woman's part" itself turns out to have been simulated, not only reveals that the "page" boy "Fidele" is the boy who has played "Innogen" throughout, but that even the voyeuristic pornographic display of Innogen's female body (and what Iachimo calls its "*natural* notes") in the scene in her "chamber" in Act 2 had been—like the images of the "simular" and "counterfeit" elsewhere in the play, including what Iachimo calls "simular proof" (5.4.200)—an elaborate simulation as well, in an English transvestite theater where "Ganymede" was not only "Jove's page" or a term for figures like Robert Carr, who began as a "page," but also a contemporary analogue of the boy player.

Like others (including feminist critics and more recently James Bromley), Michael Shapiro has argued that the cross-dressed page "Fidele" is less assertive as a "boy" than Innogen had been before the cross-dressing. Specifically, Shapiro argues that Fidele is "closer to the powerless female pages and squires of pastoral and romance or to Greene's Dorothea than she is to the enterprising and resourceful heroines who put on male clothing in novelle and many earlier Italian and English plays," the cross-dressed heroines of the play's source tales from Boccaccio's *Decameron* II.9 and the anonymous

*Frederyke of Jennen*, the saucy "Lylian page," or Shakespeare's own cross-dressed Julia, Portia, Rosalind, and even Viola.[75]

But in relation to the homoerotic attraction attached to "Fidele" the "page" (and, I would argue, the undercurrent suggestions of the Ganymede figure in those scenes), Bruce R. Smith remarks—though he does not mention Ganymede in this regard—"In his disguise as 'Fidele,' the boy actor playing Imogen works the same erotic magic on the exiles in Wales as Greene's Pleusidippus and Sidney's Pyrocles do in Arcadia," narrative romance texts that participate in the homoeroticism (and pervasive allusions to Ganymede) familiar from romance more generally, including Lodge's *Rosalynde*,[76] the source of *As You Like It*, where the "Girle-boye" Ganymede is described as "Jove's page."[77] "By Jupiter, an angel" is Belarius's response to the beautiful "boy" Fidele in *Cymbeline*, "as thunder-struck as Greene's King of Thessaly or Sidney's Kalandar"[78]—an "angel" that may well (it should be added) summon the familiar homophonic link with "ingle" in the period.[79] And Guiderius's "Were you a woman, youth, / I should woo hard" (3.6.66–67) further underscores what Smith calls "a liminal landscape where social identities, and sexual identities, dissolve in the half-light,"[80] while simultaneously foregrounding the heteronormativity in tension with it.[81]

Similarly, Roman Lucius is attracted to what he perceives when he comes upon "Fidele" the "page" and "servant" to a dead master, desiring to "see the boy's face" (4.2.358) and promising "I will not say / Thou shalt be so well mastered, but be sure / No less beloved" (4.2.381–383). And—as already observed—his suggesting a paternal role ("rather father thee than master thee," 4.2.394) would not preclude a "Ganymede" or pederastic relationship in a period when King James was fond of casting himself as "father" to his favorites. Lucius's later "The boy disdains me, / He leaves me, scorns me. Briefly die their joys / That place them on the truth of girls and boys" (5.4.105–107)—though it includes "girls" as well as "boys"—cannot help but recall Roman texts (like Martial's) where Ganymedes abound.[82] And it may be that the passivity of "Fidele" is in part a function of the ways in which this "page" becomes the focus for a male gaze that would provide the counterpart to the voyeuristic gaze upon the sleeping "female" body of "Innogen."

Commenting on Lucius's "Thy name well fits thy faith, thy faith thy name" (4.2.380) when he first encounters "Fidele" in Act 4, Martin Butler concludes in his edition that "Lucius's gloss on Fidele's name completes Innogen's transformation from faithful lover to faithful servant (without her dangerous eroticism)" (199). This appears to accord with Pisanio's earlier lines when he proposed the cross-dressing, but the eroticism continues even with the male disguise. When Pisanio proposes the cross-dressing in Act 3, he presents it in lines that include an ambiguous "Pretty and full of view":

> Th'ambassador,
> Lucius the Roman, comes to Milford Haven
> Tomorrow. Now if you could wear a mind
> Dark as your fortune is, and but disguise
> That which t'appear itself must not yet be
> But by self-danger, you should tread a course
> Pretty and full of view. (3.4.140–146)

"Self-danger" here evokes the threat of rape, while "full of view" suggests (at one level) having more opportunities to observe Posthumus, in her disguise, as well as the sense of better prospects.[83] But ironically—when dressed as a "boy"—the "view" of "Fidele" also becomes the gaze of others "he" attracts, including not only Lucius but Cymbeline himself ("Boy, / Thou hast looked thyself into my grace"; "Thou'rt my good youth, my page; / I'll be thy master," 5.4.93–94, 118–119). And in both the scene of Pisanio's cross-dressing plan and the scene where Lucius first comes upon "Fidele," allusions to Jupiter and Juno are repeated—the first in the context of Juno's anger at Jupiter's infidelities with *women* ("forget / Your laboursome and dainty trims, wherein / You made great Juno angry," 3.4.162–164), and then, immediately before Lucius comes upon the "page" and desires to "see the boy's face," in reference to "Jove's bird, the Roman eagle" (4.2.346–358).

As with *Philaster*, none of these parts of *Cymbeline* include explicit reference to Ganymede by name, in contrast to *As You Like It*, just as *Cymbeline*'s own long-acknowledged allusions to the Armada and James's controversial peace remain unspoken. But—in a play that begins with allusion to James's "Bedchamber" favorites, where Jupiter and his eagle figure in a striking dramatic descent, where the images of penetration cross the "homo/hetero divide," the "ring" of the wager plot participates in an ambiguity already foregrounded in *The Merchant of Venice*, and "Innogen" in the clothing of the "page" Fidele attracts the "view" of older male figures and is revealed in the Recognition Scene to be a boy player—we might see intimations of Ganymede in *Cymbeline* from multiple different perspectives, both within and without.

ශ

*Cymbeline*—the late play of Shakespeare that has been characterized as "much ado about everything"—gathers up many of the preoccupations of the other Shakespeare plays (and contexts) included in this book. In addition to the "arithmetic," "debitor and creditor" accounting, and (in)fidelity of an "(ac)count" it shares with *Othello*, the earlier Jacobean slander plot where Spanish "Iago" is the name corresponding to Italian "Iachimo" (and English "James"), *Cymbeline* shares with other plays its engagement with names both spoken and unspoken (or, as in *Henry V*, suppressed), as well as assumed. The name of "Fidele" that suggests not only faith but fidelity and truth simultaneously resonates with the ironies of his/her own false accounts, as well as the foregrounding in this play (and its transvestite context) of the counterfeit and "simular"; while the "Soothsayer" whose name evokes "sooth" or "truth" suits his imperial construings to the changing circumstances of the times, just as his translation or "construction" in Act 5 is open to question, like the constructions of "Cambio" in *The Taming of the Shrew*. And the unspoken name of "Ganymede" itself links *Cymbeline* to Virgil's famously homoerotic Second Eclogue,[84] cited in Chapter 3 in relation to the possibility that the "quince" may be queer; but also to *The Shrew*, whose Induction evokes what Amanda Bailey describes as "the absent-presence of the 'best known myth of homoerotic desire in early modern England,' that of Jupiter's seduction of his page Ganymede," as "Sly assumes the role of Jupiter by commanding his lady page to lie with him."[85]

*Cymbeline*'s pre-post language of "before" and "behind" (or "back door") and intimations of "preposterous venery" (including the "preposterous Italian way" associated with Aretino and others) recalls the language of the *preposterous* in *Love's Labor's Lost* and other plays in earlier chapters, but also the "sodomitical" senses of Ariosto's *I Suppositi*, the Italian source of the Bianca subplot explored in Chapter 2. And *Cymbeline*'s arresting metatheatrical moment in Act 5, with its revelation in its Recognition Scene that Innogen is a boy player, joins the foregrounding of transvestite theater and its "supposes" in other chapters, as well as the ways in which dramatic "recognition scenes" had already been ironized in relation to uncertain proofs or suppositions in *I Suppositi* and Gascoigne's *Supposes*—here in a late play where what is required is a *both-and* or double vision, just as identity and desire remain open to supposition.[86]

The simultaneous "pre" and "post" of *Cymbeline*, finally, is extraordinarily suggestive in relation to what Jonathan Gil Harris has called "Preposterous Time,"[87] and to the issue (and presumed providential teleology) of biblical typology—or the movement from "Old" Testament to "New" invoked in Berowne's sophistical defense of oath-breaking in *Love's Labor's Lost* (discussed in relation to Protestant polemics against "preposterating" the testaments, in the Introduction and first chapter, including those where such "preposteration" was assimilated to "preposterous venery," in a period when temporal and bodily "before" and "after" were routinely aligned).[88] *Cymbeline*'s own preposterous time involves not only a temporal palimpsest of contemporary Italy, "Britain," and Europe in an ancient Roman setting but a double time in which history and prophecy both cross and co-exist—in ways that also call to mind (in a different context) the history plays in Chapter 4, where Carlyle's prophecy in *Richard II* of events to follow in time from Bolingbroke's usurpation simultaneously recalls the past staging of those future events. But in a plot set in the reign of Augustus into which Christ was born that still at its end looks ahead to an epochal typological event it never reaches,[89] this late Jacobean play with its famous "anachronisms" remains both "post" and "pre," in a preposterous temporality whose vanishing point in time never comes.

# *Notes*

## INTRODUCTION

1. See Raymond Williams, *Keywords: A Vocabulary of Culture and Society* (1976; Oxford University Press, 2015), which includes a 2014 foreword by Colin MacCabe; Roland Greene, *Five Words: Critical Semantics in the Age of Shakespeare and Cervantes* (Chicago: University of Chicago Press, 2013); Leo Spitzer, *Essays in Historical Semantics* (New York: Russell and Russell, 1948); William Empson, *The Structure of Complex Words* (London: Chatto and Windus, 1951); and Martin Jay, *Cultural Semantics: Keywords of Our Time* (Amherst: University of Massachusetts Press, 1998).

2. Greene, *Five Words,* 12.

3. Unless otherwise specified, Shakespeare citations are from *The Riverside Shakespeare,* 2nd ed., ed. G. Blakemore Evans, J. J. M. Tobin, et al. (Boston: Wadsworth Cengage Learning, 1997), and italicization is my own. As in Chapter 6, the edition used in this Introduction for *Cymbeline* is *Cymbeline,* ed. Martin Butler (Cambridge: Cambridge University Press, 2005).

4. See John Michael Archer, "*Love's Labour's Lost,*" in *A Companion to Shakespeare's Works,* vol. 3: *The Comedies,* ed. Richard Dutton and Jean E. Howard (Oxford: Blackwell, 2003), 320–337, citing Jonathan Gil Harris, *Foreign Bodies and the Body Politic: Discourses of Social Pathology in Early Modern England* (Cambridge: Cambridge University Press, 1998), 79–88.

5. See Richard Rambuss, "*A Midsummer Night's Dream*: Shakespeare's Ass Play," in *Shakesqueer,* ed. Madhavi Menon (Durham, N.C.: Duke University Press, 2011), 234–244, 288, with the work of Bruce Thomas Boehrer and others cited in Chapter 3; and Jonathan Goldberg, "*Romeo and Juliet*'s Open Rs," in *Queering the Renaissance,* ed. Goldberg (Durham, N.C.: Duke University Press, 1994), 218–235.

6. See Ian Smith, "Othello's Black Handkerchief," *Shakespeare Quarterly* 64, no. 1 (2013): 1–25, and the notes to Chapter 5.

7. For the "preposterous Italian way," see Richard Brome, *Covent-Garden Weeded* (1632), with the entry on "Italian fashion" in Gordon Williams, *A Dictionary of Sexual Language and Imagery in Shakespearean and Stuart Literature,* 3 vols. (London: Athlone Press, 1994), 2:720ff.

8. See Madhavi Menon's important discussion of *Cymbeline* in chap. 2 of *Unhistorical Shakespeare: Queer Theory in Shakespearean Literature and Film* (New York: Palgrave Macmillan, 2008).

9. Amanda Bailey, *Flaunting* (Toronto: University of Toronto Press, 2007), 71–72.

10. On angels, angles, ingles (or catamites), "Ingland," and bodily "faults" of various kinds, see my *Shakespeare from the Margins* (Chicago: University of Chicago Press, 1996), 143–147.

11. See chap. 4 of my *Shakespeare from the Margins*, on female fidelity, *Merry Wives*, and "translation."

12. See Alison Thorne, "'To write and read / Be henceforth treacherous': *Cymbeline* and the Problem of Interpretation," in *Shakespeare's Late Plays: New Readings*, ed. Jennifer Richards and James Knowles (Edinburgh: Edinburgh University Press, 1999), 176–190, 189.

13. See "Preposterous Time" in Jonathan Gil Harris, *Untimely Matter in the Time of Shakespeare* (Philadelphia: University of Pennsylvania Press, 2009), 182–187.

14. See "Backedore" in Richard Huloet's *Abcedarium Anglico Latinum* (1552).

15. Angell Day, *The English Secretary . . . with a Declaration of . . . Tropes, Figures, and Schemes* (1586; rpt. London: R. Jones, 1599), 83: "*Hysteron proteron*, where that which ought to be in the first place, is put in the second."

16. Joannes Susenbrotus, *Epitome troporum ac schematum* (Zurich, [1540?]), 32–33.

17. See George Puttenham, *The Arte of English Poesie* (1589), 141, with "the Greeks call it *Histeron proteron*, we name it the Preposterous"; Elisha Coles, *An English Dictionary* (1677); and my "*Hysteron Proteron*: or the Preposterous," in *Renaissance Figures of Speech*, ed. Sylvia Adamson, Gavin Alexander, and Katrin Ettenhuber (Cambridge: Cambridge University Press, 2007), 133–145.

18. See Henry Peacham, *The Garden of Eloquence* (1577; rpt. London: R. F., 1593), 119; and *The Garden of Eloquence* (1577), sig. F4r–v, on "*Hysteron proteron*, when that is laste sayde, that was first done."

19. See Thomas Wilson, *The Arte of Rhetorique* (London: George Robinson, 1585), fols. M4r–M4v; *Proverbs or Adages, gathered out of the Chiliades of Erasmus*, trans. Richard Taverner (London, 1569).

20. See John Hart, *An Orthographie* (London 1569), concluding Epistle (n.p.); Richard Sherry, *A Treatise of Schemes and Tropes* (London: J. Day, 1550), 22.

21. See *Discoveries*, ed. Lorna Hutson, in *The Cambridge Edition of the Works of Ben Jonson*, 7 vols., ed. David Bevington, Martin Butler, and Ian Donaldson (Cambridge: Cambridge University Press, 2012), 7: 531 and 572.

22. See William Rowley and Thomas Middleton's *A Fair Quarrel* (1.1.405–408), ed. Suzanne Gossett (who dates it between 1612 and its publication in 1617), in Thomas Middleton, *The Collected Works*, ed. Gary Taylor and John Lavagnino (Oxford: Clarendon Press, 2007), 1219; Sir Roger L'Estrange, *A New Dialogue between Some Body and No Body* (1681), number 2.

23. This is part of the definition of *hysteron proteron* in *The American Heritage Dictionary of the English Language*, 4th ed. (Boston: Houghton Mifflin, 2000).

24. George Thompson, *Aimatiasis* (London, 1670), 45, 77.

25. See my *Shakespeare from the Margins*, chap. 1, which builds on Joel B. Altman's "Preposterous Conclusions: Eros, *Enargeia*, and the Composition of *Othello*," *Representations* 18 (1987): 129–157. See also Altman's *The Improbability of "Othello"* (Chicago: University of Chicago Press, 2010).

26. Thomas Wright, *The Passions of the Minde in Generall* (Urbana: University of Illinois Press, 1971), 5.

27. For a prescient treatment of "cause" (though it does not cite this particular instance), see also Lee Edelman and Madhavi Menon, "Queer Tragedy, or Two Meditations on Cause,"

in *The Oxford Handbook of Shakespearean Tragedy*, ed. Michael Neill and David Schalkwyk (Oxford: Oxford University Press, 2016), 185ff.

28. See, respectively, Polydore Vergil, *Anglica Historia*, translated by Camden in 1540 (1.39); Philip Stubbes, *The Anatomie of Abuses* (1583), sig. C2v.

29. See Stubbes, *The Second Part of the Anatomie of Abuses* (1583), sig. J2r; Rankins, *Mirror of Monsters* (1587), sig. F1r-v; Thomas Heywood, *An Apology for Actors* (1612), sig. C3r–v.

30. See Philip Massinger, *The Unnatural Combat* (2.1.180); *Beggars' Bush* (5.2.20).

31. Quoted from Section 8, Addition III, lines 8–12, in *Sir Thomas More*, ed. John Jowett (London: Bloomsbury Arden Shakespeare, 2011), 217–218. See also Jowett's comments on this soliloquy that "has plausibly been attributed to Shakespeare" (454).

32. See Stephen Greenblatt, "The Cultivation of Anxiety: King Lear and His Heirs," *Raritan* 2, no. 1 (1982): 92–114, 108.

33. See *The Poetical Works of Sir William Alexander*, 2 vols., ed. L. E. Kastner and H. B. Charlton (London: Blackwood & Sons, 1929), 2:221.

34. Thomas Adams, *The gallants burden* (London, 1612), 16v.

35. John Christopherson, *An exhortation to all menne to take hede of rebellion* (London, 1554), sigs. T1r–T2r, T6v–T7v.

36. Giacomo Affinati D'Acuto, *Il mondo al roverscio e sosopra* (Venice, 1602), 131–132.

37. See 1 Timothy 2:12–14 in *The Bible and Holy Scriptures . . . Printed at Geneva* (1561). The Bishops' Bible translation is virtually identical.

38. See Juan Luis Vives, *The Instruction of a Christen Woman* (1541), 71–72.

39. See, respectively, John Knox, *The first blast of the trumpet against the monstruous regiment of women* (Geneva, 1558); Thomas Gataker, *Marriage Duties Briefely couched togither* (London, 1620), 10; Francis Bacon, *Works* vii.33; Thomas Dekker, *The bachelers banquet* (London, 1604), chap. 12; *The life and death of Mrs. Mary Frith commonly called Mal Cutpurse* (London, 1662), 173.

40. See George Chapman, *All Fools* 3.1; John Bulwer, *Anthropometamorphosis, man transform'd, or, The artificial changeling* (London, 1650), 404–408.

41. See, respectively, George Sandys, *Ovid's Metamorphosis Englished, Mythologiz'd, and Represented in Figures*, 3rd ed. (Oxford: J. Lichfield, 1632), 336, and *Ovid's Metamorphosis Englished, Mythologized, and Represented in Figures* (London, 1640), 184; William Harvey's *Lectures on the Whole Anatomy: An Annotated Translation of "Prelectiones Anatomiae Universalis"* (1616), trans. C. D. O'Malley, F. N. L. Poynter, and K. F. Russell (Berkeley: University of California Press, 1961), 127.

42. See Alan Bray, *Homosexuality in Renaissance England* (London: Gay Men's Press, 1982).

43. See Stuart Clark, *Thinking with Demons* (Oxford: Oxford University Press, 1997), Part 1 (esp. 13–15), 91, 120. On witches (such as Medea in Ovid's *Metamorphoses* Book 7) making rivers run backward, see Reginald Scot, *The discoverie of witchcraft* (London, 1584), Book 1, chap. 4.

44. See Ben Jonson, *The Masque of Queens*, ed. David Lindley, in *The Cambridge Edition of the Works of Ben Jonson*, 3:317; Gary Wills, *Witches and Jesuits: Shakespeare's "Macbeth"* (Oxford: Oxford University Press, 1995), esp. 67–69 (with 60–61 on reversion from "baptism" to "circumcision"); Richard Brome, *The Late Lancashire Witches* (1634), sig. B4v, 1.1.256; my "Spelling Backwards," in *Rhetoric, Women and Politics in Early Modern England*, ed. Jennifer Richards and Alison Thorne (London: Routledge, 2007), 25–50.

45. *Much Ado About Nothing,* ed. A. R. Humphreys (London: Methuen, 1981), 146, has "As witches say prayers backwards to raise the devil." It is also said of Beatrice here: "If fair-fac'd, / She would swear the gentleman should be her sister."

46. See Ian Maclean, *The Renaissance Notion of Woman* (Cambridge: Cambridge University Press, 1980), 2–3, 8, 37–38; *Right and Left: Essays on Dual Symbolic Classification*, ed. R. Needham (Chicago: University of Chicago Press, 1973), 167–186; Marjorie Garber, *Vice Versa: Bisexuality and the Eroticism of Everyday Life* (New York: Simon & Schuster, 1995), chap. 12.

47. See Clark (1997: 113) on Eve as the first witch and this Ave/Eva palindrome from Robert Southwell's "The Virgins Salutation."

48. This is the gloss in William Shakespeare, *The Complete Sonnets and Poems,* ed. Colin Burrow (Oxford: Oxford University Press, 2002), 598.

49. I have discussed these lines and other preposterous inversions (including of successors and ancestors, *before* and *behind*) in *Merry Wives* in *Shakespeare from the Margins*, 34–36. See also Carolyn E. Brown's "'Preposterous' Actions and 'Tainted' Desires in *The Merry Wives of Windsor*," in *The Merry Wives of Windsor: New Critical Essays*, ed. Evelyn Gajowski and Phyllis Rackin (London: Routledge, 2015), 154–168.

50. See Pliny's *Natural History*, Book 7 (viii.45–46), with, for example, Eucharius Roeslin, *The Byrth of Mankynde* (London, 1540), sig. D3r and sig. F3r.

51. See Nashe's *Anatomie of Absurditie* (1589) in *The Works of Thomas Nashe*, 5 vols., ed. R. B. McKerrow (Oxford: Basil Blackwell, 1958), 1:36. I have discussed these contexts and descriptions of Gloucester in chap. 1 of *Margins*, 38–39, including in relation to the issue of inverted "cause" and "effect" (or "defect").

52. See, for example, Jonathan Goldberg's *Sodometries* (Stanford, Calif.: Stanford University Press, 1992; New York: Fordham University Press, 2010); and my "Preposterous Events," *Shakespeare Quarterly* 43 (Summer 1992): 186–213. For a crucial contextualization of Thersites's lines, see Mario DiGangi's *Sexual Types* (Philadelphia: University of Pennsylvania Press, 2011), 39–43.

53. See Etienne Dolet's *In Praepostera Venere Utentes*, in *Carminum Libri Quatuor* (Lyons, 1538), 2:32.

54. Browne, "Of Hares," *Pseudodoxia Epidemica*, ed. R. Robbins, 2 vols. (Oxford: Oxford University Press, 1998), 1:227, reflecting the "sed etiam *praeposterae* libidinis" of Petro Castellanus's *De Esu Carnium* 3.5 (1626).

55. See *The Essayes of Michael Lord of Montaigne*, trans. John Florio (1603); rpt. London: J. M. Dent & Sons, n.d., 1.22.

56. See Jonathan Goldberg, "*Romeo and Juliet*'s Open Rs," in *Queering the Renaissance*, on "the formations of gender difference as the homo/hetero divide imagines them" (225), with his introduction to that volume. With regard to sodomy—described as that "utterly confused category" by Michel Foucault in *The History of Sexuality,* vol. 1: *An Introduction*, trans. Robert Hurley (New York: Vintage, 1978)—see also Goldberg's *Sodometries*, including its "Introduction: 'That Utterly Confused Category,'" and Goldberg's *The Seeds of Things: Theorizing Sexuality and Materiality in Renaissance Representations* (New York: Fordham University Press, 2009), esp. chap. 2. See also, inter alia, Bray, *Homosexuality in Renaissance England*; Bruce R. Smith, *Homosexual Desire in Shakespeare's England* (Chicago: University of Chicago Press, 1991); Gregory W. Bredbeck, *Sodomy and Interpretation* (Ithaca, N.Y.: Cornell University Press, 1991); Alan Stewart, *Close Readers: Humanism and Sodomy in Early Modern England* (Princeton, N.J.: Princeton University Press, 1997); Laurie Shannon, *Sovereign Amity: Figures of Friendship in Shakespearean Contexts* (Chicago: University of Chicago Press, 2002); Mario DiGangi, *Sexual*

*Types*; Will Stockton, *Playing Dirty: Sexuality and Waste in Early Modern Comedy* (Minneapolis: University of Minnesota Press, 2011); *Sex Before Sex: Figuring the Act in Early Modern England*, ed. James M. Bromley and Will Stockton (Minneapolis: University of Minnesota Press, 2013); Valerie Traub, *The Renaissance of Lesbianism in Early Modern England* (Cambridge: Cambridge University Press, 2002), *Thinking Sex with the Early Moderns* (Philadelphia: University of Pennsylvania Press, 2016), and her introduction to *The Oxford Handbook of Shakespeare and Embodiment: Gender, Sexuality, and Race*, ed. Valerie Traub (Oxford: Oxford University Press, 2016); Jeffrey Masten, *Queer Philologies: Sex, Language, and Affect in Shakespeare's Time* (Philadelphia: University of Pennsylvania Press, 2016), including 219–221; *Queer Shakespeare: Desire and Sexuality*, ed. Goran Stanivukovic (London: Bloomsbury, 2017).

57. See Celia R. Daileader, "Back Door Sex: Renaissance Gynosodomy, Aretino, and the Exotic," *ELH* 69, no. 2 (2002): 303–334.

58. See Goldberg, *Sodometries*, 4ff., 180–181, 184, 188, 192.

59. See Michael Drayton, *Poly-Olbion* (London, 1612), 261, on Edward II "Who both his Name and Birth, by loosenes, did abuse: / Faire *Ganimeds* and Fools who rais'd to Princely places; / And chose not men for wit, but only for their faces," followed by "For that preposterous sinne wherein he did offend, / In his posteriour parts had his preposterous end" (Song XVII). The "Red-hot spit" that through his "Bowels . . . did gore" is from John Taylor's sonnet on Edward II in *A Briefe Remembrance of All The Englishe Monarchs* (London, 1618), sig. B4r. On the connection between Lucifer and "Lightborne" who administers this punishment, see, inter alia, Smith, *Homosexual Desire*, 220: "When death comes at last, the punishment suits the crime. Light-bourne (that is, *Luci-fer*, 'light-carrier'), an Italian-trained specialist in techniques of murder, designs a death that is invisible, elegantly efficient—and unmistakably allegorical. He specifically orders his accomplices to 'get me a spit, and let it be red hote' (5.5.30)." See also Masten's *Queer Philologies* for an important discussion of the differences in Marlowe's *Edward II*.

60. *The Deplorable Life and Death of Edward the Second, King of Scotland . . . Together with the Downefall of the two Unfortunate Favorits, Gaveston and Spencer* (London, 1628), stanza 17.

61. See "The Wars of the Gods" (Yale MS Beinecke Osborne b197), 111–113; Bodleian MSS Eng. poet. c.50, fol. 41v (headed "On Jove and Ganymede," 1623); Rawl. poet. 160, fol. 14; Tanner 306, fol. 261; and the text in *Texas Quarterly* 16, no. 4 (1973) supplement: 129–133, 136–141 ("Verse libels from the commonplace book of Robert Herrick, collected by Norman K. Farmer, Jr."), with Alastair Bellany, " 'Raylinge Rymes and Vaunting Verse': Libellous Politics in Early Stuart England, 1603–1628," in *Culture and Politics in Early Stuart England*, ed. Kevin Sharpe and Peter Lake (Stanford, Calif.: Stanford University Press, 1993), 285–310, 297.

62. Bellany, "Raylinge Rymes," 296; see also 301.

63. See Masten, *Queer Philologies*, chap. 6.

64. On "the *bottom of Goddes secretes*" (and 1 Corinthians 2:9), see Hannibal Hamlin, *The Bible in Shakespeare* (Oxford: Oxford University Press, 2013), 109.

65. See my "The Name of Nick Bottom," in *Autour du Songe d'une nuit d'été de William Shakespeare*, ed. Claire Gheeraert-Graffeuille and Nathalie Vienne-Guerrin (Rouen: Publications de l'Université de Rouen, 2003), 9–29.

66. See Richard Mulcaster, *The First Part of the Elementary, 1582* (Menston: Scolar Press, 1970), iv, v.

67. See Masten, *Queer Philologies*, 43, citing from Hume's dedication to King James in his unpublished *Of the Orthographie and Congruitie of the Britain Tongue*, 2 (with the editor's

errata sheet inserted after 3); 255n.21, citing *A Greek-English Lexicon,* 9th ed., comp. Henry George Liddell and Robert Scott et al. (Oxford: Clarendon, 1968), 1248–1249.

68. *Queer Philologies,* 40–41. Masten (255n.27) cites from the folio *Much Adoe* (TLN 851–855), which has "turu'd ortho-graphy" (commenting "I have myself 'righted' the writing here").

69. See *Nashe's Lenten Stuffe* (1599) in *Works,* ed. R. B. McKerrow, 3:141–226; Alain de Lille, *The Complaint of Nature,* trans. Douglas M. Moffat (Hamden, Conn.: Archon Books, 1972); J. Ziolkowski, *Alan of Lille's Grammar of Sex* (Cambridge, Mass.: Medieval Academy of America, 1985), 14–15 and passim; and Alexandre Leupin, *Barbarolexis,* trans. K. M. Cooper (Cambridge, Mass.: Harvard University Press, 1989), 60–64, 76.

70. See, respectively, *The Bible and Holy Scriptures . . . Printed at Geneva* (1561), 80–81, and its glosses on Galatians 3:3, 3:24, and 4:1–3; Miles Coverdale, trans., "The paraphrase vpon the epistle of the Apostle sainct Paule to the Galathians," in *The Seconde Tome or Volume of the Paraphrase of Erasmus upon the Newe Testament* (London, 1549), chap. 5, fol. 18r.

71. For one example among many of condemnations of the "preposterousnes" of the Roman Church and its "preposteration[s]," see Robert Parker's *A Scholasticall Discourse against Symbolizing with Antichrist in Ceremonies: Especially in the Signe of the Crosse* (1607), e.g., 146–147.

72. Quoted respectively from Henry King, *A Sermon Preached at St. Pauls March 27* (1640), in *The Sermons of Henry King,* ed. Mary Hobbs (Rutherford, NJ: Fairleigh Dickinson University Press, 1992), 227–228; and Thomas Edwards, *The Paraselene Dismantled of Her Cloud* (1699), 8.

73. See, for example, "Rome backwards" used for back-door sexual entry (or "Arsey-versey Love") and with "hole backwards" in *Ram-Alley; or Merrie-trickes, A Comedy by Lording Barry,* ed. Claude E. Jones (Louvain: Librarie Universitaire, 1952), 36.

74. John Bale, *The First Two Partes of the Actes or Vnchast Examples of the Englysh Votaryes* (1546; London, 1551), fol. 6v.

75. See *The Apology of Johan Bale agaynste a Ranke Papist* (London, 1550), on the "arse-warde procedynges" of going "preposterously to wurke" (O1r).

76. See *The Pageant of Popes* (1574), John Studley's English translation of Bale's *Acta Romanorum pontificum* (Basel: Joannes Oporinus, 1558), fol. 190r; with Bale's *The First Two Partes of the Actes or Vnchast Examples of the Englysh Votaryes* (London 1551) on the "prepost-erouse offyce of Venery" (fol. 10r).

77. See, for example, Alan Stewart's *Close Readers.*

78. Bale, *A Mysterye of inyquitie* ("Geneva" [i.e., Antwerp], 1545), sig. B2r.

79. Racialized figures for progression from Old to New Testament are used repeatedly in the period, including with regard to baptism and Acts 8:27–39 on the Ethiopian eunuch. See John Abbot, *Iesus Prefigured* (1623), 7, and other texts discussed in my "Cutting Both Ways: Bloodletting, Castration/Circumcision, and the 'Lancelet' of *The Merchant of Venice,*" in *Alternative Shakespeares 3,* ed. Diana E. Henderson (London: Routledge, 2008), 95–118, esp. 104–115. See also Ania Loomba's "Identities and Bodies in Early Modern Studies," on the Black Bride of the Song of Songs, Jeremiah 13:23 ("Can the black Moor change his skin or the leopard his spots?"), and converts to Christianity as washed "white," in Traub, *Oxford Handbook,* 236ff.

80. See *The Emblems of Thomas Palmer: Two Hundred Poosees,* ed. John Manning (New York: AMS Press, 1988), Emblem 107.

81. See also Michael Drayton's "Moone-calfe" and other texts cited in this regard in Chapter 1; Mario DiGangi, *The Homoerotics of Early Modern Drama* (Cambridge: Cambridge

University Press, 1997), 129, on the sodomitical resonances of "Hebrew" in Chapman's *Bussy D'Ambois*; *A Game at Chess: A Later Form*, ed. Gary Taylor in Middleton, *The Collected Works*, ed. Taylor and Lavagnino, 1841.

82. On these numerals as written "backward" like Arabic, see Eugene Ostashevsky, "Crooked Figures: Zero and Hindu-Arabic Notation in Shakespeare's *Henry V*," in *Arts of Calculation*, ed. David Glimp and Michelle R. Warren (New York: Palgrave Macmillan, 2004), 205–228, 225, on the *sinistrorsum* of Sacrobosco's *De Arte Numerandi* ("We writene in this art to the left side-warde, as arabiene writene, that weren fynders of this science"); and Robert Recorde, *The Ground of Artes, teachyng the worke and practise of Arithmeticke* (1541; London, 1543), 13–14, with regard to the new "Arithmetic" that "some cal . . . Arsemetrike," which teaches its users to "recken your order of places backewarde, I meane from the ryght syde towardes the lefte," reversing the familiar left-to-right spelling of the ABC, in a manual of instruction where the confused student complains that he has to learn to put "first" what he would otherwise put at the end or "last."

83. "Arsemetric[k]" and "arsmetry" remained common early modern spellings for the new arithmetic. *OED* cites, inter alia, Robert Greene's *A Looking-Glass for London and England* ([1594] 1861:132: 'Have I taught you arsmetry.'" Striking scatological applications include Geoffrey Chaucer's *The Summoner's Tale*, where (in a satire directed against fraternal orders long linked with sodomy) a "fart" is divided according to the principles of "ars-metric," and the same text of Thomas Nashe that features the bodily and scatological play on "envoy" discussed in relation to various forms of "latter end" in *Love's Labor's Lost* in Chapter 1. See Chaucer's *The Knight's Tale* for "ars-metrike" (line 1898) and *The Summoner's Tale* (line 2221) for this "fart," in F. N. Robinson, ed., *The Poetical Works of Chaucer* (London: Oxford University Press, 1957), 41, 119; and *Have with you to Saffron-walden* (1596) in Nashe, *Works*, ed. McKerrow (3:44 and 132–133).

84. On fears with regard to the so-called "infidel symbol" zero (which was written like the letter "O"), see Brian Rotman, *Signifying Nothing: The Semiotics of Zero* (1987; rpt. Stanford, CA: Stanford University Press, 1993), chap. 1; with my "Cassio, Cash, and the 'Infidel o': Arithmetic, Double-Entry Bookkeeping, and *Othello*'s Unfaithful Accounts," in *A Companion to the Global Renaissance*, ed. Jyotsna Singh (Oxford: Blackwell, 2009), 223–241; and my "*Cymbeline*: Arithmetic, Double-Entry Bookkeeping, Counts, and Accounts," *SEDERI* 23 (2013): 95–119, which also provides contemporary examples of the sexual sense of "arithmetic" in Posthumus's lines here.

85. See, for example, Gabriel Powel's commentary on Romans 1:27 in *Prodromus* (Oxford, 1602), 226, on "preposterous practices," in relation to the combination of preposterous venery with turning back from the Gospel to the carnal understandings of the Jews; William Sclater's *A Key to the Key of Scriptvre: or An Exposition with Notes, vpon the Epistle to the Romanes; the three first Chapters* (London, 1611), 1, 119, 121–122, 127, 130, 133–135, 139–140, 144, 267, 278ff., 280, 385; Thomas Wilson's *A Commentarie vpon the most Diuine Epistle of S. Paul to the Romanes* (London, 1614), 75–78, 87–88, 92–93, 103–104, 106.

86. Both are cited, for example, in relation to the "bond brat," in John Prime, *An Exposition and Observations upon Saint Paul to the Galatians* (Oxford, 1587), 239. See the Geneva gloss on Galatians 4:22 ("Abraham begate Ishmael . . . of Agar his bondmaid and begate Isaac of Sara, a free woman") and Galatians 4:24–25 (including "Agar or Sina [i.e., Sinai, where the Law of Moses was given] is a mountaine in Arabia . . . and she is in bondage with her children"): "The conclusion of the former allegorie, that we by no means procure and call backe againe the slaverie of the Law, seeing that the children of the bondmaid shall not be heirs." On

"Ishmael" as a figure for the Hebrew testament, see, inter alia, *A commentarie of M. Doctor Martin Luther vpon the Epistle of S. Paul to the Galathians . . . novv out of Latine faithfully translated into English for the vnlearned* (London, 1575).

87. See Thomas Gainsford, *The Glory of England* (1618), 205.

88. See *The Alcoran of Mahomet, Translated out of Arabique into French; by the Sieur Du Ryer . . . And newly Englished, for the satisfaction of all that desire to look into the Turkish vanities* (London, 1649), 411.

89. See, for example, William Davenant, *The Siege of Rhodes* (London, 1659), 5–6, on the Great Turk's "sensual Law"; Gainsford's *Glory of England*, 179, on Turkish "tyranny."

90. See *The Sophy* (5.1.326) in *The Poetical Works of Sir John Denham* (New Haven, Conn.: Yale University Press, 1928), 298; *Purchas his Pilgrimage* (London, 1613), 239.

91. Bartholomeus Georgijevic, *Ofspring of the house of Ottomanno*, trans. Hugh Goughe (London, 1569), sig. B4v.

92. See Sir William Alexander, *Doomes-day, or, The Great Day of the Lords Ivdgement* (London, 1614), in his *Poetical Works*, vol. 2, 18 (stanzas 45, 47), 20 (stanza 48), 24 (stanza 64), 152 (stanza 40), 192 (stanza 84), and 221 (stanza 79).

93. See, respectively, Bale, *The Actes of Englysh Votaryes* (Antwerp, 1546), 17r; Robert Burton, *The Anatomy of Melancholy* (Oxford, 1621), 537–538; Thomas Coryat, quoted in Nabil Matar, *Turks, Moors and Englishmen in the Age of Discovery* (New York: Columbia University Press, 1999), 127.

94. William Davies, *A True Relation of the Travailes and most miserable Captiuitie of William Dauies, Barber-Surgion of London* (London, 1614), chap. 2, sigs. B2v, B3v.

95. See, for example, the Prologue to *Selimus, Emperor of the Turks* (published in 1594 and often attributed to Robert Greene), in *Three Turk Plays from Early Modern England*, ed. Daniel J. Vitkus (New York: Columbia University Press, 2000), 59; George Peele's *The Battell of Alcazar, Fought in Barbarie* (London, 1594), sig. A2v.

96. See Goffe, *The Raging Turke, or Baiazet the Second* (London, 1631), usually dated ca. 1618.

97. See also Goffe's *The Courageous Turk* (usually dated from ca. 1613–1618), which underscores the unnatural family of the Turk but also demonstrates that gender trumps religion in contexts where the "bewitching" Eve could be Christian as well as Turk. See Daniel Vitkus, *Turning Turk: English Theater and the Multicultural Mediterranean* (New York: Palgrave Macmillan, 2003), 99–101, 102, 120, 123.

98. Reference to "each false preposterous way" appears in Act 5, scene 4, of Fulke Greville's *Mustapha*, in *Certain learned and elegant works of the Right Honorable Fulke Lord Brooke* (London, 1633), 156.

99. See Thomas Kyd, *The Tragedye of Solyman and Perseda*, ed. John J. Murray (London: Garland, 1991), xxxvi, with 66 (3.5.10) and 61 (3.1.148).

100. See the anonymous *Newes from the Sea, Of two notorious Pyrats Ward the Englishman and Danseker the Dutchman* (1609), chap. 9.

101. See Vitkus, *Three Turk Plays*, 236, on Scene 8 of Daborne's play and the comparison with Davies's *True Relation*, sig. B3v.

102. See my "Preposterous Conversions: Turning Turk, and Its 'Pauline' Rerighting," *JEMCS* 2, no. 1 (2002): 1–34, 25–27. Both Stuart Clark in *Thinking with Demons*—with regard to witchcraft—and James Shapiro in *Shakespeare and the Jews* (New York: Columbia University Press, 1997)—with regard to *conversos*—also suggest the threat of reversibility unsettling to any unidirectional teleology of turning or conversion.

103. Simon Shepherd's *Marlowe and the Politics of Elizabethan Theatre* (Brighton, Sussex: Harvester Press, 1986), chap. 5, discusses ways in which depictions of the Turk mirror Elizabethan concerns with succession and internecine conflicts. On Carlisle's "prophecy," see Marjorie Garber, "'What's Past Is Prologue': Temporality and Prophecy in Shakespeare's History Plays," in *Renaissance Genres,* ed. Barbara Kiefer Lewalski (Cambridge, Mass.: Harvard University Press, 1986), 301–331, 332.

104. Richard Hillman, "'Not Amurath an Amurath Succeeds': Playing Doubles in Shakespeare's Henriad," *ELR* 21, no. 2 (1991): 161–189.

105. See Harry Berger, Jr., *A Fury in the Words* (New York: Fordham University Press, 2013).

106. See Mary Thomas Crane, *Shakespeare's Brain: Reading with Cognitive Theory* (Princeton, N.J.: Princeton University Press, 2001), including 4 ("Shakespeare's mental lexicon") and 32–33.

107. See, for example, Andy Clark's *Being There: Putting Brain, Body, and World Together Again* (Cambridge, Mass.: MIT Press, 1997) and *Supersizing the Mind: Embodiment, Action, and Cognitive Extension* (Oxford: Oxford University Press, 2011), including chap. 3, Appendix (220–232, including on "socially extended cognition" 231), and 59 (on an approach that "defies any simple language of inner versus outer"); *Distributed Cognitions,* ed. G. Saloman (Cambridge: Cambridge University Press, 1993); E. Hutchins, *Cognition in the Wild* (Cambridge, Mass.: MIT Press, 1995); Kourken Michaelian and John Sutton, "Distributed Cognition and Memory Research: History and Current Directions." *Review of Philosophy and Psychology* 4, no. 1 (2013): 1–24; Evelyn Tribble, *Cognition in the Globe: Attention and Memory in Shakespeare's Theatre* (New York: Palgrave Macmillan, 2011); Ellen Spolsky, *Word vs. Image: Cognitive Hunger in Shakespeare's England* (Basingstoke: Palgrave Macmillan, 2007); special issue on Shakespeare and cognition in *College Literature* 33, no. 1 (2006), ed. Lolita Pandit and Patrick Colm Hogan; *The Extended Mind,* ed. Richard Menary (Cambridge, Mass.: MIT Press, 2010).

108. Bruce Smith, "Latin Lovers in *The Taming of the Shrew,*" in Menon, *Shakesqueer,* 343–350, 349.

109. See Goldberg, *Sodometries,* 180–182, and passim; and my "Preposterous Events," 186–213, with chap. 1 of *Shakespeare from the Margins.*

110. Traub, *Thinking Sex with the Early Moderns,* 69, also quoting from Goldberg's "After Thoughts," *South Atlantic Quarterly* 106, no. 3 (2007): 501–510, 504.

111. Laurie Shannon, "Lear's Queer Cosmos," in Menon, *Shakesqueer,* 171–178, 176.

112. See Harris, *Untimely Matter,* 182–183, citing Julia Reinhard Lupton's "*Othello* Circumcised: Shakespeare and the Pauline Discourse of Nations," *Representations* 57 (1997): 173–189. With regard to the "preposterous," Harris (232–233n.42) also cites the argument in *Queering the Middle Ages,* ed. Glenn Burger and Steven F. Kruger (Minneapolis: University of Minnesota Press, 2001), that the queer is a kind of "logic of the preposterous" that disturbs temporality and "suggests that the stabilization of a sequential 'pre' and 'post,' cause and effect, might be thought otherwise."

113. See Jonathan Goldberg and Madhavi Menon, "Queering History," *PMLA* 120, no. 5 (2005): 1608–1617; Menon, *Unhistorical Shakespeare*; Traub, *Thinking Sex with the Early Moderns,* chap. 3.

114. *Journal for Early Modern Cultural Studies* 16, no. 2 (Spring, 2016).

115. Julia Reinhard Lupton, *Thinking with Shakespeare: Essays on Politics and Life* (Chicago: University of Chicago Press, 2011).

116. See *Rethinking Feminism in Early Modern Studies: Gender, Race, and Sexuality,* ed. Ania Loomba and Melissa E. Sanchez (London: Routledge, 2016); Traub, *Oxford Handbook.* See also *A Feminist Companion to Shakespeare,* 2nd ed., ed. Dympna Callaghan (Chichester: John Wiley & Sons, 2016).

## CHAPTER 1. PREPOSTEROUS REVERSALS, LATTER ENDS

1. Evelyn Tribble cites its "uneven critical reputation" in "Pretty and Apt: Boy Actors, Skill, and Embodiment," in *The Oxford Handbook of Shakespeare and Embodiment,* ed. Valerie Traub (Oxford: Oxford University Press, 2016), 636ff. See James L. Calderwood, *Shakespearean Metadrama* (Minneapolis: University of Minnesota Press, 1971), 56 ("In perhaps no other play does language so nearly become an autonomous symbolic system whose value lies less in its relevance to reality than in its intrinsic fascination"); Jane Donawerth, *Shakespeare and the Sixteenth-Century Study of Language* (Urbana: University of Illinois Press, 1984), 153–154; Katharine Eisaman Maus, "Transfer of Title in *Love's Labor's Lost:* Language, Individualism, Gender," in *Shakespeare Left and Right,* ed. Ivo Kamps (New York: Routledge, 1991), 205–223, esp. 206–207 on "the verbal exorbitance for which *Love's Labor's Lost* has long been condemned" and (207) on the omission of the play's sexual politics in William Carroll's *The Great Feast of Language in "Love's Labor's Lost"* (Princeton, N.J.: Princeton University Press, 1976); Keir Elam's *Shakespeare's Universe of Discourse* (Cambridge: Cambridge University Press, 1984). Unless otherwise specified, Shakespeare citations are from *The Riverside Shakespeare,* 2nd ed., ed. G. Blakemore Evans, J. J. M. Tobin, et al. (Boston: Wadsworth Cengage Learning, 1997; hereafter *Riverside*), and italicization is my own.

2. For these characterizations, see Homer Swander, "*Love's Labor's Lost*: Burn the Parasols, Play the Quarto!," in *Shakesperae's Sweet Thunder,* ed. Michael J. Collins (London: Associated University Presses, 1997), 50–74, 50, 73n.1.

3. Exceptions included Herbert A. Ellis, *Shakespeare's Lusty Punning in "Love's Labour's Lost"* (Paris: Mouton, 1973), and Stephen Booth, in *King Lear, Macbeth, Indefinition, and Tragedy* (New Haven, Conn.: Yale University Press, 1983), 61–73.

4. I put "class" in scare quotes to underscore that the term in this book is used not in the classical Marxist sense but rather as a critical shorthand for position within a social hierarchy. References here are to Norbert Elias, *The History of Manners* (1939), vol. 1 of *The Civilizing Process,* trans. Edmund Jephcott (New York: Pantheon, 1978), which has been justly criticized for its emphasis on "civilizing" as a teleological history; Pierre Bourdieu, *Distinction: A Social Critique of the Judgement of Taste,* trans. Richard Nice (Cambridge, Mass.: Harvard University Press, 1984); and Kenneth Burke, "The Thinking of the Body (Comments on the Imagery of Catharsis in Literature)," in *Language as Symbolic Action* (Berkeley: University of California Press, 1966), chap. 2, 308–343.

5. See John Baret's *An Alvearie or Quadruple Dictionarie* (1580) for "Prepostere" as "Backward; overthwartly: arsieversie: contrary to al good order"; Richard Huloet's *Abcedarium* (1552), "Preposterouse, out of order, overthwharth, transverted, or last done which by rule have ben first"; Randle Cotgrave's *Dictionarie of the French and English Tongues* (1611), on *préposterer* as to "turne arsivarsie; to put the cart before the horse."

6. See Genesis 2, cited with other "thinges set in ordre" in "The fourme of the Solemnization of Matrimonie" in *The Booke of Common Prayer* (1559).

7. On "taken with the manner," see Edward J. White, *Commentaries on the Law in Shakespeare* (St. Louis: F. H. Thomas Law Book Co., 1913), 92. See also *1 Henry IV* (2.4.315).

8. Cited respectively here from *The Bible and Holy Scriptures . . . Printed at Geneva* (1561), STC 2095; and *The. holie. Bible conteynyng the olde Testament and the newe* (London, [1568]), STC 2099.

9. Helkiah Crooke, *Mikrokosmographia, a Description of the Body of Man* (1615), 282.

10. See *OED*, s.v. "manner" and "manure," and Ellis, *Shakespeare's Lusty Punning*, 157–158.

11. See *Riverside*, e.g., 226, 228, 231, 234 (on "*manu cita*—with ready hand") and 5.2.591 ("strangle serpents in his *manus*"). On the uses to which the "hand" is put, and its association with the distinguishing of "high" and "low," clean and unclean, see also *As You Like It* (3.2.49–69).

12. I use "contaminated" with the full resonance of rhetorical *contaminatio* that the play itself suggests, e.g., in the exchange on "allusion," "collusion," and "pollution" in 4.2.42–46.

13. John Hoskins, *Directions for Speech and Style* (1599), ed. Hoyt Hudson (Princeton, N.J.: Princeton University Press, 1935). See also White, *Commentaries*, 93–94, on Armado's letter and "the charging part of a common law indictment."

14. Lorna Hutson, *The Invention of Suspicion: Law and Mimesis in Shakespeare and Renaissance Drama* (Oxford: Oxford University Press, 2007), 297.

15. On varying, see T. W. Baldwin, *William Shakspere's Small Latine and Lesse Greeke*, 2 vols. (Urbana: University of Illinois Press, 1944), 2:192.

16. See David Cressy, *Literacy and the Social Order: Reading and Writing in Tudor and Stuart England* (Cambridge: Cambridge University Press, 1980); Keith Thomas, "The Meaning of Literacy in Early Modern England," in *The Written Word: Literacy in Transition*, ed. Gerd Baumann (Oxford: Oxford University Press, 1986); Adam Fox, *Oral and Literate Culture in England, 1500–1700* (Oxford: Oxford University Press, 2000), with other work on women and literacy below.

17. See Arden 3 *Love's Labour's Lost*, ed. H. R. Woudhuysen (1998; rpt. Bloomsbury Arden Shakespeare, 2014; hereafter Woudhuysen ed.), 128: "**continent canon** law or rule restricting behaviour, esp. sexual behaviour (*OED* continent *a*.3a*)."

18. See Janet Adelman, *Suffocating Mothers* (New York: Routledge, 1992), chap. 2, on the female "fault"; Gail Kern Paster, "Leaky Vessels: The Incontinent Women of City Comedy," *Renaissance Drama*, n.s. 18 (1987), 43–65, and *The Body Embarrassed* (Ithaca, N.Y.: Cornell University Press, 1993); with Mikhail Bakhtin, *Rabelais and His World*, trans. Helene Iswolsky (Bloomington: Indiana University Press, 1984). On Paster, Bakhtin, Norbert Elias, and Peter Stallybrass and Allon White's *The Politics and Poetics of Transgression* (Ithaca, N.Y.: Cornell University Press, 1986), see also the introduction to Ronda Arab's *Manly Mechanicals on the Early Modern English Stage* (Selinsgrove: Susquehanna University Press, 2011), which also draws distinctions between *Love's Labor's Lost* and *A Midsummer Night's Dream*.

19. See my "Coming Second: Woman's Place," in *Literary Fat Ladies: Rhetoric, Gender, Property* (London: Methuen, 1987; rpt. New York: Routledge, 2017), chap. 9, with 1 Timothy 2:12–14 in *The Bible and Holy Scriptures . . . Printed at Geneva* (1561), STC 2095: "I permit not a woman to teache, nether to vsurpe auctoritie ouer the man, but to be in silence. For Adam was first formed, then Eue. And Adam was not deceiued, but the woman was deceiued, and was in the transgression" (margin: "The Woman was first deceiued, and so became the instrument of Satan to deceiue the man," 89). The Bishops' Bible translation is virtually identical to the Geneva Bible's.

20. This Quarto spelling is not noted in Woudhuysen ed., 137, which prints modern "precedent," but is noted in *Riverside,* 248, and is important for its combination of meanings.

21. Berowne actually calls himself a "sheep" in this scene (4.3.7).

22. See Maus, "Transfer of Title in *Love's Labor's Lost,*" 215.

23. See Eve Rachele Sanders, *Gender and Literacy on Stage in Early Modern England* (Cambridge: Cambridge University Press, 1998), 49–56, including 53 on the Princess's "sarcastic apology for attempting to 'teach a teacher'" and the women's instructing or teaching the men as a challenging of "prevailing attitudes about gender and literacy" (55), including in their "Mock-for-Mock anti-masque" and "reversing the men's attempts to nullify the contractual document that they all had vowed, in writing, to uphold" (54). See also Kathryn M. Moncrief, "'Teach us, sweet madam': Masculinity, Femininity, and Gendered Instruction in *Love's Labor's Lost,*" in *Performing Pedagogy in Early Modern England: Gender, Instruction, and Performance,* ed. Kathryn M. Moncrief and Kathryn R. McPherson (Farnham, U.K.: Ashgate, 2011), 113–127, on the "surprising gender reversal" that "critiques the all-male educational model, as well as the early modern model that had men educating women" (127). On women, learning, and literacy more generally, see Margaret W. Ferguson, *Dido's Daughters* (Chicago: University of Chicago Press, 2003); Heidi Brayman Hackel, *Reading Material in Early Modern England* (Cambridge: Cambridge University Press, 2005); Wendy Wall, "Literacy and the Domestic Arts," *Huntington Library Quarterly* 73, no. 3 (2010): 383–412; Elizabeth Mazzola, *Learning and Literacy in Female Hands, 1520–1698* (Aldershot: Ashgate, 2013); Margaret W. Ferguson and Mihoko Suzuki, "Women's Literacies and Social Hierarchy in Early Modern England," *Literature Compass* 12/11 (2015): 575–590.

24. Sanders, *Gender and Literacy on Stage in Early Modern England,* 54.

25. See Ellis, *Shakespeare's Lusty Punning,* 188, on "shooter/suitor"; and Maus, "Transfer of Title in *Love's Labor's Lost,*" 215–216, including for the replacement of the mutilation of Philomel by hints of Actaeon, Orpheus, and the Bacchantes, below.

26. *Riverside* has "Katherine" here, based on the Quarto's speech prefix; Woudhuysen ed., 149, has "Rosaline" (based on the Folio speech prefix) and discusses the "Katherine-Rosaline" problem on 309–311. For the sexual overtones of the "Low" Countries or Netherlands, see *The Comedy of Errors* (3.2.138–139) and Chapter 5 on Brabant.

27. In the lines on the alphabet in Act 5 that involve play on the "horn-book" and hence on "sheep," if Holofernes repeats the five vowels his speaking "I" is still, when Moth interrupts, the sheep or "ewe"; and when Moth takes over as the speaking "I" and concludes the list of vowels with "U," the "you" ("ewe") he addresses is still Holofernes.

28. See Ellis, *Shakespeare's Lusty Punning,* 50, on "fit," and 132–133, on "following" and sexual "fallowing"; Helge Kökeritz, *Shakespeare's Pronunciation* (New Haven, Conn.: Yale University Press, 1953), 140–141, on "Rhyme-Rime" and "frost"; Booth, *King Lear,* 71, on "green goose."

29. See also John J. Winkler, *The Constraints of Desire* (New York: Routledge, 1990), 219.

30. On "rhymes are guards on wanton Cupid's hose: / Disfigure not his shop" (4.3.56–57), see Woudhuysen ed., 202: "**his shop** The place where Cupid does his work, and so the codpiece in his hose and the genitals in the codpiece" (*OED sb.* 3c). See also Gordon Williams, *A Dictionary of Sexual Language and Imagery in Shakespearean and Stuart Literature,* 3 vols. (London: Athlone Press, 1994), 3:1239, on "shop" as "allusive of genitals"; Burke on *rheuma* (or "stream") in *Language as Symbolic Action,* 321.

31. On cosmetics and rhetoric, see T. P. Wiseman, *Clio's Cosmetics* (London: Rowman & Littlefield, 1980); and my "Black *Hamlet*: Battening on the Moor," *Shakespeare Studies* 33

(2003): 127–164; with Kim F. Hall, "'These bastard signs of fair': Literary Whiteness in Shakespeare's Sonnets," in *Post-Colonial Shakespeares*, ed. Ania Loomba and Martin Orkin (London: Routledge, 1998), 64–83. See also Sujata Iyengar, *Shades of Difference* (Philadelphia: University of Pennsylvania Press, 2005); Farah Karim-Cooper, *Cosmetics in Shakespearean and Renaissance Drama* (Edinburgh: Edinburgh University Press, 2006); Andrea Stevens, "Cosmetic Transformations," in *Shakespeare's Theatres and the Effects of Performance*, ed. Farah Karim-Cooper and Tiffany Stern (London: Bloomsbury Arden Shakespeare, 2013), 94–117.

32. See R. Howard Bloch, *Medieval Misogyny and the Invention of Western Romantic Love* (Chicago: University of Chicago Press, 1991), chaps. 1 and 2.

33. See Maus, "Transfer of Title in *Love's Labor's Lost*," 214; David Bevington, "'Jack Hath Not Jill': Failed Courtship in Lyly and Shakespeare," *Shakespeare Survey* 42 (1990): 1–13.

34. Booth, *King Lear*, 73.

35. On this elaborate patterning, see Harry Levin, "Sitting in the Sky (*Love's Labor's Lost*, 4.3)," in *Shakespeare's "Rough Magic*," ed. Peter Erickson and Coppélia Kahn (Toronto: Associated University Presses, 1985), 113–130, esp. 120–122 (with 129).

36. On "plain plantan," Harvey, and "l'envoy" as "an address or send-off, usually placed at the end of a prose or poetical composition," see the Arden 2 *Love's Labour's Lost*, ed. Richard David (London: Methuen, 1951), 49, which notes the same wordplay on *salve* for a sore and *salve* as a greeting in Robert Greene's *Mamillia*, and the quibble from *Aristippus, or The Jovial Philosopher* (1630).

37. Woudhuysen ed. notes that "broken in a shin" could also suggest both "sexual or amatory disappointment and borrowing money" (164). See *OED*, s.v. "shin," *sb.* 2d.

38. See Thomas Nashe, *Have with you to Saffron Walden, or Gabriell Harveys Hunt is up* (1596), in *The Works of Thomas Nashe*, ed. Ronald B. McKerrow, 5 vols. (Oxford: Basil Blackwell, 1958), 3:235. Nashe's first mention of Harvey's "l'envoy" (Epistle Dedicatorie, 3:11) is accompanied by mention of "the most contemptible *Mounsier Aiaxes* of excrementall conceipts"; his second occurs in a passage on literary "presidents" which includes "iakes" and "groaning stoole." Nashe pours scorn on Harvey's "tynie titmouse lenvoy" and writes of "another *Lenvoy* for the chape of it, his *Stanza declarative, Writers post-script in meeter*, his *knitting up Cloase*, and a third *Lenvoy*, like a *fart after a good stoole*" (3:132–133). See also Nashe's treatment of Harvey's "method of Lenvoyes, Post-scripts and Preambles" (3:135); and "ware you break not your shins in the third line on preambles and postambles" and the mention of a "latter end" by Piers Pennilesse (3:117). For play on *enigma* and *enema*, see Nashe, *Works*, 3:15, with Ellis, *Shakespeare's Lusty Punning*, 125–127, 88 (Ellis, 35, also notes that *argument* in this scene can mean clyster or enema as well as vagina).

39. See Booth, *King Lear*, 72. On "Frances" as "a conventional name for a prostitute," see Woudhuysen ed., 168. On "goose" as "fool" as well as the "Winchester goose" (prostitute and venereal disease), see David ed., 50, and *OED* on the sense of "tailor's smoothing iron" (from the resemblance of the handle to the shape of a goose's neck), as in *Macbeth* 2.3.17 ("Come in taylor, here you may roast your goose"). On the suggestion in *l'envoy* of the blindworm whose opposed ends are easily confused, see Ellis, *Shakespeare's Lusty Punning*, 58–59, citing Cotgrave's "*Envoye*," which has "Looke Ennoye," whereunder we find "A certaine venemous worme, which going both wayes, and having (as a ground-worme) her head, and tayle of one bignesse, is said to have two heads," and noting both its "phallic suggestibility" and the possibility that it "suggested to Costard the dreaded clyster-pipe." Ellis further notes that "Should an envoy, or slowworm, fall in the way of a goose, it would surely end in the goose. Moreover, *oie*, or in Cotgrave *oye*, is French for goose; the word itself ends 'in the Goose.'"

Cotgrave also gives: "*Envoy*. A message, or sending; also th'Envoy, or conclusion of a Ballet, or Sonnet; in a short stanza by it self, and serving, oftentimes, as a dedication of the whole"; *Envoyé*: "A speciall messenger sent by a Prince unto his Embassador in a forreine countrey"; *Envoyé*; "Sent; delegated; addressed or directed, unto; also, cast or thrust, out." See also the "Envois" and "Seven: Postscript" sections of Jacques Derrida, *The Post Card*, trans. Alan Bass (Chicago: University of Chicago Press, 1987).

40. See, for example, *Riverside*, 223; Woudhuysen ed., 168; with Booth, *King Lear*, 70.

41. Ellis, *Shakespeare's Lusty Punning*, 57, comments on the Quarto and Folio's "no salue, in thee male" as follows: "*Male*, which most editions (notably the Arden, Penguin, and New Cambridge) see as *mail* 'wallet, budget, bag,' whence 'no salve in thee male' means 'no ointment in the bag,' almost certainly has the alternate meaning 'the male animal.' Thus Costard, apparently dreading some sort of enema, confuses *salve* 'ointment' with *salve* or *salvo* 'a discharge of firearms,' thinking of the same type of metaphor used by Mr. Thomas Brown in 'The Dispensary, A Farce' (1697)," which treats of a "Clyster-pipe" meant to "cannonade" a character's "posteriors."

42. See the argument that the "chink" in the wall is between the legs in Thomas Clayton, "'Fie What a Question's That If Thou Wert Near a Lewd Interpreter': The Wall Scene in *A Midsummer Night's Dream*," *Shakespeare Studies* 7 (1974): 101–112, with 109–110 (on Wall's "discharged" part).

43. *OED* (s.v. "envoy," 1b) for the "conclusion of a play; also a catastrophe, denouement," cites Ben Jonson's *Silent Woman* 5.3: "And then the women (as I have given the bride her instructions) to break in upon him, i' the *l'envoy*"; and Philip Massinger's *Bashful Lover* 5.1 ("Long since I look'd for this l'envoy").

44. The bodily metaphors of what can be contained or "digested" in a play are also suggested in *Henry V* (2 Chorus.31–32) and *Troilus and Cressida* (Prologue 29).

45. Berowne also underscores fears of female inconstancy in his reference to "one that will do the deed / Though Argus were her eunuch and her guard" (3.1.198–199).

46. See Ruth Nevo, *Comic Transformations in Shakespeare* (London: Methuen, 1980), 77, on "remuneration" and "guerdon" here, and Woudhuysen ed., 171, on QF's spelling "gardon" in Costard's speech.

47. On "sorrel" and "sore L," see Ellis, *Shakespeare's Lusty Punning*, 192.

48. See Margreta de Grazia, "Homonyms Before and After Lexical Standardization," *Jahrbuch der Deutschen Shakespeare-Gesellschaft West* (1990): 143–156; Donawerth, *Language*, 144–147.

49. See Nevo, *Comic Transformations*, 74, on the crossed letters, and Joel Fineman on the "logic of the post," in *Shakespeare's Perjured Eye* (Berkeley: University of California Press, 1986).

50. On the use of Spanish *oueia* (or *oveja*, for "sheep") as a mnemonic for the vowels, see F. A. Yates, *A Study of Love's Labor's Lost* (Cambridge: Cambridge University Press, 1936). On the "horn-book" as "a tablet-like rectangle of wood, to which was fixed a parchment leaf containing 'alphabets, large and small,' perhaps a table of 'vowells and syllables . . . and the Lord's Prayer,' protected by a clear, more-or-less waterproof layer of horn," see Tom Flanigan, "On Fashionable Education and the Art of Rhetoric: Reflections of a Not-Indifferent Student in *Love's Labour's Lost*," in the *Journal of the Wooden O Symposium* 5 (2005): 13–33, 18.

51. See Jeffrey Masten, *Queer Philologies: Sex, Language, and Affect in Shakespeare's Time* (Philadelphia: University of Pennsylvania Press, 2016), 27–31, citing my work on the conjunction of "paederastic . . . 'tutoring,'" and "inversion of alphabetical sequence," in *Shakespeare*

*from the Margins* (Chicago: University of Chicago Press, 1996), 30, with treatments of schoolmasters and beating in Alan Stewart, "'Traitors to Boyes Buttockes': The Erotics of Humanist Education," chap. 3 in Stewart's *Close Readers: Humanism and Sodomy in Early Modern England* (Princeton, N.J.: Princeton University Press, 1997), 84–121; Elizabeth Pittenger, "'To Serve the Queere': Nicholas Udall, Master of Revels," in *Queering the Renaissance*, ed. Jonathan Goldberg (Durham, N.C.: Duke University Press, 1994), 162–189; Wendy Wall, "'Household Stuff': The Sexual Politics of Domesticity and the Advent of English Comedy," *ELH* 65, no. 1 (1998): 1–45.

52. Masten, *Queer Philologies*, 29, 3.

53. E.g., John Lyly's *Endymion, The Man in the Moone* (1591), plays on "Mars and Ars" and "Masse and Asse" (1.3; sig. C1).

54. When Costard asks for the "head lady" (4.1.43), the Princess responds, "Thou shalt know her, fellow, by the rest that have no heads" (44–45), playing on bodily high and low, heads and maidenheads.

55. "Horace" is also exploited for the sound of "whore" and "ass" in *Titus Andronicus* (4.2.24–26): see my "Shakespeare's Sound Government: Sound Defects, Polyglot Sounds, and Sounding Out," *Oral Tradition* 24, no. 2 (2009): 359–372, 360–361. See also Jonathan Goldberg, "The Anus in *Coriolanus*," in *Historicism, Psychoanalysis, and Early Modern Culture*, ed. Carla Mazzio and Douglas Trevor (London: Routledge, 2000), 260–271; Maurice Hunt, "The Backward Voice of Coriol-anus," *Shakespeare Studies* 32 (2004): 220–239; my *Shakespeare from the Margins* (287n.27) on Erasmus's translingual play on the "anus" of "Ciceronianus" in the "Echo" Colloquy; and Sir John Harington's *Metamorphoses of Ajax* (1596) for wordplay on Aristotle's "Posterior Analytics."

56. See *Merry Wives* 3.5.73–75 ("after we had embrac'd, kiss'd, protested, and, as it were, spoke the prologue of our comedy"), with the implication of where this "prologue" will lead; and *A Midsummer Night's Dream* 1.2.9 (Bottom's "so grow to a point"), in relation to comedy's traditional concluding consummation.

57. See Cotgrave's *Dictionarie* (1611) and Claude Desainliens (or Hollyband), *A Dictionarie French and English* (1593).

58. Ingestive/digestive language also appears in Berowne's "This fellow pecks up wit as pigeons pease" (5.2.315) and Moth's "swallow'd love with singing love, sometime through [the] nose, as if you snuff'd up love by smelling love" (3.1.15–17).

59. See *Riverside* (249) for "ortagriphie" as the spelling in the First Quarto and Folio; *OED*, s.v. "ort, n." ("A fragment of food left over from a meal; fodder left by cattle; a refuse scrap; leavings. . . . Also *fig.*: a fragment, esp. of wisdom, wit, knowledge, etc. to make orts of"), citing examples that include *Timon of Athens* (1623) IV.iii.402 ("It is some poore Fragment, some slender Ort of his remainder") and beyond.

60. The Quarto has "this swaine (because of his great lim or ioynt) shall passe Pompey the great," part of the same exchange as the refrain "let it passe" and the reference to the "posterior of the day." For editorial commentary, see *A New Variorum Edition of the Plays of Shakespeare: Love's Labour's Lost*, 3rd ed., ed. Horace Howard Furness (1904; rpt. 1935), 227; Woudhuysen ed., 233. Whatever its precise meaning, *pass* here forges links with *passing* of various kinds elsewhere in this scene. On 5.1, see also Ellis, *Shakespeare's Lusty Punning*, 46–47, and Booth, *King Lear*, 73.

61. On scatology, see John W. Velz, "Scatology and Moral Meaning in Two English Renaissance Plays," *South Central Review* 1 (1984): 4–21; Robert Hornback, "Reformation Satire, Scatology, and Iconoclastic Aesthetics in *Gammer Gurton's Needle*," in *A Companion to Tudor Literature*, ed. Kent Cartwright (Oxford: Wiley-Blackwell, 2010), 309–323. On the

medieval heritage, see Susan Signe Morrison, *Excrement in the Late Middle Ages* (New York: Palgrave Macmillan, 2008); Martha Bayless, *Sin and Filth in Medieval Culture* (London: Routledge, 2013).

62. For "reverence" as slang for "excrement," see Eric Partridge, *Shakespeare's Bawdy* (New York: E. P. Dutton, 1948), with Ellis, *Shakespeare's Lusty Punning,* 86, and *As You Like It* 1.1.49–51 ("I have as much of my father in me as you, albeit I confess your coming before me is nearer to his reverence"). See also Frankie Rubinstein, *A Dictionary of Shakespeare's Sexual Puns and Their Significance*, 2nd ed. (New York: St. Martin's Press, 1995), 86–87, on "elder" as both "Ass" and "arse-related," citing French *aisne* or "eldest" and *asne* or "ass, fool," and the elderberry used as a laxative or diuretic (citing Lyly, *Alexander and Campaspe*, Epi., "Laurel for a garland, or elder for a disgrace," and *Cymbeline* 4.2.60, "let the stinking elder, grief, untwine").

63. Baret's *Alvearie or Quadruple Dictionarie* defines "Face, or visage" as the "Pars anterior." French *fesses* is the "Pars posterior." See also Ellis, *Shakespeare's Lusty Punning,* 43, on "fesse" and "confess"; Theodore B. Leinwand, "Redeeming Beggary/Buggery in *Michaelmas Term*," *ELH* 61 (1994): 53–70, 61, on "face" as "buttocks."

64. See also Ellis, *Shakespeare's Lusty Punning,* 177, 179, on the sexual suggestiveness of "pomp" or "pump."

65. A huge codpiece would also be justified by Berowne's earlier description of "Dan Cupid" as "Dread prince of plackets, king of codpieces" (3.1.184).

66. See Stephen Orgel's "Making Greatness Familiar," in *The Power of Forms in the English Renaissance*, ed. Stephen Greenblatt (Norman, OK: Pilgrim, 1982); the King's worry that the lowly actors will "*shame* us" before the "show" begins (5.2.511–513), with Ewan Fernie, *Shame in Shakespeare* (London: Routledge, 2002), 2, 57, 80, 89–90, 202, 228.

67. The wordplay here underlines the reversal involved for this social climber, as it moves from his request to the Princess to "bestow" on him the "sense of hearing"—with the familiar homophone of *earing* or "bearing"—to his focus on her "shoe" in lines that recall his earlier stooping to Jaquenetta's "foot" and "shoe" ("*Armado.* I do adore thy sweet Grace's slipper. / *Boyet.* Loves her by the foot. / *Dumaine.* He may not by the yard," 5.2.667–669).

68. See *OED,* s.v. "catastrophe, n." In Greek, "catastrophe" means "overturning" or sudden turn as well as "end," fittingly for this play of about-turns as well as sustained play on endings.

69. See Nevo, *Comic Transformations*, 85–86, who stresses (91) this ending's frustration of generic expectations, against C. L. Barber's attempt to rescue it for festive comedy in *Shakespeare's Festive Comedy* (Princeton, N.J.: Princeton University Press, 1959), 93–113; Levin, "Sitting in the Sky," 113, on its lack of "festive consummation."

70. Hutson, *Invention of Suspicion*, 302, also citing Dorothea Kehler, "Jaquenetta's Baby's Father: Recovering Paternity in *Love's Labour's Lost*," *Renaissance Papers* (1999): 45–54.

71. See "tickle your catastrophe" (*2 Henry IV* 2.1.60) and *King Lear* 1.2.134 on the "catastrophe of the old comedy." Giorgio Melchiori, ed., *The Second Part of King Henry IV* (Cambridge: Cambridge University Press, 1989), notes that "catastrophe" for posterior or "backside" was current usage. See also *OED,* s.v. "envoy," 1b, for "conclusion of a play; also a catastrophe, denouement."

72. See Burke's "The Thinking of the Body (Comments on the Imagery of Catharsis in Literature)," in *Language as Symbolic Action*, 308–343; Ellis, *Shakespeare's Lusty Punning,* on the link between "purging" and "perjury." The connection between catharsis as both dramatic process and bodily purging has also been suggested for *All's Well That Ends Well* (including the

link between "the king's nether end," the fistula, and the play's end) in Frank Whigham's "Reading Social Conflict in the Alimentary Tract: More on the Body in Renaissance Drama," *ELH* 55 (1988): 333–350, which also sees anal inversion as related to class confusion, social upstarts, and other societal disruptions. See also Will Stockton's *Playing Dirty: Sexuality and Waste in Early Modern Comedy* (Minneapolis: University of Minnesota Press, 2011).

73. See Louis A. Montrose, "'Sport by sport o'erthrown': *Love's Labour's Lost* and the Politics of Play," *Texas Studies in Literature and Language* 18, no. 4 (1977): 528–552, 543, with 542 on Marcade, who "disrupts the performance of the play," as also "breaching the play-ground's margins." For the humoral context in the period, see Gail Kern Paster, *Humoring the Body* (Chicago: University of Chicago Press, 2004); *Reading the Early Modern Passions,* ed. Paster, Katherine Rowe, and Mary Floyd-Wilson (Philadelphia: University of Pennsylvania Press, 2004).

74. See Moncrief, "'Teach us, sweet madam,'" 113–127, 125–126, also on this deferred ending's transforming the King's "single-sex paradise" into "a test of his constancy and readiness for marriage" (126); Mark Breitenberg, *Anxious Masculinity in Early Modern England* (Cambridge: Cambridge University Press, 1996), 133.

75. On the importance of Mercury for *Love's Labor's Lost,* including in relation to Marcade, see Frederick W. Clayton and Margaret Tudeau-Clayton, "Mercury, Boy Yet and the 'Harsh' Words of *Love's Labour's Lost,*" *Shakespeare Survey* 57 (2004): 209–224; Woudhuysen ed., 65–66, 109 (which prints his name as "Marcadé"); Joseph A. Porter, *Shakespeare's Mercutio* (Chapel Hill: University of North Carolina Press, 1988); Terence Hawkes, *Shakespeare's Talking Animals* (London: Edward Arnold, 1973), 69–70, which underscores Mercury's role as messenger and his links with language, writing, and "letters to write lies withal" (Thomas Nashe, *Summer's Last Will and Testament,* lines 1262ff.). In relation to the body's end, mercury was also a well-known cure or salve for venereal disease.

76. See Cynthia Lewis, "'We Know What We Know': Reckoning in *Love's Labor's Lost,*" *Studies in Philology* 105, no. 2 (2008): 245–264; and Hutson, *Invention of Suspicion,* 296–304, including on the Aquitaine debt, negotiation, and the calculations of the aristocratic men. On arithmetic as a "tool of the trades," in relation to Armado's line, *Hamlet,* and other plays, see Paula Blank, *Shakespeare and the Mismeasure of Renaissance Man* (Ithaca, N.Y.: Cornell University Press, 2006), esp. chap. 4. See also my "*Cymbeline*: Arithmetic, Double-Entry Bookkeeping, Counts, and Accounts," *SEDERI* 23 (2013): 95–119. On scatology and arithmetic as "arse-metric" and spelled "backwards" like Arabic, see my "Cassio, Cash, and the 'Infidel o': Arithmetic, Double-Entry Bookkeeping, and *Othello*'s Unfaithful Accounts," in *A Companion to the Global Renaissance,* ed. Jyotsna G. Singh (Oxford: Wiley-Blackwell, 2009), 223–241.

77. For the newly emergent humanist elites and an argument that distances Shakespeare from them, see, for example, John D. Cox, *Shakespeare and the Dramaturgy of Power* (Princeton, N.J.: Princeton University Press, 1989), esp. chaps. 3–4.

78. On the "homo/hetero divide" see Jonathan Goldberg, "*Romeo and Juliet*'s Open Rs," in *Queering the Renaissance,* ed. Goldberg, on "the formations of gender difference as the homo/hetero divide imagines them" (225). See also the discussion and bibliography in my Introduction, with Madhavi Menon, "The L Words," in *Shakesqueer: A Queer Companion to the Complete Works of Shakespeare,* ed. Madhavi Menon (Durham, N.C.: Duke University Press, 2011), 187–194; Valerie Billing, "The Queer Language of Size in *Love's Labour's Lost,*" in *Queer Shakespeare: Desire and Sexuality,* ed. Goran Stanivukovic (London: Bloomsbury Arden Shakespeare, 2017), 107–122.

79. On the anti-Petrarchanism of the play (including the role of "eyes") and its mockery of overly spiritualized notions of love, see Neal L. Goldstein, "*Love's Labour's Lost* and the Renaissance Vision of Love," *Shakespeare Quarterly* 25, no. 3 (1974): 335–350, esp. 339–340 and 342–346; Arab, *Manly Mechanicals*, 104.

80. On the "Katherine-Rosaline tangle" of 2.1 in the Quarto (where "Berowne flirts first with Katherine, then Rosaline"), see Woudhuysen ed., 309–311.

81. See John Michael Archer, *Old Worlds: Egypt, Southwest Asia, India, and Russia in Early Modern English Writing* (Stanford, Calif.: Stanford University Press, 2002), chap. 3 and 209n.56; with his earlier discussion in *Playing the Globe*, ed. John Gillies and Virginia Mason Vaughan (New York: Fairleigh Dickinson University Press, 1998), 168ff.

82. See *The Essayes of Michael Lord of Montaigne*, trans. John Florio (1603; rpt. London: J. M. Dent & Sons, n.d.), 1.22, where Florio's "preposterous" translates Montaigne's *desnaturées*; *Every Man in His Humour* (4.7.33–35), ed. David Bevington, in *The Cambridge Edition of the Works of Ben Jonson*, 7 vols., ed. David Bevington, Martin Butler, and Ian Donaldson (Cambridge: Cambridge University Press, 2012), 4:703; *Michaelmas Term*, ed. Theodore B. Leinwand, in *Thomas Middleton, The Collected Works*, ed. Gary Taylor and John Lavagnino et al. (2007; rpt. Oxford: Clarendon Press, 2010), 353 (where the gloss to this line is "Italian men were said to engage in sodomy"); *The Honest Whore, Part I*, in *The Chief Elizabethan Playwrights, Excluding Shakespeare*, ed. William Alan Neilson (Boston: Houghton Mifflin, 1911–1961), 2.1.441 (with *Thomas Middleton, The Collected Works*, 302).

83. See Celia R. Daileader, "Back Door Sex: Renaissance Gynosodomy, Aretino, and the Exotic," *ELH* 69, no. 2 (2002): 303–334; Mario DiGangi's review of her book *Eroticism on the Renaissance Stage* (Cambridge: Cambridge University Press, 1998) in *Shakespeare Quarterly* 51, no. 3 (2002): 382–384; Stockton, *Playing Dirty*, xviii–xix, 61, 123n.32; Masten, *Queer Philologies*, 187, 285n.4.

84. For a crucial contextualization of Thersites's lines, see Mario DiGangi, *Sexual Types* (Philadelphia: University of Pennsylvania Press, 2011), 39–43.

85. See, for example, William Rankins, *A Mirror of Monsters* (1587), sig. F1r–v, on the "unnaturall" monstrosity of players, "whether grounded by nature or insinuated by *some preposterous education*"; Philip Stubbes, *The Second Part of the Anatomie of Abuses* (1583), sig. J2r, which condemns such "preposterous geare, when Gods ordinance is turned topsie turuie, vpside downe," relying like other antitheatrical diatribes on the prohibition against crossdressing from Deuteronomy 22:5, and the gloss that such "were to alter ye ordre of nature, & to despise God" (Geneva Bible). Though resisting such antitheatricalism, Thomas Heywood uses the same term in arguing in *An Apology for Actors* (1612) that "To do as the Sodomites did, use preposterous lusts in preposterous habits, is in that text flatly and severely forbidden," but it is "not probable that plays were meant in that text" (sig. C3r–v).

86. See John Michael Archer, "*Love's Labour's Lost*," in *A Companion to Shakespeare's Works*, vol. 3: *The Comedies*, ed. Richard Dutton and Jean E. Howard (Oxford: Blackwell, 2003), 320–337, 321: "The word 'academe,' as modern editors realize, immediately brings to mind what Sidney's historian calls 'the dangerless Academy of Plato,' far from battle, but redolent of the 'abominable filthiness' authorized in *Phaedrus* or *The Symposium*."

87. Ellis, *Shakespeare's Lusty Punning*, 119, also sees in "Arts-man, preambulate" and its proximity to "At your sweet pleasure" (5.1.85) something that sounds like an "invitation to sodomy," and locates sodomitical references in terms such as "carriage" and "bearing" (e.g., 1.1.268). See also "secrety" (5.1.110) in the passage on the "posterior of the day."

88. Elizabeth Pentland, "Shakespeare, Navarre, and Continental History," in *Interlinguicity, Internationality, and Shakespeare*, ed. Michael Saenger (Montreal: McGill-Queen's University Press, 2014), 23–45.

89. Pentland, "Navarre," 31, citing William Warner's *Albion's England* (London, 1597), sig. P8v.

90. Pentland, "Navarre," 37, 223n.42 (citing *The Massacre at Paris: With the Death of the Duke of Guise* [London, n.d.], sig. B7r), and 45 (on Pompey the Great and Pamplona, citing François de Belleforest, *Harangues Militaires* [Paris, 1572], 1296), and Gerhard Mercator, *Historia Mundi, or Mercator's Atlas* (London, 1635).

91. Pentland, "Navarre," citing Gabriel Chappuys, *L'Histoire du Royaume de Navarre* (Paris, 1596), 127, and noting that "Elizabethans who knew their history, or followed the reports and pamphlets about Henry of Navarre" would have been aware that the conquered portion of Navarre had been formally joined to the kingdom of Castile on the feast day of Spain's patron saint.

92. Pentland, "Navarre," 40, citing from *Solyman and Perseda* (sig. A4v) and Belleforest's *Grandes Annales* (1579), "well known in England."

93. See, for example, the complaint that "Some seeke so far for outlandish English, that they forget altogether their mothers' language," in Thomas Wilson, *The Arte of Rhetorique* (1553), ed. G. H. Mair (1909), 162–163; Richard Foster Jones, *The Triumph of the English Language* (Stanford, Calif.: Stanford University Press, 1953), 102, citing Sir John Cheke's letter of 1557 to Sir Thomas Hoby ("I am of the opinion that our own tung shold be written cleane and pure, vnmixt and vnmangled with borrowing of other tvnges"), and 188, on the preface to Spenser's *The Shepheardes Calender* in 1579, where Spenser's annotator complained that "they have made our English tongue a gallimaufray or hodgepodge of al other speches"; the dedication to his translation of Philip de Mornay's *A Woorke concerning the trewnesse of the Christian Religion* (in 1587), in which Arthur Golding wrote: "great care hath been taken, by forming and deryuing of fit names and termes, out of the fountaynes of our own tongue . . . rather than by vsurping the Latine termes, or by borrowing the words of any forreine language"; and George Puttenham on "sundry languages" in his marginal note on "*Soraismus*, or the Mingle-Mangle," in *The Art of English Poesy: A Critical Edition*, ed. Frank Whigham and Wayne A. Rebhorn (Ithaca, N.Y.: Cornell University Press, 2007), 338.

94. On "French brawl" in relation to Frances Yates's argument regarding French speakers in England, see John Michael Archer, *Citizen Shakespeare: Freemen and Aliens in the Language of the Plays* (New York: Palgrave Macmillan, 2005), 35, with Yates, *A Study of Love's Labour's Lost*, 66.

95. The Russian phrase "*ponuloi nashe*" ("Have mercy on us") is used by Nashe to play on his own name in *Have With You to Saffron-Walden* (1596): "crying vpon their knees *Ponuloi nashe*, which is, in the *Russian* tongue, Haue mercie vpon us" (see also McKerrow, *Works of Thomas Nashe*, 3:4). I am indebted to Lorna Hutson for this reference. This Russian phrase also appears in Richard Hakluyt's *The principal nauigations, voyages, traffiques and discoueries of the English nation* (Oxford, 1599–1600), STC 12626a, in the section on "The maners, vsages, and ceremonies of the Russes" (321); and Samuel Purchas, *Purchas his pilgrimes* (1625), 3:229 (on "The Russian Rites": "Ghospodi Iesus Christos esine voze ponuloi nashe"). Marjorie Rubright has also pointed out to me that sixteenth-century English writer Andrew Boorde called some Slavic tongues "Doch." See M. M. Coleman, "English Interest in the Slavonic and East European Languages," *Bulletin of the American Association of Teachers of Slavic and East European Languages* 7, no. 3 (March 15, 1950): 59–60.

96. See *Riverside,* 227, including on the letter "L" and "the Roman numeral for fifty"; Williams's *Dictionary of Sexual Language and Imagery,* under "lovers alphabet" (vol. 2), which cites for "L" both Thomas Jordan's *Walks of Islington* (1641), III.2, and the double "LL" of Thomas Dekker's *Westward Ho* (1604), 2.1.99, which is put to vaginal use.

97. Florio's Italian-English *A Worlde of Wordes* (1598), has "Sorella, *a sister. Also a nunne,*" and *sorella,* like *nun,* was subjected to sexual double entendres. See Williams's *Dictionary* on "nun" and "nunnery" (2:962–964) and "sister" (3:1252–1253).

98. On angles, ingles (or catamites), and bodily "faults" of various kinds, see my *Shakespeare from the Margins,* 143–147. Archer, "*Love's Labour's Lost,*" 333, also detects "ingle" lurking in "inkle" (3.1.139).

99. For "sore-ell" (as penis), see Woudhuysen ed., 190: "An 'ell' was a measure of length and could be used to refer to a penis," so "sorrel" could suggest "a sore penis, with the implication that *thicket* refers to a vagina or to pubic hair."

100. See Archer, *Citizen Shakespeare,* 31–40.

101. See *Sir Thomas More,* ed. John Jowett (London: Bloomsbury Arden Shakespeare, 2011). On "Dutch" as a capacious term, see Marjorie Rubright, *Doppelgänger Dilemmas* (Philadelphia: University of Pennsylvania Press, 2014), 13–17, with my Chapter 5 below. On the Dutch Church Libel (1593), see Eric Griffin, "Shakespeare, Marlowe, and the Stranger Crisis of the Early 1590s," in *Shakespeare and Immigration,* ed. Ruben Espinosa and David Ruiter (Farnham, U.K.: Ashgate, 2014), 22–23; Andrew Pettegree, *Foreign Protestant Communities in Sixteenth-Century London* (Oxford: Clarendon Press, 1986), 274–275. James Shapiro also links its language to anti-Semitism in *Shakespeare and the Jews* (New York: Columbia University Press, 1996), 185.

102. See Archer, *Citizen Shakespeare,* 41, 53–54; Natasha Korda, *Labors Lost* (Philadelphia: University of Pennsylvania Press, 2011), 115–116.

103. On this exchange between Katherine and Longaville, see Woudhuysen ed., 252–253; *Love's Labour's Lost,* ed. John Kerrigan (Harmondsworth: New Penguin Shakespeare, 1982); *Riverside,* 238; with Archer, "*Love's Labour's Lost,*" 328, on "Pompion the Great."

104. On Spain as "the most mingled" of "all nations under heaven" in Edmund Spenser's *View of the State of Ireland,* see Eric Griffin, *English Renaissance Drama and the Specter of Spain* (Philadelphia: University of Pennsylvania Press, 2009), 150ff. See also Archer, "*Love's Labour's Lost,*" 328–329, on King Cophetua and "tawny" and "Dun" Armado as "half-way between European alienness and African blackness."

105. On blackness and racialized figures in this play (including its "Ethiope" references in 4.3 and black/white in relation to women), see Kim F. Hall's *Things of Darkness* (Ithaca, N.Y.: Cornell University Press, 1995), 67–69, 90–91, 130–131; Walter Cohen's introduction in the original *Norton Shakespeare* (New York: W. W. Norton, 1997), 737–738, which also includes reference to its blackamoors and Russians (and links between Russia and "*Ne-gro-Tartars*") and the third edition (New York: W. W. Norton, 2016), 803–805; Archer, "*Love's Labour's Lost,*" 329–330. Bernadette Andrea discusses Archer's influential treatment of "Negro-Tartar" in relation to the Muscovites/Russians and blackamoors in this play, in his "*Love's Labour's Lost*" and in *Old Worlds,* 124, in her "Amazons, Turks, and Tartars in the *Gesta Grayorum* and *The Comedy of Errors,*" in Traub, *Oxford Handbook,* 77–92, 79ff.

106. On the blackness of ink and (love) melancholy, as well as printing, see Carla Mazzio, "The Melancholy of Print: *Love's Labour's Lost,*" in Mazzio and Trevor, *Historicism, Psychoanalysis, and Early Modern Culture,* 186–227.

107. See Ian Smith, "The Queer Moor: Bodies, Borders, and Barbary Inns," in Singh, *Companion to the Global Renaissance*, 190–204, with his "Barbarian Errors: Performing Race in Early Modern England," *Shakespeare Quarterly* 49, no. 2 (1998): 168–186; Arthur L. Little, Jr., *Shakespeare Jungle Fever* (Stanford, Calif.: Stanford University Press, 2000); Jeffrey Masten, "Glossing and T*pping," in Traub, *Oxford Handbook*, 578–580, on "Domingo Cassedon Drago a negro" tried for "buggery"—also analyzed in Alan Bray's *Homosexuality in Renaissance England* (London: Gay Men's Press, 1982), 40ff.

108. Archer, "*Love's Labour's Lost*," 326–327. His shorter treatment of this play in *Citizen Shakespeare*, 31–39, adds more on its "Dutch" resonances, including (35–36) in Berowne's comparison of a woman to a "German clock" in 3.1.

109. Archer, "*Love's Labour's Lost*," 331. The fact that Judas Maccabeus is played by "Holofernes" also adds the "dizzying" circularity of apocryphal/biblical contexts in which Holofernes was beheaded by Judith to Judas Maccabaeus's own beheading of another enemy of the Jews (Archer, "*Love's Labour's Lost*," 332). On Holofernes as the name of Judith's enemy in the biblical apocrypha, see also Woudhuysen ed., 42. Holofernes is also the name of Gargantua's tutor in Rabelais.

110. Archer, "*Love's Labour's Lost*," 333, citing Nashe, *The Unfortunate Traveller and Other Works* (Harmondsworth: Penguin Books, 1972), 351. See also George Chapman, *Bussy d'Ambois*, ed. Maurice Evans (London: Ernest Benn, 1965), 30, noting that "Judas in tapestries was popularly represented as having red hair, and stage Jews, such as Shylock, traditionally wore red wigs."

111. Jonathan Gil Harris, *Foreign Bodies and the Body Politic: Discourses of Social Pathology in Early Modern England* (Cambridge: Cambridge University Press, 1998), 79–88.

112. Archer, "*Love's Labour's Lost*," 333, which also includes "*canus*" and "*manus*" quoted in this paragraph.

113. Ibid., citing Juvenal, *The Sixteen Satires*, trans. P. Green (Harmondsworth: Penguin Books, 1974), 148, 266, 276.

114. Archer, "*Love's Labour's Lost*," 334.

115. Ibid.

116. Ibid. See also my "Cutting Both Ways: Bloodletting, Castration/Circumicision, and the 'Lancelet' of *The Merchant of Venice*," in *Alternative Shakespeares 3*, ed. Diana E. Henderson (London: Routledge, 2008), 95–118, on the undercutting of the teleology of biblical typology in that play.

117. See Judith Hudson, "Punishing Perjury in *Love's Labour's Lost*," in *Early Modern Drama and the Bible: Contexts and Readings, 1570–1625*, ed. Adrian Streete (New York: Palgrave Macmillan, 2012), 118–136, 133.

118. See Ben Jonson, *The Masque of Queenes* (1609), sig. D1v–D2r, for the witches' "Magical Daunce, full of praeposterous change . . . making their circles backward, to the left hand" (with David Lindley's edition of this text in *The Cambridge Edition of the Works of Ben Jonson*, 3:317). On backward inversion in witchcraft discourses, see my Introduction and Stuart Clark, *Thinking with Demons* (Oxford: Clarendon, 1997), which also cites (113) the palindrome in Robert Southwell's "The Virgin's Salutation" ("Spell *Eva* back and *Ave* shall you find, / The first began, the last reverst our harmes, / An Angel's witching wordes did *Eva* blinde, / An Angel's *Ave* disinchants the charmes").

119. See Richard Mulcaster, *The First Part of the Elementary, 1582* (Menston: Scolar Press, 1970), iv, v; John Hart, *An Othographie* (London, 1569), A1. On "orthography," in addition to Masten's *Queer Philologies*, see Archer, "*Love's Labour's Lost*," 322–324, with Elam, *Shakespeare's*

*Universe of Discourse*; Jonathan Goldberg, *Writing Matter* (Stanford, Calif: Stanford University Press, 1990); William Bullokar, *Bullokars Booke at large, for the Amendment of Orthographie for English speech* (London, 1580); P. Bales, *The Writing Schoolmaster* (London, 1590).

120. See Masten, *Queer Philologies*, 43, citing from Hume's dedication to King James in his unpublished *Of the Orthographie and Congruitie of the Britain Tongue*, 2 (with the editor's errata sheet inserted after 3), 255n.21, citing *A Greek-English Lexicon*, 9th ed., comp. Henry George Liddell, Robert Scott, et al. (Oxford: Clarendon, 1968), 1248–1249.

121. *Queer Philologies*, 40–41. Masten (255n.27) cites from the Folio *Much Adoe* (TLN 851–55), which has "turu'd ortho-graphy" (commenting "I have myself 'righted' the writing here"). As noted in my Introduction, the "awkward" and "left" or "left-handed" as the inverse of the "right" also figure in "'Tis no sinister nor no awkward claim" in *Henry V* (2.4.85), in ways explored in detail in Chapter 4.

122. See *Nashe's Lenten Stuffe* (1599) in McKerrow, *Works of Thomas Nashe*, 3:141–226. For Alanus de Insulis, see J. Ziolkowski, *Alan of Lille's Grammar of Sex* (Cambridge, Mass.: Medieval Academy of America, 1985), 14–15 and passim; Alexandre Leupin, *Barbarolexis*, trans. K. M. Cooper (Cambridge, Mass.: Harvard University Press, 1989), 60–64, 76.

123. See John Bale, *The First Two Partes of the Actes or Vnchast Examples of the Englysh Votaryes* (1546; London, 1551), fol. 6v (with fol. 10r on the "preposterouse offyce of Venery"); and *The Pageant of Popes* (1574), John Studley's English translation of Bale's *Acta Romanorum pontificum* (Basel: Joannes Oporinus, 1558), fol. 190r. Alan Stewart in *Close Readers* employs the conceptual framework of the sodomitical to read the works of Bale. But the "preposterous" in Bale more comprehensively connects "sodometry," turning back to idolatry, and the prepostera-tion of the testaments he condemns as Papist reversion to Hebrew law, so it enables the percep-tion of multiple intersecting contexts (including with regard to biblical typology as proceeding "aright" or in the "right" direction from "Old" Testament to "New"). See also my Introduction.

124. See *The Apology of Johan Bale agaynste a Ranke Papist* (London, 1550), on the "arse-warde procedynges" of going "preposterously to wurke" (sig. O1r); *The Vocacyon of Johan Bale*, ed. Peter Happé and John N. King (Binghamton, N.Y.: Renaissance English Text Society, 1990), 83, on the "right handelinge" of scriptures as opposed to the "filthie buggeries" of Rome.

125. See, for example, "Rome backwards" used for backdoor sexual entry (or "Arsey-versey Love") and with "hole backwards" in *Ram-Alley; or Merrie-trickes, A Comedy by Lording Barry*, ed. Claude E. Jones (Louvain: Librarie Universitaire, 1952), 36.

126. I am citing here from *The Bible and Holy Scriptures . . . Printed at Geneva* (Geneva, 1561), STC 2095, 80–81, and its glosses on the law as a "scholemaster" in Galatians 3:24; and the image of tutoring in Galatians 4:1–3, where the Geneva gloss speaks of "the Law, which was but an abc in respect of the Gospel," and describes the Galatians as "turned backewarde to begine anew the Iewish ceremonies . . . in stede of going forward towarde Christe." The gloss in Laurence Tomson's English translation of *The Bible, that is, the Holy Scriptures contained in the Olde and New Testament* (London, 1592), STC 2157, continues the description of the "Law" as "it were an A.B.C." (587).

127. *The New Testament of our Lord Iesvs Christ*, translated out of Greeke by Theod. Beza . . . Englished by L. Tomson (London, 1589), 187v.

128. Circumcision is identified with "the sinistre rooted persuasion of the Jewes" in Miles Coverdale's translation of Erasmus's commentary on Galatians (3:1), the biblical text that describes Christians as bewitched "backward" to the Hebrew Scriptures. See "The paraphrase vpon the epistle of the Apostle sainct Paule to the Galathians," in *The Seconde Tome or Volume of the Paraphrase of Erasmus upon the Newe Testament: Conteyning the Epistles of S. Paul and the other Apostles*, trans. Miles Coverdale (London, 1549), chap. 5, fol. 18r.

129. Racialized figures for progression from Old to New Testament are used repeatedly in the period, including with regard to baptism and Acts 8 on the conversion of the Ethiopian eunuch. See John Abbot, *Iesus Prefigured* (1623), 7, and other texts discussed in relation to the importance of this racial metaphorics for *The Merchant of Venice*, in my "Cutting Both Ways," esp. 104–115. See also Ania Loomba's "Identities and Bodies in Early Modern Studies," on the Black Bride of the Song of Songs, Jeremiah 13:23 ("Can the black Moor change his skin or the leopard his spots?"), and converts to Christianity as washed "white," in Traub, *Oxford Handbook*, 236ff.

130. See, for example, Robert Parker's *A Scholasticall Discourse against Symbolizing with Antichrist in Ceremonies: Especially in the Signe of the Crosse* (1607), e.g., 146–147; and Thomas Fuller's *The Appeal of Injured Innocence* (1659), Part 2, 101 (on the "dexterous sinistrerity" of "Romish Priests" in "seducing Souls").

131. Quoted from Henry King, *A Sermon Preached at St. Pauls March 27* (1640), in *The Sermons of Henry King*, ed. Mary Hobbs (Rutherford, N.J.:Fairleigh Dickinson University Press, 1992), 227–228. I am grateful to David Cressy for this example.

132. Quoted from Thomas Edwards, *The Paraselene Dismantled of Her Cloud* (1699), 8.

133. This language was also used in polemics directed against the Ottoman Turk. See the Introduction and my "Preposterous Conversion: Turning Turk and Its 'Pauline' Rerighting," *JMCS* 2 (2002): 1–31, which cites multiple examples of Muslims or "Turks" characterized as turning back (as in Galatians) to the circumcision and bondage of the "Hebrew" testament, including John Prime's *An Exposition and Observations upon Saint Paul to the Galatians* (Oxford, 1587), 239.

134. See, respectively, Earle's *Microcosmography* (1628), sig. C13v–D2; "Moone-calfe" in Michael Drayton, *The Works of Michael Drayton*, 5 vols., ed. J. W. Hebel (Oxford: Blackwell, 1941); "*A Game at Chess*: A Later Form," ed. Gary Taylor, in Middleton, *Collected Works*, which glosses "Hebrew way" (1841) as "Hebrew (written right to left; hence 'backwards'; here alluding to alleged Italian fondness for anal intercourse)"; "backside" as "reverse side of a sheet of paper, left-hand page of an open book (but punning on 'buttocks')"; and "forward" as "(a) zealous (b) inclined to sex with the forward-facing vagina rather than the 'backside'/anus" (1868). See also Mario DiGangi, *The Homoerotics of Early Modern Drama* (Cambridge: Cambridge University Press, 1997), 129, on the sodomitical resonances of "Hebrew" in Chapman's *Bussy D'Ambois* (5.3.76).

135. See, inter alia, Ruth Mellinkoff, *The Horned Moses in Medieval Art and Thought* (Berkeley: University of California Press, 1970), passim and, e.g., 136, on the familiar figure of the horned Moses associated with the Law, the horned hat (or *pileum cornutum*), and medieval and early modern Jews depicted with horns. She also argues that "Shakespeare was aware of the multiple connotations of a horned head" (123), including with regard to Moses and the Old Testament.

136. Geneva Bible (1561), glossing "followed strange flesh" in The General Epistle of Jude 1:7 ("As Sodom and Gomorrhe, and the cities about them, which in like maner as they did, committed, and followed strange flesh, are set forthe for an ensample, and suffre the vengeance of eternal fyre"). The 1568 Bishops' Bible (STC 2099) also has "folowed straunge fleshe" in 1.7.

## CHAPTER 2. MASTERING BIANCA, PREPOSTEROUS CONSTRUCTIONS, AND WANTON SUPPOSES

1. See *The Taming of the Shrew*, ed. G. R. Hibbard (Harmondsworth: Penguin, 1968), "one who inverts the natural order of things, one who puts the cart before the horse"; Arden 2

*The Taming of the Shrew,* ed. Brian Morris (London: Methuen, 1981; hereafter Morris ed.): "*Preposterous*] literally, placing last that which should be first (*OED,* a.1)"; *The Taming of the Shrew,* ed. Ann Thompson (Cambridge: Cambridge University Press, 1984; hereafter Thompson ed.): "*Preposterous*: Used literally to mean that Hortensio puts things first which should come later"; *The Taming of the Shrew,* Signet edition, ed. Robert B. Heilman (New York: New American Library, 1966), "putting later things (*post-*) first (*pre-*)." The Arden 3 edition of *The Taming of the Shrew,* ed. Barbara Hodgdon (London: Methuen Drama, 2010; hereafter Hodgdon ed.), 219, has: "**Preposterous** literally, placing first that which should come last—in this case, music before philosophy." See also *The Taming of the Shrew,* ed. H. J. Oliver (Oxford: Oxford University Press, 1982), 57. Unless otherwise noted, the edition used is *The Riverside Shakespeare,* 2nd ed., ed. G. Blakemore Evans, J. J. M. Tobin, et al. (Boston: Wadsworth Cengage Learning, 1997; hereafter *Riverside*).

2. See Lyly's *Endymion, The Man in the Moone* (1591), Act 1, scene 3 (sig. C1); Nashe, *The Anatomie of Absurditie* (1589), sig. B2v.

3. On bawdy puns on music and musical instruments, see Laurie Maguire, "Cultural Control in *The Taming of the Shrew,*" *Renaissance Drama* 26 (1995): 83–104, esp. 87ff.

4. See Norbert Elias, *The History of Manners* (1939), vol. 1 of *The Civilizing Process,* trans. Edmund Jephcott (New York: Pantheon, 1978); Pierre Bourdieu, *Distinction: A Social Critique of the Judgement of Taste,* trans. Richard Nice (Cambridge, Mass.: Harvard University Press, 1984). I say "we *may* be distanced" because of justified critiques of the teleological bias of Elias's description of the "civilizing process" (as in Chapter 1).

5. See Maureen Quilligan, "Staging Gender: William Shakespeare and Elizabeth Cary," in *Sexuality and Gender in Early Modern Europe,* ed. James Grantham Turner (Cambridge: Cambridge University Press, 1993), esp. 216 and 219. I put "class" in scare quotes to underscore that the term is used here, as throughout, not in the classical Marxist sense but as a critical shorthand for hierarchical social position.

6. See Suzanne Hull, *Chaste, Silent and Obedient: English Books for Women, 1475–1640* (San Marino, Calif.: Huntington Library, 1982); Frank Whigham, *Ambition and Privilege* (Berkeley: University of California Press, 1984); Nancy Armstrong and Leonard Tennenhouse, *The Ideology of Conduct* (London: Methuen, 1987); Jacques Carré, *The Crisis of Courtesy* (Brill, 1994).

7. On music as primary in creation, see Joseph Barnes's *The Praise of Musicke* (Oxford, 1586): "time cannot say that hee was before [Music], or nature that she wrought without her. To prove this looke upon the frame & workmanship of the whole worlde, whether there be not above, an harmony between the spheres." For the quotation from Castiglione's *Il Cortegiano* (Venice, 1528), see *The Courtier,* Book I, trans. Thomas Hoby (London, 1561), sig. J3r.

8. Elyot, *The Book Named the Governor* (New York: Dutton Everyman's Library, 1962), 15, 20, 22.

9. Morley, *A Plain and Easy Introduction to Practical Music,* 2nd ed., ed. R. Alex Harman (New York: W. W. Norton, 1963), 298.

10. Gosson, *The Schoole of Abuse* (1587); Ferne, *The Blazon of Gentrie* (1586).

11. Morley, *Practical Music,* viii. On music as heavenly harmony (or the music of the spheres) and practical music, see John Hollander, *The Untuning of the Sky* (Princeton, N.J.: Princeton University Press, 1961). See also David Lindley, *Shakespeare and Music* (London: Thomson Learning, 2006); Christopher R. Wilson, *Shakespeare's Musical Imagery* (Continuum, 2011).

12. Cited from *Distaves and Dames,* ed. Diane Bornstein (Delmar, N.Y.: Scholars' Facsimiles and Reprints, 1978), sig. Y3, in Valerie Wayne, "Refashioning the Shrew," *Shakespeare Studies* 17 (1985): 159–187, 172, who notes that "Vives's book was the most popular conduct book for women during the Tudor period" (186n.25).

13. See Hoby, *The Courtier,* Book I, sig. J2r, with Book II, sig. M4r-v, including on music as "meete to be practised in the presence of women"; Roger Ascham, *The Schoolmaster,* ed. John E. B. Mayor (1863; rpt. New York: AMS Press, 1967), Book I, which includes "Moch Musick marreth mens maners." See also Linda Phyllis Austern, "'Sing Againe Syren': The Female Musician and Sexual Enchantment in Elizabethan Life and Literature," *Renaissance Quarterly* 42 (1989): 420–448; Maguire, "Cultural Control," 89ff.

14. Quotations are from "The fourme of the Solemnization of Matrimonie," in *The booke of common prayer, and administracion of the sacramentes, and other rites and ceremonies in the Church of England* (London, 1559), STC 16293.3—the revised text often referred to as the *Elizabethan Prayer Book,* which throughout Shakespeare's life remained more or less unchanged. See John E. Booty, *The Book of Common Prayer, 1559: The Elizabethan Prayer Book* (Charlottesville: University of Virginia Press, 2005); Morris ed., 218; Graham Holderness, "'Darkenes was before light': Hierarchy and Duality in *The Taming of the Shrew,*" in *Gender and Power in Shrew-Taming Narratives, 1500–1700,* ed. David Wootton and Graham Holderness (New York: Palgrave Macmillan, 2010), 170.

15. Quoted from "The fourme of the Solemnization of Matrimonie" (1559), which also invokes Genesis 2: "Oh God . . . whiche also after other thinges set in ordre, diddest appoynte that out of man (created after thyne own ymage and symilytude) woman shoulde take her beginninge." On male and female as first and second in Genesis 2, in contrast to the Genesis 1 "male and female created he *them,*" see my *Literary Fat Ladies: Rhetoric, Gender, Property* (London: Methuen, 1987; New York: Routledge, 2017), chap. 9.

16. See Hodgdon ed., 219.

17. For the master-schoolboy form of translation from Latin to English and back again, see chap. 4 of my *Shakespeare from the Margins* (Chicago: University of Chicago Press, 1996) on *The Merry Wives of Windsor*; with William E. Miller, "Double Translation in English Humanistic Education," *Studies in the Renaissance* 10 (1963): 163–174; Walter J. Ong, "Latin Language Study as a Renaissance Puberty Rite," in *Rhetoric, Romance, and Technology* (Ithaca, N.Y.: Cornell University Press, 1971), 113–141; Margaret Ferguson, "Translation and Homeland Insecurity in Shakespeare's *The Taming of the Shrew*: An Experiment in Unsafe Reading," in *Early Modern Cultures of Translation,* ed. Karen Newman and Jane Tylus (Philadelphia: University of Pennsylvania Press, 2015), 117–152, 130–131, including on Jeff Dolven's characterization in *Scenes of Instruction in Renaissance Romance* (Chicago: University of Chicago Press, 2007), 43–44; Marianne Montgomery, *Europe's Languages on England's Stages, 1590–1620* (Farnham: Ashgate, 2012), 105–117. See also Richard Madelaine, "'He speaks very shrewishly': Apprentice-Training and *The Taming of the Shrew,*" in Wootton and Holderness, *Gender and Power,* 70–83, 71.

18. See William Lily and John Colet, *A Shorte Introduction of Grammar* (London, 1549), fol. C7; with Jenny C. Mann, *Outlaw Rhetoric* (Ithaca, N.Y.: Cornell University Press, 2012), 149; Elizabeth Pittenger, "Dispatch Quickly: The Mechanical Reproduction of Pages," *Shakespeare Quarterly* 42, no. 4 (1991): 389–408, 404; and my *Shakespeare from the Margins,* 141–142.

19. Alison Thorne, "'To write and read / Be henceforth treacherous': *Cymbeline* and the Problem of Interpretation," in *Shakespeare's Late Plays,* ed. Jennifer Richards and James Knowles (Edinburgh: Edinburgh University Press, 1999), 176–190, 189. In my prose here, the

edition used (as in Chapter 6) is *Cymbeline,* ed. Martin Butler (Cambridge: Cambridge University Press, 2005). See also Eve Rachele Sanders on "construing" in *Love's Labor's Lost* in *Gender and Literacy on Stage in Early Modern England* (Cambridge: Cambridge University Press, 1998), e.g., 54–55; and Bruce Smith on syntax, sex, and grammatical construction in "Latin Lovers in *The Taming of the Shrew,*" in *Shakesqueer,* ed. Madhavi Menon (Durham, N.C.: Duke University Press, 2011), 343–350.

20. See chap. 4 of my *Shakespeare from the Margins*, on female fidelity, *Merry Wives*, and "translation."

21. See Ferguson, "Translation," 147–148, on the repeated "hic" in the citation of the *Heroides* in this scene as departing from Ovid's "'*Hac* ibat Simois, *haec* est Sigeia tellus; *hic* steterat Priami regia celsa senis' (my emphasis)," and (132–133) the allusion to Ovid's *Tristia* in 1.1.33 ("Ovid be an outcast quite abjured"), noted by Heather James in "Shakespeare's Learned Heroines in Ovid's Classroom," in *Shakespeare and the Classics*, ed. Charles Martindale and A. B. Taylor (Cambridge: Cambridge University Press, 2004), 66–85, 81, who also links it with the allusion in *As You Like It* (3.3) to Ovid among the Goths.

22. Thompson ed., 106, compares "Bianca's skill at 'holding off'" to that of "Cressida, who knows all about such techniques" and does not pick up on the complaint of Penelope that forms the basis of the Latin lesson; and supports Lucentio's "sure" translation of "Aeacides" as "Ajax," though as other editors point out, this is a doubtful translation instead (see below).

23. See, for example, Karen Newman's comment on Bianca's "verbatim" repetition, quoted in full later in this chapter. In "What Did Shakespeare Read?," in *The Cambridge Companion to Shakespeare*, ed. Margreta de Grazia and Stanley Wells (Cambridge: Cambridge University Press, 2001), Leonard Barkan writes, "Bianca, herself no mean pupil, returns the translation exercise, as students were expected to do," though he adds, "Her translation at least has the virtue of keeping the Latin clauses logically together" (37).

24. Colin Burrow writes in *Shakespeare and Classical Antiquity* (Oxford: Oxford University Press, 2013), 34: "Many members of Shakespeare's audience would indeed have been able to 'construe,' or translate, the passage, and some would have known it by heart, since Ovid's *Heroides* were a familiar starting point for learning classical poetry." On *The Heroycall Epistles of the learned Poet Publius Ouidius Naso,* trans. George Turberville (London, 1567), see Thomas Moisan, "Interlinear Trysting and 'Household Stuff': The Latin Lesson and the Domestication of Learning in *The Taming of the Shrew,*" *Shakespeare Studies* 23 (1995): 100–119, and Patricia B. Phillippy, "'Loytering in Love': Ovid's 'Heroides,' Hospitality, and Humanist Education in 'The Taming of the Shrew,'" *Criticism* 40, no. 1 (1998): 27–53. In *The Comedy of Errors*, Adriana's complaints against her absent husband echo Penelope's in the first epistle of the *Heroides*, including suspicion that her husband's delayed return means he has been unfaithful, and are contrasted to her sister Luciana's iteration of the Pauline counsel to wives. On the importance of the *Heroides* for Shakespeare and others, see Elizabeth D. Harvey, *Ventriloquized Voices* (New York: Routledge, 1992). Harvey (personal communication) notes that Turberville continues the Renaissance practice—not reflected in Ovid's text—of providing male responses to three of the female complaints, including Ulysses to Penelope.

25. Lucentio's counterpart in Gascoigne's *Supposes* (as in Ariosto) uses his entry into the household to lie with Bianca's counterpart. For the line of transmission through Ariosto's *I Suppositi* and Terence's *Eunuch*, see Keir Elam, "The Fertile Eunuch: *Twelfth Night*, Early Modern Intercourse, and the Fruits of Castration," *Shakespeare Quarterly* 47, no. 1 (1996): 1–36. On "stale," see Hodgdon ed., 224; Ferguson, "Translation," 133, 152; and Karen Newman, *Fashioning Femininity and English Renaissance Drama* (Chicago: University of Chicago Press,

1991), 40, on Katherine's "make a stale of me amongst these mates" (1.1.58), where "stale" is both prostitute and laughingstock and "mate" suggests husband. G. W. Pigman III in his edition of *Supposes* in George Gascoigne, *A Hundreth Sundrie Flowres* (Oxford: Clarendon Press, 2000), hereafter designated as Pigman, *Supposes*, comments (496) that when its Bianca counterpart Polynesta is called a "stal" (3.4.42–43), it could mean "whore," since, "According to the *OED*, both 'stall' and 'stale' mean, literally and figuratively, a 'decoy-bird' or a lure,' but 'stale' is also used to mean 'prostitute.'"

26. Margaret Maurer and Barry Gaines, in "Putting the Silent Woman Back into the Shakespearean *Shrew*," 101–122 of Wootton and Holderness, *Gender and Power* (110–111), prefer the unemended First Folio text here, and add that the argument I originally made in "Construing Gender: Mastering Bianca in *The Taming of the Shrew*," in *The Impact of Feminism in English Renaissance Studies*, ed. Dympna Callaghan (New York: Palgrave Macmillan, 2007), 193–209, is "even more relevant to the F1 text of the scene." Hodgdon ed., 221, notes that "Maurer argues that F's speech assignments are playable and that they have implications for Bianca's character that editorial emendation has occluded," but prints the modernized text (as I do here). See also Margaret Maurer, "The Rowe Editions of 1709/1714 and 3.1 of *The Taming of the Shrew*," in *Reading Readings*, ed. Joanna Gondris (London, 1998), 244–246; Margaret Maurer, "Constering Bianca: *The Taming of the Shrew* and *The Woman's Prize, or The Tamer Tamed*," *Medieval and Renaissance Drama* 14 (2001): 186–206; *Three Shrew Plays: Shakespeare's The Taming of the Shrew with The Anonymous The Taming of a Shrew and Fletcher's The Tamer Tamed*, ed. Barry Gaines and Margaret Maurer (Indianapolis: Hackett, 2010).

27. In Ovid, *Heroides and Amores*, with English translation by Grant Showerman (London: W. Heinemann, 1977), *Aeacides* is translated as "Achilles" every time it appears in *Heroides* (I.35; III.87; VIII.7, 33, 55). Turberville, in *Heroycall Epistles*, likewise renders *Aeacides* in Penelope's complaint as "Achylles," as he also does consistently elsewhere.

28. See also "assurance" later in this chapter. On Bianca as a "resistant student and unexpectedly accurate Latin scholar" (100), see Lynn Enterline, *Shakespeare's Schoolroom* (Philadelphia: University of Pennsylvania Press, 2012), chap. 4, which also notes (99–100) that Heather James "observes that Bianca covertly, but effectively, derails Lucentio's position of mastery in the translation 'lesson' by showing herself the better scholar of Latin grammar" ("Shakespeare's Learned Heroines," esp. 69–70). In "Interlinear Trysting," Moisan comments that Bianca's behavior in 3.1 provides "the first clear indication that she is not the passive 'blank' her name suggests and everyone, or, rather, every male, seems to suppose," and concludes that this scene "reminds its audience of what a malleable, and manipulable, a thing learning, for all of its patriachalist prescriptions, is." Vanda Zajko, in "Petruchio Is 'Kated': *The Taming of the Shrew* and Ovid," in Martindale and Taylor, *Shakespeare and the Classics*, 33–48 (39), comments that in 3.1, "it is clear that [Bianca] is as knowledgeable as" Lucentio and provides a less optimistic reading than that in Jonathan Bate's *Shakespeare and Ovid* (Oxford: Oxford University Press, 1993). See also Carole Levin and John Watkins, *Shakespeare's Foreign Worlds* (Ithaca, N.Y.: Cornell University Press, 2009), esp. 200–201, with 149 and 172, on Bianca's less than passive role; Elizabeth Mazzola, *Learning and Literacy in Female Hands, 1520–1698* (Farnham, U.K.: Ashgate, 2013), on Bianca's "artful constructions" (38–41).

29. See *Ovid's Metamorphoses: The Arthur Golding Translation 1567*, ed. John Frederick Nims (Philadelphia: Paul Dry Books, 2000), 320, Book 13, lines 27–41, where the title *Aeacides* is claimed by Ajax, who claims that Ulysses was fathered adulterously by Sisyphus rather than his supposed father Laertes. R. Warwick Bond's Arden edition (London: Methuen and Co., 1904), 73, traces awareness of this other Ovidian intertext to George Steevens's glosses on

Lucentio's "Aeacides" with Golding's translation of *Metamorphoses* XIII.27–28 ("The highest Jove of all / Acknowledgeth this AEacus, and dooth his sonne him call. / Thus am I Ajax third from Jove") and comments, "The application of the patronymic by Ovid to Peleus, Telamon, and Phocas, AEcus' sons; by Homer and Virgil to Achilles, another grandson; and by Virgil to Pyrrhus, his great-grandson, might justify Bianca's professed 'doubt,' line 55." The reason why the patronymic is open to contestation in *Metamorphoses* XIII is that Achilles was the grandson of Aeacus through his father Peleus, while Ajax was grandson to Aeacus through his father Telamon. Though Bond cites other mock translation lessons (71–72)—including in Lyly's *Mother Bombie* (3.1.139), where "Candius translates Ovid to Livia while their fathers overhear," and she responds, "'I am no Latinist, Candius, you must conster it"—Bianca with regard to the *Heroides* proves a better Latinist than her tutor, who pretends in the speech that begins "Mistrust it not" to be providing a "sure" construing of the *Heroides* (where "Aeacides" is not "Ajax").

30. The presentation of women as ostensibly passive objects is analyzed in relation to Petruchio's pun on "Kate" and "cates" (etymologically connected to "chattel" and purchases or "achats") in Natasha Korda's "Household Kates: Domesticating Commodities in *The Taming of the Shrew*," *Shakespeare Quarterly* 47, no. 2 (1996): 109–131, and her *Shakespeare's Domestic Economies* (Philadelphia: University of Pennsylvania Press, 2002), 52–75.

31. Though she does not mention Bianca's "else I promise you / I should be arguing still upon that doubt" as anticipating this moment, Holly A. Crocker writes in "Affective Resistance: Performing Passivity and Playing a-Part in 'The Taming of the Shrew,'" *Shakespeare Quarterly* 54, no. 2 (2003): 142–159, 154, that Katherine's agreeing that the "sun" is the "moon" in 4.5 is a sign that "even if she knows he is wrong, feigning agreement allows her to achieve her own desires . . . she just wants to get to Padua to escape the prison in which her husband has kept her since her wedding day."

32. Karen Newman, "Renaissance Family Politics and Shakespeare's *The Taming of the Shrew*," quoted from its reprinting in her *Essaying Shakespeare* (Minneapolis: University of Minnesota Press, 2009), 32.

33. Amy L. Smith, "Performing Marriage with a Difference: Wooing, Wedding, and Bedding in *The Taming of the Shrew*," *Comparative Drama* 36 (2002–2003): 289–320, 311.

34. Alyssa Herzog, "Modeling Gender Education in *The Taming of the Shrew* and *The Tamer Tamed*," in *Performing Pedagogy in Early Modern England*, ed. Kathryn M. Moncrief and Kathyrn R. McPherson (Farnham, U.K.: Ashgate, 2011), 191–203.

35. See Amanda Bailey's *Flaunting* (Toronto: University of Toronto Press, 2007); David Evett's "'Surprising Confrontations': Ideologies of Service in Shakespeare's England," in *Renaissance Papers* 1990, ed. Dale B. J. Randall and Joseph A. Porter, 67–78, and *Discourses of Service in Shakespeare's England* (New York: Palgrave Macmillan, 2005), which also foregrounds ways this play "entangles the roles of servants and women in a complex web of interaction," including in relation to the biblical epistles to the Ephesians and Galatians, where "the duties of wives, children, and servants are successively discussed" (48), and notes Bianca's refusal to be a "breeching scholar" (49). See also Sonya L. Brockman, "Tranio Transformed: Social Anxieties and Social Metamorphosis in *The Taming of the Shrew*," *Journal of Early Modern Studies* 4 (2015): 213–230.

36. For example, the Royal Shakespeare edition of *The Taming of the Shrew*, ed. Jonathan Bate and Eric Rasmussen (New York: Random House, 2010), 58, has "oats . . . horses i.e. the horses are more than ready to gallop (as they have been so well fed)"; *Riverside*, 159, has "i.e.

the horses are stuffed full of oats"; Morris ed., 236, has "i.e. the horses are full of oats and therefore ready for a journey. The inversion suggests that they have had more oats than they could eat" and cites the suggestion in the edition of Sir Arthur Quiller-Couch and John Dover Wilson (Cambridge: Cambridge University Press, 1928) that Grumio may have pronounced "oats" as "aits" (a sixteenth-century variant) though "such a possibility is not mentioned in Kökeritz." But H. J. Oliver's edition comments, "It is difficult to accept that the words mean only that the horses have eaten their fill of oats and are therefore ready" (and notes that "No relevant proverb is recorded"); David Bevington's text in *The Taming of the Shrew: Texts and Contexts,* ed. Frances E. Dolan (Boston: Bedford/St. Martin's, 1996; hereafter Dolan ed.), 99, has that it is "a comic inversion"; Thompson ed., 109, has "Either a deliberate slip of the tongue (motivated by the 'preposterous' situation) or an ironic reference to the fact that these broken-down horses have been incapable of eating a normal feed"; Hodgdon ed., 237, has "deliberately inverted nonsense talk; making sense of it requires reversing subject and object—i.e. the horses have eaten the oats and thus are ready to travel." *The Norton Shakespeare,* 3rd ed., ed. Stephen Greenblatt et al. (New York: W. W. Norton, 2016), 389, has "Either Grumio gets it the wrong way around, or he is joking about the great quantity of oats the horses have eaten."

37. On the gamut as a symbol of "order and degree in the universe," in texts such as Mersenne's *Traité de L'Harmonie Universelle* (1627) and Joseph Barnes's *The Praise of Musicke* (1586), see John H. Long, *Shakespeare's Use of Music* (Gainesville: University of Florida Press, 1961), esp. chap 3.

38. See also my *Shakespeare from the Margins,* 33, on Lucentio's "*ad imprimendum solum*"— a line that Hodgdon ed., 277, glosses as Latin for "'with the sole right to print,' a formula denoting a monopoly of publication"; Oliver, *Shrew* ("The bridegroom's right to the bride is similarly to be a monopoly," 209); Hibbard, *Shrew,* on printing as "stamping one's own image on [a woman] by getting her with child," with Margreta de Grazia, "Imprints: Shakespeare, Gutenberg and Descartes," in *Alternative Shakespeares 2,* ed. Terence Hawkes (London: Routledge, 1996), 65–95, esp. 74–82.

39. *The Anatomie of Abuses* (1583), sig. C2v. On sumptuary legislation and Petruchio's "parodic spectacle of sumptuary tradition," see Brockman, "Tranio Transformed," 217ff., esp. 219. On Grumio, see also Bailey, *Flaunting,* 57–59.

40. On "the slippage of the word 'groom' in late sixteenth-century usage," see Mazzola, *Learning and Literacy,* 23.

41. On the Induction, see also Dolan ed., *Shrew,* 6; Julia Reinhard Lupton, *Thinking with Shakespeare* (Chicago: University of Chicago Press, 2011), 39; Bailey, *Flaunting,* esp. 68–72. Thompson ed., 8, 46, comments that Sly's "Look in the chronicles; we came in with Richard Conquerer" (Ind. 1:3–5) is curiously evocative of the anecdote recorded in John Manningham's diary in 1601 about Shakespeare and Burbage that ends with "William the Conqueror was before Richard the Third" (8).

42. See, inter alia, Smith, "Performing Marriage," 296–298; Crocker, "Affective Resistance"; Herzog, "Modeling Gender Education," 193–194; Ferguson, "Translation," 126–129.

43. Stubbes, *The Second Part of the Anatomie of Abuses* (1583), sig. J2r; Rankins, *Mirror of Monsters* (1587), sig. F1r–v. Both employ the same term as Thomas Heywood would in arguing in *An Apology for Actors* (1612) that "To do as the Sodomites did, use preposterous lusts in preposterous habits, is in that text flatly and severely forbidden," but it is "not probable that plays were meant in that text" (sig. C3r–v).

44. See Thompson ed., 65–66, on this line from Terence's *The Eunuch* (1.1.29–30) but cited from Lily's *Latin Grammar* (1542), "a work well-known to every Elizabethan schoolboy."

45. See chap. 2 of my *Shakespeare from the Margins* on the biblical and commercial senses of "redemption" in *The Comedy of Errors.*

46. On the gender inversions that include not only Dido "Queen of Carthage" and her sister Anna, but also the Folio's "*captam*" (rather than *captum*), see Moisan, "Interlinear Trysting," 107–108, who reads the Folio's *captam* as meaningful rather than assuming that it is an error (as many editors do). The commercial sense of "*cambio*" (along with its other meaning of "exchange" or substitution of place) is also stressed in contemporary translingual dictionaries. For example, John Baret's *An Alvearie, or Triple Dictionarie, in Englishe, Latin, and French* (1574) has "Cambio" for "to change money"; John Florio's Italian-English *Queen Anna's New World of Words* (1611) has "Cambio, *a change, an exchange, a stead*" as well as "Cambio di denari *an exchange of money*" and "Cambio secco, *an exchange among Marchants so called, when no money but bare billes passe from one to another.*"

47. See 4.2.45 and 4.4.6, with Thompson ed., 96, on the possible pun on "case."

48. See also *Pericles* ("Thou that beget'st him that did thee beget," 5.1.195).

49. On primero and "card of ten," see Thompson ed., 96; Hodgdon ed., 218.

50. See Pigman, *Supposes,* 29–30 (where the text of 3.2 includes both reference to primero and fear that "one mischance or other wyll come and turne it topsie turvie," 3.2.20–21); and Pigman's gloss (493), which also cites Ariosto's "della bassetta o della zarra' (*SP*); 'Tara' (*SV*)," where "*SP*" designates the prose version of *I Suppositi* and "*SV*" its later verse version.

51. Hodgdon ed., 212, also notes "vied" in 2.1.313 of her text as a reference to primero.

52. See Bailey, *Flaunting,* 60–68, on the "braving servant" and repeated wordplay on "face" and "brave," including in the Tailor Scene (66–68) and in relation to Tranio and Grumio. In addition, when Lucentio demands that "philosophy" come *before* "music," Hortensio responds, "Sirrah, I will not bear these braves of thine" (3.1.15).

53. "Countenance" is also used later when the Pedant (counterfeiting the identity of Lucentio's father) accuses the real father of using means to "cozen somebody . . . under my countenance" (5.1.39) and when Lucentio admits that he exchanged places with his servant, who "did bear my countenance in the town" (5.1.126).

54. See *OED,* s.v. "shrew," n.2 and adj. (used for both male and female); *OED,* s.v. "shrewd," adj., which cites, among other examples, *Troilus and Cressida* (1.2: "He has a shrow'd wit"), *Henry VI Part 1* (1.2) on "women" as "shrewd tempters with their tongues," *The Taming of the Shrew* (1.2) on "shrowd" Xantippe, and *Much Ado About Nothing* (2.1) on Beatrice's "shrewd . . . tongue."

55. Keith Thomas, "Age and Authority in Early Modern England," *Proceedings of the British Academy* 62 (1976): 205–248, 211.

56. Quoted from Stephen Greenblatt, "The Cultivation of Anxiety: King Lear and His Heirs," *Raritan* 2, no. 1 (1982): 92–114, 108 (on the period's "deep gerontological bias"). See also 101 (on the "world turned upside down" in which Lear has made his daughters his mothers) and 109 (on the parallel with Gremio's "Your father were a fool / To give thee all").

57. Coppélia Kahn, "The Absent Mother in *King Lear,*" in *Rewriting the Renaissance,* ed. Margaret W. Ferguson et al. (Chicago: University of Chicago Press, 1986), 33–49, 44, with reference to Greenblatt's *Raritan* article.

58. See *OED,* s.v. "assurance," n.: "4. *Law.* The securing of a title to property; the conveyance of lands or tenements by deed; a legal evidence of the conveyance of property"; Oliver,

*Shrew,* 153, on "assure" as "guarantee or convey by deed to (*OED* 3)"; Hodgdon ed., 215, on "assure" as "guarantee, secure, ensure (*OED v.* 1c, 5); legally convey or assign to (*OED v.* 3)."

59. See the gloss on "doing" in Hodgdon ed., 196.

60. See Moisan, "Interlinear Trysting," 110.

61. See *The Proverbs, Epigrams and Miscellanies of John Heywood,* ed. John S. Farmer (New York: Barnes & Noble, 1966), 41, 208.

62. John Lyly, *Midas* (London, 1592), Act 1, scene 2 (sig. A3r). This passage (where the opening speech prefix—corrected and expanded in my block quotation to *Licio*—is *Lit.*) continues with "*Li.* That is when those two genders are at iarre, but when they belong both to one thing, then. / *Pet.* What then? / *Li.* Then they agree like the fiddle and the stick."

63. See Lyly's already cited *Endymion* (1591), 1.3 (sig. Cr); the discussion of the "latter end" of "Jud-as" in *Love's Labor's Lost* in Chapter 1; my *Shakespeare from the Margins* (25) on "backare" in Lyly's *Midas*; and Ferguson, "Translation," 141–143, including on "same-sex antics" (142) in relation to "*baccare*/backare" (within the context of the name "Licio" in *Midas* that is also used as Hortensio's alias in the Second Folio text of Shakespeare's *Shrew*).

64. See J. Ziolkowski, *Alan of Lille's Grammar of Sex* (Cambridge, Mass.: The Medieval Academy of America, 1985), 14–15 and passim; Alexandre Leupin, *Barbarolexis,* trans. K. M. Cooper (Cambridge, Mass.: Harvard University Press, 1989), 60–64, 76.

65. John Grange, *The Golden Aphroditis* (London, 1577), sig. D3r.

66. See Sandys, *Ovid's Metamorphosis Englished, Mythologized, and Represented in Figures* (London, 1640), 184; Browne, "Of Hares," *Pseudodoxia Epidemica,* 2 vols., ed. R. Robbins (Oxford: Oxford University Press, 1998), 1:227, with the "sed etiam *praeposterae* libidinis" of Petro Castellanus's *De Esu Carnium* 3.5 (1626), one of Browne's principal sources.

67. See Thompson ed., 45: "*Litio* Shakespeare took the name for Hortensio's alias from Gascoigne's *Supposes.* It is spelt 'Litio' and 'Lisio' in F but many editors follow F2's 'Licio.'" Hodgdon ed. adopts F2's "Licio" (citing Kittredge as predecessor) and cites Margaret Ferguson's 2007 MLA conference paper ("The tutors' nicknames") on Lyly's "backare" passage. Interestingly, as noted above, the opening speech prefix for "Licio" in that passage is "*Lit.*" (*Midas,* sig. A3r).

68. See John Fletcher, *The Woman's Prize; or, the Tamer Tamed* (ca. 1611), with Gordon Williams, *A Dictionary of Sexual Language and Imagery in Shakespearean and Stuart Literature,* 3 vols. (London: Athlone Press, 1994), vol. 1, under "fiddle" for these citations as well as Aretino's *Ragionamenti* 1.2.48 ("*cassa de la viola*") and the "fiddlestick" and "consort" of *Romeo and Juliet* (3.1). Williams also cites *Comforts of Whoreing* (1694), 29, on a prostitute satisfying her client "as if she had a Fidle in her Commodity." See also *OED,* s.v. "minikin."

69. On the *cinaedus,* see, for example, Amy Richlin, *The Garden of Priapus* (Oxford: Oxford University Press, 1992); Richlin's "Not Before Homosexuality: The Materiality of the *Cinaedus* and the Roman Law Against Love Between Men," *Journal of the History of Sexuality* 3, no. 4 (1993): 523–573; David M. Halperin, "Forgetting Foucault: Acts, Identities, and the History of Sexuality," *Representations* 63 (Summer 1998): 93–120; Anthony Corbeill, *Nature Embodied: Gesture in Ancient Rome* (Princeton, N.J.: Princeton University Press, 2004), 110–111, 121–122, 124; *Same-Sex Desire and Love in Greco-Roman Antiquity and in the Classical Tradition of the West,* ed. Beert C. Verstraete (London: Routledge, 2005); Craig A. Williams, *Roman Homosexuality,* 2nd ed. (Oxford: Oxford University Press, 2010).

70. See *The Essayes of Michael Lord of Montaigne,* 3 vols., trans. John Florio (London, n.d.), 3:66–67; Martial, *Epigrams* VII:lvii, 8.

71. *The Cambridge Edition of the Works of Ben Jonson*, 7 vols., ed. David Bevington, Martin Butler, and Ian Donaldson (Cambridge: Cambridge University Press, 2012), 2:171.

72. Ibid., 2:80.

73. Ibid., 2:87.

74. Ibid., 2:114.

75. Ibid., 2:35.

76. On "spit in the hole," see Ferguson, "Translation," 135.

77. See Thomas Moisan, "'Knock Me Here Soundly': Comic Misprision and Class Consciousness in Shakespeare," *Shakespeare Quarterly* 42, no. 3 (1991): 276–290, 278–283; Bailey, *Flaunting*, 55–56, who also stresses how "Grumio achieves his goal by choosing to perform his submission in histrionic fashion" (55), and other forms of "resistance."

78. See Frankie Rubinstein, *A Dictionary of Shakespeare's Sexual Puns and Their Significance*, 2nd ed. (New York: St. Martin's Press, 1989), 142; Ferguson, "Translation," 123–125. Williams, *Dictionary*, 2:766–767, also cites the spelling "nock."

79. See John Bale, *The First Two Partes of the Actes or Vnchast Examples of the Englysh Votaryes* (1546; London, 1551), fol. 6v; *Acta Romanorum pontificum* (Basel, 1558), trans. John Studley as *The Pageant of Popes* (1574), fol. 190r.

80. See "Backedore" in Richard Huloet's *Abcedarium Anglico Latinum* (1552).

81. On the ambiguities involving Tranio at the end, see Brockman, "Tranio Transformed," esp. 227–229; with Evett, *Service*, 47ff., and his discussion of Tranio's earlier role as wily servant, recalling Roman New Comedy, and the ambiguities of his position (including 65ff.).

82. In *The Invention of Suspicion* (Oxford: Oxford University Press, 2007), 288–289, Lorna Hutson comments: "In *The Taming of the Shrew* the indulgence with which Ariosto and Gascoigne regard Polynesta's affair with the disguised Erostrato translates into the disturbing implication that Bianca, wooed similarly by Lucentio, will prove adulterously inclined as a wife. We are all married, Petruchio tells Lucentio at the end of the play, but 'you are sped'; that is, you have been brought to the destiny of cuckoldry." She cites for this meaning of "sped" Christopher Marlowe's *Doctor Faustus* (4.2.3) where "Faustus conjures up horns upon the heads of the courtiers of the German Emperor, Charles, and one of them observes, 'we are all sped.'"

83. On *The Woman's Prize; or, the Tamer Tamed*, see Hodgdon ed., 73–74; and Dolan ed. (who remarks that it "suggests that not all Shakespeare's contemporaries assumed that Petrucchio had triumphed decisively," 73).

84. On Katherine's final speech, see, inter alia, Dolan ed., 32–37; Wayne, "Refashioning," 172–174; Bailey, *Flaunting*, 72ff., including on the "language of service" (74); Ferguson, "Translation," 118–119; the review of criticism in Levin and Watkins, *Shakespeare's Foreign Worlds*, 169–170, 173–176, 203–206; and Nathanial B. Smith, "Speaking Medicine: A Paracelsian Parody of the Humors in *The Taming of the Shrew*," in *Disability, Health, and Happiness in the Shakespearean Body*, ed. Sujata Iyengar (New York: Routledge, 2015), 204–209; with Lupton, *Thinking with Shakespeare*, chap. 2; Mazzola, *Learning and Literacy*, 20–21, 24, 34, 41 (on "Petruchio's script"), 64.

85. See Hodgdon ed., 305, 306–308, 118–131, who also cites Margie Burns, "The Ending of *The Shrew*," in *The Taming of the Shrew: Critical Essays*, ed. Dana E. Aspinall (New York: Routledge, 2002), 84–105. (Hodgdon also discusses the anonymous play *The Taming of a Shrew* in her introduction, 7–18, and includes a facsimile in her Appendix 3.) On the ambiguities of the restoration of "customary order" at the end, see also Evett, *Service*, 45ff., who further

remarks, "The closing lines of the play are oddly inconclusive" and "imply a question whether Kate's transformation is for real" (in Lucentio's " 'Tis a wonder . . . she will be tam'd so").

86. See Lorna Hutson, " 'Che indizio, che prova . . . ?' Ariosto's Legal Conjectures and the English Renaissance Stage," in *Renaissance Drama,* New Series, 36/37 (2010): 179–205, including on "The Crisis of Conjecture" in relation to Ariosto's *I Suppositi* and also Gascoigne's *Supposes* (1566), which she describes as "as overtly skeptical as Ariosto's original" (191); Ariosto's treatment of the expected New Comedy "Recognition Scene" and its ostensibly clear "proofs" (195ff.); and the ways that *The Taming of the Shrew* (199ff.) complicates its own ending, including in relation to Katherine's final speech, commenting on "the desire of so many critics and audiences, traditional and feminist, to believe that Katherina's opacity constitutes proof of our exclusion from a profound intimacy with her husband, to which no other can have access" as well as the fact that "generations of readers of Shakespeare have been so ready to believe in Petruchio and Kate's postmarital romance" (202–203).

87. Ariosto's *I Suppositi* is cited only elliptically as Gascoigne's source (often in a single sentence) in the editions of Oliver (44), Hodgdon (64), Dolan (7), Thompson (10, 14), and the 2016 *Norton Shakespeare* (345); in Cecil C. Seronsy's " 'Supposes' as the Unifying Theme in *The Taming of the Shrew,*" *Shakespeare Quarterly* 14, no. 1 (1963): 15–30, 16. Richard Hosley's "Sources and Analogues of *The Taming of the Shrew,*" *Huntington Library Quarterly* 27, no. 3 (1964): 289–308, just mentions it as part of a sentence on Gascoigne (303) and another that includes the name Lizio (305). Ferguson, "Translation," briefly mentions Ariosto (but reverses the order of the prose and verse versions, 301n.53). Ariosto is missing from the discussion of "Supposes" and Gascoigne in Margaret Lael Mikesell, " 'Love Wrought These Miracles': Marriage and Genre in *The Taming of the Shrew,*" *Renaissance Drama* 20 (1989): 141–167. Exceptions to the more general ignoring of Ariosto include Lorna Hutson's 2010 article (cited above) and her *Invention of Suspicion,* Levin and Watkins's *Shakespeare's Foreign Worlds,* and Keir Elam's " 'Wanton pictures': The Baffling of Christopher Sly and the Visual-Verbal Intercourse of Early Modern Erotic Arts," in Michele Marrapodi, ed., *Shakespeare and the Italian Renaissance* (Farnham, U.K.: Ashgate, 2014), 123–146, which also includes Aretino. But Elam's focus is the Induction rather than the rest of *The Shrew,* as it is in his " 'Most truly limned and living in your face': Looking at Pictures in Shakespeare," in *Speaking Pictures,* ed. Virginia Mason Vaughan et al. (Madison: Fairleigh Dickinson University Press, 2010), 63–89, 65–66, 71. With regard to Shakespeare's use of Ariosto rather than simply of Gascoigne's translation, George W. Pigman III has noted in a private communication that "One way to argue for direct use of Ariosto might be to indicate that . . . Gascoigne left out more of Ariosto's two prologues than any other part of the play and that it's the prologues that contain the wildest play with *suppositi,*" though given Shakespeare's penchant for wordplay hints from Gascoigne might have sufficed. Naseeb Shaheen, in "Shakespeare's Knowledge of Italian," *Shakespeare Survey* 47 (1994): 161–169, argues for Shakespeare's use of various sources in Italian, including Geraldi Cinthio's *Hecatommithi* for *Othello* (which had no English translation until 1753, though he may also have used a 1583 French translation), Cinthio's Italian-only play *Epitia* in *Measure for Measure,* and Curzio Gonzaga's Italian-only play *Gl'Inganni* in *Twelfth Night.* E. A. J. Honigmann, ed., *Othello* (1997; London: Bloomsbury Arden Shakespeare, 2016), 375–397, does not agree with Shaheen that Shakespeare would have had to depend on Bandello's Italian as source for the ending of that play, but does argue that he used Cinthio's Italian in *Othello.* Elam assumes (as I do) that Shakespeare "must have read *I suppositi* in the original Italian as well as in Gascoigne's translation" (Elam, " 'Wanton pictures,' " 127).

88. On the legal (with other) senses of Ariosto's *I Suppositi*, see Hutson, "'Che indizio, che prova . . . ?,'" esp. 190–196; and *Invention of Suspicion*, esp. 192ff. and 199ff.

89. See *OED*, s.v. "suppose, v.": "15. *trans.* To substitute (something, esp. a child) by artifice or fraud. Cf. earlier suppone v. 4; also supposition n. 4a, supposititious adj. 1. *Obs.*" and "16. To put, place, or add below something; to append. Chiefly *fig.* or in figurative contexts. *Obs.*)." See also *Lexicons of Early Modern English* (*LEME*) for the sense of "place under" as well in Plautus as "substitute."

90. Cotgrave, *A Dictionarie of the French and English Tongves* (1611).

91. See Gascoigne, *A Hundreth Sundrie Flowres*, ed. G. W. Pigman III, 470–471. Ariosto's prose *I Suppositi* was originally staged at the palace of the Duke of Ferrara; then in 1519 in Rome, in the presence of Pope Leo X, with a new prologue; and was rewritten in unrhymed verse between 1528 and 1531. The first edition of the prose version was published around 1509; the second in Rome in 1524, with nine other editions (all following the second) appearing between 1525 and 1542. The verse version was first printed in Venice in 1551 and reprinted in a collection of Ariosto's plays in 1562. Pigman comments, "No other edition of either version was published in Italy during Gascoigne's lifetime," and adds that in 1552, *La Comedie Des Supposez*, with "a French prose translation on facing pages did appear in Paris, but I know of no convincing evidence that Gascoigne used it." Gascoigne's English translation *Supposes* (1566) was first performed at Gray's Inn. See also Hutson, *Invention of Suspicion*, 128, 146.

92. I quote the Italian text from Ludovico Ariosto, *Le Commedie*, ed. Andrea Gareffi (Turin: Utet, 2007), *I Suppositi in prosa*, 282; with *The Comedies of Ariosto*, trans. and ed. Edmond M. Beame and Leonard G. Sbrocchi (Chicago: University of Chicago Press, 1975), 53. Emphasis mine, as elsewhere in this chapter.

93. See Martial, *Epigrammata* (XII:43—"molles Elephantidos libelli"), and Suetonius, *Duodecim caesares, Tiberius* (cap. xliii).

94. Elam in "'Wanton pictures,'" 127, for example, has "Benign auditors, do not interpret this *supposing* in the wrong way," rather than Beame and Sbrocchi's "substitutions," and assumes allusion to "sodomies" in the title of *I Suppositi.*

95. Translation from Bette Talvacchia, *Taking Positions: On the Erotic in Renaissance Culture* (Princeton, N.J.: Princeton University Press, 1999), 245n.21; with verse Italian text *I Suppositi in versi*, from Ariosto, *Le Commedie*, ed. Gareffi, 350.

96. Beame and Sbrocchi, *Comedies of Ariosto,* 95, have: "although I speak to you about substitution, my substitutions are not like those ancient ones that Elephantis depicted in various actions, forms, and manners and that have lately reappeared in our own day in the holy city of Rome." "Supposes" is also another possible translation.

97. For the controversial history of the publication of *I modi* and the addition of Aretino's *Sonetti lussuriosi* (or "Lascivious Sonnets"), see Talvacchia, *Taking Positions*, chap. 1.

98. Talvacchia, *Taking Positions*, 55. She also notes that a modern editor of Aretino "states that the name *I suppositi* was also given to *I modi*, although I have not found this mentioned in any other source" (245n.21).

99. Giulio Romano, Pietro Aretino, et al., *I Modi: The Sixteen Pleasures, An Erotic Album of the Italian Renaissance*, ed. Lynne Lawner (Evanston, IL: Northwestern University Press, 1988), 28.

100. Beame and Sbrocchi, *Comedies of Ariosto,* 95–96.

101. The prose *I Suppositi* in Ludovico Ariosto, *Commedie*, ed. Cesare Segre (Turin: Einaudi, 1976), 62, has for its title, if taken "*in mala parte*: in cattivo senso, interpretando 'supporre' come 'sottoporsi ad amori contro natura'" (or the Pauline *contra naturam*).

102. For "Non pigliate, benigni auditori, questo supponere in mala parte: che bene in altra guisa si suppone che non lasciò ne li suoi lascivi libri Elefantide figurato," Beame and Sbrocchi translate "in mala parte" as "in a bad sense" (*Comedies of Ariosto,* 53).

103. Ariosto, *Le Commedie,* ed. Gareffi: "*Li Suppositi*: il titolo vale tanto 'sostituiti,' quanto un'allusione oscena" (281).

104. Ibid., verse *I Suppositi,* 351; Beame and Sbrocchi, *Comedies of Ariosto,* 95.

105. Beame and Sbrocchi, *Comedies of Ariosto,* 95, with their "substitution" supplemented by my also-possible "supposition." Italian text is from Gareffi's edition of the verse *I Suppositi,* 350.

106. Sergio Costola, "The Politics of a Theatrical Event: The 1509 Performance of Ariosto's *I suppositi,*" *Mediaevalia* 33 (2012): 195–228, 213, and 223n.51.

107. Costola, "1509 Performance," 224n.59. Hutson's *Invention of Suspicion* quotes a similar argument from Costola's doctoral dissertation (University of California at Los Angeles, 2002).

108. Italian text from Ariosto, *Le Commedie,* ed. Gareffi, *I Suppositi in prosa,* 282; trans. Beame and Sbrocchi, 53. The Italian texts cited reflect the variant use of "gioveni" and "giovani."

109. Beame and Sbrocchi, *Comedies of Ariosto,* 53.

110. Ariosto, *Le Commedie,* ed. Gareffi, 349, notes that "*soppongano*" in its "Che talora I fanciulli si soppongano / A nostra etade, e per adietro siano / Stati non meno più volte sopposiiti" involves wordplay on "*supporre*" as substitute (the identity of a person) and "sottoporre (porre sotto, con sottintesi osceni)," or the obscene meaning of place *under.*

111. Ibid., verse Prologue (351). The young "supposing" the old would reverse the more accepted sexual roles in which the young were "supposed." See, inter alia, Guido Ruggiero, *Machiavelli in Love* (Baltimore: Johns Hopkins University Press, 2007).

112. Laura Giannetti, *Lelia's Kiss: Imagining Gender, Sex, and Marriage in Italian Renaissance Comedy* (Toronto: University of Toronto Press, 2009), 165, citing from Ariosto's *Commedie,* ed. Segre, 62. Giannetti (personal communication) has noted that the non-professional actors playing its female parts would have been adolescent male youths ("di prima barba"), able to "play all women parts appropriately (voice etc.)." See also chap. 3 of *Lelia's Kiss.*

113. *Lelia's Kiss,* 270n.33: "Ma voi ridete, oh che cosa da ridere / havete da me udita? Ah ch'io mi imagino / Donde cotesto riso dee procedere. / Voi vi pensate che qualche sporcitia / Vi voglia dire o farvene spettacolo," citing the Prologue from *I suppositi. Comedia di M. Lodovico Ariosto, da lui medesimo riformata e ridotta in versi* (Venice: Giolito de' Ferrari, 1551), sig. C3r.

114. See ibid., 165, 270n.35: "Lettera di Alfonso Paolucci ad Alfonso I d'Este, dell' 8 Marzo 1519," in *Il teatro italiano, II: La commedia del Cinquecento,* ed. Davico Bonino, 431–433, 432. Giannetti (166) also cites this letter on the Nuncio Lanfranco Spinola, who complained that "in the presence of so great a Majesty there were received words that were not honest."

115. I owe this reference to a personal communication from Laura Giannetti. Ariosto, *Le Commedie,* ed. Gareffi, prose *I Suppositi* (312) has: "NEBBIA: Donde diavolo esci tu? / PASIFILO: Di casa vostra, per l'uscio di drieto" (or "dietro").

116. Gareffi's edition of the prose *I Suppositi* (305) has: "aperto: sodomita, che si accompagna a 'giovani di prima barba,' come dirà dopo."

117. Gareffi's edition of the prose version has: "Che tu patisci una certa infermità, a cui giova et è appropriato rimedio a stare con li giovani di prima barba." Beame and Sbrocchi, *Comedies of Ariosto,* note (97): "The last line of Dulippo is somewhat more precise and more

vulgar in the 1525 prose edition: 'Because you suffer a certain infirmity in your behind for which a good and appropriate remedy is to be with adolescent boys.' "

118. Giannetti, *Lelia's Kiss*, 166, 270n.37.

119. Pigman, *Supposes*, 491.

120. Morris ed., 79, notes "J. W. Cunliffe's discovery that [Gascoigne] used not only the original prose version of the play but a later verse rendition, made between 1528 and 1531, and used them simultaneously." See J. W. Cunliffe, ed., *Supposes and Jocasta* (Boston: D. C. Heath, 1906), 109–111; Gascoigne's *Supposes*, ed. Donald Beecher and John Butler (Ottawa: Dovehouse Editions, 1999), 64–65: "Gascoigne made continuous use of both, choosing between their readings according to his own preferences"; *Early Plays from the Italian*, ed. R. Warwick Bond (Oxford: Oxford University Press, 1911), xx: "*Supposes* is closely translated, with but slight additions, from the two forms of Ariosto's *I Suppositi*"; Pigman, *Supposes*, 472: [Gascoigne] "made extensive use of both Ariosto's prose and verse versions. . . . It is often very difficult to tell which version he is following because Ariosto's verse is usually very close to his prose," though he adds (474) that "Gascoigne appears to follow *SV* more frequently than *SP*." Elam, " 'Wanton Pictures,' " 128, is in error that the verse *I Suppositi* was "apparently not consulted by Gascoigne."

121. Pigman, *Supposes*, 478, which also includes Gascoigne's variations on "supposes" and "supposed."

122. See her 2010 article and *Invention of Suspicion* (chaps. 3 and 4).

123. See Pigman, *Supposes*, 2.4.79 and 491: "Gascoigne's joke: 'Rosso rasto o Arosto' (*SP*); 'Arosto, o rospo, o grosco' (*SV*)"; Hutson, *Invention of Suspicion*, 190.

124. See 2.3.9–10 (in Pigman, *Supposes*, 23) with gloss (489); Beecher and Butler, *Supposes*, on "purse" here as "scrotum" as well as "female genitalia" (167).

125. See entries on "nose" in Williams's *Dictionary*, 2:954–956, and his *A Glossary of Shakespeare's Sexual Language* (London: Athlone Press, 1997), 218–219, citing examples from *Antony and Cleopatra, Troilus and Cressida, All's Well That Ends Well, Othello,* and the Quarto of *The Merry Wives of Windsor*; Celia R. Daileader, "Back Door Sex: Gynosodomy, Aretino, and the Exotic," *ELH* 69, no. 2 (2002): 303–334, 308, and 329n.21, on "nose" and *ars* or ass in Middleton's *More Dissemblers Besides Women*. Pigman, *Supposes*, 492, cites the corresponding line in Ariosto's verse *I Suppositi* ("Si ben forse rompere / Ch'io non possa di poi seder"), and comments that "Gascoigne is more explicitly crude but thereby eliminates the homoerotic suggestion of the Italian." But given the sense of "nose" as "penis" in other English writing (including Shakespeare), the sexual sense may be registered in Gascoigne's line as well.

126. Quoted from Beecher and Butler, *Supposes*, 151, who gloss Gascoigne's scatological addition (175). See also Hutson, *Invention of Suspicion*, 201. Pigman's unmodernized edition (53) has "*Li.* He hath a moulde there in deede: and an hole in an other place too, I woulde your nose were in it" (5.5.132–133), also citing (506) Ariosto's " 'Il segno v'ha, v'havessi'egli / Cosi' (*SV*)."

127. Pigman, *Supposes*, 58.

128. See Hutson, " 'Che indizio, che prova . . . ?' " and *Invention of Suspicion*, 193, 201–202.

129. Ariosto, *Le Commedie*, ed. Gareffi, 384; Beame and Sbrocchi, *Comedies of Ariosto*, 97: "CLE. Young men? What for? DUL. Imagine it yourself."

130. Pigman, *Supposes*, 26; Beecher and Butler, *Supposes*, 117.

131. See Andrew Gurr, "The Many-Headed Audience," *Essays in Theatre* (1982): 52–62, 49–50; Talvacchia, *Taking Positions*, 66–69, on the references in Jonson; Elam, " 'Wanton Pictures,' " 130–133.

132. See Elam, "'Wanton Pictures,'" 123–146.

133. See ibid., 139–142; Michele Marrapodi's "The Aretinean Intertext and the Heterodoxy of *The Taming of the Shrew*," in *Shakespeare and the Italian Renaissance*, ed. Marrapodi, 235–255 (though I disagree with his exclusively hetero-reading of *The Shrew*'s ending in contrast to *Il Marescalco*).

134. Bailey, *Flaunting*, 71–72, quoting from Bruce R. Smith on Ganymede in *Homosexual Desire in Shakespeare's England* (1991; rpt. Chicago: University of Chicago Press, 1994), 192.

135. Hodgdon ed., 140.

136. See Bruce Smith, "Latin Lovers," in Menon, *Shakesqueer*, esp. 349–350.

137. See Ferguson, "Translation," 150, on "treble jars," with 134–135 on "breeching scholar," and 144 on the final scene's "bush."

138. Editorial glosses on "butt" in Bianca's "Head, and butt!" (5.2.40) include "buttock" (Hodgdon ed., 295, citing *OED* n.3); "tail, bottom" (Thompson ed., 147; Dolan ed., 133). "Bush" is glossed as having bawdy undertones as "pubic hair" (Thompson ed., 148; Dolan ed., 133), and in these lines where Bianca's "I mean to shift my bush" is accompanied by a "bow" that suggests a phallic arrow, "Bianca's allusion shifts the sense of the previous word-play to archery—flight and butt shooting, where *butt* = the goal or target" (Hodgdon ed., 295). This image is then picked up in Petruchio's "You hit the white" (to Lucentio in the play's final lines), which is not only Italian for Bianca's name but "white" as the center of the target in archery (Dolan ed., 138; Hodgdon ed., 305, including in a sexual sense) and "wight" (glossed as a "man" in Michael Neill's Oxford edition of *Othello* on the wordplay on "white" in *Othello* 2.1). See *Othello, the Moor of Venice*, ed. Michael Neill (Oxford: Oxford University Press, 2006), 249. The connection through archery between "butt" and "white" in this final scene of Shakespeare's *Shrew* thus joins the double meaning of "butt" as "buttock."

## CHAPTER 3. MULTILINGUAL QUINCES AND *A MIDSUMMER NIGHT'S DREAM*

1. See *The Riverside Shakespeare*, 2nd ed., ed. G. Blakemore Evans, J. J. M. Tobin, et al. (Boston: Wadsworth Cengage Learning, 1997; hereafter *Riverside*), from which citations in this chapter are taken unless otherwise noted (including that edition's spelling of "Thisby" for the character based on Ovid's Thisbe): "Quince's name is probably a form of *quoins* or *quines*, wedge-shaped pieces of wood used in carpentry" (259). See also Harold F. Brooks's Arden 2 edition (London: Routledge, 1979), on "Peter Quince" as "From 'quines' or 'quoins': wooden wedges used by carpenters" (3); R. A. Foakes's edition (Cambridge: Cambridge University Press, 1984), 57 ("'Quince' suggests quoins, or wedges used in carpentry"); Peter Holland's edition (Oxford: Oxford University Press, 1995), 147 ("**Quince** from 'quines' or 'quoins,' wooden wedges used by carpenters"). Margreta de Grazia's "Imprints: Shakespeare, Gutenberg and Descartes," in *Alternative Shakespeares 2*, ed. Terence Hawkes (London: Routledge, 1996), 253n.22, notes that "'Peter' Quince finds his way into women's corners or quoins, the metal or wooden shanks used to fill up gaps," in analyzing the importance of coining, stamping, the *cuneus* or wedge, and the mechanics of the "imprint" to the play (65–95).

2. Important earlier discussions of some of the traditions surrounding the quince have not been reflected in editorial glossing. See especially Rev. Henry N. Ellacombe, *The Plant-Lore & Garden-Craft of Shakespeare*, 2nd ed. (London: Simpkin, Marshall & Col, 1884), 234–236; Raymond B. Waddington, "Two Notes Iconographic on *A Midsummer Night's Dream*," *English Language Notes* 26, no. 1 (1988): 12–17; J. Barry Webb, *Shakespeare's Imagery of Plants*

(Hastings, U.K.: Cornwallis Press, 1991), 145. See also, in a different context, Robert Palter, *The Duchess of Malfi's Apricots and other Literary Fruits* (Columbia: University of South Carolina Press, 2002). Since the publication of my "(Peter) Quince: Love Potions, Carpenter's Coigns and Athenian Weddings," *Shakespeare Survey* 56 (2003): 39–54, that earlier version of this chapter has been cited for "quince" in Vivian Thomas and Nicki Faircloth, *Shakespeare's Plants and Gardens: A Dictionary* (London: Bloomsbury Arden Shakespeare, 2014), 282, and *A Midsummer Night's Dream*, ed. Sukanta Chaudhuri (London: Bloomsbury Arden Shakespeare, 2017), 119.

3. Minsheu, *Ductor in Linguas* (London, 1617), 437.

4. On Crete (including the Minotaur and the "bottom" or "clue" given by Ariadne to Theseus), see Anne E. Witte, "Bottom's Tangled Web: Texts and Textiles in *A Midsummer Night's Dream*," *Cahiers Élisabéthains*, no. 56 (October 1999): 25–39.

5. Sebastián de Covarrubias, *Diccionario de la lengua castellana o espanola* (1611), "Membrillo": "La etimologia de membrillo traen algunos del diminutivo de la palabra membrum, por cierta semejança que tienen los más de ellos con el miembro genital y femineo."

6. See Luis de Góngora, *Romances*, ed. Antonio Carreño (Madrid: Ediciones Cátedra, 1982), no. 34 (234: "En las ruinas ahora / del sagrado Tajo, viendo / debajo de los membrillos / engerirse tantos miembros": "In the ruins now / of the sacred Tajo, seeing / below the quinces [*membrillos* or little members] / so many members being eaten") and no. 36 (242, where the editor glosses "membrillos" by reference to Covarrubias's etymologizing and cites the "membrillo toledano" or quince of Toledo from Cervantes's *El Licenciado Vidriera* in *Novelas ejemplares*, ed. Harry Siebet). On the "membrillo" or quince of Cervantes's "The Glass Graduate," see Paul Julian Smith, *Writing in the Margin: Spanish Literature of the Golden Age* (Oxford: Oxford University Press, 1988), esp. 197–198; and Maria Antonia Garcés, *The Phantom of Desire: A Cervantine Erotics* (Johns Hopkins doctoral dissertation, 1994), who comments (143) that "Toledo was celebrated for its whores, considered the best in the Peninsula."

7. On this "covert description of an aged female's pudendum," see Louise O. Vasvari, "Vegetal-Genital Onomastics in the *Libro de buen amor*," *Romance Philology* (1988–1989): 16; Francis Lee Utley, *The Crooked Rib: An Analytical Index to the Argument About Women in English and Scots Literature to the End of the Year 1568* (Columbus: Ohio State University, 1944), 213, who notes that this verse was erroneously "ascribed by Stow to Chaucer [in Stowe's *Chaucer* of 1561]."

8. See Pliny, *Natural History* 15.11 ("in bed-chambers also they are to garnish the images standing about the beds-head and sides"), cited here from *The Historie of the World: Commonly called, The Naturall Historie of C. Plinius Secundus*, 2 vols., trans. Philemon Holland (London, 1635), 1:436; Eugene Stock McCartney, "How the Apple Became the Token of Love," in *Transactions and Proceedings of the American Philological Association* 56 (1925): 70–81.

9. See Thomas Thomas, *Dictionarivm Lingvae Latinae et Anglicanae* (London, 1587); and Randle Cotgrave's *Dictionarie* for "Pomme d'or. *The golden apple, amorous apple, apple of Loue; the Quince hath also been called, Pomme d'or*"; and "Pomme d'amours. *The raging, or mad, apple; also, the amorous apple, apple of Loue, golden apple.*"

10. Ellacombe, *Plant-Lore & Garden-Craft*, 234–235. Sir Thomas Browne (341) notes that we may "read in Pierius, that an Apple was the Hieroglyphicke of Loue, and that the Statua of Venus was made with one in her hand."

11. See Virgil, *Eclogues, Georgics, Aeneid I–VI*, trans. H. Rushton Fairclough, revd. G. P. Goold (Cambridge, Mass.: Harvard University Press, 1999), for the quinces of the homoerotic Eclogue 2.51 ("Come hither lovely boy. . . . My own hands will gather quinces, pale with tender

down," the Loeb translation, 34–35, of Corydon's "Huc ades, o formose puer . . . ipse ego cana legam tenera lanugine mala")—on which see also below, on the use of Latin *lanugine* ("downy") both for the quince (as in this famous homoerotic text) and for a youth's first beard; and Eclogue 3 (Loeb trans., 42–43): "Malo me Galatea petit lasciva puella, / et fugit ad salices, et se cupit ante videri" ("Galatea, saucy girl, pelts me with an apple, then runs off to the willows—and hopes I saw her first"). The "apple" of the lascivious Galatea is identified as a quince or "Cydonian apple" in the *Vertumnus* of Joan Goropius Becanus, cited in Covarrubias's *Tesoro de la lengua castellana o española* (Madrid, 1611), under "Membrillo": "Juan Goropio, en su *Vertumno*, fol. 72, declarando aquel verso de Virgilio: *Malo me Galatea petit, etc., et se cupitante videri*, da a entender esto, infamando al membrillo por su forma, y concluye: *An hic non videmus clarissima indicia, cotoneum apud nos quoque eiusdem rei, cuius apud graecos symbolum fuisse, si ex eius quidem nomine vile scortum hactenus nominetur*," the *scortum* that was a familiar term for the female genitalia. See Garcés, *Phantom*, 151, 162.

12. See Vives's *Convivium*, which is also included in *Tudor School-Boy Life: The Dialogues of Juan Luis Vives*, trans. Foster Watson (London: J. M. Dent, 1908), 136; and the excerpt from Eden's translation in *The Literature of Renaissance England*, ed. John Hollander and Frank Kermode (New York: Oxford University Press, 1973), 44–45.

13. Marcel Detienne, *Dionysos Slain*, trans. Mireille Muellner and Leonard Muellner (Baltimore: Johns Hopkins University Press, 1979), 42–43, 103n.125.

14. See *The. xv. bookes of P. Ouidius Naso, entytuled Metamorphosis*, trans. Arthur Golding (London, 1567), Book 10, 133v, on Atalanta who until then "shonnne[d] husbanding" (132r), in the story told by Venus herself in the midst of the narrative of Venus and Adonis. In Theocritus 3:40–42, the golden apples fill Atalanta with the "madness of Eros" analyzed by Detienne, who discusses the "wild copulation" of Hippomenes and Atalanta and their subsequent metamorphosis into lions—linking this Ovidian story with those of Hippolytus and Adonis killed by the boar. On the conflation of Atalanta and Hippolyta in *MND* 4.1.111–113 and *TNK* 1.1.79, see Jonathan Bate, *Shakespeare and Ovid* (Oxford: Clarendon Press, 1993), 137; John Fletcher and William Shakespeare, *The Two Noble Kinsmen*, ed. Lois Potter (Walton-on-Thames, U.K.: Thomas Nelson and Sons, 1997), 146; *The Two Noble Kinsmen*, ed. Eugene Waith (Oxford: Oxford University Press, 1994), 85.

15. The quotation on its apple and pear shapes is from Rembert Dodoens, *Histoire des Plantes* (1557), translated by Henry Lyte in 1578; on its "Coten" suit from Henry Buttes, *Dyets dry Dinner* (1599). Buttes's aligning of *cotoneum* ("quince") with "coten" (or "cotton") also joins a set of interconnections in the period between not only wool but also cotton and the quince's famously "downy" (*lanugine*) covering. Thomas Thomas's Latin-English *Dictionarium* (1587) for "*Lanuginosus*" has "Mossie, full of soft cotton, soft like cotton or wool, couered with soft haire," and for "*Lanugo,-inus*" (from which *lanugine* in both Minsheu's Quince entry and Virgil's homoerotic Eclogue 2 comes) "the soft wooll, cotton, or furre in fruites and hearbs" as well as facial hair (on which see more below). John Florio's Italian-English *A Worlde of Wordes* (1598) has for Italian *Lanugine* not only soft or downy facial hair but "Also the soft wooll, cotton or furre in fruites or hearbs" (as well as for *Cotone*, "cotton, bumbace, a nappe, or a thrum"). Claude Hollyband's *A Dictionarie of French and English* (1593) describes "the downe on some fruits, as on Peaches and Quinces, like a fine cotton." John Parkinson's *Paradisi in Sole: Paradisus Terrestris OR A Garden of Pleasant Flowers* contrasts the English quince that "no man can endure to eat it . . . rawe" with the "Portingall Apple quince" which is "so pleasant being fresh gathered, that it may be eaten like vnto an Apple without offence." For the quince's

ability to restore hair lost by the "mange" (as Pliny's translation renders it), see Pliny, *Natural History* Book 23:54.

16. *Minerva Britanna or a Garden of Heroical Deuises, furnished, and adorned with Emblemes and Impresa's of sundry natures, Newly devised, moralized, and published*, by Henry Peacham (London, 1612).

17. *The Lives of the Noble Grecians and Romanes, compared together by that graue learned Philosopher and Historiographer, Plutarke of Chaeronea: Translated out of Greeke into French by* IAMES AMYOT, *Abbot of Bellozane, Bishop of Auxerre, one of the Kings priuy counsel, and great Amner of Fraunce, and out of French into Englishe, by Thomas North* (London, 1579), 98.

18. *Roman Questions* is cited from Holland's translation of *The Philosophie, commonlie called, the Morals written by the learned Philosopher* PLUTARCH *of Chaeronea. Translated out of Greeke into English, and conferred with the Latine translations and the French, by* PHILEMON HOLLAND (London, 1603), 872. The 1623 Folio here has "Odours, odours," the 1600 First Quarto "Odours, odorous."

19. *Conjugal Precepts* is characterized in volume 3 of Foucault's *The History of Sexuality* (Part 5, "The Wife") as marking "a changing attitude towards self and sexuality articulated by writers of the early Christian era," the "art of conjugality" that would become "an integral part of the cultivation of the self."

20. See the introduction to *The Flower of Friendship: A Renaissance Dialogue Contesting Marriage* by Edmund Tilney, ed. Valerie Wayne (Ithaca, N.Y.: Cornell University Press, 1992), on the pervasive influence of Plutarch's "Precepts" of wedlock in sixteenth-century treatments of marriage and (155) on Tilney's recall of the "Solon" of Plutarch's *Lives* ("Furthermore, he tooke awaye all joynters and dowries in other mariages, and willed that the wives should bring their husbands but three gownes only . . . that man and woman should marye together for issue, for pleasure, and for love, but in no case for money"). On *De institutione Christianae feminae*, by Spanish humanist Juan Luis Vives (1523)—translated as *A Very Frutefull and Pleasant Boke Called the Instruction of a Christen Woman* by Richard Hyrd—see also *Distaves and Dames: Renaissance Treatises For and About Women*, ed. Diane Bornstein (Delmar, N.Y.: Scholars' Facsimiles & Reprints, 1978), xvii–xix. *A Mery Dialogue* is available in *Tudor Translations of the Colloquies of Erasmus (1536–1584)*, ed. Dickie A. Spurgeon (Delmar, N.Y.: Scholars' Facsimiles & Reprints, 1972), 245–283. On Erasmus's "*Eulalia*" as "sweetly speaking," see *The Colloquies of Erasmus*, trans. Craig R. Thompson (Chicago: University of Chicago Press, 1965), 114, with Wayne's introduction, 23.

21. See, for example, the 1554 Italian treatise *Delle Nozze* (On weddings), from Fausto da Longiano, which repeats Solon's precept on the eating of a quince ("un pomo cotogno") to make the mouth more "odorous" (*odorato*) or sweet-smelling: *Delle Nozze. Trattato del Fausto da Longiano, in cui si leggono i riti, i costumi, gl'instituti, le cerimonie, et le solennità di diuersi antichi popoli, onde si sono tratti molti problemi; & aggiuntiui, i precetti matrimoniali di Plutarco* (1554).

22. See Robert Aulotte, *Amyot et Plutarque: La tradition des Moralia au XVIe siècle* (Geneva: Librairie Droz, 1965), who cites all editions of Plutarch available in Latin and the vernaculars, including (Appendix II, 241) a Venetian translation in 1585 by Marc'Antonio Gandino, dedicated to his nephew on the occasion of his marriage.

23. Aulotte, *Amyot et Plutarque*, esp. 60–63, 348–350, and chap. 4.

24. See Martha Hale Shackford, *Plutarch in Renaissance England with Special Reference to Shakespeare* (n.p., 1929), 5, and chaps. 2–4, for the influence of individual parts of the *Moralia* and its translation in whole or in part, including the 1542 Basel Latin edition translated by

various scholars, including Erasmus, Budé, Melanchthon, and Poliziano and the 1570 edition of Xylander (Wilhelm Holtzman), professor of Greek at Heidelberg, who "published the Greek text with a Latin version of all the works" (17).

25. See Shackford, *Plutarch in Renaissance England*, esp. 31ff., and Gabriel Harvey, *Foure Letters and Certeine Sonnets*, Bodley Head Quarto (London, 1923), 17, 41, 95.

26. The quotation (slightly modernized) is from John Lyly, *Euphues and His England* (1580), STC (2nd ed.) 17070, 129. For this text of Lyly—who (as Shackford comments in *Plutarch in Renaissance England*, 27) was second only to North as an intermediary between Plutarch and English readers—see also John Lyly, *Eupheus and his England*, in *The Complete Works of John Lyly*, ed. R. Warwick Bond (Oxford: Clarendon Press, 1902), 2:223. Bond observes (537) of "*Euphues to Philautus*: this letter is largely borrowed from the *Coniugalia Praecepta* of Plutarch, with amplifications by Lyly . . . and some borrowings from Edmund Tylney's *Flower of Friendship*, which bears as title to the book proper, 'A brief and pleasant discourse of duties in Mariage,' and is itself indebted to the *Coniug. Praecepta*. From the words 'Helen gaped for goods,' p. 225 . . . Lyly seems to have used Xylander's translation (Basileae, 1570, fol.) ('Inhiabat opibus Helena,' p. 146), from which therefore I quote."

27. See the reference to nuptial posts and wool in *Roman Questions*, with *Poems Written by Mr William Cartwight* (London, 1651), in *The Plays and Poems of William Cartwright*, ed. G. Blakemore Evans (Madison: University of Wisconsin Press, 1951), 540.

28. See Erwin Panofsky, *Studies in Iconology* (1939; rpt. New York: Harper and Row, 1962), 163, with Figure 121 of the painting from Vienna, Kunsthistorisches Museum, no. 233; Panofsky's *Problems in Titian, Mostly Iconographic* (New York: New York University Press, 1969), 131, 138; and for more on the quince associated with Venus and marriage, Guy de Tervarent, *Attributs et Symboles dans l'Art profane* (Geneva: Librairie E. Droz, 1958), 103.

29. Edgar Wind, *Bellini's Feast of the Gods: A Study in Venetian Humanism* (Cambridge, Mass.: Harvard University Press, 1948), 36–37, 40, identifies the central couple (where the female figure is "holding the quince, the symbol of matrimony," 40) with Alfonso d'Este and his wife Lucrezia Borgia. The source for the painting is the story in Ovid's *Fasti* (I.391–440 and VI.319–348) of Priapus's interruption by the braying of Silenus's ass just as he is about to rape a sleeping nymph, an interruption for which the ass is sacrificed.

30. Cited from Andrea Alciato, *Emblemata* (Lyons, 1550), translated and annotated by Betty I. Knott, with an introduction by John Manning (Hants, England: Scolar Press, 1996), 218. This is also the Latin text and translation for this Lyons, 1550, *Cotonea* emblem on the Glasgow University Emblem website at http://www.emblems.arts.gla.ac.uk/alciato/emblem.php?id=A50a203, which includes the 1550 illustration of a quince tree with its fruit, and the footnote to Solon's mandate that it is from Plutarch's *Coniugalia praecepta* (in his *Moralia*).

31. *Omnia Andreae Alciati V. C. Emblemata: Cum commentariis, qvibvs Emblematum omnium aperta origine, mens auctoris explicatur, & obscura omnia dubiaque illustrantur; per CLAVDIVM MINOEM* (Antwerp, 1577).

32. *Emblemes d'Alciat, de noueeau Trãslatez en Frãçois vers pour vers iouxte les Latins. Ordonnez en lieux comuns, auec briefues expositions, & Figures nouuelles appropriés aux derniers Emblemes*. A Lyon Chez Gvill Roville. 1549, 254 ("Le Coing"). One example among many of the tradition that includes both bride and groom is provided by the Italian *Diverse Imprese Accommodate a diuerse moralità, con versi che i loro significati dichiarono. Tratte da gli Emblemi dell'Alciato* (Lyon, 1549), which has "li sposi" (or "newlyweds").

33. See, for example, the commentary by Mignault in the Antwerp 1577 edition, 619.

34. See, respectively, *ICONOLOGIA overo Descrittione dell'Imagini Vniversali cavate dall'Antichità et da altri Luoghi* de Cesare Ripa Perugin (Roma, 1593), and the 1603 edition.

35. See also Claude Hollyband, *A Dictionarie French and English* (1593), on "Vne pomme de coing, a Quince"; "Vn cognier, a Quince tree."

36. All of these variant spellings and historical instances are readily accessible in the corresponding *OED* entries.

37. Randle Cotgrave, *A Dictionarie of the French and English Tongues* (London, 1611), s.v. "*coing.*"

38. See Helge Kökeritz, *Shakespeare's Pronunciation* (New Haven, Conn.: Yale University Press, 1953), 100.

39. On "the *bottom of Goddes secretes*" and 1 Corinthians 2:9, see Hannibal Hamlin, *The Bible in Shakespeare* (Oxford: Oxford University Press, 2013), 109.

40. Kökeritz, *Shakespeare's Pronunciation*, 119, 331.

41. On sexual double entendres in the names of the artisan-players, see, inter alia, Wolfgang Franke, "The Logic of *Double Entendre* in *A Midsummer Night's Dream*," *Philological Quarterly* 58, no. 3 (1979): 282–297.

42. F. W. Clayton, "The Hole in the Wall: A New Look at Shakespeare's Latin Base for 'A Midsummer Night's Dream,'" The Jackson Knight Memorial Lecture, delivered at the University of Exeter, June 13, 1977 (1979), 9.

43. Clayton, "Hole in the Wall," 9. On Ovid's *ad busta Nini* and English "ninny," see Margaret Tudeau-Clayton, "Scenes of Translation in Jonson and Shakespeare: *Poetaster, Hamlet,* and *A Midsummer Night's Dream,*" *Translation and Literature* 11, no. 1 (2002): 1–23, 11.

44. See Jonathan Bate and Eric Rasmussen's RSC edition of William Shakespeare, *Complete Works* (Houndmills, U.K.: Macmillan, 2007), 374; and single-play RSC *A Midsummer Night's Dream* (Houndmills, U.K.: Macmillan, 2008; New York: Random House, 2008), 27.

45. See The New Oxford Shakespeare edition of William Shakespeare, *The Complete Works (Modern Critical Edition),* ed. Gary Taylor, John Jowett, Terri Bourus, and Gabriel Egan (Oxford: Oxford University Press, 2016), 1089.

46. See *The Norton Shakespeare,* 3rd ed., ed. Stephen Greenblatt et al. (New York: W. W. Norton, 2016), 1037–1044, 1054, 1401 (hereafter referred to as *Norton Shakespeare*).

47. See Laurie Shannon, *Sovereign Amity: Figures of Friendship in Shakespearean Contexts* (Chicago: University of Chicago Press, 2002), 68; and (further on the issue of consent) Julia Reinhard Lupton, *Thinking with Shakespeare* (Chicago: University of Chicago Press, 2011), esp. 103; with Amanda Bailey, "Personification and the Political Imagination of *A Midsummer Night's Dream,*" in Valerie Traub, ed., *The Oxford Handbook of Shakespeare and Embodiment* (Oxford: Oxford University Press, 2016).

48. See Jonathan Goldberg, "*Romeo and Juliet*'s Open Rs," in *Queering the Renaissance,* ed. Goldberg (Durham, N.C.: Duke University Press, 1994), 218–235, 225. In *Sodometries* (Stanford, Calif.: Stanford University Press, 1992), 158, Goldberg also cautions against concluding that "anal sex marks the difference between hetero-and homosexuality." The *Riverside* gloss for "open-arse" has "another name for the medlar, with allusion to the female pudenda" (1113); the *Norton Shakespeare,* 986, has for "medlar": "a fruit thought to resemble the female sexual organs or the anus"; and notes the wordplay on "pop her in" for the "pear from Poperinghe in Flanders."

49. Laura Giannetti Ruggiero, "The Forbidden Fruit or the Taste for Sodomy in Renaissance Italy," *Quaderni d'italianistica* 27, no. 1 (2006): 31–52, 44, 47.

50. For the "preposterous Italian way" and other examples of "Italian" back-door entry, see Gordon Williams, *A Dictionary of Sexual Language and Imagery in Shakespearean and Stuart Literature,* 3 vols. (London: Athlone Press, 1994), 2:721; Celia R. Daileader, "Back Door Sex: Renaissance Gynosodomy, Aretino, and the Exotic," *ELH* 69, no. 2 (2002): 303–334.

51. See Alan Sinfield on Oberon and the Indian votaress's "lovely boy" in his "Intertextuality and the Limits of Queer Reading in *A Midsummer Night's Dream* and *The Two Noble Kinsmen,*" in his *Shakespeare, Authority, Sexuality* (London: Routledge, 2006), 68–85, 77–79; and Richard Rambuss, "*A Midsummer Night's Dream*: Shakespeare's Ass Play," in *Shakesqueer,* ed. Madhavi Menon (Durham, N.C.: Duke University Press, 2011), 234–244, including Thisby's "I kiss the wall's hole" as an "arse-kiss" (240). See also Thomas Clayton, "'Fie What a Question's That If Thou Wert Near a Lewd Interpreter': The Wall Scene in *A Midsummer Night's Dream,*" *Shakespeare Studies* 7 (1974): 101–112; James M. Bromley, "Rimming the Renaissance," in *Sex Before Sex: Figuring the Act in Early Modern England,* ed. James M. Bromley and Will Stockton (Minneapolis: University of Minnesota Press, 2013).

52. See, inter alia, Bruce R. Smith, *Homosexual Desire in Shakespeare's England* (Chicago: University of Chicago Press, 1994), 89ff.; Stephen Guy-Bray, *Homoerotic Space* (Toronto: University of Toronto Press, 2002), 43ff.; Will Fisher, "'Wantoning with the Thighs': The Socialization of Thigh Sex in England, 1590–1730," *Journal of the History of Sexuality,* 24, no. 1 (2015): 1–24, 20 (which also mentions Solon in Plutarch's *Eroticus*—on the love of boys—and the "quivering thigh" of Rosaline in *Romeo and Juliet,* on 3 and 18–19, respectively). With regard to Corydon's address to the "lovely boy" in Eclogue 2.51 ("*Huc ades, o formose puer . . . ipse ego cana legam tenera lanugine mala,*" or "Come hither lovely boy. . . . My own hands will gather quinces, pale with tender down"), Barbara Weiden Boyd, in "*Cydonea Mala*: Virgilian Word-Play and Allusion," *Harvard Studies in Classical Philology* 87 (1983): 169–174, not only discusses the connection between these lines, Cydonia in Crete and "the Cretans' reputation for youthful homosexuality" but also notes (170) that "down-covered fruits (*tenera lanugine mala*) are a particularly suitable gift for a youth whose beard has just begun (*tenera lanugine malae*)." This connection also appears repeatedly in early modern texts, including interlingual dictionaries: Thomas's Latin-English *Dictionarium* (1587) and Florio's Italian-English *Worlde of Wordes* (1598), to cite just two of many examples, include this soft hair on the face (as well as on the fruit) in their definitions of Latin *lanuginosus* and *lanugo* and Italian *lanugine* respectively.

53. The discussion in my Introduction involves Jeffrey Masten's brilliant work in chap. 6 of *Queer Philologies: Sex, Language, and Affect in Shakespeare's Time* (Philadelphia: University of Pennsylvania Press, 2016) on the logic of the "fundament," which escapes the binary opposition of *before* and *after,* as well as a binary understanding of "preposterous" erotic logics. See also Rambuss, "Shakespeare's Ass Play," 238, on Bottom as "a hybrid genus that straddles species."

54. Bailey, "Personification and the Political Imagination of *A Midsummer Night's Dream,*" 400–418, 415, which also discusses a father's power to "figure" and "disfigure" and the issue of "consent" (407–408).

55. See Rambuss, "Shakespeare's Ass Play," 288; Bruce Thomas Boehrer, "Bestial Buggery in *A Midsummer Night's Dream,*" in *The Production of English Renaissance Culture,* ed. David Lee Miller et al. (Ithaca, N.Y.: Cornell University Press, 1994); Boehrer's *Shakespeare Among the Animals* (New York: Palgrave, 2002) and "Economies of Desire in *A Midsummer Night's Dream,*" *Shakespeare Studies* 32 (2004): 99–117. On this play's multiple erotic investments, see also, inter alia, Valerie Traub, *The Renaissance of Lesbianism in Early Modern England* (Cambridge: Cambridge University Press, 2002); Kathryn Schwarz, *Tough Love: Amazon Encounters*

*in the English Renaissance* (Durham, N.C.: Duke University Press, 2000) and *What You Will: Gender, Contract, and Shakespearean Social Space* (Philadelphia: University of Pennsylvania Press, 2011); Mario DiGangi, *Sexual Types* (Philadelphia: University of Pennsylvania Press, 2011), esp. 75–84, 162–164 (including on Oberon and the changeling boy); Arthur L. Little, Jr., on the "queer marriage" of Titania and her votaress, in "'A Local Habitation and a Name': Presence, Witnessing, and Queer Marriage in Shakespeare's Romantic Comedies," in *Presentism, Gender, and Sexuality in Shakespeare,* ed. Evelyn Gajowski (New York: Palgrave Macmillan, 2009), 207–236, e.g., 227. See also Kirk Quinsland, "The Sport of Asses: *A Midsummer Night's Dream,*" in *Queer Shakespeare: Desire and Sexuality,* ed. Goran Stanivukovic (London: Bloomsbury Arden Shakespeare, 2017), 69–85.

56. See my Introduction above and Masten's *Queer Philologies,* chap. 6.

57. On "disfigure" in 3.1, see also Robert Weimann, *Author's Pen and Actor's Voice* (Cambridge: Cambridge University Press, 2000), 82–85.

58. See Tiffany Stern, *Rehearsal from Shakespeare to Sheridan* (Oxford: Clarendon Press, 2000), 30, citing *A Midsummer Night's Dream,* ed. Peter Holland, 90–92: "As Peter Holland explains, the kind of acting group depicted in *A Midsummer Night's Dream* never actually existed at all: the classical play put on by Quince and his company is unlike anything that their counterparts ever performed, for though groups of workers did mount productions, they never, to our knowledge, presented English versions of classical stories."

59. The quotation is from Annabel Patterson, *Shakespeare and the Popular Voice* (Oxford: Blackwell, 1989), 58.

60. On this mispunctuated Prologue, see, inter alia, Ronda Arab's *Manly Mechanicals on the Early Modern English Stage* (Selinsgrove: Susquehanna University Press, 2011), 108–109.

61. See Laurie Shannon, *The Accommodated Animal: Cosmopolity in Shakespearean Locales* (Chicago: University of Chicago Press, 2013), 216–217, on "night-rule."

62. The tragic death of Hippolytus is one of the most memorable moments of Book 15 of Ovid's *Metamorphoses* as well as the subject of Seneca's *Hippolytus,* which Jonathan Bate notes was "was one of the best-known classical tragedies in the sixteenth century," in his introduction to the RSC single-play edition (7). I see the end of this play as much more shadowed by its evocation of the tragic issue of this marriage than Peter Holland does in "Theseus' Shadows in *A Midsummer Night's Dream,*" *Shakespeare Survey* 47 (1994): 139–151, 142–146, which also notes the play's choice of Chaucer's "Hippolyta" over "Antiopa" from North's Plutarch (143).

## CHAPTER 4. "NO SINISTER NOR NO AWKWARD CLAIM"

1. T. W. Craik, ed., *King Henry V* (London: Routledge/Arden Shakespeare, 1995), 152, citing Edward Hall, *The Union of the Two Noble and Illustre Families of Lancaster and York,* 1548, ed. H. Ellis (1809), 113, and Raphael Holinshed, *The Chronicles of England, Scotland and Ireland,* 2nd ed. (1587; rpt. 1808, 6 vols.), 3:583—the editions used unless otherwise noted. Unless otherwise specified, Shakespeare citations are from *The Riverside Shakespeare,* 2nd ed., ed. G. Blakemore Evans, J. J. M. Tobin, et al. (Boston: Wadsworth Cengage Learning, 1997; hereafter *Riverside*), and italicization is my own.

2. "Our bending author" (Epilogue 2) is a phrase *Riverside* (1015) has trouble glossing—"bending: bowing (?) or stooped with the labor of composition (?)"—but which also suggests the regressive curving back to the theatrically earlier plays of the son it pointedly recalls as

having come *before*. Christopher Pye, *The Regal Phantasm* (London: Routledge, 1990), 41, suggests the "male homoerotic resonances" in "bending."

3. See E. M. W. Tillyard, *Shakespeare's History Plays* (London: Chatto & Windus, 1944; rpt. New York: Macmillan, 1947), 183. I use "tetralogy" in the sense used, for example, in Janette Dillon's *Shakespeare and the Staging of English History* (Oxford: Oxford University Press, 2012), 129–130 (though I would add that it is important to see the further discussion below of the other versions of plays she refers to here by their 1623 Folio titles): "The sequence in which the First Tetralogy (composed of the three parts of *Henry VI* and *Richard III*) was written remains controversial. (The term 'First Tetralogy,' furthermore, is sometimes used to imply the view that the four plays were planned as a sequence; but here I use the terms 'First Tetralogy' and 'Second Tetralogy' without that implication, merely to distinguish the two groups of four into which these eight plays fall.)" With regard to the *Henry V* Epilogue's "Which oft our stage hath shown" (13), Richard Dutton in *Shakespeare, Court Dramatist* (Oxford: Oxford University Press, 2016), 209–210, argues that earlier versions of the Henry VI plays were revised by Shakespeare from 1594 onwards and that "A revised sequence of *Henry VI* plays [for the Chamberlain's Men] might have been a welcome novelty—and of a piece with other evidence we have seen that the tetralogies tracing the histories of the Houses of Lancaster and York were revised to make them run more smoothly as sequences," adding that "it is difficult to resist the conclusion that the plays of both tetralogies were mainstays of the Chamberlain's Men's repertoire in a four-year window, *c.* 1596–1600, very possibly in various sequences: 'as oft our stage hath shown,' says the chorus at the end of F *Henry V*" (see also 184–185). Gary Taylor and Rory Loughnane, in "The Canon and Chronology of Shakespeare's Works," chapter 25 of *The New Oxford Shakespeare: Authorship Companion* ed. Gary Taylor and Gabriel Egan (Oxford: Oxford University Press, 2017), 493–499, 513–517, argue that the original versions of *Henry VI Part 2* and *Henry VI Part 3* were written by Shakespeare, Christopher Marlowe, and most likely another as-yet-anonymous author (*ca.* 1590 and late 1590 respectively) and that the original version of *Henry VI Part 1* was written by Thomas Nashe, Marlowe, and another as-yet anonymous author (by March, 1592) and later adapted by Shakespeare (who may or may not have been an original co-author). They conclude that Shakespeare revised all three of the Henry VI plays between 1594 and 1597 (most likely 1595) to create a unified tetralogy (with *Richard III*) for the Chamberlain's Men; so that by the time of the Epilogue to *Henry V* (which they date in its Folio version as 1599 [527]) all three Henry VI plays were part of a more unified tetralogy. See also the discussion of the 1594 Quarto and 1595 Octavo counterparts to *2 Henry VI* and *3 Henry VI* respectively, later in this chapter.

4. Tillyard, *History Plays*, 149, speculates that Shakespeare "may well have written early versions of the plays of the second tetralogy, *Richard II*, *Henry IV*, and *Henry V*, now lost but recast in the plays we have."

5. See Marjorie Garber, "Descanting on Deformity: Richard III and the Shape of History," in her *Shakespeare's Ghost Writers* (New York: Methuen, 1987), 52, with her "'What's Past Is Prologue': Temporality and Prophecy in Shakespeare's History Plays," in *Renaissance Genres*, ed. Barbara Kiefer Lewalski (Cambridge, Mass.: Harvard University Press, 1986), 301–331, on the reversed order of the two tetralogies.

6. By referring to "the plays of the son, Henry VI," I am deliberately not suggesting that *Henry VI Part I* was composed before the plays known in the 1623 Folio as *Henry VI Parts 2* and *3*. Though the matter remains under debate (as does the issue of original authorship), many believe that *1H6* was composed after the others (perhaps as an intended "prequel" since the other two plays had already been so popular on stage, in some version). See, inter alia, the

Royal Shakespeare edition of *Henry VI Parts I, II, and III*, ed. Jonathan Bate and Eric Rasmussen (New York: Random House, 2012), viii–x; *The Norton Shakespeare*, 3rd ed., ed. Stephen Greenblatt et al. (New York: W. W. Norton, 2016), 182, 190–191, 273–274, 424–425. See also Taylor and Loughnane, "Canon and Chronology," e.g. 494, 516 (with 506 on "mid-to-late 1592" as their "best guess" date for *Richard III* and 512 on "mid-1595" as their "best guess" date for *Richard II*); below on the 1594 Quarto and 1595 Octavo counterparts to *2 Henry VI* and *3 Henry VI* respectively.

7. For echoes of *Richard III* in *Henry V*, see Pye, *Phantasm*, 42; my *Shakespeare from the Margins* (Chicago: University of Chicago Press, 1996), chap. 1, which also includes the "preposterous" with regard to Gloucester, the future Richard III.

8. See Garber, "What's Past Is Prologue," 322. See also the pre-1595 dating of the earliest versions of the Henry VI plays in Taylor and Loughnane's "Canon and Chronology," and 1595 as their "best guess" for the date when Shakespeare revised all three plays (494–499, 513–517), with their discussion of *Richard II* (512–513). With regard to the date of the 1623 Folio *Henry V* (whose prologue, epilogue and choruses are not in the 1600 Quarto), James Shapiro in *A Year in the Life of William Shakespeare: 1599* (New York: HarperCollins, 2005), 87ff., argues for 1599, prior to the publication of the "stripped-down" Quarto version in 1600 (91). Richard Dutton, in "'Methinks the truth should live from age to age': The Dating and Contexts of *Henry V*," *Huntington Library Quarterly* 68 (2005): 173–204, argues for a date soon after the battle of Kinsale (1601), and consequently allusion to Mountjoy rather than Essex in the Chorus to Act 5. See also Stephen Orgel's review of Shapiro's book in *TLS*, 19 August 2005, 11. Dutton's argument (revisited in his *Shakespeare, Court Dramatist*, where he also argues that the Henry VI plays were revised into part of a first tetralogy before *Henry V*) has been countered by other scholars who argue for the 1599 date for the Folio *Henry V*, including Douglas Bruster and Geneviève Smith in "A New Chronology for Shakespeare's Plays," in *Digital Scholarship in the Humanities* (formerly *Literary and Linguistic Computing*) (December, 2014): 1–20; Taylor and Loughnane, "Canon and Chronology," 527. With regard to performance of the Folio *Henry V*, critics have also countered Andrew Gurr's argument in his edition of *The First Quarto of King Henry V* (Cambridge: Cambridge University Press, 2000), ix, that "the Folio text, with its famous Choruses and speeches such as Henry's exhortation to his troops before Harfleur, was unlikely to have been heard at the Globe at any time before 1623," as well as Lukas Erne's in *Shakespeare as Literary Dramatist* (Cambridge: Cambridge University Press, 2003), 224, that the Chorus as a role may have been written primarily to be read rather than acted. James P. Bednarz, in "When Did Shakespeare Write the Choruses of *Henry V*?" *Notes and Queries* 53 (December 2006): 486–489, argues that "the Chorus was already part of a version acted in 1599" (486), noting a parody of *Henry V*'s choruses in Ben Jonson's *Every Man Out of His Humour* (1599; First Quarto registered in April of 1600). And Bednarz's argument in "Dekker's Response to the Chorus of *Henry V* in 1599," *Notes and Queries* (2012), 63–68, "corroborates that analysis with evidence from two contemporaneous plays by Thomas Dekker that the Chorus was indeed a feature of Shakespeare's drama in 1599." In noting examples of the detachability of such features, Tiffany Stern writes in *Documents of Performance in Early Modern England* (Cambridge: Cambridge University Press, 2009), 108–109, that the Folio's prologue, epilogue, and choruses (missing from the 1600 Quarto) are "less likely to be additions to *Henry V* than sections removed from it," adding that "James Bednarz produces parallels between *Henry V*'s prologue and chorus and Ben Jonson's *Every Man Out of his Humour* (1600) that date the stage-orations and chorus to 1599, overturning recent ideas that the passages entered the play late." Brian Walsh also counters Gurr and Erne, as well as Dutton and Orgel, in his

*Shakespeare, the Queen's Men, and the Elizabethan Performance of History* (Cambridge: Cambridge University Press, 2009), 183–184, arguing that "the fact that the lines do not appear in the first print editions does not indicate that they were not said on stage in 1599." See also Bednarz's review of Walsh's 2009 book in *Modern Philology* 110, no. 4 (2013): 243–247, esp. 245–246.

9. This is the *Riverside* text. The 1623 Folio (F1) has: "*Dead March./ Enter the Funerall of King Henry the Fift, attended on by/ the Duke of Bedford, Regent of France; the Duke/ of Gloster, Protector; the Duke of Exeter War-/ wicke, the Bishop of Winchester, and / the Duke of Somerset.*" See Garber, "What's Past Is Prologue," 324; Philip Edwards, *Threshold of a Nation* (Cambridge: Cambridge University Press, 1979), chap. 5; Moody E. Prior, *The Drama of Power* (Evanston, Ill.: Northwestern University Press, 1973), 334–335ff.; John Cox, *Shakespeare and the Dramaturgy of Power* (Princeton, N.J.: Princeton University Press, 1989), esp. 82ff.; Phyllis Rackin, *Stages of History* (Ithaca, N.Y.: Cornell University Press, 1990), 29, 82–85, 149ff.; Graham Holderness, *Shakespeare: The Histories* (New York: St. Martin's Press, 2000), 140–141; Pye, *Phantasm*, 19–20; Walsh, *Performance of History*, 110–113, 206; Tobias Döring, *Performances of Mourning in Shakespearean Theatre and Early Modern Culture* (New York: Palgrave Macmillan, 2006); Dillon, *Staging*, 1, 5ff.

10. On the historical Fastolf, see *The First Part of King Henry VI*, ed. Michael Hattaway (Cambridge: Cambridge University Press, 1990), 64.

11. See Pye, *Phantasm*, 42, with Garber on Richard III as "crooked," in *Ghost Writers*, 45.

12. Pye, *Phantasm*, 20.

13. On this parable, see Andrew Gurr, "*Henry V* and the Bees' Commonwealth," *Shakespeare Survey* 30 (1977): 61–72; *King Henry V*, ed. Andrew Gurr (Cambridge: Cambridge University Press, 1992; updated edition, 2005), 21; Dermot Cavanagh, "Georgic Sovereignty in *Henry V*," *Shakespeare Survey* 63 (2010): 119. All subsequent references to Gurr's edition of *Henry V* will be to this 2005 update.

14. See *Riverside*, 987; "unnaturally" in Gurr, *Henry V*, 110; *Henry V*, ed. Gary Taylor (1982; Oxford: Oxford University Press, 2008), 136; *Norton Shakespeare*, 3rd ed., 1560; and The New Oxford Shakespeare edition of William Shakespeare, *The Complete Works*, ed. Gary Taylor, John Jowett, Terri Bourus, and Gabriel Egan (Oxford: Oxford University Press, 2016), 1551. For the Old Cambridge gloss cited here, see *Henry V*, ed. John Dover Wilson (Cambridge: Cambridge University Press, 1947), 197.

15. On the implications of sodomy in the denunciation of Scroop, see Pye, *Phantasm*, 135; Jonathan Goldberg, *Sodometries* (Stanford, Calif.: Stanford University Press, 1992), 175.

16. "Cryptic" is used by Herschel Baker in *Riverside*, 988, and Rackin, *Stages*, 169. Gurr, *Henry V*, 112, comments: "This is the nearest the play comes to an explicit acknowledgement of the non-commercial motive that Cambridge had for the conspiracy. The intention is explained in *3H6* 1.1, especially 26–7." (Gurr's glosses to specific lines help to counter his emphasis on the only-later "corrective" provided by the *Oldcastle* play). Taylor, *Henry V*, also cites the earlier plays of Henry VI: "Some of Shakespeare's audience presumably realized that what Cambridge intended was to make Edmund Mortimer king (the beginning of the Yorkist claim to the throne, dramatized in *Henry VI*)."

17. Craik, *Henry V*, 177, quoting Holinshed, *Chronicles*, 3:548. See also Richard Dutton, *Shakespeare, Court Dramatist*, 195.

18. Hall, *Union*, fol. xliiii (v). Craik, *Henry V*, 180, cites Holinshed, *Chronicles*, 3.548, on the Cambridge rebellion as kindling a "fire" which "ceassed not to increase, till at length"

Henry V's "line and stocke was cleane consumed to ashes." See also Peter Saccio, *Shakespeare's English Kings* (1977; rpt. Oxford: Oxford University Press, 2000), 74.

19. See Nashe, *Pierce Pennilesse his supplication to the Divell*, in *The Works of Thomas Nashe*, ed. Ronald B. McKerrow, 5 vols. (1904; rpt. Oxford: B. Blackwell, 1958),1:212, and inter alia on this passage, Dermot Cavanagh, "History, Mourning and Memory in *Henry V*," in *Shakespeare's Histories and Counter-Histories*, ed. Dermot Cavanagh, Stuart Hampton-Reeves, and Stephen Longstaffe (Manchester: Manchester University Press, 2006), 38ff.; Jean-Christophe Mayer, "The Decline of the Chronicle and Shakespeare's History Plays," *Shakespeare Survey* 63 (2010): 12–23, 19–20. There has been debate with regard to both Nashe and Henslowe here. Janette Dillon, in *Staging* (2), notes that Nashe may have had a hand in writing the play—something that might mean that he exaggerated its popularity. But Michael Taylor, ed., *Henry VI Part 1* (Oxford: Oxford University Press, 2003), 2–3, argues that "Nashe's emphasis on the popularity of the play in 1592 . . . squares with the information we find in the account book, rather misleadingly called *Diary*, of the theatre manager Philip Henslowe." Taylor and Loughnane ("Canon and Chronology," 515–517) argue as follows with regard to Nashe, Henslowe, and the earliest staged version of what later became the Folio's *1 Henry VI*: "Nashe clearly alludes to the play in *Pierce Penniless (*entered in the Stationers' Register on 8 August 1592): 'How would it haue ioyed braue Talbot (the terror of the French) to thinke that after he had lyne two hundred yeare in his Tombe, hee should triumphe againe on the Stage, and haue his bones newe embalmed with the teares of ten thousand spectators at least (at seuerall times), who, in the Tragedian that represents his person, imagine they behold him fresh bleeding' (McKerrow and Wilson 1958, 1:212). Since London theatres were closed because of plague from 23 June until January 1593, Nashe's allusion dates the first performance no later than June 1592. Philip Henslowe's *Diary* identifies a 'Harey the vj', first performed at his Rose Theatre on 3 March 1592. . . . Henslowe's play, belonging to Strange's Men, was performed thirteen or fourteen times during the spring and early summer, to exceptionally large audiences; most critics accept that Nashe alludes to the same play which Henslowe records" ("Canon and Chronology," 515).

Though they initially state that they "accept, as did virtually all critics before Peter Alexander (1929), that Henslowe's 'harey the vj' is, either in its entirety or at least for the most part, the *1 Henry VI* of the Shakespeare Folio" (516), Taylor and Loughnane then add, "But none of the foregoing evidence establishes that Henslowe's 'harey vj' was identical to the text printed in 1623," and since "Many of the exact details of Shakespeare's alterations of the original 'harey the vj' will remain uncertain, even when larger chunks of added text can be attributed confidently," it is "safer to say 'adapted by Shakespeare' than 'with added scenes by Shakespeare.'" They then conclude that Shakespeare's adaptation or revision of "all three Henry VI plays occurred at the same time, as part of the process of creating a unified tetralogy for the Chamberlain's Men" in the 1590s (with their earlier-stated "best guess" date as 1595), but "whereas Shakespeare seems, in the case of *2 Henry VI* and *3 Henry VI*, to have been an original collaborator as well as a later adapter, in *1 Henry VI* he does not seem to have been part-author of the original" (516–517). On the echo of the line from *3 Henry VI* in *Greene's Groatsworth of Wit*, see John D. Cox and Eric Rasmussen's Arden 3 edition of *King Henry VI Part 3* (London: Thomson Learning, 2001), 6, 45–47. Though Taylor and Loughnane in "Canon and Chronology" join some other scholars in questioning whether Robert Greene himself authored this text, they do agree (498) that it suggests a performance of some version of *3 Henry VI* prior to June 1592 (which may have been the 1595 Octavo version discussed later in this chapter): "A line from the play . . . present in both the 1595 and the 1623 texts, was parodied in *Greene's*

*Groatsworth of Wit* (STC 12245; entered in the Stationers' Register on 20 September 1592, and allegedly written shortly before Robert Greene's death on 3 September 1592). As the theatres were closed between 23 June and the composition of the pamphlet, the allusion almost certainly dates performances of *3 Henry VI* before June 1592."

20. See Gurr, *Henry V*, 19, with *A Critical Edition of "1 Sir John Oldcastle,"* ed. Jonathan Rittenhouse (New York: Garland, 1984). Gurr (19) also notes that this play "rubbed in the Chamberlain's Men's hasty change of his name to Falstaff, for which they had apologised in the Epilogue to *2 Henry IV*," and represented Oldcastle "not as a clown but as the Lollard martyr, enemy of the Catholic Church and loyal friend of the king that Foxe's *Acts and Monuments* made him." On Oldcastle, see, inter alia, Gary Taylor, "The Fortunes of Oldcastle," *Shakespeare Survey* 38 (1985): 85–100; bibliography in Bradley Greenburg, " 'O for a muse of fire': *Henry V* and Plotted Self-Exculpation," *Shakespeare Survey* 36 (2008): 182–206, 205. See also James J. Marino, *Owning William Shakespeare: The King's Men and Their Intellectual Property* (Philadelphia: University of Pennsylvania Press, 2011), chap. 4.

21. Gurr, *Henry V*, 20, citing from Act 3 of Anthony Munday et al., *The First Part of . . . the Life of Sir John Oldcastle* (1600).

22. Gurr, *Henry V*, 21.

23. Italics mine. See *Norton Shakespeare*, 2nd ed., 1476 (identical to the 1997 first edition, 1449–1450).

24. See *Norton Shakespeare*, 3rd ed., 1533–1540, 1558–1562.

25. *The Life of Henry V*, ed. Barbara A. Mowat and Paul Werstine (1995; rpt. New York: Simon & Schuster, 2009), 60. This edition's genealogy of "The Line of Edward III" (lix)—though it includes Richard II (from his first son Edward the Black Prince) and the Henries descended from John of Gaunt (Edward III's fourth son), as well as Aumerle and Richard Earl of Cambridge (as grandfather of Edward IV and Richard III)—completely omits the higher line (and female claim) through Edward III's third son that gave Cambridge and his heirs their right to the throne already repeatedly foregrounded in the Henry VI plays. Michael Neill's "*Henry V:* A Modern Perspective" in this edition does, however, mention (260–261) the Henry VI plays in regard to the Epilogue and hints in the Rebellion Scene (267–268) to "better-informed playgoers of the intrafamilial struggles that motivated Cambridge and of the dynastic dispute that would ultimately lead to Cambridge's Yorkist descendants deposing Henry's own son."

26. See *Henry V*, ed. Jonathan Bate and Eric Rasmussen (New York: Modern Library, 2007, 2010), xvi. This omission is particularly striking because it would further illustrate their reading of the ironies of Henry V's rhetoric of right as son of a usurper.

27. See Nicholas Grene, *Shakespeare's Serial History Plays* (Cambridge: Cambridge University Press, 2002), 163, with 164 ("Writing *Richard II* in 1595, Shakespeare could gesture back to the sequence of plays on the reigns of Henry VI and Richard III, reassembled and produced by the Chamberlain's Men in 1594 after the re-opening of the theatres, the sequence 'which oft our stage hath shown' "—a reference to the Epilogue of *Henry V* but without followup with regard to the dramatization in those earlier plays of the motive behind the Cambridge rebellion), and passim.

28. Garrett A. Sullivan, Jr., *Memory and Forgetting in English Renaissance Drama* (Cambridge: Cambridge University Press, 2005). The chapter on "Sleep, history and 'life indeed' in Shakespeare's *1* and *2 Henry IV* and *Henry V*" in Sullivan's *Sleep, Romance and Human Embodiment: Vitality from Spenser to Milton* (Cambridge: Cambridge University Press, 2012) comments

on memories of Falstaff "haunting *Henry V*" (96) but does not mention the Henry VI plays that also haunt it.

29. See Shapiro, *A Year in the Life of William Shakespeare: 1599*, 90. *Forgetting in Early Modern English Literature and Culture: Lethe's Legacies*, ed. Christopher Ivic and Grant Williams (London: Routledge, 2004) has only one paragraph on *Henry V* (5), which stresses memory and fogetting, but with no mention of the Henry VI plays.

30. *Shakespeare, Memory and Performance*, ed. Peter Holland (Cambridge: Cambridge University Press, 2006), introduction.

31. Warren Chernaik, *Cambridge Introduction to Shakespeare's History Plays* (Cambridge: Cambridge University Press, 2007), 167. No mention of the Henry VI plays or their strategic forgetting in *Henry V* is made in either Greenburg's "'O for a muse of fire,'" which treats *Henry V* as "a play enacted in the shadow of *1 and 2 Henry IV*" (185), or Isabel Karremann's "Rites of Oblivion in Shakespearian History Plays," *Shakespeare Survey* 63 (2010): 24–36.

32. See Lina Perkins Wilder, *Shakespeare's Memory Theatre: Recollection, Properties, and Character* (Cambridge: Cambridge University Press, 2010), chap. 3 (83–106), 91, on "a remembering theatrical community," and Anthony B. Dawson's "The Arithmetic of Memory: Shakespeare's Theatre and the National Past," *Shakespeare Survey* 52 (1999): 54–67. Her "Henry plays" chapter does not mention the Epilogue's backward recollection of the Henry VI plays, though she contrasts Henry V's "future mnemonics" and "Prince Hal's forward-looking hermeneutics" to "looking backward" (citing Robert Hapgood's "Shakespeare's Thematic Modes of Speech: 'Richard II' to 'Henry V,'" *Shakespeare Survey* 20 [1967]: 41–49). Her discussion of "theatrical memory" in *Henry V* is restricted to Falstaff and the plays of the second tetralogy. Neema Parvini's *Shakespeare's History Plays: Rethinking Historicism* (Edinburgh: Edinburgh University Press, 2012) devotes an entire chapter (7) to the Henry VI plays that foregrounds York's higher right to the throne and is more sympathetic to him than many critics, but does not include analysis of the importance of those plays to *Henry V*.

33. See Lees-Jeffries, *Shakespeare and Memory* (Oxford: Oxford University Press, 2013), 71, 80.

34. Karl P. Wentersdorf, "The Conspiracy of Silence in *Henry V*," *Shakespeare Quarterly* 27, no. 3 (1976): 264–287. Wentersdorf's article is not cited in the bibliography of either the Oxford 1982 *Henry V* edition of Gary Taylor or the 1995 Arden 3 *Henry V* edition of T. W. Craik—an omission reflected in the bulk of the criticism of the play as well. The present chapter builds on Wentersdorf's much briefer argument and examples.

35. Jonathan Baldo, "Wars of Memory in *Henry V*," *Shakespeare Quarterly* 47, no. 2 (1996): 132–159, 140. Though he stresses memories of historical rather than theatrical events, Baldo also notes that in the Rebellion Scene, "Edmund Mortimer, whose claim to the throne the traitors Cambridge, Scrope, and Grey were advancing, would have been remembered by the vast majority of Shakespeare's audience, since he inaugurates the Yorkist claim to the throne, dramatized in the popular *Henry VI* plays," though "in *Henry V* he is erased," and that "Cambridge's line indirectly pointing out his true motive—'For me, the gold of France did not seduce' (2.2.151)—is the closest the play comes to recalling the rival claimant to the English throne" (citing in this regard Wentersdorf's "Conspiracy of Silence"). See also Baldo's chapter of the same title in *Memory in Shakespeare's Histories: Stages of Forgetting in Early Modern England* (New York: Routledge, 2012), 102–130, 108–109.

36. Editors comment on Shakespeare's "mistake"—like that of the chroniclers—in confusing "Edmund Mortimer" with the imprisoned Sir John Mortimer and the "Edmund Mortimer" recognized by Richard II as heir. See Hattaway, *The First Part of King Henry VI*, 113;

Andrew S. Cairncross, *The Second Part of King Henry VI* (London: Methuen, 1957), 105, 49; *King Henry VI Part 2,* ed. Ronald Knowles (London: Bloomsbury Arden Shakespeare, 1999), 213, with Gillian West, "Shakespeare's Edmund Mortimer," *NQ* 223 (1988): 463–465. *The Second Part of Henry VI,* ed. Michael Hattaway (Cambridge: Cambridge University Press, 1991), 119, notes that "Salisbury, like the chroniclers [i.e., Hall, *Union,* 246; Holinshed, *Chronicles,* 3:263] confuses the fifth Earl of March with his uncle, Sir Edmund Mortimer (1374–1409). This Mortimer was captured by Glendower, but after Bullingbrook had made no effort to ransom him, joined the side of Glendower whose daughter he married." However, in *dramatic* terms, it is important to note that Shakespeare's *theatrical* conflation means that the imprisoned Mortimer who speaks in *1 Henry VI* of the "suppressed" right of Cambridge and his son is the *same* Mortimer who appears later, as a *younger* man, in *Henry IV Part 1* as Richard II's designated heir and "rightful owner" of the English crown, i.e., the suppressed dynastic right behind the Cambridge rebellion in *Henry V.* In *Henry IV Part I,* the threat he poses to the "ingrate and cank'red Bullingbrook" who trembles "at the name of Mortimer . . . proclaim'd, / By Richard" as the "next of blood" (1.3.137–146), since he should himself be Bolingbroke's "king" (4.3.93–95), can be more elliptically summoned in part because it had already been set forth at length in the earlier plays. On Mortimer's genealogy in the context of a different reading from mine, see Walsh, *Performance of History,* 120–124. As noted earlier, Taylor and Loughnane ("Canon and Chronology," 493–496, 513) give 1595 as their "best guess" date for Shakespeare's revision or adaptation of the earlier Henry VI plays, to be part of a tetralogy (with *Richard III*) for the Chamberlain's Men. They give a date range of 1595–1597 ("best guess," mid-1595) for *Richard II* (512) and 1596–1597 ("best guess," late 1597) for *Henry IV Part 1* (522–523), which was entered in the Stationers' Register on February 25, 1598, and published in 1598.

37. See also Rackin, *Stages,* 168–169.

38. Henry Ansgar Kelly, *Divine Providence in the England of Shakespeare's Histories* (Cambridge, Mass.: Harvard University Press, 1970), 49–50, notes that Yorkist chroniclers also characterized the Lancastrian usurpation as an inversion of the "right." The Yorkist text "A Political Retrospect" proclaimed that "unrightful heirs by wrong alliance / Usurping this royaume caused great adversity" and celebrated the righting of these wrongs when Cambridge's grandson Edward IV replaced Henry V's son and successor, Henry VI: "Scripture saith, 'Heritage holden wrongfully / Shall never chieve ne with the third heir remain,'/ As hath be verified late full plain. / Whereas three kings have reigned by error, / The third put out, and the right brought again." See "A Political Retrospect," ed. Thomas Wright, in *Political Poems, RS* 14.2 (London, 1861), 267–270, 267.

39. On "grandfather" here, see *King Henry VI Part 1,* ed. Edward Burns (London: Bloomsbury Arden Shakespeare, 2000), 183: "Clarence was actually, in modern terms, Richard's great-great-grandfather, but the Elizabethans used terms for family relationship much more loosely—so adding to the confusion of later readers and audiences."

40. See the *Riverside* note (647): "The King restores to Richard not only the earldom of Cambridge (which he inherited from his father) but also the dukedom of York (which he inherited from his father's elder brother, who had been killed at Agincourt)."

41. Although *1 Henry VI* is only in the Folio, there are other 1590s texts for the plays the Folio calls *The second Part of Henry the Sixt, with the death of the Good Duke* HVMFREY and *The third Part of Henry the Sixt, with the death of the Duke of* YORKE—respectively the 1594 Quarto of *The First part of the Contention betwixt the two famous Houses of Yorke and Lancaster, with the death of the good Duke Humphrey: And the banishment and death of the Duke of Suffolke, and the Tragicall end of the proud Cardinall of Winchester, with the notable Rebellion of Iacke Cade:*

*And the Duke of Yorkes first claime unto the Crowne* (London, 1594), STC 26099; and the 1595 Octavo of *The true Tragedie of Richard Duke of Yorke, and the death of good King Henrie the Sixt, with the whole contention betweene the two Houses Lancaster and Yorke,as it was sundrie times acted by the Right Honourable the Earle of Pembrooke his seruants* (London, 1595), STC 21006. On the 1595 Octavo text, see, inter alia, Cox and Rasmussen, *3H6,* 149–150, 256, which also cites Peter W. M. Blayney's "The Publication of Playbooks," in *A New History of Early English Drama,* ed. John D. Cox and David Scott Kastan (New York: Columbia Unversity Press, 1997), 383–422. Richard Dutton, in *Shakespeare, Court Dramatist,* 200–210, argues that the 1594 Quarto and 1595 Octavo represent legitimate early versions later expanded by Shakespeare "with court performance in mind," as part of his revision of all three Henry VI plays prior to the reference to them in the Epilogue of *Henry V.* See also Taylor and Loughnane, "Canon and Chronology," 493–499, 513–517. Arguing for the performance of their Folio versions in the 1590s, Randall Martin, in his edition of *Henry VI Part Three* (Oxford: Oxford University Press, 2001), 126–127, notes the appearance in the Folio text of *2 Henry VI* and *3 Henry VI* of "the names of actors believed to be associated with particular companies during the 1590s; John Holland and George Bevis in Part Two, and (more certainly) Gabriel Spencer, John Sincklo (or Sincler), and Humphrey Jeffes in Part Three" (130). See also Dutton, *Shakespeare, Court Dramatist,* 209; Cox and Rasmussen, *3H6,* 167–173; Marino, *Owning,* 50ff. on Sincklo; and Taylor and Loughnane, "Canon and Chronology," 499, who suggest that reference to Spencer, Sinc[k]lo, and Jeffes ("all active in the mid-1590s") helps date the Folio *3 Henry VI* to prior to late 1597. For every quotation in this chapter from the Folio (or Folio-based) texts, the endnotes give the variants in the 1594 Quarto and 1595 Octavo texts (where equivalent lines exist), also designated as Q and O. Although it cannot be certain on which dates the different versions were performed, it is important to note (in relation to what is suppressed or omitted in *Henry V* with regard to the higher right of Cambridge and his heirs to the throne of England as well as France, through the female from the Earl of March and Edward III's third son Lionel) that these Quarto and Octavo texts of the Henry VI plays also repeatedly stress this claim. In *The End Crowns All* (Princeton, N.J.: Princeton University Press, 1991), Barbara Hodgdon even argues that the 1594 Quarto is more "Yorkist" than the Folio *2 Henry VI*: "Less hesitantly than the ambiguous 'Lancastrian' Folio, Quarto relocates 'true' right in York," 67; see also 66.

42. 1594 Q has: "Cold newes for me,for I had hope of *France,* / Euen as I haue of fertill England. / A day will come when *Yorke* shall claime his owne."

43. Like the Folio, 1594 Q also has "Nor shall proud *Lancaster* vsurpe my right."

44. The parallel lines in the 1594 Q have that he said that "the Duke of Yorke was lawfull heire vnto the Crowne, and that your grace was an usurper." In the earlier part of this scene (corresponding to *Riverside* 1.3.25–32), the 1594 Q has the apprentice say: "my maister said, that the Duke of *Yorke* was true heire vnto the Crowne,and that the King was an vsurer" (sig. B2r). When his malapropism "usurer" is corrected by Queen Margaret ("An vsurper thou wouldst say"), he responds, "I forsooth an vsurper." Though there are minor differences between the 1594 Q and the Folio here, the charge that the current Lancastrian king Henry VI is a usurper and Richard, Duke of York, the true heir to the crown is the same.

45. "Title / Which is infallible, to England's Crowne" (the Folio text here) is not verbatim in the 1594 Q, but Q correspondingly has as its preface to the genealogy to follow, York saying to Warwick and Salisbury: "Let me reueale vnto your honours here, / The right and title of the house of Yorke, / To Englands Crowne by liniall desent."

46. Even the garbled genealogy of York in the 1594 Q—which led Peter Alexander to conclude that it was a botched memorial reconstruction—does not obscure the fact (as Steven Urkowitz pointed out) that Q's genealogy, however error-filled, makes clear the higher right of Cambridge's son York (through his mother to Lionel Duke of Clarence, Edward III's third son, as opposed to John of Gaunt, Edward III's fourth son): see Knowles, *King Henry VI Part 2*, 128. The 1594 Q also includes York's narrative of Bolingbroke's murder of Richard II (which ends with "and so by Richards death came the house of Lancaster vnto the Crowne") and Warwick's conclusion after hearing York's speech: "What plaine proceedings can be more plaine, hee claimes it from Lyonel Duke of Clarence,the third sonne to Edward the third, and Henry from Iohn of Gaunt the fourth sonne. So that till Lyonels issue failes, his should not raigne. It failes not yet, but florisheth in thee & in thy sons, braue slips of such a stock. Then noble father, kneele we both togither, and in this priuate place, be we the first to honor him with birthright to the Crown"—a speech which is immediately followed in Q by both Warwick and his father Salisbury saying "Long liue Richard Englands royall King" to York.

47. See Hattaway, *The Second Part of King Henry VI* (120); and Cairncross's Arden 2 gloss (50), on "plain proceedings," the phrase used in both the 1594 Q and the Folio, as is Warwick's conclusion concerning York's "birthright to the crown." "Plain proceedings" may be heard ironically by modern ears, but legal arguments based on genealogy were also prominently registered in *Edward III*, the anonymous play first printed in 1596 that is now considered to have been contributed to by Shakespeare (and is included in *Riverside*). It opens with extended discussion of Edward's genealogical "pedigree" (1.1.5) as giving him "right" (34) and "sovereignty" (50) as "inheritor to France" (16) through female descent—providing a counterpart to the Salic Law Scene of *Henry V*—while its reference to "John of Valois" as having "indirectly" climbed to the French throne (37) though the male line provides an ironic counterpart to Henry V's usurper-father's reference to his "indirect crook'd ways" to the crown in *Henry IV Part 2* (4.5.184).

48. These lines are not in 1594 Q, but Q ends with the returned York speaking of "faint-heart Henry" who "did vsurpe our rights." See below.

49. This quotation is not in 1594 Q.

50. This quotation is not in 1594 Q, but it is not germane to the higher claim of Cambridge's heir that is suppressed in the later *Henry V*.

51. Though this wording is not in 1594 Q, it ends with the returned York determined to regain the "rights" that Henry VI has usurped ("our great honour,that so long we lost, / Whilst faint-heart Henry did vsurpe our rights").

52. See Charles Ross, *Richard III* (Berkeley: University of California Press, 1981), 4–5; and the discussion below of the Chorus to Act 5 of *Henry V*, which envisages returns from both Ireland and France.

53. 1594 Q does not have these Folio-based lines, but it does have York's "Resigne thy Crowne proud Lancaster to me, / That thou vsurped hast so long by force, / For now is Yorke resolu'd to claime his owne, / And rise aloft into faire Englands Throane."

54. Neither "justice and true right" (5.2.25) nor Salisbury's lines quoted here (5.1.175–178) are in 1594 Q, but Q clearly ends with Salisbury's loyalty to York's cause ("Well hast thou fought this day,thou valiant Duke, / And thou braue bud of Yorkes encreasing house, / The small remainder of my weary life, / I hold for thee") and with Warwick's final lines celebrating York's victory.

55. For the text from Hall's *Union*, see *Narrative and Dramatic Sources of Shakespeare*, ed. Geoffrey Bullough (London: Routledge and Kegan Paul, 1960), 3:172–175. *The Third Part of*

*King Henry VI,* ed. Michael Hattaway (Cambridge: Cambridge University Press, 1993), 72, has that "Shakespeare seems to have read York's oration in Holinshed" (Holinshed, *Chronicles,* 3:262–264) and notes specific echoes. York's oration (263) includes "my most deerest lord and father [i.e., Cambridge], so farre set foorth that right and title, that he lost his life & worldlie ioy at the towne of Southampton, more by power than indifferent iustice"—a very different perspective on the executions of Cambridge and the conspirators than in the Rebellion Scene of *Henry V.*

56. The 1595 Octavo scene is virtually the same as F1. Henry's "And kneel for grace and mercy at my feet" is not in O, but it does have "Thou factious duke of Yorke,descend my throne, / I am thy soueraigne" and York's "Thou art deceiu'd: I am thine . . . / Twas mine inheritance as the kingdome is" (which is even stronger than F's "the Earledome," i.e., of March). O has York determined "To take possession of my right" (F, "to take possession of my Right"). Both have Henry VI admit "I know not what to say,my Titles weake" (F1; Octavo, "I know not what to saie my titles weake"), and both have Exeter's "His is the right, and therefore pardon me" in response to the king's "Art thou against vs, Duke of *Exceter*?" (Octavo; Folio has "His is the right,and therefore pardon me").

57. The 1595 Octavo has "I am the sonne of Henrie the Fift who tamde the *French,* / And made the Dolphin stoope, and seaz'd vpon their / Townes and prouinces."

58. The 1595 Octavo passage is essentially the same, but importantly precedes Henry's "Think'st thou, that I will leaue my Kingly Throne, / Wherein my Grandsire and my Father sat?' "' (which is the beginning of his speech in the Folio text) with lines that include his reference to York's "right" ("Suppose by right and equitie thou be king, / Thinkst thou that I will leaue my kinglie seate / Wherein my father and my grandsire sat?"). The Octavo here also has (1) "seate" instead of F1's "Throne" in Henry's opening line; (2) "My titles better farre than his" instead of F1's "My Title's good,and better farre then his"; (3) "soueraigne" rather than F1's "King" in York's " 'Twas by rebellion against his king"; (4) "Then am I lawfull king For *Richard* / The second in the view . . ." instead of F1's lineation ("And if he may,then am I lawfull King: / For *Richard,*in the view . . ."); (5) "the Crowne" at the end of the line of Exeter that appears in F1 as "his Crowne"; (6) "must" rather than F1's "should" in Exeter's "But that the next heire should succeed and reigne." It does not have the last two quoted lines here, but it does have Exeter say with regard to York "His is the right. . . ."

59. This scene also underscores the reversibility of each's faction's claim to the "natural" ("Whom should he follow but his *natural* king?"). Henry VI "unnaturally" (1.1.194) disinherits his own sons, the "unnatural" (218) act to which his son responds, "Father, you cannot disinherit me. / If you be king, why should not I succeed?" (1.1.226–227).

60. See Craik, *Henry V,* 351.

61. See Garber, "What's Past Is Prologue," 323.

62. Taylor, *Henry V,* 136, has "natural (for devils)"; Gurr, *Henry V,* 110—citing F's "an naturall" and F2's "a natural"—has "What is natural for devils is monstrous for humans. The F compositor seems to have wavered between 'natural' and 'unnatural.' "

63. Dillon, *Staging,* 42, notes that "Holinshed also draws the parallel with the mockery of Christ." See also Paul Strohm, "York's Paper Crown: 'Bare Life' and Shakespeare's First Tragedy," *Journal of Medieval and Early Modern Studies* 36, no. 1 (2006): 75–101, including on the implications of the 1595 Octavo title (*The true Tragedie of Richard Duke of Yorke . . .* ).

64. See Desmond Seward, *Richard III* (London: Country Life Books, 1983), 23; with John Watts's entry on Richard Duke of York (1411–1460) in the *Dictionary of National Biography* (Oxford: Oxford University Press, 2004).

65. This progression is reflected in his hailing (by Warwick) as "No longer Earl of March, but Duke of York; / The next degree is England's royal throne" (*3H6* 2.1.192–193).

66. In *1 Henry IV* the usurping "counterfeit" king also has "many marching in his coats" (5.3.25).

67. See my *Shakespeare from the Margins*, chap. 4, on "conveyance" and "convey" as steal as well as transfer or transport.

68. For "fine" as "end," see, for example, *Hamlet* 5.1.106 ("the fine of his fines"); *Love's Labor's Lost* 5.2.487 ("vara fine"); *All's Well That Ends Well* 3.7.33, 4.3.52, 5.3.215. See also *The Comedy of Errors* 4.4.41 ("*respice finem*, respect your end"). Gurr, *Henry V*, 87, glosses "fine" as "i.e. refine, make perfect."

69. Kelly, *Providence*, 168: "the theme of the deprived line of March-York is rather prominent in the *Mirror*'s treatment, especially in the tragedies of the two Mortimers, Cambridge, and York, and on the Lancastrian side, in those of Somerset and Henry VI." The monology of the Lancastrian Edmund, Duke of Somerset, added to the 1563 edition of *The Mirror for Magistrates*, also underscores the Lancastrian kings' descent "from the heyre male," as opposed to the Yorkist claim "from the heyre female." See *The Mirror for Magistrates*, ed. Lily B. Campbell (Cambridge: Cambridge University Press, 1938), 399.

70. See Craik, *Henry V*, 136, on Numbers 27:8 ("If a man dye and haue no sonne, ye shall turne his inheritaunce vnto his daughter") with Holinshed, *Chronicles*, 3:546: "The archbishop further alledged out of the booke of Numbers this saieng: When a man dieth without a sonne, let the inheritance descend to his daughter. At length, hauing said sufficientlie for the proofe of the kings iust and lawfull title to the crowne of France, he exhorted him to aduance foorth his banner to fight for his right, to conquer his inheritance, to spare neither bloud, sword, nor fire, sith his warre was iust, his cause good, and his claime true."

71. Kelly, *Providence*, 40, citing from Sir Henry Ellis, ed. *The Chronicle of John Hardyng* (London, 1812), 15–17.

72. Holinshed, *Chronicles*, 3:66.

73. For Holinshed on Scroop as Henry's "bedfellow," see *Narrative and Dramatic Sources of Shakespeare*, 4 vols., ed. Geoffrey Bullough (London: Routledge and Kegan Paul, 1962), 4:384.

74. Saccio, *English Kings*, 73. The rebel Scroop may also have been influenced by his wife Joan Holland (formerly the second wife of Edmund, Duke of York) and her links with her stepson the Earl of Cambridge.

75. See Saccio, *English Kings*, 55; Kenneth Bruce McFarlane, *Lancastrian Kings and Lollard Knights* (Oxford: Clarendon Press, 1972), 103–104.

76. See McFarlane, *Lancastrian Kings*, 107.

77. See Saccio, *English Kings*, 68, on his elevation to the earldom of Cambridge.

78. Taylor, *Henry V*, 149.

79. See Craik, *Henry V*, 190; Gurr, *Henry V*, 118.

80. *OED* defines the heraldic "bend" as "two parallel lines drawn from the dexter chief to the sinister base of the shield. . . . *Bend sinister*: a similar ordinary drawn in the opposite direction: one of the marks of bastardy." See also Taylor, *Henry V*, 113; *Norton Shakespeare*, 3rd ed., 1565.

81. *OED* cites 1600 W. CLARKE in Archpr. Controv. (Camden) I.168, on "indirecte and sinisterous proceedings"; and Ben Jonson's *Staple of News* v.ii ("You told me you had got a growen estate, By griping means, sinisterly").

82. See *OED* 2. "Sinisterly" (#3), citing 1581 G. PETTIE's translation of Guazzo's *Civile Conversation* (1586), 1.13b—"The mallice of men is so greate, that they . . . think sinisterlie and preposterouslie of all the good deedes which are wrought."

83. See *OED*, citing 1530 PALSGRAVE 305/2 ("Awkwar leftehanded, gauche"); *OED*, "awk" ("turned the wrong way, back foremost"), citing 1530 PALSGRAVE 196 ("Auke stroke, *revers*"); 1440 PROMP. PARV. 18 ("Awke or wronge, sinister"); 1567 MAPLET Gr. Forest 25 ("A preposterous maner in judging, and an awk wit").

84. See Philemon Holland, trans., *The Philosophie, commonlie called, the Morals,* trans. Philemon Holland (London, 1603), 148 ("ignorant and untaught persons many times when fortune presenteth herselfe unto them on the right hand, receive her awkly, turning to the left side undecently").

85. Under "awkly," as "in the wrong direction, in backhanded or left-handed wise; hence, sinisterly, unluckily," *OED* cites Golding's *Trogus Pomp.* (1564), 18, on Egyptians: "They write their letter aukelie [i.e., backwards, from right to left]." See also my Introduction on Hebrew and Arabic described in the period as spelled "backward" or *sinistrorsum.*

86. *OED* cites both under "awkward" as "Turned the wrong way, averted, back-handed; not straightforward, oblique."

87. Taylor, *Henry V*, 151. Both *Norton Shakespeare,* 3rd ed. (1565), and the Royal Shakespeare edition, ed. Bate and Rasmussen, have "oblique" (40) for "awkward." New Folger (74) has "perverse; oblique." The New Oxford Shakespeare *Complete Works*, ed. Gary Taylor et al. (1557), has: "**awkward** oblique"; "**sinister** deceitful, misleading; illegitimate"; "**evenly derived** directly descended"; "**indirectly** by crooked means."

88. *Riverside*: "truly descended" (990). Gurr (120), Craik (193), Taylor (151), Bate and Rasmussen (40), and *Norton Shakespeare*, 3rd ed. (1565), have "directly descended." New Folger (74) has "directly, justly, accurately" for "evenly."

89. On this contradictory logic, see Pye, *Phantasm*, 27–28.

90. See Gurr, *Henry V*, 120; sig. E2v of *The Famous Victories of Henry the fifth* (London, 1598). On the latter, which is generally assumed to have been performed in the 1580s, see, inter alia, Walsh, *Performance of History*, chap. 2; Janet Clare, "Medley History: *The Famous Victories of Henry the Fifth* to *Henry V*," *Shakespeare Survey* 63 (2010): 102–113.

91. See Hattaway, *The First Part of King Henry VI*, 120, and 63 on the Exeter of *1H6* (the same historical figure as the Exeter of *Henry V*).

92. On the importance of the Infanta's claim through descent from John of Gaunt's first marriage to Blanche of Lancaster, in contrast to the Tudor-Stuart descent from Gaunt's Beaufort offspring, see Richard Dutton, "Shakespeare and Lancaster," *Shakespeare Quarterly*, 49, no. 1 (1998): 1–21, and other works cited on this issue in Chapter 5.

93. The notorious "mistake" in which Bolingbroke is elided in representing Edward III as Henry V's "grandfather" (e.g., *H5*, 4.7.92: "Your grandfather of *famous memory*") may be part of this play's simultaneous calling attention to what it suppresses. For the historical Henry V's attempts to align himself with Richard II, see McFarlane, *Lancastrian Kings*, 104–105.

94. See, inter alia, Annabel Patterson, *Shakespeare and the Popular Voice* (Cambridge: Cambridge University Press, 1989), 88–91; and Neill, in Mowat and Werstine, *Henry V* (266–67), who also comments on the "crowns" of 4.4 as a term that "confuses the King's regal ambition with Pistol's mercenary desire for gold" (264).

95. Gurr, *Henry V*, 165. By contrast, most critics, including Cavanagh, in "History, Mourning and Memory," 43, and Anny Crunelle Vanrigh, in "*Henry V* as Royal Entry," *SEL Studies in English Literature, 1500–1900* 47, no. 2 (2007): 355–377, 367, make no mention of the

striking theatrical remembrance in this speech of the major figures from the Henry VI plays. Richard Dutton's recent *Shakespeare, Court Dramatist* (184–185) does, however, note that the inclusion of Warwick, Talbot, Salisbury, and others in the St. Crispin's Day speech of the Folio's *Henry V* does emphasize its recall of those earlier plays.

96. See Gurr, *Henry V*, 77, 173.

97. See ibid., 116.

98. Ibid. has "Holinshed (3.553) wrongly says that he was at Agincourt and commanded the rear-guard (see 3.3.51–6n., 52n, 3.6.5n), but rightly says that he was at Troyes (3.572). He appears also in *1H6*."

99. Taylor, *Henry V*, 229. See also Hodgdon, *End*, 54.

100. See Saccio, *English Kings*, 70; Craik, *Henry V*, 116. Craik also comments (290) in his gloss on Warwick's name in the St. Crispin's Day speech, "He was not at Agincourt . . . but his prominence in the French wars of *1H6*, like Talbot's . . . may have led to the combination of their names in this line."

101. See Gurr, *Henry V*, 173: "The Warwick in this list is most likely the anachronistic 'kingmaker' Warwick of the Henry VI plays." The "kingmaker" Warwick had also been (with his father Salisbury) the audience for York's presentation of his higher right through the female in *2 Henry VI*, as well as a key figure in the opening scene of *3 Henry VI*, where York sits on the throne of Henry V's son. On the confusion and conflation of the two Warwicks, see also Hattaway, *The Second Part of King Henry VI*, 77, 85, 102; Knowles, *King Henry VI Part 2*, 147: "Shakespeare slightly confused this Warwick with his father-in-law, Richard de Beauchamp, Earl of Warwick (1382–1439) of *1H6*, some of whose military triumphs are claimed by 'the kingmaker' (*2H6* 1.1.116–19)." Taylor, *Henry V*, comments with regard to the Warwick of this play (227): "Shakespeare (and his audience) could easily confuse this Earl of Warwick with his more famous son, 'the Kingmaker.' "

102. See Craik, *Henry V*, 116; Gurr, *Henry V*, 75, 173.

103. Taylor, *Henry V*, 233, emends to "once more come" on the grounds that the "Folio's come againe is awkwardly redundant and unmetrical"; but this (to my mind) underscores the importance of "come again" here.

104. E.g., Gurr, *Henry V*, 170; see also Craik, *Henry V*, 296.

105. Memories of the suppressed March-York claim may also be evoked when "Charles Duke of Orleance" is cited among French prisoners taken at Agincourt (4.8.76), since he was not only husband to Isabella (the widow of Richard II who returned to France after the usurpation and killing of Richard) but also a prisoner whose long imprisonment in England in the *aftermath* of Agincourt had already been cited in a prominent passage of *1Henry VI* (3.3.69–70), along with the figure of Burgundy. See *Henry V*, ed. J. H. Walter (London: Methuen, 1969). 4.

106. See Holinshed, *Chronicles*, 3:83; Gurr, *Henry V*, 77.

107. See Walter, *Henry V*, 122, and *The Chronicles of Enguerrand de Monstrelet*, 2 vols., trans. Thomas Johnes (London: Routledge, 1867), 1:346 ("the duke of Alencon gave him a blow on the helmet that struck off part of his crown"). The "Suffolk" who died at Agincourt was the third earl, Michael de la Pole, who was Earl of Suffolk for only a month between the death of his father the second earl and his own death.

108. This is the "Suffolk" that Shakespeare also (unhistorically) makes the lover of Henry VI's wife Margaret. On the antagonism between York and Suffolk, see Cox, *Dramaturgy of Power*, 84ff. Parvini, *History Plays*, 136, also notes that, in *2 Henry VI*, when "Suffolk issues the assassination order, York promptly leaks the information to his co-conspirators, Salisbury and Warwick, who in turn promptly tell the King."

109. See Wilson, *Henry V*, 175; Taylor, *Henry V*, 241; Gurr, *Henry V*, 184; Craik, *Henry V*, 307.

110. See the *Henry V* editions of Walter, 122; Taylor, 241; Gurr, 183; Craik, 306. According to Johnes, *Monstrelet* (1:343), this York was (as Gurr notes, 77), "a fat man who, leading the English van, was trampled and suffocated in the press of the first confrontation" at Agincourt.

111. See Taylor, *Henry V*, 242.

112. Shapiro (*A Year in the Life*, 90) notes that Essex was himself descended from the Earl of Cambridge. Though commentators differ over whether it is Essex or Mountjoy who is evoked in these lines, it remains a return from *Ireland* that is alluded to in this Chorus on Henry's return from *France*.

113. See Gurr, *Henry V*, 198.

114. For the link between Julius Caesar and Bolingbroke, see Hall, *Union*, 247, where in his oration to Parliament, York says, "I will not molest you . . . nor troble you with the continual warre, which happened emonge the Romaines, when Iulius Cesar toke upon hym, without lawe or aucthoritie, the name and stile of Emperor: but I put you in remembrance of our awne nacion, what mischiefe, strife and misery succeded in theis realme, by the iniurious usurpacions."

115. Wordplay on "salt" and "leek" and the "law Salique" is suggested in Frankie Rubinstein, *A Dictionary of Shakespeare's Sexual Puns and their Significance*, 2nd ed. (New York: St. Martin's Press, 1995), 145 ("Leek"); and is not implausible given the "leak" sounded in "leek" and the re-emerging problem of the Law Salique in the immediately following Wooing Scene. See my "Uncertain Unions: Welsh Leeks in *Henry V*," in *British Identities and English Renaissance Literature*, ed. David J. Baker and Willy Maley (Cambridge: Cambridge University Press, 2002), 81–100.

116. See Craik, *Henry V*, 342.

117. See Gurr, *Henry V*, 21 (where Gurr continues: "This weakness in the treaty, . . . with its restoration of the legal position that Edward III had fought for, is camouflaged in the play by the game of Henry's betrothal to Katherine. But it remains as a feature to justify the final Chorus lamenting the brevity of Henry's triumph. And the Dauphin's absence from the final act as the dispossessed heir, despite his presence in the earlier versions and his pre-existing return on stage in *1 Henry VI* at Rheims to reclaim the French crown, makes the omission as pointed as the omission of the Cambridge claim. Dynastic title was an insoluble and recurrent problem").

118. See *Riverside*, 712, on "the Dauphin Charles, who succeeded his father as King of France in 1422, a few months after Henry V's death." In the *Henry VI* plays, the Dauphin (or Dolphin) is shown as "with one Joan de Pucelle join'd" (*1H6* 1.4.101) and described in *2 Henry VI* as having "prevail'd beyond the seas" (1.3.125), in lines that refer to him as Dauphin even after he became King Charles VII of France, because "the English considered Henry VI the rightful king of France" (*Riverside*, 674).

119. On the homoerotic overtones with regard to the boy actor playing Katherine, see Pye, *Phantasm*, 31–33. See also Jonathan Goldberg, *Sodometries*, 157–159, where he also cautions against concluding that "anal sex marks the difference between hetero- and homosexuality" (158).

120. See Michael Neill, "Broken English and Broken Irish: Nation, Language, and the Optic of Power in Shakespeare's Histories," *Shakespeare Quarterly* 45, no. 1 (1994): 1–32, 22, on the recollections of "Petruchio's conquest of another Kate."

121. Henry's "sold my farm to buy my crown" (5.2.125–126) also ironically recalls the former Bolingbroke's "purchased" in the deathbed speech of *Henry IV Part 2* on his "indirect crook'd ways" to the "crown" (4.5.184, 199).

122. See also Henry's earlier "France being ours, we'll bend it to our awe, / Or break it all to pieces" (1.2.224–225).

123. See Neill, "Broken English," e.g., 11. The pun on "pale" in the French king's final speech in *Henry V* ("whose very shores look pale," 5.2.350) also recalls both the French and Irish "pales."

124. Holinshed, *Chronicles*, 3:267.

125. See Jean E. Howard and Phyllis Rackin, *Engendering a Nation* (London: Routledge, 1997), esp. 212–215.

126. On witchcraft in *Henry VI Parts 1 and 2*, see Jean E. Howard, *The Stage and Social Struggle in Early Modern England* (London: Routledge, 1994), 135ff.; Jean-Christophe Mayer, *Shakespeare's Hybrid Faith* (New York: Palgrave Macmillan, 2006), chap. 1. See also Rackin, *Stages*, 198–199; Howard and Rackin, *Engendering*, chap. 12, including 204–205 on Margaret of Anjou and Joan of Arc—on whom see also Katherine Eggert, *Showing Like a Queen* (Philadelphia: University of Pennsylvania Press, 2000), chap. 3, and Kathryn Schwarz, *Tough Love: Amazon Encounters in the English Renaissance* (Durham, N.C.: Duke University Press, 2000), chap. 2; Dillon, *Staging*, 70, 100ff. Gurr, *Henry V*, 215, remarks of Henry's "cannot see many a fair French city for one fair French maid that stands in my way" (*H5* 5.2.318) that "this anticipates *1H6* where Joan of Arc successfully led the fight against the English," but in the dramatic ordering (in a way suggested by "led"), it is a recall of the earlier plays of that other "maid" rather than an anticipation. See also Eggert on the other aftermath of Henry V's wooing, the second marriage of Katherine to Owen Tudor that culminated in the Tudor line (*Showing Like a Queen*, 96, 105).

127. Burgundy also married his sister Anne to the Duke of Bedford, Henry V's younger brother, joining the houses of Lancaster and Burgundy. (For a different aspect of Burgundy's importance, see Richard Dutton, "The Dating and Contexts of *Henry V*," 173–204.)

128. On Burgundy, see also Craik, *Henry V*, 117: "Philip (1396–1467), who succeeded his father John in 1419 (see 5.2.7n.). . . . He appears also in *1H6*"; and Hattaway, *The First Part of King Henry VI*, 65, concerning the same Burgundy in that play: "Philip the Good who, by the Treaty of Troyes (1420), became an ally of the English; with Bedford, he was named co-regent of France by Henry V. After 1435, however, he transferred his allegiance to Charles VII."

129. The Dauphin's urging of La Pucelle to "enchant" Burgundy with her "words" (*1H6* 3.3.40) is also preposterously echoed in the Wooing Scene's evocation of witchcraft.

130. The concluding language of marital "union" in *Henry V* also "preposterously" recalls the end of *Richard III*, where this apocalyptic language is used for the marriage of Richmond and Elizabeth of York (Edward IV's daughter, another female link with a more legitimate claim than Tudor Richmond's). But in the reversed tetralogies, both senses of an "ending" are undermined—in *Henry V* by the curving back to the Henry VI plays the Epilogue recalls and in *Richard III* by the reversed dramatic order in which this triumphant ending leads into the beginning of the history of discord and civil war in *Richard II*.

## CHAPTER 5. WHAT'S IN A NAME?

Note to epigraph: *Othello, the Moor of Venice: Texts and Contexts*, ed. Kim F. Hall (Boston: Bedford/St. Martin's, 2007), 205.

Unless otherwise specified, Shakespeare citations are from *The Riverside Shakespeare*, 2nd ed., ed. G. Blakemore Evans, J. J. M. Tobin, et al. (Boston: Wadsworth Cengage Learning, 1997; hereafter *Riverside*).

1. *Putting History to the Question* (New York: Columbia University Press, 2000), 32.

2. On Iago and Sant'Iago or Santiago (including with regard to King James, at whose court *Othello* was performed in 1604), see Samuel L. Macey, "The Naming of the Protagonists in Shakespeare's *Othello*," *Notes & Queries* n.s. 25 (1978): 143–145; Barbara Everett, "'Spanish' Othello: The Making of Shakespeare's Moor," *Shakespeare Survey* 35 (1982): 101–112; Frederick M. Burelbach, "Name-Play and Internationalism in Shakespearean Tragedy," *Literary Onomastics Studies* 12 (1985): 137–151; Eric J. Griffin, *English Renaissance Drama and the Specter of Spain* (Philadelphia: University of Pennsylvania Press, 2009), where chap. 6 revises his "Un-Sainting James: Or, *Othello* and the 'Spanish Spirits' of Shakespeare's Globe," *Representations* 62 (Spring 1998): 58–99; *Othello, the Moor of Venice,* ed. Michael Neill (Oxford: Oxford University Press, 2006), 194; Hall, *Othello*, 204–205. On Roderigo's Spanish name (evoking El Cid, a legendary fighter against the Moors), see Everett, "'Spanish' Othello," 103; Griffin, *Specter*, 184ff.; Hall, *Othello*, 204.

3. See Thomas Dekker, *The vvhore of Babylon* (London, 1607), with Frank R. Ardolino, "'In Saint Iagoes Parke': Iago as Catholic Machiavel in Dekker's *The Whore of Babylon*," *Names: Journal of the American Name Society* 30, no. 1 (1982): 1–4; Frances E. Dolan, *Whores of Babylon* (1999; rpt. Notre Dame University Press, 2005), 53–55. Griffin, *Specter*, 196–199, also discusses *Blurt, Master Constable* (1603), including (199) its "refashioning of Santiago" as the "scatologically low Don Dego" (i.e., Don Diego, another version of "James").

4. Brabantio is not glossed except as a Venetian senator and Desdemona's father in M. R. Ridley's Arden 2 *Othello* (London: Methuen, 1958); Barbara A. Mowat and Paul Werstine's New Folger edition (New York: Washington Square Press, 1993); Norman Sanders's New Cambridge edition (1984; rev. ed. Cambridge: Cambridge University Press, 2003); or Neill, *Othello*.

5. See *William Shakespeare, The Complete Works*, ed. Stanley Wells, Gary Taylor, John Jowett, and William Montgomery (1986; 2nd ed. Oxford: Clarendon Press, 2005), 874 ("BRABANZIO, Desdemona's father, a Senator of Venice") and the same name and gloss repeated in the 2016 New Oxford Shakespeare, *The Complete Works*, ed. Gary Taylor et al. (Oxford: Oxford University Press, 2016), 2115; *The Norton Shakespeare,* 3rd ed., Stephen Greenblatt et al. (New York: W. W. Norton, 2016), 2084 ("BRABANZIO, father to Desdemona"). Andrew Davies's 2001–2002 television adaptation of *Othello* has "James Brabant" and "Dessie Brabant."

6. Griffin, "Un-Sainting James," 72 (in Griffin, *Specter*, 183).

7. Griffin, "Un-Sainting James," 94n.73 (in Griffin, *Specter*, 256n.74).

8. Burelbach, "Name-play," 146–147: "English sympathies toward Brabant would have been transferred to its namesake Brabantio, even though this character is set in opposition to Othello and made to look a little foolish. We must remember that Brabantio had been Othello's friend before his daughter's elopement and had often invited Othello to his home. Brabantio's mixed emotions between his friendship for Othello and his protectiveness of Desdemona echo the linguistic, political, and religious divisions within Brabant. Moreover, Brabantio is losing his daughter, his *daimon* or vital spirit, to a Moor, and the Moors were associated with Spain. He is aroused to this loss by Iago, a man with a Spanish name. When called before the Duke, Desdemona says that she perceives 'a divided duty' (I.iii.181) between her father and her husband, possibly another echo of the divisions within Brabant."

9. See Neill, *History*, 32, including on "Cassio" possibly sounded as "Cashio," from "Italian *casso* = cashiered *cashiering*."

10. The Induction to the Booke, Thomas Dekker, *The Seven deadly Sins of London* (1606), sig. Av.

11. See Vaughan, *Othello: A Contextual History* (Cambridge: Cambridge University Press, 1994), chap. 1; *Actes and monuments* (1583), STC (2nd ed.) 11225, which is filled with references to Brabant, Brabanters, and "Brabant" names, including Brabantinus. On Brabant Senior as Jonson in *Jack Drum's Entertainment* (1601), see James P. Bednarz, "Representing Jonson: *Histriomastix* and the Origin of the Poets' War," *Huntington Library Quarterly* 54 (1991): 1–30.

12. See *Othello*, ed. E. A. J. Honigmann (1997; rev. ed. London: Bloomsbury Arden Shakespeare, 2016), 338; *A Critical Edition of the Anonymous Elizabethan Play The Weakest Goeth to the Wall*, ed. Jill L. Levenson (London: Garland, 1980).

13. Neill, *Othello*, 263, citing Sanders edition, 100. *OED*, s.v. "cashier," *v*.5.

14. See Williams, *A Briefe Discourse of Warre* (1590) STC (2nd ed.) 25733, e.g., 22; Neill, *Othello*, 200; Charles Edelman, *Shakespeare's Military Language* (2000; rpt. London: Continuum, 2004), 76–77.

15. See *King Henry V*, ed. T. W. Craik (London: Arden Shakespeare, 1995), 117, 330, 345; Edward Sugden, *A Topographical Dictionary to the Works of Shakespeare and His Fellow Dramatists* (Manchester: Manchester University Press, 1925), 72, who notes that in 1477, "by the marriage of Mary of Burgundy to the Emperor Maximilian, [Brabant] passed to the house of Austria, and through Charles V became part of the Spanish dominions"; Susan Doran, *England and Europe, 1485–1603* (1986; 2nd ed. London: Longman, 1996), on Philip II's father Charles V as "duke of Burgundy (1506), king of Spain (1516), ruler of the Austrian Habsburg Lands (1516) and Holy Roman Emperor (1519)"; Doran's *The Tudor Chronicles* (New York: Metro Books, n.d.), 29, for the painting of Maximilian and Mary with their grandsons (later Charles V and Ferdinand I, ruler of Habsburg lands in central Europe). On Burgundy in the genealogy of Habsburg rulers, see also J. H. Elliott, *Imperial Spain, 1469–1716* (1963; rev. ed. London: Penguin, 2002), 135–137; William S. Maltby, *The Reign of Charles V* (New York: Palgrave Macmillan, 2002), chap. 1; Martin van Gelderen, *The Political Thought of the Dutch Revolt, 1555–1590* (Cambridge: Cambridge University Press, 1992), 16ff.; Graham Darby, "Narrative of Events," in *The Origins and Development of the Dutch Revolt*, ed. Darby (London: Routledge, 2001), 8ff.; Susan Doran, *Elizabeth I and Foreign Policy, 1558–1603* (London: Routledge, 2000), 4, who notes that a "new dimension to Anglo-Habsburg tensions arose" when Henry VIII "discarded his wife, Catherine of Aragon, the aunt of Charles V"; but (4–5) that the long-standing tradition of "Anglo-Burgundian commerce" (11), which centrally involved trade in cloth, continued. As noted in Carole Levin and John Watkins, *Shakespeare's Foreign Worlds* (Ithaca, N.Y.: Cornell University Press, 2009), 64, Philip II's name was a reminder that "he was the heir and descendent of Philip the Good, the same duke of Burgundy who figures as a pivotal character in *1 Henry VI*" (as well as the Wooing Scene of *Henry V*, on which see my Chapter 4).

16. "Waterish Burgundy" (1.1.260: *Riverside* 1.1.258, "wat'rish Burgundy") evokes his "wishy-washy" nature (*King Lear*, ed. R. A. Foakes [London: Arden Shakespeare, 1997], 175) *and* the Low Countries abounding in water. In *3 Henry VI*, Edward escapes to "Burgundy" (4.6.79) and returns to England with the "desired help from Burgundy" (4.7.6): "Edward from Belgia / With hasty Germans and blunt Hollanders / Hath pass'd in safety through the Narrow Seas [i.e., the English Channel]" (4.8.1–3); in "doubtless Burgundy will yield him help, / And we shall have more wars before't be long" (4.6.90–91), "wars" would have a striking resonance in the 1590s, when England was mired in the Low Countries' wars against the Habsburg power in Brabant. See also *Henry VI, Part 3*, ed. Randall Martin (Oxford: Oxford University Press, 2001), 195, on George and Richard, who historically "fled with their mother for safety to the

Netherlands to stay with the Duchess of Burgundy," and on "soldiers" sought by George from his "aunt, Duchess of Burgundy" (2.1.145–147 in his edition), with his Appendix A on 2.1.143–147; *Richard III*, ed. James R. Siemon (London: Arden Shakespeare, 2009), 194 and 409, with Clarence's dream of being "embarked to cross to Burgundy" (1.4.10–11), and Margaret of York as Duchess of Burgundy; 5.3.324n. on support for Richmond by Charles, Duke of Burgundy.

17. See Sugden, *Dictionary*, 55 ("Belgia"): "Belgia commonly stands for the Netherlands generally, though it is more properly confined to the Spanish Netherlands"; Marjorie Rubright, "Going Dutch in London City Comedy: Economies of Sexual and Sacred Exchange in John Marston's *The Dutch Courtesan* (1605)," *English Literary Renaissance* 40, no. 1 (2010): 88–112, and her *Doppelgänger Dilemmas: Anglo-Dutch Relations in Early Modern English Literature and Culture* (Philadelphia: University of Pennsylvania Press, 2014), chap. 1. Edmund Spenser's allegory of the Lady "Belgia" in *The Faerie Queene*, Book V, Cantos x–xi (to xi: stanza 35), includes not only the "fell Tyrant" Philip II (V.x.8) but also the fall of Antwerp (V.x.25ff.), Elizabeth's declaration of war in the Treaty of Nonsuch (V.x.16), and her refusing of sovereignty of the Netherlands when it was offered (V.xi.16).

18. See John R. Hale, in *The Art of War and Renaissance England* (Washington, D.C.: Folger Shakespeare Library, 1961), 26.

19. On the "preposterous" in *Othello*, see my *Shakespeare from the Margins* (Chicago: University of Chicago Press, 1996), chap. 1, which builds on Joel B. Altman's "Preposterous Conclusions: Eros, *Enargeia*, and the Composition of *Othello*," *Representations* 18 (1987): 129–157; Altman's *The Improbability of Othello* (Chicago: University of Chicago Press, 2010), esp. chap. 6; Will Stockton's "Chasing Chastity: The Case of Desdemona," in *Rethinking Feminism in Early Modern Studies*, ed. Ania Loomba and Melissa E. Sanchez (London: Routledge, 2016), 205; and Jonathan Gil Harris's prescient discussion of "Preposterous Time" in his *Untimely Matter in the Time of Shakespeare* (Philadelphia: University of Pennsylvania Press, 2009), 182–187. In addition to what he calls "a preposterous temporality in which 'before' and 'after' are simultaneous" (184), Harris notes Iago's own linear oppositions—something I would argue is characteristic as well of Brabantio's invocation of the backward (or "preposterous") spells of witchcraft. See also Lee Edelman and Madhavi Menon's "Queer Tragedy, or Two Meditations on Cause," in *The Oxford Handbook of Shakespearean Tragedy*, ed. Michael Neill and David Schalkwyk (Oxford: Oxford University Press, 2016), 285–297: 286–294 on "cause" with regard to *Othello* (including "the tragedy of *Othello* is queer because it removes itself from the realm of the causal," 294)—which is highly suggestive in relation to Brabantio's invoking of witchcraft as the cause of his daughter's elopement with a Moor (though they do not mention it).

20. See Stallybrass, "Patriarchal Territories: The Body Enclosed," in *Rewriting the Renaissance*, ed. Margaret Ferguson et al. (Chicago: University of Chicago Press, 1986), 123–142; Michael Neill, "Changing Places in *Othello*," *Shakespeare Survey* 37 (1984): 115–131; my *Shakespeare from the Margins*, 246, 362n.50.

21. See Sugden's *Dictionary* on "Brabant," "Antwerp," "Bergen-op-Zoom," "Breda," "Brussels," "Burse," "Tilmont," "Low Countries," "Netherlands."

22. See Bartholomaeus Anglicus, *Batman vppon Bartholome* (1582), STC 1538; William Cuningham, *The cosmographical glasse* (1559), STC 6119, Book 5; Lisa Jardine, *Worldly Goods* (New York: W. W. Norton, 1996), 112, on Medici bank agents; Jerry Brotton, *The Renaissance Bazaar* (Oxford: Oxford University Press, 2002), 114; with Jardine and Brotton, *Global Interests* (Ithaca, N.Y.: Cornell University Press, 2000).

23. See Jardine, *Worldly Goods*, chap. 3, on Christophe Plantin and other Antwerp printers, and Rubright, *Dilemmas*, 9, on books and printing linking England and the Low Countries.

24. Prefatory pages to Abraham Ortelius, *Theatrum orbis terrarum Abrahami Orteli Antuerp. geographi regii. / The theatre of the vvhole world: set forth by that excellent geographer Abraham Ortelius* (London, 1606 [i.e., 1608?]), STC (2nd ed.) 18855. On Ortelius, see Jerry Brotton, *A History of the World in Twelve Maps* (New York: Penguin, 2012), 10, 15, 236, 258, 263–265.

25. Abraham Ortelius, *An epitome of Ortelius his Theater of the vvorld* . . . (London, [i.e., Antwerp], 1601), STC (2nd ed.) 18857, 38–39.

26. See Francesco Guicciardini, *The historie of Guicciardin containing the warres of Italie and other partes*, trans. Geoffrey Fenton (London, 1579).

27. See *The description of the Low countreys and of the prouinces thereof, gathered into an epitome out of the historie of Lodouico Guicchardini* (1593), STC (2nd ed.) 12463, 22–33, 25v.

28. *The Perspective of the World*, vol. 3 of *Civilization and Capitalism, 15th–18th Century*, trans. Sian Reynolds (New York: Harper & Row, 1984), 143. Braudel also notes that "Antwerp was in fact as much the successor to Venice as to Bruges." See also Peter Burke, *Antwerp* (Ghent: Snoeck-Ducaju & Zoon, 1993); Guido Marnef, *Antwerp in the Age of Reformation* (Baltimore: Johns Hopkins University Press, 1996).

29. Andrew Boorde, *The fyrst boke of the introduction of knowledge* (London, [1555?]), STC (2nd ed.) 3383, chap. 10.

30. *The glasse of gouernement* (London, 1575), STC (2nd ed.) 11643a, sig. A3.

31. *Thomas Lord Cromwell* (London, 1602), STC (2nd ed.) 21532, sig. Bv.

32. See David Eltis, *The Military Revolution in Sixteenth-Century Europe* (1998; rpt. London: I. B. Tauris, 1995), 13, 109; Lindsay Boynton, *The Elizabethan Militia, 1558–1638* (London: Routledge & Kegan Paul, 1967), 57; Paul E. J. Hammer, *Elizabeth's Wars* (New York: Palgrave Macmillan, 2003), 56, 67; R. B. Wernham, *Before the Armada* (New York: W. W. Norton, 1966), esp. 201–203, 278–279.

33. Ian Blanchard, entry on "Gresham, Sir Thomas" (ca. 1518–1579), *Dictionary of National Biography* (Oxford: Oxford University Press, 2004), hereafter *DNB*. See also Blanchard's *The International Economy in the "Age of the Discoveries," 1470–1570: Antwerp and the English Merchants' World* (Stuttgart: Franz Steiner Verlag, 2009); M. J. Rodríguez-Salgado, *The Changing Face of Empire* (Cambridge: Cambridge University Press, 1988), 186.

34. Sullivan, *The Rhetoric of Credit* (London: Associated University Presses, 2002), 64.

35. See Lyly's *Euphues and his England* (1580), STC 17070; Raphael Holinshed, *Chronicles* ([London], 1587), STC 13569 (235); Georgijevic, *The ofspring of the house of Ottomanno* (1569), STC 11746; de Nicolay, *The nauigations, peregrinations and voyages, made into Turkie*, 37; Jerome Turler, *The traueiler* (1575), STC 24336 (177). On Elizabeth's visit in 1571, see John Stow's *Survey of London* (1598).

36. See John Schofield, "The Topography and Buildings of London, c. 1600," in *Material London, ca. 1600*, ed. Lena Cowen Orlin (Philadelphia: University of Pennsylvania Press, 2000), 317, on "Hendrick van Paesschen of Antwerp." See also *The Royal Exchange*, ed. Ann Saunders (London: London Topographical Society, 1997).

37. Rubright, *Dilemmas*, 170–172, who also notes that "English artisans and bricklayers . . . incensed at the loss of potential income" protested the use of "foreign labor" (170) and that "the original name stuck and the building was called both the Royal Exchange and Gresham's Burse until its fiery demise" (172).

38. See *The Three Ladies of London* in *Three Renaissance Usury Plays*, ed. Lloyd Kermode (Manchester: Manchester University Press, 2009), 160 (on "Usury" and the "Exchange" in

Scene 17, lines 9–10), and 29–33 on Wilson's Low Countries visit and association with Leicester and Leicester's Men.

39. Thomas Nashe, *Pierce Penilesse, His Supplication to the Divell* (1592), ed. G. B. Harrison (New York: Barnes and Noble, 1966), 13–14.

40. Kermode's edition in *Three Renaissance Usury Plays*, cited from here, which also notes the play's sexual wordplay on "account" (173), comments (193) that the Spanish galleys' fear of being "drowned" (1.3.249) because of a storm on the Mediterranean would have reminded the audience of England's "miraculous escape" from "the vastly superior Spanish Armada of 1588," which was undone by "bad weather." On Haughton's play, see also Rubright, *Dilemmas*, 45, 60, 90, 98, 119, 125–126, 128–129; Jean E. Howard, *Theater of a City* (Philadelphia: University of Pennsylvania Press, 2007), esp. 38–49; Natasha Korda, *Labors Lost* (Philadelphia: University of Pennsylvania Press, 2011), chap. 2; A. J. Hoenselaars, *Images of Englishmen and Foreigners in the Drama of Shakespeare and His Contemporaries* (London, 1992), 53–58.

41. Rubright, *Dilemmas*, 176: see also 175–184 on James's entry, the Dutch arch, and Thomas Dekker's "The Magnificent Entertainment: Given to King James (1604)," and 13–17 on "Dutch" as a capacious term, with Andrew Pettegree, *Foreign Protestant Communities in Sixteenth-Century London* (Oxford: Clarendon Press, 1986), 13, 102. Griffin, *Specter*, 205, notes James's appropriation of Sant'Iago in his coronation on St. James's Day, anniversary of the coronation of the previous "English" king, Philip of Spain.

42. Rubright, *Dilemmas*, 180; see also 177 on the architect Conraet Jansen (or Coenraet Janszoon); *The Dramatic Works of Thomas Dekker*, vol. 2 (Cambridge: Cambridge University Press, 1955), 231–252.

43. Rubright, *Dilemmas*, 182–183.

44. See Thomas Heywood, *If you know not me, you know no bodie: Or, The troubles of Queen Elizabeth* (1605), STC (2nd ed.) 13328, sig. B3r; *The second part of, If you know not me, you know no bodie VVith the building of the Royall Exchange: and the famous victorie of Queene Elizabeth, in the yeare 1588* (1606), STC (2nd ed.) 13336, sig. F3r–v.

45. Howard, *Theater*, 55. See also Vanessa Harding's "London, Change and Exchange," in *The Culture of Capital: Property, Cities, and Knowledge in Early Modern England*, ed. Henry S. Turner (New York: Routledge, 2002), 133–134.

46. Howard, *Theater*, 55.

47. See Howard, *Theater*, 56ff., 229–230.

48. See Raymond De Roover, *Business, Banking, and Economic Thought in Late Medieval and Early Modern Europe*, ed. Julius Kirshner (Chicago: University of Chicago Press, 1974), 128; Alfred W. Crosby, *The Measure of Reality: Quantification and Western Society* (Cambridge: Cambridge University Press, 1997), 205, on the need to control "lieutenants."

49. Michele Jaffe, *The Story of O* (Cambridge, Mass.: Harvard University Press, 1999), 63.

50. See David Murray, *Chapters in the History of Bookkeeping, Accountancy, & Commercial Arithmetic* (1930; rpt. New York: Narno Press, 1978), 202–206. On the transmission of double-entry through Antwerp to England, see Sullivan, *Credit*, 13.

51. On Valentin Mennher de Kempten's treatise as "known and often quoted in England," see Murray, *Chapters*, 208, with 212 and 228 on Weddington and de Raeymaker.

52. See my "Cassio, Cash, and the 'Infidel o': Arithmetic, Double-Entry Bookkeeping, and *Othello*'s Unfaithful Accounts," in *A Companion to the Global Renaissance*, ed. Jyotsna Singh (Oxford: Blackwell, 2009), 223–241, which also cites contemporary identifications of the female "count" with the account books of "debitor and creditor"; the combination in Shakespeare's Sonnet 136 of "account" with "things of great receipt," "nothing," "a treasure," and a

female "will"; "lenders' books" juxtaposed with "brothels" and "plackets" in *King Lear* (3.4.96–97); and the combination of account book and female "(ac)count" in "I see, lady, the gentleman is not in your books" in *Much Ado About Nothing* (1.1.79), as well as the figure of Desdemona as a "book" in *Othello* (e.g., 4.2.71).

53. On the theater and brothel district as a locus of "debitor and creditor" accounting and arithmetic, see Linda Woodbridge, *English Revenge Drama* (Cambridge: Cambridge University Press, 2010), 65ff.

54. See Nashe, *The vnfortunate traueller. Or, The life of Iacke Wilton* (London, 1594), STC (2nd ed.) 18380, sig. Br; Eric Ives, *The Life and Death of Anne Boleyn* (Oxford: Blackwell, 2004), 18ff. On Brabant (including Brussels) in relation to Charles V and his aunt Margaret of Austria, see James D. Tracy, *Emperor Charles V, Impresario of War* (Cambridge: Cambridge University Press, 2002), 1–24.

55. See John Bale, *A mysterye of inyquyte* (1545), STC (2nd ed.) 1303, 41: "Good Wyllyam Tyndale was done to death also at Vylforde in Braban"; *The whole workes of W. Tyndall, Iohn Frith, and Doct. [Robert] Barnes, three worthy martyrs* (1573), STC (2nd ed.) 24436, for the illustration of "The Martyrdome and burning of William Tyndall in Brabant" after "The Preface to the Reader"; Peter Happé, *DNB* entry on "Heywood, John (*b.* 1496/7, *d.* in or after 1578)," which also notes that Heywood wrote Burleigh from Mechelen in Brabant in 1575, joined his son Ellis Heywood in Antwerp in 1576, and with Ellis fled to Catholic Louvain in 1578, where both died.

56. See John Stow, *The chronicles of England* (1580), STC (2nd ed.) 23333; Jardine, *Worldly Goods*, 386, on Philip's entry into Antwerp; Rodríguez-Salgado, *Empire*, 202, on Mary's bitterness at his absence, and 298ff. on his negotiations with the Turk. On the loss of Calais, see also Hammer, *Elizabeth's Wars*, 50–51.

57. See Jardine, *Worldly Goods*, 387–395. On the Tunis tapestries, see also Jardine and Brotton, *Global Interests*, 85–86.

58. Rodríguez-Salgado, *Empire*, 197.

59. See ibid., 320, and 339–56 on Philip's hesitancy to leave his center of power in Brussels for Spain. He finally did in 1559.

60. On refugees and immigrants from the Low Countries, see Laura Hunt Yungblut, *Strangers Settled Here Amongst Us* (London: Routledge, 1996), 21 and passim; *Returns of Strangers in the Metropolis, 1593, 1627, 1635, 1639*, ed. Irene Scouloudi (London: Huguenot Society, 1985); *Immigrants in Tudor and Early Stuart England*, ed. N. Goose and Lien Luu (Brighton: Sussex Academic Press, 2005); Joseph Ward, "Fictitious Shoemakers, Agitated Weavers and the Limits of Popular Xenophobia in Elizabethan London," in *From Strangers to Citizens*, ed. Randolph Vigne and Charles Littleton (Brighton: Sussex Academic Press, 2001), 80–87; Lien Bich Luu, "'Taking the Bread out of Our Mouths': Xenophobia in Early Modern London," *Immigrants and Minorities* 19 (2000): 1–22. See also Steve Rappaport, *Worlds Within Worlds* (Cambridge: Cambridge University Press, 1989); Ian W. Archer, *The Pursuit of Stability* (Cambridge: Cambridge University Press, 1991); John Michael Archer, *Citizen Shakespeare* (New York: Palgrave Macmillan, 2005); Lloyd Edward Kermode, *Aliens and Englishness in Elizabethan Drama* (Cambridge: Cambridge University Press, 2009); A. J. Hoenselaars, *Englishmen and Foreigners*. On "Dutch" as including immigrants from Brabant, see Rubright, *Dilemmas*, 13–17.

61. Rubright, *Dilemmas*, 9, with 244n.26. See also Raymond Fagel, "Immigrant Roots: The Geographical Origins of Newcomers from the Low Countries in Tudor England," in Goose and Luu, *Immigrants*, 48; Michael Wyatt, *The Italian Encounter with Tudor England* (Cambridge: Cambridge University Press, 2005), 151. On the Dutch Church of Austin Friars,

see Pettegree, *Communities*; Rubright, *Dilemmas*, 12, 13, 92, 94, 177, 246n.43, 247n.44; Charles G. D. Littleton, "The Strangers, Their Churches and the Continent: Continuing and Changing Connexions," in Goose and Luu, *Immigrants*, 177–191.

62. Rubright, *Dilemmas*, 86. See Pettegree, *Communities*, 3.

63. Jacob Selwood, *Diversity and Difference in Early Modern London* (Farnham, U.K.: Ashgate, 2010), 19; see also 59.

64. Eric Griffin, "Shakespeare, Marlowe, and the Stranger Crisis of the Early 1590s," in *Shakespeare and Immigration*, ed. Ruben Espinosa and David Ruiter (Farnham, U.K.: Ashgate, 2014), 22–23, citing "A Libell, fixte upon the French Church Wall. Anno 1593." See also Pettegree, *Communities*, 274–275; A. Spicer, "'A Place of refuge and sanctuary of holy Temple': Exile Communities and the Stranger Churches," in Goose and Luu, *Immigrants*, 91–109, 92.

65. On the 1566 petition (or "Request"), followed by the "Iconoclastic Fury" or *Beeldenstorm*, see Darby, "Narrative," 17ff.; Geoffrey Parker, *The Dutch Revolt*, rev. ed. (Harmondsworth: Penguin, 1985), 68–78; van Gelderen, *Dutch Revolt*, 38ff.; Jonathan I. Israel, *The Dutch Republic* (1995; rpt. Oxford: Clarendon Press, 1998), chap. 7; James D. Tracy, *The Founding of the Dutch Republic* (Oxford: Oxford University Press, 2008), 68 ff.; Maarten Prak, *The Dutch Republic in the Seventeenth Century* (Cambridge: Cambridge University Press, 2005), 7–24.

66. Susan Doran, "The Politics of Renaissance Europe," in *Shakespeare and Renaissance Europe*, ed. Andrew Hadfield and Paul Hammond (London: Thomson Learning, 2005), 21–52, at 44. See also Doran's *England and Europe*, 68–78ff., in the larger context of England's relations with Spain between 1564 and 1585, including Hawkins's slaving voyages, Philip II's listening to "Thomas Stukeley's plans for an invasion of Ireland," and the Sea Beggars ("Exiles from the Netherlands who attacked the ships and supporters of the duke of Alva," 128).

67. On Spain's far-flung engagements, including in the Americas, see Anthony Pagden, *Lords of All the World* (New Haven, Conn.: Yale University Press, 1995), 71, 32ff., chap. 3; Elliott, *Imperial Spain*, 181ff., chaps. 5–8; J. H. Elliott, *Spain and Its World, 1500–1700* (New Haven, Conn.: Yale University Press, 1989); R. J. W. Evans, *The Making of the Habsburg Monarchy, 1550–1700* (Oxford: Clarendon Press, 1979), chap. 1; William S. Maltby, *The Rise and Fall of the Spanish Empire* (New York: Palgrave Macmillan, 2008). On the Moriscos, see Elliott, *Spain*, 235–241; L. P. Harvey, *Muslims in Spain, 1500–1614* (Chicago: University of Chicago Press, 2005), chap. 6; Barbara Fuchs, *Exotic Nation* (Philadelphia: University of Pennsylvania Press, 2009).

68. Parker, *The Dutch Revolt*, 85. See also Elliott, *Imperial Spain*, 231–233; Israel, *Dutch Republic*, 137–154.

69. Hale, *Art of War*, 10.

70. Geoffrey Parker, *The Army of Flanders and the Spanish Road, 1567–1659* (1972; 2nd ed. Cambridge: Cambridge University Press, 2004), 28. See also the following in Darby, *Dutch Revolt*: Henk van Nierop, "The Nobles and the Revolt" (48–66: 32), and Fernando González de León and Geoffrey Parker, "The Grand Strategy of Philip II and the Revolt of the Netherlands" (107–132).

71. Parker, *Army of Flanders*, 195. On Alva (or Alba), see also R. B. Wernham, *The Making of Elizabethan Foreign Policy, 1558–1603* (Berkeley: University of California Press, 1980), esp. 34–40; Wernham, *Before the Armada*, 289–321; Hammer, *Elizabeth's Wars*, 81–91.

72. Brian M. Downing, *The Military Revolution and Political Change* (Princeton, N.J.: Princeton University Press, 1992), 220 (and 78).

73. Israel, *Dutch Republic*, 184. See also I. A. A. Thompson, "'Money, Money, and Yet More Money!': Finance, the Fiscal State, and the Military Revolution: Spain 1500–1650," in

*The Military Revolution Debate*, ed. Clifford J. Rogers (Boulder, Colo.: Westview Press, 1995), 273–298, 276, and passim.

74. See Elliott, *Imperial Spain*, 263–264; Parker, *Army of Flanders*, 198–199; Hammer, *Elizabeth's Wars*, 89, on Alba's hope to "crush the Dutch" before the "combined cost" of war against the Turks and the Dutch "drove the Spanish monarchy into bankruptcy" (89). On the Breda talks, see Israel, *Dutch Republic*, 184; Geoffrey Parker, *Spain and the Netherlands, 1559–1659* (Glasgow: William Collins Sons, 1979), 70.

75. Quoted from Sir Lewis Lewkenor, *A discourse of the vsage of the English fugitiues, by the Spaniard* (1595), STC (2nd ed.) 15562, sig. I—which was expanded in *The estate of English fugitiues vnder the king of Spaine and his ministers* (1595), STC (2nd ed.) 15564. Roderick Clayton's *DNB* entry on "Lewknor, Sir Lewes (*c.* 1560–1627)" says he was "probably the anonymous author" of this text, as well as translator of Gasparo Contarini's. But Albert J. Loomie, S. J., *The Spanish Elizabethans* (New York: Fordham University Press, 1963), 10, ascribed it to Lewis Lewkenor's cousin Samuel Lewkenor, who had served as a Spanish soldier in the Netherlands.

76. See Anon., *The edict and decree of Phillip King of Spaine published and proclaimed by the said king, touching the exchaungings and leuyings of moneys, by him made & passed with marchants. . . . First translated out of Spanish, and now out of French into English by W. P.* (London, 1597), STC (2nd ed.) 22992.3. On Philip II's third (1596) Decree of Bankruptcy, see Elliott, *Imperial Spain*, 287–290.

77. See Parker, *Dutch Revolt*, 102–103. On Alva, see also Lisa Jardine, *The Awful End of Prince William the Silent* (New York: Harper, 2005), chap. 1; Hammer, *Elizabeth's Wars*, 81–91.

78. On James's *Lepanto*—cited in Richard Knolles's dedication to James of his *Generall Historie of the Turkes* (1603), an acknowledged influence on *Othello*—see Emrys Jones, "'Othello,' 'Lepanto' and the Cyprus Wars," *Shakespeare Survey* 21 (1968): 47–52, 48; Griffin, "Un-sainting James," 63–64, and *Specter*, 174–175.

79. Doran, "Renaissance Europe," 45. See also William S. Maltby, *Alba: A Biography of Fernando Alvarez de Toledo, Third Duke of Alba, 1507–1582* (Berkeley: University of California Press, 1983); Henry Kamen, *The Duke of Alba* (New Haven, Conn.: Yale University Press, 2004).

80. On Alba, see William S. Maltby, *The Black Legend in England* (Durham, N.C.: Duke University Press, 1971), 48–50; Israel, *Dutch Republic*, chap. 8. On St. Geertruidenberg and the sack of Mechelen, see Israel, *Dutch Republic*, 30, 178, 234, 246, 278, 546, 704, 1021; Geoffrey Parker, *The Grand Strategy of Philip II* (New Haven, Conn.: Yale University Press, 1998) 127, and *Dutch Revolt*, 162, 182, 222, 231.

81. On Vilvoorde, see Parker, *Dutch Revolt*, 214. On Grave, see Israel, *Dutch Republic*, 273; Hammer, *Elizabeth's Wars*, 127–128. On the 1602 Hoogstraten mutiny, see R. B. Wernham, *The Return of the Armadas* (Oxford: Clarendon Press, 1994), 390. See also Paul C. Allen, *Philip III and the Pax Hispanica, 1598–1621* (New Haven, Conn.: Yale University Press, 2000), 89, 123 (on Hoogstraten), and 125–127, 281n.40 (on the 1603 siege of 's-Hertogenbosch).

82. On Don John of Austria's appointment, entry, and problems after his arrival, see Elliott, *Imperial Spain*, 265–265; Israel, *Dutch Republic*, 186–187; Tracy, *Founding*, 135ff.; van Gelderen, *Dutch Revolt*, 47ff.; Darby, "Narrative," 19ff.

83. See Wernham, *Return*, 12–18, on the Lopez plot (with 16 on this other plot). William Camden's *The historie of the life and reigne of that famous princesse Elizabeth* (1634) describes this plot (involving Edmund Yorke and Richard Williams, "hired to kill the Queene, by Ibarra, and suborned to that also by the turne-coates in the Low Countries," 105) immediately after the Lopez plot (103–105) involving the Count of Fuentes and Esteban de Ibarra, Philip's chief

ministers in Brussels, and his account of "Parsons the Iesuit" and "Genealogical phantasies" behind the Spanish Infanta's right to England's crown (102–103).

84. See Wernham, *Return*, 62 ff., on Calais, and his chaps. 6–8 on Cadiz, chap. 12 on the 1597 Armada scare, and chap. 14 on Vervins and Elizabeth's insistence on direct negotiation with the archduke Albert.

85. On Archduke Albert of Austria and the Infanta Isabella, see Elliott, *Imperial Spain*, 290; Israel, *Dutch Republic*, 254–259, 270, 387–388, 400–402. Chapter 4 of Jane Pettegree's *Foreign and Native on the English Stage, 1588–1611* (New York: Palgrave Macmillan, 2011)—in addition to citing the Dutch revolt of 1566, relations between England, Spain, and the Turk, James's peace with Spain, Essex, and other relevant issues and texts—relates the Infanta to the "Isabella" of Marlowe's *Edward II* and the Armada (91), but does not include *Othello*. On the importance for Shakespeare of the Infanta's claim through John of Gaunt's first marriage to Blanche of Lancaster, in contrast to the Tudor-Stuart descent from the Beaufort offspring of Gaunt and his mistress Catherine Swynford (later legitimized but still bearing the taint of bastardy reflected in Gloucester's insulting of the Beaufort Winchester as "bastard of my grandfather"—i.e., Gaunt—in *1 Henry VI*, 3.1.42), see Chapter 4 above and Richard Dutton, "Shakespeare and Lancaster," *Shakespeare Quarterly* 49, no. 1 (1998): 1–21, with 15–16 on Parson's book, which "achieved a fair circulation, as we see in the number of attempts to repudiate it," though "Parliament made it high treason to possess a copy." Dutton notes that James "wrote *The Trew Law of Free Monarchies* (1598) at least partly in repudiation of it."

86. Doran in *James VI and I: Ideas, Authority, and Government*, ed. Ralph Houlbrooke (Aldershot: Ashgate, 2006), 32. See also Pauline Croft, "*Rex Pacificus*, Robert Cecil, and the 1604 Peace with Spain," in *The Accession of James I*, ed. Glenn Burgess et al. (New York: Palgrave Macmillan, 2006), 143–144, on Cecil and James's concerns over the Infanta's claim, and her position across the Channel in Brussels after 1599.

87. Wernham, *Return*, 266–268.

88. Ibid., 320 (see also 293 and chaps. 18–19). On England, Spain, the Low Countries, and the rebellion in Ireland, see also Croft, "*Rex Pacificus*," 143–145.

89. Citations and details from Paul E. J. Hammer's 2004 *DNB* entry on "Devereux, Robert, second earl of Essex (1565–1601)." See also Hammer's *The Polarisation of Elizabethan Politics: The Political Career of Robert Devereux, 2nd Earl of Essex, 1585–1597* (Cambridge: Cambridge University Press, 1999). For the quotation from "An Apologie of the Earle of Essex . . . 1598 (London, 1603), D3r, see Rubright, *Dilemmas*, 78, who accompanies it by maps showing the geographical proximity of the Spanish-occupied Low Countries to England (75–81).

90. Wernham, *Return*, 352. On Essex in relation to the Infanta's claim, see also Jean-Christophe Mayer, *Shakespeare's Hybrid Faith* (New York: Palgrave Macmillan, 2006), 122–127.

91. Wernham, *Return*, 357. See also 407–415 on Cecil's continuing denial of support for her claim (and his favoring of James), and the Infanta's reluctance to press this claim between 1602 and James's peace with Spain in 1604.

92. Neill, *Othello*, 404.

93. Wernham, *Return*, 334.

94. Quoted from D. J. B. Trim's *DNB* entry on "Norris [Norreys], Sir John (c. 1547x50–1597)." On Norris, see also John S. Nolan's *Sir John Norreys and the Elizabethan Military World* (Exeter: Exeter University Press, 1997) and "The Militarization of the Elizabethan State," *Journal of Military History* 58, no. 3 (1994): 391–420, 396–397; R. B. Wernham, *After the Armada* (Oxford: Clarendon Press, 1984), esp. 19–21, 36–37, 58–64, 67–69, 215, 228, 154, 171–172, 275–283; Wernham, *Return*, esp. 127–138; Hammer, *Elizabeth's Wars*, esp. 113–114, 120–129, 156ff.,

177–184, 209–210, 77 (on Norris's role in Ireland, a problem for England that was repeatedly triangulated with Spain and the Low Countries); 56, 105, 113 (on English military involvement in the Low Countries in the late 1570s despite "Elizabeth's own profound reluctance to become too openly involved").

95. John Polemon, *The second part of the booke of battailes* (1587), STC (2nd ed.) 20090. On Don John (Don Juan) and Gembloux, see also Tracy, *Founding*, 157–160.

96. Parker, *Spain and the Netherlands*, 89. See also Israel, *Dutch Republic*, 194 (with 184–205 on Brabant and the Low Countries from 1576 to 1579).

97. Parker, *Army of Flanders*, 202. On Don John's seizing of the "citadel at Namur," see also van Gelderen, *Dutch Revolt*, 47.

98. On the 1581 designation of Alençon (Anjou) as "prince and lord of the Netherlands," his entry into Antwerp as "Duke of Brabant," and subsequent events, see Hammer, *Elizabeth's Wars*, 105–115; Jardine, *Prince William*, 42–46, 126; with Jardine and Brotton, *Global Interests*, 125, 128; Tracy, *Founding*, 4, 140–146; Israel, *Dutch Republic*, 209–215; Wernham, *Before the Armada*, 321–336, 358–369; Parker, *Dutch Revolt*, 205–206; Colin Martin and Geoffrey Parker, *The Spanish Armada*, rev. ed. (Manchester: Manchester University Press, 1999), 52–53; Darby, "Narrative," 21ff.; van Gelderen, *Dutch Revolt*, 53–55.

99. STC (2nd ed.) 11310, Preface, sig. A3v. The title page also has "Translated out of Frenche by Arthur Golding, according to the copie printed by Plantine at Antwerpe, his highnesse printer." Golding had earlier translated from French *A iustification or cleering of the Prince of Orendge agaynst the false sclaunders, wherewith his ilwillers goe about to charge him wrongfully* (1575), STC (2nd ed.) 25712.

100. See Israel, *Dutch Republic*, 213; Jardine, *Awful End*, on the 1584 assassination of William of Orange.

101. See *A tragicall historie of the troubles and ciuile warres of the lowe Countries* (1583), STC (2nd ed.) 17450.3, title page and 138. See also Pierre Loyseleur, *A treatise against the proclamation published by the King of Spayne* (Delft [i.e., London], 1584), STC 15208, on "the treatie helde at Breda, about the question of religion" (sig. I2); *The second admonition, sent by the subdued prouinces to Holland hereby to entice them by faire-seeming reasons, groundlesse threates, and unlike examples to make peace with the Spaniards. With the Hollanders aunswer to the same. Translated out of Dutch into English by H. W.* (1598), STC (2nd ed.) 18467, on "deceitfull trickes" in "the treatise of peace at Breda" (14). See also van Gelderen, *Dutch Revolt*, 44–45; Parker, *Army of Flanders*, 113, 198–199; Israel, *Dutch Republic*, 183–184.

102. See Lewkenor's *A discourse*, e.g., sig. G3r; Wernham, *After the Armada*, 208–209. Darby, "Narrative," has that Parma "took Maastricht and 's Hertogenbosch in 1579, Courtrai in 1580 and Breda in 1581" (21).

103. Eltis, *Military Revolution*, 118. See also Israel, *Dutch Republic*, 233–234; Wernham, *After the Armada*, chap. 2 ("Victory at Bergen-op-Zoom," 23–47).

104. Hammer, *Elizabeth's Wars*, 172.

105. See Parker, *Spain and the Netherlands*, 108, 115, 116 (on the Zichem mutiny); 111 (on the mutinies in Diest), with 119 (on Groningen and Grave). See also Wernham, *After the Armada*, 213, 320 (on Diest) and (on Grave) 210, 214, 348, 486, with Wernham's *Return*, 389, 411–412. For events of the 1590s, see also Israel, *Dutch Republic*, chap. 12.

106. Doran, "Renaissance Europe," 49–50. Henry J. Webb writes in *Elizabethan Military Science: The Books and the Practice* (Madison: University of Wisconsin Press, 1965), 77: "Elizabeth's troops . . . made glorious names for themselves at Turnhout, Nieuport, and Ostend." On the English victory at Turnhout, see also *European Warfare, 1350–1750*, ed. Frank Tallett

and D. J. B. Trim (Cambridge: Cambridge University Press, 2010), 228; Wernham, *Return*, 143–147.

107. Doran, "Renaissance Europe," 49–50. Flushing was where Marlowe was arrested in 1592.

108. Nick de Somogyi, *Shakespeare's Theatre of War* (Aldershot: Ashgate, 1998), 6, 91–92. See also James Shapiro, *A Year in the Life of William Shakespeare: 1599* (New York: Harper Collins, 2005), 186–187, on the Turnhout play.

109. D. J. B. Trim, *DNB* entry on "Norris [Norreys], Sir John (*c.* 1547x50–1597)."

110. Quoted from the Draft Calendar of Patent Rolls, 1584–1585, List and Index Society 241, 1990, 194, in D. J. B. Trim's *DNB* entry on Norris. Nolan writes in *Sir John Norryes,* "By the end of May 1585, Walsingham had agreed . . . to send 2000 men to relieve the siege of Antwerp," and "eventually it was agreed that Elizabeth would aid the Dutch Republic" by sending substantial English forces. On the Treaty of Nonsuch and siege of Zutphen, see James McDermott, *England and the Spanish Armada* (New Haven, Conn.: Yale University Press, 2005), 159–160, with chap. 8. On 1584–1586 and its aftermath, see also Hammer, *Elizabeth's Wars*, 128–130, with chap. 4, and 112–113; Wernham, *Before the Armada*, 367–372, and chap. 27; Parker, *Spain and the Netherlands*, 5–36, 51; Tracy, *Founding*, 221–228; Israel, *Dutch Republic*, 219–228, 235, 293.

111. Simon Adams's *DNB* entry on "Dudley, Robert, earl of Leicester (1532/3–1588)." On Leicester and the Low Countries, see Wernham, *Before the Armada*, esp. 369, 372, 374–379, 386–393, 395; Israel, *Dutch Republic*, esp. 220–239, 277–278; Tracy, *Founding*, 220ff.; Simon Adams, *Leicester and the Court* (Manchester: Manchester University Press, 2002); Hammer, *Elizabeth's Wars*, 87, 102–105, 112, 118, 124ff., which includes the cash crises involved in England's engagement in the Low Countries after 1585 (132ff., 169ff.), in ways suggestive for the emphasis in *Othello* on mercenaries, money, and "cashiered" soldiers.

112. D. J. B. Trim's *DNB* entry on "Vere [de Vere], Sir Francis." See also Clifford J. Rogers, "Tactics and the Face of Battle," in Tallett and Trim, *European Warfare*, 228.

113. Nolan, "Militarization," 401–402. On Vere and his brothers, see also Hammer, *Elizabeth's Wars* (172–174, including the tension between the new military science and "old-style soldiers," suggestive for *Othello* 1.1; with 195–197, 202–206, 220–228); Wernham, *After the Armada*, 208, 302–304, 347–348, 397–399, 422–423; Clements R. Markham, *The Fighting Veres* (Boston, 1888); Allen, *Philip III*, 16, 22, 46–47, 67–68. In 1609, Cyril Tourneur, who saw service in the Low Countries, wrote a *Funerall Poeme upon the Death of the most Worthy and True Souldier, Sir Francis Vere.*

114. On events in Ireland and the Battle of Kinsale, with the siege at Ostend by the forces of Archduke Albert and the Infanta Isabella (ruling from Brussels), see Wernham, *Return*, chaps. 22–24; with Hammer, *Elizabeth's Wars*, chap. 6, 182ff., 206–214, 216–235 (which also includes England's transatlantic conflicts with Spain). See also Andrew Hadfield on *Othello*'s "significant Irish dimension," in *Literature, Travel, and Colonial Writing in the English Renaissance* (Oxford: Oxford University Press, 1998), 217ff.; Willy Maley, "*Othello* and the Irish Question," in *Celtic Shakespeare,* ed. Willy Maley and Rory Loughnane (Farnham, U.K.: Ashgate, 2013), 121–138.

115. See Allen, *Philip III*, chap. 3, on Albert's siege of Ostend, England's distraction by the Essex rebellion (61), the Battle of Kinsale and Spain's 1601 attempted invasion of Ireland (72–73), and the Infanta's claim to the English throne (74, 83–84, 101), ultimately abandoned in favor of peace with James (chap. 4), in the context of Spain's far-flung engagements, including with the Turk.

116. Willem Schrickx, "Elizabethan Drama and Anglo-Dutch Relations," in *Reclamations of Shakespeare*, ed. A. J. Hoenselaars (Amsterdam: Editions Rodopi, 1994), 21–32, 27–28. See also 30 on the archduke alluded to in *All's Well That Ends Well* (1.2.5), and St. James or Sant'-Iago (as "St. Jacques") in that play; 26–27 on the archduke and Vere in relation to Ostend, in the opening of Cyril Tourneur's *The Atheist's Tragedy*.

117. John Manningham, *Diary*, quoted in Schrickx, "Elizabethan Drama," 28. On Vere's parley with the archduke, see also Wernham, *Return*, 388 ff.

118. STC (2nd ed.) 24651. Schrickx, "Elizabethan Drama," 27–28, argues that this pamphlet's author was Cyril Tourneur.

119. *A dialogue and complaint made vpon the siedge of Oastend*, sig. A2. The first two anonymous reports in this paragraph (STC 18892.3 and 18893) were translated out of Dutch. *A dialogue and complaint*, STC (2nd ed.) 18892, was translated out of French. The cost of the siege was also foregrounded in other texts, e.g., Anon., *Further newes from Ostend* (London, 1601), STC (2nd ed.) 18894 (sig. A3).

120. See, for example, Anon., *Further newes from Ostend*. Archduke Albert was also well known from reports—including Anon., *A true relation of the famous & renowmed [sic] victorie latelie atchieued by the counte Maurice of Nassau, . . . against the arch-duke Albertus* (London, 1600), STC (2nd ed.) 17679, which like *A short report* (1602) STC (2nd ed.) 17675 was translated from the Dutch.

121. http://special.lib.gla.ac.uk/exhibns/month/mar2004.html.

122. Croft, "*Rex Pacificus*," 149 (see also 143–144). On the key role of Archduke Albert and the Infanta, see also Doran in Houlbrooke, *James VI*, 42; Allen, *Philip III*, chap. 5. Griffin, *Specter*, 171–172, relates *Othello* to James's peace negotiations with Spain, but does not mention that the governors of the Spanish Netherlands in Brabant were central to this peace.

123. Hammer, *Elizabeth's Wars*, 234–235.

124. See Hale, *Art of War*, 26; Tracy, *Founding*, 150. See also Bert S. Hall, *Weapons and Warfare in Renaissance Europe* (Baltimore: Johns Hopkins University Press, 1997); Eltis, *Military Revolution*, chap. 4; and the debate that followed Geoffrey Parker's *The Military Revolution* (1988; 2nd ed. Cambridge: Cambridge University Press, 1996), including in Roberts, *Military Revolution Debate*. Hammer's last chapter in *Elizabeth's Wars* critiques particulars of the "military revolution" arguments of Parker and Eltis.

125. Willy Maley's *DNB* entry on "Rich, Barnaby (1542–1617)" records similarities "noted between Rich's first military tract and *The Arte of Warre* (1560), Peter Whitehorne's translation of Machiavelli." See Niccolò Machiavelli, *Art of War*, trans. Ellis Farnesworth (1965; rev. ed. New York: Da Capo Press, 2001), introduction by Neal Wood. On Whitehorne's translation, see Timothy J. Reiss, "Calculating Humans: Mathematics, War, and the Colonial Calculus," 148–151, and Patricia Cahill, "Killing by Computation: Military Mathematics, the Elizabethan Social Body, and Marlowe's *Tamburlaine*," 166–186, 180–181, in *Arts of Calculation*, ed. David Glimp and Michelle R. Warren (New York: Palgrave Macmillan, 2004). See also Steven A. Walton, "The Mathematical and Military Sciences in Renaissance England," *Endeavour* 24, no. 4 (2000): 152–156. On Northumberland, see Nina Taunton, *1590s Drama and Militarism* (Aldershot: Ashgate, 2001), 42, 40, 149.

126. See *Instructions for the Warres*, trans. Paul Ive (1589), STC 1708.5; M. Biddle, introduction to Ive's *The practice of fortification* (Farnborough: Gregg Publishing, 1972); Reiss, "Calculating," 137–163, 145, on Fourquevaux, *Instructions*. On Whitehorne's Machiavelli, Niccolò Tartaglia's *Nova Scientia* (1537), Albrecht Dürer's *Befestigung der Stett, Schloß und Flecken* (1527),

Paul Ive, Northumberland, and others, see Steven A. Walton, "State Building Through Building for the State: Foreign and Domestic Expertise in Tudor Fortification," *Osiris* 25, ed. Eric H. Ash (2010): 66–84. See also J. R. Hale, *Renaissance Fortification: Art or Engineering?* (London: Thames and Hudson, 1977).

127. On Marlowe's use of Ive, see Michael Hattaway, "Blood Is Their Argument: Men of War and Soldiers in Shakespeare and Others," in *Religion, Culture, and Society in Early Modern Britain*, ed. Anthony Fletcher and Peter Roberts (Cambridge: Cambridge University Press, 1994), 84–101, 89; Patricia Cahill, "Marlowe, Death-Worlds, and Warfare," in *Christopher Marlowe in Context*, ed. Emily C. Bartels and Emma Smith (Cambridge: Cambridge University Press, 2013), 169–180: 173, 176, and 169 on *Tamburlaine*'s evoking of "siege tactics like those ruthlessly used by the Spanish and the Dutch in the Low Countries," where "Many English soldiers saw such tactics first-hand" while "others read about them in early modern English works on warfare" (169). See also David R. Lawrence, *The Complete Soldier: Military Books and Military Culture in Early Stuart England, 1603–1645* (Leiden: Brill, 2009), 313–370.

128. Stephen Johnston's *DNB* entry on "Ive, Paul (d. 1604)." Murray, *Chapters*, 213, notes that Stevin "began life as a book-keeper and cashier at Antwerp." On links between military science and accounting, see Patricia A. Cahill's *Unto the Breach* (Oxford: Oxford University Press, 2008), 99, with 18, 93–94.

129. Hale, *Art of War*, 38. See also Fernando González de León, *The Road to Rocroi: Class, Culture and Command in the Spanish Army of Flanders, 1567–1659* (Leiden: Brill, 2009). On Hoby's translation of Mendoza's treatise, see Barbara Fuchs, *The Poetics of Piracy* (Philadelphia: University of Pennsylvania Press, 2013), 19–23.

130. Hale, *Art of War*, 38. On Fluellen, see Edelman, *Military Language*, 356.

131. D. J. B. Trim's *DNB* entry on "Williams, Sir Roger (1539/40–1595)." See also Wernham's *Elizabethan Foreign Policy*, 3, 21, 25, and *After the Armada*, 9–10, 128, 528, 532; McDermott, *Spanish Armada*, 220, 359; Hammer, *Elizabeth's Wars*, 90–92, 129, 135, 142, 161, 177–178, 180, 195, 257.

132. See Webb, *Military Science*, 86, 70; Williams, *A briefe discourse of warre*, 23ff., which also refers to cashiered or "cashed souldiers," "cashed Officers," and "cashed" military companies in the passage that begins "to speake troth, the *Spanish* discipline is verie gratefull vnto the men of warre" (22).

133. Parker, *Spain and the Netherlands*, 91: "Three of the best military writers of the reign of Elizabeth—William Garrard, Humphrey Barwick, and Sir Roger Williams—had all served in the Spanish Army of Flanders for several years and held up its practices as examples to others." See also Hale, *Art of War*, 30, on William Clowes, the London surgeon who accompanied Leicester's troops to the Low Countries in 1585.

134. G. Geoffrey Langsam, *Martial Books and Tudor Verse* (New York: Columbia University King's Crown Press, 1951), 24. Though the title page to Garrard's *Arte of Warre*, "Corrected and finished by Captaine *Hichcock*. *Anno*. 1591," states that it is "drawne out of all our late and forraine seruices, by *William Garrard* Gentleman, who serued the King of Spayne in his warres fourteene yeeres," Webb writes in *Elizabethan Military Science* that it includes "wholesale borrowing from Digges' *Stratioticos*, Styward's *Pathwaie to Martiall Discipline*, and Fourquevaux's *Instructions for the Warres*" (or what Iago in *Othello* 1.1 terms "bookish theoric").

135. See Giles Clayton, *The approued order of martiall discipline* (1591), STC (2nd ed.) 5376.2 (sig. B1); Webb, *Military Science*, 55, on Sutcliffe as "judge-advocate general under Leicester in the Low Countries"; Robert Barret, *The theorike and practike of moderne vvarres* (1598), STC 1500, sig. ¶2*r*.

136. Stephen Johnston, *DNB* entry on "Digges, Thomas (*c.* 1546–1595)." Leonard Digges, *An arithmeticall militare treatise, named Stratioticos . . . augmented, digested, and lately finished, by Thomas Digges, his sonne* (London, 1579), STC (2nd ed.) 6848, was expanded in *An Arithmetical Warlike Treatise Named Stratioticos* (London, 1590), STC 6849. See also Taunton, *Militarism*, 8, on Thomas Digges and Leicester; Cahill, "Killing by Computation," on *Stratioticos* and other texts cited here; Edelman, *Military Language*, 357–358, on *Stratioticos* and *Othello.*

137. On Wilson, see the *DNB* entry by Susan Doran and Jonathan Woolfson on "Wilson, Thomas (1523/4–1581)"; Wernham, *Before the Armada*, 314; McDermott, *Spanish Armada*, 117, 130, 347n.3. For Chapman, see "Hymnus in Cynthiam," in *The Poems of George Chapman*, ed. Phyllis Brooks Barlett (1941; rpt. New York, 1962: lines 328–333). On Anjou declared Duke of Brabant, see *Four Revenge Tragedies*, ed. Katharine Eisaman Maus (Oxford: Oxford University Press, 1995), 181–183 (1.1.145, 1.1.196), 378. For Whetstone, see M. Eccles, "Whetstone's death," *TLS*, 27 August 1931, 648.

138. Geffrey Gates, *The Defence of Militarie Profession* (1579), STC 11683, 15, 21.

139. Raphael Lyne, *DNB* entry on "Churchyard, Thomas (1523?–1604)."

140. On this Churchyard treatise, see McDermott, *Spanish Armada*, 109.

141. Emanuel van Meteren's Latin *Historia Belgica* was also a source for other English writers, including William Camden. The updated translation, completed by Churchyard with Robinson's assistance, was published in 1602 as *A true discourse historicall, of the succeeding gouernours in the Netherlands, and the ciuill warres there begun in the yeere 1565 with the memorable seruices of our honourable English generals, captaines and souldiers, especially vnder Sir Iohn Norice knight, there performed from the yeere 1577 vntill the yeere 1589 and afterwards in Portugale, France, Britaine and Ireland, vntill the yeere 1598,* STC (2nd ed.) 17846. On this 1602 translation as "one of the most curious potpourries in historical literature," see Maltby, *Black Legend*, 57.

142. Hall, *Othello*, 203. See also Daniel Vitkus, *Turning Turk* (New York: Palgrave Macmillan, 2003).

143. Parker, *Spain and the Netherlands*, 110, 117, 118. See also Israel, *Dutch Republic*, 183–184.

144. Israel, *Dutch Republic*, 185. On the 1576 sack of Antwerp, see also Wernham's *Elizabethan Foreign Policy*, 48ff., and *Before the Armada*, 328ff.; Parker, *Army of Flanders*, 116–118, 173; Cahill, *Breach*, chap. 5; Maltby, *Black Legend*, 51–52; Andrew Pettegree, "Religion and the Revolt," in Darby, *Dutch Revolt*, 67–83; Tallett and Trim, *European Warfare*, 164; Darby, "Narrative," 19.

145. S. M. Pratt, "Antwerp and the Elizabethan Mind," *Modern Language Quarterly* 24 (1963): 53–60.

146. See de Somogyi, *Theatre of War*, 62, quoting from *Doctor Faustus* here; Langsam, *Martial Books*, 139–140; Pratt, "Antwerp," 56, on Nashe. On Giambelli's "fireships," see Parker, *Grand Strategy*, 229; and below.

147. Doran, "Renaissance Europe," 45–46. In *England and Europe*, Doran places the 1576 sack of Antwerp (74) in the context of Elizabeth's lack of official military engagement on the side of the rebels against Spanish occupation of the Low Countries—evaluating (71–73) the arguments of R. B. Wernham, C. Wilson's *Queen Elizabeth and the Revolt of the Netherlands* (London: Macmillan, 1970), and Wallace T. MacCaffrey's *Queen Elizabeth and the Making of Policy, 1572–88* (Princeton: Princeton University Press, 1981)—and the role of Don John and Anjou in the years following the sack (74ff.). See also Cahill, *Breach*, 173, with Maltby, *Black Legend*; Griffin, *Specter*, 2, 8–17, 24–25, 47, 104–106, 160, 196, 205, 208–210, 213; Griffin's "From Ethos to Ethnos: Hispanizing 'the Spaniard' in the Old World and the New," *CR: The*

*New Centennial Review* 2, no. 1 (Spring 2002): 69–116; Fuchs, *Poetics of Piracy*, 8, 64, 95, 132n.9, on the Black Legend.

148. Laurie Shannon, "Poetic Companies: Musters of Agency in George Gascoigne's 'Friendly Verse,'' *GLQ* 10, no. 3 (2004): 453–483, 456 (see also 453: Gascoigne "was a mercenary and may have in fact been a spy"). See Jones, " 'Othello,' 'Lepanto' and the Cyprus Wars," 52, on his 1572 Mountacute Masque, which incorporated "a dramatic eyewitness account of the sea-fight" at Lepanto; Linda Bradley Salamon, "Blackening 'the Turk' in Roger Ascham's *A Report of Germany* (1553)," in *Rereading the Black Legend*, ed. Margaret R. Greer et al. (Chicago: University of Chicago Press, 2007), 270–292, 291–292.

149. Charles T. Prouty, *George Gascoigne* (New York: Columbia University Press, 1942), 238. See also Cahill, *Breach*, 169; Pratt, "Antwerp," 55.

150. These and other quotations are from George Gascoigne, *The spoyle of Antwerpe. Faithfully reported, by a true Englishman, who was present at the same* (1576), STC (2nd ed.) 11644. See also de Somogyi, *Theatre of War*, 32–33; George Gascoigne, *Complete Works*, ed. John W. Cunliffe, Cambridge English Classics (Cambridge: Cambridge University Press, 1910), II, 599.

151. Rubright's *Dilemmas* (235–239) stresses that Gascoigne's focus on Antwerp's Burse emphasizes parallels with London, while his being "taken for a Walloon" (C3v), or French-speaking Dutch Protestant of Antwerp, underscores the "English double vision on Dutchness" (237–238).

152. Cahill, *Breach*, 169.

153. Ibid., 169–170.

154. Pratt, "Antwerp," 54. See also Doran, "Renaissance Europe," 45; Cahill, *Breach*, 170.

155. Norris's ballad (STC 18656) is cited as 1577 in Doran, "Renaissance Europe," 46. On the possibility that it might be a response to the 1585 fall of Antwerp instead, see Pratt, "Antwerp," 54–55.

156. De Somogyi, *Theatre of War*, 31–32.

157. See Barnabe Riche, *Allarme to England* (1578), STC (2nd ed.) 20979, with Doran, "Renaissance Europe," 46; de Somogyi, *Theatre*, 31–32; Cahill, *Breach*, 170ff.

158. Churchyard STC 5239, sig. H2v (60).

159. STC 11683. See also de Somogyi, *Theatre of War*, 31–32.

160. Quotations are from Cahill, *Breach*, 174, 205, who also cites Anna E. C. Simoni, *The Ostend Story* ('t Goy-Houten: HES and DeGraaf, 2003). See also *A True Historie of the Memorable Siege of Ostend, and what passed on either side*, trans. Edward Grimestone (1604); Allen, *Philip III*, 65, 76, 79, 109, 123–125, 131, 136, 139; Vin Nardizzi, "The Wooden Matter of Human Bodies: Prothesis and Stump in *A Larum for London*," in *The Indistinct Human in Renaissance Literature*, ed. Jean E. Feerick and Vin Nardizzi (New York: Palgrave Macmillan, 2012), 119–136.

161. See Roslyn L. Knutson, "Filling Fare: The Appetite for Current Issues and Traditional Forms in the Repertory of the Chamberlain's Men," *Medieval and Renaissance Drama in England* 15 (2002): 57–76, 64, which also cites fears of Spanish invasion "illustrated by documents in the Elizabethan state papers in 1599, plus the correspondence of John Chamberlain and the *Annals* of John Stow." As Wernham's *Return* makes clear, however, there were multiple "Armada" invasion scares in the 1590s, so the 1599 scare is not definitive for dating the first performance of *A Larum for London*. Cahill, *Breach*, 171, points out that "the title page of its first printing in 1602, which promises a narrative about 'the ventrous actes and valorous deeds of the lame Soldier,' advertises that the drama 'hath been played by the right Honorable the

Lord Charberlaine [*sic*] his Servants'" (i.e., Shakespeare's company) and cites W. W. Greg, *A Larum for London 1602* (Oxford: Malone Society Reprints, 1913; hereafter MSR), for its performance "sometime between the autumn of 1594 when the company ceased to be associated with Philip Henslowe and the spring of 1600 when the play was first entered into the Stationers' Register." Cahill also cites Laurie Maguire, "A Stage Property in *A Larum for London*," *Notes and Queries* 231, ser. 3 (1986): 371–373, for the suggestion that it may be the same as the lost play "the Sege of London," which is listed in Henslowe's diary as having had eleven performances between 1594 and 1596. See also Shapiro, *A Year in the Life*, 181–184, on *A Larum for London* and fears of Spanish invasion in 1599.

162. Quoting here from Cahill, *Breach*, 175, 166.

163. Maltby, *Black Legend*, 51–53.

164. Quoted from Knutson, "Filling Fare," 66. Unless otherwise noted, quotations from the play are from *A Larum for London, or the Siedge of Antwerpe. VVith the ventrous actes and valorous deeds of the lame Soldier. As it hath been playde by the right Honorable the Lord Charberlaine his Seruants* (1602), STC (2nd ed.) 16754.

165. On the play's references to Antwerp's Burse, see also Howard, *Theater*, 50.

166. Quotations from the 1602 text here are from sig. B1r–B2v; sig. D2r; sig. C2r–C3r; and sig. B4r. See Cahill, *Breach*, 172; with Yungblut, *Strangers*, 41, on 1593 London flysheets against "you beastly brutes the Belgians, or rather drunken drones and faint-hearted Flemings," and Pettegree, *Communities*, 300, on attempts by the Dutch church in London to counter this reputation.

167. De Somogyi, *Theatre of War*, 32–33, citing C. Patrides, "'The Bloody and Cruell Turke': The Background of a Renaissance Commonplace," *Studies in the Renaissance* 10 (1963):126–135, and R. Howell, "The Sidney Circle and the Protestant Cause in Elizabethan Foreign Policy," *Renaissance and Modern Studies* 19 (1975): 31–46. See also de Somogyi, *Theatre of War*, 31, 34, 49–50.

168. De Somogyi, *Theatre of War*, 33, quoting (with line numbers) from the MSR text of *A Larum for London* (see his 51n.11).

169. Ibid., 33–34, quoting from the MSR text.

170. Ibid., 49–50.

171. See Neill, *Othello*, 267; Honigmann, *Othello* (196: "take up arms; revolt" for "rise"); Griffin, *Specter*, 203. Othello calls the alarm bell a "dreadful bell" (2.3.175). See also Neill, *Othello*, 261, on "the familiar erotic vocabulary of warfare" in "alarum to love" and Desdemona's "eye" as sounding "a *parley* to provocation" (2.3.22–23).

172. Anita Auer and Marcel Withoos, "Social Stratification and Stylistic Choices in Thomas Dekker's *The Shoemaker's Holiday*," in *English Text Construction* 6, no. 1 (2013) [ed. Ton Hoenselaars and Dirk Delabastita]: 134–157, 151. "Fill up the cannikin drink" is the translation of the stage-Dutch here ("Tap eens de cannikin / Drincke") provided in Rubright, *Dilemmas*, 97–98.

173. *Sir Thomas More*, ed. John Jowett (London: Bloomsbury Arden Shakespeare, 2011), notes that this later dating (as opposed to earlier in the 1590s) would put it in the period of James's "peace with Catholic Spain" (361), as well as after the Treaty of Vervins (429–430), Kinsale, and Haughton's *Englishmen for My Money* (425). Though he does not mention Brabant, Jowett (454) also cites a connection in language between *Sir Thomas More* and *Othello*.

174. See Jones, "'Othello,' 'Lepanto' and the Cyprus Wars," 47–58, with Griffin, *Specter*, 174–175 ("Even as it evokes the Holy League's 1572 triumph at Lepanto, *Othello*'s storm and bonfires also conjure England's own triumph, its 1588 'deliverance' from Philip's Armada"). See

also Hall, *Othello*, 205; Boynton, *Elizabethan Militia*, 196–197; Wernham's *Return*, 185; Hammer's *Elizabeth's Wars*, 204, on the storm that contributed to the failure of the 1597 Armada as well. In "Preposterous Nature in Shakespeare's Tragedies," in Neill and Schalkwyk, *Shakespearean Tragedy*, 105–119, Philip Armstrong also cites the parallels between the 1588 Armada storm and the tempest that defeats the threatened Turkish invasion in *Othello* (107–108), though he does not develop the implications of the two citations of the "preposterous" in that play (simply citing Neill, *Othello*, 219; and briefly noting "the tendency for nature" to "err, stray or drift from its course; to reverse, invert or disrupt its supposedly conventional order").

175. See Tracy, *Founding*, 223–225; Elliott, *Imperial Spain*, 288–290; Wernham, *Before the Armada*, chaps. 27 and 28; McDermott, *Spanish Armada*, chaps. 8 and 9. On the "Armada paradigm," see Fuchs, *Poetics of Piracy*, 9, 11, 89, 125–126.

176. Quoted in Parker, *Grand Strategy*, 225. See 217 on Walsingham's plan for "securing 'intelligence at Brussells,'" and 221ff. on Elizabeth's ambassador in Paris, Sir Edward Stafford, whose false reports regarding Spanish intentions (including that the Armada was aiming for Algiers) are reminiscent of the false reports of "Signior Angelo" about the Turkish fleet in *Othello* (1.3.14–19). On Stafford, see also Wernham, *Before the Armada*, 334, 396–398; James McDermott's *DNB* (2004) entry on "Stafford, Sir Edward (1552–1605)"; McDermott, *Spanish Armada*, 194ff.

177. See http://www.luminarium.org/renlit/tilbury.htm.

178. Parker, *Grand Strategy*, 201–202. On Allen, see also McDermott, *Spanish Armada*, 106–107, 112, 166, 197, 298, 302; Wernham, *Before the Armada*, 338–339, 363.

179. Parker, *Grand Strategy*, 192. See also E. A. Pears, "The Spanish Armada and the Ottoman Porte," *English Historical Review* 7 (1893): 439–466; S. A. Skilliter, *William Harborne and the Trade with Turkey, 1578–1582* (Oxford: Oxford University Press for the British Academy, 1977).

180. See Hammer, *Elizabeth's Wars*, 171–172; Eltis, *Military Revolution*, 118.

181. Wernham's *Before the Armada* also notes that pre-Armada peace negotations provided England with "up-to-date information about Parma's preparations" from his center in Brabant and stresses the influence of "veteran officers from the Low Country wars" (400) in the preparation for England's defenses. See also *England, Spain, and the "Gran Armada," 1585–1604*, ed. M. J. Rodríguez-Salgado and Simon Adams (Edinburgh: John Donald, 1991).

182. Hammer, *Elizabeth's Wars*, 151–152. Wernham, *Before the Armada*, 407, notes that as a result of the fireships, "in the ensuing panic the Armada lost all formation."

183. McDermott, *Spanish Armada*, 267–268.

184. Walton, "Tudor Fortification," 79–80. On Bedwell, see also Walton's "Mathematical and Military Sciences," 152–156; Stephen Johnston's *DNB* entry on "Bedwell, Thomas (c. 1547–1595)."

185. Martin and Parker, *Spanish Armada*, 173–174, 54 (see 53 on Giambelli's "fireships" at Antwerp in 1585). On Giambelli's "hellburners of Antwerp" and "the terror of his name" to the Spanish, see also Garrett Mattingly, *The Armada* (Boston: Houghton Mifflin, 1959), 323–324.

186. Triangulations between Spain, England, and the Low Countries continued in the years leading up to *Othello*, not only in relation to the "Turk" but also to "Moors." Elizabeth's edicts in 1599 and 1601 regarding the "great number of negars and blackamoors which are crept into the realm since the troubles between her Highness and the King of Spain" included "refugee Moors from Spain." From 1602 to 1604, when the French spy Saint-Estienne was in London "attempting to persuade the English government to give assistance to the rebelling

Moors of Valencia," Robert Cecil was "forced to decide that in view of his new King's pro-Spanish policy he could do no more for the rebels than give money and advise application to their other, because similarly Protestant, ally, Holland." See Everett, "'Spanish' Othello," 104, citing *The Calendar of Manuscripts . . . The Marquis of Salisbury* (1906), part ix, 569, and Henry Charles Lea, *The Moriscos of Spain* (1901), 287, respectively.

187. See Cahill, "Marlowe," 171; Walton, "Mathematical and Military Sciences," 156.

188. See, for example, *1 Henry VI* 1.4.61, 4.2.19; *3 Henry VI* 1.2.52; and Henry S. Turner, *The English Renaissance Stage* (Oxford: Oxford University Press, 2006), on this passage in *2 Henry IV*.

189. See Cahill, "Marlowe," 174–175 (on the Damascus virgins) and 176 on "Jacob's staff."

190. Neill, *Othello,* 294, 296.

191. Susan Frye, *Pens and Needles* (Philadelphia: University of Pennsylvania Press, 2010).

192. Jane Schneider, "Fantastical Colors in Foggy London: The New Fashion Potential of the Late Sixteenth Century," in *Material London, ca. 1600,* ed. Lena Cowen Orlin, 109–127, 117 (see also 115 and 122). On Antwerp as a center of silk production, and central to the transmission of luxury textiles between Venice and London, see also Derek Keene, "Material London in Time and Space," in this Orlin volume, 63 and 65.

193. Howard, "Women, Foreigners, and the Regulation of Urban Space in *Westward Ho,*" in Orlin, *Material London,* 155. Howard also notes the disruption of the Antwerp trade in the 1560s.

194. Rubright, *Dilemmas,* 13, citing this 1593 London record from Scouloudi, *Returns,* 199.

195. See Lien Bich Luu, *Immigrants and the Industries of London, 1500–1700* (Aldershot: Ashgate, 2005; New York Routledge, 2016), 119–120. See also Selwood, *Diversity,* 33–36; Yungblut, *Strangers,* 106–107; Linda Levy Peck, *Consuming Splendor: Society and Culture in Seventeenth-Century England* (Cambridge: Cambridge University Press, 2005), esp. chap. 2; Lien Bich Luu, "Assimilation or Segregation: Colonies of Alien Craftsmen in Elizabethan London," in *The Strangers' Progress,* ed. Randolph Vigne and Graham C. Gibbs (London: Huguenot Society, 1995), 160–172.

196. Korda, *Labors Lost,* 99–100, citing C. W. Chitty, "Aliens in England in the Sixteenth Century," *Race* 8 (1966–1967): 129–145, 131, 133. See B. A. Holderness, "The Reception and Distribution of the New Draperies in England," in *The New Draperies in the Low Countries and England, 1300–1800,* ed. N. B. Harte (Oxford: Oxford University Press, 1997), 217–243, 217.

197. Korda, *Labors Lost,* 113, who also cites Scouloudi, *Returns,* 208, 219, on the Widow Stedon and Dionis Welfes.

198. Korda, *Labors Lost,* 114, citing John Stow, *The Annales, or A Generall Chronicle of England . . . Continued and Augmented . . . Unto the Ende of This Present Yeere 1614* (London, 1615), 869.

199. See Korda, *Labors Lost,* 94–95ff., on cloth and the suspect honesty of women, in relation to London's suburbs; 254n.84 on *The Dutch Courtesan.* See also Rubright, *Dilemmas* (esp. 41ff., 46ff.) with her "Going Dutch," 88–112, which stresses the role of the Family of Love in relation to the Low Countries; Howard, *Theater,* 151 ff., who observes that "Freevill positions the Dutch not as fellow allies in a Protestant cause, but as inhabitants of a convenient buffer zone keeping Spanish troops from attacking England," and relates this play to the "burgeoning global economy" (157); the University of York's website for *The Dutch Courtesan,* where

Michael Cordner's "Franceschina's Voice" notes that it "received its first performances in the midst of a mini-fad for plays about Italian, usually Venetian, courtesans."

200. See Korda, *Labors Lost*, 93; and 94, quoting from Edward Grimeston, *A Generall Historie of the Netherlands . . . out of the Best Authors That Have Written of That Subject* (London, 1608), sig. B6r, 496, and 1193; Korda, 255n.86.

201. Korda, *Labors Lost*, 94. Korda's survey includes the lost play by John Day and William Haughton, *The Proud Woman of Antwerp* (122); "Tannekin" the Dutch immigrant starch-woman in Thomas Dekker, Henry Chettle, and William Haughton's *The Pleasant Comodie of Patient Grissil* (1600), 133 ff.; and the "chaste industry and domestic virtue of Dutch women" in *The London Prodigall*, ascribed to Shakespeare on the title page of its 1605 Quarto (137 ff.).

202. Quoted from Dympna Callaghan, "Looking Well to Linens: Women and Cultural Production in *Othello* and Shakespeare's England," in *Marxist Shakespeares*, ed. Jean E. Howard and Scott Cutler Shershow (New York: Routledge, 2001), 53–81, 39. On Callaghan and other treatments of the handkerchief, see also Harris, *Untimely Matter*, chap. 6, with my Introduction.

203. See Whetstone's *Heptameron of Civil Discourses* (1582), Y1v (marginal note); and his *Aurelia* (1593), 7th Day.

204. Frye, *Pens and Needles*, 164–165, 167.

205. Rubright, *Dilemmas*, 1–2, citing *The Roaring Girl*, ed. Paul A. Mulholland (Manchester: Manchester University Press, 1987), 2.1.226–228, 302–305.

206. Frye, *Pens and Needles*, 165. On Mistress Openwork, see also Natasha Korda, "Coverture and Its Discontents: Legal Fictions on and off the Early Modern English Stage," in *Married Women and the Law*, ed. Tim Stretton and Krista J. Kesselring (Montreal: McGill-Queen's University Press, 2013), 45–63: 55–57.

207. Korda, *Labors Lost*, 116. See 115 on "Dutch" stereotypes in *Merry Wives* deflected onto Falstaff.

208. See Rymer, *A Short View of Tragedy* (London, 1693), 138; Callaghan, "Linens," 56ff., 72. See also *Much Ado About Nothing* on Beatrice and Benedick as "between the sheet" (2.3.137), and Autolycus's "My traffic is sheets; when the kite builds, look to lesser linen" (*The Winter's Tale* 4.3.23–24). On the strawberry as symbol of both fertility and deceit, see Neill, *Othello*, 155, with Frye, *Pens and Needles*, 172.

209. See Frye, *Pens and Needles*, 175ff., on the purse that "lewdly suggests not only Iago's and Roderigo's body parts that 'purse'—the forehead, lips, and anus—but also Desdemona's vagina" (with 172–173 on the control of the reading of female textiles assumed by the men in *Othello*).

210. Callaghan, "Linens," 74.

211. See Sandra K. Fischer, *Econolingua* (Wilmington: University of Delaware Press, 1985), 60.

212. Callaghan, "Linens," 61.

213. Lynda E. Boose, "Othello's Handkerchief: The Recognizance and Pledge of Love," *English Literary Renaissance* 5 (1975): 360–374.

214. Callaghan, "Linens," 64. On "courtesan," see Valerie Wayne, "The Sexual Politics of Textual Transmission," in *Textual Formations and Reformations*, ed. T. Berger and L. Maguire (Wilmington: University of Delaware Press, 1999).

215. Sugden's *Dictionary*, 320, notes the prevalence of "camp followers" in the Low Countries' campaigns as English soldiers' most proximate contemporary experience.

216. See Giraldi Cinthio, *Gli Hecatommithi* (III, 7), trans. Bruno Ferraro, in Neill, *Othello*, 434–444, esp. 439. Richard Andrews has suggested in a private communication that the fact that it is given in Cinthio to a woman to copy because she is expert at doing embroidery on *tela de rensa* (a fine type of linen cloth for luxury use)—defined in an entry in Treccani's online dictionary where the word *candido* is used—may indicate that it was white (i.e., *candido*), but there is nothing certain in Cinthio's text regarding its color.

217. See, respectively, Ian Smith, "Othello's Black Handkerchief," *Shakespeare Quarterly* 64, no 1 (2013): 1–25, with Michael Neill's "Othello's Black Handkerchief: Response to Ian Smith," *Shakespeare Quarterly* 64, no. 1 (2013): 26–31; and Smith's more recent "Seeing Blackness: Reading Race in *Othello*," in Neill and Schalkwyk, *Shakespearean Tragedy*, 405–420: 413. See also Natasha Korda, "Shakespeare's Laundry: Feminist Futures in the Archive," in Loomba and Sanchez, *Rethinking Feminism*, 93–111: 106.

218. See my "What's in a Name: and More," *SEDERI* 11 (2002): 101–149: 106ff., on Latin *morus* as "mulberry tree," "fool," and "black," which also includes Erasmus's referring to Thomas More (or Moore) as *Niger* as well as contemporary associations of the mulberry or "Moor-tree" with Moors. The reminder of the mulberry tree in these lines also imports a sense of *Othello* as a racialized version of the Pyramus and Thisbe story of tragic lovers central to *Romeo and Juliet* and *A Midsummer Night's Dream*. See my *Shakespeare from the Margins*, 275n.11; with Sujata Iyengar, "Why Ganymede Faints and the Duke of York Weeps: Passion Plays in Shakespeare," *Shakespeare Survey* 67 (2014): 265–278, esp. 266. On the color black associated with Habsburg Spain (as well as Spanish rule in Brabant), see also *Spanish Fashion at the Courts of Early Modern Europe*, 2 vols, ed. José Luis Colomer and Amalia Descalzo (Madrid: Centro de Estudios Europa Hispánica, 2014).

219. See Williams, *Dictionary*, 3:1439–1440 ("Turk"); and "She can turn, and turn" (*Othello* 4.1.253) in Vitkus, *Turning Turk*, 54.

220. See Yachnin's "Magical Properties: Vision, Possession, and Wonder in 'Othello,'" *Theatre Journal* 48, no. 2 (1996): 197–208, 202; expanded in *Staged Properties in Early Modern English Drama*, ed. Jonathan Gil Harris and Natasha Korda (Cambridge: Cambridge University Press, 2006). See also Andrew Sofer, *The Stage Life of Props* (Ann Arbor: University of Michigan Press, 2003), 18ff.; and Ariane M. Balizet, *Blood and Home in Early Modern Drama* (London: Routledge, 2014).

221. See Hall, *Othello*, 233.

222. Everett, "'Spanish' Othello," 104.

223. Jones, "'Othello,' 'Lepanto' and the Cyprus Wars," 49.

## CHAPTER 6. INTIMATIONS OF GANYMEDE IN *CYMBELINE*

1. See, inter alia, Leah S. Marcus, *Puzzling Shakespeare* (Berkeley: University of California Press, 1988), 119; David Bergeron, "*Cymbeline*: Shakespeare's Last Roman Play," *Shakespeare Quarterly* 31 (1980): 31–41, 35. Unless otherwise specified, citations of this play are from *Cymbeline*, ed. Martin Butler (Cambridge: Cambridge University Press, 2005; hereafter Butler ed.), which retains the Folio's name Iachimo but changes Imogen to Innogen (familiar from *Cymbeline*'s sources and Simon Forman's account, as well as the name of the wife of Leonato in *Much Ado About Nothing*). *The Riverside Shakespeare*, 2nd ed., ed. G. Blakemore Evans and J. J. M. Tobin et al.(Boston: Wadsworth Cengage LearningH, 1997; hereafter *Riverside*), is cited for other Shakespeare plays.

2. See my "Romance and Empire: Anachronistic *Cymbeline*," in *Unfolded Tales*, ed. G. M. Logan and G. Teskey (Ithaca, N.Y.: Cornell University Press, 1989), 189–207, 193–194, on Jupiter's prophecy and the ultimately tragicomic shape of the travails of both Aeneas and Posthumus. As Colin Burrow points out in *Shakespeare and Classical Antiquity* (Oxford: Oxford University Press, 2013), 88, when Innogen as Cymbeline's heir is replaced at the end by the king's newfound sons, Posthumus (unlike Aeneas) is no longer in a position to become progenitor of an imperial line.

3. See the topical argument regarding Jupiter's descent with lightning and James's admonitions to the 1606–1607 Parliament in Marcus, *Puzzling Shakespeare*, 119, 123, 137.

4. See, inter alia, Glynne Wickham, "Riddle and Emblem: A Study in the Dramatic Structure of *Cymbeline*," in *English Renaissance Studies: Presented to Dame Helen Gardner in Honour of Her Seventieth Birthday* (Oxford: Oxford University Press, 1980), 95–113: "Jupiter, as *deus ex machina* within the play, signifies the will of Divine Providence."

5. Marcus, *Puzzling Shakespeare*, 137.

6. Ibid., 139. The reference in this block quotation from Marcus to "throwne" or "rent asunder in contrary sences like the old Oracles of the Pagan gods" is from James's own 1604 speech before Parliament, discussed in *Puzzling Shakespeare*, 111.

7. Ibid., 140.

8. For these and other wager stories, see Valerie Wayne, "Romancing the Wager: *Cymbeline*'s Intertexts," in *Staging Early Modern Romance*, ed. Mary Ellen Lamb and Valerie Wayne (London: Routledge, 2009), 163–187.

9. Heather James's *Shakespeare's Troy: Drama, Politics, and the Translation of Empire* (Cambridge: Cambridge University Press, 1997) makes no mention, in its treatment of *Cymbeline* or elsewhere, of the figure of Ganymede in relation to Troy and the translation of empire in the *Aeneid* or other familiar sources. Similarly, Colin Burrow's discussion of *Cymbeline* in his chapter on Virgil in *Shakespeare and Classical Antiquity*, 83–91, makes no mention of Trojan Ganymede or his relation to Virgil's narrative of Aeneas (or the play). Although he does not mention the *raptus* of Ganymede, Goran V. Stanivukovic—in " 'The city's usuries': Commerce and *Cymbeline*," *Quidditas* 19 (1998): 229–243 (239)—notes the use of "raps" as a verb elsewhere in *Cymbeline*: "During her first conference with Iachimo . . . Imogen questions Iachimo's emotional state: 'What, dear sir, Thus *raps* you?' (1.7.50, emphasis added). She uses *raps* here in the sense in which it is commonly glossed, as 'transports.' But *rap* also implies *rape*, as it might be suggested in the form *rap's*, which is how the First Folio reads at this point."

10. See John Boswell, *Christianity, Social Tolerance, and Homosexuality* (Chicago: University of Chicago Press, 1980), 251, with 260 on Servius's influential commentary on Virgil, which stresses (as Ovid's *Metamorphoses* 10.155–161 does) Juno's outrage at Ganymede's replacement of Hebe as cupbearer to the gods; and James M. Saslow, *Ganymede in the Renaissance: Homosexuality in Art and Society* (New Haven, Conn.: Yale University Press, 1986), 3, on Ovid's *Metamorphoses* 10.155–161 and Virgil's *Aeneid* 5.250–257 in particular, and passim on other sources, including Ovid, *Fasti* 6.43; Lucian, *Dialogues of the Gods* 8.5; Martial; Achilles Tatius, *Leucippe and Clitophon*; Statius, *Thebaid*; and the influential *Ovide moralisé* and *Ovidius moralizatus*. Ovid's *Fasti* 6.43 (for the month of June named after Juno) stresses Jupiter's *raptus* of Ganymede as one of the two reasons for Juno's anger against the Trojans. Saslow also traces the divergence between the transcendent tradition emanating from Xenophon's *Symposium* (8:28–30) in which Ganymede's elevation to heaven is viewed "as a spiritual allegory representing the ascent of the pure, questing soul toward knowledge of the divine" (also acknowledged in Plato's *Phaedrus* 255) and the very different tradition from Plato's *Laws* (1:636D), where the

myth is presented as "invented by the Cretans to justify their predilection for pederasty," together with the satirical contexts of Euripides and Martial's bawdy Epigrams (Saslow, *Ganymede in the Renaissance,* 4). On historical traditions from classical to English Renaissance, including Pliny, Alciati, and others, see Leonard Barkan, *Transuming Passion: Ganymede and the Erotics of Humanism* (Stanford, Calif.: Stanford University Press, 1991). Barkan's entry on Ganymede in *The Classical Tradition,* ed. Anthony Grafton, Glenn W. Most, and Salvatore Settis (Cambridge, Mass.: Harvard University Press, 2010), 385–386, stresses that the allusion to Ganymede in Book 1 of the *Aeneid* underscored that Jupiter's elevation of the beautiful boy "helped produce the rage of Juno, that in turn caused the Trojan War"; describes the medieval tradition—including the Dream of the Eagle in Dante's *Purgatorio*—and Ganymede in the NeoPlatonism of Renaissance Florence as "the perfect exemplar of the ladder of love, making the transit from earthbound carnality to ecstatic spiritual union with the divine" (though remarking that "the story never quite loses its associations with erotic heterodoxy"); and includes the well-known paintings by Michelangelo and Correggio. See also the opening chapter ("Christ's Ganymede") of Richard Rambuss, *Closet Devotions* (Durham, N.C.: Duke University Press, 1998), 11–71, which includes the Christian devotional tradition.

11. See Virgil, *Aeneid* 1.27–28, where the causes of Juno's anger against Troy (given as the reason for her persecution of Aeneas on his journey to found Rome) are the judgment of Paris and honors given to "ravished Ganymede" (*rapti Ganymedis honores*).

12. See Ovid, *Metamorphoses,* trans. Arthur Golding (1567), ed. John Frederick Nims (Philadelphia: Paul Dry Books, 2000), 296 ("Faire Ganymed who Jupiter did ravish as his joy," 11.871).

13. Quoted from Ovid, *Metamorphoses* 10.161–167, trans. Golding, ed. Nims, 253. The Loeb edition of Ovid, *Metamorphoses,* 2 vols., trans. Frank Justus Miller (Cambridge, Mass.: Harvard University Press, 1968), 75, has: "The king of the gods once burned with love for Phrygian Ganymede, and something was found which Jove would rather be than what he was. Still he did not deign to take the form of any bird save only that which could bear his thunderbolts. Without delay he cleft the air on his lying wings and stole away the Trojan boy, who even now, though against the will of Juno, mingles the nectar and attends the cups of Jove." See also Mario DiGangi, *The Homoerotics of Early Modern Drama* (Cambridge: Cambridge University Press, 1997), on texts from the 1590s that bring "Orpheus's misogyny and homoeroticism more directly to the fore" (45ff.) and his "Queering the Shakespearean Family," *Shakespeare Quarterly* 47, no. 3 (1996): 269–290.

14. Edmund Spenser, *The Faerie Queene,* ed. A. C. Hamilton (London: Longman, 1977), 3.12.7–8, cited in DiGangi, *Homoerotics,* 32. See Butler ed., 11–13, on Spenser's importance for the play in other respects.

15. DiGangi, *Homoerotics,* 34.

16. Bruce R. Smith, *Homosexual Desire in Shakespeare's England* (1991; rpt. Chicago: University of Chicago Press, 1994), 191–192, 195–196.

17. Michael B. Young, *King James and the History of Homosexuality* (New York: New York University Press, 2000), 72, quoting William Prynne (London, 1633; Garland facsimile edition, New York, 1974), 208–209, 213.

18. See DiGangi, *Homoerotics,* 35, citing and quoting respectively from Thomas Cooper, *Dictionarium Historicum & Poeticum . . .* in *Thesaurus Linguae Romanae & Britannicae . . .* (London, 1565), sig. J4r, and Christopher Marlowe, *Dido, Queen of Carthage,* in *Christopher Marlowe: The Complete Plays,* ed. J. B. Steane (Harmondsworth: Penguin, 1986), including I.I.sd, I.I.51.

19. See DiGangi, *Homoerotics*, 171, quoting from *Shakespeare's Ovid: Being Arthur Golding's Translation of the Metamorphoses*, ed. W. H. D. Rouse (Carbondale: Southern Illinois University Press, 1961), book 10, line 167.

20. See John Mason, *The Turke. A Worthie Tragedie* (London, 1610), sig. Cr3.

21. DiGangi, *Homoerotics*, 35–36. DiGangi also cites Marlowe's *Edward II* (1592), where Queen Isabella finds a model in Juno: "Like frantic Juno will I fill the earth / With ghastly murmur of my sighs and cries; / For never doted Jove on Ganymed / So much as he on cursed Gaveston"; John Marston's *The Malcontent* (1603), where the court favorite is accused of precipitating conjugal rupture ("Duke's Ganymede, Juno's jealous of thy long stockings"); and Marston's *The Scourge of Villainy* (1598) in relation to the spread of pederasty: "Marry, the jealous queen of air doth frown, / That Ganymede is up, and Hebe down." For the later Caroline history of the Ganymede figure, see Mario DiGangi's *Sexual Types: Embodiment, Agency, and Dramatic Character from Shakespeare to Shirley* (Philadelphia: University of Pennsylvania Press, 2011), 192ff.

22. Saslow, *Ganymede*, 116.

23. Though he does not pursue its wider implications for *Cymbeline*, Martin Butler notes the parallel with Heywood in his gloss on the descent of Jupiter in *Cymbeline*'s final act (Butler ed., 219): "The play's spectacular high point, especially since Jupiter descends on an eagle, rather than a throne as in other theophanies. The actor would have been lowered on a mechanism worked from a winch hidden in the roof above the Globe stage. Such effects were uncommon at the indoor Blackfriars playhouse and more in vogue at the open-air theatres. For example, in Thomas Heywood's *The Golden Age* (ca. 1609–1611), staged at the Red Bull, Jupiter and Ganymede ascend to heaven on an eagle; in *The Silver Age* (ca. 1610–1612) he 'descends in his majesty, his thunderbolt burning', though not on an eagle (Heywood, III, 78, 154)." Though he does not discuss *Cymbeline*, Bruce R. Smith, in "Rape, Rap, Rupture, Rapture: R-Rated Futures on the Global Market," *Textual Practice* 9, no. 3 (1995): 421–443, 432–433, links Jupiter and Ganymede in Heywood's *The Golden Age* to Shakespeare's earlier *Coriolanus*, where the Ganymede story is evoked in lines on "Boy" and Jupiter's "eagle" (5.6.113–117), as well as citing the parallel between the biblical stories of Enoch and Elijah ("rapt in to heaven") and the transcendent Xenophon tradition reflected in George Sandys's commentary on Ovid (Smith, "Rape," 426).

24. Jeffrey Masten, *Queer Philologies: Sex, Language, and Affect in Shakespeare's Time* (Philadelphia: University of Pennsylvania Press, 2016), chap. 4, part of which is an updated revision of his earlier treatment of *Philaster* in "Editing Boys: The Performance of Genders in Print," in *From Performance to Print in Shakespeare's England,* ed. Peter Holland and Stephen Orgel (Basingstoke: Palgrave Macmillan, 2006), 113–134. Masten observes that "the boy Bellario" is "the object of concerted erotic interest in *Philaster*, and not only *from* Philaster" (*Queer Philologies,* 115), since he is the object of erotic interest for both men and women. For an earlier reading of *Philaster* that argues that "homoeroticism is invoked in a way that implicitly denigrates and disavows it," including in relation to "the institutional heteroeroticism of the ending," see Nicholas F. Radel, "Fletcherian Tragicomedy, Cross-Dressing, and the Constriction of Homoerotic Desire in Early Modern England," *Renaissance Drama,* n.s. 26 (1995): 53–82 (67, 68). I do not agree with the statement in Michael Shapiro's discussion of *Philaster*—in his *Gender in Play on the Shakespearean Stage* (Ann Arbor: University of Michigan Press, 1994)—that "*Cymbeline* insulates Fidele from suggestions of sexual intimacy," which he contrasts with *Philaster*, which places the "boy" Bellario, "even though (or precisely because) his gender is uncertain, in situations that recall the page-master-mistress triangle in *Twelfth Night*" (189); or

his more idealizing view of *Cymbeline*'s Jupiter as embodying "the watchful and benevolent eye of Eternity" (192). James M. Bromley's discussion of *Philaster* in *Intimacy and Sexuality in the Age of Shakespeare* (Cambridge: Cambridge University Press, 2012), 83–86, does not include comparison with *Cymbeline.*

25. Cited by Masten from Francis Beaumont and John Fletcher, *Philaster, or, Love Lies A-Bleeding,* Arden Early Modern Drama, ed. Suzanne Gossett (London: A&C Black, 2009).

26. Masten, *Queer Philologies,* 120, citing Stephen Orgel, *Impersonations: The Performance of Gender in Shakespeare's England* (Cambridge: Cambridge University Press, 1996), 163n.8.

27. In relation to book culture in particular, Masten (*Queer Philologies,* 132) notes that "the first two editions of *Philaster* were printed 'for *Thomas Walkley*, and [were] to be sold'—strangely enough—'at his shop at the *Eagle and Child* in Brittaines Bursse' (in 1620, also 1622)." That is, both the "Boy Quarto and the Bellario Quarto . . . were sold at what must have resonated as the sign of the Rape of Ganymede, this story of both pedagogical uplift and homoerotic ravishment and adoption." And he goes on to record that this was "not an unfamiliar sign either before or after" Walkley, since there are "several imprints of Thomas Creede printing and selling at this sign in 1600, 'in the Old Change . . . neare Old Fish-streete,'" there is "a golden eagle and child in Pater Noster Row in 1590," and books continued to be published under the "Ganymedic sign" for years after *Philaster,* making clear "the ubiquity in this culture of this sign of the Ganymedic child ('sign' in all the senses of that word)" (132). Masten's discussion in *Queer Philologies* also cites from his earlier "Ben Jonson's Head," *Shakespeare Studies* 23 (2000): 160–168.

28. Gossett's edition of *Philaster* cites from Masten's "Editing Boys," 113–134.

29. Gossett also observes that "King James's penchant for young men was well known at court" in her gloss on Hylas and Hercules (256, glossing 5.4.104), and her introduction discusses topics that link this play to James and his court.

30. In relation to the much-debated order of these two plays, Gossett concludes (7) that *Philaster* came before rather than after *Cymbeline,* and that Shakespeare could have seen it in manuscript even before performance. See also Suzanne Gossett, "Taking *Pericles* Seriously," in *Early Modern Tragicomedy,* ed. Subha Mukherji and Raphael Lyne (Cambridge: D. S. Brewer, 2007), 101–114, 107.

31. See Michael Drayton, *Englands heroicall epistles* (1597), STC 7193, 18, for Queen Isabella's complaint against "that girle-boy, wanton *Gaueston*" she calls a "shamelesse *Ganimed.*" See also DiGangi, *Homoerotics,* 103.

32. For these and other biographical details, see R. E. Schreiber, "The First Carlisle: Sir James Hay, First Earl of Carlisle as Courtier, Diplomat and Entrepreneur, 1580–1636," *Transactions of the American Philosophical Society* 74, no. 7 (1984): 1–202; and his 2004 *Oxford Dictionary of National Biography* entry on "Hay, James, first earl of Carlisle (*c.* 1580–1636)."

33. Quoted from Appendix A (189–191) of the Arden 2 edition of *Cymbeline,* ed. J. M. Nosworthy (London: Methuen, 1955).

34. See Wickham, "Riddle and Emblem," 95–113; with Geoffrey Bullough, *Narrative and Dramatic Sources of Shakespeare*, vol. 8 (London: Routledge and Kegan Paul; New York: Columbia University Press, 1975), 11–12, 46–50. Wickham also notes that the 1607 wedding of Haie's (i.e., Hay's) Jacobean descendant to the daughter of an English peer "was regarded at Court as itself so important an emblem of James's unifying and pacifying policies (to be matched where possible by similar marriages between Protestants and Catholics) as to warrant celebration with a nuptual Masque," commissioned from Thomas Campion and Inigo Jones (and printed in 1607), where Campion concludes his dedicatory poem to James with: "who can wonder then

If he that marries kingdomes, marries men?" Wickham argues that this wedding is reflected in the "Imogen-Posthumus" story and final act of *Cymbeline*, together with confirmation of James's broader "Union" policy.

35. John Kerrigan, *Archipelagic English* (Oxford: Oxford University Press, 2008), 133, 140.

36. See also Marcus, *Puzzling Shakespeare*, 131: "The riddle of the man and two boys in the narrow lane who save the Britons from the Romans is taken from Scots history and was an exploit actually performed by three Scotsmen named Hay—the ancestors of James I's favorite Lord Hay, one of the Scots who, like Posthumus in the play, had to contend with insular British prejudice." She does not follow up this topical connection, though she does mention that Gentleman of the Bedchamber was "a position monopolized by Scotsmen even in James I's court at Whitehall during the early years of his reign" (125).

37. See Martin Butler, "Ben Jonson and the Limits of Courtly Panegyric," in *Culture and Politics in Early Stuart England,* ed. Kevin Sharpe and Peter Lake (Stanford, Calif.: Stanford University Press, 1993), 91–115, 110; and Curtis Perry, *Literature and Favoritism in Early Modern England* (Cambridge: Cambridge University Press, 2006), 135, for Francis Osborne on Hay as a "Monster in Excess." On James's English favorite, the "handsome Sir Philip Herbert," who was promoted to the Bedchamber in 1605 (and one of the two brothers to whom Heminges and Condell dedicated the Shakespeare First Folio), see, inter alia, Peter R. Roberts, "The Business of Playing and the Patronage of Players at the Jacobean Courts," in *James VI and I: Ideas, Authority, and Government,* ed. Ralph Houlbrooke (Aldershot: Ashgate, 2006), 81–105, 97. Sir Philip Herbert became Earl of Pembroke in 1630, after his brother's death. See also Kerrigan, *Archipelagic English*, 137, on Pembrokeshire as the setting of *Cymbeline*'s Welsh scenes.

38. See the entry on "knights of the battle" in Charles Edelman, *Shakespeare's Military Language: A Dictionary* (London: Athlone Press, 2000), in relation to the inflation of honors at James's court; and the gloss in Butler ed., 225, which emphasizes that "in 1610 there would have been an implicit contrast with the changing conventions of courtly honour, in which knighthood was a mark of status increasingly divorced from military service," a stark contrast to the military valor at the "narrow lane" that distinguishes these three from such "carpet knights."

39. See, inter alia, John Cramsie, "The Philosophy of Imperial Kingship and the Interpretation of James VI and I," in Houlbrooke, *James VI and I*, 43–60, 58, on complaints about Scots in the Bedchamber (with 57 on Samuel Lewkenor and Xenophon's *Cyropaedia*).

40. See R. Malcolm Smuts, *Court Culture and the Origins of a Royalist Tradition in Early Stuart England* (Philadelphia: University of Pennsylvania Press, 1987), 80.

41. See Young, *King James*, 81. See also *The vvhore of Babylon As it was acted by the Princes Seruants. Written by Thomas Dekker* (London, 1607), where St. James's Park in London is referred to as "Sant'Iagoes park" (a fascinating aligning of James with the patron saint of Spain, only a few years after his 1604 peace with Spain and performance of *Othello* at James's court, and a reminder that the names of Iago and Iachimo in *Cymbeline* are Spanish and Italian counterparts of "James").

42. See Neil Cuddy, "The Revival of the Entourage: The Bedchamber of James I, 1603–1625," in *The English Court from the Wars of the Roses to the Civil War*, ed. David Starkey (Harlow, U.K.: Longman Group, 1987), 173–225, esp. 189–190, 202–204, 212. See also Young, *King James*, 28–29, on the "strong resentment against the Scots who monopolized the Bedchamber" and contemporary concern that any money James received from Parliament would be "frittered away on the Scots at court" ("he also used royal revenues to pay off the personal

debts of the Bedchamber Scots"; "In 1607 he paid off the debts of three of these insiders amounting to £44,000").

43. Quoted from Alan Stewart, *The Cradle King: The Life of James VI & I, the First Monarch of a United Great Britain* (New York: St. Martin's Press, 2003), 258. See also Jonathan Goldberg, *James I and the Politics of Literature* (Stanford, Calif.: Stanford University Press, 1989), 19.

44. See, inter alia, Young, *King James*, 150–151.

45. Stewart, *The Cradle King*, 260 ff., goes on to discuss the later history of Carr and Frances Howard (already lovers by late 1609), the divorce case that enabled them to marry in 1613, and the Overbury murder that ultimately meant Carr's fall—the latter events that post-dated *Cymbeline* itself.

46. Stewart, *The Cradle King*, 258. Stewart also quotes Lord Thomas Howard's communication to Sir John Harington, recorded in Harington's *Nugae Antiquae* (390–397), which he sees as dated ca. 1607, soon after James's infatuation with Carr began, in which Howard observes that Carr was now "most likely to win the Prince's [James's] affection, and does it wondrously in a little time. The Prince leaneth on his arm, pinches his cheek, smoothes his ruffled garment, and, when he looketh at Carr, directeth discourse to diverse others. This young man doth much study all art and device: he hath changed his tailors and tiremen many times, and all to please the Prince, who laugheth at the long grown fashion of our young courtiers, and wisheth for change every day," in the midst of other comments on fashionable garments at court (Stewart, *The Cradle King*, 258). On James's relationship to Carr—and the tensions it caused within his family—see also David M. Bergeron, *Royal Family, Royal Lovers: King James of England and Scotland* (Columbia: University of Missouri Press, 1991), 82 ff. Bergeron also records the comments on negative views of James in England by 1607, by the Venetian ambassador.

47. See Young, *King James*, 42. On the identification of Ganymede with a "smooth" beardlessness, see also, inter alia, Saslow, *Ganymede*, e.g., 158–159; and my "Barbers and Barbary: Early Modern Cultural Semantics," *Renaissance Drama* (Fall 2004): 201–244. Marston's *Malcontent* (1600–1604) calls the "Dukes Ganimed" a "smooth chinned Catamite" (1.2.9), and an "imberbis juvenis" or beardless youth (2.1.142–146) is called "Ganymede" in Middleton's *A Mad World, My Masters* (ca. 1606). James's male favorites were likewise characterized as "smooth-faced," as Harington in *Nugae Antiquae* describes Carr, who was also portrayed by Francis Osborne as retaining his attractiveness to the king "before he had either Wife or Beard" (see Young, *King James*, 74).

48. Perry, *Literature and Favoritism*, 116, citing Henry Peacham, *Minerva Britanna or A garden of heroical devises* (London, 1612), 48; and also citing DiGangi, *Homoerotics*, 103–107. See also Bergeron, *Royal Lovers*, 65.

49. Curtis Perry, "The Politics of Access and Representations of the Sodomite King in Early Modern England," *Renaissance Quarterly* 53, no. 4 (2000): 1054–1083, 1072–1073. Perry here also cites the "volume entitled *Corona Regia*—falsely attributed on its title page to Isaac Casaubon, the humanist scholar in residence in James's court, but actually published overseas by a satirist and smuggled into England in 1615," which "makes explicit allusions to the king's sodomitical bedchamber" and in which "The epithet 'Magnus Cubicularius tuus" (your Knight of the Bedchamber) is added to cap a list of Carr's honorific titles, where it is intended at once to convey a hint of sodomy and to satirize the puffed-up importance of the king's lofty intimates." See also Winfried Schleiner, "Scioppius' Pen against the English King's Sword: The Political Function of Ambiguity and Anonymity in Early Seventeenth-Century Literature,"

*Renaissance and Reformation* o.s. 26 (1990): 271–284; and Schleiner, "'A Plott to have his nose and eares cut of': Schoppe as Seen by the Archbishop of Canterbury," *Renaissance and Reformation* 19, no. 4 (1995): 69–86.

50. See Saslow, *Ganymede*, 23–25; Barkan, *Transuming Passion*, 24–26. See also DiGangi, *Homoerotics*, 185n.13: "Several emblematists, including the influential Alciatus, 'translated Ganymede's abduction by Zeus as the *sursum corda* or elevation of heart, mind, or soul, or joy and rapture in God or the love of God,'' quoting from Lorrayne Y. Baird-Lange, "Victim Criminalized: Iconographic Traditions and Peacham's Ganymede," in *Traditions and Innovations: Essays on British Literature of the Middle Ages and the Renaissance*, ed. David G. Allen and Robert A. White (Newark: University of Delaware Press, 1990), 231–250, 241.

51. See DiGangi, *Homoerotics*, 107, 103.

52. See also Thomas Dekker's *Satiromastix*, where "Joves page / Sweet Ganimed fills Nectar" (5.2.1–2, 5–6), with DiGangi, *Homoerotics*, 86–87, 50–63; and the suggestive remarks on the "absent-presence" of the Ganymede / Jupiter story in the Induction of *The Taming of the Shrew*, in Amanda Bailey's *Flaunting: Style and the Subversive Male Body in Renaissance England* (Toronto: University of Toronto Press, 2007), 71–72, cited in the conclusion to this chapter, though she does not mention *Cymbeline* in this regard.

53. See *Queering the Renaissance*, ed. Jonathan Goldberg (Durham, N.C.: Duke University Press, 1994), 2, 225.

54. Gina Bloom's excellent discussion of penetration through the ear in *Cymbeline*, including with regard to Innogen, Iachimo, and Cloten, also cites these lines on the penetration/"infection" of Posthumus's ear by a "false Italian" but does not develop their sexual/bodily implications. See Bloom, *Voice in Motion: Staging Gender, Shaping Sound in Early Modern England* (Philadelphia: University of Pennsylvania Press, 2007), 136–141.

55. Stanivukovic, "'The city's usuries,'" 241. I would add that the image of "counterfeiting" (associated with the female "c[o]unt" and infidelity in Posthumus's "woman's part" speech) also resonates with the associations Will Fisher discusses in "Queer Money," *ELH* 66, no. 1 (Spring 1999): 1–23, as in the "counterfeit coins" of Peacham's Ganymede emblem.

56. See "Italian fashion" in Gordon Williams, *A Dictionary of Sexual Language and Imagery in Shakespearean and Stuart Literature*, 3 vols. (London: Athlone Press, 1994), 2:720ff.; with Richard Brome, *Covent-Garden Weeded* (1632), in *Five New Playes* (1659), 13 ("preposterous Italian way"); Middleton's *Michaelmas Term* 3.1.20 ("'tis such an Italian world, many men know not before from behind"), with *A Mad World, My Masters*, 3.3.66 ("after the Italian fashion, backward"), in *Thomas Middleton, The Collected Works*, ed. Gary Taylor and John Lavagnino et al. (2007; rpt. Oxford: Clarendon Press, 2010), 353 and 436; *The Honest Whore, Part I*, in *The Chief Elizabethan Playwrights, Excluding Shakespeare*, ed. William Alan Neilson (Boston: Houghton Mifflin, 1911–1961), 2.1.441 (with *Thomas Middleton, The Collected Works*, 302); Celia R. Daileader, "Back Door Sex: Renaissance Gynosodomy, Aretino, and the Exotic," *ELH* 69, no. 2 (2002): 303–334.

57. See John Bale, *The First Two Partes of the Actes or Vnchast Examples of the Englysh Votaryes* (London, 1551),fol. 6v; "Roma amor est. Amor est? qualis? Praeposterus," in *The Pageant of Popes* (1574), John Studley's English translation of Bale's *Acta Romanorum pontificum* (Basel: Joannes Oporinus, 1558), fol. 190r; Lording Barry, *Ram-Alley; or merrie-tricks* (1611), sig. E2v. See also my Introduction to this book.

58. See Philemon Holland's 1606 translation of Suetonius's *History of Twelve Caesars*, 2 vols., ed. Charles Whibley (London: David Nutt, 1899), 1.45 (49), 1.49 (51), 1.48–49, 16. N. K. Hayles in "Sexual Disguise in *Cymbeline*," *Modern Language Quarterly* 41, no. 3 (1980): 231–

247—a very different reading that stresses the paternal and views Innogen/Fidele's androgyny within a NeoPlatonic framework—sees Lucius as vicariously becoming "the kind father whom Imogen had earlier lacked" (240). She also reads the lines in which Cymbeline says to Lucius "Thy Caesar knighted me; my youth I spent / Much under him" (3.1.67–68) as potentially suggesting that "Caesar is a father figure for Cymbeline, who seems to feel genuine regret that the decision not to pay tribute has divided him from his earlier mentor" (245).

59. See my *Shakespeare from the Margins* (Chicago: University of Chicago Press, 1996), chap. 1; and the Introduction and subsequent chapters in this book. On Thersites's "preposterous discoveries" in *Troilus and Cressida*, see the important discussion in Mario DiGangi's *Sexual Types*, 39–43.

60. See my "Spelling Backwards," in *Rhetoric, Women and Politics in Early Modern England*, ed. J. Richards and A. Thorne (London: Routledge, 2007), 25–50, 27–28.

61. See Joel Fineman on the "logic of the post," in *Shakespeare's Perjured Eye* (Berkeley: University of California Press, 1986). In addition to Leah Marcus's discussion of the "Post Nati" in *Puzzling Shakespeare* (124–148, 150–155), see also (inter alia) Bradin Cormack, *A Power to Do Justice* (Chicago: University of Chicago Press, 2007), chap. 5, and Marie Theresa O'Connor, "A British People: *Cymbeline* and the Anglo-Scottish Union Issue," in *Shakespeare and the Law*, ed. Bradin Cormack, Martha C. Nussbaum, and Richard Strier (Chicago: University of Chicago Press, 2013), 231–255.

62. See, inter alia, Marjorie Garber, "'What's Past Is Prologue': Temporality and Prophecy in Shakespeare's History Plays," in *Renaissance Genres*, ed. Barbara Kiefer Lewalski (Cambridge, Mass.: Harvard University Press, 1986), 301–331; my *Shakespeare from the Margins*, chap, 1, which also discusses the temporally "preposterous" lines in *The Winter's Tale* (5.2.139–140, 148).

63. Ros King, *Cymbeline: Constructions of Britain* (Aldershot: Ashgate, 2005), 102.

64. See King, *Cymbeline*, 102–104. I am citing her examples without subscribing to her particular conclusions.

65. In *Late Shakespeare: A New World of Words* (1997; rpt. Oxford: Clarendon Press, 2006), Simon Palfrey says of this scene that "intimations of buggery . . . linger to stain even the ragged threesome's heroics" (99). Criticism in the 1990s also addressed the link between war and denigration of the other: see, for example, Gregory W. Bredbeck's *Sodomy and Interpretation* (Ithaca, N.Y.: Cornell University Press, 1991) and the chapters on *Troilus and Cressida* in Valerie Traub's *Desire and Anxiety* (New York: Routledge, 1992). Although her recent *Thinking Sex with the Early Moderns* (Philadelphia: University of Pennsylvania Press, 2016) does not include *Cymbeline*, Traub's focus on opacity (introduced in her opening chapter, "Thinking Sex: Knowledge, Opacity, History") is highly suggestive for what I am calling "intimations of Ganymede" in this chapter. See also her discussion of Laurie Shannon's *Sovereign Amity: Figures of Friendship in Shakespearean Contexts* (Chicago: University of Chicago Press, 2002), and Shannon's "Queerly Philological Reading," paper presented at the "Lesbianism in the Renaisssance" seminar, Shakespeare Association of America, Minneapolis, 2002.

66. See Linda Woodbridge, "Palisading the Elizabethan Body Politic," *Texas Studies in Literature and Language* 33, no. 3 (Fall 1991): 327–354.

67. Quoted from Bromley, *Intimacy and Sexuality*, 65–78, who notes (76) the repeated references to the posterior (echoing the earlier reference to the "backside" of the "town") in "the backs of Britons [were] seen, all flying / Through a strait lane" (5.3.6–7) and "the strait pass was dammed / With dead men hurt behind" (5.3.11–12)—a reversal, he notes, of the frequent casting of the narrow lane as a penetration of the female body—and the defense of

the lane that "miraculously closes off these male bodies to penetration and submission to Roman invaders," when "the Britons penetrate the now cowardly Romans" ("Having found the back door open / Of the unguarded hearts, heavens, how they wound!," 5.3.45–46). But Bromley also observes Cymbeline's own final "submission to Caesar" in an ending that recalls his earlier "Caesar knighted me; my youth I spent / Much under him; of him I gathered honour"; and the future to come after the play when Arviragus "returns Britain to Roman submission" (77).

68. Stanivukovic, "'The city's usuries,'" 237. His terming Iachimo a "dry usurer" calls upon the contemporary notion of "dry exchange," for which he had earlier (216) cited Raymond de Roover, "What Is Dry Exchange? A Contribution to the Study of English Mercantilism," in *Business, Banking, and Economic Thought in Late Medieval and Early Modern Europe: Selected Studies of Raymond de Roover*, ed. Julius Kirshner (Chicago: University of Chicago Press, 1974). For classical Latin *anus* as "ring," see, inter alia, *OED* anus, *n.*

69. Bromley also argues that the play works to restrict the homoerotic implications of the cross-dressed "Fidele." He writes that "Unlike Viola in *Twelfth Night*, Rosalind in *As You Like It*, and Portia in *The Merchant of Venice*, who each achieve an arguable measure of temporary empowerment when in male disguises, Innogen is severely physically weakened in her cross-dressed state to the point of nearly dying" (73). He also adds that in disguise, "Innogen stages a version of the male submission the play rejects" and that "Shakespeare stifles the homoerotic responses generated by the cross-dressed heroine to create non-standard erotic pairings" (73)—replacing them by familial ones, both when Guiderius says that if Fidele "were . . . a woman," he "should woo hard" (3.6.66–67) and again (in another rewriting of the "eroticized submission that is so threatening in this play") when Lucius "redefines Fidele's service to him as a father-son relationship" (Bromley, *Intimacy and Sexuality*, 73–75), though (as I have noted elsewhere) King James liked to represent himself as a "father" to his favorites.

70. For the wordplay on *ring* and *anus* at the end of *The Merchant of Venice*, see Orgel, *Impersonations*, 76.

71. See Tina Mohler, "'What Is Thy Body but a Swallowing Grave . . .?': Desire Underground in *Titus Andronicus*," *Shakespeare Quarterly* 57, no. 1 (Spring 2006): 23–44, 37. Mohler also cites the derivation of English *anus* from the Latin for "ring," in *Webster's Third New International Dictionary of the English Language, Unabridged*, ed. Philip Babcock Gove (Springfield, Mass.: G. and C. Merriam, 1981), and the *Oxford Latin Dictionary*, ed. P. G. W. Glare (New York: Oxford University Press, 1982). The discussion of the boy's voice "cracked within the ring" (*Hamlet* 2.2.428) in Bloom, *Voice in Motion*, 37–39, is also more tangentially suggestive in this regard.

72. The introduction to *The Woman's Part: Feminist Criticism of Shakespeare*, ed. Carolyn Ruth Swift Lenz, Gayle Greene, and Carol Thomas Neely (Urbana: University of Illinois Press, 1980), 3–14, contrasts this moment in Act 4, scene 4, of *The Two Gentlemen of Verona* with Posthumus's misogynist outburst against "the woman's part" in *Cymbeline* (2.5.20ff.), but does not foreground the relation of the former to the context of English transvestite theater or what Phyllis Rackin in *Shakespeare and Women* (Oxford: Oxford University Press, 2005), 74, calls "the doubly gendered identity of the boy actors who dressed as women to play their parts."

73. Clare R. Kinney's reading of these metatheatrical lines has a very different emphasis: "In Act 5's labyrinthine (one might almost say Sidneian) denouement, she is nearly slapped into silence by her own husband, as if she were an intrusive actor in an important scene ('Shall's have a play of this?' shouts Posthumus. 'Thou scornful page, / There lie thy part!' [5.4.228–229]). But Innogen doesn't die, and if you hit her she gets up again and discloses her gendered

identity and keeps on speaking 'the woman's part'—the part that Posthumus had once desired be excised from himself (2.5.19–32), the 'speaking part' that he is not, however, allowed to banish from the world of this romance." See Clare R. Kinney, "Undoing Romance: Beaumont and Fletcher's Resistant Reading of *The Countess of Pembroke's Arcadia*," in *Staging Early Modern Romance*, ed. Mary Ellen Lamb and Valerie Wayne, 203–218 (215). In stressing this moment as a transvestite theatrical moment, what I suggest is that the audience is asked to see *double*, both active heroine *and* boy player. "Page" also plays on printed page, in this play where "Richard du Champ" may well evoke the name of the famous printer Richard Field. On homoeroticism in relation to Fidele/Innogen, see also Valerie Wayne's recent essay "The Gendered Text and Its Labour," in *The Oxford Handbook of Shakespeare and Embodiment: Gender, Sexuality, and Race*, ed. Valerie Traub (Oxford: Oxford University Press, 2016), 549–568, esp. 565–568. Stephen Guy-Bray does not mention the doubleness of "Fidele" or the final scene's transvestite metatheatrical moment in his "Locating Queerness in *Cymbeline*," in *Queer Shakespeare: Desire and Sexuality*, ed. Goran Stanivukovic (London: Bloomsbury Arden Shakespeare, 2017), 123–136.

74. On the Jailer's invoking of "debitor and creditor" accounting in relation to the "true" and the pervasive language of debitor and creditor or double-entry accounting throughout *Cymbeline* (including in the debts "uncrossed" in a ledger in 3.3.26, the "inventory" taken by Iachimo in the scene in Innogen's bedchamber in 2.2, and the "circumstances" he presents to Posthumus in 2.4), see my "*Cymbeline*: Arithmetic, Double-Entry Bookkeeping, Counts, and Accounts," *SEDERI* 23 (2013): 95–119, which also provides contemporary examples of the sexual sense of "arithmetic" in Posthumus's lines here. For this shared language in *Othello*, see Chapter 5, and my "Cassio, Cash, and the 'Infidel o': Arithmetic, Double-entry Bookkeeping, and *Othello*'s Unfaithful Accounts," in *A Companion to the Global Renaissance*, ed. Jyotsna Singh (Oxford: Blackwell, 2009), 223–241, which also cites contemporary identifications of the female "count" with the account books of "debitor and creditor"; the combination in Shakespeare's Sonnet 136 of "account" with "a treasure," "things of great receipt," "nothing," and a female "will"; lenders' books juxtaposed with "brothels" and "plackets" in *King Lear* (3.4.96–97); and the combination of account book and female "(ac)count" in "I see, lady, the gentleman is not in your books" in *Much Ado About Nothing* (1.1.79).

75. See Shapiro, *Gender in Play*, 174–179.

76. See Smith, *Homosexual Desire*, 152, alluding to Robert Greene's *Menaphon* (1589), where (it should be noted) Pleusidippus is gazed upon "as wanton *Jove* gazed on *Phrygian Ganimede* in the fields of *Ida*" (Smith, *Homosexual Desire*, 137), and Sir Philip Sidney's *The Countesse of Pembroke's Arcadia* (*The New Arcadia*) and *The Countess of Pembroke's Arcadia* (*The Old Arcadia*).

77. See *Narrative and Dramatic Sources of Shakespeare*, 2 vols., ed. Geoffrey Bullough (London: Routledge and Kegan Paul, 1958), 159–160.

78. Smith, *Homosexual Desire*, 153.

79. On "angel" and "ingle" (catamite/Ganymede or boy lover), see my *Shakespeare from the Margins*, 143–147, 325–326; and the Introduction here.

80. Smith, *Homosexual Desire*, 153. See also Shapiro, *Gender in Play*, 180ff.

81. See Bromley's reading of "Fidele," in relation to the "family feeling" that reshapes the homoerotic in these scenes (*Intimacy and Sexuality*, esp. 73–74).

82. See also Alan Sinfield's *Shakespeare, Authority, Sexuality* (New York: Routledge, 2006), chap. 7 ("Near Misses: Ganymedes and Page Boys"), 125, which only marginally cites *Cymbeline* but briefly stresses the homoerotic relation between "master" and "page" in Lucius's line.

83. Butler ed., 163.

84. On the importance of Virgil's Second Eclogue in relation to early modern homoeroticism, see, for example, Bruce R. Smith, *Homosexual Desire*, 89ff.; Stephen Guy-Bray, *Homoerotic Space* (Toronto: University of Toronto Press, 2002), 43ff.; Will Fisher, "'Wantoning with the Thighs': The Socialization of Thigh Sex in England, 1590–1730," *Journal of the History of Sexuality* 24, no. 1 (2015): 1–24, 20.

85. Bailey, *Flaunting*, 71–72, quoting from Bruce R. Smith on Ganymede in *Homosexual Desire*, 192.

86. Madhavi Menon's discussion of *Cymbeline* in Chapter 2 of *Unhistorical Shakespeare: Queer Theory in Shakespearean Literature and Film* (New York: Palgrave Macmillan, 2008) is exceptionally suggestive in this regard, in addition to other aspects of the play.

87. See the section on "Preposterous Time" in Jonathan Gil Harris, *Untimely Matter in the Time of Shakespeare* (Philadelphia: University of Pennsylvania Press, 2009), 182–187.

88. See my Introduction and Chapter 1 on the combination of temporal and bodily in examples such as the entry on "Backedore" in Richard Huloet's *Abcedarium Anglico Latinum* (1552); and on the preposterating of the biblical testaments in the work of John Bale and others, with *The Apology of Johan Bale agaynste a Ranke Papist* (London, 1550) on the "arsewarde procedynges" of going "preposterously to wurke" (sig. O1r).

89. See in this regard the suggestive analysis of *Cymbeline* in Jane Pettegree's *Foreign and Native on the English Stage, 1588–1611* (New York: Palgrave Macmillan, 2011), esp. 154–156 and 160–164; and (though he does not mention *Cymbeline*) Harris's *Untimely Matter* on Christian typology and "Preposterous Time" (esp. 183).

# Index

Hull, Suzanne: 82, 95, 322n6

invasion (and fears of): 5–7, 25, 28, 187, 213–216, 222, 224, 228–233, 248, 251, 253, 259–263, 289, 372n161

posterior: 7, 12, 19, 27, 33, 56–60, 62, 64, 66, 75, 303n59, 316n87, 385n67

# *Acknowledgments*

During this book's gestation and completion, I have accrued many debts of different kinds, which it is a pleasure to acknowledge here. I am grateful to Stanford University for supported leaves and the opportunity to engage with generations of students, from undergraduates and Ph.D.s to postdoctoral fellows; and to Stanford Library staff, including John E. Mustain and Glen Worthey. I am thankful for years of engagement with colleagues past and present, including John Bender, Eavan Boland, Terry Castle, Margaret Cohen, Sandra Drake, Dan Edelstein, Harry Elam, Michele Elam, Paula Findlen, Shelley Fisher Fishkin, Denise Gigante, Roland Greene, Monika Greenleaf, Shirley Heath, Blair Hoxby, Nicholas Jenkins, Adam Johnson, Gavin Jones, Andrea Lunsford, Mark McGurl, Jisha Menon, Paula Moya, Sianne Ngai, Stephen Orgel, David Palumbo-Liu, Peggy Phelan, Mary Louise Pratt, Vaughn Rasberry, David Riggs, Nancy Ruttenburg, José David Saldívar, Ramón Saldívar, Jennifer Summit, Elizabeth Tallent, Elaine Treharne, Blakey Vermeule, and Alex Woloch. I am indebted to the Huntington Library and the Folger Shakespeare Library for support during periods of research, and in particular to Georgianna Ziegler, Barbara Mowat, Betsy Walsh, and the Folger staff who were key to that research when I was a Senior Fellow at the Folger; and to the staff at the Huntington, the Folger, the National Portrait Gallery in London, the National Gallery in Washington, DC, the Kunsthistorisches Museum in Vienna, and the Koninklijke Bibliotheek, National Library of the Netherlands, for assistance and particular illustrations.

At the University of Pennsylvania Press, I am grateful beyond words to Jerome Singerman, who has been supportive of this project from its inception and an exemplary editor at every turn; to Hannah Blake for crucial assistance at key times; and to my wonderful managing editor Noreen O'Connor-Abel for her unfailing support, understanding, and good cheer. I am thankful as well to the two anonymous readers for the Press, whose comments were invaluable in the process of revision.

I also owe so much to friends and fellow scholars whose wisdom, counsel, and critical engagements have in different ways been crucial in the development of this book, including Albert Russell Ascoli, Shaul Bassi, James Bednarz, Jerry Brotton, Douglas Bruster, Dympna Callaghan, Anthony Corbeill, Karen Cunningham, Adhaar Noor Desai, Lynn Enterline, Will Fisher, Susan Frye, Barbara Fuchs, Maud Gleason, Kim F. Hall, Timothy Hampton, Philip Hardie, Margo Hendricks, Robert Henke, Stephen Hinds, Peter Holland, Jean Howard, Lorna Hutson, Sujata Iyengar, Natasha Korda, Arthur L. Little, Jr., Ania Loomba, Rory Loughnane, Laurie Maguire, Jenny C. Mann, Jeffrey Masten, Michael Neill, Richard Rambuss, Eric Rasmussen, Laura Giannetti Ruggiero, Melissa E. Sanchez, Emma Smith, Ian Smith, Tiffany Stern, Valerie Traub, Jesús Tronch Pérez, Paul Werstine, and Paul Yachnin. And I owe a particular debt of gratitude to those who read and provided invaluable comments on individual chapters in progress, who (with other interlocutors) bear no responsibility for the book's errors and omissions, which are my own: Jonathan Baldo, Alessandro Barchiesi, Patricia Cahill, Mario DiGangi, Andrew Hadfield, Willy Maley, Randall Martin, George W. Pigman III, Marjorie Rubright, Philip Schwyzer, Goran Stanivukovic, and Valerie Wayne.

I am at the same time grateful for the opportunities to share my work and thinking in invited talks and keynote speeches at the School of Criticism and Theory, Yale University, Wellesley College, MIT, New York University, CUNY Graduate Center, McGill University, McMaster University, the Peter Wall Institute of Advanced Studies at the University of British Columbia, the South California Renaissance Association, the Newberry Library, the University of Hawaii, the University of Alabama, the University of California at Los Angeles, the University of California at Irvine, the University of California at Berkeley, the Shakespeare Association of America, the Group for Early Modern Cultural Studies, the University of Pennsylvania conference on "Historicizing Sex," the Department of English at Cornell University (as the annual Paul Gottschalk Lecturer), and the University of Toronto (as the annual Northrop Frye Professor Lecturer). In relation to my developing work on early modern contexts and Shakespeare's language (including its multilingual dimensions), I am also very grateful for the opportunity to address international audiences at the Shakespeare's Globe Theatre in London, the Passmore Edwards Symposium at Oxford, the London Renaissance Seminar, and the Shakespeare Institute, and on other particular occasions at the Universities of Oxford, Cambridge, London, Exeter, Sussex, Southampton, Hull, York, Glasgow, and Strathclyde in the United Kingdom; the Shakespeare's Globe Conference in Venice; La Sociedad Española de Estudios Renacentistas Ingleses; the German Shakespeare Society; La Société française Shakespeare; Université de Paris III (Sorbonne Nouvelle); the Centre National de la Recherche Scientifique; Université Paul Valéry-Montpellier III; University of Caen; University of Rouen; University of Bucharest; University of Vienna; University of Dubrovnik and University of Split in Croatia; Charles University in Prague; the Universities of Geneva and Basel in Switzerland; the University of Szeged, Hungary; the University of Sydney, Australia; the "Shakespeare and Philosophy in a Multicultural World" conference in Budapest; the "Theater Without Borders" conference in Istanbul; the Shakespeare Association of Australia and New Zealand; the Oxford University Interdisciplinary Conference on "Blood," and the 2014 Paris conference on the 450th anniversary of Shakespeare's birth.

The first three chapters of this book include revisions and expansions of previously published work. Chapter 1 is a substantially revised and expanded version of "Preposterous Reversals: *Love's Labor's Lost*," which appeared in *Modern Language Quarterly* 54, no. 4 (1993). The first section of Chapter 2 is from "Construing Gender: Mastering Bianca in *The Taming of the Shrew*," in *The Impact of Feminism in English Renaissance Studies*, ed. Dympna C. Callaghan (New York: Palgrave Macmillan, 2007), which is substantially revised and expanded here. And I am grateful to Cambridge University Press for permission to use portions of "(Peter) Quince: Love Potions, Carpenter's Coigns and Athenian Weddings," from *Shakespeare Survey* 56 (2003) in revised and expanded form as well.

As always—as throughout my years as a scholar, writer, and teacher—I have a tremendous ongoing debt of gratitude for the love and support of my children Jackie and Josh, and my now-extended family, including daughter-in-law Maria Granberg, son-in-law Craig Hargett, and my wonderful granddaughter Emma Elizabeth Parker Hargett, whose limericks, nonsense verses, and emojis have kept me smiling and guessing. To them—and another grandchild on the way—this book is affectionately dedicated.